T0137005

Lecture Notes in Computer Science 14111

Founding Editors

Gerhard Goos
Juris Hartmanis

The series Lecture Notes in Computer Science (LNCS), including its subseries Lecture Notes in Artificial Intelligence (LNAI) and Lecture Notes in Bioinformatics (LNBI), has established itself as a medium for the publication of new developments in computer science and information technology research, teaching, and education.

LNCS enjoys close cooperation with the computer science R & D community, the series counts many renowned academics among its volume editors and paper authors, and collaborates with prestigious societies. Its mission is to serve this international community by providing an invaluable service, mainly focused on the publication of conference and workshop proceedings and postproceedings. LNCS commenced publication in 1973.

Osvaldo Gervasi · Beniamino Murgante ·
Ana Maria A. C. Rocha · Chiara Garau ·
Francesco Scorza · Yeliz Karaca ·
Carmelo M. Torre
Editors

Computational Science and Its Applications – ICCSA 2023 Workshops

Athens, Greece, July 3–6, 2023
Proceedings, Part VIII

Springer

Editors
Osvaldo Gervasi ⓘD
University of Perugia
Perugia, Italy

Beniamino Murgante ⓘD
University of Basilicata
Potenza, Italy

Ana Maria A. C. Rocha ⓘD
University of Minho
Braga, Portugal

Chiara Garau ⓘD
University of Cagliari
Cagliari, Italy

Francesco Scorza ⓘD
University of Basilicata
Potenza, Italy

Yeliz Karaca ⓘD
University of Massachusetts Medical School
Worcester, MA, USA

Carmelo M. Torre ⓘD
Polytechnic University of Bari
Bari, Italy

ISSN 0302-9743   ISSN 1611-3349 (electronic)
Lecture Notes in Computer Science
ISBN 978-3-031-37125-7   ISBN 978-3-031-37126-4 (eBook)
https://doi.org/10.1007/978-3-031-37126-4

This Springer imprint is published by the registered company Springer Nature Switzerland AG
The registered company address is: Gewerbestrasse 11, 6330 Cham, Switzerland

Preface

These 9 volumes (LNCS volumes 14104–14112) consist of the peer-reviewed papers from the 2023 International Conference on Computational Science and Its Applications (ICCSA 2023) which took place during July 3–6, 2023. The peer-reviewed papers of the main conference tracks were published in a separate set consisting of two volumes (LNCS 13956–13957).

The conference was finally held in person after the difficult period of the Covid-19 pandemic in the wonderful city of Athens, in the cosy facilities of the National Technical University. Our experience during the pandemic period allowed us to enable virtual participation also this year for those who were unable to attend the event, due to logistical, political and economic problems, by adopting a technological infrastructure based on open source software (jitsi + riot), and a commercial cloud infrastructure.

ICCSA 2023 was another successful event in the International Conference on Computational Science and Its Applications (ICCSA) series, previously held as a hybrid event (with one third of registered authors attending in person) in Malaga, Spain (2022), Cagliari, Italy (hybrid with few participants in person in 2021 and completely online in 2020), whilst earlier editions took place in Saint Petersburg, Russia (2019), Melbourne, Australia (2018), Trieste, Italy (2017), Beijing, China (2016), Banff, Canada (2015), Guimaraes, Portugal (2014), Ho Chi Minh City, Vietnam (2013), Salvador, Brazil (2012), Santander, Spain (2011), Fukuoka, Japan (2010), Suwon, South Korea (2009), Perugia, Italy (2008), Kuala Lumpur, Malaysia (2007), Glasgow, UK (2006), Singapore (2005), Assisi, Italy (2004), Montreal, Canada (2003), and (as ICCS) Amsterdam, The Netherlands (2002) and San Francisco, USA (2001).

Computational Science is the main pillar of most of the present research, industrial and commercial applications, and plays a unique role in exploiting ICT innovative technologies, and the ICCSA series have been providing a venue to researchers and industry practitioners to discuss new ideas, to share complex problems and their solutions, and to shape new trends in Computational Science. As the conference mirrors society from a scientific point of view, this year's undoubtedly dominant theme was the machine learning and artificial intelligence and their applications in the most diverse economic and industrial fields.

The ICCSA 2023 conference is structured in 6 general tracks covering the fields of computational science and its applications: Computational Methods, Algorithms and Scientific Applications – High Performance Computing and Networks – Geometric Modeling, Graphics and Visualization – Advanced and Emerging Applications – Information Systems and Technologies – Urban and Regional Planning. In addition, the conference consisted of 61 workshops, focusing on very topical issues of importance to science, technology and society: from new mathematical approaches for solving complex computational systems, to information and knowledge in the Internet of Things, new statistical and optimization methods, several Artificial Intelligence approaches, sustainability issues, smart cities and related technologies.

In the workshop proceedings we accepted 350 full papers, 29 short papers and 2 PHD Showcase papers. In the main conference proceedings we accepted 67 full papers, 13 short papers and 6 PHD Showcase papers from 283 submissions to the General Tracks of the conference (acceptance rate 30%). We would like to express our appreciation to the workshops chairs and co-chairs for their hard work and dedication.

The success of the ICCSA conference series in general, and of ICCSA 2023 in particular, vitally depends on the support of many people: authors, presenters, participants, keynote speakers, workshop chairs, session chairs, organizing committee members, student volunteers, Program Committee members, Advisory Committee members, International Liaison chairs, reviewers and others in various roles. We take this opportunity to wholehartedly thank them all.

We also wish to thank our publisher, Springer, for their acceptance to publish the proceedings, for sponsoring part of the best papers awards and for their kind assistance and cooperation during the editing process.

We cordially invite you to visit the ICCSA website https://iccsa.org where you can find all the relevant information about this interesting and exciting event.

July 2023

Osvaldo Gervasi
Beniamino Murgante
Chiara Garau

Welcome Message from Organizers

After the 2021 ICCSA in Cagliari, Italy and the 2022 ICCSA in Malaga, Spain, ICCSA continued its successful scientific endeavours in 2023, hosted again in the Mediterranean neighbourhood. This time, ICCSA 2023 moved a bit more to the east of the Mediterranean Region and was held in the metropolitan city of Athens, the capital of Greece and a vibrant urban environment endowed with a prominent cultural heritage that dates back to the ancient years. As a matter of fact, Athens is one of the oldest cities in the world, and the cradle of democracy. The city has a history of over 3,000 years and, according to the myth, it took its name from Athena, the Goddess of Wisdom and daughter of Zeus.

ICCSA 2023 took place in a secure environment, relieved from the immense stress of the COVID-19 pandemic. This gave us the chance to have a safe and vivid, in-person participation which, combined with the very active engagement of the ICCSA 2023 scientific community, set the ground for highly motivating discussions and interactions as to the latest developments of computer science and its applications in the real world for improving quality of life.

The National Technical University of Athens (NTUA), one of the most prestigious Greek academic institutions, had the honour of hosting ICCSA 2023. The Local Organizing Committee really feels the burden and responsibility of such a demanding task; and puts in all the necessary energy in order to meet participants' expectations and establish a friendly, creative and inspiring, scientific and social/cultural environment that allows for new ideas and perspectives to flourish.

Since all ICCSA participants, either informatics-oriented or application-driven, realize the tremendous steps and evolution of computer science during the last few decades and the huge potential these offer to cope with the enormous challenges of humanity in a globalized, 'wired' and highly competitive world, the expectations from ICCSA 2023 were set high in order for a successful matching between computer science progress and communities' aspirations to be attained, i.e., a progress that serves real, place- and people-based needs and can pave the way towards a visionary, smart, sustainable, resilient and inclusive future for both the current and the next generation.

On behalf of the Local Organizing Committee, I would like to sincerely thank all of you who have contributed to ICCSA 2023 and I cordially welcome you to my 'home', NTUA.

On behalf of the Local Organizing Committee.

Anastasia Stratigea

Organization

ICCSA 2023 was organized by the National Technical University of Athens (Greece), the University of the Aegean (Greece), the University of Perugia (Italy), the University of Basilicata (Italy), Monash University (Australia), Kyushu Sangyo University (Japan), the University of Minho (Portugal). The conference was supported by two NTUA Schools, namely the School of Rural, Surveying and Geoinformatics Engineering and the School of Electrical and Computer Engineering.

Honorary General Chairs

Norio Shiratori	Chuo University, Japan
Kenneth C. J. Tan	Sardina Systems, UK

General Chairs

Osvaldo Gervasi	University of Perugia, Italy
Anastasia Stratigea	National Technical University of Athens, Greece
Bernady O. Apduhan	Kyushu Sangyo University, Japan

Program Committee Chairs

Beniamino Murgante	University of Basilicata, Italy
Dimitris Kavroudakis	University of the Aegean, Greece
Ana Maria A. C. Rocha	University of Minho, Portugal
David Taniar	Monash University, Australia

International Advisory Committee

Jemal Abawajy	Deakin University, Australia
Dharma P. Agarwal	University of Cincinnati, USA
Rajkumar Buyya	Melbourne University, Australia
Claudia Bauzer Medeiros	University of Campinas, Brazil
Manfred M. Fisher	Vienna University of Economics and Business, Austria
Marina L. Gavrilova	University of Calgary, Canada

| Sumi Helal | University of Florida, USA and University of Lancaster, UK |
| Yee Leung | Chinese University of Hong Kong, China |

International Liaison Chairs

Ivan Blečić	University of Cagliari, Italy
Giuseppe Borruso	University of Trieste, Italy
Elise De Donker	Western Michigan University, USA
Maria Irene Falcão	University of Minho, Portugal
Inmaculada Garcia Fernandez	University of Malaga, Spain
Eligius Hendrix	University of Malaga, Spain
Robert C. H. Hsu	Chung Hua University, Taiwan
Tai-Hoon Kim	Beijing Jaotong University, China
Vladimir Korkhov	Saint Petersburg University, Russia
Takashi Naka	Kyushu Sangyo University, Japan
Rafael D. C. Santos	National Institute for Space Research, Brazil
Maribel Yasmina Santos	University of Minho, Portugal
Elena Stankova	Saint Petersburg University, Russia

Workshop and Session Organizing Chairs

| Beniamino Murgante | University of Basilicata, Italy |
| Chiara Garau | University of Cagliari, Italy |

Award Chair

| Wenny Rahayu | La Trobe University, Australia |

Publicity Committee Chairs

Elmer Dadios	De La Salle University, Philippines
Nataliia Kulabukhova	Saint Petersburg University, Russia
Daisuke Takahashi	Tsukuba University, Japan
Shangwang Wang	Beijing University of Posts and Telecommunications, China

Local Organizing Committee Chairs

Anastasia Stratigea	National Technical University of Athens, Greece
Dimitris Kavroudakis	University of the Aegean, Greece
Charalambos Ioannidis	National Technical University of Athens, Greece
Nectarios Koziris	National Technical University of Athens, Greece
Efthymios Bakogiannis	National Technical University of Athens, Greece
Yiota Theodora	National Technical University of Athens, Greece
Dimitris Fotakis	National Technical University of Athens, Greece
Apostolos Lagarias	National Technical University of Athens, Greece
Akrivi Leka	National Technical University of Athens, Greece
Dionisia Koutsi	National Technical University of Athens, Greece
Alkistis Dalkavouki	National Technical University of Athens, Greece
Maria Panagiotopoulou	National Technical University of Athens, Greece
Angeliki Papazoglou	National Technical University of Athens, Greece
Natalia Tsigarda	National Technical University of Athens, Greece
Konstantinos Athanasopoulos	National Technical University of Athens, Greece
Ioannis Xatziioannou	National Technical University of Athens, Greece
Vasiliki Krommyda	National Technical University of Athens, Greece
Panayiotis Patsilinakos	National Technical University of Athens, Greece
Sofia Kassiou	National Technical University of Athens, Greece

Technology Chair

Damiano Perri	University of Florence, Italy

Program Committee

Vera Afreixo	University of Aveiro, Portugal
Filipe Alvelos	University of Minho, Portugal
Hartmut Asche	University of Potsdam, Germany
Ginevra Balletto	University of Cagliari, Italy
Michela Bertolotto	University College Dublin, Ireland
Sandro Bimonte	CEMAGREF, TSCF, France
Rod Blais	University of Calgary, Canada
Ivan Blečić	University of Sassari, Italy
Giuseppe Borruso	University of Trieste, Italy
Ana Cristina Braga	University of Minho, Portugal
Massimo Cafaro	University of Salento, Italy
Yves Caniou	Lyon University, France

Ermanno Cardelli	University of Perugia, Italy
José A. Cardoso e Cunha	Universidade Nova de Lisboa, Portugal
Rui Cardoso	University of Beira Interior, Portugal
Leocadio G. Casado	University of Almeria, Spain
Carlo Cattani	University of Salerno, Italy
Mete Celik	Erciyes University, Turkey
Maria Cerreta	University of Naples "Federico II", Italy
Hyunseung Choo	Sungkyunkwan University, Korea
Rachel Chieng-Sing Lee	Sunway University, Malaysia
Min Young Chung	Sungkyunkwan University, Korea
Florbela Maria da Cruz Domingues Correia	Polytechnic Institute of Viana do Castelo, Portugal
Gilberto Corso Pereira	Federal University of Bahia, Brazil
Alessandro Costantini	INFN, Italy
Carla Dal Sasso Freitas	Universidade Federal do Rio Grande do Sul, Brazil
Pradesh Debba	The Council for Scientific and Industrial Research (CSIR), South Africa
Hendrik Decker	Instituto Tecnológico de Informática, Spain
Robertas Damaševičius	Kausan University of Technology, Lithuania
Frank Devai	London South Bank University, UK
Rodolphe Devillers	Memorial University of Newfoundland, Canada
Joana Matos Dias	University of Coimbra, Portugal
Paolino Di Felice	University of L'Aquila, Italy
Prabu Dorairaj	NetApp, India/USA
Noelia Faginas Lago	University of Perugia, Italy
M. Irene Falcao	University of Minho, Portugal
Cherry Liu Fang	U.S. DOE Ames Laboratory, USA
Florbela P. Fernandes	Polytechnic Institute of Bragança, Portugal
Jose-Jesus Fernandez	National Centre for Biotechnology, CSIS, Spain
Paula Odete Fernandes	Polytechnic Institute of Bragança, Portugal
Adelaide de Fátima Baptista Valente Freitas	University of Aveiro, Portugal
Manuel Carlos Figueiredo	University of Minho, Portugal
Maria Celia Furtado Rocha	PRODEB–PósCultura/UFBA, Brazil
Chiara Garau	University of Cagliari, Italy
Paulino Jose Garcia Nieto	University of Oviedo, Spain
Raffaele Garrisi	Polizia di Stato, Italy
Jerome Gensel	LSR-IMAG, France
Maria Giaoutzi	National Technical University, Athens, Greece
Arminda Manuela Andrade Pereira Gonçalves	University of Minho, Portugal

Andrzej M. Goscinski	Deakin University, Australia
Sevin Gümgüm	Izmir University of Economics, Turkey
Alex Hagen-Zanker	University of Cambridge, UK
Shanmugasundaram Hariharan	B.S. Abdur Rahman University, India
Eligius M. T. Hendrix	University of Malaga, Spain and Wageningen University, The Netherlands
Hisamoto Hiyoshi	Gunma University, Japan
Mustafa Inceoglu	EGE University, Turkey
Peter Jimack	University of Leeds, UK
Qun Jin	Waseda University, Japan
Yeliz Karaca	University of Massachusetts Medical School, Worcester, USA
Farid Karimipour	Vienna University of Technology, Austria
Baris Kazar	Oracle Corp., USA
Maulana Adhinugraha Kiki	Telkom University, Indonesia
DongSeong Kim	University of Canterbury, New Zealand
Taihoon Kim	Hannam University, Korea
Ivana Kolingerova	University of West Bohemia, Czech Republic
Nataliia Kulabukhova	St. Petersburg University, Russia
Vladimir Korkhov	St. Petersburg University, Russia
Rosa Lasaponara	National Research Council, Italy
Maurizio Lazzari	National Research Council, Italy
Cheng Siong Lee	Monash University, Australia
Sangyoun Lee	Yonsei University, Korea
Jongchan Lee	Kunsan National University, Korea
Chendong Li	University of Connecticut, USA
Gang Li	Deakin University, Australia
Fang Liu	AMES Laboratories, USA
Xin Liu	University of Calgary, Canada
Andrea Lombardi	University of Perugia, Italy
Savino Longo	University of Bari, Italy
Tinghuai Ma	Nanjing University of Information Science & Technology, China
Ernesto Marcheggiani	Katholieke Universiteit Leuven, Belgium
Antonino Marvuglia	Research Centre Henri Tudor, Luxembourg
Nicola Masini	National Research Council, Italy
Ilaria Matteucci	National Research Council, Italy
Nirvana Meratnia	University of Twente, The Netherlands
Fernando Miranda	University of Minho, Portugal
Giuseppe Modica	University of Reggio Calabria, Italy
Josè Luis Montaña	University of Cantabria, Spain
Maria Filipa Mourão	Instituto Politécnico de Viana do Castelo, Portugal

Giuseppe A. Trunfio	University of Sassari, Italy
Pablo Vanegas	University of Cuenca, Equador
Marco Vizzari	University of Perugia, Italy
Varun Vohra	Merck Inc., USA
Koichi Wada	University of Tsukuba, Japan
Krzysztof Walkowiak	Wroclaw University of Technology, Poland
Zequn Wang	Intelligent Automation Inc, USA
Robert Weibel	University of Zurich, Switzerland
Frank Westad	Norwegian University of Science and Technology, Norway
Roland Wismüller	Universität Siegen, Germany
Mudasser Wyne	SOET National University, USA
Chung-Huang Yang	National Kaohsiung Normal University, Taiwan
Xin-She Yang	National Physical Laboratory, UK
Salim Zabir	France Telecom Japan Co., Japan
Haifeng Zhao	University of California, Davis, USA
Fabiana Zollo	University of Venice "Cà Foscari", Italy
Albert Y. Zomaya	University of Sydney, Australia

Workshop Organizers

Advanced Data Science Techniques with Applications in Industry and Environmental Sustainability (ATELIERS 2023)

Dario Torregrossa	Goodyear, Luxemburg
Antonino Marvuglia	Luxembourg Institute of Science and Technology, Luxemburg
Valeria Borodin	École des Mines de Saint-Étienne, Luxemburg
Mohamed Laib	Luxembourg Institute of Science and Technology, Luxemburg

Advances in Artificial Intelligence Learning Technologies: Blended Learning, STEM, Computational Thinking and Coding (AAILT 2023)

Alfredo Milani	University of Perugia, Italy
Valentina Franzoni	University of Perugia, Italy
Sergio Tasso	University of Perugia, Italy

Advanced Processes of Mathematics and Computing Models in Complex Computational Systems (ACMC 2023)

Yeliz Karaca	University of Massachusetts Chan Medical School and Massachusetts Institute of Technology, USA
Dumitru Baleanu	Cankaya University, Turkey
Osvaldo Gervasi	University of Perugia, Italy
Yudong Zhang	University of Leicester, UK
Majaz Moonis	University of Massachusetts Medical School, USA

Artificial Intelligence Supported Medical Data Examination (AIM 2023)

David Taniar	Monash University, Australia
Seifedine Kadry	Noroff University College, Norway
Venkatesan Rajinikanth	Saveetha School of Engineering, India

Advanced and Innovative Web Apps (AIWA 2023)

Damiano Perri	University of Perugia, Italy
Osvaldo Gervasi	University of Perugia, Italy

Assessing Urban Sustainability (ASUS 2023)

Elena Todella	Polytechnic of Turin, Italy
Marika Gaballo	Polytechnic of Turin, Italy
Beatrice Mecca	Polytechnic of Turin, Italy

Advances in Web Based Learning (AWBL 2023)

Birol Ciloglugil	Ege University, Turkey
Mustafa Inceoglu	Ege University, Turkey

Blockchain and Distributed Ledgers: Technologies and Applications (BDLTA 2023)

Vladimir Korkhov	Saint Petersburg State University, Russia
Elena Stankova	Saint Petersburg State University, Russia
Nataliia Kulabukhova	Saint Petersburg State University, Russia

Bio and Neuro Inspired Computing and Applications (BIONCA 2023)

Nadia Nedjah	State University of Rio De Janeiro, Brazil
Luiza De Macedo Mourelle	State University of Rio De Janeiro, Brazil

Choices and Actions for Human Scale Cities: Decision Support Systems (CAHSC–DSS 2023)

Giovanna Acampa	University of Florence and University of Enna Kore, Italy
Fabrizio Finucci	Roma Tre University, Italy
Luca S. Dacci	Polytechnic of Turin, Italy

Computational and Applied Mathematics (CAM 2023)

Maria Irene Falcao	University of Minho, Portugal
Fernando Miranda	University of Minho, Portugal

Computational and Applied Statistics (CAS 2023)

Ana Cristina Braga	University of Minho, Portugal

Cyber Intelligence and Applications (CIA 2023)

Gianni Dangelo	University of Salerno, Italy
Francesco Palmieri	University of Salerno, Italy
Massimo Ficco	University of Salerno, Italy

Conversations South-North on Climate Change Adaptation Towards Smarter and More Sustainable Cities (CLAPS 2023)

Chiara Garau	University of Cagliari, Italy
Cristina Trois	University of kwaZulu-Natal, South Africa
Claudia Loggia	University of kwaZulu-Natal, South Africa
John Östh	Faculty of Technology, Art and Design, Norway
Mauro Coni	University of Cagliari, Italy
Alessio Satta	MedSea Foundation, Italy

Computational Mathematics, Statistics and Information Management (CMSIM 2023)

Maria Filomena Teodoro	University of Lisbon and Portuguese Naval Academy, Portugal
Marina A. P. Andrade	University Institute of Lisbon, Portugal

Computational Optimization and Applications (COA 2023)

Ana Maria A. C. Rocha	University of Minho, Portugal
Humberto Rocha	University of Coimbra, Portugal

Computational Astrochemistry (CompAstro 2023)

Marzio Rosi	University of Perugia, Italy
Nadia Balucani	University of Perugia, Italy
Cecilia Ceccarelli	University of Grenoble Alpes and Institute for Planetary Sciences and Astrophysics, France
Stefano Falcinelli	University of Perugia, Italy

Computational Methods for Porous Geomaterials (CompPor 2023)

Vadim Lisitsa	Russian Academy of Science, Russia
Evgeniy Romenski	Russian Academy of Science, Russia

Workshop on Computational Science and HPC (CSHPC 2023)

Elise De Doncker	Western Michigan University, USA
Fukuko Yuasa	High Energy Accelerator Research Organization, Japan
Hideo Matsufuru	High Energy Accelerator Research Organization, Japan

Cities, Technologies and Planning (CTP 2023)

Giuseppe Borruso	University of Trieste, Italy
Beniamino Murgante	University of Basilicata, Italy
Malgorzata Hanzl	Lodz University of Technology, Poland
Anastasia Stratigea	National Technical University of Athens, Greece
Ljiljana Zivkovic	Republic Geodetic Authority, Serbia
Ginevra Balletto	University of Cagliari, Italy

Gender Equity/Equality in Transport and Mobility (DELIA 2023)

Tiziana Campisi	University of Enna Kore, Italy
Ines Charradi	Sousse University, Tunisia
Alexandros Nikitas	University of Huddersfield, UK
Kh Md Nahiduzzaman	University of British Columbia, Canada
Andreas Nikiforiadis	Aristotle University of Thessaloniki, Greece
Socrates Basbas	Aristotle University of Thessaloniki, Greece

International Workshop on Defense Technology and Security (DTS 2023)

Yeonseung Ryu	Myongji University, South Korea

Integrated Methods for the Ecosystem-Services Accounting in Urban Decision Process (Ecourbn 2023)

Maria Rosaria Guarini	Sapienza University of Rome, Italy
Francesco Sica	Sapienza University of Rome, Italy
Francesco Tajani	Sapienza University of Rome, Italy

Carmelo Maria Torre	Polytechnic University of Bari, Italy
Pierluigi Morano	Polytechnic University of Bari, Italy
Rossana Ranieri	Sapienza Università di Roma, Italy

Evaluating Inner Areas Potentials (EIAP 2023)

Diana Rolando	Politechnic of Turin, Italy
Manuela Rebaudengo	Politechnic of Turin, Italy
Alice Barreca	Politechnic of Turin, Italy
Giorgia Malavasi	Politechnic of Turin, Italy
Umberto Mecca	Politechnic of Turin, Italy

Sustainable Mobility Last Mile Logistic (ELLIOT 2023)

Tiziana Campisi	University of Enna Kore, Italy
Socrates Basbas	Aristotle University of Thessaloniki, Greece
Grigorios Fountas	Aristotle University of Thessaloniki, Greece
Paraskevas Nikolaou	University of Cyprus, Cyprus
Drazenko Glavic	University of Belgrade, Serbia
Antonio Russo	University of Enna Kore, Italy

Econometrics and Multidimensional Evaluation of Urban Environment (EMEUE 2023)

Maria Cerreta	University of Naples Federico II, Italy
Carmelo Maria Torre	Politechnic of Bari, Italy
Pierluigi Morano	Polytechnic of Bari, Italy
Debora Anelli	Polytechnic of Bari, Italy
Francesco Tajani	Sapienza University of Rome, Italy
Simona Panaro	University of Sussex, UK

Ecosystem Services in Spatial Planning for Resilient Urban and Rural Areas (ESSP 2023)

Sabrina Lai	University of Cagliari, Italy
Francesco Scorza	University of Basilicata, Italy
Corrado Zoppi	University of Cagliari, Italy

Gerardo Carpentieri   University of Naples Federico II, Italy
Floriana Zucaro   University of Naples Federico II, Italy
Ana Clara Mourão Moura   Federal University of Minas Gerais, Brazil

Ethical AI Applications for a Human-Centered Cyber Society (EthicAI 2023)

Valentina Franzoni   University of Perugia, Italy
Alfredo Milani   University of Perugia, Italy
Jordi Vallverdu   University Autonoma Barcelona, Spain
Roberto Capobianco   Sapienza University of Rome, Italy

13th International Workshop on Future Computing System Technologies and Applications (FiSTA 2023)

Bernady Apduhan   Kyushu Sangyo University, Japan
Rafael Santos   National Institute for Space Research, Brazil

Collaborative Planning and Designing for the Future with Geospatial Applications (GeoCollab 2023)

Alenka Poplin   Iowa State University, USA
Rosanna Rivero   University of Georgia, USA
Michele Campagna   University of Cagliari, Italy
Ana Clara Mourão Moura   Federal University of Minas Gerais, Brazil

Geomatics in Agriculture and Forestry: New Advances and Perspectives (GeoForAgr 2023)

Maurizio Pollino   Italian National Agency for New Technologies,
                                Energy and Sustainable Economic
                                Development, Italy
Giuseppe Modica   University of Reggio Calabria, Italy
Marco Vizzari   University of Perugia, Italy
Salvatore Praticò   University of Reggio Calabria, Italy

Geographical Analysis, Urban Modeling, Spatial Statistics (Geog-An-Mod 2023)

Giuseppe Borruso   University of Trieste, Italy
Beniamino Murgante   University of Basilicata, Italy
Harmut Asche   Hasso-Plattner-Institut für Digital Engineering
                            Ggmbh, Germany

Geomatics for Resource Monitoring and Management (GRMM 2023)

Alessandra Capolupo   Polytechnic of Bari, Italy
Eufemia Tarantino   Polytechnic of Bari, Italy
Enrico Borgogno Mondino   University of Turin, Italy

International Workshop on Information and Knowledge in the Internet of Things (IKIT 2023)

Teresa Guarda   Peninsula State University of Santa Elena,
                            Ecuador
Modestos Stavrakis   University of the Aegean, Greece

International Workshop on Collective, Massive and Evolutionary Systems (IWCES 2023)

Alfredo Milani   University of Perugia, Italy
Rajdeep Niyogi   Indian Institute of Technology, India
Valentina Franzoni   University of Perugia, Italy

Multidimensional Evolutionary Evaluations for Transformative Approaches (MEETA 2023)

Maria Cerreta   University of Naples Federico II, Italy
Giuliano Poli   University of Naples Federico II, Italy
Ludovica Larocca   University of Naples Federico II, Italy
Chiara Mazzarella   University of Naples Federico II, Italy

Stefania Regalbuto   University of Naples Federico II, Italy
Maria Somma   University of Naples Federico II, Italy

Building Multi-dimensional Models for Assessing Complex Environmental Systems (MES 2023)

Marta Dell'Ovo   Politechnic of Milan, Italy
Vanessa Assumma   University of Bologna, Italy
Caterina Caprioli   Politechnic of Turin, Italy
Giulia Datola   Politechnic of Turin, Italy
Federico Dellanna   Politechnic of Turin, Italy
Marco Rossitti   Politechnic of Milan, Italy

Metropolitan City Lab (Metro_City_Lab 2023)

Ginevra Balletto   University of Cagliari, Italy
Luigi Mundula   University for Foreigners of Perugia, Italy
Giuseppe Borruso   University of Trieste, Italy
Jacopo Torriti   University of Reading, UK
Isabella Ligia   Metropolitan City of Cagliari, Italy

Mathematical Methods for Image Processing and Understanding (MMIPU 2023)

Ivan Gerace   University of Perugia, Italy
Gianluca Vinti   University of Perugia, Italy
Arianna Travaglini   University of Florence, Italy

Models and Indicators for Assessing and Measuring the Urban Settlement Development in the View of ZERO Net Land Take by 2050 (MOVEto0 2023)

Lucia Saganeiti   University of L'Aquila, Italy
Lorena Fiorini   University of L'Aquila, Italy
Angela Pilogallo   University of L'Aquila, Italy
Alessandro Marucci   University of L'Aquila, Italy
Francesco Zullo   University of L'Aquila, Italy

Modelling Post-Covid Cities (MPCC 2023)

Giuseppe Borruso	University of Trieste, Italy
Beniamino Murgante	University of Basilicata, Italy
Ginevra Balletto	University of Cagliari, Italy
Lucia Saganeiti	University of L'Aquila, Italy
Marco Dettori	University of Sassari, Italy

3rd Workshop on Privacy in the Cloud/Edge/IoT World (PCEIoT 2023)

Michele Mastroianni	University of Salerno, Italy
Lelio Campanile	University of Campania Luigi Vanvitelli, Italy
Mauro Iacono	University of Campania Luigi Vanvitelli, Italy

Port City Interface: Land Use, Logistic and Rear Port Area Planning (PORTUNO 2023)

Tiziana Campisi	University of Enna Kore, Italy
Socrates Basbas	Aristotle University of Thessaloniki, Greece
Efstathios Bouhouras	Aristotle University of Thessaloniki, Greece
Giovanni Tesoriere	University of Enna Kore, Italy
Elena Cocuzza	University of Catania, Italy
Gianfranco Fancello	University of Cagliari, Italy

Scientific Computing Infrastructure (SCI 2023)

Elena Stankova	St. Petersburg State University, Russia
Vladimir Korkhov	St. Petersburg University, Russia

Supply Chains, IoT, and Smart Technologies (SCIS 2023)

Ha Jin Hwang	Sunway University, South Korea
Hangkon Kim	Daegu Catholic University, South Korea
Jan Seruga	Australian Catholic University, Australia

Spatial Cognition in Urban and Regional Planning Under Risk (SCOPUR23)

Domenico Camarda	Polytechnic of Bari, Italy
Giulia Mastrodonato	Polytechnic of Bari, Italy
Stefania Santoro	Polytechnic of Bari, Italy
Maria Rosaria Stufano Melone	Polytechnic of Bari, Italy
Mauro Patano	Polytechnic of Bari, Italy

Socio-Economic and Environmental Models for Land Use Management (SEMLUM 2023)

Debora Anelli	Polytechnic of Bari, Italy
Pierluigi Morano	Polytechnic of Bari, Italy
Benedetto Manganelli	University of Basilicata, Italy
Francesco Tajani	Sapienza University of Rome, Italy
Marco Locurcio	Polytechnic of Bari, Italy
Felicia Di Liddo	Polytechnic of Bari, Italy

Ports of the Future - Smartness and Sustainability (SmartPorts 2023)

Ginevra Balletto	University of Cagliari, Italy
Gianfranco Fancello	University of Cagliari, Italy
Patrizia Serra	University of Cagliari, Italy
Agostino Bruzzone	University of Genoa, Italy
Alberto Camarero	Politechnic of Madrid, Spain
Thierry Vanelslander	University of Antwerp, Belgium

Smart Transport and Logistics - Smart Supply Chains (SmarTransLog 2023)

Giuseppe Borruso	University of Trieste, Italy
Marco Mazzarino	University of Venice, Italy
Marcello Tadini	University of Eastern Piedmont, Italy
Luigi Mundula	University for Foreigners of Perugia, Italy
Mara Ladu	University of Cagliari, Italy
Maria del Mar Munoz Leonisio	University of Cadiz, Spain

Smart Tourism (SmartTourism 2023)

Giuseppe Borruso	University of Trieste, Italy
Silvia Battino	University of Sassari, Italy
Ainhoa Amaro Garcia	University of Alcala and University of Las Palmas, Spain
Francesca Krasna	University of Trieste, Italy
Ginevra Balletto	University of Cagliari, Italy
Maria del Mar Munoz Leonisio	University of Cadiz, Spain

Sustainability Performance Assessment: Models, Approaches, and Applications Toward Interdisciplinary and Integrated Solutions (SPA 2023)

Sabrina Lai	University of Cagliari, Italy
Francesco Scorza	University of Basilicata, Italy
Jolanta Dvarioniene	Kaunas University of Technology, Lithuania
Valentin Grecu	Lucian Blaga University of Sibiu, Romania
Georgia Pozoukidou	Aristotle University of Thessaloniki, Greece

Spatial Energy Planning, City and Urban Heritage (Spatial_Energy_City 2023)

Ginevra Balletto	University of Cagliari, Italy
Mara Ladu	University of Cagliari, Italy
Emilio Ghiani	University of Cagliari, Italy
Roberto De Lotto	University of Pavia, Italy
Roberto Gerundo	University of Salerno, Italy

Specifics of Smart Cities Development in Europe (SPEED 2023)

Chiara Garau	University of Cagliari, Italy
Katarína Vitálišová	Matej Bel University, Slovakia
Paolo Nesi	University of Florence, Italy
Anna Vaňová	Matej Bel University, Slovakia
Kamila Borsekova	Matej Bel University, Slovakia
Paola Zamperlin	University of Pisa, Italy

Smart, Safe and Health Cities (SSHC 2023)

Chiara Garau	University of Cagliari, Italy
Gerardo Carpentieri	University of Naples Federico II, Italy
Floriana Zucaro	University of Naples Federico II, Italy
Aynaz Lotfata	Chicago State University, USA
Alfonso Annunziata	University of Basilicata, Italy
Diego Altafini	University of Pisa, Italy

Smart and Sustainable Island Communities (SSIC_2023)

Chiara Garau	University of Cagliari, Italy
Anastasia Stratigea	National Technical University of Athens, Greece
Yiota Theodora	National Technical University of Athens, Greece
Giulia Desogus	University of Cagliari, Italy

Theoretical and Computational Chemistry and Its Applications (TCCMA 2023)

Noelia Faginas-Lago	University of Perugia, Italy
Andrea Lombardi	University of Perugia, Italy

Transport Infrastructures for Smart Cities (TISC 2023)

Francesca Maltinti	University of Cagliari, Italy
Mauro Coni	University of Cagliari, Italy
Francesco Pinna	University of Cagliari, Italy
Chiara Garau	University of Cagliari, Italy
Nicoletta Rassu	University of Cagliari, Italy
James Rombi	University of Cagliari, Italy

Urban Regeneration: Innovative Tools and Evaluation Model (URITEM 2023)

Fabrizio Battisti	University of Florence, Italy
Giovanna Acampa	University of Florence and University of Enna Kore, Italy
Orazio Campo	La Sapienza University of Rome, Italy

Urban Space Accessibility and Mobilities (USAM 2023)

Chiara Garau	University of Cagliari, Italy
Matteo Ignaccolo	University of Catania, Italy
Michela Tiboni	University of Brescia, Italy
Francesco Pinna	University of Cagliari, Italy
Silvia Rossetti	University of Parma, Italy
Vincenza Torrisi	University of Catania, Italy
Ilaria Delponte	University of Genoa, Italy

Virtual Reality and Augmented Reality and Applications (VRA 2023)

Osvaldo Gervasi	University of Perugia, Italy
Damiano Perri	University of Florence, Italy
Marco Simonetti	University of Florence, Italy
Sergio Tasso	University of Perugia, Italy

Workshop on Advanced and Computational Methods for Earth Science Applications (WACM4ES 2023)

Luca Piroddi	University of Malta, Malta
Sebastiano Damico	University of Malta, Malta
Marilena Cozzolino	Università del Molise, Italy
Adam Gauci	University of Malta, Italy
Giuseppina Vacca	University of Cagliari, Italy
Chiara Garau	University of Cagliari, Italy

Sponsoring Organizations

ICCSA 2023 would not have been possible without the tremendous support of many organizations and institutions, for which all organizers and participants of ICCSA 2023 express their sincere gratitude:

Springer Nature Switzerland AG, Switzerland
(https://www.springer.com)

Computers Open Access Journal
(https://www.mdpi.com/journal/computers)

National Technical University of Athens, Greece
(https://www.ntua.gr/)

University of the Aegean, Greece
(https://www.aegean.edu/)

University of Perugia, Italy
(https://www.unipg.it)

University of Basilicata, Italy
(http://www.unibas.it)

Monash University, Australia
(https://www.monash.edu/)

Kyushu Sangyo University, Japan
(https://www.kyusan-u.ac.jp/)

University of Minho, Portugal
(https://www.uminho.pt/)

Universidade do Minho
Escola de Engenharia

Referees

Francesca Abastante	Turin Polytechnic, Italy
Giovanna Acampa	University of Enna Kore, Italy
Adewole Adewumi	Algonquin College, Canada
Vera Afreixo	University of Aveiro, Portugal
Riad Aggoune	Luxembourg Institute of Science and Technology, Luxembourg
Akshat Agrawal	Amity University Haryana, India
Waseem Ahmad	National Institute of Technology Karnataka, India
Oylum Alatlı	Ege University, Turkey
Abraham Alfa	Federal University of Technology Minna, Nigeria
Diego Altafini	University of Pisa, Italy
Filipe Alvelos	University of Minho, Portugal
Marina Alexandra Pedro Andrade	University Institute of Lisbon, Portugal
Debora Anelli	Polytechnic University of Bari, Italy
Mariarosaria Angrisano	Pegaso University, Italy
Alfonso Annunziata	University of Cagliari, Italy
Magarò Antonio	Sapienza University of Rome, Italy
Bernady Apduhan	Kyushu Sangyo University, Japan
Jonathan Apeh	Covenant University, Nigeria
Daniela Ascenzi	University of Trento, Italy
Vanessa Assumma	University of Bologna, Italy
Maria Fernanda Augusto	Bitrum Research Center, Spain
Marco Baioletti	University of Perugia, Italy

Ginevra Balletto	University of Cagliari, Italy
Carlos Balsa	Polytechnic Institute of Bragança, Portugal
Benedetto Barabino	University of Brescia, Italy
Simona Barbaro	University of Palermo, Italy
Sebastiano Barbieri	Turin Polytechnic, Italy
Kousik Barik	University of Alcala, Spain
Alice Barreca	Turin Polytechnic, Italy
Socrates Basbas	Aristotle University of Thessaloniki, Greece
Rosaria Battarra	National Research Council, Italy
Silvia Battino	University of Sassari, Italy
Fabrizio Battisti	University of Florence, Italy
Yaroslav Bazaikin	Jan Evangelista Purkyne University, Czech Republic
Ranjan Kumar Behera	Indian Institute of Information Technology, India
Simone Belli	Complutense University of Madrid, Spain
Oscar Bellini	Polytechnic University of Milan, Italy
Giulio Biondi	University of Perugia, Italy
Adriano Bisello	Eurac Research, Italy
Semen Bochkov	Ulyanovsk State Technical University, Russia
Alexander Bogdanov	St. Petersburg State University, Russia
Letizia Bollini	Free University of Bozen, Italy
Giuseppe Borruso	University of Trieste, Italy
Marilisa Botte	University of Naples Federico II, Italy
Ana Cristina Braga	University of Minho, Portugal
Frederico Branco	University of Trás-os-Montes and Alto Douro, Portugal
Jorge Buele	Indoamérica Technological University, Ecuador
Datzania Lizeth Burgos	Peninsula State University of Santa Elena, Ecuador
Isabel Cacao	University of Aveiro, Portugal
Francesco Calabrò	Mediterranea University of Reggio Calabria, Italy
Rogerio Calazan	Institute of Sea Studies Almirante Paulo Moreira, Brazil
Lelio Campanile	University of Campania Luigi Vanvitelli, Italy
Tiziana Campisi	University of Enna Kore, Italy
Orazio Campo	University of Rome La Sapienza, Italy
Caterina Caprioli	Turin Polytechnic, Italy
Gerardo Carpentieri	University of Naples Federico II, Italy
Martina Carra	University of Brescia, Italy
Barbara Caselli	University of Parma, Italy
Danny Casprini	Politechnic of Milan, Italy

Omar Fernando Castellanos Balleteros	Peninsula State University of Santa Elena, Ecuador
Arcangelo Castiglione	University of Salerno, Italy
Giulio Cavana	Turin Polytechnic, Italy
Maria Cerreta	University of Naples Federico II, Italy
Sabarathinam Chockalingam	Institute for Energy Technology, Norway
Luis Enrique Chuquimarca Jimenez	Peninsula State University of Santa Elena, Ecuador
Birol Ciloglugil	Ege University, Turkey
Elena Cocuzza	Univesity of Catania, Italy
Emanuele Colica	University of Malta, Malta
Mauro Coni	University of Cagliari, Italy
Simone Corrado	University of Basilicata, Italy
Elisete Correia	University of Trás-os-Montes and Alto Douro, Portugal
Florbela Correia	Polytechnic Institute Viana do Castelo, Portugal
Paulo Cortez	University of Minho, Portugal
Martina Corti	Politechnic of Milan, Italy
Lino Costa	Universidade do Minho, Portugal
Cecília Maria Vasconcelos Costa e Castro	University of Minho, Portugal
Alfredo Cuzzocrea	University of Calabria, Italy
Sebastiano D'amico	University of Malta, Malta
Maria Danese	National Research Council, Italy
Gianni Dangelo	University of Salerno, Italy
Ana Daniel	Aveiro University, Portugal
Giulia Datola	Politechnic of Milan, Italy
Regina De Almeida	University of Trás-os-Montes and Alto Douro, Portugal
Maria Stella De Biase	University of Campania Luigi Vanvitelli, Italy
Elise De Doncker	Western Michigan University, USA
Luiza De Macedo Mourelle	State University of Rio de Janeiro, Brazil
Itamir De Morais Barroca Filho	Federal University of Rio Grande do Norte, Brazil
Pierfrancesco De Paola	University of Naples Federico II, Italy
Francesco De Pascale	University of Turin, Italy
Manuela De Ruggiero	University of Calabria, Italy
Alexander Degtyarev	St. Petersburg State University, Russia
Federico Dellanna	Turin Polytechnic, Italy
Marta Dellovo	Politechnic of Milan, Italy
Bashir Derradji	Sfax University, Tunisia
Giulia Desogus	University of Cagliari, Italy
Frank Devai	London South Bank University, UK

Piero Di Bonito	University of Campania Luigi Vanvitelli, Italy
Chiara Di Dato	University of L'Aquila, Italy
Michele Di Giovanni	University of Campania Luigi Vanvitelli, Italy
Felicia Di Liddo	Polytechnic University of Bari, Italy
Joana Dias	University of Coimbra, Portugal
Luigi Dolores	University of Salerno, Italy
Marco Donatelli	Università of Insubria, Italy
Aziz Dursun	Virginia Tech University, USA
Jaroslav Dvořak	Klaipeda University, Lithuania
Wolfgang Erb	University of Padova, Italy
Maurizio Francesco Errigo	University of Enna Kore, Italy
Noelia Faginas-Lago	University of Perugia, Italy
Maria Irene Falcao	University of Minho, Portugal
Stefano Falcinelli	University of Perugia, Italy
Grazia Fattoruso	Italian National Agency for New Technologies, Energy and Sustainable Economic Development, Italy
Sara Favargiotti	University of Trento, Italy
Marcin Feltynowski	University of Lodz, Poland
António Fernandes	Polytechnic Institute of Bragança, Portugal
Florbela P. Fernandes	Polytechnic Institute of Bragança, Portugal
Paula Odete Fernandes	Polytechnic Institute of Bragança, Portugal
Luis Fernandez-Sanz	University of Alcala, Spain
Maria Eugenia Ferrao	University of Beira Interior and University of Lisbon, Portugal
Luís Ferrás	University of Minho, Portugal
Angela Ferreira	Polytechnic Institute of Bragança, Portugal
Maddalena Ferretti	Politechnic of Marche, Italy
Manuel Carlos Figueiredo	University of Minho, Portugal
Fabrizio Finucci	Roma Tre University, Italy
Ugo Fiore	University Pathenope of Naples, Italy
Lorena Fiorini	University of L'Aquila, Italy
Valentina Franzoni	Perugia University, Italy
Adelaide Freitas	University of Aveiro, Portugal
Kirill Gadylshin	Russian Academy of Sciences, Russia
Andrea Gallo	University of Trieste, Italy
Luciano Galone	University of Malta, Malta
Chiara Garau	University of Cagliari, Italy
Ernesto Garcia Para	Universidad del País Vasco, Spain
Rachele Vanessa Gatto	Università della Basilicata, Italy
Marina Gavrilova	University of Calgary, Canada
Georgios Georgiadis	Aristotle University of Thessaloniki, Greece

Ivan Gerace	University of Perugia, Italy
Osvaldo Gervasi	University of Perugia, Italy
Alfonso Giancotti	Sapienza University of Rome, Italy
Andrea Gioia	Politechnic of Bari, Italy
Giacomo Giorgi	University of Perugia, Italy
Salvatore Giuffrida	Università di Catania, Italy
A. Manuela Gonçalves	University of Minho, Portugal
Angela Gorgoglione	University of the Republic, Uruguay
Yusuke Gotoh	Okayama University, Japan
Mariolina Grasso	University of Enna Kore, Italy
Silvana Grillo	University of Cagliari, Italy
Teresa Guarda	Universidad Estatal Peninsula de Santa Elena, Ecuador
Eduardo Guerra	Free University of Bozen-Bolzano, Italy
Carmen Guida	University of Napoli Federico II, Italy
Kemal Güven Gülen	Namık Kemal University, Turkey
Malgorzata Hanzl	Technical University of Lodz, Poland
Peter Hegedus	University of Szeged, Hungary
Syeda Sumbul Hossain	Daffodil International University, Bangladesh
Mustafa Inceoglu	Ege University, Turkey
Federica Isola	University of Cagliari, Italy
Seifedine Kadry	Noroff University College, Norway
Yeliz Karaca	University of Massachusetts Chan Medical School and Massachusetts Institute of Technology, USA
Harun Karsli	Bolu Abant Izzet Baysal University, Turkey
Tayana Khachkova	Russian Academy of Sciences, Russia
Manju Khari	Jawaharlal Nehru University, India
Vladimir Korkhov	Saint Petersburg State University, Russia
Dionisia Koutsi	National Technical University of Athens, Greece
Tomonori Kouya	Shizuoka Institute of Science and Technology, Japan
Nataliia Kulabukhova	Saint Petersburg State University, Russia
Anisha Kumari	National Institute of Technology, India
Ludovica La Rocca	University of Napoli Federico II, Italy
Mara Ladu	University of Cagliari, Italy
Sabrina Lai	University of Cagliari, Italy
Mohamed Laib	Luxembourg Institute of Science and Technology, Luxembourg
Giuseppe Francesco Cesare Lama	University of Napoli Federico II, Italy
Isabella Maria Lami	Turin Polytechnic, Italy
Chien Sing Lee	Sunway University, Malaysia

Marcelo Leon	Ecotec University, Ecuador
Federica Leone	University of Cagliari, Italy
Barbara Lino	University of Palermo, Italy
Vadim Lisitsa	Russian Academy of Sciences, Russia
Carla Lobo	Portucalense University, Portugal
Marco Locurcio	Polytechnic University of Bari, Italy
Claudia Loggia	University of KwaZulu-Natal, South Africa
Andrea Lombardi	University of Perugia, Italy
Isabel Lopes	Polytechnic Institut of Bragança, Portugal
Immacolata Lorè	Mediterranean University of Reggio Calabria, Italy
Vanda Lourenco	Nova University of Lisbon, Portugal
Giorgia Malavasi	Turin Polytechnic, Italy
Francesca Maltinti	University of Cagliari, Italy
Luca Mancini	University of Perugia, Italy
Marcos Mandado	University of Vigo, Spain
Benedetto Manganelli	University of Basilicata, Italy
Krassimir Markov	Institute of Electric Engineering and Informatics, Bulgaria
Enzo Martinelli	University of Salerno, Italy
Fiammetta Marulli	University of Campania Luigi Vanvitelli, Italy
Antonino Marvuglia	Luxembourg Institute of Science and Technology, Luxembourg
Rytis Maskeliunas	Kaunas University of Technology, Lithuania
Michele Mastroianni	University of Salerno, Italy
Hideo Matsufuru	High Energy Accelerator Research Organization, Japan
D'Apuzzo Mauro	University of Cassino and Southern Lazio, Italy
Luis Mazon	Bitrum Research Group, Spain
Chiara Mazzarella	University Federico II, Naples, Italy
Beatrice Mecca	Turin Polytechnic, Italy
Umberto Mecca	Turin Polytechnic, Italy
Paolo Mengoni	Hong Kong Baptist University, China
Gaetano Messina	Mediterranean University of Reggio Calabria, Italy
Alfredo Milani	University of Perugia, Italy
Alessandra Milesi	University of Cagliari, Italy
Richard Millham	Durban University of Technology, South Africa
Fernando Miranda	Universidade do Minho, Portugal
Biswajeeban Mishra	University of Szeged, Hungary
Giuseppe Modica	University of Reggio Calabria, Italy
Pierluigi Morano	Polytechnic University of Bari, Italy

Filipe Mota Pinto	Polytechnic Institute of Leiria, Portugal
Maria Mourao	Polytechnic Institute of Viana do Castelo, Portugal
Eugenio Muccio	University of Naples Federico II, Italy
Beniamino Murgante	University of Basilicata, Italy
Rocco Murro	Sapienza University of Rome, Italy
Giuseppe Musolino	Mediterranean University of Reggio Calabria, Italy
Nadia Nedjah	State University of Rio de Janeiro, Brazil
Juraj Nemec	Masaryk University, Czech Republic
Andreas Nikiforiadis	Aristotle University of Thessaloniki, Greece
Silvio Nocera	IUAV University of Venice, Italy
Roseline Ogundokun	Kaunas University of Technology, Lithuania
Emma Okewu	University of Alcala, Spain
Serena Olcuire	Sapienza University of Rome, Italy
Irene Oliveira	University Trás-os-Montes and Alto Douro, Portugal
Samson Oruma	Ostfold University College, Norway
Antonio Pala	University of Cagliari, Italy
Maria Panagiotopoulou	National Technical University of Athens, Greece
Simona Panaro	University of Sussex Business School, UK
Jay Pancham	Durban University of Technology, South Africa
Eric Pardede	La Trobe University, Australia
Hyun Kyoo Park	Ministry of National Defense, South Korea
Damiano Perri	University of Florence, Italy
Quoc Trung Pham	Ho Chi Minh City University of Technology, Vietnam
Claudio Piferi	University of Florence, Italy
Angela Pilogallo	University of L'Aquila, Italy
Francesco Pinna	University of Cagliari, Italy
Telmo Pinto	University of Coimbra, Portugal
Luca Piroddi	University of Malta, Malta
Francesco Pittau	Politechnic of Milan, Italy
Giuliano Poli	Università Federico II di Napoli, Italy
Maurizio Pollino	Italian National Agency for New Technologies, Energy and Sustainable Economic Development, Italy
Vijay Prakash	University of Malta, Malta
Salvatore Praticò	Mediterranean University of Reggio Calabria, Italy
Carlotta Quagliolo	Turin Polytechnic, Italy
Garrisi Raffaele	Operations Center for Cyber Security, Italy
Mariapia Raimondo	Università della Campania Luigi Vanvitelli, Italy

Bruna Ramos	Universidade Lusíada Norte, Portugal
Nicoletta Rassu	University of Cagliari, Italy
Roberta Ravanelli	University of Roma La Sapienza, Italy
Pier Francesco Recchi	University of Naples Federico II, Italy
Stefania Regalbuto	University of Naples Federico II, Italy
Rommel Regis	Saint Joseph's University, USA
Marco Reis	University of Coimbra, Portugal
Jerzy Respondek	Silesian University of Technology, Poland
Isabel Ribeiro	Polytechnic Institut of Bragança, Portugal
Albert Rimola	Autonomous University of Barcelona, Spain
Corrado Rindone	Mediterranean University of Reggio Calabria, Italy
Maria Rocco	Roma Tre University, Italy
Ana Maria A. C. Rocha	University of Minho, Portugal
Fabio Rocha	Universidade Federal de Sergipe, Brazil
Humberto Rocha	University of Coimbra, Portugal
Maria Clara Rocha	Politechnic Institut of Coimbra, Portual
Carlos Rodrigues	Polytechnic Institut of Bragança, Portugal
Diana Rolando	Turin Polytechnic, Italy
James Rombi	University of Cagliari, Italy
Evgeniy Romenskiy	Russian Academy of Sciences, Russia
Marzio Rosi	University of Perugia, Italy
Silvia Rossetti	University of Parma, Italy
Marco Rossitti	Politechnic of Milan, Italy
Antonio Russo	University of Enna, Italy
Insoo Ryu	MoaSoftware, South Korea
Yeonseung Ryu	Myongji University, South Korea
Lucia Saganeiti	University of L'Aquila, Italy
Valentina Santarsiero	University of Basilicata, Italy
Luigi Santopietro	University of Basilicata, Italy
Rafael Santos	National Institute for Space Research, Brazil
Valentino Santucci	University for Foreigners of Perugia, Italy
Alessandra Saponieri	University of Salento, Italy
Mattia Scalas	Turin Polytechnic, Italy
Francesco Scorza	University of Basilicata, Italy
Ester Scotto Di Perta	University of Napoli Federico II, Italy
Nicoletta Setola	University of Florence, Italy
Ricardo Severino	University of Minho, Portugal
Angela Silva	Polytechnic Institut of Viana do Castelo, Portugal
Carina Silva	Polytechnic of Lisbon, Portugal
Marco Simonetti	University of Florence, Italy
Sergey Solovyev	Russian Academy of Sciences, Russia

Maria Somma	University of Naples Federico II, Italy
Changgeun Son	Ministry of National Defense, South Korea
Alberico Sonnessa	Polytechnic of Bari, Italy
Inês Sousa	University of Minho, Portugal
Lisete Sousa	University of Lisbon, Portugal
Elena Stankova	Saint-Petersburg State University, Russia
Modestos Stavrakis	University of the Aegean, Greece
Flavio Stochino	University of Cagliari, Italy
Anastasia Stratigea	National Technical University of Athens, Greece
Yue Sun	European XFEL GmbH, Germany
Anthony Suppa	Turin Polytechnic, Italy
David Taniar	Monash University, Australia
Rodrigo Tapia McClung	Centre for Research in Geospatial Information Sciences, Mexico
Tarek Teba	University of Portsmouth, UK
Ana Paula Teixeira	University of Trás-os-Montes and Alto Douro, Portugal
Tengku Adil Tengku Izhar	Technological University MARA, Malaysia
Maria Filomena Teodoro	University of Lisbon and Portuguese Naval Academy, Portugal
Yiota Theodora	National Technical University of Athens, Greece
Elena Todella	Turin Polytechnic, Italy
Graça Tomaz	Polytechnic Institut of Guarda, Portugal
Anna Tonazzini	National Research Council, Italy
Dario Torregrossa	Goodyear, Luxembourg
Francesca Torrieri	University of Naples Federico II, Italy
Vincenza Torrisi	University of Catania, Italy
Nikola Tosic	Polytechnic University of Catalonia, Spain
Vincenzo Totaro	Polytechnic University of Bari, Italy
Arianna Travaglini	University of Florence, Italy
António Trigo	Polytechnic of Coimbra, Portugal
Giuseppe A. Trunfio	University of Sassari, Italy
Toshihiro Uchibayashi	Kyushu University, Japan
Piero Ugliengo	University of Torino, Italy
Jordi Vallverdu	University Autonoma Barcelona, Spain
Gianmarco Vanuzzo	University of Perugia, Italy
Dmitry Vasyunin	T-Systems, Russia
Laura Verde	University of Campania Luigi Vanvitelli, Italy
Giulio Vignoli	University of Cagliari, Italy
Gianluca Vinti	University of Perugia, Italy
Katarína Vitálišová	Matej Bel University, Slovak Republic
Daniel Mark Vitiello	University of Cagliari

Plenary Lectures

A Multiscale Planning Concept for Sustainable Metropolitan Development

Pierre Frankhauser

Théma, Université de Franche-Comté, 32, rue Mégevand, 20030 Besançon, France
pierre.frankhauser@univ-fcomte.fr

Keywords: Sustainable metropolitan development · Multiscale approach · Urban modelling

Urban sprawl has often been pointed out as having an important negative impact on environment and climate. Residential zones have grown up in what were initially rural areas, located far from employment areas and often lacking shopping opportunities, public services and public transportation. Hence urban sprawl increased car-traffic flows, generating pollution and increasing energy consumption. New road axes consume considerable space and weaken biodiversity by reducing and cutting natural areas. A return to "compact cities" or "dense cities" has often been contemplated as the most efficient way to limit urban sprawl. However, the real impact of density on car use is less clear-cut (Daneshpour and Shakibamanesh 2011). Let us emphasize that moreover climate change will increase the risk of heat islands on an intra-urban scale. This prompts a more nuanced reflection on how urban fabrics should be structured.

Moreover, urban planning cannot ignore social demand. Lower land prices in rural areas, often put forward by economists, is not the only reason of urban sprawl. The quality of the residential environment comes into play, too, through features like noise, pollution, landscape quality, density etc. Schwanen et al. (2004) observe for the Netherlands that households preferring a quiet residential environment and individual housing with a garden will not accept densification, which might even lead them to move to lower-density rural areas even farther away from jobs and shopping amenities. Many scholars emphasize the importance of green amenities for residential environments and report the importance of easy access to leisure areas (Guo and Bhat 2002). Vegetation in the residential environment has an important impact on health and well-being (Lafortezza et al. 2009).

We present here the Fractalopolis concept which we developed in the frame of several research projects and which aims reconciling environmental and social issues (Bonin et al., 2020; Frankhauser 2021; Frankhauser et al. 2018). This concept introduces a multiscale approach based on multifractal geometry for conceiving spatial development for metropolitan areas. For taking into account social demand we refer to the fundamental work of Max-Neef et al. (1991) based on Maslow's work about basic human needs. He introduces the concept of satisfiers assigned to meet the basic needs of "Subsistence, Protection, Affection, Understanding, Participation, Idleness, Creation, Identity and Freedom". Satisfiers thus become the link between the needs of everyone and society and may depend on the cultural context. We consider their importance, their location and their accessibility and we rank the needs according to their importance for individuals or households. In order to enjoy a good quality of life and to shorten trips and to reduce automobile use, it seems important for satisfiers of daily needs to be easily accessible. Hence, we consider the purchase rate when reflecting on the implementation of shops which is reminiscent of central place theory.

The second important feature is taking care of environment and biodiversity by avoiding fragmentation of green space (Ekren and Arslan 2022) which must benefit, moreover, of a good accessibility, as pointed out. These areas must, too, ply the role of cooling areas ensuring ventilation of urbanized areas (Kuttler et al. 1998).

For integrating these different objectives, we propose a concept for developing spatial configurations of metropolitan areas designed which is based on multifractal geometry. It allows combining different issues across a large range of scales in a coherent way. These issues include:

- providing easy access to a large array of amenities to meet social demand;
- promoting the use of public transportation and soft modes instead of automobile use;
- preserving biodiversity and improving the local climate.

The concept distinguishes development zones localized in the vicinity of a nested and hierarchized system of public transport axes. The highest ranked center offers all types of amenities, whereas lower ranked centers lack the highest ranked amenities. The lowest ranked centers just offer the amenities for daily needs. A coding system allows distinguishing the centers according to their rank.

Each subset of central places is in some sense autonomous, since they are not linked by transportation axes to subcenters of the same order. This allows to preserve a linked system of green corridors penetrating the development zones across scales avoiding the fragmentation of green areas and ensuring a good accessibility to recreational areas.

The spatial model is completed by a population distribution model which globally follows the same hierarchical logic. However, we weakened the strong fractal order what allows to conceive a more or less polycentric spatial system.

We can adapt the theoretical concept easily to real world situation without changing the underlying multiscale logic. A decision support system has been developed allowing to simulate development scenarios and to evaluate them. The evaluation procedure is based on fuzzy evaluation of distance acceptance for accessing to the different types of amenities according to the ranking of needs. We used for evaluation data issued from a great set of French planning documents like Master plans. We show an example how the software package can be used concretely.

References

Bonin, O., et al.: Projet SOFT sobriété énergétique par les formes urbaines et le transport (Research Report No. 1717C0003; p. 214). ADEME (2020)

Daneshpour, A., Shakibamanesh, A.: Compact city; dose it create an obligatory context for urban sustainability? Int. J. Archit. Eng. Urban Plann. 21(2), 110–118 (2011)

Ekren, E., Arslan, M.: Functions of greenways as an ecologically-based planning strategy. In: Çakır, M., Tuğluer, M., Fırat Örs, P.: Architectural Sciences and Ecology, pp. 134–156. Iksad Publications (2022)

Frankhauser, P.: Fractalopolis—a fractal concept for the sustainable development of metropolitan areas. In: Sajous, P., Bertelle, C. (eds.) Complex Systems, Smart Territories and Mobility, pp. 15–50. Springer, Cham (2021). https://doi.org/10.1007/978-3-030-59302-5_2

Frankhauser, P., Tannier, C., Vuidel, G., Houot, H.: An integrated multifractal modelling to urban and regional planning. Comput. Environ. Urban Syst. 67(1), 132–146 (2018). https://doi.org/10.1016/j.compenvurbsys.2017.09.011

Guo, J., Bhat, C.: Residential location modeling: accommodating sociodemographic, school quality and accessibility effects. University of Texas, Austin (2002)

Kuttler, W., Dütemeyer, D., Barlag, A.-B.: Influence of regional and local winds on urban ventilation in Cologne, Germany. Meteorologische Zeitschrift, 77–87 (1998) https://doi.org/10.1127/metz/7/1998/77

Lafortezza, R., Carrus, G., Sanesi, G., Davies, C.: Benefits and well-being perceived by people visiting green spaces in periods of heat stress. Urban For. Urban Green. 8(2), 97–108 (2009)

Max-Neef, M. A., Elizalde, A., Hopenhayn, M.: Human scale development: conception, application and further reflections. The Apex Press (1991)

Schwanen, T., Dijst, M., Dieleman, F. M.: Policies for urban form and their impact on travel: The Netherlands experience. Urban Stud. 41(3), 579–603 (2004)

Graph Drawing and Network Visualization – An Overview – (Keynote Speech)

Giuseppe Liotta

Dipartimento di Ingegneria, Università degli Studi di Perugia, Italy
giuseppe.liotta@unipg.it

Abstract. Graph Drawing and Network visualization supports the exploration, analysis, and communication of relational data arising in a variety of application domains: from bioinformatics to software engineering, from social media to cyber-security, from data bases to powergrid systems. Aim of this keynote speech is to introduce this thriving research area, highlighting some of its basic approaches and pointing to some promising research directions.

1 Introduction

Graph Drawing and Network Visualization is at the intersection of different disciplines and it combines topics that traditionally belong to theoretical computer science with methods and approaches that characterize more applied disciplines. Namely, it can be related to Graph Algorithms, Geometric Graph Theory and Geometric computing, Combinatorial Optimization, Experimental Analysis, User Studies, System Design and Development, and Human Computer Interaction. This combination of theory and practice is well reflected in the flagship conference of the area, the *International Symposium on Graph Drawing and Network Visualization*, that has two tracks, one focusing on combinatorial and algorithmic aspects and the other on the design of network visualization systems and interfaces. The conference is now at its 31st edition; a full list of the symposia and their proceedings, published by Springer in the LNCS series can be found at the URL: http://www.graphdrawing.org/.

Aim of this short paper is to outline the content of my Keynote Speech at ICCSA 2023, which will be referred to as the "Talk" in the rest of the paper. The talk will introduce the field of Graph Drawing and Network Visualization to a broad audience, with the goal to not only present some key methodological and technological aspects, but also point to some unexplored or partially explored research directions. The rest of this short paper briefly outlines the content of the talk and provides some references that can be a starting point for researchers interested in working on Graph Drawing and Network Visualization.

2 Why Visualize Networks?

Back in 1973 the famous statistician Francis Anscombe, gave a convincing example of why visualization is fundamental component of data analysis. The example is known as the *Anscombe's quartet* [3] and it consists of four sets of 11 points each that are almost identical in terms of the basic statistic properties of their x– and y– coordinates. Namely the mean values and the variance of x and y are exactly the same in the four sets, while the correlation of x and y and the linear regression are the same up to the second decimal. In spite of this statistical similarity, the data look very different when displayed in the Euclidean plane which leads to the conclusion that they correspond to significantly different phenomena. Figure 1 reports the four sets of Anscombe's quartet. After fifty years, with the arrival of AI-based technologies and the need of explaining and interpreting machine-driven suggestions before making strategic decision, the lesson of Anscombe's quartet has not just kept but even increased its relevance.

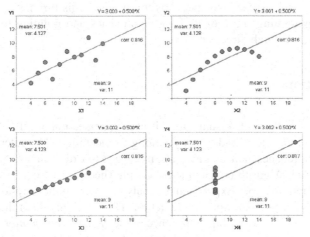

Fig. 1. The four point sets in Anscombe's quartet [3]; the figure also reports statistical values of the x and y variables.

As a matter of fact, nowadays the need of visualization systems goes beyond the verification of the accuracy of some statistical analysis on a set of scattered data. Recent technological advances have generated torrents of data that area relational in nature and typically modeled as networks: the nodes of the networks store the features of the data and the edges of the networks describe the semantic relationships between the data features. Such networked data sets (whose algebraic underlying structure is a called graph in discrete mathematics) arise in a variety of application domains including, for example, Systems Biology, Social Network Analysis, Software Engineering, Networking, Data Bases, Homeland Security, and Business Intelligence. In these (and many other) contexts, systems that support the visual analysis of networks and graphs play a central role in critical decision making processes. These are human-in-the-loop processes where the continuous interaction between humans (decision makers) and data mining or optimization algorithms (AI/ML components) supports the data exploration, the development of verifiable theories about the data, and the extraction of new knowledge that is used to make strategic choices. A seminal book by Keim et al. [33] schematically represents the human-in-the-loop approach to making sense of networked data sets as in Fig. 2. See also [46–49].

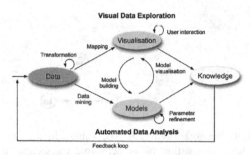

Fig. 2. Sense-making/knowledge generation loop. This conceptual interaction model between human analysts and network visualization system is at the basis of network visual analytics system design [33].

To make a concrete application example of the analysis of a network by interacting with its visualization, consider the problem of contrasting financial crimes such as money laundering or tax evasion. These crimes are based on relevant volumes of financial transactions to conceal the identity, the source, or the destination of illegally gained money. Also, the adopted patterns to pursue the illegal goals continuously change to conceal the crimes. Therefore, contrasting them requires special investigation units which must analyze very large and highly dynamic data sets and discover relationships between different subjects to untangle complex fraudulent plots. The investigative cycle begins with data collection and filtering; it is then followed by modeling the data as a social network (also called *financial activity network* in this context) to which different data mining and data analytic methods are applied, including graph pattern matching, social network analysis, machine learning, and information diffusion. By the network visualization system detectives can interactively explore the data, gain insight and make new hypotheses about possible criminal activities, verify the hypotheses by asking the system to provide more details about specific portions of the network, refine previous outputs, and eventually gain new knowledge. Figure 3 illustrates a small financial activity network where, by means of the interaction between an officer of the Italian Revenue Agency and the MALDIVE system described in [10] a fraudulent pattern has been identified. Precisely, the tax officer has encoded a risky relational scheme among taxpayers into a suspicious graph pattern; in response, the system has made a search in the taxpayer network and it has returned one such pattern. See, e.g., [9, 11, 14, 18, 38] for more papers and references about visual analytic applications to contrasting financial crimes.

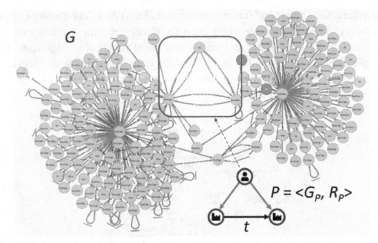

Fig. 3. A financial activity network from [10]. The pattern in the figure represents a SuppliesFromAssociated scheme, consisting of an economic transaction and two shareholding relationships.

3 Facets of Graph Drawing and Network Visualization

The Talk overviews some of the fundamental facets that characterize the research in Graph Drawing and Network Visualization. Namely:

– Graph drawing metaphors: Depending on the application context, different metaphors can be used to represent a relational data set modeled as a graph. The talk will briefly recall the matrix representation, the space filling representation, the contact representation, and the node-link representation which is, by far, the most commonly used (see, e.g., [43]).
– Interaction paradigms: Different interaction paradigms have different impacts on the sense-making process of the user about the visualized network. The Talk will go through the full-view, top-down, bottom-up, incremental, and narrative paradigms. Pros and cons will be highlighted for each approach, also by means of examples and applications. The discussion of the top-down interaction paradigm will also consider the hybrid visualization models (see, e.g., [2, 24, 26, 28, 39]) while the discussion about the incremental paradigm will focus on research about graph storyplans (see, e.g., [4, 6, 7]).
– Graph drawing algorithms: Three main algorithmic approaches will be reviewed, namely the force-directed, the layered), and the planarization-based approach; see, e.g., [5]. We shall also make some remarks about FPT algorithms for graph drawing (see, e.g., [8, 19, 20, 25, 27, 40, 53]) and about how the optimization challenges vary when it is assumed that the input has or does not have a fixed combinatorial embedding (see, e.g., [12, 13, 16, 17, 23]).
– Experimental analysis and user-studies: The Talk will mostly compare two models to define and experimentally validate those optimization goals that define a "readable"

network visualization, i.e. a visualization that in a given application context can easily convey the structure of a relational data set so to guarantee efficiency both in its visual exploration and in the elaboration of new knowledge. Special focus will be given to a set emerging optimization goals related to edge crossings that are currently investigated in the graph drawing and network visualization community unedr the name of "graph drawing beyond planarity" (see, e.g., [1, 15, 29, 35]).

The talk shall also point to some promising research directions, including: (i) Extend the body of papers devoted to user-studies that compare the impact of different graph drawing metaphors on the user perception. (ii) Extend the study of interaction paradigms to extended reality environments (see, e.g., [21, 30, 36, 37]); (iii) Engineer the FPT algorithms for graph drawing and experimentally compare their performances with exact or approximate solutions; and (iv) Develop new algorithmic fameworks in the context of graph drawing beyond planarity.

We conclude this short paper with pointers to publication venues and key references that can be browsed by researchers interested in the fascinating field of Graph Drawing and Network Visualization.

4 Pointers to Publication venues and Key References

A limited list of conferences where Graph Drawing and Network Visualization papers are regularly part of the program includes *IEEE VIS, EuroVis, SoCG, ISAAC, ACM-SIAM SODA, WADS,* and *WG.* Among the many journals where several Graph Drawing and Network Visualization papers have appeared during the last three decades we recall *IEEE Transactions on Visualization and Computer Graphs, SIAM Journal of Computing, Computer Graphics Forum, Journal of Computer and System Sciences, Algorithmica, Journal of Graph Algorithms and Applications, Theoretical Computer Science, Information Sciences, Discrete and Computational Geometry, Computational Geometry: Theory and Applications, ACM Computing Surveys,* and *Computer Science Review.* A limited list of books, surveys, or papers that contain interesting algorithmic challenges on Graph Drawing and Network Visualization include [5, 15, 22, 29, 31–35, 41–45, 50–52].

References

1. Angelini, P., et al.: Simple k-planar graphs are simple (k+1)-quasiplanar. J. Comb. Theory, Ser. B, **142**, 1–35 (2020)
2. Angori, L., Didimo, W., Montecchiani, F., Pagliuca, D., Tappini, A.: Hybrid graph visualizations with chordlink: Algorithms, experiments, and applications. IEEE Trans. Vis. Comput. Graph. **28**(2), 1288–1300 (2022)
3. Anscombe, F.J.: Graphs in statistical analysis. Am. Stat. **27**(1), 17–21 (1973)
4. Di Battista, G., et al.: Small point-sets supporting graph stories. In: Angelini, P., von Hanxleden, R. (eds.) Graph Drawing and Network Visualization. GD 2022, LNCS, vol. 13764, pp. 289–303. Springer, Cham (2022). https://doi.org/10.1007/978-3-031-22203-0_21

5. Battista, G.D., Eades, P., Tamassia, R., Tollis, I.G.: Graph Drawing: Algorithms for the Visualization of Graphs. Prentice-Hall, Hoboken (1999)
6. Binucci, C., et al.: On the complexity of the storyplan problem. In: Angelini, P., von Hanxleden, R. (eds.) Graph Drawing and Network Visualization. GD 2022. LNCS, vol. 13764, pp. 304 318. Springer, Cham (2023). https://doi.org/10.1007/978-3-031-22203-0_22
7. Borrazzo, M., Lozzo, G.D., Battista, G.D., Frati, F., Patrignani, M.: Graph stories in small area. J. Graph Algorithms Appl. **24**(3), 269–292 (2020)
8. Chaplick, S., Giacomo, E.D., Frati, F., Ganian, R., Raftopoulou, C.N., Simonov, K.: Parameterized algorithms for upward planarity. In: Goaoc, X., Kerber, M. (eds.) 38th International Symposium on Computational Geometry, SoCG 2022, June 7–10, 2022, Berlin, Germany, LIPIcs, vol. 224, pp. 26:1–26:16. Schloss Dagstuhl - Leibniz-Zentrum für Informatik (2022)
9. Didimo, W., Giamminonni, L., Liotta, G., Montecchiani, F., Pagliuca, D.: A visual analytics system to support tax evasion discovery. Decis. Support Syst. **110**, 71–83 (2018)
10. Didimo, W., Grilli, L., Liotta, G., Menconi, L., Montecchiani, F., Pagliuca, D.: Combining network visualization and data mining for tax risk assessment. IEEE Access **8**, 16073–16086 (2020)
11. Didimo, W., Grilli, L., Liotta, G., Montecchiani, F., Pagliuca, D.: Visual querying and analysis of temporal fiscal networks. Inf. Sci. **505**, 406–421 (2019)
12. W. Didimo, M. Kaufmann, G. Liotta, and G. Ortali. Didimo, W., Kaufmann, M., Liotta, G., Ortali, G.: Rectilinear planarity testing of plane series-parallel graphs in linear time. In: Auber, D., Valtr, P. (eds.) Graph Drawing and Network Visualization. GD 2020. LNCS, vol. 12590, pp. 436–449. Springer, Cham (2020). https://doi.org/10.1007/978-3-030-68766-3_34
13. Didimo, W., Kaufmann, M., Liotta, G., Ortali, G.: Rectilinear planarity of partial 2-trees. In: Angelini, P., von Hanxleden, R. (eds.) Graph Drawing and Network Visualization. GD 2022. LNCS, vol. 13764, pp. 157–172. Springer, Cham (2023). https://doi.org/10.1007/978-3-031-22203-0_12
14. Didimo, W., Liotta, G., Montecchiani, F.: Network visualization for financial crime detection. J. Vis. Lang. Comput. **25**(4), 433–451 (2014)
15. Didimo, W., Liotta, G., Montecchiani, F.: A survey on graph drawing beyond planarity. ACM Comput. Surv. **52**(1), 4:1–4:37 (2019)
16. Didimo, W., Liotta, G., Ortali, G., Patrignani, M.: Optimal orthogonal drawings of planar 3-graphs in linear time. In: Chawla, S. (ed.) Proceedings of the 2020 ACM-SIAM Symposium on Discrete Algorithms, SODA 2020, Salt Lake City, UT, USA, January 5–8, 2020, pp. 806–825. SIAM (2020)
17. Didimo, W., Liotta, G., Patrignani, M.: HV-planarity: algorithms and complexity. J. Comput. Syst. Sci. **99**, 72–90 (2019)
18. Dilla, W.N., Raschke, R.L.: Data visualization for fraud detection: practice implications and a call for future research. Int. J. Acc. Inf. Syst. **16**, 1–22 (2015)
19. Dujmovic, V., et al.: A fixed-parameter approach to 2-layer planarization. Algorithmica **45**(2), 159–182 (2006)
20. Dujmovic, V., et al.: On the parameterized complexity of layered graph drawing. Algorithmica **52**(2), 267–292 (2008)

21. Dwyer, T., et al.: Immersive analytics: an introduction. In: Marriott, K., et al. (eds.) Immersive Analytics, LNCS, vol. 11190, pp. 1–23. Springer, Cham (2018)
22. Filipov, V., Arleo, A., Miksch, S.: Are we there yet? a roadmap of network visualization from surveys to task taxonomies. Computer Graphics Forum (2023, on print)
23. Garg, A., Tamassia, R.: On the computational complexity of upward and rectilinear planarity testing. SIAM J. Comput. 31(2), 601–625 (2001)
24. Di Giacomo, E., Didimo, W., Montecchiani, F., Tappini, A.: A user study on hybrid graph visualizations. In: Purchase, H.C., Rutter, I. (eds.) Graph Drawing and Network Visualization. GD 2021. LNCS, vol. 12868, pp. 21–38. Springer, Cham (2021). https://doi.org/10.1007/978-3-030-92931-2_2
25. Giacomo, E.D., Giordano, F., Liotta, G.: Upward topological book embeddings of dags. SIAM J. Discret. Math. 25(2), 479–489 (2011)
26. Giacomo, E.D., Lenhart, W.J., Liotta, G., Randolph, T.W., Tappini, A.: (k, p)-planarity: a relaxation of hybrid planarity. Theor. Comput. Sci. 896, 19–30 (2021)
27. Giacomo, E.D., Liotta, G., Montecchiani, F.: Orthogonal planarity testing of bounded treewidth graphs. J. Comput. Syst. Sci. 125, 129–148 (2022)
28. Giacomo, E.D., Liotta, G., Patrignani, M., Rutter, I., Tappini, A.: Nodetrix planarity testing with small clusters. Algorithmica 81(9), 3464–3493 (2019)
29. Hong, S., Tokuyama, T. (eds.) Beyond Planar Graphs. Springer, Singapore (2020). https://doi.org/10.1007/978-981-15-6533-5
30. Joos, L., Jaeger-Honz, S., Schreiber, F., Keim, D.A., Klein, K.: Visual comparison of networks in VR. IEEE Trans. Vis. Comput. Graph. 28(11), 3651–3661 (2022)
31. Jünger, M., Mutzel, P. (eds.) Graph Drawing Software. Springer, Berlin (2004). https://doi.org/10.1007/978-3-642-18638-7
32. Kaufmann, M., Wagner, D. (eds.): Drawing Graphs, Methods and Models (the book grow out of a Dagstuhl Seminar, April 1999), LNCS, vol. 2025. Springer, Berlin (2001). https://doi.org/10.1007/3-540-44969-8
33. Keim, D.A., Kohlhammer, J., Ellis, G.P., Mansmann, F.: Mastering the Information Age - Solving Problems with Visual Analytics. Eurographics Association, Saarbrücken (2010)
34. Keim, D.A., Mansmann, F., Stoffel, A., Ziegler, H.: Visual analytics. In: Liu, L., Özsu, M.T. (eds.) Encyclopedia of Database Systems, 2nd edn. Springer, Berlin (2018)
35. Kobourov, S.G., Liotta, G., Montecchiani, F.: An annotated bibliography on 1-planarity. Comput. Sci. Rev. 25, 49–67 (2017)
36. Kraus, M., et al.: Immersive analytics with abstract 3D visualizations: a survey. Comput. Graph. Forum 41(1), 201–229 (2022)
37. Kwon, O., Muelder, C., Lee, K., Ma, K.: A study of layout, rendering, and interaction methods for immersive graph visualization. IEEE Trans. Vis. Comput. Graph. 22(7), 1802–1815 (2016)
38. Leite, R.A., Gschwandtner, T., Miksch, S., Gstrein, E., Kuntner, J.: NEVA: visual analytics to identify fraudulent networks. Comput. Graph. Forum 39(6), 344–359 (2020)

39. Liotta, G., Rutter, I., Tappini, A.: Simultaneous FPQ-ordering and hybrid planarity testing. Theor. Comput. Sci. **874**, 59–79 (2021)
40. Liotta, G., Rutter, I., Tappini, A.: Parameterized complexity of graph planarity with restricted cyclic orders. J. Comput. Syst. Sci. **135**, 125–144 (2023)
41. Ma, K.: Pushing visualization research frontiers: essential topics not addressed by machine learning. IEEE Comput. Graphics Appl. **43**(1), 97–102 (2023)
42. McGee, F., et al.: Visual Analysis of Multilayer Networks. Synthesis Lectures on Visualization. Morgan & Claypool Publishers, San Rafael (2021)
43. Munzner, T.: Visualization Analysis and Design. A.K. Peters visualization series. A K Peters (2014)
44. Nishizeki, T., Rahman, M.S.: Planar Graph Drawing, vol. 12. World Scientific, Singapore (2004)
45. Nobre, C., Meyer, M.D., Streit, M., Lex, A.: The state of the art in visualizing multivariate networks. Comput. Graph. Forum **38**(3), 807–832 (2019)
46. Sacha, D.: Knowledge generation in visual analytics: Integrating human and machine intelligence for exploration of big data. In: Apel, S., et al. (eds.) Ausgezeichnete Informatikdissertationen 2018, LNI, vol. D-19, pp. 211–220. GI (2018)
47. Sacha, D., et al.: What you see is what you can change: human-centered machine learning by interactive visualization. Neurocomputing **268**, 164–175 (2017)
48. Sacha, D., Senaratne, H., Kwon, B.C., Ellis, G.P., Keim, D.A.: The role of uncertainty, awareness, and trust in visual analytics. IEEE Trans. Vis. Comput. Graph. **22**(1), 240–249 (2016)
49. Sacha, D., Stoffel, A., Stoffel, F., Kwon, B.C., Ellis, G.P., Keim, D.A.: Knowledge generation model for visual analytics. IEEE Trans. Vis. Comput. Graph. **20**(12), 1604–1613 (2014)
50. Tamassia, R.: Graph drawing. In: Sack, J., Urrutia, J. (eds.) Handbook of Computational Geometry, pp. 937–971. North Holland/Elsevier, Amsterdam (2000)
51. Tamassia, R. (ed.) Handbook on Graph Drawing and Visualization. Chapman and Hall/CRC, Boca Raton (2013)
52. Tamassia, R., Liotta, G.: Graph drawing. In: Goodman, J.E., O'Rourke, J. (eds.) Handbook of Discrete and Computational Geometry, 2nd edn., pp. 1163–1185. Chapman and Hall/CRC, Boca Raton (2004)
53. Zehavi, M.: Parameterized analysis and crossing minimization problems. Comput. Sci. Rev. **45**, 100490 (2022)

Understanding Non-Covalent Interactions in Biological Processes through QM/MM-EDA Dynamic Simulations

Marcos Mandado

Department of Physical Chemistry, University of Vigo, Lagoas-Marcosende s/n, 36310 Vigo, Spain
mandado@uvigo.es

Molecular dynamic simulations in biological environments such as proteins, DNA or lipids involves a large number of atoms, so classical models based on widely parametrized force fields are employed instead of more accurate quantum methods, whose high computational requirements preclude their application. The parametrization of appropriate force fields for classical molecular dynamics relies on the precise knowledge of the non-covalent inter and intramolecular interactions responsible for very important aspects, such as macromolecular arrangements, cell membrane permeation, ion solvation, etc. This implies, among other things, knowledge of the nature of the interaction, which may be governed by electrostatic, repulsion or dispersion forces. In order to know the balance between different forces, quantum calculations are frequently performed on simplified molecular models and the data obtained from these calculations are used to parametrize the force fields employed in classical simulations. These parameters are, among others, atomic charges, permanent electric dipole moments and atomic polarizabilities. However, it sometimes happens that the molecular models used for the quantum calculations are too simple and the results obtained can differ greatly from those of the extended system. As an alternative to classical and quantum methods, hybrid quantum/classical schemes (QM/MM) can be introduced, where the extended system is neither truncated nor simplified, but only the most important region is treated quantum mechanically.

In this presentation, molecular dynamic simulations and calculations with hybrid schemes are first introduced in a simple way for a broad and multidisciplinary audience. Then, a method developed in our group to investigate intermolecular interactions using hybrid quantum/classical schemes (QM/MM-EDA) is presented and some applications to the study of dynamic processes of ion solvation and membrane permeation are discussed [1–3]. Special attention is paid to the implementation details of the method in the EDA-NCI software [4].

References

1. Cárdenas, G., Pérez-Barcia, A., Mandado, M., Nogueira, J.J.: Phys. Chem. Chem. Phys. **23**, 20533 (2021)
2. Pérez-Barcia, A., Cárdenas, G., Nogueira, J.J., Mandado, M.: J. Chem. Inf. Model. **63**, 882 (2023)

3. Alvarado, R., Cárdenas, G., Nogueira, J.J., Ramos-Berdullas, N., Mandado, M.: Membranes **13**, 28 (2023)
4. Mandado, M., Van Alsenoy, C.: EDA-NCI: A program to perform energy decomposition analysis of non-covalent interactions. https://github.com/marcos-mandado/ EDΛ NCI

Contents – Part VIII

**Urban Regeneration: Innovative Tools and Evaluation Model
(URITEM 2023)**

Urban Space Accessibility and Mobilities (USAM 2023)

Virtual Reality and Augmented Reality and Applications (VRA 2023)

**Workshop on Advanced and Computational Methods for Earth
Science Applications (WACM4ES 2023)**

Smart Tourism (SmartTourism 2023)

The Concept of Smart Marinas for the Implementation of Croatian Nautical Tourism

Andrea Gallo(✉)

University of Trieste, 34127 Trieste, Italy
andrea.gallo3@phd.units.com

Abstract. The present paper proposes to frame the analysis of the recreational boating tourism system for the coastal area of Croatia through an analysis of the system of ports and marinas, focusing on the implementation of sustainable development strategies from an environmental perspective by implementing the concept of "green ports" through the investigation of spatial components, energy management, water and waste management. Nautical tourism represents an extremely central component to the economy of coastal areas, which is why this contribution is structured through an initial overview of the marinas present in the area, the services offered, and tourist flows, focusing subsequently on the infrastructural aspects related to the energy and environmental efficiency of different port systems.

Keywords: Smart Ports · Green Ports · Smart Tourism · Croatia

1 Introduction

Tourist ports and marinas represent key infrastructure in the development of nautical tourism. However, the increasing attention paid to environmental issues is reflected in a growing focus on adopting technologies, systems, and solutions capable of reducing the negative externalities produced by different port systems [1]. In the process of optimizing performance, environmental issues related to energy supply [2], safety, waste management, and port operations will therefore have to be addressed [3].

In recent years, there has been a gradual and steady increase in demand for nautical tourism in the coastal and island areas of Croatia, abruptly interrupted by the pandemic but resumed from 2021. This represents an extremely important driving force for the local economy, generating an impact of over 125 million euros [4], subject inevitably to seasonal fluctuations. However, the increase in demand for nautical tourism has led, in the summer periods, to congestion of ports and marinas due to the greater number of boats present, leading to an increase in different factors of environmental pollution both in terms of emissions and in reference to waste disposal, atmospheric pollution, and groundwater pollution [5] and to a complex management of energy and water consumption, resulting in increased costs for both boat owners and marina managers [6].

O. Gervasi et al. (Eds.): ICCSA 2023 Workshops, LNCS 14111, pp. 3–16, 2023.
https://doi.org/10.1007/978-3-031-37126-4_1

It should be emphasized that the economic and environmental components must go hand in hand in the optimal management of the Croatian marine infrastructure system, finding sustainable management models both from an economic and environmental perspective, pursuing environmental sustainability goals. To this end, the idea is that marinas adopt smart and low environmental impact solutions to improve processes in the transition to "green marinas" [7]. Such a transformation must be supported by the implementation of infrastructural and technological systems and by optimizing operational processes. In this context, marinas that are able to minimize time and optimize spatial and resource utilization will become more attractive [8], as well as an optimal waste management and accurate use of energy resources. These different factors represent the main challenges to be addressed in the market of recreational nautical tourism [9].

2   The Insular and Coastal Croatian Context

The Croatian geographical context has intrinsic characteristics that are ideal for the development of nautical tourism. The coastline is extremely rugged, constantly opening up to beaches and suggestive coves from a landscape point of view, where natural amenities combine with excellent hospitality services for recreational tourists. The infrastructure network of ports, marinas and other moorings for various boats is capillary distributed throughout the coastal and insular area [10]. In this context, nautical tourism represents an important driving force for the local economy, but to preserve the environment and try

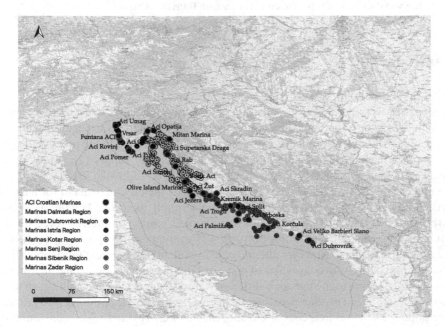

Fig. 1. Definition of the Study area and the Croatian Marinas. Source: Personal Elaboration on Framesport data. Author: Andrea Gallo

to mitigate the negative externalities generated by high volumes of tourist flows, it will be essential to act on different critical elements in order to improve the sustainability of these value creation processes [11].

This paper will consider the seven coastal administrative regions, highlighted in the map in Fig. 1, which will now be introduced briefly [12]:

Istrian Region (Istria) – located on the north-western tip of Croatia, bordering Slovenia and Italy. It has an area of about 2,820 km^2 and includes the city of Pula and the historic town of Rovinj.

Littoral-Mountainous Region (Primorje-Gorski Kotar) – northwest of Dalmatia and bordering Slovenia. It covers an area of about 3,590 km^2 and includes the city of Rijeka and the islands of Krk, Rab, and Cres.

Lika-Senj Region (Lika-Senj) – located northeast of Dalmatia, characterized by a mountainous topography, and includes a series of national parks, including the Plitvice Lakes National Park, covering an area of about 5,350 km^2.

Zadar Region (Zadarska županija) – located in the central part of the Croatian Adriatic coast and includes the city of Zadar, one of the oldest historic cities in Croatia, covering an area of about 3,640 km^2.

Šibenik-Knin Region (Šibensko-Kninska županija) – located on the central coast of Dalmatia, includes the city of Šibenik, as well as the Krka National Park and the Kornati Islands archipelago.

Split-Dalmatia Region (Splitsko-Dalmatinska županija) – located in the southern part of Dalmatia, with an area of 2,940 km^2, it is the most populous region of Croatia and includes the city of Split, as well as numerous islands such as Hvar, Brač, and Vis.

Dubrovnik-Neretva Region (Dubrovačko-Neretvanska županija) – located in the southernmost part of Croatia, bordering Montenegro, with a slightly smaller area than the other coastal regions at 1,780 km^2, it includes the city of Dubrovnik, one of the most famous and popular tourist destinations in Croatia, declared a UNESCO World Heritage Site, as well as the Mljet National Park.

Croatia is located on the eastern shore of the Adriatic Sea basin: due to its position within the Mediterranean Sea [13], it is becoming a primary tourist area for all of continental Europe [14].

All of these factors highlight how recreational tourism in Croatia has an extremely significant impact on the region in terms of its economic benefits, particularly with regards to the development of logistical infrastructure related to the various port systems, marinas, and moorings. It is estimated that the economic benefits of the industry in 2021 amounted to €125.5 million, with the regions of Zadar (19.5%), Sibenik (26.4%), and Split and Dalmatia (22.3%) contributing over 68% of the total. Data by the Croatian National Bureau of Statistics[1], suggests that in 2021 given, the total number of vessels in transit exceeded 210,000 units, with 67% being sailboats and 32% motor yachts. These figures highlight how environmental and panoramic factors, coupled with the existing infrastructure, have generated significant tourism flows for all coastal and island regions of Croatia. Furthermore, the Croatian statistical office estimates a total of 1,831 employees in the sector, with a total number of available moorings and docks amounting

---

[1] https://dzs.gov.hr/en accessed in data 21/03/2023.

to 18,942, capable of accommodating all types of vessels in terms of size, tonnage, and draft, as shown in the table below (Table 1).

Table. 1. Overview of Croatian touristic marinas infrastructure. Source: Croatian National Bureau of Statistics

Capacity of Nautical Port for Croatian Costal and Insular area	
Water Surface area (m^2)	4,643,877
Total number of moorings	18,942
Of that for ships:	
Under 6 m long	1,049
6–8 m	1,532
8–10 m	2,440
10–12 m	4,666
12–15 m	5,848
15–20 m	2,455
over 20 m	952
(m)	73,705
Number of employed persons	1,831
Of that with seasonal jobs	374

To fully understand the geographical context of Croatia's coastal area, we can compare Croatia with other European countries in the Mediterranean area such as Greece, Italy, Spain, and Turkey. From this analysis, it is evident that the tendency for recreational tourism in the Croatian area also arises from various intrinsic geomorphological characteristics of the analyzed area, such as the length of the coastline, the large number of islands, and the ruggedness of the coast. For the Mediterranean area, Greece has the longest coastline (approximately 13,670 km), followed by Italy (7,600 km), and in third place, we find the Croatian coast with 6,278 km, higher than that of Turkey (5,190 km) and Spain (2,580 km) [13]. With regard to the island context, Croatia is second only to Greece (3,053 islands) with 1,246 islands covering an area of 3,259 km^2 and an island coastline length of 4,398 km [13]. The land coastline thus represents about 29% of the Croatian coastal context. These data highlight how, compared to other Mediterranean countries, the geographical conditions are absolutely favorable for significant development of nautical tourism. These factors, combined with a multitude of bays, islands, and coves, are capable of making navigation interesting and represent a component to consider in choosing tourist itineraries [15, 16]. The combination of the maritime space and small and large urban settlements where different ports and marinas are located, represents a fertile ground for proactive development, due to the economic impact on the city fabric. Historic waterfront and cultural tourism: the case of Dubrovnik [17]. Inevitably, picturesque landscapes of fishing villages along the Croatian coast and on numerous islands represent an important attraction for nautical tourism. These villages usually still retain their traditional charm and offer visitors an authentic experience of Croatian coastal life [18]. The analysis of the geographical context cannot overlook considerations of a geomorphological, biological, and climatic nature, where the mild climate, medium-intensity winds, and a large number of protected bays, deep seabeds and great marine biodiversity are certainly driving factors in the development of Croatian nautical tourism.

3   The Concept of Smart Marinas

The implementation of smart technologies in ports has led to the need for similar solutions in marinas, giving rise to the concept of the smart marina. To tackle the challenges faced by marinas, innovative technology-based solutions are being developed and implemented [7]. The concept of the smart marina has been derived from the smart port concept, which has been adapted to meet the specific needs of the nautical tourism market. Ports are also becoming increasingly conscious of their relationship with the local community in terms of environmental quality, living standards, and port development [19, 20]. The primary challenge faced by marinas is the effective handling and organization of vessels' arrival, departure, and maintenance. By adopting innovative management strategies and smart technologies, marinas can increase productivity, optimize capacity utilization, and reduce associated costs. Automated machinery can replace human workers, reducing human errors, safety issues, and congestion, resulting in increased service quality, safety, and security in the marina [21]. Additionally, the implementation of smart marina solutions can provide marina operators with valuable data insights that can help them make informed decisions regarding their operations. For instance, data on visitor patterns, vessel occupancy, and energy consumption can be used to optimize the use of resources and reduce waste [22].

Furthermore, smart marina solutions can also improve the overall customer experience by providing convenient and efficient services, such as automated check-ins and digital payment systems. The adoption of smart marina solutions is also in line with the growing trend towards sustainable and eco-friendly practices in the tourism industry [23]. By monitoring and reducing energy consumption and emissions, marinas can contribute to the overall reduction of the industry's environmental impact. In addition, the implementation of smart waste management systems can help address the issue of marine litter and protect the local ecosystem [22]. The emergence of smart technologies in ports has led to the need for similar solutions in marinas, giving rise to the concept of the smart marina.

By adopting innovative management strategies and smart technologies, marinas can increase productivity, optimize capacity utilization, and reduce associated costs while contributing to sustainable and eco-friendly practices in the tourism industry. Moreover, the smart marina concept can also enhance safety and security in the marina by providing real-time monitoring and alerts for potential hazards, such as bad weather conditions or intruders. This can help prevent accidents and ensure the safety of both vessels and visitors [24]. The implementation of smart marina solutions can also benefit the local economy by attracting more visitors and boosting tourism. By providing high-quality and convenient services, marinas can enhance the overall tourist experience and increase the likelihood of repeat visits.

In addition, the use of smart technologies can also create new job opportunities in the fields of technology and data management. It is worth noting that the smart marina concept is not without its challenges [25]. The implementation of new technologies and management strategies can be costly and require significant investment [26]. The adoption of new practices may require changes to the existing regulatory framework, which can be a time-consuming process.

Overall, the smart marina concept offers many benefits for marina operators, visitors, and the environment [27]. As the tourism industry continues to evolve and embrace new technologies, it is likely that the adoption of smart marina solutions will become increasingly common.

4 Materials and Data Collection

The analysis of functionality parameters of Croatian tourist marinas are instrumental in assessing the attractiveness and environmental sustainability of these destinations through the elaboration of a matrix. The data presented in this section refer to the services and characteristics of five different marinas characterized by the road accessibility, despite the fact that Betina marina is located on the island of Murter and not on the mainland. However, road accessibility on the island is provided by the Tisno Bridge, effectively making this marina comparable to its predecessors.

The information presented derive from the analysis of the information provided by the online systems of the different marinas[2], as well as information presented as part of the European Project FrameSPort[3], which is available online and from the "Portolano[4]", an online database that gives a wide range of information related to ports and marinas.

Primarily, the focus of the analysis will be on the size of the marinas, in terms of operational capacity, number of berths available, and size of boats moored. Those informations are presented in Table 2.

Looking at the data provided for these marinas, we can draw some considerations about marinas this different marinas presented: as first, the size and facilities of a marina can greatly impact its capacity and ability to accommodate different types and sizes of boat, observing how the maximum boat length and vessel tonnage that those marinas can accommodate is an important consideration for boat owners when choosing a marina to moor their boats. Depending on the size and type of boat, some marinas may not be suitable due to restrictions in size and tonnage. And it is possible also to take in to consider that the width of a marina's entrance is also an important factor, especially for larger boats. A wider entrance allows for easier and safer navigation for larger boats, making it easier to access the marina and reducing the risk of accidents or damage to boats.

---

[2] https://aci-marinas.com/it/marina access on 26/03/2023.

[3] https://www.italy-croatia.eu/web/framesport/docs-and-tools last access on 26/03/2023.

[4] https://www.tuttobarche.it/ricerca-rade-e-porti last access on 26/03/2023.

Table 2. Infrastructural characteristics of the marinas under analysis. Source: Online web-page of marinas. Source: [28]

Marinas	Nr. of Berths (< 11 m)	Nr. of Berths (> 11 m)	Total number of moorings	Max boat lenght	Max vessel tonnage	Width of port's entrance
ACI Umag	340	20	360	60	500	60
Aci Veljko Barbieri Slano	40	130	170	15	150	70
ACI Betina	295	0	295	15	80	30
ACI Milna	327	13	340	20	40	600
Marina Veruda	380	250	630	40	NA	20

After the overview of the marinas analyzed in terms of mooring capacity based on the size of the boats and a screening of some characteristics, we will now analyze in detail the different services offered by these ports in the following table (Table 3).

Table 3. Servicies provided by different marinas: Source: FramesSport Project [28]

Marinas	ACI Umag	Marina Veruda	ACI Veljko Barbieri Slano	ACI Milna	ACI Betina
Fuel Station	Yes	Yes	Yes	Yes	Yes
Docking Service	No	No	Yes	Yes	Yes
Reception Office	Yes	Yes	Yes	Yes	No
Night security service	No	No	Yes	No	No
Presence of the custom	Yes	No	No	No	No
Car parking	Yes	Yes	Yes	No	No
Emergency defribillators	No	No	No	No	No
Grocery store	Yes	Yes	Yes	Yes	Yes
Services for straightening ropes	No	No	Yes	No	No
Engine maintenance service	No	No	Yes	No	No

(*continued*)

Table 3. (*continued*)

Marinas	ACI Umag	Marina Veruda	ACI Veljko Barbieri Slano	ACI Milna	ACI Betina
Toilets	Yes	Yes	Yes	Yes	Yes
Laundry	Yes	Yes	Yes	Yes	Yes
Water filtrartion sistem	Yes	Yes	Yes	Yes	Yes
Differentiated waste collection	Yes	Yes	Yes	Yes	Yes
Smart booking	Yes	Yes	Yes	Yes	Yes
Free Wifi	Yes	Yes	Yes	Yes	Yes
Boat rent service	Yes	Yes	Yes	Yes	Yes
Lowering and raising the vessel into the sea	No	Yes	Yes	No	Yes
Vessel Storage place	No	Yes	Yes	No	Yes
Crane Lift service	No	Yes	Yes	No	Yes
Final Marks	60%	70%	90%	55%	65%

In the previous table, some of the main services offered by the different marinas were presented, where it is essential to emphasize some key services that are fundamental in terms of attracting tourist flows. Marinas are in fact nodes of sea/land connection; therefore, it is evident that the presence of a parking area to leave vehicles parked during the period spent at sea, the presence of crane lift services to put boats into the water, and finally access ramps to the sea represent indispensable services for the attractiveness of a recreational marina.

Finally, data related to the accessibility of the marinas under analysis will be considered, considering both the distance to major strategic infrastructures such as hospitals and fire stations and the distance to major transportation services and logistical nodes: thus analyzing the distance in terms of minutes of car-driving distance to the airports, bus stops and distance to highways. These data are presented in the following table (Table 4).

The set of data presented will be useful to the development of a matrix of attractiveness of tourist marinas, presented in the next section, borrowing some considerations treated for the marinas of Sardinia, in the case of the Metropolitan City of Cagliari in the paper of Mundula et al. (2020) [29]. Here, will be take in consideration the intrinsic characteristics of the different marinas, the range of services offered and aspects of road accessibility and services of proximity as hospitals and fireworks stations, to the elaboration of an "Attractiveness Matrix".

Table 4. Servicies provided by different marinas: Source: FramesSport Project [28]

	Distance from railway stop	Distance from Airport	Distance from the bus station	Distance to highway	Distance to the Firework station	Distance from the nearest hospital
ACI Umag	20	65	1	8	1	3
Aci Veljko Barbieri Slano	10	10	10	5	5	5
ACI Betina	50	40	15	15	15	15
ACI Milna	65	70	10	17	17	10
Marina Veruda	5	10	5	7	5	15

5 Methodology

This paper proposes to develop an attractiveness matrix of the different Croatian marine tourism destinations, based on two fundamental aspects: the first related to the services offered to tourists within the marinas, aimed at improving performance in terms of efficiency, safety, environmental sustainability [30], and smartness, while the second refers to the degree of accessibility for the different marinas [31], which therefore considers not only the availability of berths but also takes into consideration factors related to the geographical location of the different marinas in relation to the main logistical needs.

To be able to structure the accessibility matrix of the marine tourism destinations, 20 different key services proposed by the different marinas were taken as parameters, assigning a value of 5% to each service offered. For accessibility, an index was constructed, called "Marina-accessibility index" [33]. The elaboration of this Index derives from the application of the Simpson formula to the dataset presented [32] in Table 2 and Table 4. The aggregation of the information provided into this different tables we can obtain an extremely accurate overview of the accessibility level of different marinas. For this reason, it was decided to adopt the Simpson Index formula to construct the accessibility index. The Simpson Index has found wide application in statistics in the analysis of various characteristics of a finite population, finding its greatest application in the study of biodiversity in biology [32]. By analogy, we propose to adopt this index in port contexts, where it is assumed that, by combining the different characteristics of marinas, it is able to provide an accurate representation of the level of accessibility and centrality of tourist systems.

To calculate the "Marinas_accessibility Index", the Simpson formula was used, as shown below, in the following equation:

$$\text{Marina\_Accessibility Index} = 1 - \frac{\sum n(1-n)}{N(1-N)} \tag{1}$$

where "n" is number of individuals of each species and "N" represent total number of individuals of all species [32].

6   Results and Discussion

It seems that the study is focusing on the evaluation of small tourist marinas in Croatia and their relationship with the different services provided. The study is attempting to identify a representative index that can measure the interrelationship between the marinas and the services, and then use this index to create a matrix of attractiveness for the various small tourist ports.

The study is also introducing the concept of the Marinas: Accessibility Index, which appears to be a metric used to evaluate the centrality level of the marinas based on their location and other features [33]. Overall, it seems that the study is trying to provide a comprehensive evaluation of small tourist marinas in Croatia and their relationship with the surrounding services and amenities. The resulting matrix of attractiveness may be useful for tourists and investors alike in determining which marinas are the most desirable and offer the best value. Below, the accessibility matrix elaborated through the use of the two different indicators is represented. On the two axes there will be the indicator of the services offered by the different marinas, based on the data presented before and on the other will be the marinas_accessibility index, based on the Simpson Index as presented previously [34] (Fig. 2).

The results obtained show that all the marinas under analysis occupy the suboptimal position of the proposed attractiveness matrix, except for the degree of acceptability of the. Marina Veruda as presented in the following table (Table 5):

These results are in line with expectations as only large marinas were considered in this elaboration and with an extremely aligned offer in terms of services, accessibility, and smartness. We can also note that the Marina ACI Milna is the most lacking in terms of services offered, but without missing the offer of basic services.

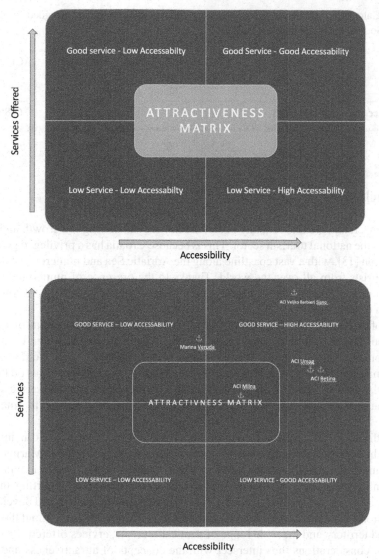

Fig. 2. The Attractiveness Matrix based on the different indicator of Services offered by marinas and the so-called Marinas_Accessibility Index (Fig. A), and the localization of the different marinas on the Matrix (Fig. B). Source: Personal Elaboration.

Table 5. Calculation of the marina:accessibility index and the services provided by different marinas. Source: Elaboration of the Author.

	ACI Betina	Marina Veruda	ACI Veljko Barbieri Slano	ACI Milna	ACI Umag
marina_accessibility index	0,6948	0,4947	0,7721	0,7100	0,6785
Services	60%	75%	90%	55%	60%

7 Conclusions

Marinas in Croatia are undoubtedly one of the key factors driving the growth and development of the national tourism sector. This is because Croatia has a privileged geographical location [13], with a vast coastline along the Adriatic Sea and numerous islands that attract tourists from all over the world. Thanks to the presence of numerous marinas, nautical tourism has become a major source of income for many coastal towns and islands in Croatia [15].

One of the distinguishing features of Croatian marinas is their widespread distribution throughout the coastal and island territory. There are marinas everywhere along the coast, from the largest (of which the marinas in ACI Milna, Betina, Veljko Barbieri Slano Umag, and Veruda have been analyzed in detail), to the small marinas on the most remote islands. This means that tourists wishing to explore the Croatian coast can easily rent a boat or yacht and sail along the coast, stopping at various ports and marinas along the way.

In addition to this, the presence of marinas throughout the country is also an important factor in the economic development of Croatian coastal towns and islands. Marinas attract tourists and consequently other tourist services, such as restaurants, souvenir stores, hotels, and private accommodation, thus creating new jobs and supporting the local economy. Marinas in Croatia thus represent key drivers for the growth and development of the national tourism sector, due to their widespread distribution throughout the coastal and island territory and the wide range of nautical tourism services offered.

These considerations thus intersect with the concepts of attractiveness and smartness for different marinas, where a wide range of services assisted by a wide range of special features implies that a given marina is more or less attractive and efficient. These considerations were highlighted through the development of a matrix of attractiveness for different marinas, taking a sample of five different large marinas for analysis: the choice fell on the marinas of Milna, Betina, Veljko Barbieri Slano Umag and Veruda because of the wide range of services offered and the availability of the different data used in particular in the marinas_accessibility index presented earlier.

Thus, the Croatian Tourism System sees tourist marinas as an important channel of development for the coastal economy, an asset to be preserved and implemented as much in terms of aspects related to accessibility, service offerings as in terms of environmental sustainability, trying to adopt strategies to mitigate the negative externalities generated by these key nautical tourism infrastructures.

References

1. Molavi, A., Lim, G.J., Race, B.: A framework for building a smart port and smart port index. Int. J. Sustain. Transp. **14**(9), 686–700 (2020)
2. Lamberti, T., Sorce, A., Di Fresco, L., Barberis, S.: Smart port: exploiting renewable energy and storage potential of moored boats, pp. 1–3. In: OCEANS 2015-Genova. IEEE (2015)
3. Bucak, U., Kuleyin, B.: Evaluation of green performance indicators' priority perception in terms of sustainable port concept a comparative analysis for Turkish ports. In: Conference: 1st International Congress on Ship and Marine Technology: Green Technologies At İstanbul, pp. 249–260 (2016)
4. Croatian Bureau of Statistics: Natucal Tourism – Capacity and turnover of Ports, first release (2021)
5. Tselentis, V., Papadimitriou, S., Tzannatos, E.: Environmental management and monitoring for sustainable development in marinas. FME Trans. **44**(3), 305 (2016)
6. Shin, I.S., Kim, B.S.: Development smart yacht operational system and marina control system for navigational safety. Int. J. Infor. Electr. Eng. **4**(1), 16 (2014)
7. Karaś, A.:. Smart port as a key to the future development of modern ports. TransNav: Int. J. Marine Navig. Safety Sea Transp. **14**(1) (2020)
8. Battino, S., del Mar Muñoz Leonisio, M.: Smart ports from theory to practice: a review of sustainability indicators. In: Computational Science and Its Applications–ICCSA 2022 Workshops, Malaga, Spain, 4–7 Jul 2022, Proceedings, Part V, pp. 185–195. Springer International Publishing, Cham (2022)
9. Acciaro, M., et al.: Environmental sustainability in seaports: a framework for successful innovation. Marit. Policy Manage. **41**(5), 480–500 (2014)
10. Corluka, G., Mikinac, K., Milenkovska, A.: Classification of tourist season in costal tourism. UTMS J. Econ. **7**(1), 71–83 (2016)
11. Mikulić, J., Kožić, I.: An exploratory assessment of tourism sustainability in Croatian coastal destinations. EFZG Working Paper Series (4), 1–12 (2011)
12. Favro, S., Saganić, I.: Natural characteristics of Croatian littoral area as a comparative advantage for nautical tourism development. Geoadria **12**(1), 59–81 (2007)
13. Krstinić Nižić, M., Drpić, D.: Model for sustainable tourism development in Croatia. Tourism in Southern and Eastern Europe, pp. 159–173 (2013)
14. Luković, T., Favro, S.: Strategic and tactical plans as part of controlling in marina management. In: 6th Paneuropean shipping conference, Split (2005)
15. Horak, S., Marusic, Z., Favro, S.: Competitiveness of Croatian nautical tourism. Tour. Mar. Environ. **3**(2), 145–161 (2006)
16. Razović, M., Tomljenović, R.: Development model of tourism on Croatian open-sea islands. Tourism Int. Interdiscip. J. **63**(1), 19–36 (2015)
17. Bunja, D.: Modernizing the Croatian tourism industry. Int. J. Contemp. Hosp. Manag. **15**(2), 126–128 (2003)
18. Douaioui, K., Fri, M., Mabrouki, C.: Smart port: design and perspectives. In: 2018 4th International Conference on Logistics Operations Management (GOL) IEEE, pp. 1–6 (2018)
19. Dragović, B., Tzannatos, E., Tselentis, V., Meštrović, R., Škurić, M.: Ship emissions and their externalities in cruise ports. Transp. Res. Part D: Transp. Environ. **61**, 289–300 (2018)
20. Borruso, G., Balletto, G., Milesi, A., Ladu, M.: Cartography and security. Port security: trends and perspectives. In: Gervasi, O., et al. (eds.) ICCSA 2021. LNCS, vol. 12958, pp. 252–261. Springer, Cham (2021). https://doi.org/10.1007/978-3-030-87016-4_19

21. Balletto, G., Milesi, A., Ladu, M., Borruso, G.: A dashboard for supporting slow tourism in green infrastructures. A methodological proposal in Sardinia (Italy). Sustainability **12**(9), 3579 (2020)
22. Mundula, L., Ladu, M., Balletto, G., Milesi, A.: Urban and territorial accessibility. A new role for the marinas. In: Innovation in Urban and Regional Planning: Proceedings of the 11th INPUT Conference, vol. 1, pp. 665–663. Springer International Publishing, Cham (2021)
23. Min, H.: Developing a smart port architecture and essential elements in the era of Industry 4.0. Marit. Econ. Logist. **24**(2), 189207 (2022)
24. Maglić, L., Grbčić, A., Gundić, A.: Application of smart technologies in Croatian marinas. Trans. Marit. Sci. **10**(1), 178–188 (2021)
25. Karayel, G.K., Javani, N., Dincer, I.: Sustainable marina concept with green hydrogen utilization: a case study. Sustain. Energy Technol. Assess. **54**, 102900 (2022)
26. Martínez-Vázquez, R.M., de Pablo Valenciano, J., Milán-García, J.: Impact analysis of marinas on nautical tourism in Andalusia. J. Mar. Sci. Eng. **10**(6), 780 (2022)
27. Radulovic, A.:Smart Technology Applied in The Management of Yachting Marinas. *International Journal of Maritime Engineering, 164*(A1) (2022),
28. FrameSPort Project Framework initiative fostering the sustainable development of Adriatic small ports, ICT platform 1st updating report – Marinas, W.P. 3, Deliverables: 3.2.2 (2022)
29. Mundula, L., Ladu, M., Balletto, G., Milesi, A.: Smart marinas. the case of metropolitan city of Cagliari. In: Gervasi, O., et al. (eds.) ICCSA 2020. LNCS, vol. 12255, pp. 51–66. Springer, Cham (2020). https://doi.org/10.1007/978-3-030-58820-5_5
30. Balletto, G., Ladu, M., Milesi, A., Borruso, G.: A methodological approach on disused public properties in the 15-minute city perspective. Sustainability **13**(2), 593 (2021)
31. Rodrigo González, A., González-Cancelas, N., Molina Serrano, B., Orive, A.C.: Preparation of a smart port indicator and calculation of a ranking for the Spanish port system. Logistics **4**(2), 9 (2020)
32. Comer, D., Greene, J.S.: The development and application of a land use diversity index for Oklahoma City OK. Appl. Geogr. **60**, 46–57 (2015)
33. Balletto, G., Borruso, G., Campisi, T., Meloni, I., Scappini, B.: City form, mobility and University students in post pandemic era. In: Gervasi, O., et al. (eds) Computational Science and Its Applications – ICCSA 2021. ICCSA 2021. Lecture Notes in Computer Science, vol. 12952, 267–281. Springer, Cham (2021)
34. Roh, S., Thai, V.V., Wong, Y.D.: Towards sustainable ASEAN port development: challenges and opportunities for Vietnamese ports. Asian J. Shipping Logistics **32**(2), 107–118 (2016)

A Decade Bibliometric Analysis of Decision Making in Tourism and Hospitality

Tutut Herawan[1]([✉]), Sholahuddin Arsyad[2], Wahyu Indro Widodo[3],
Assyifa Shafia Adiyanti[1], Damiasih Damiasih[1], Rakhmat Ashartono[1],
and Eka Novita Sari[4]

[1] Sekolah Tinggi Pariwisata Ambarrukmo Yogyakarta, Jalan Ringroad Timur No. 52,
Bantul, Daerah Istimewa Yogyakarta 55198, Indonesia
{tutut,damiasih}@stipram.ac.id

[2] Universitas Bina Darma, Jl. Jenderal Ahmad Yani No.3, Kota Palembang,
Sumatera Selatan 30111, Indonesia
shola.arsyad@binadarma.ac.id

[3] Lembaga Kajian Pariwisata Indonesia, Babadan, Sewon, Bantul, Daerah
Istimewa Yogyakarta 55185, Indonesia

[4] AMCS Research Center, Jalan Griya Taman Asri, Yogyakarta 55512, Indonesia

Abstract. We identify the evolution of decision making in tourism and hospitality researches from 2013 to 2023, such as: source, document type, journal name, publisher name, topic trends, and author collaborations. Bibliometric analysis was used to analyze 217 articles published from 2013 to 2023. We use the combination of decision making + tourism + hospitality as our main keywords in searching related article titles, abstracts, and keywords to get metadata, where the Scopus database is the main source. The tools used in this bibliometric analysis are Harzing's Publish or Perish for importing source data from Scopus database and further used for citation and metrics analysis. Furthermore, we employ VoS Viewer for data visualization. The results indicate that most related articles to are published in scientific journals, compared to other publication outlets e.g., book chapter, conference proceedings and book. Related articles published in scientific journals have received the highest citations compared to others. Based on network and overlay visualization, the most dominant terms (often appearing) are "Tourism", "Decision Making", and "Hospitality Industry".

Keywords: Bibliometric analysis · Decision making · Tourism · Publish or Perish · VoS Viewer

1 Introduction

Tourism recently has become a major big socio-economic phenomenon which involve an elaborate set of interactions between tourists, tour operators, academia, governments, and local communities. In tourism and hospitality sectors, decision making has played an important role in assisting all tourism stake holders, including tourists and business operators. The rapid development of information technology has influenced people in making decision regarding tourism choices.

© The Author(s), under exclusive license to Springer Nature Switzerland AG 2023
O. Gervasi et al. (Eds.): ICCSA 2023 Workshops, LNCS 14111, pp. 17–36, 2023.
https://doi.org/10.1007/978-3-031-37126-4_2

Many works on decision making in tourism and hospitality fields exist. The use of internet, technology, data science, big data, and artificial intelligence has attracted many scholars in assisting tourism decision makers. Zsarnoczky [1] studied on how artificial intelligence can affect the tourism industries Ivanov & Webster [2] proposed a conceptual framework in incorporating robots, many methods of artificial intelligence and service automation in travel, tourism, and hospitality companies. Samara, *et al.* [3] presented a survey and review on artificial intelligence and big data in tourism. Höpken, *et al.* [4] presented a study in the prediction of tourist arrival using big data analytics and soft computing method based on artificial neural network model. Wu, *et al.* [5] presented a survey on distributed linguistic representations in decision making including applications in hotel selection. They highlight some research opportunities involving data science and explainable artificial intelligence. Mak, *et al.* [6] presented a study on decision-making process involving community participation for sustainable tourism development, where the case study was taken in rural areas of Hong Kong, China. Karl [7] presented the effect of risk and uncertainty in travel decision from the perspective tourist and destination. Yu *et al.* [8] adopted MCDM model in selecting hotel with linguistic distribution assessments. Nilashi *et al.* [9] determined factors which influence the decision in medical tourism to Malaysia using DEMATEL-Fuzzy TOPSIS approach. Pantano *et al.* [10] developed a novel recommender system to facilitate tourists in making a decision through open data analyses. Karl *et al.* [11] examine the tourist's decision-making process for destination choice through travel risks. Stylos [12] studied the evolution of technology for tourism decision-making. McCartney & McCartney [13] presented a research framework on a service-robot for the hospitality and tourism industry. Pappas & Glyptou [14] presented insights from Greece toward accommodation decision-making during the COVID-19 pandemic.

On the other side, to understand the current state of researches on tourism and hospitality, many study has been proposed by many scholars, where they use meta-analysis and bibliometric approach. Niñerola, *et al.* [15] presented their results of a bibliometric analysis on the topic of tourism research on sustainability. Nusair [16] presented a bibliometric analysis from 2002 to 2018 on the development of a comprehensive social media research based on life cycle framework in hospitality and tourism. Palácios, *et al.* [17] presented a bibliometric analysis of trust in the field of hospitality and tourism. Sigala [18] presented a bibliometric analysis of existing researches on tourism and Covid-19 pandemic. Manosso & Domareski Ruiz [19] presented bibliometric analysis, systematic and integrative review on existing researches of sentiment analysis in tourism. Pandey & Joshi [20] presented research trends for past 25-years using bibliometric analysis on the topic of tourism destination choice. Habibi, *et al.* [21] studied medical tourism researches using bibliometric approach. Pahrudin, *et al.* [22] presented a bibliometric study on the role of tourism management and marketing toward sustainable tourism. Qiao, *et al.* [22] presented a bibliometric review in understanding family tourism. Kalia, *et al.* [23] presented a bibliometric analysis in the last three decades on the trends and the emerging research directions of digital tourism. Lopes, *et al.* [24] presented a bibliometric analysis on tourism and land planning in natural spaces. Gomes, *et al.* [25] presented a bibliometric analysis on the tourism industry 4.0 and further they highlighted the future challenges. Vatankhah, *et al.* [26] presented a bibliometric analysis on the application of MCDM techniques in hospitality and tourism research.

Motivated from aforementioned works [15–26], we present a bibliometric analysis on decision making in Tourism and Hospitality. Unlike previous works, we use the Scopus database from 2013 to 2023. We not only present the publication source, document type, journal name and rank, publisher name and rank, topic trends, and author collaborations, but also, visualize them. Finally, we discuss some of the research challenges to be explore in future.

The remainder of the paper is organized as follows. In Sect. 2, we describe our proposed research method. Section 3 presents our obtained results and following by complete discussion. Finally, we conclude our work and highlight future work in Sect. 4.

2 Proposed Method

In this paper, we adopt bibliometrics analysis method [27–33] which consists of five stages, namely: Determining the keywords, initial searching and repair searching results; Compiling preliminary data statistics (before and after repairing) and saving in RIS format; Enter RIS data into Publish or Perish; Analysis of publications sources and citations; and finally visualize the results using VoS Viewer. Figure 1 below depicts the flow chart of our proposed method.

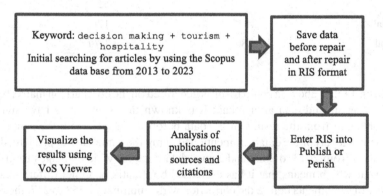

Fig. 1. Flow chart of the proposed method

3 Results and Discussion

This section explains the obtained results of this work, which includes publications and citations, visualizations, authors and networks, research locations and research domains.

3.1 Publications and Citations

For knowing comparison of the citation matrix on the data taken via Scopus, then researcher make the table in which containing number article, number citation, number citations per year, number authors per year, H index, G index, normal hI, and hI yearly at the beginning search and on results repair. Comparison data matrix in result search start and result search after repair could be seen in Table 1.

Table 1. Comparison Matrix

Data	Initial Search Results	Search Results Repair
Database	Scopus	Scopus
Year publishing	(2013–2023)	(2013–2023)
Year citation	10	10
Number of Articles	258	217
Number citation	3698	3268
Number Citation per Year	369.80	326.80
Number Authors per Year	2.94	2.85
H index	30	29
G index	56	52
hI Normal	18	17
hI Annual	1.80	1.70

Based on Table 1 above, a comparison is generated on the comparison matrix between data before repair and data after repair. It is known that some parts have significant changes obtained from the results of the data before the repair with the data after the repair. There is a part of the database mentioned using the same via Scopus with the year of publication from 2013 to 2023 and author data per year which changes from 2.94 to 2.85 per year which means that it has decreased by 9 authors. Other differences are in the number of documents before the correction with a number of 258 to 217, the number of citations that were previously 3698 to 3268, the average citation for the previous year 326.80 to 326.80 after making repairing, the H index amounted to 30 before the repairing to 29 after repairing and G index experienced a data reduction of 4 which before the repairing amounted to 56 to 52. As for the explanation of the statistics of publication per year is described in Table 2.

Table 2. The statistics descriptive of publication

Year	TP	% (N = 217)	NCP	TC	C/P	C/CP
2013	11	0.05	9	986	89.64	109.56
2014	8	0.04	4	75	9.38	18.75
2015	7	0.03	6	223	31.86	37,17
2016	14	0.06	13	259	18.50	19.92
2017	27	0.12	23	407	15.07	17.70
2018	22	0.10	17	296	13.45	17.41
2019	27	0.12	26	399	14.78	15.35
2020	17	0.08	13	216	12.71	16.62
2021	33	0.15	22	305	9.24	13.86
2022	46	0.21	23	101	2.20	4.39
2023	5	0.02	1	1	0.20	1,00
	217	100%				

Note: TP = total number of publications; NCP = number cited publications; TC = total quotes; C/P = average citations per publication; C/CP = average citation per cited publication

Table 2 above shows publication statistics data obtained for 10 years, from 2013 to 2023. In the first year of 2013, there were a total of 11 publications with 9 of the total citations of 986. Then in the following year, namely 2014, it was found to have a total of 8 publications from the results of 4 publication citations out of a total of 75 citations. In 2015 there were 7 total publications which had 6 citations that had been published, and a total of 223 citations. In 2016 it doubled from the previous year where there were 14 total publications, 13 citations published, with a total of 259 citations. Then in 2017 also experienced an increase in the total number of publications from previous years, which increased by 13 documents to 27 total publication documents with the number of citations increasing also to 23 which became a significant addition of documents with a total acquisition of 407 citations documents so that it became the second total cited document after the first year in 2013. However, in 2018 there was a decrease in the total number of publications by 0.10% or to 22 total documents with publication citations decreasing to 17 from a total citation of 296 documents. That way in 2019 it experienced an increase that returned to the previous 2 years, namely with a total of 27 publications which increased by 0.12% with a total of 26 publication citations out of a total of 399 or became the third in the total citations of the last 10 years. In 2020, it received a significant decline, which was at 17 of the total number of publications, with a total of 13 publication citations out of a total of 216 document citations, then in 2021 it increased with a total of 33 documents, with 22 citations out of a total of 305 citied documents. In 2022, it increased by the second order after 2013, and increased from the previous year by 0.21% with the number of citations published as many as 23 with a total of 101 citations. And in the last year, namely 2023, there are only 5 total publication documents, out of 1 each of the number of citation and station documents published. This is because the search for new documents is carried out during the last 3 months of 2023. Figure 2 as follow depicts the bar chart of publication and citations.

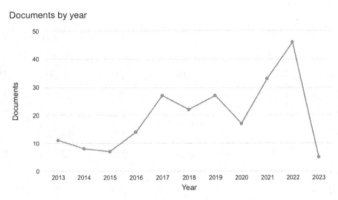

Documents by year

Fig. 2. Publication from 2013–2023

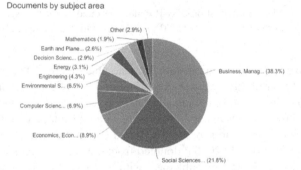

Documents by subject area

Fig. 3. Documents by subject area from 2013–2023

In Fig. 2 above, there is a graph showing documentation data published at intervals between 2013–2023. As shown in the diagram above and in the previous table, it is known that the peak of the most total publications is in 2022 with a total of 46 documents or an increase of 21% from previous years. Meanwhile, in the following year in 2023 it is the lowest total publicans with the acquisition of 5 documents or with a percentage of only 2% from previous years. Meanwhile, in Fig. 3 above, the data of the document by the subject area is presented. The diagram is dominated by blue color where there is Business, Management, and Accounting data with a total publication of 160 documents or 38.3% of the total data. In addition, in other subject areas obtained from Social Sciences represented by red color which is the second most documents with 21.8% or with 91 publication documents. Other subject areas are filled with Economics, Econometrics and Finance as much as 8.9%, Computer Science as much as 6.9%, Environmental Science as much as 6.5%, then in Engineering with 4.3%, Energy with 3.1%, Decision Sciences 2.9%, Earth and Planetary Sciences as much as 2.6% and the last subject with the acquisition of other documents which have 2.9% and the least document, namely

Mathematics with 1.9%. The conclusion is that from the many subject areas obtained, the most widely used documents are on the subjects of Business, Management, and Accounting. Figure 4 and Table 3 as follow depicts and describe the document type, respectively.

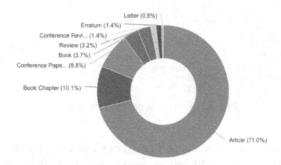

Fig. 4. Documents type

Table 3. Document type

Type	Number	Percentage
Article	154	0.71
Book Chapter	22	0.10
Conference Paper	19	0.09
Book	8	0.04
Reviews	7	0.03
Conference Review	3	0.01
Erratum	3	0.01
Letter	1	0.00
	217	100%

From both Fig. 4 and Table 3 above, the analysis results obtained based on the type of document from the Scopus database include Article, Book Chapter, Conference Paper, Book, Review, Conference Review, Erratum, and Letter. It is mentioned in the table above, that the most document type gains are obtained in Article types as many as 154 documents or 71% of the total 217 documents. Then followed by the Book Chapter document type as much as 10.1% or with 22 documents, then in third place with the Conference Paper type as much as 19 or 8.8% rounded up to 9%. Review document type with 7 documents, then 3 documents each are taken for Conference Review and Erratum type documents. And the last or the least type of use is obtained from the document type, namely 1 Letter type document. Figure 5 as follow depicts the documents per year by source.

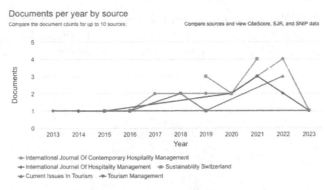

Documents per year by source

Compare the document counts for up to 10 sources.   Compare sources and view CiteScore, SJR, and SNIP data

-●- International Journal Of Contemporary Hospitality Management
-●- International Journal Of Hospitality Management   -●- Sustainability Switzerland
-●- Current Issues In Tourism   -●- Tourism Management

Fig. 5. Documents per year by source

From Fig. 5 above, the International Journal of Contemporary Hospitality Management published articles from 2014 and increased until 2022. Furthermore, the International Journal of Hospitality Management published a journal from 2013 to 2023 but decreased from 2021 to 2023. In the next source, Sustainability Switzerland with green lines began publishing journals in 2019 to 2021. Source: Current Issues in Tourism with purple line color from 2015 to 2022 and the last one is Tourism Management with orange line color starting in 2015 to 2023. Table 4 as follow describes the sources type of publication.

Table 4. Sources type of publication

Type	Number	Percentage
Journal	165	0.76
Book	24	0.11
Conference Proceedings	16	0.07
Book Series	12	0.06
	217	100%

In Table 4 above, data is presented in the form of document analysis or data based on the type of source. Obtained from the Scopus database, document types are classified with several source type areas in the last 10 years between 2013–2023 that international journals of contemporary hospitality management have experienced a significant increase every year starting from 2016 to 2022 and with a surge in current issues in tourism in 2019 to 2022. We obtained source types based on the Journal with the acquisition of 165 data sources or 76%, Book as much as 11% or 24 sources, Conference Proceedings as many as 16 types of sources, and Book Series with the acquisition of 12 of the totals of 217 data sources obtained. Figure 6 as follow depicts the documents by affiliation.

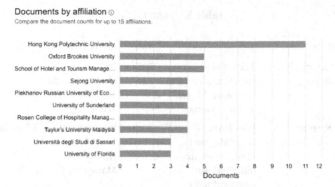

Fig. 6. Documents by affiliation

Figure 6 above displays the number of documents by affiliation. Based on the results of analysis from the Scopus database, it was found that Hong Kong Polytechnic University had the highest number of documents with 11 documents, then Oxford Brookes University and The Hong Kong Polytechnic University School of Hotel and Tourism Management with 5 documents each. As for the other affiliation, it has an average of 4 documents and 3 documents. Table 5 as follow describes the list of top 20 cited articles in the related field.

Table 5. Top 20 cited articles

Citation	Authors	Title	Year	Journal Name	Publisher
792	D. Leung, R. Law, H. van Hoof, D. Buhalis	Social Media in Tourism and Hospitality: A Literature Review	2013	Journal of Travel and Tourism Marketing	Taylor and Francis
136	G. Abrate, G. Viglia	Strategic and tactical price decisions in hotel revenue management	2016	Tourism Management	Elsevier
115	L. Kwok, K.L. Xie, T. Richards	Thematic framework of online review research: A systematic analysis of contemporary literature on seven major hospitality and tourism journals	2017	International Journal of Contemporary Hospitality Management	Emerald

(continued)

Table 5. (*continued*)

Citation	Authors	Title	Year	Journal Name	Publisher
95	E. Varkaris, B. Neuhofer	The influence of social media on the consumers' hotel decision journey	2017	Journal of Hospitality and Tourism Technology	Emerald
92	M. Singal	How is the hospitality and tourism industry different? An empirical test of some structural characteristics	2015	International Journal of Hospitality Management	Elsevier
90	F. Altuntas, M.S. Gok	The effect of COVID-19 pandemic on domestic tourism: A DEMATEL method analysis on quarantine decisions	2021	International Journal of Hospitality Management	Elsevier
77	S. Ham, H. Han	Role of Perceived Fit With Hotels' Green Practices in the Formation of Customer Loyalty: Impact of Environmental Concerns	2013	Asia Pacific Journal of Tourism Research	Taylor and Francis
65	H. Han, J. Hwang	Multi-dimensions of the perceived benefits in a medical hotel and their roles in international travelers' decision-making process	2013	International Journal of Hospitality Management	Elsevier
55	N. Pappas	Hotel decision-making during multiple crises: A chaordic perspective	2018	Tourism Management	Elsevier

(*continued*)

Table 5. (*continued*)

Citation	Authors	Title	Year	Journal Name	Publisher
51	H.-F. Luoh, S.-H. Tsaur, Y.-Y. Pliers	Empowering employees: Job standardization and innovative behavior	2014	International Journal of Contemporary Hospitality Management	Emerald
50	M. Mariani, M. Ek Styven, J.K. Ayeh	Using Facebook for travel decision-making: an international study of antecedents	2019	International Journal of Contemporary Hospitality Management	Emerald
47	B. Liu, L. Pennington-Gray	Bed bugs bite the hospitality industry? A framing analysis of bed bug news coverage	2015	Tourism Management	Elsevier
44	G. McCartney, A. McCartney	Rise of the machines: towards a conceptual service-robot research framework for the hospitality and tourism industry	2020	International Journal of Contemporary Hospitality Management	Emerald
44	I.P. Soler, G. Fond	Hedonic price models with geographically weighted regression: An application to hospitality	2018	Journal of Destination Marketing and Management	Elsevier
44	L. Parte-Esteban, P. Alberca-Oliver	Determinants of technical efficiency in the Spanish hotel industry: regional and corporate performance factors	2015	Current Issues in Tourism	Routledge
43	N. Stylos, J. Zwiegelaar, D. Buhalis	Big data empowered agility for dynamic, volatile, and time-sensitive service industries: the case of tourism sector	2021	International Journal of Contemporary Hospitality Management	Emerald

(*continued*)

Table 5. (*continued*)

Citation	Authors	Title	Year	Journal Name	Publisher
43	A. Farmaki	Tourism and hospitality internships: A prologue to career intentions?	2018	Journal of Hospitality, Leisure, Sport and Tourism Education	Elsevier
42	M. Peters, A. Kallmuenzer, D. Buhalis	Hospitality entrepreneurs managing quality of life and business growth	2019	Current Issues in Tourism	Routledge
40	M. Guix, M.J. Bonilla-Priego, X. Fonts	The process of sustainability reporting in international hotel groups: an analysis of stakeholder inclusiveness, materiality and responsiveness	2018	Journal of Sustainable Tourism	Routledge
38	T. Zhang, Z.A. Shaikh, A.V. Yumashev, M. ChÅ'ad	Applied model of E-learning in the framework of education for sustainable development	2020	Sustainability (Switzerland)	MDPI

Table 5 presents a list of the top 20 articles cited from various related fields. The document created by Leung, *et al.* in the Journal of Travel and Tourism Marketing published in 2013 by Taylor and Francis, with the title "Social Media in Tourism and Hospitality: A Literature Review" is the document with the highest number of citations, up to792 with a number of information about Content analysis on the articles was analyzed from the point of view of consumers and suppliers, and found that consumer-centered studies generally focused on the use and impact of social media in the research phase of travelers' travel planning process. Meanwhile, the least citation i.e., 38 citations were obtained with the title "Applied model of E-learning in the framework of education for sustainable development" which was written by Zhang, *et al.* published in 2020 by Sustainability (Switzerland) MDPI. Table 6 as follow describes the top five publisher on the related field.

Table 6. Top five publishers

No	Publisher	Number of Articles	Percentage
1	Emerald	43	32
2	Elsevier	37	28
3	Routledge	24	18
4	Taylor and Francis	15	11
5	Springer	14	11
		133	100%

In Table 6, the top publisher was Emerald with the total articles 43 with a percentage of 32%, and in the last place with 14 articles or 11% is achieved by Springer publisher from the total number of articles as many as 133 published documents. Table 7 as follow describes the top five journals on the related field.

Table 7. Top five journals ranking

No	Journal Name	Number of Articles	Percentage
1	International Journal of Contemporary Hospitality Management	16	33
2	International Journal of Hospitality Management	11	22
3	Sustainability (Switzerland)	9	18
4	Tourism Management	7	14
5	Current Issues in Tourism	6	12
		49	100%

From Table 7 above, it is stated that the International Journal of Contemporary Hospitality Management has 16 publications with a percentage of 33% and the last number of publications is in the journal Current Issues in Tourism with a percentage of 12% with 6 articles from a total of 49 articles.

3.2 Visualization Topics Use VoS Viewer

Figure 7 below shows visualization of topic areas using network visualization from VoS Viewer.

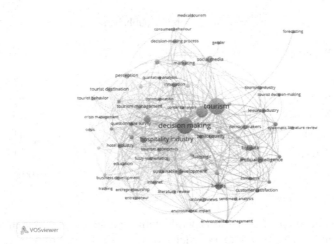

Fig. 7. Visualization topic area using network visualization (Color figure online)

From Fig. 7 above, 8 clusters with different node colors are formed. The number of items obtained from mapping images with visualization of the topic area are described by colors as follows:

a. Red color contains 15 items: Decision making, Tourism Industry, Tourism decision-making, Leisure Industry, Decision Makers, Systematic, Big Data, Artificial Intelligence, Commerce, Customer Satisfaction, Hotels, and so on.
b. Green color contains 14 items: Service Quality, Fuzzy Logic, Tourism Economics, Fuzzy Mathematics, Sustainable Development, Internet, Sentiment Analysis, Online Reviews, and so on.
c. Blue color contains 11 items: Qualitative Analysis, Innovation, Communication, Content Analysis, Questionnaire Survey, Hotel Industry, and so on.
d. Yellow color contains 10 items: Perception, Tourist Destination, Tourist Behavior, Crisis Management, Crisis, Tourism Management, and so on.
e. Purple color contains 9 items: Tourism, social media, Consumer Behavior, Decision Making Process, Forecasting, and so on.
f. Light Blue color contains 8 items: Education, Business, Development, Training, Entrepreneurship, Entrepreneur, Literature Review, and so on.
g. Orange color contains 2 items: Marketing and Medical Tourism.
h. Chocolate color contains 2 items: Investment and Forecasting

Figure 8 as follow describes the visualization topic area using overlay visualization from Vos Viewer.

In Fig. 8, the application of this mapping is based on the color of the item. As seen in the dark color indicator with a dark blue base owned in 2018 and 2019 where the color shows the darker the color produced, the longer the time presented. The dark colors include "Marketing", "Questionnaire survey", and "Education". Then in 2019 there are "Decision Making", "Hotels", and "Hospitality Industry". Meanwhile, in 2020 and 2021 and above, the colors tend to be brighter, namely "Tourism", "Hotel Industry",

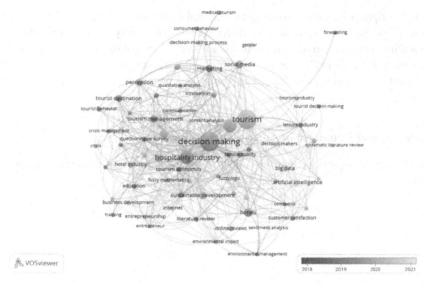

Fig. 8. Visualization topic area using overlay visualization (Color figure online)

and "Entrepreneur". Then continued for the latest years, namely "Artificial Intelligence", "Sentiment Analysis" and "Innovation".

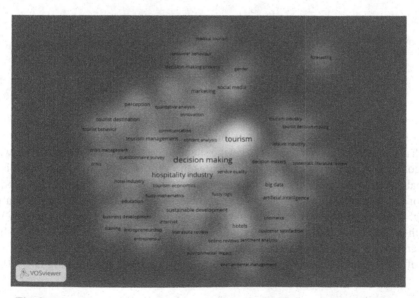

Fig. 9. Visualization topic area using density visualization (Color figure online)

Figure 9 as above describes the visualization topic area using density visualization from Vos Viewer. It presents an overview of the topic area of density visualization. In this case it is mentioned that the presented indicator with a bright color. It is intended that items with bright colors are interpreted by the number of topics taken as research material and have a widely used level of density. As for the level of density that is quite a little given symbol with the provision of color tends to be darker. Some of the items that researchers still use include "Tourism", "Decision Making", and "Hospitality Industry". As for items rarely used by researchers include "Environmental Management", "Forecasting", and "Gender".

3.3   Author and Relationship Among Authors

Figure 10 below depicts overlay visualization of the author and co-author using VoS Viewer.

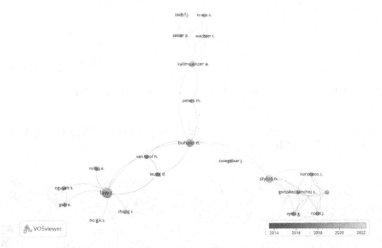

Fig. 10. Visualization of the author and co-author overlay

In Fig. 10 above, it is a mapping of the author visualization and co-author overlay which is analyzed using Vos Viewer to get the shape of the author's visualization network. The color of the nodes on each author indicates the year of publication in the published journal, while the number of nodes indicates the number of documents uploaded and the size of the network connecting with other authors. Based on the results of the analysis in Fig. 10, there are four authors who have greater links than other authors, namely Law R with 8 links who published their writings on average in 2016, Buhalis D with 7 links with an average publication year in 2017, Stylos N 7 links with an average publication year of 2020. And Kallmuenzer A with 6 links that published their writing in 2020.

3.4   Research Locations and Research Domains

Figure 11 below depicts the network visualization of the author-based countries. Meanwhile, Table 8 below describes the number of documents along with the country of origin and with their respective research domain.

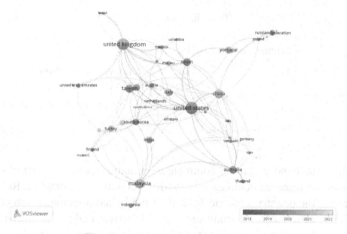

Fig. 11. Visualization of the country

Table 8. Top 10 Country of location research and research domain

No	Country	Number of Articles	Research domain
1	United States	36	Decision making, tourism, hospitality industry, hospitality, social media, entrepreneurship, machine learning
2	United Kingdom	30	Decision making, tourism, hospitality, social media, hospitality industry, consumption behavior, sustainability
3	Malaysia	19	Decision making, tourism, hospitality, hospitality industry, machine learning, tourism development, tourist destination
4	China	18	Decision making, tourist destination, medical tourism, hospitality, tourism development, sustainability
5	Spain	14	Decision making, tourism, hospitality industry, hospitality, environmental management, hotel industry
6	Taiwan	14	Decision making, hospitality industry, social media, performance, sustainability, hotels
7	Australia	13	Decision making, social networking (online), tourism, affect-driven behavior
8	Italy	12	Decision making, hotels, hospitality industry, tourism development

(continued)

Table 8. (*continued*)

No	Country	Number of Articles	Research domain
9	India	11	Decision making, tourist destination, tourism, hospitality, social media
10	Portugal	11	Decision making, tourism, hospitality industry, customer satisfaction

Based on Table 8 above, a more complete explanation of the number of documents published based on research domains from various countries is obtained. Related to the previous picture, the country with the 36th most published documentation comes from the United States with research domain keywords "Decision making", "tourism", "hospitality industry", "hospitality", "social media", "entrepreneurship", "machine learning". Then followed by neighboring countries, namely the United Kingdom with 30 documents, Malaysia 19 documents, China with 18 documents, Spain and Taiwan with 14 documents or with the acquisition of the same documents, Australia with 13 documents, Italy with 12 documents, and with the last position being in India along with Portugal having 11 documents published. The most widely used domains in Table 8 are "Decision Making", "Tourism", and "Hospitality Industry".

4   Conclusion and Suggestions

We have successfully presented a bibliometric analysis on decision making in tourism and hospitality from 2013 to 2023. Our bibliometric study has shown in helping researchers to determine the characteristics of scientific production, including what, who, how, how, and where, it was published. Our bibliometric study contributes theoretically in determining the characteristics and evolution of scientific publication in the related field. Therefore, the results of this work can be a guideline for future researchers who are researching new topics in decision making in tourism and hospitality. Finally, the most found topics "Decision Making", "Tourism", and "Hospitality Industry" can help the researchers to come up with alternative ideas of researches.

Since the coverage of Scopus database is larger than that ISI WoS database, thus it is recommended for future work to explore the WoS database which contain mostly reputable publication in doing bibliometric analysis for the same topic. For more comparison results involving different sources, it is also suggested to explore other databases such as Google, EBSCO, and ProQuest.

Acknowledgment. This research is fully supported by Sekolah Tinggi Pariwisata Ambarrukmo Yogyakarta (STIPRAM), Indonesia.

References

1. Zsarnoczky, M.: How does artificial intelligence affect the tourism industry? VADYBA **31**(2), 85–90 (2017)
2. Ivanov, S., Webster, C.: Conceptual framework of the use of robots, artificial intelligence and service automation in travel, tourism, and hospitality companies. In: Robots, Artificial Intelligence, and Service Automation in Travel, Tourism and Hospitality. Emerald (2019)
3. Samara, D., Magnisalis, I., Peristeras, V.: Artificial intelligence and big data in tourism: a systematic literature review. J. Hosp. Tour. Technol. **11**(2), 343–367 (2020)
4. Höpken, W., Eberle, T., Fuchs, M., Lexhagen, M.: Improving tourist arrival prediction: a big data and artificial neural network approach. J. Travel Res. **60**(5), 998–1017 (2021)
5. Wu, Y., et al.: Distributed linguistic representations in decision making: taxonomy, key elements and applications, and challenges in data science and explainable artificial intelligence. Inf. Fusion **65**, 165–178 (2021)
6. Mak, B.K., Cheung, L.T., Hui, D.L.: Community participation in the decision-making process for sustainable tourism development in rural areas of Hong Kong China. Sustainability **9**(10), 1695 (2017)
7. Karl, M.: Risk and uncertainty in travel decision-making: tourist and destination perspective. J. Travel Res. **57**(1), 129–146 (2018)
8. Yu, S.M., Wang, J., Wang, J.Q., Li, L.: A multi-criteria decision-making model for hotel selection with linguistic distribution assessments. Appl. Soft Comput. **67**, 741–755 (2018)
9. Nilashi, M., et al.: Factors influencing medical tourism adoption in Malaysia: a DEMATEL-Fuzzy TOPSIS approach. Comput. Ind. Eng. **137**, 106005 (2019)
10. Pantano, E., Priporas, C.V., Stylos, N., Dennis, C.: Facilitating tourists' decision making through open data analyses: a novel recommender system. Tour. Manag. Persp. **31**, 323–331 (2019)
11. Karl, M., Muskat, B., Ritchie, B.W.: Which travel risks are more salient for destination choice? An examination of the tourist's decision-making process. J. Destin. Mark. Manag. **18**, 100487 (2020)
12. Stylos, N.: Technological evolution and tourist decision-making: a perspective article. Tourism Rev. **75**(1), 273–278 (2020)
13. McCartney, G., McCartney, A.: Rise of the machines: towards a conceptual service-robot research framework for the hospitality and tourism industry. Int. J. Contemp. Hosp. Manag. **32**(12), 3835–3851 (2020)
14. Pappas, N., Glyptou, K.: Accommodation decision-making during the COVID-19 pandemic: complexity insights from Greece. Int. J. Hosp. Manag. **93**, 102767 (2021)
15. Niñerola, A., Sánchez-Rebull, M.V., Hernández-Lara, A.B.: Tourism research on sustainability: a bibliometric analysis. Sustainability **11**(5), 1377 (2019)
16. Nusair, K.: Developing a comprehensive life cycle framework for social media research in hospitality and tourism: a bibliometric method 2002–2018. Int. J. Contemp. Hosp. Manag. **32**(3), 1041–1066 (2020)
17. Palácios, H., de Almeida, M.H., Sousa, M.J.: A bibliometric analysis of trust in the field of hospitality and tourism. Int. J. Hosp. Manag. **95**, 102944 (2021)
18. Sigala, M.: A bibliometric review of research on COVID-19 and tourism: reflections for moving forward. Tour. Manag. Perspect. **40**, 100912 (2021)
19. Manosso, F.C., Domareski Ruiz, T.C.: Using sentiment analysis in tourism research: A systematic, bibliometric, and integrative review. J. Tour. Herit. Serv. Mark. **7**(2), 17–27 (2021)
20. Pandey, K., Joshi, S.: Trends in destination choice in tourism research: a 25-year bibliometric review. FIIB Bus. Rev. **10**(4), 371–392 (2021). https://doi.org/10.1177/23197145211032430

21. Habibi, A., Mousavi, M., Jamali, S.M., Ale Ebrahim, N.: A bibliometric study of medical tourism. Anatolia **33**(3), 415–425 (2022)
22. Pahrudin, P., Liu, L.W., Li, S.Y.: What is the role of tourism management and marketing toward sustainable tourism? A bibliometric analysis approach. Sustainability **14**(7), 4226 (2022)
23. Qiao, G., Cao, Y., Chen, Q., Jia, Q.: Understanding family tourism: a perspective of bibliometric review. Front. Psychol. **13** (2022). https://doi.org/10.3389/fpsyg.2022.937312
24. Kalia, P., Mladenović, D., Acevedo-Duque, Á.: Decoding the trends and the emerging research directions of digital tourism in the last three decades: a bibliometric analysis. SAGE Open **12**(4), 21582440221128180 (2022)
25. Lopes, E., Araújo-Vila, N., Perinotto, A.R.C., Cardoso, L.: Tourism and land planning in natural spaces: bibliometric approach to the structure of scientific concepts. Land **11**(11), 1930 (2022). https://doi.org/10.3390/land11111930
26. Vatankhah, S., Darvishmotevali, M., Rahimi, R., Jamali, S.M., Ale Ebrahim, N.: Assessing the application of multi-criteria decision making techniques in hospitality and tourism research: a bibliometric study. Int. J. Contemp. Hosp. Manag. **35**(7), 2590–2563 (2023). https://doi.org/10.1108/IJCHM-05-2022-0643
27. Setyanto, T.J., Purnama, Y., Kherenhapukh, W.: A bibliometric analysis of pilgrimage tourism researches from 2012 to 2022. Int. J. Adv. Contemp. Islamic Stud **1**(1) (2023)
28. Nayan, N.A.M., Ghazali, N.A., Sayuthi, A.S.M., Sarizan, N.M.: Bibliometric analysis of lectin in cancer research. Int. J. Adv. Pub. Health **4**(2) (2023)
29. Gomes, S., Lopes, J.M., Ferreira, L.: Looking at the tourism industry through the lenses of industry 4.0: a bibliometric review of concerns and challenges. J. Hosp. Tour. Insights 1–22 (2023)
30. Oktaviani, A.D., Anggrayni, R., Della Sari, F., Megawanti, P. (2022). Bibliometric analysis of the mathematical learning method during the covid-19 pandemic. Int. J. Adv. Math. Comput. Sci. **3**(3)
31. Sari, I.R., Basuki, E.A., Kunda, E.E.: A decade analysis on sustainable tourism in Indonesia: bibliometric approach. Int. J. Adv. Psychol. Hum. Sci. **4**(5) (2023)
32. Widodo, W.I., et al.: A decade analysis on big data for tourism: bibliometric approach. Int. J. Adv. Data Sci. Intell. Anal. **2**(2) (2022)
33. Kiswantoro, A., et al.: A Bibliometric Analysis of Risk Management in Homestay Researches. Int. J. Adv. Manag. Bus. Intell. **4**(1) (2023)

Smart Touristic Ports – The Emergence of Sustainable Marinas from Smart Conversion. What Future for Sardinians Ports

Brunella Brundu⬤, Silvia Battino⬤, and Stefano Carboni(✉)⬤

DiSea – University of Sassari, 07100 Sassari, Sardinia, Italy
{brundubr,sbattino,scarboni2}@uniss.it

Abstract. Among the sectors covered by Blue Growth, the Europe 2020 strategy to foster sustainable growth in the marine and maritime sectors, coastal tourism represents an important sector of the tourism industry. The Region of Sardinia recently launched the Regional Plan for the Tourist Port Network as a fundamental tool for strategic planning of the sector, in order to better exploit the islands strategic position in the Mediterranean. However, the potential of ports is not always expressed by the territories in which they are located for various reasons, economic, political, administrative, etc. Competition will therefore take place if all the potential is balanced according to the peculiarities of the territories and the dictates of the most advanced multi-sectoral policies. In this context, the focus will be on the strategy that conceives the future of ports, in particular of the Sardinian Region, considering a smart, green and integrated approach for a better management, accessibility and safety of marinas and surrounding areas.

Keywords: Smart tourism · Marinas · Smart ports · Sardinia

1 Introduction

The 'blue planet' represents a vital resource for all countries of the world. The transition to a sustainable, green and smart world therefore also affects marine and coastal landscapes. The United Nations during the Rio de Janeiro +20 Conference in 2012, introduced for the first time the concept of a 'Blue economy' in which seas and oceans are considered key resources for achieving sustainability goals [1]. The benefits for local communities are undoubted, but at the same time the negative impacts (land use, pollution, water consumption, physical and socio-cultural pressures) are different.

Indeed, for the better management of coastal territories, the European Commission on February 20, 2014, released the 'Strategy for more Growth and Jobs in Coastal and

This study is developed in the Research Project "Tourism, accessibility, and digitalization for sustainable transformation of internal areas", Department of Economics and Business – University of Sassari. This paper is the result of the joint work of the authors. In particular: paragraphs 1, 2 and 3 have been written by Silvia Battino, paragraphs 4 and 6 by Brunella Brundu and paragraph 5 by Stefano Carboni.

Maritime Tourism,' which aims, through 14 action steps, to sustainably promote the growth of the sector by helping coastal regions and entrepreneurs achieve the goals of the blue economy [2].

Port areas (industrial, commercial, tourist, etc.) are its pillars, and their operation is fundamental for moving goods and people and connecting even the most peripheral and insular areas. The many and varied activities carried out in the ports are a driving force for the socio-economic development of the coastal regions involved [3]. With specific reference to the activities related to the tourism sector, in particular, coastal and maritime tourism, besides representing one of the oldest forms of tourism, has become one of the main areas of growth in this sector and accounts for 44% of Gross Value Added (GVA) and 63% of employment in the European blue economy [4, 5]. Along with its 70,000 km of coastline, Europe is one of the main destinations for boaters. The more than 4,500 marinas offer around 1.75 million berths for a total of 6.3 million boats [6, 7]. This diversified 'ecosystem' crossed every day by significant flows of people and goods must today survive according to the rules of sustainability. The latter must be followed by an innovative approach in which Information Communication Technologies (ICTs) represent the tools that can improve and optimize the competitiveness and activities of all operators involved.

In this scenario, we will focus on the strategy that conceives the future of ports considering the combination of three elements: smart, green and integrated that will allow better management, accessibility and safety of marinas and surrounding areas. On this line of research, the article consists of three more paragraphs in addition to this first introductory paragraph: 2. Objectives and methods, 3. Related works, 4. Some of the policies dedicated and implemented at local level, 5. Sardinia's smart tourist ports, 6. Conclusions. After a brief literature review on nautical tourism, this research focuses on the case study of the Region of Sardinia (Italy), which aims, by adopting a smart and sustainable approach, to enhance the network of its marinas to improve its position in the Mediterranean tourism context.

2 Objectives and Methods

The purpose of this article is to understand the importance of adopting policies and actions aimed at following the sustainable approach and the use of new technologies capable of helping tourist port realities to design 'new' cohesive and smart spaces. The redevelopment of infrastructural spaces and the creation of new resources and services for tourism is outlined as a strategy capable of satisfying, in the long term, the different users (residents and tourists) and improving the competitiveness and image of the territories involved.

The first part of the work begins with a brief review of the literature on the concept of nautical tourism and the different declinations of this complex tourism typology. The second part is dedicated to the case study of Sardinia, an island at the centre of the Mediterranean, which is working to pursue innovative initiatives and projects to improve the network of its marinas.

3 Related Works

Nautical tourism is a form of tourism generally identified in places where water is the main resource for bringing to fruition a variety of recreational and sporting activities. The multifunctional nature of these recreational activities, which can be achieved by enjoying the landscapes of the sea, lakes, rivers, and other aquatic environments, does not facilitate the definitional framing of the concept of nautical tourism [8]. A recent study (2021) by Martínez Vázquez, Milán García and De Pablo Valenciano [9] reported that, although there are different schools of thought on the definition of the term, the sea, the boat and the marina seem to stand out as peculiar elements of this type of tourism. Therefore, considering the broader meaning of the term, it is necessary to include the concept of nautical yachting, which is expressed through the activities (tourist and non-tourist) carried out with a recreational boat. Luković, acquiring the more general characteristics of the 'tourism' term, seems to summarize these attributes by defining nautical tourism as "a sum of poly-functional activities and relations that are caused by the tourists boaters' stay within or out of the ports of nautical tourism, and by the use of vessels or other objects related to the nautical and tourist activities, for the purpose of recreation, sports, entertainment or other needs" [10, p. 400]. In the following, we will focus on the leading role of port facilities in Italian nautical tourism. Italy, with its 7,500 km of coastline and rooted maritime culture, qualifies as one of the most important nautical tourism destinations internationally. Considering the data extrapolated from the report for the year 2021 by Confindustria Nautica of the approximately 1,622 marinas and multi-purpose ports (ports and small ports, industrial and commercial ports, canal ports and docks) distributed along the Mediterranean coasts, as many as 547 are concentrated on Italian territory, followed by the coastal regions of France (400) and Spain (370). Port structures count 148,634 berths, of which as many as 46,251 are to be subject to marinas which have an average number of berths (526) more than double that of multipurpose ports (223). Among the regional classifications, Sardinia holds first place for the number of berths (21,709), followed by Liguria (21,577) and Sicily (17,875). More specifically on the distribution of berths in marinas, about half are concentrated in four regions (Liguria, Sardinia, Friuli Venezia Giulia, Tuscany) [11]. Each individual infrastructure may be operated in the public, private or mixed form, and represents a simple 'boat park', but also a 'seaside plaza' destined to connect the sea with the mainland by welcoming yachtsmen and tourists seeking tourist-recreational experiences [12, 13]. In addition to yachtsmen and tourists, the actors of this organized space between 'land and sea' are the service providers in the port area and the residents who use or can use the services present. Technical, commercial and tourist services in all types of port must be organized and managed with a view to maximum functionality while also integrating the environmental and socio-economic resources of the surrounding area into the network. The activation of 'new' territorial aggregations for local development is in line with the objectives of the blue economy, which in Italy is implemented in the National Recovery and Resilience Plan (PNRR – Piano Nazionale di Ripresa e Resilienza). The Plan provides for a series of investments and strategic actions oriented towards a green, circular and smart development to increase the competitiveness and qualification of the activities related to the sea. The valorization of the tourist port system must necessarily pass through the adoption of a smartness approach in which the role of innovative technological tools is essential to create cohesive spaces [3, 14].

4 Some of the Policies Dedicated and Implemented at Local Level

In March 2023, the Ministry of Tourism presented the Strategic Tourism Plan 2023–2027 to Federalberghi and the other organizations dedicated to it, indicating the sea as one of the three pillars on which to support the strategic strengthening of Italian tourism (ferries, island tourism, cruise ships, etc.) and the driving factor of the entire industry. At the moment it seems difficult to calculate the flows that may be generated on Mediterranean passenger routes due to multiple variables, to be identified mainly in the post-Covid flows and the war in Ukraine, although a general increase in the qualitative standards of the offer is considered very likely [15].

The Tenth Report on the Sea Economy (2022) [16] explains Italy's contribution to the European Union's Blue Economy, and in the ranking by incidence of employment and of blue economy enterprises on the regional total, it places Sardinia in second place with 6.6% and 7%, undoubtedly an excellent position but far behind Liguria, which has a value of 11.9% and 10.3% respectively. Of course, there can be many explanations, but it is perplexing that a region located in the centre of the western Mediterranean, with the highest perimeter compared to the other Italian regions bordering the sea (just under 1900 km), is not able to exploit the advantages of blue growth activities to a greater extent. Morphological, structural, political, social, etc., these are the causes presented throughout Sardinian history and which still constitute problems that are far from being resolved.

The multiple activities covered by the nautical industry make it a sector of great importance for the regional economy with which it is strategically connected to the tourist market. Ports are increasingly becoming places of penetration and vehicles for further recreational activities and tourist products and assets located in more inland areas and of which, the tourist who is increasingly well-informed and also eager for new experiences, seizes the opportunities for knowledge and enjoyment.

The island is the second region nationwide, after Sicily, for the number of active ports and berths. In recent years, also due to the pandemic period, more and more tourists, including yachtsmen, have chosen Sardinia's coasts, the preferred areas being in the north, in the Provinces of Olbia and Sassari, on the Costa Smeralda, the Maddalena Archipelago and the Capo Caccia protected area. In particular, in the north-eastern part 'there are 43.48% of the ports in the whole of Sardinia, the highest number of berths on the island and 66% of maxi-yacht and giga-yacht berths' [11, 17, p. 5].

The Region of Sardinia, however, is certainly not unaware of the importance of policies and directives devised at various levels; among the latest documents produced is the Regional Plan for the network of tourist ports (Delib.G.R. no. 47/52 of 24.9.2020), which is of interest for the topic dealt with in this paper.

The Plan's objective is the construction of the island's network of tourist ports and is divided into a Vision and a Mission. The former, considering the island's strategic position at the centre of the Mediterranean and the quality of both services and environmental value of Sardinia as a whole, would like to lead it to be a privileged destination for leisure navigation. The Mission aims to 'implement a capillary system of access points to the hinterland to favor the overall tourist fruition of the regional territory' [18, p. 17].

Achieving these goals requires planning the existing ports, identifying their criticalities and reorganizing their logic for a well-defined offer of a product that is not only nautical but more broadly tourist. In fact, the document states that "port facilities dedicated to nautical pleasure boating do not 'dilute' each other, in the sense that they constitute a whole but not a system" [18, p.19]. The criticalities are innumerable if the real goal is a high target, in line with the dictates of environmental and structural policies indicated by the increasingly dense directives governing the subject.

The Marina Network Plan has used the Strategic Plan for the Development and Marketing of Tourism in Sardinia (STP) – Destination Sardinia 2018 – 2021, and the Regional Landscape Plan as the planning tools of greatest interest [19]. The TSP clearly includes the "Nautical Product" in which it specifies that the Network is dedicated to the promotion of both Sardinian nautical tourism and the inland territory with its specificities. It also highlights the weakness of the shipbuilding industry, which would allow the mooring and maintenance of boats during the winter with an estimated loss, according to the Ports Network, of 60–70% of the potential market that is currently directed to destinations such as Palma or Menorca in the Balearic Islands.

The Regional Landscape Plan (PPR) indicates the planning/design framework of each Plan intervention in terms of constraints and prescriptions to be respected. As is well known, Sardinia's PPR, approved by DGR no. 36/7 of 05/09/2006 and currently being updated, represents the First Homogeneous Territorial Area, and is composed of 27 landscape areas made up of the coastal municipalities hosting all the ports on the island, including marinas [20].

More recently, the Ministry of Sustainable Infrastructures and Mobility, transposed Directive 2014/89/EU through Legislative Decree No. 201/2016 and formulated three Italian Maritime Spatial Plans, traceable to the three sub-regions referred to in the Marine Strategy (Art. 4 of Directive 2008/56/EU):

- the Western Mediterranean Sea;
- the Adriatic Sea;
- the Ionian and Central Mediterranean Sea.

The indications provided by the plans are defined at a strategic and guideline level and each one is based on the characteristics of its own sub-area; Sardinia belongs to the "Ionian and Central Mediterranean Sea" region (2022). The reference time horizon of the Plan is 2032, extendable, according to the needs that may arise, to 2050 [21].

In the "Ionian and Central Mediterranean Sea" region, improved port energy efficiency is desired in order to achieve a conversion to "green ports" and a reduction in pollution in these areas. Finally, the coexistence of various maritime uses and the protection of habitats and species is an obligation. The sub-area in which the island is framed is MO/7 Territorial Waters Sardinia. The Plan states that the general and transversal

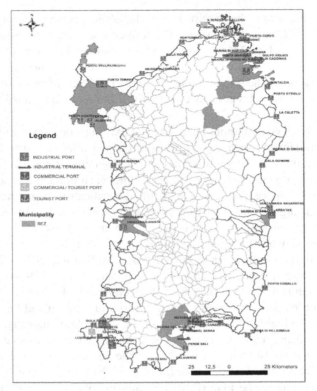

Fig. 1. The main ports in Sardinia and the municipalities over which a SEZ falls. Source: Own elaboration on Sardinia Geoportal data.

objective of the Region of Sardinia is sustainable development, in concert and in compliance with the United Nations 2030 Agenda, the National Strategy for Sustainable Development and the Regional Strategy for Sustainable Development (SRSvS) [21, p. 118]. Among the thirty specific objectives, it identifies Maritime Transport and Ports and Coastal and Maritime Tourism, in addition to the other activities covered by Blue Growth.

While focusing on Sardinia's marinas, this work cannot ignore the island's 'Strategic Development Plan' (2021) [22], which also includes Special Economic Zones (SEZs) in some areas. The Plan proposes a SEZ configured as a 'network' in the coastal area, conceived according to national dictates in which a SEZ is 'also made up of areas that are not territorially adjacent as long as they present an economic-functional nexus, and which include at least one port area…'. These areas are also represented by ports that "present a strategic relevance for the activities of territorial specialization that are intended to strengthen and demonstrate a functional economic link with the port area". The countries in which SEZs are located have clearly demonstrated the importance of the contribution they make to the entire economy. The SEZ that the Plan proposes for the coastal area has, as already stated, a 'network' configuration; it includes the ports of Cagliari, Olbia, Oristano, Porto Torres, Portovesme and Arbatax, to which other ports or industrial areas may be later connected (Fig. 1[1]). These are port areas that often host further typologies within them, such as, for example, marinas, areas that can convey tourism and tourists towards more inland places or act as a land link between the various seaside areas, places in any case a hinge between sea and land [23].

The PNRR's "Investments and reforms for the port" report (2022) [24], set itself the goal of improving competitiveness through four key points: strengthening the powers of port authorities for strategic planning; improving the processes for planning and awarding port concessions; improving port energy efficiency and cold-ironing; and developing a National Logistics Platform capable of making information content and processes related to port and retro-port activities interoperable. Sardinia, in addition to other projects, is seeing the financing of on-shore power supply plants in many of its most important ports (Olbia – Golfo Aranci – Santa Teresa Gallura – Porto Torres – Portovesme – Cagliari Porto Storico – Cagliari Porto Canale), the objective being to power the ships at berth from dockside installations that allow the engines of the vessels to be switched off with a consequent zero impact on the atmosphere.

5 Sardinia's Smart Tourist Ports

Tourist ports represent one of the main elements of nautical tourism [25] and, by creating demand, they contribute to the development of the local economy [26].

The Region of Sardinia, which aims to strengthen the network of its marinas, is adopting a smart and sustainable approach in order to improve its position in the Mediterranean tourist context [27]. Tourist ports create demand for nautical tourism and are of fundamental importance for the territory of Sardinia, in which the tourist offer is strongly seasonal and of a seaside type. It is essential to protect and apply efficient strategies at the regional level that are capable of offering adequate services and that can satisfy the tourist demand dedicated to this segment.

In a recent report on tourism, drawn up by the Bank of Italy (Banca d'Italia), it is possible to observe that the revenues from international travel in Italy amounted to 21.3 billion euros in 2021, with a tourist presence of around 26 million individuals [28].

These data show that Sardinia is in a context of high tourist levels and the data relating to tourist movements on the island show that the region has contributed decisively to such large numbers of tourists at a national level in 2021 and 2022.

Investigating the specific case of Sardinian ports, the data provided by the Sardinian Sea Port System Authority (Autorità di Sistema Portuale del mare di Sardegna) show that 2.3 million passengers were welcomed by the ports of the region in 2022, of which

---

[1] Figure 1 identifies the island's major tourist ports and the multifunctional ports located in the most economically dynamic municipalities and benefiting from the projects financed by the PNRR (only the port of Oristano is absent from such funding). The Regional Plan for the Tourist Port Network, however, identifies a further 79 port facilities for nautical pleasure boating under public or mixed management to be developed to complete the Network, some of which already meet the Plan's requirements, while others need upgrading and restructuring. Finally, it recognizes 7 New Port Facilities (NPS) located in territorial areas that, despite offering a qualified tourist offer (landscape, environmental and historical-cultural emergencies), do not enjoy adequate use.

1.9 million from June 1st to September 20th [29]. The most significant period, in terms of tourist flow, is the month of September, in which 275,196 visits were registered. Thus showing an increase of 16.8% compared to the previous year in which 235,613 tourists were registered in the ports of the island [30].

The impact that the large number of tourists, generated by the marinas, creates on the economic development of surrounding urban areas, enhancing its local resources [31] is also of considerable interest. It must therefore be considered that these places must be able to welcome and host all the tourists who go there through a Smart management of the port [32, 33].

By examining the tourist ports of Sardinia, it is possible to observe the data relating to the pleasure craft registered in the Registers of the Peripheral Maritime Offices, the kilometers of coastline, the berths per coast and then comparing them with the data relating to the other Italian provinces (Table 1).

Table 1. Nautical pleasure craft registered in the Registers of the Peripheral Maritime Offices, kilometers of coastline, berths by coastline as of December 31st 2021. Source: Own elaboration on Ministry of Infrastructure and Sustainable Mobility data, 2021.

Region	Units registered with Maritime Offices	Coastline (Km)	Berths per km of coastline
Abruzzo	557	138	12.5
Campania	8,088	522	31.2
Calabria	1,045	796	6.5
Emilia-Romagna	3,434	122	43.4
Friuli-Venezia Giulia	3,569	94	167.9
Lazio	8,378	363	22.9
Liguria	18,141	389	63.9
Marche	2,531	188	24.6
Molise	65	36	16.3
Puglia	2,507	1,015	14.4
Sardinia	4,012	1,851	9.4
Sicily	4,109	1,473	11.0
Tuscany	8,610	561	34.3
Veneto	4,165	140	44.9
Total	**69,211**	**7,688**	**20.4**

Sardinia, with its 1,851 km of coastline, is the region with the largest coastline in Italy. However, it should focus on the availability of berths by exploiting precisely the high extension of its coasts.

Furthermore, it was possible to investigate the data relating to the number of parking places by type of structure, in such a way as to be able to compare the data relating to tourist ports with two other types, commercial ports and mooring points (Table 2). Comparing the data of Sardinia with those of the other regions of Italy, it can be observed that the number of berths in the tourist ports of Sardinia is the highest compared to the other regions of Italy, thus representing 17.5% of the number of berths throughout Italy.

Table 2. Number of berths by region and type of structure as of September 30th 2021. Source: Own elaboration on Ministry of Infrastructure and Sustainable Mobility data, 2021.

Region	Tourist Port	Commercial Ports	Mooring Points
Abruzzo	140	1,584	–
Campania	5,555	5,220	5,530
Calabria	3,195	1,251	739
Emilia-Romagna	2,483	1,519	1,293
Friuli-Venezia Giulia	10,136	1,177	4,471
Lazio	2,645	2,811	2,845
Liguria	10,623	6,077	8,159
Marche	3,908	200	524
Molise	434	153	–
Puglia	4,558	3,490	6,563
Sardinia	12,584	3,087	1,798
Sicily	4,971	5,548	5,670
Tuscany	6,973	3,235	9,031
Veneto	3,684	1,239	1,362
Total	**71,889**	**36,591**	**47,985**

Since the economy linked to tourist ports is essential for the economy of a country like Italy, it is necessary to plan sustainable development strategies [34] that take into account green policies within tourist ports, and how the care and conservation of the existing greenery is fundamental in the planning process [35]. It is therefore necessary to manage this aspect through an approach aimed at protecting the marine environment by eliminating or reducing the activities that cause pollution [31].

An action that can be done, aimed at mitigating pollution levels and keeping the waters of tourist ports clean, can be achieved by introducing laws that further promote the protection of marine waters [36]. It should also be remembered that sustainable development strategies can be more effective if adopted at the national level [37] thus the success of a sustainable strategy applied in a single tourist port can be replicated in other tourist ports across the country as well, to be able to generate an increase in the quality of port services at a national level.

A constant analysis of the water will then be necessary, especially in the summer period, in which a greater concentration of boats and yachts could worsen their quality compared to the rest of the year.

Tourist ports need dredging of the seabed which can however pollute the waters in which the works take place. Also in this case, sustainable alternatives can be chosen such as the seabed remodeling plant based on the principle of ejectors, which let the removal of sand accumulated in the seabed of the port with zero environmental impact [38].

Within the theme of the sustainability of a tourist port, it must be considered that the boats and port equipment will inevitably pollute the marine waters [39]. The engines of boats and yachts that remain in operation during mooring, in order to power the electronic devices used in tourist boats, generate pollution of both the water and the surrounding air [40].

Solutions that make it possible to satisfy the needs of tourists and at the same time protect the territory from pollution must be adopted, in order to preserve a cleaner sea for future generations [41].

As a response to the issue of environmental sustainability within ports, cold ironing is introduced, which is an innovative energy supply system [42] aimed at reducing water and air pollution near ports [43], caused by the engines of ships and boats during mooring [44, 45].

Through this process it is possible to have electricity in the docks [46] so that parked yachts and boats no longer need to keep their engines running while moored [47], as they will be able to use electricity directly from the pier [48].

It has been ascertained that, thanks to the electrical infrastructure of the port docks, it is possible to obtain a reduction of CO_2 equal to 50%, 99% of CO and over 50% of N_2O [49].

Obviously, in order to maximize this system, the electricity used for the energy supply of ships should be produced from renewable sources, for example from solar panels, wind or photovoltaic plants [50].

The electricity produced can also be stored in lithium-ion batteries [51] in order to have energy available when it is not possible to receive it from wind and photovoltaic plants.

It has been observed that cold ironing is also convenient in economic terms, taking into account the fuel savings and wear of the engines [52] of boats and yachts.

Cold ironing is spreading in the major ports worldwide, especially in North America, Northern Europe [53] and in Italy as well, such as in Venice, as part of the "green ports" project [54].

The implementation of this system can also be implemented in the tourist ports of Sardinia which, as observed in this work, are of considerable importance at a national level, taking into account that they have the largest number of berths in Italy.

6 Conclusions

It is now well understood that the economy of the sea is of particular importance in Sardinia. The geopolitical context could also favor the shift in global maritime routes and finally grant it the importance that its geographical position should guarantee. The driving sectors (tourism, transport, logistics, etc.), however, must be combined with the often critical nature of the sectors themselves and the dictates of the imperative policies of environmental and landscape sustainability of their development. The island's strong vocation for tourism increasingly has indirect effects on other sectors of the economy, such as, for example, agriculture and culture, which place the region in a very low position compared to the regions of the European Union considered on the basis of per capita GDP (177/244).

The greatest criticality, in addition to the now very heavy population deficit, is linked to the port and airport infrastructure, for external connections, which are the gateways to the entire region, but also roads for the penetration of the innermost areas. Sardinia is thus condemned to a perennial, historical and bivalent isolation: difficult accessibility to internal areas and isolation with respect to the peninsula due not only to insularity, but above all to the problems of territorial continuity. The White Paper on Sardinia's infrastructural priorities (2022) [55] reports on all these critical issues and sets two macro objectives: upgrading the main road and rail network and taking care of the secondary road network; connecting Sardinia to the peninsula and to the national and international markets through additional and stronger connections to ports and airports for both freight and passenger transit. However, the commitment to connect the island with itself and to the outside world requires further medium- and long-term projects; there are now many unfinished works that are more than a decade old. Or else an obsolete railway network, for which the White Paper calls for a modern and capillary one that "cancels the gap created by the lack of connections between the island's main ports and airports" [55, p. 30] in order to "interconnect them and link them to the main towns and centres of major tourist attraction" [55, p. 51]. Finally, enhancing the network of marinas is also a strategic regional asset for economic and social development. The policies examined in this paper, although for lack of space they are briefly mentioned, explain what can be achieved at various levels for the needs of our economy but also of our planet. The idea of increasingly exploiting Sardinia's geographic position as the centre of the Mediterranean is not only, though undoubtedly an economic issue, but also the possibility of servicing an ever-growing number of logistical chains by virtue of the various ports dedicated to them, and offering moorings and other types of tourism in and from ports reserved to this segment of the economy.

The future developments of this research envisage the structure of models, not only to bring the ports up to set standards, but which initially involve, organize and revitalize at least the hinterlands and the first belt areas of these systems. These already exist in the hinterlands of Sardinia's major ports, but all the others need a territorial identification, such as a brand, to make them attractive and dynamic for the development of 'new' economic segments.

References

1. United Nations: Blue Economy Concept Paper (2012). https://sustainabledevelopment.un. org/content/documents/2978BEconcept.pdf
2. European Commission: A European Strategy for more Growth and Jobs in Coastal and Maritime Tourism. COM (2014) 86 final, Brussels (2014). https://eur-lex.europa.eu/legal-content/ EN/TXT/PDF/?uri=CELEX:52014DC0086
3. Battino, S., Muñoz Leonisio, M.M.: Port Authorities and smartness: the training policies of Spain's smart ports. J. Reading 2(11), 195–208 (2022)

4. Commission, E.: The EU blue economy report 2022. Publications Office of the European Union, Luxembourg (2022)
5. Orams, M.: Marine Tourism: Development, Impacts and Management. Routledge, Abingdon (2002)
6. European Boating Industry: Nautical tourism in Europe. https://europeanboatingindustry.eu/eu-affairs/eu-issues/tourism
7. Mundula, L., Ladu, M., Balletto, G., Milesi, A.: Smart marinas. The case of metropolitan city of Cagliari. In: Gervasi, O., et al. (eds.) ICCSA 2020, LNCS 12255, pp. 51–66. Springer Nature, Switzerland (2020)
8. Benevolo, C.: Problematiche di sostenibilità nell'ambito del turismo nautico in Italia. Impresa-Progetto Electron. J. Manag. **2**, 1–17 (2011)
9. Martínez Vázquez, R.M., Milán García, J., De Pablo Valenciano, J.: Analysis and trends of global research on nautical, maritime and marine tourism. J. Marine Sci. Eng. **9**(1), 93 (2021)
10. Luković, T.: Nautical tourism and its function in the economic development of Europe. In: Kasimoglu, M. (eds.) Visions for Global Tourism Industry – Creating and Sustaining Competitive Strategies, pp. 399–430. IntechOpen, London (2012)
11. Confindustria Nautica: Boating in figures. Industry statistics for 2021. Fondazione Edison, Milano (2022). https://lanauticaincifre.it/pubblicazioni/. The data do not include the 237 berthing points in Italy with seasonal facilities whose infrastructures are not permanent as they may be removed in winter (quays and wharves, equipped beaches and boat launch ramp).
12. Fortezza, F.: La nautica da diporto: reti produttive, risorse umane e sfide strategiche. Il comparto nella Provincia di Pesaro-Urbino. Franco Angeli, Milano (2009)
13. Spinelli, R., Benevolo, C.: Towards a new body of marine tourism research: a scoping literature review of nautical tourism. J. Outdoor Recreat. Tour. **40**, 100569 (2022)
14. de la Peña Zarzuelo, I.: Cybersecurity in ports and maritime industry: reasons for raising awareness on this issue. Transp. Policy **100**, 1–4 (2021). https://doi.org/10.1016/j.tranpol.2020.10.001
15. Acciaro, M.: Recenti sviluppi dell'economia del mare. In: Il mare che verrà. Analisi strategica sulle opportunità del Mar Mediterraneo. Centro Giuseppe Bono SEACS, pp. 102–122 (2023)
16. INFORMARE (eds.): X Rapporto Economia del Mare 2022. Azienda Speciale della Camera di commercio di Frosinone e Latina, Alatri (2022)
17. Benelli, G., Calatola, R., Ezza, A., Giovanelli, L., Morandi, F., Usai, A.: La Nautica in Sardegna: le prospettive di crescita di un sistema economico territoriale tra industria e turismo. Dipartimento di Scienze Economiche e Aziendali. Università degli Studi di Sassari (2022)
18. Regione Sardegna: Piano Regionale della rete della portualità turistica. Assessorato dei lavori pubblici, Allegato alla Delib. G.R. n. 47/52 del 24.09.2020 (2020). https://portal.sardegnasira.it/-/piano-regionale-della-rete-di-portualita-turistica-prrpt-avviata-la-valutazione-ambientale-strategica
19. Regione Sardegna: Destinazione Sardegna 2018–2021. Piano Strategico di Sviluppo e Marketing Turistico della Sardegna, F-Tourism and Marketing, Torino (2018)
20. Brundu, B., Battino, S.: Riflessioni sul piano paesaggistico regionale della Sardegna: il contributo delle aree interne. Documenti Geografici **2**, 71–89 (2021)
21. MIMS (Ministero delle Infrastrutture e della mobilità sostenibili): I Piani dello Spazio Marittimo italiani Area Marittima "Tirreno-Mediterraneo Occidentale". Sintesi (Agosto 2022)
22. Regione Sardegna: Pianificazione dello spazio marittimo: documento di posizionamento della Regione Autonoma della Sardegna (2021)
23. Zunica, M.: Per un approccio con l'interfaccia terra-mare. Quaderni del Dipartimento di Geografia, pp. 3–15. Padova (1986)
24. MIMS (Ministero delle Infrastrutture e della Mobilità Sostenibili): Investimenti e riforme del PNRR per la portualità (2022)

25. Martín, R., Yepes, V.: Assessing the relationship between landscape and management within marinas: the managers' perception. Land **11**(7), 961 (2022). https://doi.org/10.3390/land11 070961
26. Teo, T.W., Choy, B.H.: In: Tan, O.S., Low, E.L., Tay, E.G., Yan, Y.K. (eds.) Singapore Math and Science Education Innovation. ETLPPSIP, vol. 1, pp. 43–59. Springer, Singapore (2021). https://doi.org/10.1007/978-981-16-1357-9_3
27. Balletto G., Milesi A., Ladu, M., Borruso, G.: Networks for reinventing the past. The case of the Santa Barbara Walk (Sardinia, Italy). In: 23rd IPSAPA/ISPALEM International Scientific Conference Napoli (Italy), 4th–5th Jul 2019
28. Banca d'Italia: Indagine sul turismo internazionale. Statistiche - Banca d'Italia (2022)
29. Regione Sardegna: Turismo, estate record per la Sardegna e la stagione continua. Cagliari (2022). https://www.regione.sardegna.it/j/v/2568?s=441458&v=2&c=3692&t=1
30. Regione Sardegna: Turismo, la Sardegna cresce e a giugno supera i livelli pre-Covid. Cagliari (2022). https://www.regione.sardegna.it/j/v/2568?s=437493&v=2&c=3692&t=1
31. Gambino, S.: Nuove forme di turismo per l'Area costiera nebroidea: il ruolo del porto turistico di Capo d'Orlando – New forms of tourism for the Nebrodi coastal area: the role of tourist port of Capo d'Orlando. Bollettino dell'Associazione Italiana di Cartografia **164**, 62–72 (2018)
32. Łapko, A.: Age simulation suits in education and training of staff for the nautical tourism sector. Sustainability **15**(4), 3803 (2023)
33. Radulovic, A.: Smart technology applied in the management of yachting marinas. Int. J. Maritime Eng. **164**(A1), 81–90 (2022)
34. Di Bella, A.: Boutique festival e innovazione turistica: il caso della Sicilia. Rivista Geografica Italiana **1**, 75–94 (2023)
35. Locci, E.: Birth of tourism in southern Sardinia Santa Margherita di Pula. Eur. J. Hospitality Tourism Res. **10**(3), 13–22 (2022)
36. Leonardi, R., Abondio, I., Campolo, F., Fabris, E., Pedersoli, M., Tropea, M.F.: Commentario alle leggi sull'ambiente – Articoli da 53 a 176. Key editore, Milano (2023)
37. Idris, H.: Southeast asian port development: policy and initiatives towards achieving 2030 agenda on sustainable development goals. Akademika **92**(2), 129–142 (2022)
38. Pellegrini, M., Saccani, C.: Tecnologie innovative ad eiettori per la gestione sostenibile di fondali costieri, bocche portuali e porti turistici. In: Gestione sostenibile dei sedimenti e crescita blu in ambito costiero e nei medi e piccoli porti, Tavolo Nazionale Erosione Costiera. Ecomondo Scientific Technical Committee, ISPRA, GNRAC, 2019, pp. 379–385 (2019)
39. Tong, L., Zhang, C., Peng, Z., Wang, L.: Spatial–temporal distribution characteristics and correlation analysis of air pollutants from ships in inland ports. Sustainability **14**(21), 14214 (2022)
40. Barberi, S., Sambito, M., Neduzha, L., Severino, A.: Pollutant emissions in ports: a comprehensive review. Infrastructures **6**(8), 114 (2021)
41. Łapko, A., Hącia, E., Wieczorek, R.: Collection of waste from passenger ships and its impact on the functioning of tourist port city Świnoujście. Sustainability **13**(4), 1–16 (2021)
42. Chica, M., Martínez-López, A., Romero-Filguiera, A.: Specific environmental charges to boost Cold Ironing use in the European Short Sea Shipping, Transport and Environment. Transport. Res. Part **94**, 102775 (2021)
43. Martínez-López, A., Romero, A., Orosa, J.A.: Assessment of cold ironing and LNG as mitigation tools of short sea shipping emissions in port: a Spanish case study. Appl. Sci. **11**(5), 1–16 (2021)
44. D'Agostino, F., Schiapparelli, G.P., Dallas, S., Spathis, D., Georgiou, V., Prousalidis, J.: On estimating the port power demands for cold ironing applications. In: IEEE Electric Ship Technologies Symposium (ESTS), Arlington, VA, USA, pp. 1–5 (2021)
45. Zis, T.: Prospects of cold ironing as an emissions reduction option. Transport. Res. Part A Policy Pract. **119**, 82–95 (2019)

46. Bakar, N.N.A., Bazmohammadi, N., Vasquez, J.C., Guerrero, J.M.: Electrification of onshore power systems in maritime transportation towards decarbonization of ports: a review of the cold ironing technology. Renew. Sustain. Energy Rev. **178**, 113243 (2023)

47. Colarossi, D., Principi, P.: Feasibility study of a cold ironing system and district heating in port area. Firenze University Press **178**, 113243 (2020)

48. Spengler, T., Tovar, B.: Potential of cold-ironing for the reduction of externalities from in-port shipping emissions: the state-owned Spanish port system case. J. Environ. Manage. **279**, 111807 (2021)

49. La Gazzetta Marittima: I porti e l'ambiente (2018). https://www.lagazzettamarittima.it/2017/09/27/remtech-i-porti-e-lambiente/

50. Sifakis, N., Vichos, E., Smaragdakis, A., Zoulias, E., Tsoutsos, T.: Introducing the cold-ironing technique and a hydrogen-based hybrid renewable energy system into ports. Int. J. Energy Res. **46**(14), 20303–20323 (2022)

51. Capraram G., Martirano, L., Kermani, M., de Mesquita Sousa, D., Barilli R., Armas, V.: Cold Ironing and Battery Energy Storage System in the Port of Civitavecchia. In: 2022 IEEE International Conference on Environment and Electrical Engineering and 2022 IEEE Industrial and Commercial Power Systems Europe, pp. 1–6. Prague, Czech Republic (2022)

52. Piccoli, T., Fermeglia, M., Bosich, D., Bevilacqua, P., Sulligoi, G.: Environmental assessment and regulatory aspects of cold ironing planning for a maritime route in the Adriatic Sea. Energies **14**(18), 5836 (2021). https://doi.org/10.3390/en14185836

53. Innes, A., Moison, J.: Identifying the unique challenges of installing cold ironing at small and medium ports – The case of Aberdeen. Transp. Res. Part D: Transp. Environ. **62**, 298–313 (2018)

54. di Venezia, A.P.: Comunicato stampa: Enel consegna all'Autorità Portuale di Venezia il cold ironing per l'area di Marittima, Iniziative "verdi" per il porto, a beneficio della città (2011)

55. CCIAA Sardegna: Libro Bianco sulle priorità infrastrutturali della Sardegna. Uniontrasporti (2022). https://www.caor.camcom.it/notizie/libro-bianco-delle-priorita-infrastrutturali-della-sardegna

Assessing Management Effectiveness: Manglares El Salado Fauna Production Reserve Study Case

Miriam Vanessa Hinojosa-Ramos[1] (ID), Marcelo León[2]([⊠]) (ID), Paulina León[3] (ID),
Ricardo Arevalo[4] (ID), and Carlos Redroban[2] (ID)

[1] Instituto Superior Tecnológico Vicente Rocafuerte, Guayaquil, Ecuador
[2] Universidad ECOTEC, Samborondon, Ecuador
marceloleon11@hotmail.com
[3] Universidad de Málaga, Malaga, Spain
[4] Universidad Técnica Particular de Loja, Loja, Ecuador

Abstract. The Manglares El Salado Fauna Production Reserve in Guayaquil, Ecuador has not updated its Management Plan since 2013 and none of the management actions have been carried out. In this sense, is vital to assess its management effectiveness through two methodologies, in order to study whether this natural space has the ideal conditions to promote ecotourism activities. From the results obtained, Manglares El Salado Fauna Production Reserve evidenced a moderately satisfactory, which means that this protected area possessed many resources and means for its management but lacked elements to reach a minimum acceptable level. In the national scope, Control and Surveillance and Biodiversity Management programs were the most worrying due to their low management effectiveness levels. Also, Planning, Inputs and Processes areas registered the same preoccupying scenario.

Keywords: Management Effectiveness Evaluation · Fauna Production Reserve · Protected areas

1 Diagnosis of the Current Situation

The Manglares El Salado Fauna Production Reserve (RPFMS by its acronym in Spanish) is part of the National System of Protected Areas and is located at northwest of the estuary of the Gulf of Guayaquil and southwest of the city of Guayaquil. It was categorized as a reserve on 15 November 2002 by Ministerial Agreement No. 142, and in 2007 its boundaries were rectified, adding Manglares of Puerto Hondo. At present, according to the last rectification made in 2017, the RPFMS has 15,535.56 hectares of extension [1].

In the perimeter of the reserve, some housing developments stand out, such as Cooperativa Puerto del Sol, Puerto Azul and Bello Horizonte; as well as industrial warehouses, the International Port Terminal (IPT) dock, the Puerto Hondo Spa and Recreational Centre, and the Intervention and Rescue Group (IRG) camp [2].

The RPFMS is made up of salt marshes, remnants of tropical dry forest, mangrove forest and three estuaries: Mongón, Plano Seco and Salado. Its flora and fauna accumulate

O. Gervasi et al. (Eds.): ICCSA 2023 Workshops, LNCS 14111, pp. 51–63, 2023.
https://doi.org/10.1007/978-3-031-37126-4_4

48 plant species, 79 bird species, 12 mammals, 7 amphibians and reptiles, 20 fishes, 18 mollusks and 13 crustaceans [3]. Thus, the RPFMS has provided economic resources to the inhabitants of its shores, with artisanal fishing as the main source of income [1].

Furthermore, it has an appreciable ecotourism potential based on a great variety of attractions and resources that are currently not adequately valued, in order to be considered a local ecotourism pole. One of the consequences of this undervaluation is the low number of visitors, which could be increased through the implementation of diversification options for tourists, with new ideas, recommendations and proposals for tourism development in the area and, specifically, in the community of Puerto Hondo [4].

According to the World Tourism Organization, tourism comprises "activities undertaken by people during their travels and stays in places other than their usual environment for a consecutive period of time of less than one year, for leisure, business or other purposes" [5]. Tourism has therefore become one of the most important industries worldwide. In our country, the 2018 figures reflect that the tourism balance grew compared to 2017, leaving a positive balance according to the Central Bank of Ecuador. In addition, tourism contributed to the Ecuadorian economy, maintaining it as the third source of non-oil income, after bananas and shrimp. Even in the nine national holidays of 2018, the economic dynamization was 425.8 million dollars, with Carnival being the busiest [6].

Although tourism has diversified over time in order to satisfy a growing demand from travelers according to their preferences and the search for new experiences, the health emergency resulting from the COVID pandemic19 has significantly limited and conditioned global tourism; as mentioned, it is a reality that domestic visitors prefer fun activities in the first place, followed by visits to protected areas and to a lesser extent by the practice of sports, according to the Integrated Tourism Marketing Plan of Ecuador "PIMTE 2014", as shown in Table 1.

Table 1. Activity preferences of domestic visitors (Source: [7]).

Activities	Total visitors	Percentage
Playing sports	326,317	12.2
Observing flora and fauna	79,232	3.0
Visiting, naturalizing in protected areas	695,169	26.1
Visiting communities	4,473	0.2
Visiting shamans, healers	1,608	0.1
Visiting archaeological and historical sites	77,126	2.9
Fun	1'214,990	45.6
Gastronomy	170,882	6.4
Making purchases	52,381	2.0
Other	44,137	1.7
Total	2'666,315	100.0

Coincidentally, the PIMTE 2014 reflects that at the national level the most marketed tourism product is ecotourism and nature tourism, while in the international market this product is the second, constituting 21% of the supply [7]. As highlighted in the Strategic Plan for the Development of Sustainable Tourism for Ecuador "PLANDETUR 2020", our country has a privileged position to develop tourism thanks to its mega biodiversity housed in its protected areas [8].

This natural wealth contrasts with unsustainable consumption and production systems that threaten the integrity of Ecuadorian ecosystems. This reality presents an enormous challenge in order to accelerate the introduction of best practices such as cleaner production, eco-efficiency and the application of more environmentally responsible behavior [8].

On the other hand, in the technical report of the Marine and Coastal Biodiversity Conservation Project of Ecuador, it was found that the management plan for the Manglares El Salado Fauna Production Reserve is out of date, despite the fact that the year it was created (2008) was mentioned as the last update [9]. In 2013, the Reserve's Management Plan was updated, reinforcing, complementing and restructuring what was stated in the 2008 Plan, through the following analyses: physical-climatic; biological and ecosystemic; socio-economic and cultural; basic services and infrastructure; land use; socio-organizational; and socio-environmental conflicts. In terms of the initial proposal, the

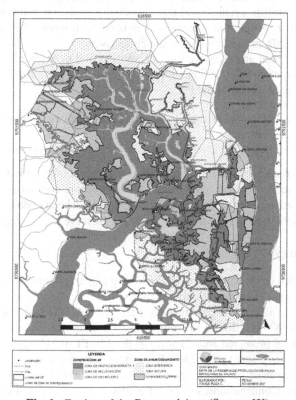

Fig. 1. Zoning of the Protected Area (Source: [3]).

reserve's programs were adjusted to the following: Biodiversity Protection; Research and Monitoring; Education, Communication and Public Relations; Public Use; Sustainable Development; and Organizational Development. In addition, the zoning proposed in 2006 was changed from 6 to 5 zones: Strict Conservation (ZCE); Multiple Use (ZUM); Tourism and Recreation Use (ZUTYR); Ecological Restoration (ZRE); and, Sensitive to Industrial Use and Domestic Discharges (ZSUIDD), as shown in Fig. 1 [3].

Therefore, in 2013, according to experts in the area, reserve's management plan update was documented; however, the new management plan has not yet been implemented [3]. To date, as an updated management plan has not been carried out, there have been no periodic evaluations of management effectiveness of the protected area, which does not allow us to have a perspective of the obstacles it faces.

Protected areas Management Effectiveness Evaluation serves multiple purposes, among which the following are specified [10]:

- Document the management of the Protected Area (PA), as it describes and systematizes the state of the area. It constitutes an "institutional memory" and makes it possible to collect and make reliable data available;
- Improve the planning and decision-making process by identifying lessons learned that can be used to improve future planning and management;
- Stimulate management excellence through adaptive management by comparing the progress of Coastal Marine Protected Area (CMPA) management over time;
- Enable APMC staff to evaluate and take ownership of the continuous improvement process. In other words, the information is used to improve the performance of protected area staff, both individually and collectively;
- Promote the efficient and effective use of resources and investments;
- Increase participation by enabling support to be obtained from interest groups and the most significant actors in the PA;
- Identify work priorities;
- Develop policies that promote the adoption of best practices in the protected area;
- Continuous improvement;
- Increase transparency in the use of information and enable accountability.

Given that tourism is one of the main sources of development in Ecuador; protected areas are natural spaces that have the conditions to promote ecotourism activities; and that the management plan for the area in question has not yet been updated, it is necessary to carry out an evaluation of the effectiveness of the Reserve's management.

2 Methodology

The research carried out had the aim of evaluating management effectiveness of the protected area. In this study case, working together with Reserve staff, two methodologies were used for the Evaluation of Management Effectiveness, the first is an adaptation of the World Bank - WWF Alliance instrument used to evaluate the management effectiveness of terrestrial protected areas, known as the METT questionnaire (Management Effectiveness Tracking Tool) [10]. The METT questionnaire consists of 34 questions, with a maximum score of 138 points, corresponding to 100%, distributed in six scopes: Context, Planning, Contributions, Product, Results and Consequences, as indicated in Table 2.

Table 2. Distribution and maximum score of METT survey questions by Scope (Source: [9]).

Scope	Questions	Supplementary questions	Maximum Score
Context	1–7	1.a, 3.a, 3.b, 5.a, 5.b	26
Planning	8–9	9.a, 9.b, 9.c, 9.d, 9.c, 9.f, 9.g, 9.h	14
Contributions	10–12	10.a, 11.a, 12.a, 12.b	14
Product	13–19	14.a, 15.a, 19.a, 19.b	25
Results	20–27	20.a, 20.b, 20.c, 20.d, 20.e, 20.f, 20.g, 21.a, 21.b, 21.c	33
Consequences	28–34	31.a, 31.b, 31.c, 31.d, 34.a, 34.b	26
		Total	138

The second methodology contemplates the evaluation of the management effectiveness of the State Natural Areas Heritage (PANE by its acronym in Spanish) through a methodological guide [11]. The following forms were used in this study: Form 1 (General Data), Form 3 (Evaluation of Management Effectiveness); and Form 4 (Strategic Actors of the protected area).

Form 1 includes name and category of the protected area, subsystem to which it belongs, legal document of creation, surface of the area, land tenure details, geographical location, number of staff, annual budget accrued at the end of the fiscal year and other nominations of the protected area.

Form 3 consists of 44 questions with four multiple choices (0 to 3) and its questions correspond in part to an equivalence with the METT indicators plus some additional questions elaborated for the PANE, which allow a better reflection of the reality of protected areas. Each question represents an indicator, which are coded and of which there are two additional indicators Impact or Result that are considered referential and are not evaluated numerically (EV1 and EV2), so they do not affect the total evaluation score.

Due to the nature of the protected area that is the object of this study case, as the public use and tourism program is not applied, 7 indicators associated with this program are discarded, leaving form 3 with a total of 35 indicators or questions, with a maximum score of 105 points. Tables 3 and 4 show the distribution and maximum score of the survey questions by program and scope.

Table 3. Distribution and maximum score of PANE survey questions by Program (form 3) (Source: [11]).

Program	Questions	Maximum Score
Administration and Planning	3 - 16	42
Control and Surveillance	17 - 23	21

(*continued*)

Table 3. (*continued*)

Program	Questions	Maximum Score
Environmental Communication, Education and Participation	24 - 30	21
Biodiversity Management	38 - 44	21
	Total	105

Table 4. Distribution and maximum score of PANE survey questions by Scope (form 3) (Source: [11]).

Scope	Questions	Maximum Score
Context	10, 14, 15, 16, 19, 20	18
Planning	3, 4, 5, 6, 11, 13, 39, 43	24
Inputs	8, 30, 18, 21, 22, 23, 38, 44	24
Processes	9, 12, 26, 17, 40, 42	18
Products	7, 24, 25, 27, 28, 29, 41	21
	Total	105

Form 4 measures the perception of the protected area's strategic stakeholders. The aim of this external assessment is to contrast the self-assessment of each area with the external perception. The questions correspond to 29 indicators also found in form 3, which are classified by type of stakeholder.

For the present case of study, only the communities were considered, so the evaluation was reduced to 13 questions addressed to the representatives of the inhabitants inside or on the borders of the protected area. Of the 13 questions, only 12 were considered, as the one related to the public use and tourism program was discarded, as shown in Table 5.

Table 5. Distribution of PANE survey questions for strategic stakeholders (form 4) (Source: [11]).

Actors	Questions
Communities	24, 25, 26, 27, 28, 29, 18, 20, 40, 42, 1, 2

3   Analysis and Results

3.1   World Bank – WWF Methodology

Table 6 presents the comparative summary of the Management Effectiveness Assessment, considering its different scopes, the years and the entities that carried out the measurement.

Table 6. Comparative summary of Management Effectiveness Evaluation.

Scope	BID 2009	MAE 2009	PCBMC 2015	PCBMC 2016	ISTVR 2019
Context	0	9	17	18	18
Planning	4	3	13	12	9
Contributions	3	1	10	6	6
Product	0	2	17	14	13
Results	0	0	15	13	15
Consequences	7	4	21	14	12
MEE (Pts)	**14**	**19**	**93**	**77**	**73**
MEE (%)	**10.14%**	**13.77%**	**67.39%**	**55.80%**	**52.90%**

Figure 2 shows the variation that the Management Effectiveness Evaluation has undergone, according to the different years and entities in charge of the measurement. It is notable that its lowest values occurred in 2009, with an upturn in 2015; however, from 2015 onwards, the trend has been decreasing considering the current measurement carried out by this study.

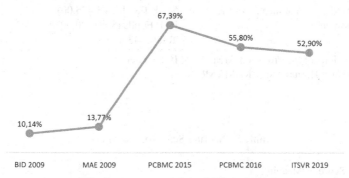

Fig. 2. MEE trend from 2009 to 2019.

3.2 PANE Methodology

Prior to the calculation of the management effectiveness assessment, form 1 was filled in, reflecting the information in Table 7.

As part of the process of obtaining the Management Effectiveness Assessment percentage for a protected area, it is necessary to score each of the indicators that make up Form 3 according to the scoring scale shown in Table 8. This table contains the scale from 0 to 3 and its respective meaning interpreted in the context in which it is being used.

Table 7. RPFMS General Data.

Item	Detail
Name and category	Manglares El Salado Fauna Production Reserve
Subsystem	State
Legal document of creation (Date and number)	No. 5 15 November 2002 Official Register 142; 22–01-2003
Total area	15,535.56 ha (20% Land and 80% Marine)
Land tenure	State (92%) Private (8%)
Geographical location	It is located at the northern Gulf of Guayaquil Province: Guayas; Canton: Guayaquil
Number of staff	Head of area (1) Technicians (1) Park Rangers (11) Administrative staff (0)* *The technician carries out the administrative activity together with the head of the protected area due to lack of personnel
Annual accrued budget at the end of the fiscal year of assessment	MAE Funds ($ 3,475.00) FAP Funds ($ 40,000.00) Total ($43,475.00)
Other nominations of the Protected Area (UNESCO World Heritage Site, RAMSAR Site, etc.)	It does not have

Table 8. Scoring Scale for indicators.

Score	Meaning
0	No progress or minimal progress
1	Shows some level of progress
2	Corresponds to good progress, with room for improvement
3	Optimal situation

With the individual results of the indicators, three ways of analysis are defined: the first considering the total percentage of the Management Effectiveness Evaluation of a protected area, the second with the percentage of Management Effectiveness Evaluation by Management Programs, and the third, taking into consideration the percentage of Management Effectiveness Evaluation by Management Scopes.

Based on the corresponding expressions, the calculations for the Management Effectiveness Evaluation (MEE) in the RPFMS protected area, which is the subject of this research, were computed, obtaining the following results.

Total percentage of MEE in protected area:

$$\% \text{ MEE in PA} = \frac{\sum_{i=1}^{35} p_i}{(35)(3)} * 100 = \frac{49}{105} * 100 = 46.66\% \tag{1}$$

where p_i is the score obtained in each of the 35 indicators

Percentage of MEE by Management Programs:

Administration and Planning

$$\% \text{ MEE in PA} = \frac{\sum_{i=1}^{14} app_i}{(14)(3)} * 100 = 52.38\% \tag{2}$$

where app_i is the score obtained in each of the 14 indicators of this program

Control and Surveillance.

$$\% \text{ MEE in PA} = \frac{\sum_{i=1}^{7} cvp_i}{(7)(3)} * 100 = 42.86\% \tag{3}$$

where cvp_i is the score obtained in each of the 7 indicators of this program.

Environmental Communication, Education and Participation

$$\% \text{ MEE in PA} = \frac{\sum_{i=1}^{7} ecepp_i}{(7)(3)} * 100 = 52.38\% \tag{4}$$

where $ecepp_i$ is the score obtained in each of the 7 indicators of this program

Biodiversity Management

$$\% \text{ MEE in PA} = \frac{\sum_{i=1}^{7} bmp_i}{(7)(3)} * 100 = 33.33\% \tag{5}$$

where bmp_i is the score obtained in each of the 7 indicators of this program

Figure 3 shows the percentages achieved by each of the programs considered in the PANE methodology.

Percentage of MEE by Management Scopes:

Context

$$\% \text{ MEE in PA} = \frac{\sum_{i=1}^{6} cp_i}{(6)(3)} * 100 = 50.00\% \tag{6}$$

where cp_i is the score obtained in each of the 6 indicators of this scope

Planning

$$\% \text{ MEE in PA} = \frac{\sum_{i=1}^{8} pp_i}{(8)(3)} * 100 = 45.83\% \tag{7}$$

where pp_i is the score obtained in each of the 8 indicators of this scope

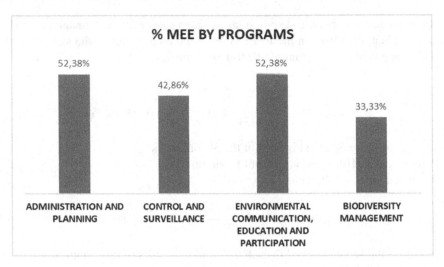

Fig. 3. MEE by Management Programs.

Inputs

$$\% \text{ MEE in PA} = \frac{\sum_{i=1}^{8} ip_i}{(8)(3)} * 100 = 41.67\% \tag{8}$$

where ip_i is the score obtained in each of the 8 indicators of this scope
Processes

$$\% \text{ MEE in PA} = \frac{\sum_{i=1}^{6} procp_i}{(6)(3)} * 100 = 44.44\% \tag{9}$$

where $procp_i$ is the score obtained in each of the 6 indicators of this scope
Products

$$\% \text{ MEE in PA} = \frac{\sum_{i=1}^{7} prodp_i}{(7)(3)} * 100 = 52.38\% \tag{10}$$

where $prodp_i$ is the score obtained in each of the 7 indicators of this scope

Figure 4 shows the percentages achieved by each of the scopes considered in the PANE methodology.

As part of this methodology, the strategic stakeholders of the protected area are also evaluated with form 4, proceeding to obtain the perceptions of the head of the Puerto Hondo community that adjoins the RPFMS. The also president of the Association of Small Farmers of Puerto Hondo, answered the 12 corresponding questions, in order to make comparisons between this external and internal perception on the management of the protected area. Figure 5 shows the results of the aforementioned comparison.

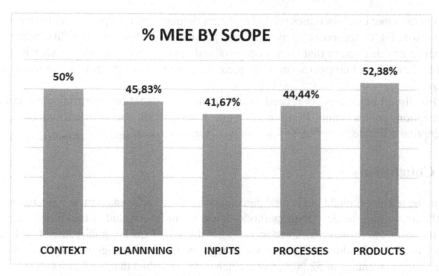

Fig. 4. MEE by Management Scopes.

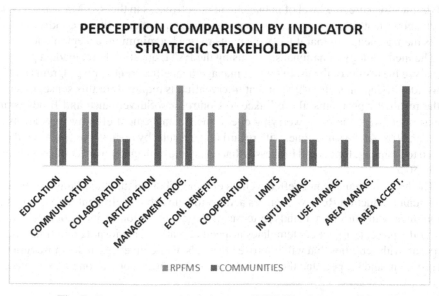

Fig. 5. Perception comparison between RPFMS and Communities.

From Fig. 5, it can be established that, in the indicators related to participation in management decision-making or planning processes in the reserve, with the existence of specific actions for the sustainable management of resources; and, with the level of acceptance of the protected area, the perception of the community or external perception is high.

On the other hand, in issues related to the participation of area personnel to improve the well-being of the community, with the provision of economic benefits, with the presence of other actors that support control and surveillance activities; and, with the current condition of conservation of the area, the perception of the external community is low.

Finally, in other aspects related to environmental education, environmental communication, collaboration, limits and on-site management, the internal and external perception coincide.

4 Conclusions

From the results obtained in the total percentage levels of the Management Effectiveness Evaluation, using the described methodologies, it can be concluded that in both cases similar results were obtained, since according to the METT questionnaire, the Manglares El Salado Fauna Production Reserve was categorized with a Management Effectiveness Evaluation percentage of 52.90%, from which it is established that the factors and means that make the management of the area possible are being adequately attended to, with room for improvement. Similarly, when analyzing the results of the total levels with the PANE questionnaire, the level of management effectiveness in the RPFMS was 46.66%, which shows that the area possesses many resources and means that are indispensable for its management, but that it lacks elements to reach a minimum acceptable level.

The methodology of national scope, using the PANE questionnaire, made it possible to analyze the results of the evaluation of management effectiveness by programs and by areas, identifying those in which urgent intervention is required. In this sense, in terms of the results by programs, those linked to Control and Surveillance and Biodiversity Management were the most worrying due to their management effectiveness levels of less than 50%. At the same time, with regard to the results by area, it was precisely those related to Planning, Inputs and Processes that registered management effectiveness levels below 50%.

The levels of management effectiveness obtained showed that the Manglares El Salado Fauna Production Reserve requires actions to help achieve efficient management in accordance with current demands in terms of the conservation of its resources, which is why the present project contemplates a specific, realistic, achievable and time-bound proposal, with activities that will improve the levels of effectiveness in the most vulnerable programs and scopes; and therefore, the management and operation of the protected area.

References

1. Quinteros, A., Castro, J., León, F.: La Reserva de Producción Faunística Manglares El Salado (RPFMS) de Guayaquil, como recurso turístico sostenible. Rev. Caribeña Ciencias Soc. (2017). ISSN: 2254
2. Aguirre, J., Troya, M.: Propuesta de diseño de rutas turísticas acuáticas o marino-fluviales en la Reserva de Producción Faunística Manglares El Salado. ESPOL (2015)
3. Ministerio del Ambiente: Actualización del Plan de Manejo de la Reserva de Producción de Fauna Manglares El Salado (en revisión). Guayaquil, Ecuador (2013)

4. Zúñiga, G.: Descripción y Propuesta de Desarrollo del Área Turística: Puerto Hondo – Cerro Blanco, Vía E 40. ESPOL (2009)
5. Sancho, A.: Unidad 1 El turismo como actividad económica. Introd. al Tur (1998)
6. Ministerio de Turismo: El turismo ecuatoriano creció un 11% en 2018. In: Noticias. https://www.turismo.gob.ec/el-turismo-ecuatoriano-crecio-un-11-en-2018/ (2019)
7. Ministerio de Turismo: Tourism & Leisure Advisory Services, Fondo de Promoción Turística. Plan Integral de Marketing Turístico de Ecuador PIMTE 2014 (2009)
8. Ministerio de Turismo: Diseño del Plan Estratégico de Desarrollo de Turismo Sostenible para Ecuador PLANDETUR 2020 (2007)
9. León, M., Cornejo, G., Calderon, M., Gonzalez-Carrion, E., Florez, H.: Effect of deforestation on climate change: a co-integration and causality approach with time series. Sustainability **14**(18), 11303 (2022)
10. Paguay, J.: Evaluación de la Efectividad de Manejo de AMCP's del Ecuador Continental. Ecuador (2016)
11. Stolton, S., Hockings, M., Dudley, N., MacKinnon, K., Whitten, T.: Cómo informar sobre los avances en el manejo de áreas protegidas individuales (2003)
12. MAE: Evaluación de Efectividad de Manejo del Patrimonio de Áreas Naturales del Estado – Guía Metodológica. Quito, Ecuador (2014)

Smart and Slow Tourism in Protected Natural Context

Silvia Battino[1](✉) ⓘ, Giuseppe Borruso[2] ⓘ, and Ginevra Balletto[3] ⓘ

[1] DiSea - University of Sassari, 07100 Sassari, Sardinia, Italy
sbattino@uniss.it
[2] Deams - University of Trieste, 34127 Trieste, Italy
giuseppe.borruso@deams.units.it
[3] DICAAR - University of Cagliari, 07100 Cagliari, Sardinia, Italy
balletto@unica.it

Abstract. The manuscript comes from the interdisciplinary research carried out in the field of tourism in Sardinia, with particular attention to elements such as the environmental pressure of the sector, the drive towards slow tourism and sustainable mobility which, even in areas with even in highly urbanized areas, it can represent a different and seasonally adjusted way of appreciating, safeguarding and experiencing a territory.

The opportunity is to unite different observation points, from the land and sea sides of Sardinia, in the northeastern part already widely characterized by over tourism and take advantage of geographical information tools such as GIS and WebGIS, for sharing information and the enhancement of slow tourism.

Case studies are presented in the manuscript in the Tavolara Punta Coda Cavallo protected marine area and in the La Maddalena Archipelago National Park, where the perspective of active under tourism is privileged as an alternative to over tourism, for the sustainable use of landscapes unique. Furthermore, the case studies constitute experiences to discover landscapes through the integration of mobile spatial geographic tools (smartphones). Finally, through ad hoc applications (weather and atmospheric conditions, as well as apps for enjoying outdoor activities), a sharing map was created, also with external users, through the MyMaps platform, to support sustainable tourism.

Keywords: Protected natural areas · Smart and slow tourism · Smart Community

1 Introduction

In[1] the context of different spatial scales, achieving the sustainability goal of the 2030 Agenda emerges as both a necessary, and in some respects restrictive, policy to transform and improve the landscape balance of the regions involved. This need is strongly

---

[1] This study is developed in the context of the working group 'Grupo de Trabajo en Conflictos socio-espaciales del Turismo, G.T. COTUR' of the RIIR (Red Iberomericana de Investigación en Imaginarios y Representaciones). This paper is the result of the joint work of the authors. In particular: paragraphs 1 and 2 have been written by Silvia Battino, paragraph 3 and subparagraphs 3.1 and 3.2 by Giuseppe Borruso and paragraphs 4 an 5 by Ginevra Balletto.

© The Author(s), under exclusive license to Springer Nature Switzerland AG 2023
O. Gervasi et al. (Eds.): ICCSA 2023 Workshops, LNCS 14111, pp. 64–74, 2023.
https://doi.org/10.1007/978-3-031-37126-4_5

emphasized in the United Nations Environment Programme (UNEP) report 'Making peace with nature' (2021) [1] in which biodiversity loss, climate change and pollution are the most urgent environmental problems that require addressing. The idea therefore seems to be emerging that more careful planning of territories, with particular regard to the expansion and valorization of protected areas, is an essential element in improving the use of resources and avoiding uncontrolled over-exploitation. The UN definition, contained in the Convention on Biological Diversity (CBD) that came into force on 29 December 1993, emphasizes the importance of preserving natural balances, but at the same time consolidates the intention to also safeguard and enhance cultural and economic resources [2, 3]. Within the European community, the most recent interest and actions aimed at protecting fragile ecosystems stem from the 'Biodiversity strategy for 2030', which aims to increase protected areas by approximately 30 per cent of the land surface and 30 percent of the marine areas by 2030 [4]. The restoration of biodiversity is based on the active involvement of multiple local actors (resident communities, businesses, researchers, public institutions) who are motivated to create collaborative networks capable of reducing the gaps in the territory. Biodiversity restoration relies on the active involvement of multiple local actors (communities, businesses, researchers, public institutions) who are motivated to create collaborative networks capable of reducing the gaps in the territory. Considering data from the World Database of Protected Areas (WDPA) as of April 2023, there are 176,550 protected areas in Europe covering a land area (including inland waters) of 3,805,373 square kilometers and a marine area of 1,572,026 square kilometers [5]. An important tool devised by the EU authorities to guide protection actions on the territory is the Natura 2000 Network. The ecological network was established by the Habitats Directive 92/43/EEC and together with the Birds Directive 79/409/EEC (amended by Directive 2009/147/EEC) ensures the balance of natural habitats of threatened or rare species of flora and fauna. The Network consists of Sites of Community Interest (SCI), Special Areas of Conservation (SAC) and Special Protection Areas (SPA) [6, 7].

In Italy (December 2022) there are 2,639 sites belonging to the network, which guarantee the protection of approximately 132 habitats, 92 species of flora and 120 species of fauna [7]. In addition to the areas falling within the scope of this ecological network, the classification of Italy's protected areas is regulated by Law No. 394/1991 in Article 2, which identifies them as: National Parks; Regional Natural Parks; Nature Reserves; Protected Marine Areas and Other Protected Natural Areas. These areas cover 20% of the land surface and 11% of the sea surface and specifically there are 843 protected areas of which: 25 National Parks, 148 State Nature Reserves, 134 Regional Nature Reserves, 365 Regional Nature Reserves and 171 other Protected Areas of different classifications and denominations.

In order to respond to the stimuli of Community policies and strategies, Italy too is oriented towards activating 'new' economic models starting from the most vulnerable areas in which tourism can act as a valid support to the valorization, not only of the natural component, but also of the economic, social and cultural one [8, 9].

The manuscript, after a review of the literature concerning the combination of protected areas and slow tourist use in an intelligent perspective, aims to analyze using hybrid maps (traditional and digital) of two areas under protection in the north-east area:

the National Park' La Maddalena Archipelago and Tavolara-Punta Coda Cavallo Marine Protected Area.

In addition to the Introduction, the paper consists of four other paragraphs: 2. Related works; 3. Materials and methodology, 3.1. Study area and 3.2 Methodology; 4. Results and Discussion and 5. Conclusions and future developments.

2 Related Works

The interaction between tourism and biodiversity conservation in protected areas is complex. It is well-established that organizing spaces in a sustainable tourism way using ecotourism or slow tourism implies a low-impact use of resources while creating 'new' employment, better infrastructure and more socio-economic opportunities for local communities. Certainly, in addition to the positive aspects, when a destination experiences increased intensity of tourism development, pressure on ecosystems increases and negative externalities (ex: pollution, loss of biodiversity, land use change etc.) become evident if it is not effectively managed and monitored [10]. Thus, the increased potential conflict between maintaining a healthy natural environment and economic development pushes different local actors to formulate a sustainable offer, but also to adopt an innovative approach to strike a balance between tourism and nature conservation [11].

Concerning the first aspect, i.e., formulating a sustainable supply of tourism goods and services, the drives from globally adopted policies and strategies are many. Among the various indications, the input of the World Tourism Organization through the publication of the report "Rethinking Tourism: from Crisis to Transformation" in 2022 [12], pushes different countries to seek 'new' economic models to improve the resilience of territories [13]. This vision has also been contributed to by recent (post-Covid era) changes in the demand of tourists more inclined to experience places of 'proximity' motivated mainly by the need to find new balances, to undertake outdoor vacations based on the enjoyment of the natural resource [8, 14, 15]. The contemporary tourist shows increasing fascination with living 'non-ordinary' experiences, but which allow one to slowly traverse different landscapes [16]. This slow philosophy of travel combined with the visit of protected areas induces a non-invasive fruition of the territory, choosing low environmental impact modes of travel on specially created or 'recovered' routes that represent the essence of the place [17–19]. Sustainability is also prefigured in the different interaction with the indigenous community that is experienced by guests with greater awareness and a stronger thirst for knowledge of identities [20, 21].

Moving through protected landscapes slowly must also be planned through the adoption of an innovative approach (second aspect mentioned above). The smart paradigm offers an interesting choice of useful technological solutions to create a better balance between tourism practices and area protection. Trends in future technological transformation for the purpose of optimal management of protected areas include the use of Artificial Intelligence (AI), Big Data, Internet of Things (IoT), Augmented Reality (AR) and Virtual Reality (VR). These technologies can help the protected areas to improve methodologies regarding, for example, the management and monitoring of natural and cultural resources, tracking the movement of wildlife or tourist flows within the considered area [22]. The use of Geographic Information Systems (GIS), GPS, and public participation to collect geographic information can support local agencies to plan and manage recreational routes and different transportation patterns useful in predicting and mitigating potential impacts generated by increased visitation [11, 23, 24].

3 Materials and Methods

In the context of the outlined tendencies, the article aims to present some experiences of slow fruition in Sardinia (Region of Italy) and in particular the Tavolara-Punta Coda Cavallo Marine Protected Area and the National Park of the La Maddalena Archipelago in the northeast area of the Island will be considered.

3.1 Study Area

The Region of Sardinia in Italy, the Mediterranean's second-largest island, is a well-established tourist destination on a national and international scale that attracts tourists seeking a primarily seaside vacation [25]. Thus, the coastal landscape is the island space most traversed, consumed and transformed by a significant flow of guests who count in 2021 2,500,000 arrivals and 10,600,000 stays [26]. In particular, it is northern Sardinia, that is the historical region of Gallura, that polarizes supply and demand. The area with a surface area of 2,442.16 sq. km has 460 km of coastline consisting of a succession of cliffs alternating with fine sandy beaches. These beaches present a scarce width that makes them unsuitable to bear the tourist load that is concentrated almost exclusively during the summer season with negative consequences especially for the natural environment. A coastal heritage rich in biodiversity and cultural values that has been under a protection regime through the establishment of several Protected Areas (PAs). The ecological network officially managed to conserve nature, ecosystem services and cultural values is configured in a National Park of the La Maddalena Archipelago (1994) and a Tavolara-Punta Coda Cavallo Marine Protected Area (1997) to which is added the 'Natura 2000' network with eight Sites of Community Interest (SCIs), four Special Protection Areas (SPAs), eight Special Areas of Conservation (SACs), two Important Bird Areas (IBAs) and four Natural Monuments.

In our study we will consider the first two PAs mentioned above.

The La Maddalena Archipelago National Park, falling within the municipality having the same name, covers a land area of 5,134 ha and a sea area of 15,046 ha (Fig. 1). In 2021, the 10,687 residents [27] were joined by 203,981 presences and 52,212 arrivals attracted not only by the beauty of its seaside resources, but also by its rich biodiversity and sites of historical and artistic cultural interest. The institution of the Tavolara-Punta Coda Cavallo Marine Protected Area, consisting of 15,000 ha of sea and 40 km of coastline, is also part of the safeguarding and sustainable development of the area. The management of the area has involved since 2004 the coastal municipalities of Olbia, Loiri Porto San Paolo and San Teodoro with a predominantly seaside tourist vocation in which resides a population of 69,363 inhabitants [27] that in 2021 hosted 271,236 arrivals for a total of 1,115,127 presences [28].

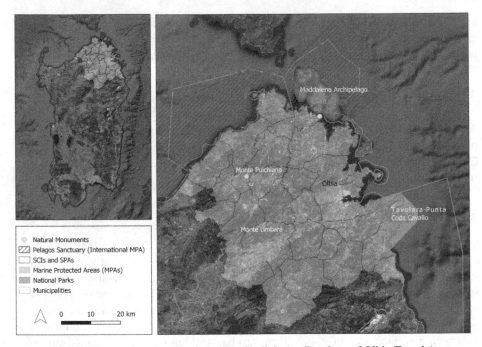

Fig. 1. The protected areas of northern Sardinia (ex-Province of Olbia-Tempio).

3.2 Methodology

The aim of the paper is to consider these protected spaces, not as physical support to the organization of recreational activities, but as a primary resource capable of attracting an 'alternative' demand. In fact, the safeguard itineraries of these areas are born to preserve the landscape, but at the same time contribute to strengthening the identity and promotion of the places [29]. Enhancement from a sustainable tourism perspective is achieved by integrating interactive geographic data acquisition and mapping tools (MyMaps platform) to create a multimedia cartography aimed at sustainable tourism enjoyment. In particular, digital tracks (GPS tracks classified according to walking, biking, kayaking, swimming, etc.) left by the smart community moving, presumably with greater awareness, through different areas and sites of natural and cultural interest are to be analyzed. There are many websites (ex: strava.org; trekkingitalia.org, Escursionismo.it etc.) or applications for mobile devices (ex: Viewranger; Wikiloc; Map My Tracks; Oruxmaps; Bergfex etc.) that allow users to upload their hiking or training activities and share their experiences. The visualization of the tracks, single or as heatmaps, is made possible by the different platforms that are thus configured as interesting tools capable of providing appreciable insights into the different phenomena observed for better planning and management of protected areas included [30]. These traces represent voluntary geographic information (Volunteered Geographic Information - VGI), the production of which over the years has become a phenomenon that has aroused the interest of the scientific community, due to the bottom-up geographic and cartographic contribution.

Digital traces thus contribute to implementing territorial knowledge, thanks to the smart community, producer and user of geographical information. In particular, digital traces assume a progressive role in the planning and also in the management of protected areas. In particular, the qualitative information of the heatmaps (raster images), i.e. without associated metadata, provides important insights for the representation of the observed phenomenon. Table 1 shows the methodological framework.

Table 1. Methodological framework. Source: All authors.

Step	Phenomenon - Digital track	Spatial Dimension - Park and protected areas	References
01	Input - Observation	Digital track (GPS) and Heatmap	Malek et al. (2010) Criscuolo et al. (2014) Ladu et al. (2019) Tarachucky et al. (2021)
02	Representation of the phenomenon in the spatial dimension	Overlapping Layers	
03	Output - Hybrid Map	Traditional Thematic Cartography and Volunteered Geographic Information (VGI)	

Table 2. Methodological framework of acquisition - processing - return of data.. Source: All authors.

Phase 1	Phase 2	Phase 3	Phase 4	Phase 5
Data acquisition hardware device/platform/app identification - tracking software	Tracking routes	Route correction in GoogleMaps / QGIS environment	File processing in kml format for sharing on Google MyMaps platform - Google Earth web	Google MyMaps platform deployment and integration with additional multimedia information

The authors then investigated and then tested the density of the digital traces of the smart community (Strava community) and the relative spatial distribution of the complex protected environmental system of the La Maddalena National Park, obtaining the following hybrid maps (Fig. 2).

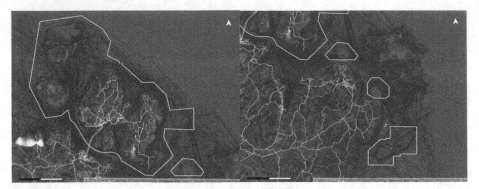

Fig. 2. La Maddalena National Park and digital traces of the smart community. Source: Strava.org.

The method used for the elaboration of Fig. 2 therefore consists in a hybridization of the traditional thematic cartography with the voluntary digital one, which constitutes the sensitive part of the data, because it is imbued with significance, enriching the map with contents.

This hybridization is also reflected in the methods of returning geographic information through different methods and platforms, favoring, in particular, the use of low-cost instruments normally available, such as mobile devices (smartphones) and freely usable apps (such as training apps sports) and popular search engines (e.g. Google Dashboard with location history). In this case, the work developed required the collection of various geographical contents and the creation of ad hoc information layers. In particular, it was necessary to use the GPS tracks relating to the individual routes under study (Table 2).

These traces were recorded using the GPS chipsets present in commercial smartphones, and the traces recorded by them during the various routes. In this case, during the data acquisition operations, various activity tracking apps were used, ultimately focusing on Strava and linking the data collection to the Google profile which, through the 'location history' service, allows observing the places visited and the different routes taken. The 'double tracking' allows, in fact, to activate the systematic acquisition of position data, effectively improving the positioning accuracy. Furthermore, since, in this specific case, we are dealing with routes carried out at sea, therefore outdoors and with a limited, if any, presence of natural obstacles to satellite signals, the positioning of the routes is fairly high for the purposes set by this research, i.e. corresponding to an accuracy of around 5m. As will be evident in the discussion of the case study and the results obtained, during the data processing phase, steps were taken to correct position tracking errors, reconstructing the routes on the basis of the cartography used as backgrounds during processing (e.g. Google Maps; OpenStreetMap; Geoportal of the Autonomous Region of Sardinia).

A phase following the acquisition of geographical data and their correction, concerned the return by means of the Google MyMaps platform.

The use of this platform is useful for a dual purpose. On the one hand, allowing simultaneous and concurrent access to the same data for their processing and cartographic dressing, as well as, on the other hand, representing a starting point for information dissemination activities to a wider audience, given the possibility of inserting and in the places visited multimedia references, such as images, videos, websites, as well as the possibility of incorporating MyMaps projects into specific web pages.

4   Discussion and Results

The work developed in different directions, aimed at the acquisition of voluntary geo-referenced information. In particular, the coastal and naturalistically protected areas of northern Sardinia constitute the case study. The work involved carrying out field investigation in 2022, as highlighted in Table 3. The field investigation concerned slow mobility in water, by canoe (La Maddalena Archipelago, Tavolara-Punta Coda Cavallo, Teulada) and walk mobility (Valle della Luna, Santa Teresa di Gallura).

Table 3. Data acquisition and field investigation activities

Period	Place	Way of travel
23 april 2022	Maddalena Park	canoe
24 april 2022	Santa Teresa di Gallura - Valle della Luna and Capo Testa	walk
4 june 2022	San Teodoro - Tavolara - Porto Taverna	canoe

In the field activities, the paths were traced using a GNSS receiver mounted on a smartphone in order to trace the paths and subsequently process them in the GIS environment and import them in the Google MyMaps environment, as well as for the subsequent dissemination and dissemination of the results. The work therefore involved tracing the routes using a popular sports activity tracking app (Strava.org), integrated with the mobility data collection system developed by Google (Location History). These systems allow you to acquire and track position data thanks to the GPS chipset present in popular smartphones and to give you a recording cadence useful for carrying out physical activity. Both platforms (Strava and Google) were used in order to integrate the information left out by one of the two systems in conditions of low satellite or mobile network signal coverage. In both cases, in fact, a loss of coverage can result in an incompletely correct recording of the journey undertaken.

In fact, it was necessary to intervene ex post in the elaboration of the sections in the 'Parco di La Maddalena'. This was organized in three different sections (Palau - Santa Trinità beach; Santa Trinità beach - La Maddalena; La Maddalena - Palau). The first required an important reworking, with a reconstruction of the route thanks also to the points acquired, but discarded by the algorithms of the apps and platforms used, for the correct manual reconstruction.

All the above activities were then aggregated in the MyMaps digital environment in order to create a multimedia cartography aimed at the slow tourist use of protected natural contexts (Fig. 3).

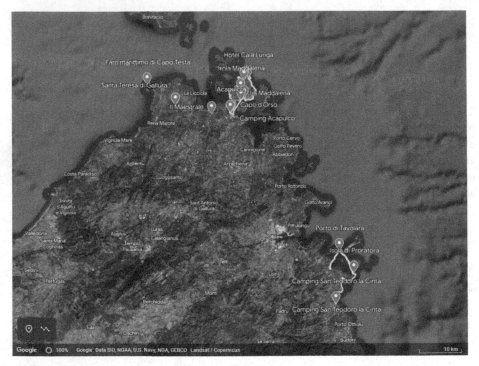

Fig. 3. MyMaps: Slow tourism 2022. Source: All Authors, link: https://bit.ly/Turismo_Lento.

The research carried out therefore represented an opportunity to combine tourist use activities with low environmental impact (walk and canoe) in contact with nature, with opportunities for knowledge and use of the territory, thanks to the privileged observation point characterized by the coastal navigation of proximity, remote shooting integrated with those on the ground (or on the sea), slow pedestrian mobility. This making possible a sustainable tourist use of protected and protected areas and contexts, through participation in initiatives carried out with respect for the environment.

5 Conclusion and Future Developments

The over tourism in Sardinia requires a renewed approach between: governance, innovation, technology, accessibility and sustainability, through active participation, which is the key to building a new way of conceiving travel in a sustainable and safe way, respecting the contexts and appreciating local cultures and traditions and providing proactive economic and social benefits in preserving the environment. In particular, digital tourism services represent the most dynamic component of tourism [31].

Furthermore, the implementation of technologies within reach of 'smartphones' allows tourism - understood as an experiential moment at the service of culture, the territory and its resources - to balance fruition and protection. In particular, hybrid maps, the result of the contribution of voluntary geographical information - bottom-up - through the digital traces of the smart community, understood as producer and user of geographical information, contribute to spreading knowledge and collective responsibility in sensitive contexts (Natura 2000 sites, protected areas, parks, etc.).

The experience gained in the development of MyMaps slow tourism 2022 can be considered a positive result, which can be deduced from the progressive increase in views. In this framework, future scenarios open up which see the authors engaged in the development and construction of similar voluntary maps in other sensitive contexts of Sardinia to promote a wider project called 'Slow tourism around Sardinia'.

References

1. United Nations Environment Programme: Making Peace with Nature: A scientific blueprint to tackle the climate, biodiversity and pollution emergencies, UNEP, Nairobi (2021). Available at: https://www.unep.org/resources/making-peace-nature
2. Geldmann, J., Manica, A., Burgess, N.D., Coad, L., Balmford, A.: A global-level assessment of the effectiveness of protected areas at resisting anthropogenic pressures. PNAS **116**(46), 23209–23215 (2019)
3. Lopoukine, N.: Editorial: what does Target 11 really mean? Parks **18**, 5–8 (2012)
4. European Commission: Biodiversity Strategy 2030. Available at: https://environment.ec.eur opa.eu/strategy/biodiversity-strategy-2030_en
5. UNEP-WCMC: Protected Area Profile for Europe dal World Database on Protected Areas (2023). Available at: www.protectedplanet.net
6. European Environment Agency: An introduction to Europe's Protected Areas (2020). Available at: https://www.eea.europa.eu/themes/biodiversity/europe-protected-areas
7. Ministero dell'Ambiente e della Sicurezza Energetica: Rete Natura (2000). Available at: https://www.mase.gov.it/pagina/rete-natura-2000
8. González Rosales, V.M., López Torres, V.G.: Turismo en Áreas Naturales Protegidas: una discusión sobre su pertinencia. Revista Iberoamericana Ambiente & Sustentabilidad **4**, 1–13 (2021)
9. Cardillo, M.C.: L'area marina protetta e la riserva naturale statale delle isole di Ventotene e Santo Stefano tra salvaguardia ambientale e sostenibilità turistica. Geotema **67**, 29–37 (2023)
10. Burbano, D.V., Valdivieso, J.C., Izurieta, J.C., Meredith, T.C., Quiroga Ferri, D.: 'Rethink and reset' tourism in the Galapagos Islands: Stakeholders' views on the sustainability of tourism development. Annals of Tourism Research Empirical Insights 3(2), 100057 and 1–12 (2022)
11. Mandić, A.: Nature-based solutions for sustainable tourism development in protected natural areas: a review. Environment Systems and Decisions **39**(3), 249–268 (2019). https://doi.org/10.1007/s10669-019-09718-2
12. UNWTO: Rethinking Tourism: from Crisis to Transformation (2022). Available at: https://www.unwto.org/world-tourism-day-2022
13. Balletto, G., Borruso, G., Murgante, B., Milesi, A., Ladu, M.: Resistance and Resilience. A Methodological Approach for Cities and Territories in Italy. In: Gervasi, O., et al. (eds.) ICCSA 2021. LNCS, vol. 12952, pp. 218–229. Springer, Cham (2021). https://doi.org/10.1007/978-3-030-86973-1_15
14. Baba, C.A., Stăncioiu, A.F., Gabor, M.R., Alexe, F.A., Oltean, F.D., Dinu, A.C.: Considerations Regarding the Effects of COVID-19 on the Tourism Market, pp. 271–284. Theor. Appl. Econ, XXVII (2020)
15. Corbisiero, F., Monaco, S., Ruspini, E.: Millennials. Generation Z and the Future of Tourism. Channel View Publications, Bristol (2022)

16. Lois-González, R.C., Santos Solla, M.X.: New trends in Urban and Cultural Tourism: the Model of Santiago de Compostela. In: Lois-González, R.C., et al. (eds.) New Tourism in the 21st Century: Culture, the City, Nature and Spirituality, pp. 209–234. Scholars Publishing, Cambridge, Newcastle upon Tyne (2014)

17. Privitera, D.: Turismo lento e territori insulari. Il caso studio Favignana. Bollettino della Associazione Italiana di Cartografia **169**, 145–163 (2020)

18. Krasna, F.: Dal turismo "mordi e fuggi" allo slow tourism: viaggiando su strade blu negli USA. Bollettino della Associazione Italiana di Cartografia **173**, 31–43 (2021)

19. Ladu, M., Battino, S., Balletto, G., Amaro García, A.: Green infrastructure and slow tourism: a methodological approach for mining heritage accessibility in the sulcis-iglesiente bioregion (Sardinia, Italy). Sustainability **15**(4665), 1–24 (2023)

20. Gardner, N.: A manifesto for slow travel. Hidden Europe Magazine **25**(1), 10–14 (2009)

21. Manthiou, A., Klaus, P., Luong, V.H.: Slow tourism: Conceptualization and interpretation – A travel vloggers' perspective. Tour. Manage. **93**(104570), 1–15 (2022)

22. Radun, V., Bartula, M.: Applying technologies of the fourth industrial revolution – the future of ecotourism and tourism of protected areas. In: The Seventh International Scientific Conference, The Future of Tourism (TISC 2022) – Thematic Proceedings **7**(1), pp. 630-647. University of Kragujevac, VrnjačkaBanja (2022)

23. Wolf, I., Wohlfart, T., Brown, G., Lasa, A., Torland, M.: Monitoring and management of mountain biking through public participation geographic information systems. In: Reimann, M., Sepp, K., Parna, E., Tuula, R. (eds.) Proceedings of the 7th international conference on monitoring and management of visitors in recreational and protected areas, pp. 158–160. Tallinn University, Institute of Health Sciences and Sports, Alfapress (Verlag), Tallin (2014)

24. Campelo, M.B., Nogueira Mendes, R.M.: Comparing webshare services to assess mountain bike use in protected areas. J. Outdoor Recreat. Tour. **15**, 82–88 (2016)

25. Battino, S.: Turismo sostenibile in Gallura: prospettiva vincente o modello illusorio? I principali caratteri distintivi del cuore turistico della Sardegna. Patron editore, Bologna (2014)

26. Istat: I dati sul turismo a livello comunale (2022). Available at: http://dati.istat.it/

27. Istat: I dati sulla popolazione residente (2022). Available at: https://demo.istat.it

28. Regione Sardegna: Statistiche sul turismo (2022). Available on: http://www.sardegnastatist iche.it/argomenti/turismo/

29. Gavinelli, D., Zanolin, G.: Paesaggio e tutela della biodiversità. Le prospettive di una proficua sinergia per lo sviluppo locale nelle aree protette. In: Castiglioni, B., Puttilli, M., Tanca, M. (eds.) Oltre la convenzione. Pensare, studiare, costruire il paesaggio vent'anni dopo, pp. 292–301. Società Studi Geografici, Firenze (2021)

30. Cui, N., Malleson, N., Houlden, V., Comber, A.: Using vgi and social media data to understand urban green space: a narrative literature review. International Journal of Geo-Information **10**(7), 1–23 (2021)

31. Battino, S., Balletto, G., Borruso, G., Donato, C.: Internal Areas and Smart Tourism. Promoting Territories in Sardinia Island. In: Gervasi, O., et al. (eds.) ICCSA 2018. LNCS, vol. 10964, pp. 44–57. Springer, Cham (2018). https://doi.org/10.1007/978-3-319-95174-4_4

Spatial Energy Planning, City and Urban Heritage (Spatial_Energy_City 2023)

Conservation and Regeneration for a Sustainable and Circular City

Mara Ladu[✉]

DICAAR - Department of Civil and Environmental Engineering and Architecture,
University of Cagliari, 09100 Cagliari, Italy
mara.ladu@unica.it

Abstract. Conservation and regeneration approaches on existing buildings are the result of a system of attributes and values recognized by the human culture, which results in a framework of rules and practices that differ in different contexts. In the contemporary condition marked by the paradigm of sustainability, conservation planning is required to face the challenges of climate change, through the promotion of circular development and social inclusion, as well as the protection of ecosystems and biodiversity. The circular economy, which is based on the principles of recovery, recycling, reuse and sharing, in line with the sustainable development goals of the 2030 Agenda, offers the opportunity to rethink development models, in urban areas and beyond. Within this framework, the study proposes a systematization of the literature review which classifies taxonomies of values and methods to assess sustainability and circularity in urban planning and design at different urban scales. The proposed conceptual scheme is the first step for the definition of a new system of values of the existing building stock, which prove to be fundamental to guide urban transformations in the Green New Deal.

Keywords: Conservation Planning · Urban Regeneration · Circular City

1 Introduction

Urban conservation and regeneration play a fundamental role in pursuing the sustainable development goals [1]. According to the Circularity Gap Report 2021, the building sector is responsible for about 39% of carbon dioxide emissions dispersed in the environment [2]. Nowadays, the need that represents the largest resource and emissions footprint is for construction and maintenance of residential houses, especially in lower income nations [3]. The construction sector represents a significant component of the national GDP, especially in Italy, where the investment in real estate, in terms of redevelopment and energy efficiency, is still considered one of the main levers for re-launching the economy.

Although the first definition of sustainable development dates to several decades ago, and many initiatives and policies have been promoted to implement this international strategy, an effective integration of sustainability in contemporary society has not yet been achieved. In Italy, for example, the sustainable management of existing buildings

O. Gervasi et al. (Eds.): ICCSA 2023 Workshops, LNCS 14111, pp. 77–88, 2023.
https://doi.org/10.1007/978-3-031-37126-4_6

is threatened by complete demolition, often preferred to a comprehensive renovation based on additions, stratifications, or partial demolitions.

Several categories of existing buildings are in danger of being in Italy:

- residential housing built after the Second World War, especially during the 60s and 70s of the Italian economic boom [4–6] (Fig. 1), often characterized by poor architectural quality: although not the oldest in Europe, the Italian residential building stock needs interventions aimed at responding to the new standards, improving its environmental performance (Fig. 2);
- brownfield sites and all the buildings falling within "transformation areas", where the urban design should define a new physical and value dimension;
- ancient cores and historic urban areas protected by conservation planning tools which sometimes allows the demolition of certain buildings in favor of a restoration in harmony with the characteristics of the landscape, without paying enough attention to the ecological value of the building stock.

In this sense, the integration of a sustainability and circularity paradigm in urban governance and spatial planning requires updating the system of values recognized to the built environment, which should guide any decision-making process [7, 8] and affirm a sustainable conservation and regeneration of existing buildings, understood as a resource and social, environmental, and economic capital.

However, the integration of sustainable development goals in urban conservation still represents an important challenge for contemporary society [9, 10]. The need to update architectural and urban conservation approaches is expressed in the UNESCO Recommendation on the Historic Urban Landscape [11], which states: «The historic urban landscape is the urban area understood as the result of a historic layering of cultural and natural values and attributes, extending beyond the notion of "historic centre" or "ensemble" to include the broader urban context and its geographical setting»

According to this perspective, historical urban areas are dynamic organisms, the result of a stratification of values and attributes. This particular attention to the intangible component (values) provides the base to conserve the city as a palimpsest, where the ancient core is only a part [12]. The "landscape approach" introduced by the UNESCO Recommendation is a holistic and multidisciplinary approach to recognize, conserve, and manage historic urban areas [13] within a more complex strategy of sustainable urban development [14]. This involves a new approach to conservation. The action on the built environment (reuse, restoration, renovation, demolition) derives from an analysis of a renewed system of values, which should consider the possibility of recovering, reusing, and recycling building materials, in line with the pillars of the circular economy [15].

At the same time, the landscape dimension, which consider urban areas as the result of a stratification process still ongoing, a direct testimony of the past and, at the same time, a palimpsest for future generations, defines the conceptual framework to ensure better integration between contemporary architectures and the pre-existing one [46]. However, significant difficulties persist today in assessing the level of sustainability and circularity of interventions on the built environment.

Within this framework, starting from an analysis of housing regeneration schemes aimed at improving the performance of buildings and relative living conditions, the paper proposes a systematization of the literature review which classifies methods to assess

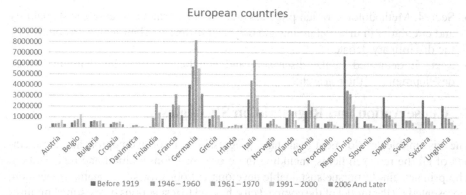

Fig. 1. Age categorization of housing stock in Europe. The EU countries with the oldest housing stock are the United Kingdom and France. Source: [4].

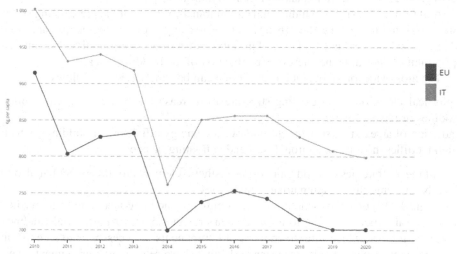

Fig. 2. Greenhouse gas emissions by households for heating and cooling in the EU in 2020 (in kg per capita). Source: [4].

the level of circularity at different urban scales. The circularity matrix is the first step for the definition of a new system of values of the existing building stock, which prove to be fundamental to update the paradigm of architectural and urban conservation in line with the Sustainable Development Goals (SDGs) of the UN Agenda 2030 [16] and the new vision of the European Green Deal [17].

After the introduction, the paper is organized as follows:

- Sect. 2: Materials, which focuses on conservation and regeneration strategies, according to the Historic Urban Landscape approach.
- Sect. 3: Case Study, where two housing regeneration schemes in Europe are analyzed.

- Sect. 4: Methodology, which proposes a conceptual scheme to assess sustainability and circularity in urban planning and design at different urban scales, as codified by the disciplinary debate.
- Sect. 5: dedicated to the discussion and conclusions, together with the future developments of the research.

2 Conservation and Regeneration Strategies

The sustainable development goals have progressively informed approaches and methods of all the research fields, including those of urban conservation and regeneration. The primary aim to pursue sustainable development objectives in a spatial dimension, represented by the model of the compact city, has led to test actions on existing buildings oriented towards the architecture stratification [18]. Several studies investigate innovative design solutions ascribable to the stratification model, understood as a third way between integral conservation and tout court demolition.

Addition to an existing building and partial transformation of the pre-existing structure contribute to shaping the urban layout of the city. In many cases, the addition, which transforms the material fabric of the city with zero soil consumption, becomes an opportunity to promote the energy requalification of the building stock.

The most widespread operations in Europe can be summarized as follows:

- physical elevation of an existing structure to increase the living area, which often modifies or replaces the roofs.
- addition of an existing structure to improve the energy efficiency of buildings, which often modifies the envelope through suspended floating facades.

All these strategies can add unique and aesthetic elements to the project but also to the urban setting, thus shaping urban morphology.

Angi, B. [19] proposes adaptive, interdisciplinary, and integrated modifications, i.e., architectural, structural and performance design strategies. Some of these are also defined as retrofit actions, which refer to addition of components or accessories to an existing building to meet new performance standards, first those relating to environmental performance. These operations, especially if carried out on large real estate complexes such as those of social housing, usually adopt prefabricated and pre-assembled elements [20] also to reduce the costs and times of the intervention, as well as the additional load on the structure.

The stratification models involve design solutions that may require partial demolition of existing buildings to improve their intrinsic and extrinsic characteristics, respectively in terms of a new flexibility of the living space and of a greater accessibility. In this sense, these strategies shape the dynamic nature of the city image [21], with its tangible and intangible values.

Considering this assumption, a critical reflection on the possible forms of demolition is needed, within a more general framework which assesses both the creative role and the possible environmental, economic, and social impacts. In this regard, Bracchi P. [22] proposes a conceptual framework for three types of demolition: "Measuring distances" (separate, reduce, insert); "Design absences" (subtract, include, connect); "Recompose memories" (stratify, recompose).

These design solutions, that lie between integral conservation and complete demo-lition, inform conservation and regeneration processes to respond to the needs of contemporary society.

3   Case Study

The literature review highlights how the action on the built environment significantly affects the development of sustainable and circular cities [3]. In particular, the architec-tural and energy renovation of "big size architectures", such as social housing districts, could prove to be strategic for achieving the objectives of environmental, economic, and social sustainability.

Significant regeneration schemes of this type of architecture, based on adaptive solutions, have been implemented in European countries and beyond [19].

Park Hill, a housing estate in Sheffield, South Yorkshire, England, is one of the most emblematic social housing schemes built between the 1950s and 1960s, a true urban landmark of the city (Fig. 3).

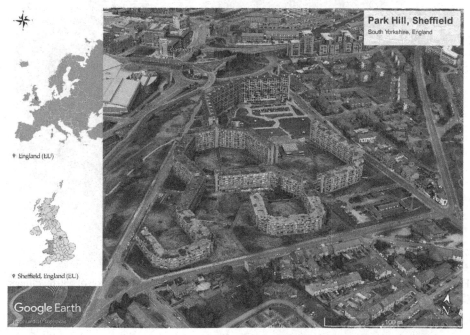

Fig. 3. Park Hill, housing estate in Sheffield, South Yorkshire, England. Form listing to renovation. Source: Google Earth.

Designed by Ivor Smith and Jack Lynn, in 1998 it received the status of Grande II* listed building for its architectural interest and for its historical value: Park Hill is the first demolition project of post-war slum clearance to have been completed in Great

Britain, as well as one of the most ambitious programs launched in the context of urban policies focused on the inner cities renaissance.

The typological and morphological redevelopment scheme of the Northern Block of the complex started in 2008. The first aim of preserving the original architectural qualities and adapting buildings to the new standards of livability and design, consisted of various interventions [23]: partial demolition, particularly on the fronts; rehabilitation of the load-bearing structure; reorganization of living spaces in line with the principles of energy efficiency.

Switching to the French context, the redevelopment scheme of 530 social housing apartments in the Grand Parc district of Bordeaux (2017), designed by the famous architects Anne Lacaton and Jean-Philippe Vassal, in collaboration with Christophe Hutin and Frédéric Druot [24], implements some of the main goals and targets of the sustainable regeneration of the built environment (Fig. 4).

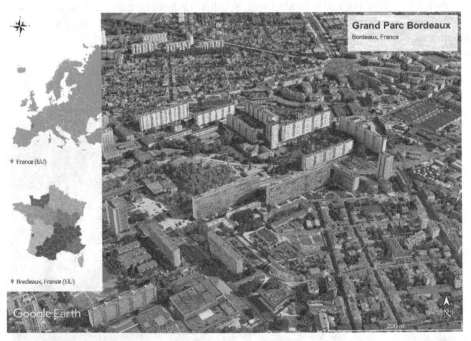

Fig. 4. Quartier du Grand Parc - Lacaton & Vassal, Druot, Hutin. Transformation of 530 dwellings (2017). Bordeaux, France. Source: Google Earth.

It is a large housing estate developed in the 1960s, in a modernist style. In recent years, the building obsolescence had made it eligible for demolition. However, this scenario was never implemented, in favor of the redevelopment scheme which applies the principles proper of the professional activity of Lacaton & Vassal, winners of the Pritzker Prize 2021 [25]. Firstly, the systemic approach to sustainability [26], which led to test technological innovation in response to environmental and social needs and adopt a design able to shape a concept that incorporates ideals of democracy and social justice. This approach is reflected in the primary choice to renovate the social housing district also by the addition of o architectural elements [27]: better living conditions are achieved through the addition of external to internal structural connections such as balconies in each apartment, which improves the use of natural light and, consequently, reduces energy consumption and costs.

The project is sustainable in environmental terms, considering the reuse and improvement of existing buildings performance, but also in social terms, both for the recognition of the historical values of the buildings and the attention in guaranteeing the permanence of the inhabitants during the renovation stages.

It is in line with the objectives of the *Rénovation énergétique et réhabilitation lourde des logements sociaux* (Energy renovation and major rehabilitation of social housing) [28], an important policy introduced by the French government to finance the major restructuring of social housing (reconfiguration of their typology or even improvement the accessibility) coupled with a global thermal renovation (in terms of energy performance), also supporting a new industrial production chain in these sectors. It means that major restructuring or rehabilitation operations that profoundly transform the asset (retention of only the building envelope; addition of an elevator/modification of the stairwells; modification of housing typologies, etc.) are associated with ambitious renovation to increase the energy performance, in line with policies launched at an international level [29].

Applications can be submitted by subjects closely involved in the management of social housing, in order generate the greatest benefits for the local community: low-rent housing organizations; semi-public companies; other bodies benefiting from project management approval; public establishments of an administrative nature under the supervision of local authorities and housing managers; municipalities managing social rental housing.

This policy has already financed the rehabilitation of 37,501 housing units in 2021, integrating major restructuring or rehabilitation associated with energy renovation. In the same year, the number of beneficiary housing units grew thanks to a further national call for projects of renovation of the social rental stock, *MassiRéno*, which made it possible to finance the renovation of 2,605 housing units.

However, although some experiences may be considered best practice, the definition of indexes and key performance indicators conceived as assessment tools to measure the sustainability of the action on the built environment and the circularity of the previous and post conditions (ex-ante and ex-post intervention), still represents one of the main issues.

4 Framework to Assess Sustainability in Urban Planning and Design

The literature review highlighted that the definition of methods to assess the degree of sustainability and circularity of interventions on the built environment continues to be one of the main issues. The methodology is aimed to develop a conceptual scheme based on a systematization of the literature review which classifies recent studies that develop sets of indicators to assess the sustainability at different urban scales: urban planning, urban regeneration projects and architecture renewal (Fig. 5).

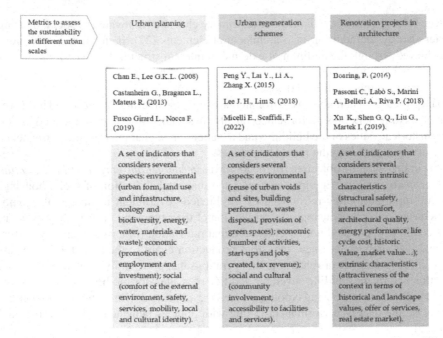

Metrics to assess the sustainability at different urban scales	Urban planning	Urban regeneration schemes	Renovation projects in architecture
	Chan E., Lee G.K.L. (2008) Castanheira G., Braganca L., Mateus R. (2013) Fusco Girard L., Nocca F. (2019)	Peng Y., Lai Y., Li A., Zhang X. (2015) Lee J. H., Lim S. (2018) Micelli E., Scaffidi, F. (2022)	Doaring, P. (2016) Passoni C., Labò S., Marini A., Belleri A., Riva P. (2018) Xu K., Shen G. Q., Liu G., Martek I. (2019).
	A set of indicators that considers several aspects: environmental (urban form, land use and infrastructure, ecology and biodiversity, energy, water, materials and waste); economic (promotion of employment and investment); social (comfort of the external environment, safety, services, mobility, local and cultural identity).	A set of indicators that considers several aspects: environmental (reuse of urban voids and sites, building performance, waste disposal, provision of green spaces); economic (number of activities, start-ups and jobs created, tax revenue); social and cultural (community involvement, accessibility to facilities and services).	A set of indicators that considers several parameters: intrinsic characteristics (structural safety, internal comfort, architectural quality, energy performance, life cycle cost, historic value, market value...); extrinsic characteristics (attractiveness of the context in terms of historical and landscape values, offer of services, real estate market).

Fig. 5. Conceptual scheme to assess the degree of sustainability of urban regeneration at different urban scales according to the literature review.

Studies that define metrics to assess sustainability in urban planning, essential for supporting the idea of sustainable cities [30, 31], consider several aspects: environmental (urban form, land use, infrastructure, ecology and biodiversity, energy, water, materials, and waste); economic (employment promotion and investment); social (comfort of the urban and rural context, safety, services, mobility, local and cultural identity) [32]. Other studies, starting from the results of questionnaires submitted to planners, real estate entrepreneurs and the local communities, identified the main factors underlying the improvement of the social sustainability of urban redevelopment projects [33], which can be summarized as follows: the satisfaction welfare requirements; the conservation of resources and the surrounding environment; the creation of places that respond to the needs of daily life; the urban development model. These assessments, which should inform the strategies and planning choices to implement sustainable and circular cities, are also the base to define actions to conserve and enhance the built environment [34].

The review of international research focused on the definition of metrics to assess the level of sustainability of urban regeneration schemes [41] includes studies concerning several aspects: the social impact of urban regeneration processes [15, 35]; the economic feasibility [36]; the environmental value of the built environment [37, 38].

Other studies adopt a systemic approach to define matrices [39, 40] or circularity indices [42].

Finally, other research focused on the definition of indicators to support decision-making processes aimed at evaluating the opportunity of demolishing the existing buildings in urban renewal projects [43], taking into consideration several parameters, affecting the intrinsic and extrinsic characteristics of the buildings. The first ones include structural safety, internal comfort, architectural quality, energy performance, life cycle cost, historical value, market value, etc. The second ones include the attractiveness of the context, in terms of historical and landscape values, the number and variety of surrounding services and the real estate market [44]. Moreover, the list of sustainable building certifications such as LEED and WELL, testifies to the great attention towards a design capable of reducing environmental impacts in favoring more sustainable and circular production and consumption models. In Italy, one of the most important policies is that of the Minimum Environmental Criteria (MEC), i.e. green criteria designed to prompt public bodies to purchase green goods and services, with the lowest possible environmental impact throughout their life-cycle, in line with the European legislative framework [45].

All these studies offer the opportunity to implement the system of values of the built environment, to assess the sustainability of ex ante and ex post conditions, to guide planning decisions (conservation, transformation, total or partial demolition) according to the life cycle approach.

5 Discussion and Conclusions

The present study proposed three interrelated topics which contribute to the project of the sustainable and circular city: the updating of the system of values of the built environment; the innovation in technique, materials, and design to conserve and regenerate the building stock; the development of metrics to assess the degree of sustainability and circularity in planning decisions, urban design schemes and architectural renewal.

System of values, methods of intervention and metrics should converge to affirm a culture of recovery and transformation in the construction sector.

Recent studies confirm the role of the circular economy paradigm and of spatial energy planning in urban governance. European cities are characterized by specific trends to steer the circular transition, as well as important challenges still outstanding to shift the paradigm from linear to circular systems.

Within this complex scientific-disciplinary debate the methodology proposed a conceptual scheme to assess the degree of sustainability and circularity of urban regeneration plans and projects. The framework is based on a systematization of the literature review which classifies recent studies that develop sets of indicators to assess the sustainability at different urban scales: urban planning, urban regeneration projects and architecture renewal.

Although important goals have been achieved, there are still few codified methods. In Italy, the definition of Minimum Environmental Criteria (MEC) represents an important milestone. However, the definition of metrics to assess all three dimensions of the sustainability of urban regeneration schemes is still a challenge.

Social housing complexes are often threatened by demolition and consequent relocation of various groups of residents, without consider the impact in social, economic, and environmental terms. Yet, the regeneration of "big size architectures", such as social housing districts, could prove to be strategic for achieving the sustainable development goals. In this sense, the definition of matrices represents a real tool to support urban governance and planning.

Within this framework, the future steps of the research will be dedicated to the implementation of the set of key performance indicators to assess and monitor performance of urban regeneration schemes, with particular attention to those relating to the large public and private real estate complexes, which prove to be fundamental to guide urban transformations and ecological transition in the Green New Deal.

References

1. Badami, A.: La rigenerazione urbana di Aalborg: un modello di sviluppo sostenibile per il futuro delle città. Franco Angeli, Milano (2022)
2. Circle Economy: The Circularity Gap Report 2021 (2021). https://www.circularity-gap.world/2021
3. Circle Economy: The Circularity Gap Report 2022, pp. 1–64, Rep. Circle Economy. Amsterdam (2022)
4. Eurostat Homepage, https://ec.europa.eu/eurostat/cache/digpub/housing/index.html?lang=en&lang=en, last accessed 11 April 2023
5. Osservatorio del mercato immobiliare (OMI): Statistiche catastali 2019. Catasto edilizio urbano (2020)
6. CRESME e Consiglio nazionale degli architetti, pianificatori, paesaggisti e conservatori (CNAPPC): Chi ha progettato l'Italia? Ruolo dell'architettura nella qualità del paesaggio edilizio italiano (2017)
7. Gasparoli, P.: Processi di cura del costruito storico tra esigenze di conservazione e necessità di trasformazione. In: Minelli C., Pianazza A., Segala P., et al. (eds.) Quale cura per i territori storici. Riflessioni sulle prospettive di poter operare perché il fare umano sia integrativo e non distruttivo della bellezza del mondo, pp. 75–95. Nardini Editore (2018)
8. Ladu, M., De Montis, T.: Il valore della qualità architettonica e urbana nel restauro: il fenomeno del non finito sardo e le buone pratiche per una ripartenza. In: Atti della Biennale BRAU5 - Congresso Itinerante della 5a Biennale del Restauro Architettonico e Urbano. 15 Aprile - 4 Maggio 2021, Brasile, Cipro, Egitto, Grecia, Italia, Siria, pp. 651–661. CICOP Italia ONLUS (2021)
9. Huuhka, S., Vestergaard, I.: Building conservation and the circular economy: a theoretical consideration. Journal of Cultural Heritage Management and Sustainable Development **10**(1), 29–40 (2020)
10. Foster, G.: Circular economy strategies for adaptive reuse of cultural heritage buildings to reduce environmental impacts. Resour. Conserv. Recycl. **152**, 10450 (2020)
11. UNESCO: Recommendation on the Historic Urban Landscape, including a glossary of definitions (2011)
12. Bandarin, F., Oers, R.V.: The Historic Urban Landscape: Managing Heritage in an Urban Century. Wiley-Blackwell, Chichester (2012)
13. Guzmán, P.C., Roders, A.P., Colenbrander, B.J.F.: Measuring links between cultural heritage management and sustainable urban development: An overview of global monitoring tools. Cities **60**(A), 192–201 (2017)
14. Veldpaus, L.: Historic urban landscapes: framing the integration of urban and heritage planning in multilevel governance. Technische Universiteit Eindhoven, Eindhoven (2015)

15. Girard, L.F., Gravagnuolo, A.: Circular economy and cultural heritage/landscape regeneration. Circular business, financing and governance models for a competitive Europe. BDC. Bollettino Del Centro Calza Bini **17**(1), 35–52 (2017)
16. United Nations: Transforming our World: The 2030 Agenda for Sustainable Development, Resolution adopted by the General Assembly on 25 September 2015 A/RES/70/1 (2015)
17. European Commission: Communication from the Commission. The European Green, 11 December 2019. COM (2019) 640 final (2019)
18. Spinelli, A.: Nuove strategie d'intervento sul patrimonio costruito. La prefabbricazione leggera nella valorizzazione del tessuto edilizio esistente. In: Atti del convegno Abitare il nuovo/abitare di nuovo ai tempi della crisi, Vol. 2 (2012)
19. Angi, B.: Amnistia per l'esistente: Strategie architettoniche adattive per la riqualificazione dell'ambiente costruito, Vol. 2, LetteraVentidue Edizioni (2016)
20. Mangialardo, A., Micelli, E.: Off-site retrofit to regenerate multi-family homes: evidence from some European experiences. In: International Symposium on New Metropolitan Perspectives, pp. 629–636. Springer, Cham (2018)
21. Choay, F.: Del destino della città. Alinea editrice, Firenze (2008)
22. Bracchi, P.: Costruire la demolizione. In: Bertelli, G. (ed.) Paesaggi fragili, pp. 363–377 (2018)
23. English Heritage (EH): Constructive Conservation in practice. English Heritage, London (2008)
24. Lacaton & Vassal Homepage: https://www.lacatonvassal.com/index.php?idp=80, last accessed 11 April 2023
25. Biagi, M.: Un intervento esemplare–Lacaton & Vassal, Fréderic Druot, Christophe Hutin, Trasformazione di 530 alloggi negli edifici G, H e I del quartiere Grand Parc, Bordeaux, Francia. Casabella, n. 878, ottobre 2017, pp. 48–56 (2017)
26. Mattioli, C.: Verso un'architettura circolare. Officina, Trimestrale di architettura, tecnologia e ambiente, n. 33 aprile-maggio-giugno 2021, Ecolomia, pp. 54–55 (2021)
27. Moratilla, J.M.: Lacaton & Vassal: Condiciones abiertas para el cambio permanente. Entrevista con Anne Lacaton. In: Materia Arquitectura (18), pp. 6–21 (2021)
28. Ministère Charge Du Logement: Plan de relance: restructuration lourde et renovation thermique de logements locatifs sociaux criteres d'eligibilite des operations en 2022 et regles de financement (2022)
29. Masse, S.: Du patrimoine du xxe siècle à l'architecture contemporaine remarquable. L'action du ministère de la Culture français en faveur de la reconnaissance et de la sauvegarde de l'architecture récente. In: Situ. Revue des patrimoines 47 (2022)
30. Ladu, M.: Patrimonio immobiliare pubblico. Prospettive di rigenerazione per una città accessibile e di prossimità. UNICApress, Cagliari (2022)
31. Balletto, G.: Some reflections between city form and mobility. TeMA - Journal of Land Use, Mobility and Environment, pp. 7–15 (2022)
32. Castanheira, G., Braganca, L., Mateus, R.: Defining best practices in Sustainable Urban Regeneration projects. In: Portugal sb13 - contribution of sustainable building to meet EU 20–20–20 targets, pp. 435–442 (2013)
33. Chan, E., Lee, G.K.L.: Critical factors for improving social sustainability of urban renewal projects. Soc Indic Res **85**, 243–256 (2008)
34. Giorgi, S., Lavagna, M., Campioli, A.: Circular economy and regeneration of building stock: policy improvements, stakeholder networking and life cycle tools. In: Regeneration of the Built Environment from a Circular Economy Perspective, pp. 291–301. Springer, Cham (2020)
35. Bottero, M., Datola, G.: Addressing social sustainability in urban regeneration processes. An application of the social multi-criteria evaluation. Sustainability **12**(18), 7579 (2020)

36. Mangialardo, A., Micelli, E.: Off-site retrofit to regenerate multi-family homes: evidence from some European experiences. In: International Symposium on New Metropolitan Perspectives, pp. 629–636. Springer, Cham (2018)

37. Lee, G.K., Chan, E.H.: Indicators for evaluating environmental performance of the Hong Kong urban renewal projects. Facilities (2009)

38. Balletto, G., Borruso, B., Mei, G., Milesi, A.: Recycled aggregates in constructions. A case of circular economy in Sardinia (Italy), in Tema. Journal of Land Use, Mobility and Environment 14(1), 51–68 (2021)

39. Peng, Y., Lai, Y., Li, X., Zhang, X.: An alternative model for measuring the sustainability of urban regeneration: The way forward. J. Clean. Prod. 109, 76–83 (2015)

40. Lee, J.H., Lim, S.: An analytic hierarchy process (AHP) approach for sustainable assessment of economy-based and community-based urban regeneration: The case of South Korea. in Sustainability 10(12), 4456 (2018)

41. Micelli, E., Scaffidi, F.: Sustainability in Urban Regeneration: Real or Propaganda?. In: et al. Urban Regeneration Through Valuation Systems for Innovation. Green Energy and Technology. Springer, Cham (2022)

42. Balletto, G., Ladu, M., Camerin, F., Ghiani, E., Torriti, J.: More Circular City in the Energy and Ecological Transition: A Methodological Approach to Sustainable Urban Regeneration. Sustainability 14(22), 14995 (2022)

43. Giammetti, M.T., Rigillo, M.: Gestione del rifiuto da demolizione nel progetto di rigenerazione urbana. In: TECHNE: Journal of Technology for Architecture & Environment, p. 22 (2021)

44. Xu, K., Shen, G.Q., Liu, G., Martek, I.: Demolition of existing buildings in urban renewal projects: A decision support system in the China context. In: Sustainability 11(2), p. 491 (2019)

45. Direttiva 2010/31/UE del Parlamento Europeo e del Consiglio del 19 maggio 2010 sulla prestazione energetica nell'edilizia (rifusione), Gazzetta Ufficiale delle Comunità europee L. 153/13 del 18.6.2010

46. Russo, V.: Antico, moderno, contemporaneo. Note dalla riflessione sul restauro di Giulio Carlo Argan, in Atti del Convegno «Antico e Nuovo. Architetture e Architettura» a cura di In: Ferlenga, A., Vassallo, E., Schellino, F. (eds) (Venezia 31 marzo – 3 aprile 2004), vol. I, pp. 431–441. Università IUAV di Venezia, Il Poligrafo, Padova (2007)

Problem Setting on Energy Risk and Climate Change Adaptation: Topics and Tools

Roberto De Lotto[1]([✉]) [iD], Ilaria Delponte[2] [iD], Elisabetta Venco[1] [iD], Caterina Pietra[1] [iD], and Valentina Costa[2] [iD]

[1] Department of Civil Engineering and Architecture - DICAr, University of Pavia, 27100 Pavia, Italy
uplab@unipv.it
[2] Civil Chemical and Environmental Engineering Department, University of Genoa, 16145 Genoa, Italy

Abstract. Energy risk management and climate change adaptation strategies have long been targeted as individual and independent challenges, having emerged separately along the European Union (EU) and international agenda and policy history. Nevertheless, the most recent EU initiative in this field, the Global Covenant of Mayors (GCoM), faces mitigation and adaptation strategies simultaneously within the framework of the Sustainable Energy and Climate Action Plans (SECAP) design. A similar approach may lead to a re-definition of energy-related and climate change vulnerability and consequently to developing multi-risk territorial analysis. This would require building a complex and detailed knowledge of the territorial context, thus developing a strongly data-driven local risk and vulnerability assessment (RVA). Moreover, it must be remembered that SECAPs are drawn at the municipal scale, where geometry shows to be extremely various, and large metropolitan areas, as well as fragmented hamlets, coexist. This integrated approach may prove to be particularly critical for small municipalities. The present contribution aims at providing a methodology to plan mitigation and adaptation of local actions based on land use municipal assets and consequent multi-risk territorial mapping.

Keywords: Energy Risk · Multi-risk analysis · Sustainable Energy and Climate Action Plans

1 Introduction

Increasing territorial resilience within urban contexts represents one of the main challenges that cities are currently facing [1, 2]. Regarding urban risk assessment, energy- and climate-related components have been traditionally targeted individually and independently, having emerged at different times along EU and international agenda and policy history [3, 4].

Although both mitigation and adaptation actions have been considered complementary and necessary initiatives to reduce Climate Change impact on the environment [5]

O. Gervasi et al. (Eds.): ICCSA 2023 Workshops, LNCS 14111, pp. 89–103, 2023.
https://doi.org/10.1007/978-3-031-37126-4_7

during the last decades, they have been pursued separately and at different paces [6]. Priority has been long identified with Greenhouse Gases (GHG) emissions reduction to limit and act on the magnitude of climate change drivers before focusing on adapting as well the human environment to reduce Climate Change impacts on everyday life [7].

This time shift represents only one of the several dissimilarities between mitigation and adaptation strategies: the spatial and temporal scale of impacts of the actions, benefits, cost assessment methodologies, stakeholders, and actors involved, above all [8].

Despite deep and substantial differences, both energy- and climate- related actions need to be implemented within the same territorial framework so that interactions are no longer deniable [9–12]. Urban areas are simultaneously the main centers for GHG emissions production and the most vulnerable sites in case of extreme weather events [13].

According to the need to develop integrated initiatives targeting both mitigation and adaptation goals within limited and densely built contexts, scholars started to argue about ways to balance and combine local actions to cope with present and future challenges effectively and synergically [14, 15]. Developing synergies, indeed, requires more than the simple simultaneous design and implementation of actions [16]; a strong effort should be addressed towards a re-definition of urban vulnerability and risk concepts, towards a multi-layered and comprehensive approach.

As far as urban risk definition is concerned, energy and climate goals have been targeted as separate risks affecting the same territorial context, deriving from the action of different hazards (H), acting on different vulnerabilities (V) and exposures (E):

$$R_{energy} = H_{energy} + V_{energy} + E_{energy}$$

$$R_{climate} = H_{climate} + V_{climate} + E_{climate}$$

The traditional approach leads to a double risk assessment where consequent actions are developed independently and indifferently to potential overlaps and conflicts.

A multi-risk approach, on the other hand, could help in highlighting synergies and critical points when risk assessment layers – descending from vulnerabilities and exposures mapping – need to match with underlying urban and landscape assets [17–19].

Developing a multi-risk analysis would require building a strong, deep, and punctual knowledge of territorial context and collecting a significant amount of data, in order to implement several indicators' sets able to evaluate and monitor local response and capacity over time [20, 21].

Resilience-oriented urban planning implies relevant human and material resources to support similar data-driven processes' implementation [22, 23]. Nevertheless, according to cities' pivotal role within the global socio-economic system and the subsidiarity principle, municipal scale has been pinpointed as the most suitable for developing such planning activity. Proximity, context knowledge, accountability towards the local community, as well as the direct capacity to implement local and place-based actions led to a municipality leadership as far as mitigation and adaptation actions' planning is concerned [24–27].

Municipal scale variability in the population, territorial extension, and consequent administrative structure may undermine widespread and shared implementation of similar activities, making small municipalities unable to cope with such challenges [28].

This element proved to be significantly critical within the framework Covenant of Mayors' (CoM) initiative that started in 2008 to support municipality-led, voluntary, and bottom-up actions across the EU – and beyond with the Global Covenant of Mayors since 2015- through the design of Sustainable Energy and Climate Action Plans (SECAPs).

Among more than 11 000 signatories, beyond 65% were small municipalities with fewer than 10 000 inhabitants [29]. Despite initial enthusiastic participation, signatories faced several issues in SECAPs' design, implementation, and monitoring steps, so many have not yet submitted their local proposal [30].

Even though Joint Research Centre (JRC) in its guide for SECAP development provides a simpler methodology to be implemented by medium and small-sized centers [31], a strongly data-driven approach hampers the mitigation and adaptation capacity of the tiniest municipalities.

This paper aims to provide a multi-risk approach to be developed within the SECAP planning framework that, based on the municipal scale of the initiative, targets small municipalities with a simpler methodology based on land use of municipal assets (Sect. 2). Specifically, energy risk will be addressed in 2.1 and climate risk in 2.2. In the discussion, the authors highlight potential drivers and barriers to implementing such a multi-risk approach for adaptation and energy-related action planning at the local scale, also in light of new normative updates (Sect. 3). Finally, some considerations on the implementation of SECAPs and future challenges in multi-risk planning are reported in the conclusions (Sect. 4).

2 Methodology

The urban environment (generally the territory) is recognized as a highly multi-risk environment addressing air pollution, noise, waste, road accidents, heat island effects, climate, natural hazards, etc. Those multiple risk sources may cause damage of different degrees to the system's users at once, also generating cascading effects and mutual intensification of adverse effects. Therefore, a global vision of safety needs to be developed. The latter should be considered as a fundamental objective of urban planning, public space design, technological network planning, and mobility, as well as a design assessment criterion.

To effectively support decision-making actions, distinguishing among the possible measures and activities to manage risks is fundamental. Indeed, risk management refers to applying specific policies by exploring new opportunities to prevent new conflicts on the one hand and to reduce losses, accidents, and disasters on the other, looking to strengthen overall resilience [32–34]. It is intended to develop a systematic approach and practice that manages uncertainty to mitigate potential harm and loss. Risk management includes risk assessment, analysis, and communication.

Conducting a risk analysis establishes a risk picture, highlights different alternatives and solutions, detects the critical factors, conditions, activities, systems, components, etc., and finally shows the impact of multiple measures on risk [35].

Risk assessment establishes a methodology to evaluate risks' nature and extent through analyzing eventual hazards and testing existing vulnerability conditions "that together could potentially harm exposed people, property, services, livelihoods and the environment on which they depend" [33]. More technically, risk assessments (with related risk mapping) take into consideration: detailed features of hazards such as their location, intensity, frequency, and probability; the exposure and vulnerability study that deals with the physical, social, health, economic, and environmental components; and the estimation of the effectiveness of existing and alternative response capabilities in relation to likely risk scenarios.

Finally, risk communication is linked to a highly complex and interdisciplinary academic field that works to provide a real-time exchange of information, advice, and opinions between targeted experts, official institutions, and people who are threatened (due to a hazard) putting in danger their survival, health, economic or social wellbeing. The main objective consists in enabling people at risk to decide for their safety and mitigate hazard's effects by reaching protective and preventive measures [36, 37]. Moreover, risk communication is conceived to support a positive change in people's behavior to reduce potential threats in the long term [38].

In this regard, the SECAP tool can be detected as part of the overall risk management framework (Fig. 1). In particular, the latter represents an evaluation tool that can estimate the shift towards a low-carbon economy and climate-proof cities [39].

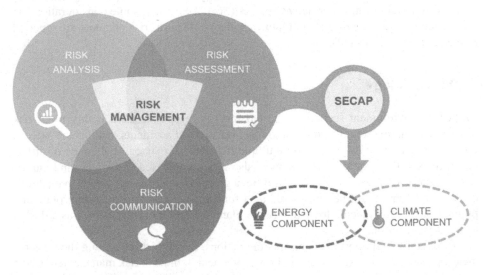

Fig. 1. SECAP within risk management framework (authors).

Given the numerous definitions in the literature, Risk represents the probability that a potentially harmful phenomenon can occur in a certain place and at a specific time, causing an expected damage value. Dealing with the concept of risk and its related evaluation process means taking into consideration several components: the triggering event, thus the hazard source, the probability of this occurring, the context in which it could take place, the elements involved, and the damage that these elements may undergo [40–46]. Besides, many social and natural sciences fields are also involved (for example, engineering, economics, political science, sociology, psychology, and philosophy), making this topic extremely multi-inter and trans-disciplinary.

The Risk equation proposed by Dilley [47] links four main parameters (Exposure, Vulnerability, Hazard, Risk), which depend on the time (t) variable. This formulation is one of the most significant, highlighting the most evident relationships between the urban environment and urban planning:

- H (hazard) is the probability that a given calamitous event will occur within a specific period and in a particular area;
- V (vulnerability) refers to the degree of loss produced on a certain element or group of elements exposed to risk; the term represents the weakness of physical and social systems against specific dangers;
- E (exposure) represents the set of elements exposed to risk in a specific area (population, movable and immovable property, economic activities, public services, etc.). Exposure can also be seen as the overlap of the spatial and temporal distribution of human goods and dangerous phenomena;
- R (risk) is the expected total number of human losses, injuries, property damage, and business interruption due to a particular phenomenon [48].

The methodology correlates the two main components within the SECAP framework (energy and climate). It analyzes them from the point of view of risk assessment focusing on the hazard factor of risk equation, examining causes and possible interrelation (such as secondary and tertiary events, compounding, and cascading effects) among them. Thus, through a synthetic and structured representation, it is possible to define that (Fig. 2):

1. The Energetic Risk can be evaluated and analyzed considering the following factors:
   i. The issue related to energy shortage (reduction of primary sources, socio-political issues at the international level, high costs);
   ii. The level of access to energy compared on both the specific economic and the overall system spheres ("energy inequalities" due to social/cultural components, economic status, technological gap);
   iii. Energy literacy (in terms of knowledge, attitudes, and behavior that allow people to translate knowledge of what energy is, which are its production processes and sources, uses, and conservation strategies, into concrete actions), which is in turn linked to scientific and financial literacy [49, 50];
   iv. The set of infrastructure opportunities (network grids and production plants) that can be developed at different scales.

These assumptions let the SECAP tool be interpreted as the one able to reduce the mentioned Energetic Risk by enabling some given actions:

- The definition and systematization of the overall and detailed needs and vulnerabilities;
- The processing of needs, vulnerabilities, and exposures related to each urban and economic sector within the global framework;
- The population's direct involvement;

• Communication and training events.

2. The Climate Risk can be evaluated and analyzed considering the following factors:
   i. The level of greenhouse gas emissions;
   ii. The natural risk effects deriving from extreme weather events and climate change.

These assumptions let the SECAP tool be interpreted as the one able to reduce the mentioned Climate Risk by enabling some given actions:

• The targeting of dedicated responses to these risks:

   i. Emissions' reduction;
   ii. Extreme events defense;
   iii. Energy poverty alleviation.

• The population's direct involvement;
• Communication and training events.

Hence: SECAP is a multi-risk response tool (with different weights depending on context and objectives), which is also transcalar since its initiative is taken at the EU level, later implemented by municipalities, often supported and coordinated by regional agencies and/or administrations, that may represent the first step towards an integrated and multi-risk approach to energy and climate planning.

Despite climate risk having been mainstreamed into an initially energy risk-led planning program -the so-called Sustainable Energy Action Plan (SEAP) initiative- progressive evolution of SECAPs may lead to a more holistic methodology to face multi-risk assessment.

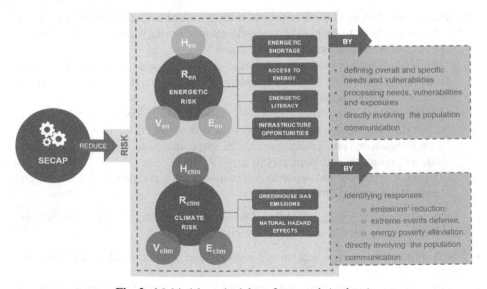

Fig. 2. Multi-risk methodology framework (authors).

The two risk components previously discussed are explained in more detail below, particularly concerning the possible hazards' sources that trigger them.

2.1 Energy Risk

Energy Risk is understood as a highly multi-disciplinary concept. Indeed, it integrates topics deriving from technology, economy, social science, environment, politics, and geopolitics, as it is displayed in Table 1, which overall denotes a sustainable-oriented approach [51]. For this reason, dealing with quantitative evaluation of energy risk means reasoning on multiple methodological approaches, particularly considering its significant set of qualitative dimensions [52, 53].

Moreover, energy production determines specific social costs and Energy Risk is considered part of them. Those social costs refer to air and water pollution, land abuse, depletion of natural resources, and other factors [54, 55].

Human health is equally affected, and the most significant threat deriving from energy systems is mainly linked either to industrial and occupational risk or pollution effects. Nevertheless, the loss' extent can be perceived differently; indeed, an industrial accident involving one individual does not have the same impact on the public as on hundreds of people [56, 57].

Table 1. Energy risk main causes (authors).

Main category	Sources
Environmental	Natural disasters Energy production (production process, type, and method of production) External factors Raw material and fuel production Materials Component fabrication Plant construction and maintenance Transportation
Economical	Market Client-related Project-related Contractor-related Performance-related Cost High price volatility Time and quality
Social	Technology Political organization Culture Energy literacy Not equal access to energy

2.2 Climate Risk

Natural hazards involve many processes that can be physical, chemical, and biological. Such processes can determine, among others, volcanic eruptions, earthquakes, landslides, and floods which consistently affect the Earth's surface. Their origin can depend on deep internal or external forces (i.e., the energy from the Sun that can generate violent storms, flooding, and coastal erosion).

Climatological hazards result from long-lived, meso to macro-scale atmospheric processes ranging from intra-seasonal to multi-decadal climate variability [58]. Overall, climate risks derive from climate-related hazards, vulnerability, and societal exposure. Temperature change, precipitation intensity, windstorms, sea-level rise, salinity, and water temperature can be listed as the main drivers of climate-related hazards. The latter are affected by natural variability and anthropogenic climate change.

In this case, vulnerability and exposure rely on socio-economic factors, including socio-economic development pathways, societal adaptation and mitigation measures, and governance.

Climate change-related hazards are associated with various events that cause many direct and indirect repercussions to people. Indeed, such hazards influence many sectors, as shown in Table 2; moreover, due to great countries' involvement in the global world economy, it becomes easy to detect several pathways for transboundary impacts [59].

Table 2. CoM Risk assessment components (LIFE Adaptate Projects).

CoM Climate Hazards	Local Vulnerabilities	Impacted sectors
Extreme heat	Socio-economic	Buildings
Extreme cold	Physical/Environmental	Transport
Heavy precipitation: rainfall, snowfall, fog, or hail		Energy
Floods: flash/surface flood, river flood, coastal flood, groundwater flood, or permanent inundation		Water
Droughts and water scarcity		Wastes
Storms: severe wind, tornado, cyclone (hurricane/typhoon), tropical or extratropical storm, storm surge, or lightning/thunderstorm		Land Planning
Mass movement: landslide, avalanche, rockfall, or subsidence		Agriculture and Forestry

(continued)

Table 2. (*continued*)

Wildfires: forest or land fire		Environment and Biodiversity
Chemical change: saltwater intrusion, ocean acidification, or atmospheric CO2 concentrations		Health
Biological hazards: water-borne disease, vector-borne disease, airborne disease, or insect infestation		Civil Protection and Emergency

3 Discussion

Today the link between energy consumption, global warming, climate change, environmental pollution, and biodiversity loss is evident. In this respect, the international scientific community has identified numerous initiatives and specific rules intending to establish a new balance between the environment and human activities (including energetic supplies and protection against climate change to slow and reduce them).

Some of the most relevant actions come from the energy sector, in particular from the definition of Energy Communities (ECs). From the European legislative point of view, the creation of ECs provides a responsive tool to restructure the energy systems by allowing citizens to participate actively in the ecological transition. Indeed, through the "Clean energy for all Europeans package" (2019), the Directive on common rules for the Internal Electricity Market (EU 2019/944), and the Renewable Energy Directive (2018/2001/EU, RED II) the EU sets the general framework of ECs and strengthens the role of renewable sources as the primary source of energy (for electricity and heating) production.

The Italian legislation introduced the definitions of renewable energy communities through the *Decreto Milleproroghe* ("Thousand-extension" Decree-Law, 2020) that transposes the RED II directive by encouraging the large-scale development of ECs. Additionally, the National Recovery and Resilience Plan (2021) outlines, among the others, the objectives of making Italy more resilient to the inevitable climate change and its system safer and more sustainable in the long term by ensuring its competitiveness. Moreover, it refers to energy transition, resilience, and territory, specifically with Mission 2 – Green revolution and ecological transition and its components C1, C2, C3, and C4.

At the regional level, i.e., in 2022 Lombardy Region defined a law for the Promotion and development of a system of Renewable Energy Communities (CER) at the regional scale to reach an energy independence. The Region intends to take an active role in the promotion of ECs establishing the so-called Lombardy Regional Energy Community (CERL).

At the local level, already existing since the 1990s, there are the former Municipal Energy Plans, today SECAP Sustainable Energy and Climate Action Plans. The latter materialize the objectives of the National and Community directives to have a sustainable energy supply and to identify the potential for action existing in the municipality in terms of energy and, therefore, to use energy most rationally and efficiently possible, to encourage and increase the use of renewable energy sources to reduce emissions of CO_2.

Focusing on climate risk, to support national and local implementation of the Sendai Framework, in 2017, the United Nation Office for Disaster Risk Reduction – UNDRR created guidelines on National Disaster Risk Assessment (NDRA) as a policy guide and a practical reference to introduce government, authorities, stakeholders, and scholars to policy, process, and the high-level technical requirements for a holistic national disaster risk assessment. In this framework, SECAP fits perfectly [32, 60].

It is crucial to notice that in urban areas, in case of slow natural phenomena (drought, climate change, environmental degradation, desertification), the complex urban system proves to be capable of modifying its main components (physical and functional) and adapting the urban structure and the different subjects involved [61]. It also requires the ability to accommodate very quick modifications of external (global geo-political and socio-economic situations) and internal (social and organizational scenario) conditions.

Urban planning tools are essential in planning and implementing SECAP strategies and actions at the municipal planning level, becoming the substantial and procedural focus. Through the diversified panorama of laws on territorial planning characterizing the various Italian regions, some points referring to SECAPs can be traced transversally:

- The urban fabric and urban functions are analyzed as part of the strategic component of the plan (influences on the general strategies about energy and climate change adaptation actions for the new settlements or regeneration area), and as a component of the private city with a specific normative system (influences on the local and private management);
- The technological, infrastructural system is analyzed as elements under the public management and as technical elements (energy grids, recharge stations, energy cabins, and so on);
- Mobility issues through specific (sustainable) mobility plans define the general strategies for sustainable mobility and address the practical design of soft mobility and the urban road system and cycle paths.

Furthermore, even the municipal emergency plans (or civil protection plans) include these elements to pay attention to, as a study of the context, therefore like an analysis of risk scenarios and preventive and emergency procedures.

In its substantive and procedural structuring, the proposed method allows an objective quantification of the climate risk and energy in the different portions of the territory. Therefore, the most at-risk areas are highlighted, identifying for the public administrations the possibility of prioritizing interventions on a municipal scale. It follows that this approach makes it possible to reconcile the need for political-social-economic choices that each municipality is called to make for the current and strategic management of its territory with the scientific objectivity dictated by the method itself. Furthermore, the vision on a local or municipal scale makes it possible to establish local-punctual actions, even on individual buildings or portions of infrastructure, in a general framework by defining a "system of actions" that considers the complex dynamic nature that characterizes urban contexts.

4 Conclusions

Building more resilient urban environments requires a deep change in how risk is defined and faced. The present contribution investigated the potential of a re-definition of urban risk concept through a multi-risk approach, able to mainstream both energy and climate components.

The multifaceted nature of urban risk implies targeting risk assessment, prevention, and management planning through a flexible, holistic, and multi-level approach.

Traditional allocation of competencies and sectorial planning activities and tools may prove unable to cope with climate change evolution and uncertainties. Following SECAPs' municipality-led initiative scheme, the proposed methodology suggests local urban plans as pivotal tools to foster multi-level and cross-sectoral approaches toward risk assessment.

As previously stated, being risk the result of hazards' impact on territorial assets and vulnerabilities – both in its energy and climate drivers – its modelling, analysis, as well as mitigation and adaptation strategies need to be developed at the same scale at which considered phenomena occur, as risk assessment requires taking into account its various and peculiar nature, features and causes. Similar considerations initially led the EU initiative to downscale from global energy and climate scenarios to local actions such as the Covenant of Mayors and SECAPs' implementation.

A multi-risk assessment should involve multiple governance and territorial scales, indeed. Strong network, exchange, and cooperation should interlink EU, National, Regional, and Local scales, as far as different hazards may concern different geographical and administrative entities, thus insisting on the same territory.

The unpredictable evolution of climate and socio-economic environment, as well as specific features and various risks require developing a deep background of territorial knowledge where different layers overlap, thus highlighting potential synergies and conflicts. Therefore, integrated reading and interpretation of the context are necessary to assess local vulnerabilities' components. This represents a particularly challenging task as far as multiple risks are concerned and urban assets provide an extensive range of variables and factors related to different morphology, uses, and urban fabrics, as briefly introduced in the previous section.

Consequently, similar knowledge could be deepened and collected on a quite wide scale due to the need for significant human, technological, and economic resources. Research centers, universities, and administrations should be involved in developing structured and synthetic descriptions of the territorial asset that need to improve their resilience and response to multi-risk challenges.

Nevertheless, the effectiveness of the actions requires local participation as well. Solutions should be tailored according to punctual criticalities and needs; local stakeholders and communities are essential to down-scale general goals and strategies to match top-down knowledge with bottom-up experience. Exposure enters multi-risk assessment through the closer reading of micro-dynamics.

In this direction, the present work aims to underline the crucial role urban plans may play. They may act as contact points where general goals and policies meet with local communities' needs, will, and ambitions, thus targeting solutions that aim to reach higher objectives through tangible, place-based, and practical actions. They could represent the foundation for a multi-level and multi-disciplinary approach leading to tailored resilient solutions able to face multi-risk challenges, starting from their potential as supporting tools for SECAPs implementation, especially as far as small municipalities are concerned.

SECAP initiative represents the first step towards this mindset change, according to its EU-Local dual nature and its integration of energy and climate actions, simultaneously targeting mitigation and adaptation goals. Future challenges will therefore address:

- Further widening of territorial risks to be included within assessment procedures, thus adding new layers to local, territorial framework analysis;
- Relevant participation of small municipalities requires an intermediate governance level, where mesoscale stakeholders, such as regional agencies and research centers, act as link between local and higher scales. A similar contribution is, therefore, pivotal to fostering cooperation and collaboration and supporting smaller municipalities in the implementation phases, thus reducing the percentage of actions that remain on paper.

From a methodological and scientific point of view, a comprehensive re-definition of urban risk that needs to be translated into preventive and managing strategies and actions requires several sectorial plans and visions to be mainstreamed into a more comprehensive framework, thus targeting advanced smoothing of traditional barriers among different sectors, mitigation and adaptation planning.

Competencies and know-how should therefore converge into the wider borders of territorial multi-risk assessment and planning, thus enhancing comparing and prioritizing interventions to be implemented according to their overall impacts on the urban ecosystem.

Finally, building such a complex, integrated, multi-disciplinary, and multi-layer territorial knowledge would represent a massive challenge in terms of background standardization of methodology and tools, requiring strong efforts of coordination and cooperation to develop structured and shared layering asset able to convey a holistic, rich and synthetic reading of the local context.

A similar approach may prove highly relevant regarding resource allocation within the National Resilience and Recovery Plan framework, as far as energy risk and climate change represent key challenges and drivers.

References

1. Heinzlef, C., Serre, D.: Urban resilience: From a limited urban engineering vision to a more global comprehensive and long-term implementation. Water Security 11, 100075 (2020). https://doi.org/10.1016/j.wasec.2020.100075
2. Rizzi, P., Graziano, P., Dallara, A.: A capacity approach to territorial resilience: The case of European regions. Ann. Reg. Sci. 60, 285–328 (2018). https://doi.org/10.1007/s00168-017-0854-1
3. Pielke, R.A., Jr.: Rethinking the role of adaptation in climate policy. Glob. Environ. Chang. 8(2), 159–170 (1998). https://doi.org/10.1016/S0959-3780(98)00011-9
4. Burton, I.: Deconstructing adaptation... and reconstructing. Delta 5(1), 14–15 (1994)

5. United Nations: United Nations Framework Convention on Climate Change. Rio de Janeiro (1992)
6. Pittock, A.B., Jones, R.N.: Adaptation to what and why? Environ. Monit. Assess. **61**, 9–35 (2000). https://doi.org/10.1023/A:1006393415542
7. Kates, R.W.: Climate change 1995: impacts, adaptations, and mitigation. Environment: Science and Policy for Sustainable Development **39**(9), 29–33 (1997). https://doi.org/10.1080/00139159709604767
8. Klein, R.J., Schipper, E.L.F., Dessai, S.: Integrating mitigation and adaptation into climate and development policy: three research questions. Environ. Sci. Policy **8**(6), 579–588 (2005). https://doi.org/10.1016/j.envsci.2005.06.010
9. Kane, S., Shogren, J.F.: Linking adaptation and mitigation in climate change policy, pp. 75–102. Springer Netherlands (2000)
10. McEvoy, D., Lindley, S., Handley, J.: Adaptation and mitigation in urban areas: synergies and conflicts. In: Proceedings of the Institution of Civil Engineers-Municipal Engineer, vol. 159, no. 4, pp. 185–191. Thomas Telford Ltd (2006)
11. Solecki, W., et al.: A conceptual framework for an urban areas typology to integrate climate change mitigation and adaptation. Urban Climate **14**, 116–137 (2015). https://doi.org/10.1016/j.uclim.2015.07.001
12. Pasimeni, M.R., Valente, D., Zurlini, G., Petrosillo, I.: The interplay between urban mitigation and adaptation strategies to face climate change in two European countries. Environ. Sci. Policy **95**, 20–27 (2019). https://doi.org/10.1016/j.envsci.2019.02.002
13. Rosenzweig, C., Solecki, W., Hammer, S.A., Mehrotra, S.: Cities lead the way in climate–change action. Nature **467**(7318), 909–911 (2010). https://doi.org/10.1038/467909a
14. Laukkonen, J., Blanco, P.K., Lenhart, J., Keiner, M., Cavric, B., Kinuthia-Njenga, C.: Combining climate change adaptation and mitigation measures at the local level. Habitat Int. **33**(3), 287–292 (2009). https://doi.org/10.1016/j.habitatint.2008.10.003
15. Hamin, E.M., Gurran, N.: Urban form and climate change: Balancing adaptation and mitigation in the US and Australia. Habitat Int. **33**(3), 238–245 (2009). https://doi.org/10.1016/j.habitatint.2008.10.005
16. Landauer, M., Juhola, S., Klein, J.: The role of scale in integrating climate change adaptation and mitigation in cities. J. Environ. Planning Manage. **62**(5), 741–765 (2019). https://doi.org/10.1080/09640568.2018.1430022
17. Di Mauro, C.: Regional vulnerability map for supporting policy definitions and implementations. In: ARMONIA conference "multi-hazards: challenges for risk assessment, mapping and management". Barcelona (2006)
18. Gallina, V., Torresan, S., Critto, A., Sperotto, A., Glade, T., Marcomini, A.: A review of multi-risk methodologies for natural hazards: Consequences and challenges for a climate change impact assessment. J. Environ. Manage. **168**, 123–132 (2016). https://doi.org/10.1016/j.jenvman.2015.11.011
19. Gallina, V., Torresan, S., Zabeo, A., Critto, A., Glade, T., Marcomini, A.: A multi-risk methodology for the assessment of climate change impacts in coastal zones. Sustainability **12**(9), 3697 (2020). https://doi.org/10.3390/su12093697
20. Carpignano, A., Golia, E., Di Mauro, C., Bouchon, S., Nordvik, J.P.: A methodological approach for the definition of multi-risk maps at regional level: first application. J. Risk Res. **12**(3–4), 513–534 (2009). https://doi.org/10.1080/13669870903050269
21. Terzi, S., Torresan, S., Schneiderbauer, S., Critto, A., Zebisch, M., Marcomini, A.: Multi-risk assessment in mountain regions: A review of modelling approaches for climate change adaptation. J. Environ. Manage. **232**, 759–771 (2019). https://doi.org/10.1016/j.jenvman.2018.11.100

22. Khazai, B., Bendimerad, F., Cardona, O.D., Carreño, M.L., Barbat, A.H., Buton, C.G.: A guide to measuring urban risk resilience: Principles, tools and practice of urban indicators. Earthquakes and Megacities Initiative (EMI), The Philippines (2015)
23. Hurlımann, A., Moosavi, S., Browne, G.R.: Urban planning policy must do more to integrate climate change adaptation and mitigation actions. Land Use Policy **101**, 105188 (2021) https://doi.org/10.1016/j.landusepol.2020.105188
24. Arentsen, M., Bellekom, S.: Power to the people: local energy initiatives as seedbeds of innovation? Energy, Sustainability and Society **4**(1), 1–12 (2014). https://doi.org/10.1186/2192-0567-4-2
25. Measham, T.G., et al.: Adapting to climate change through local municipal planning: barriers and challenges. Mitig. Adapt. Strat. Glob. Change **16**, 889–909 (2011). https://doi.org/10.1007/s11027-011-9301-2
26. Pasquini, L., Ziervogel, G., Cowling, R.M., Shearing, C.: What enables local governments to mainstream climate change adaptation? Lessons learned from two municipal case studies in the Western Cape. South Africa. Climate and Development **7**(1), 60–70 (2015). https://doi.org/10.1080/17565529.2014.886994
27. Westerhoff, L., Keskitalo, E.C.H., Juhola, S.: Capacities across scales: local to national adaptation policy in four European countries. Climate Policy **11**(4), 1071–1085 (2011). https://doi.org/10.1080/14693062.2011.579258
28. Fekete, A., Damm, M., Birkmann, J.: Scales as a challenge for vulnerability assessment. Nat. Hazards **55**, 729–747 (2010). https://doi.org/10.1007/s11069-009-9445-5
29. Joint Research Centre: Covenant of Mayors, Signatories, https://eu-mayors.ec.europa.eu/en/signatories#signatoryListMap
30. Santopietro, L., Scorza, F., Rossi, A.: Small Municipalities Engaged in Sustainable and Climate Responsive Planning: Evidences from UE-CoM. In: Gervasi, O., et al. (eds.) ICCSA 2021. LNCS, vol. 12957, pp. 615–620. Springer, Cham (2021). https://doi.org/10.1007/978-3-030-87013-3_47
31. Bertoldi, P.: Guidebook 'How to develop a Sustainable Energy and Climate Action Plan (SECAP)'. Publication Office of the European Union (2018)
32. Sendai Framework for Disaster Risk Reduction, https://www.undrr.org/quick/11409, last accessed 29 March 2023
33. United Nations Office for Disaster Risk Reduction, https://www.undrr.org/quick/11409, last accessed 29 March 2023
34. UNDRR: Terminology on Disaster Risk Reduction, www.undp.org/sites/g/files/zskgke326/files/migration/ge/GE_isdr_terminology_2009_eng.pdf, last accessed 29 March 2023
35. Aven, T.: What is risk analysis? John Wiley & Sons, Hoboken, New Jersey, USA (2015)
36. Risk communications and community engagement (RCCE), https://www.who.int/emergencies/risk-communications, last accessed 29 March 2023
37. EFSA reports set to inspire future risk communications in Europe, https://www.efsa.europa.eu/en/news/efsa-reports-set-inspire-future-risk-communications-europe, last accessed 29 March 2023
38. Rickard, L.N.: Pragmatic and (or) Constitutive? On the Foundations of Contemporary Risk Communication Research, Risk Analysis **41**, 466–479 (2021)
39. Scorza, F., Santopietro, L.: A systemic perspective for the Sustainable Energy and Climate Action Plan (SECAP). Eur. Plan. Stud. (2021). https://doi.org/10.1080/09654313.2021.1954603
40. UNDRO (United Nations Disaster Relief Coordinator): Natural Disasters and Vulnerability Analysis. Office of the United Nations Disaster Relief Coordinator, Geneva (1982)
41. UNDHA (United Nations Department of Humanitarian Affairs): Internationally agreed glossary of basic terms related in disaster management. UN Department of Humanitarian Affairs, Geneva (1992)

42. Burton, I., Kates, R.W., White, G.F.: The Environment as Hazard, 2nd edn. Oxford University Press, New York, NY (1993)

43. Adams, J.: Risk. UCL Press, London (1995)

44. UNI EN ISO 12100/2003 Sicurezza del macchinario. Concetti fondamentali, principi generali di progettazione, https://store.uni.com/uni-11230-2007, last accessed 27 March 2023

45. UNI 11230/2007 Gestione del rischio – Vocabolario, https://store.uni.com/uni-11230-2007, last accessed 27 March 2023

46. UNDP (United Nations Development Programme): Human development Report 2005. International cooperation at a crossroads. Aid, trade, and security in an equal world. New York, NY (2005)

47. Dilley, M., et al.: Natural Disaster Hotspots: A Global Risk Analysis. International Bank for Reconstruction and Development. The World Bank and Columbia University, Washington, DC (2005)

48. Venco, E.M.: La pianificazione preventiva per la riduzione del rischio: definizione di scenari preventivi nel contesto della città flessibile e resiliente. Santarcangelo di Romagna, Maggioli Editore (2017)

49. Brounen, D., et al.: Energy literacy, awareness, and conservation behaviour of residential households. Energy Economics 38, 42–50 (2013). https://doi.org/10.1016/j.eneco.2013.02.008

50. Martins, A., et al.: Energy literacy: What is out there to know? Energy Rep. 6, 454–459 (2020). https://doi.org/10.1016/j.egyr.2019.09.007

51. Rawat, A., Gupta, S., Joji Rao, T.: Risk analysis and mitigation for the city gas distribution projects. Int. J. Energy Sect. Manage. 15(5), 1007–1029 (2021). https://doi.org/10.1108/IJESM-10-2020-0001

52. Escribano, G., García-Verdugo, J.: Energy security, energy corridors and the geopolitical context: a conceptual approach. In: Marín-Quemada, J.M., García-Verdugo, J., Escribano, G. (eds.) Energy security for the EU in the 21st Century. markets, geopolitics and corridors. Routledge: Oxford and New York (2012)

53. Munoz, B., García-Verdugo, J., San-Martín, E.: Quantifying the geopolitical dimension of energy risks: A tool for energy modelling and planning. Energy 82, 479–500 (2015). https://doi.org/10.1016/j.energy.2015.01.058

54. Bohi, D.R., Toman, M.A.: The economics of energy security. Kluwer Academic Publishers, Boston (1996)

55. Yergin, D.: Ensuring energy security. Foreign Aff 85(2), 69e82 (2006)

56. Inhaber, H.: Energy Risk Assessment. Gordon and Breach Science Publichers, London (1982)

57. Burger, M., Graeber, B., Schindlmayr, G.: Managing Energy Risk: An Integrated View on Power and Other Energy Markets. John Wiley & Sons Ltd., Chichester, West Sussex, UK (2014)

58. Guha-Sapir, D., Hoyois, P., Below, R.: Annual Disaster Statistical Review 2014: the numbers and trends. CRED, Brussels (2015)

59. Tuhkanen, H., Piirsalu, E.: Overview of climate risk drivers, hazards and consequences. CASCADE – Community Safety Action for Supporting Climate Adaptation and Development, https://www.cascade-bsr.eu/sites/cascade-bsr/files/publications/cascade_overview_of_climate_drivers_and_hazards_final_version_0.pdf, last accessed 07 April 2023

60. UNISDR Local Government powers for Disaster Risk Reduction: a study on local-level authority and capacity for resilience, https://www.undrr.org/quick/11634, last accessed 07 April 2023

61. Jha, A.K., Miner, T.W., Stanton-Geddes, Z.: Building Urban Resilience: Principles, Tools and Practice. Directions in Development. (Eds.). World Bank: Washington, DC. (2013)

The Role of Spatial Circular Planning in Urban Governance. A Set of Indicators to Evaluate Performance in Urban Regeneration

Ginevra Balletto[✉] and Mara Ladu

DICAAR - Department of Civil and Environmental Engineering and Architecture,
University of Cagliari, 09100 Cagliari, Italy
{balletto,mara.ladu}@unica.it

Abstract. Cities are strategic places for development, but also places where many environmental, social, and economic problems arise. The scenario that by 2050 two thirds of the world's population will live in cities confirms that cities will still be responsible for growing consumption and, consequently, for a significant production of waste. Within this worrying situation, the principles of the Circular Economy (recovery, recycling and sharing) offers the opportunity to rethink the way goods and services are produced and used, exploring new approaches to ensure long-term prosperity. These principles find direct application in energy planning and urban governance at different scales.

In this framework, the manuscript proposes a methodology for the evaluation of a set of indicators capable of measuring the degree of circularity in the various urban scales (from small to extra large), with particular attention to energy performance.

Keywords: Energy Transition · Energy planning · Circular City

1   Introduction

The Circular City is based on the dynamic principles of the circular economy, a concept that is still complex and controversial today. Although it is not possible to declare a universal definition of Circular Economy, precisely due to its dynamic and constantly evolving nature, the scientific debate agrees on how the circular city aims to eliminate waste and emissions, as well as to provide services through the combined digital-ecological transition to ensure prosperity, improve the livability and resilience of communities [1]. An effective use of resources, as much as possible on local production, using renewable natural resources, is at the core of the circular city, which evolves between the concepts of sharing, efficiency and protection [2]. It is not a new urban model: the origins date back to the first phases of the industrial revolution, then re-emerge in the contemporary industrial phase 4.0.

Linear, circular and mixed economic models have developed, spread and alternated throughout history (Fig. 1).

© The Author(s), under exclusive license to Springer Nature Switzerland AG 2023
O. Gervasi et al. (Eds.): ICCSA 2023 Workshops, LNCS 14111, pp. 104–118, 2023.
https://doi.org/10.1007/978-3-031-37126-4_8

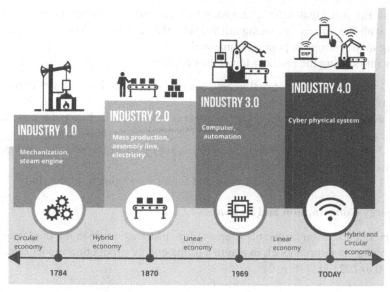

Fig. 1. Industrial phases and models based on circular, linear and hybrid economy. Author: G. Balletto.

The proto-industrial phase was characterized by a Circular Economy (proximity materials, spoliation of monuments). In the various industrial phases, from 1.0 to 3.0, a linear economy prevailed, which neglects the environmental and social impacts of the process: production based on the use of natural resources regardless of their effective long-term availability; growing energy production capacities; significant production of waste and waste. Finally, the 4.0 phase is characterized by a hybrid economy in which the paradigm of the linear economy coexists with that of the circular economy characterized by Recovery, Recycling, Reuse and Sharing. This last phase introduced renewable energy, secondary raw materials, sharing mobility, hybridizing the linear economy with the circular one.

The circular city model offers the opportunity to rethink the way we produce and use goods and services by exploring new ways to ensure long-term prosperity [3]. In the city, it may be applied through the reduction of urban enclaves [4], the reuse and regeneration of the built environment [5], in particular the unused public real estate asset [6], where the opportunities of the Circular City are concentrated [7]: from the sequestration of CO_2 to the use of recycled materials; from the implementation of proximity networks to the production of renewable energy, seizing the opportunities of the Renewable Energy Communities (REC) [8].

The manuscript proposes a set of indicators to represent the circular city, in quantitative-qualitative terms, at different urban scales, within a broader research on the circular city which investigates the role of the regeneration of the built environment, in particular of the public city [9], in sustainable urban planning. In this sense, the manuscript investigates the relationship between city and energy, health and mobility [10], with the aim of proposing advances in the research field of the circular city according to the European policies framework.

After introducing the research topic, the contribution develops as follows:

- Sect. 1.1 analyzes the relationship between energy consumption and resources, with particular reference to the Italian context;
- Sect. 2 focuses on the ecological and energy transition in European and national policies;
- Sect. 3 proposes a methodology to define a set of KPI to assess the circularity of urban governance at different urban scales;
- Sect. 4 is dedicated to the conclusions and future development of the study.

1.1 Energy Consumption and Resources

Energy production from renewable sources plays a strategic role in the implementation of the circular economy model, in contrast to the energy production model established from 1800 to 2021 [11] (Fig. 2).

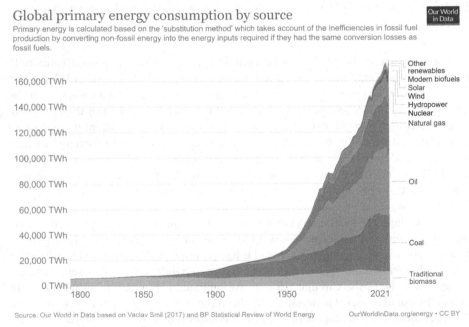

Fig. 2. Global primary energy consumption source. Sources: [11].

The issue of energy production, like that of the Circular City, requires a global scale of analysis and intervention. Studies show that in 1980 and 2021, in various parts of the world, energy consumption derives from the use of non-renewable sources. The situation is different in European Union as a part of consumption, albeit small, is attributable to the production of energy from renewable sources [11] (Fig. 3a, b).

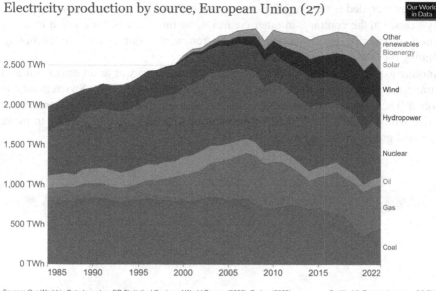

Electricity production by source, European Union (27)

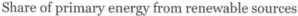

a.

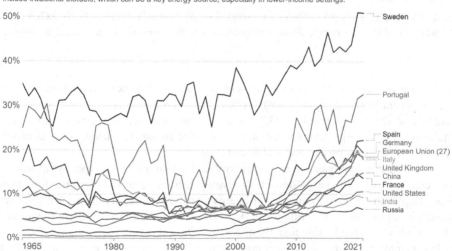

b.

Fig. 3. a. Electricity production by source and shar electricity production from renewable (EU27). Sources: [11]. **b.** Share of primary energy from renewable sources. Sources: [11].

Italy has recorded a very modest energy renewal and a slow transition in the last twenty years. On the contrary, in other countries, an impetus has been given to a real transition by favoring electrification based on renewable sources and, consequently, eliminating the consumption of primary resources.

Another aspect to consider is that the energy vector is part of an international grid that connects all states. Italy, for example, exchanges with France, with Switzerland and vice versa. There are no governmental problems, they are just international agreements that arise with the European Union, with the need to create the possibilities to move services and goods, including energy (Fig. 4).

Fig. 4. CLIMATE, INFRASTRUCTURE AND ENVIRONMENT EXECUTIVE AGENCY / ENERGY - PCI Transparency platform - Projects of common interest – Interactive map. Source: [12].

Among the indexes for evaluating the environmental efficiency of an energy system or more generally, of the overall energy system for the production of goods and services, there is also the carbon intensity [13]. A low carbon intensity corresponds to a high efficiency of the energy transformation system. The Italian Electricity map platform (Fig. 5a, b) represents production and distribution.

The particular coal, gas and oil are energy-dense sources. In Europe, the transition from coal to gas (both energy-dense). It developed because gas is compressible, thus responding to the growing demand for energy. Analyzing the condition of the Italian regions, it can be seen that Sardinia still depends on coal, therefore the carbon intensity is high with a high production and distribution inefficiency.

In this framework, the circular economy makes it possible to balance the demand for energy and to introduce the principle of circularity in the production of energy and its distribution to meet the needs of communities by reducing impacts. Energy production from renewable sources represents the first objective to be pursued, which requires a progressive convergence between urban planning and energy planning.

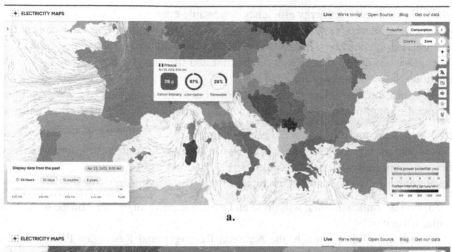

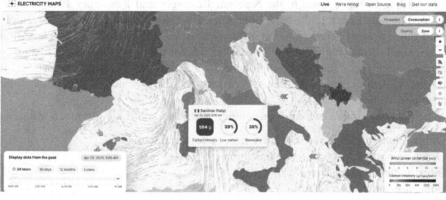

Fig. 5. a. Electricity Maps, production and distribution. Source: [13]. **b.** Electricity Maps, production and distribution. Sardinia case. Source: [13].

2   The Ecological and Energy Transition in European and National Policies

The European Green Deal launched by the European Commission in December 2019, is a set of policy initiatives with the overarching aim of making the European Union (EU) climate neutral in 2050 and the first continent to have a zero-climate impact.

The primary objective of the European sustainable development strategy is to drive the green transition of the member countries, thus achieving the international commitments established by the Paris Agreement and the 2030 Agenda for Sustainable Development (UN – HABITAT). According to the legally binding targets established by the European Climate Law, the Member States are bound to raise the EU's ambition on reducing greenhouse gas emissions to at least 55% below 1990 levels by 2030.

In this sense, the integrated National Energy and Climate Plans (NECPs) for the period from 2021 to 2030, represents a set of policy initiatives adopted by each country in the following sectors: energy efficiency, renewable energies, reduction of greenhouse gas emissions, interconnections, research and innovation. Among these, the clean energy transition, i.e. the decarbonization of the EU energy system, represents one of the main challenges, considering that energy production and use account for more than 75% of greenhouse gas emissions of the EU [14].

The transition takes place through a series of actions responding to three principles of a social, economic and environmental nature, which may be summarized as follows:

- ensuring secure and affordable EU energy supplies;
- developing an energy sector based largely on renewable sources to improve energy efficiency, especially of existing buildings;
- developing a fully integrated, interconnected and digitized energy market.

This is the framework that will drive an integral transformation of Europe towards a circular economy.

According to this approach, the National Recovery and Resilience Plan (NRRP) presented by Italy as part of the Next Generation EU (NGEU) programme, is developed around three strategic axes shared at a European level: digitalization and innovation, ecological transition, and social inclusion [15]. This is a unique opportunity to address and resolve the social and economic damage caused by the pandemic, as well as to overcome structural gaps in the Italian economy, reducing territorial, generational and gender inequalities.

The Plan aims to lead a long-term ecological transition of Italy through 6 missions:

1. Digitization, innovation, competitiveness, culture and tourism.
2. Green revolution and ecological transition.
3. Infrastructures for sustainable mobility.
4. Education and research.
5. Cohesion and inclusion.
6. Health.

With a total of € 68.6 billion allocated, the mission 2 is the one funded with the most resources with the main goals of improving the sustainability and resilience of the economic system and ensuring a fair and inclusive environmental transition through specific actions: waste recycling enhancement; reduction in drinking water leakage on water networks; increase in the number of more efficient private and public buildings; support for research on the use of hydrogen in industry and transport.

Most of these goals testify the role of the circular economy paradigm and of spatial energy planning in urban governance. Recent studies show that European cities are characterized by specific trends to steer the circular transition, as well as important challenges still outstanding [16]. Cities differ in the initiatives adopted in the various sectors. A significant set of policies refers to: circular infrastructure and construction to close material loops; public procurement to reduce their environmental footprint; local food systems more regenerative; raising awareness of citizens. At the same time, cities still face several issues like overcoming capacity and resource limitations, securing political support, measuring circularity, shifting the paradigm from linear to circular systems.

According to the system of indicators carried out by the EU to monitor member states in 4 areas (Production and consumption; Waste management; Secondary raw materials; Competitiveness and innovation) [17], several studies focused on the definition of indexes and related key performance indicators to assess the circularity of urban policies and projects, at the urban [18] and regional scale [19].

Within this research field, the paper proposes a set of key performance indicators (KPIs) to assess the level of circularity of regeneration projects at different urban scales, in order to fill the gap in data collection and monitoring frameworks, thus supporting urban governance in the energy and ecological transition.

3 Method

The methodology develops a set of key performance indicators (KPIs) to assess the level of circularity of interventions in the different urban scales (USs), according to the interpretative review of the literature [16, 18]. Starting from the results of a previous research [7], which identified the 7 pillars of the Circular Economy - Adaptive and resilient; Culture & society; Health and wellness; Renewable energy; Recycled materials; Protects biodiversity; Innovation & Value -, declined by 4 focuses - Green and recycled materials; CO_2 uptake; Renewable energy & REC; Proximity -, the study proposes a set of KPIs and related units of measurement (um) for the following USs (Fig. 6, Fig. 7): Small scale - Building area; Medium scale - Cluster or District; Large scale - Metropolitan City; X Large scale - Regions.

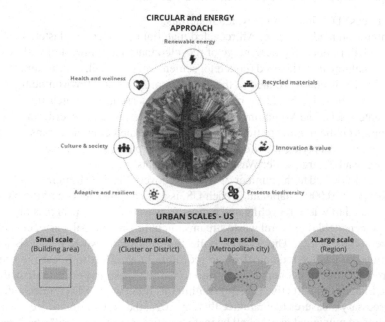

Fig. 6. Pillars of the circular and energy approach (Author: Balletto G., 2023).

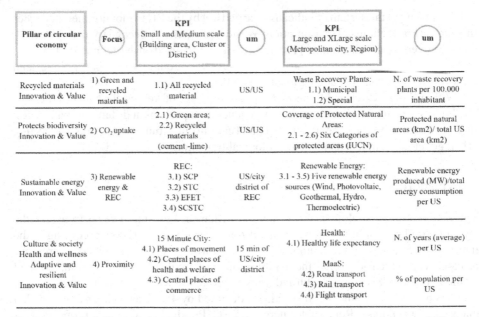

Pillar of circular economy	Focus	KPI Small and Medium scale (Building area, Cluster or District)	um	KPI Large and XLarge scale (Metropolitan city, Region)	um
Recycled materials Innovation & Value	1) Green and recycled materials	1.1) All recycled material	US/US	Waste Recovery Plants: 1.1) Municipal 1.2) Special	N. of waste recovery plants per 100.000 inhabitant
Protects biodiversity Innovation & Value	2) CO$_2$ uptake	2.1) Green area; 2.2) Recycled materials (cement -lime)	US/US	Coverage of Protected Natural Areas: 2.1 - 2.6) Six Categories of protected areas (IUCN)	Protected natural areas (km2)/ total US area (km2)
Sustainable energy Innovation & Value	3) Renewable energy & REC	REC: 3.1) SCP 3.2) STC 3.3) EFET 3.4) SCSTC	US/city district of REC	Renewable Energy: 3.1 - 3.5) Five renewable energy sources (Wind, Photovoltaic, Geothermal, Hydro, Thermoelectric)	Renewable energy produced (MW)/total energy consumption per US
Culture & society Health and wellness Adaptive and resilient Innovation & Value	4) Proximity	15 Minute City: 4.1) Places of movement 4.2) Central places of health and welfare 4.3) Central places of commerce	15 min of US/city district	Health: 4.1) Healthy life expectancy MaaS: 4.2) Road transport 4.3) Rail transport 4.4) Flight transport	N. of years (average) per US % of population per US

Fig. 7. Matrix of pillars of circular economy, focuses, literature, and key performance indicators (KPIs) of Circular city. Authors: G Balletto and M. Ladu (2023).

The proposed KPIs for the different USs are as follows:

1) KPIs Focus (1) - Green and recycled materials.

Small and medium scale: All recycled material (as concrete, plaster, steel).

The KPI refers to the percentage of recycled material of the total, with reference to each building material used (concrete, cement, plaster, steel, aluminium, etc..) [20, 21]. The KPI is closely related to the concepts of Minimum Environmental Criteria [22], which in Italy should be respected in all interventions which involve public real estate assets. The Minimum Environmental Criteria are green criteria introduced to support public administrations in implementing the ecological transition phase, which requires applying the life-cycle approach in public governance.

Large and XLarge scale: Waste Recovery Plants.

The KPI related to the number of Waste Recovery Plants (Municipal and Special) [23, 24] per 100.000 inhabitant, in each US, is a direct consequence of the basic concepts related to waste, recycling and recovery, as well as of the progress in the waste management field for several waste streams, including municipal waste, construction and demolition waste. The separate collection of specific waste materials and sets ambitious targets for municipal waste recycling in an effort to boost the transition towards the circular economy, according to the European targets established by the Waste Framework Directive [25, 26]. Within this framework, EU countries shall take the necessary measures to guarantee that, by 2025, the preparation for re-use and the recycling of municipal waste shall be increased to a minimum of 55%, 60% and 65% by weight by 2025, 2030 and 2035 respectively.

2) KPIs Focus (2) - CO$_2$ uptake.

Small and medium scale: Green areas and Recycled materials (cement-lime) [27].

The KPIs are important parameters to be considered in the renovation projects of the existing building stock and in the urban regeneration projects of public and private real estate complexes.

Large and XLarge scale: Coverage of Protected Natural Areas.

Protected Natural Areas include both Natura 2000 sites (Special Protection Areas-SPAs; Sites of Community Importance-SCIs; Special Areas of Conservation-SACs) and those areas established at national and regional level, according to the related law [28, 29]. Although the classification of protected natural areas differs in different countries, the International Union for Conservation of Nature (IUCN) identified six different protected area categories based on management objectives. This is a fundamental attempt to describe and categorize the different management approaches in individual sites [30].

The Common Database on Designated Areas (CDDA) [31] collects the main data referring to the protected area in European countries. It is the official source from Europe to the World Database of Protected Areas (WDPA). The share of terrestrial protected areas in 2021 amounted to 26.4%, of which 18.5% falling within Natura 2000 sites, while 7.9% in areas established at national or regional level [31].

In this sense, the coverage of protected natural areas in relation to the total US area represents an important parameter to be considered to ensure high levels of CO_2 uptake and environmental protection in metropolitan cities and regions.

3) KPIs Focus (3) - Renewable Energy & REC.

Small and medium scale: Renewable Energy Communities-REC [32, 33].

As discussed in previous research [7], the set of indicators which support the project of Renewable Energy Communities-REC can be summarized as follows:

- Self-consumed over the total energy produced over a set period in the city district - SCP
- Shared energy over total energy consumption of the community over a set period in the city district - STC
- Ratio between energy fed to the grid and energy withdrawn from the grid over a set period - EFET
- Ratio between the sum of self-consumed and shared energy over the total energy consumption of the community over a set period – SCSTC

Large and XLarge scale: Renewable Energy.

The set of indicators refers to the amount of renewable energy produced from renewable sources (wind, photovoltaic, geothermal, hydro, thermoelectric) in relation to the total energy consumed in each US. The indicator monitors the results of energy transition policies in different contexts and at different scales [34], according to the objectives of the European Green Deal and the Recovery and Resilience Plans.

4) KPIs Focus (4) - Proximity.

Small and medium scale: 15 min City.

The 15 min city indicators refer to an urban planning model aimed at guaranteeing citizens high levels of accessibility to the main urban facilities, which can be reached on foot or by bike within 15 min [35, 36]. The promotion of a slow and sustainable mobility stimulates virtuous and healthy lifestyles, as well as reducing polluting emissions from transport systems. In this sense, the 15 min City arises from awareness of the value of good behavioral practices and motor activity for the so-called culture of healthy living.

Large and XLarge scale: Health and Mobility as a Service (MaaS).

In particular, Health has declined according to the concept of Healthy life expectancy [37], while Mobility according to the framework that may be adopted in a Mobility as a Service (MaaS) [38, 39]. KPIs are the direct consequence of a new awareness that considers health, well-being and sustainable mobility as a conceptual unicum.

According to recent studies, the transport system is one of the most polluting factors worldwide. Therefore, favoring the transition towards sustainable transport systems is a precondition to protect the environment and people's health.

The new frontier of MaaS addresses sustainable mobility issues, particularly on travel users' behaviors, transport systems organization and new technologies and innovation services. This approach identifies and designs the actions that can facilitate the adoption of Mobility as a Service to better integrate the different transportation services (public transport, sharing mobility, ride hailing) and give tourists and non-residents the opportunity to easily plan, book and pay for multiple types of mobility services. For this reason, the present study considers the percentage of the population which uses transport systems (Road, Rail, Flight) [19] per US. This policy is functional to safeguard public health and well-being through the environmental sustainability of living spaces, which means the development of practices and policies for several aspects: life-improvement, as life expectancy; quality of public services and inclusiveness; social innovation and sustainable mobility.

The proposed Matrix of pillars of circular economy, focuses, literature, and key performance indicators (KPIs) is applicable for both ex-ante and ex-post scenarios in the different USs. However, it is important to underline that the set of KPIs contributes to the achievement of the circular city's objectives only if considered in a comprehensive and integrated manner.

4   Discussion and Conclusions

The ecological transition, at local, metropolitan, and regional level, represents a real opportunity to achieve the sustainable development goals and targets, including the European ambition on reducing dependence on fossil fuels and greenhouse gas emissions by 2050.

The need to define metrics to assess the degree of circularity of regeneration projects stimulates several studies involved in the definition of indicators and indices which also allow to test and monitor the effects of policies and projects oriented towards the application of the circular economy paradigm.

Following a comprehensive literature review on the challenge of the circular city in the ecological transitions, with particular attention to the energy transition and its possible integration within urban planning processes, the methodology develops a set of key performance indicators (KPIs) of the 7 pillars of the Circular Economy, declined by

4 focuses, to assess the level of circularity of interventions in the different urban scales (USs).

The study and the proposed methodology derive from previous research that developed a method to calculate the Circular City Index as a first attempt to evaluate benefits of the comprehensive regeneration of clusters of public buildings, which refer to the Small scale - Building area, and the Medium scale - Cluster or District.

From the Small and Medium scale to the Large and X Large scale, the focus becomes Metropolitan Cities and Regions.

As a matter of fact, the ambitious objectives of the European Green Deal require a multidimensional approach which led to consider several aspects and different geographical and administrative contexts. In this sense, the selected KPIs - All recycled materials & Waste Recovery Plants; Green areas and Recycled materials & Coverage of Protected Natural Areas; Renewable Energy Communities-REC & Renewable energy; 15 min City & Health and Mobility as a Service (MaaS) - define a Matrix of pillars of circular economy. However, the set of KPIs contributes to the achievement of the circular city's objectives only if considered according to an integrated approach.

The future steps of the research will be dedicated to the implementation of the set of KPIs aimed at building a Circular Index (CI) for each US, capable of measuring the degree of circularity of policies and projects at different scales.

The possibility to assess ex-ante conditions and ex-post scenarios drives future actions and monitor performance such as benefits for the environment and well-being and health of communities, according to the UN-Habitat Agenda 2030.

Acknowledgments. This study was supported by Projects Ecosystem of Innovation for Next Generation Sardinia (e.INS) - approved by MUR, prot. n. 1056 of 23/06/2022.

This paper is the result of the joint work of the authors. In particular: Section 1 and Section 1.1 have been written by G. Balletto; Section 2 by M. Ladu; Section 3 and Section 4 by G. Balletto and M. Ladu.

Glossary

CDDA   Common Database on Designated Areas
CI   Circular Index
EFET   Ratio between energy fed to the grid and energy withdrawn from the grid over a set period
EU   European Union
IUCN   International Union for Conservation of Nature
KPI   Key Performance Indicator
MaaS   Mobility as a Service
NECP   National Energy and Climate Plan
NGEU   Next Generation EU
NRRP   National Recovery and Resilience Plan
PREA   Publi c Real-Estate Assets
REC   Renewable Energy Communities
SCSTC Ratio between the sum of self-consumed and shared energy over the total energy consumption of the community over a set period

SCP Self-consumed over the total energy produced over a set period in the city district
STC Shared energy over total energy consumption of the community over a set period in the city district
US Urban Scale
WDPA World Database of Protected Areas

References

1. Kirchherr, J.: Circular economy and growth. A critical review of "post-growth" circularity and a plea for a circular economy that grows. Resources, Conservation and Recycling **179**, 1–2 (2022)
2. Paiho, S., et al.: Towards circular cities—Conceptualizing core aspects. Sustain. Cities Soc. **59**, 102143 (2020)
3. Harris, S., Weinzettel, J., Bigano, A., Källmén, A.: Low carbon cities in 2050? GHG emissions of European cities using production-based and consumption-based emission accounting methods. J. Clean. Prod. **248**, 119206 (2020)
4. Balletto, G., Ladu, M., Milesi, A., Camerin, F., Borruso, G.: Walkable city and military enclaves. Analysis and decision-making approach to support the proximity connection in urban regeneration. Sustainability **14**(1), 457 (2022)
5. Girard, L.F.: The evolutionary paradigm and the circular economy model: the horizon 2020 clic research outcomes. BDC. Bollettino Del Centro Calza Bini **22**(1), 11–21 (2022)
6. Ladu, M.: Patrimonio immobiliare pubblico. Prospettive di rigenerazione per una città accessibile e di prossimità. UNICApress, Cagliari (2022)
7. Balletto, G., Ladu, M., Camerin, F., Ghiani, E., Torriti, J.: More circular city in the energy and ecological transition: a methodological approach to sustainable urban regeneration. Sustainability **14**(22), 14995 (2022)
8. Gerundo, R., Marra, A., Grimaldi, M.: A preliminary model for promoting energy communities in urban planning. International Symposium: New Metropolitan Perspectives, pp. 2833–2840. Springer, Cham (2022)
9. Balletto, G., Mundula, L., Milesi, A., Ladu, M.: Cohesion Policies in Italian Metropolitan Cities. Evaluation and Challenges. In: Gervasi, O., et al. (eds.) ICCSA 2020. LNCS, vol. 12255, pp. 441–455. Springer, Cham (2020). https://doi.org/10.1007/978-3-030-58820-5_33
10. Beniamino, M., et al.: A methodological proposal to evaluate the health hazard scenario from COVID-19 in Italy. Environ. Res. **209**, 112873 (2022)
11. Our World in Data: https://ourworldindata.org/energy-production-consumption, last accessed April 2023
12. European Commission: CLIMATE, INFRASTRUCTURE AND ENVIRONMENT EXECUTIVE AGENCY ENERGY. PCI Transparency platform. Projects of common interest – Interactive map, https://ec.europa.eu/energy/infrastructure/transparency_platform/map-viewer/main.html, last accessed April 2023
13. Electricity maps: https://app.electricitymaps.com/map, last accessed April 2023
14. Tutak, M., Brodny, J., Bindzár, P.: Assessing the level of energy and climate sustainability in the european union countries in the context of the european green deal strategy and agenda 2030. Energies **14**, 1767 (2021)
15. MEF: Circular no. 34 of 17 October 2022. Methodological Guidelines for the reporting and transmission of the common indicators - Attachment to the circular no. 34 of 17 October 2022 (2022)

16. ICLEI: Circular Cities Declaration Report 2022. ICLEI – Local Governments for Sustainability – European Secretariat Leopold Ring 3, 79098. Freiburg, Germany (2022)
17. Eurostat - EU key indicators: https://ec.europa.eu/eurostat/web/main/home, last accessed April 2023
18. Muscillo, A., et al.: Circular City Index: An Open Data Analysis to Assess the Urban Circularity Preparedness of Cities to Address the Green Transition—A Study on the Italian Municipalities. arXiv Preprint, arXiv:2109.10832 (2021)
19. European Commission: EU Regional Competitiveness Index 2.0 2022 edition. Publications Office of the European Union, Luxembourg (2023)
20. Omer, M.M., Rahman, R.A., Almutairi, S.: Construction waste recycling: Enhancement strategies and organization size. Phys. Chem. Earth Parts A/B/C 126, 103114 (2022)
21. Balletto, G., Borruso, G., Mei, G., Milesi, A.: Strategic circular economy in construction: case study in sardinia, Italy. J. Urban Plan. Dev 147, 05021034 (2021)
22. Ministero dell'ambiente e della Tutela del Territorio e del Mare. Decreto 11 Gennaio 2017. Adozione dei Criteri Ambientali Minimi per Gli Arredi per Interni, per L'edilizia e per i Prodotti Tessili
23. Ferronato, N., Rada, E.C., Portillo, M.A.G., Cioca, L.I., Ragazzi, M., Torretta, V.: Introduction of the circular economy within developing regions: a comparative analysis of advantages and opportunities for waste valorization. J. Environ. Manage. 230, 366–378 (2019)
24. Di Foggia, G., Beccarello, M.: Designing waste management systems to meet circular economy goals: The Italian case. Sustainable Production and Consumption 26, 1074–1083 (2021)
25. Directive 2008/98/EC of the European Parliament and of the Council of 19 November 2008 on waste and repealing certain Directives (Text with EEA relevance)
26. 2011/753/EU: Commission Decision of 18 November 2011 establishing rules and calculation methods for verifying compliance with the targets set in Article 11(2) of Directive 2008/98/EC of the European Parliament and of the Council (notified under document C 8165 (2011)
27. Shafique, M., Xue, X., Luo, X.: An overview of carbon sequestration of green roofs in urban areas. Urban For. Urban Green 47, 126515 (2020)
28. Vimal, R., Navarro, L.M., Jones, Y., Wolf, F., Le Moguédec, G., Réjou-Méchain, M.: The global distribution of protected areas management strategies and their complementarity for biodiversity conservation. Biol. Cons. 256, 109014 (2021)
29. Oberč, B.P., de Jong, R., Demozzi, T., Battioni Romanelli, B.: Towards acircular economy that begins and ends in nature. IUCN, European Regional Office (2022)
30. IUCN: Protected areas programme. Vol 14 No 3 PROTECTED AREA CATEGORIES, 2004 (2004)
31. European Environment Agency: Homepage, https://www.eea.europa.eu/en, last accessed April 2023
32. Carrus, A.S., Galici, M., Ghiani, E., Mundula, L., Pilo, F.: Multi-energy planning of urban district retrofitting. In: Proceedings of the 2021 International Conference on Smart Energy Systems and Technologies (SEST). Vaasa, Finland, 6–8 September 2021
33. Ghiani, E., Giordano, A., Nieddu, A., Rosetti, L., Pilo, F.: Planning of a smart local energy community. The case of Berchidda municipality (Italy). Energies 12, 4629 (2019)
34. Terna spa. Homepage, https://www.terna.it/it, last accessed April 2023
35. Moreno, C., Allam, Z., Chabaud, D., Gall, C., Pratlong, F.: Introducing the "15-Minute City": Sustainability, resilience and place identity in future post-pandemic cities. Smart Cities 4, 93–111 (2021)

36. Balletto, G., Ladu, M., Milesi, A., Borruso, G.: A methodological approach on disused public properties in the 15-minute city perspective. Sustainability **13**(2), 593 (2021)
37. BES2021_byIstat, https://public.tableau.com/app/profile/istat.istituto.nazionale.di.statistica/viz/BES2021_/Regione?publish−yes, last accessed April 2023
38. Zhang, H., Song, X., Shibasaki, R.: (eds.) Big data and mobility as a service. Elsevier (2021)
39. Hensher, D.A., Mulley, C., Ho, C., Wong, Y., Smith, G., Nelson, J.D.: Understanding Mobility as a Service (MaaS): Past, present and future. Elsevier (2020)

Theoretical and Computational Chemistry and Its Applications (TC-CMA 2023)

Protein Tetrahedral Networks
by Invariant Shape Coordinates

Lombardi Andrea$^{(\boxtimes)}$, Noelia Faginas-Lago, and Leonardo Pacifici

Dipartimento di Chimica, Biologia e Biotecnologie, Università di Perugia,
Perugia, Italy
{andrea.lombardi,noelia.faginaslago}@unipg.it
http://www.chm.unipg.it/gruppi?q=node/48

Abstract. Representations of large molecules, typically proteins or DNA, for classification purposes, are commonly obtained by molecular networks. These are usually made up by a set of specific atoms (e.g. C_α atoms in the amino acids) of the molecule plus a neighbourhood criterium, that establishes links between the centers, so building the network. The main objectve of such approaches is the discrimination of structures, the induction of grouping of them, depending on the basis of structural molecular properties. Here we propose applications of invariant shape coordinates as parameters for the construction of enhanced molecular networks for protein classification.

Keywords: Protein structure classification · Hyperspherical coordinates · Invariant shape coordinates

1 Introduction

Proteins are complex molecules, whose structures can hardly be put into clear relationships with the corresponding biological functions, unless a number of proper classification schemes, on the basis of conveniently chosen chemical and physical properties, are made available. The availability of large sets of geometries, continuously fed by newly experimentally determined structures, allows to work on sufficiently large amounts of data to test new approaches to classification. Depending on the choice of parameters, the schematic representation adopted for the molecules (e.g. molecular networks) can be varied, and different classifications can be induced by application to large set of structures, revealing hidden patterns. Deep learning based methods, in particular, so helpful in unveiling patterns and regularities, could greatly benefit of alternative representations of the data structures used to feed neural networks [1,2].

A valid alternative for a set of suitable structural parameters for molecular networks, i.e. a mathematical object made up by a set of atoms or atom goups (nodes) with some closeness notion to establish links, is provided by hyperspherical coordinates, as traditionaly used in quantum reactive scattering calculations, or in their extention to the classical molecular dynamics of many-body systems

O. Gervasi et al. (Eds.): ICCSA 2023 Workshops, LNCS 14111, pp. 121–132, 2023.
https://doi.org/10.1007/978-3-031-37126-4_9

L. Andrea et al.

(more suited for application to large biomolecules). The fundamental feature of the quantum hyperspherical dynamics are the hyperspherical function basis sets [3–5] for three and four-atom collisions (see e.g [6–11]). Among the several variants of hyperspherical coordinates, the so called "symmetric" ones are characterized by invariance with respect to all the available product channels of a given system of atoms (as common in multi-channel processes). The same hyperspherical basis functions can be properly combined in finite sums to represent the intermolecular and intramolecular interactions. For theory and applications of the classical hyperspherical coordinates see Refs. [12,13,13–18,18–20,20–22,22–39].

The classical formulation of the hyperspherical coordinates introduces a partition of the degrees of freedom in terms of shape coordinates, ordinary rotation and kinematic rotation angles [8,40–44], for which the contributions to the kinetic energy can be calculated separately, as a function of time [8,41]. Moreover, the shape coordinates are such that to be invariant with respect to both types of rotations [40,45–50]. Using shape coordinates, invariant shape parameters can be defined, to be used for systematic classification of protein structures.

The paper is organized as follows. In Sect. 2 a definition of molecular networks is provided. In Sec 3 the theory of the hyperspherical coordinates, shape parameters and deformation indexes is succinctly resumed and alternative molecular networks, based on the local tetrahedral geometry of amino acids in proteins, are introduced. An example of application to representative protein structures is illustrated in Sect. 4. Sect. 5 draws conclusions and anticipates perspective applications.

2 Molecular Networks

In the context of the classification of proteins, it is possible to represent them schematically in the form of a graph. A graph is a network made up of vertices (or nodes) and edges (or links), an example of which is shown in Fig. 1, where, specifically, the vertices could represent amino acids and the links correspond to van der Waals type interactions or chemical bonds. Graphs of this type are called amino acid networks. The most common amino acid networks are the α carbon networks and the atomic distance networks. In such networks, for example, the nodes represent single C_α atoms, present in the various amino acid residues, or the atoms present in the various amino acids, except the hydrogen atoms. In both cases, two nodes are connected if the distance between them is less than a certain threshold value. In principle, network nodes can represent group of atoms, for example portions of each amino acid, and in these case the possibility of adding additional information to the node can be exploited to increase the informatio content of the network itself. In the next sections we will illustrate how a network of tetrahedral units can be constructed to represent a protein structure, by hypersherical shape coordinates.

3   Methodology

The $N-1$ Jacobi vectors $\mathbf{Q}_\alpha$, where $\alpha = 1, \cdots, N-1$, are the starting point to obtain the hyperspherical coordinates of a system of N particles. These vectors are combinations of the position vectors of the N particles of a system in the center of mass reference frame, which are denoted as $\mathbf{r}_\alpha$ [40] and are the starting point to generate hyperspherical coordinates by a bijective mapping in the Euclidean space. The combination coefficients are a function of the masses of the individual atoms, for details see next Sect. 3.1. As a generalization of spherical coordinates, the hyperspherical ones have an hyperradius ρ, modulus of a vector spanning the $3N-3$ dimensional configuration space, with Cartesian components equivalent to the Jacobi vector ones. The remaining $3N-4$ "hyperangles", mathematically define the hyperspherical coordinates. Many set of angles can be chosen, here we focus on the so called "symmetric" hyperspherical coordinates. These are obtained by a matrix transformation known as *singular value decomposition*, acting over a position matrix containing column-wise the Cartesian vectors of the particle in the system. A brief description is in the following section.

3.1   Properties of the Hyperspherical Coordinates

The *singular value decomposition* [51] is a theorem valid for any 3 x N position matrix constructed starting from a given set of N vectors, by arranging them column-wise.

Given $N \geq 2$ particles with masses $m_1, \cdots, m_N$ and radial position vectors in the center of mass reference frame, $\mathbf{r}_1, \cdots, \mathbf{r_N}$, a corrsponding set of mass *scaled* radii vectors, $\mathbf{q}_\alpha = (m_\alpha/M)^{1/2}\mathbf{r}_\alpha$ $(1 \leq \alpha \leq N)$, can be obtained, where $M = \sum_\alpha^N m_\alpha$ is the total mass of the system.
The $3 \times N$ position matrix is denoted by Z and its columns are the mass scaled vectors whose components denoted as q_{ij}:

$$Z = \begin{pmatrix} q_{1,1} & q_{1,2} & \cdots & q_{1,N} \\ q_{2,1} & q_{2,2} & \cdots & q_{2,N} \\ q_{3,1} & q_{3,2} & \cdots & q_{3,N} \end{pmatrix}. \tag{1}$$

The orthogonal matrix R^t (transpose of a matrix $R \in O(3)$) can act on the position matrix Z by left-multiplication performing rotations in the three-dimensional physical space. Also, an orthogonal matrix $K \in O(N)$ can act on the position matrix by right-multiplication, again rotating the coordinate frame, but in the so called *kinematic space* [7,41], $Z' = ZK$.

Allowed K matrices have typically the following form:

$$K = \begin{pmatrix} k_{1,1} & k_{1,2} & \cdots & (m_1/M)^{1/2} \\ k_{2,1} & k_{2,2} & \cdots & (m_2/M)^{1/2} \\ \cdots & \cdots & \cdots & \cdots \\ k_{N,1} & k_{N,2} & \cdots & (m_N/M)^{1/2} \end{pmatrix} \tag{2}$$

such matrices applied to the Z matrix generate a subset of all the possible Cartesian frames. Note that the last column of such Z matrices are identically zero, as a consequence of the separation of the motion of the center of mass, therefore the number of degrees of freedom is reduced to $3N - 3$. The matrix Z with one less column is called *reduced position matrix*.

The sets of $(N\text{-}1)$ Jacobi and related vectors always generate reduced matrices.

The possible different linear combinations of the N Cartesian particle position vectors satisfying the Jacobi vector definition, all generated as a function of the particle masses [40,52] are such that some of them resemble the asymptotic (reactive) channels of the system; it is well known that properly defined kinematic rotations smoothly connect them.

The *singular value decomposition* applied to the $3 \times n$ position matrix Z (where $n = N$ or $n = N - 1$) results in a product of three matrices:

$$Z = R \Xi K^t \tag{3}$$

where $R \in O(3)$ and $K \in O(n)$ are 3×3 and $3 \times n$ orthogonal matrices, respectively. The elements of the $3 \times n$ matrix Ξ are zeroes, with the possible exception of the three diagonal entries, $\Xi_{11} = \xi_1, \Xi_{22} = \xi_2, \Xi_{33} = \xi_3$, which are subjected to the inequality $\xi_1 \geq \xi_2 \geq \xi_3 \geq 0$.

The values ξ_i, $(i = 1, 2, 3)$ are called the *singular values* of the matrix Z and are uniquely determined, although the factors R and K in Eq. 3 are not. If $N \leq 3$ and Z is the full $3 \times N$ position matrix, then the smallest singular value ξ_3 is necessarily zero. The hyperradius and the ξ's are connected as follows [40,41]:

$$\xi_1^2 + \xi_2^2 + \xi_3^2 = \rho^2. \tag{4}$$

It has to be noted that the ξ's are invariant under both ordinary rotations in the three-dimensional physical space and kinematic rotations [7,8,41,53]. This invariance makes the ξ's appropriate as coordinates for molecular dynamics [40,54–57] and for the study of the minimum energy structures of N-particle systems.

In the special case $n = N - 1 = 3$, the matrix Z represents four particles or four center systems and the R and K matrices cannot be chosen to be *special orthogonal* ($R \in SO(3)$ and $K \in SO(n)$), but have to be just orthogonal matrices ($O(3)$). Accordingly, if the determinant of Z is lower than zero, its sign depends on the sign of the product of the ξ's, implying $\xi_3 \leq 0$. This fact is directly connected to the mirror image and chirality sign of the system [45,58,59].

3.2 Shape Coordinates and Tetrahedral Networks

The singular values (ξ_1, ξ_2, ξ_3) (shape coordinates), invariant under kinematic and ordinary rotations [60], can be put into relationship to the moments of inertia of the system:

$$
\begin{aligned}
\frac{I_1}{M} &= \xi_2^2 + \xi_3^2 \\
\frac{I_2}{M} &= \xi_1^2 + \xi_3^2 \\
\frac{I_3}{M} &= \xi_1^2 + \xi_2^2
\end{aligned}
\tag{5}
$$

where I_1, I_2 and I_3 are the moments of inertia in the principal axis reference frame. This clarifies why the ξs are referred to as shape coordinates: they contain information about the distribution of the masses with respect to the principal axis frame. From Eq. 4 one obtains:

$$
I_1 + I_2 + I_3 = 2M\rho^2.
\tag{6}
$$

the square of the hypperadius of the hyperspherical coordinates. The values of the ξ's also determine whether the system is an asymmetric, symmetric or a spherical rotor. for spherical top configurations $\xi_1 = \xi_2 = \xi_3$, prolate and oblate tops one has $\xi_3 = \xi_2 < \xi_1$ and $\xi_1 = \xi_2 > \xi_3$ respectively.

As Cartesian variables, the three ξ's can be represented on a sphere, in terms of the hyperradius and two angles θ and ϕ, as follows [40]:

$$
\begin{aligned}
\xi_1 &= \rho \sin\theta \cos\phi \\
\xi_2 &= \rho \sin\theta \sin\phi \\
\xi_2 &= \rho \cos\theta
\end{aligned}
\tag{7}
$$

As anticipated in previous section, the special case of a four-atom (or four-center) system is symmetric and the three ξs can be tought of as representative of the shape of a tetrahedron. Accordingly, a complex protein structure can be represented as a set of tetrahedral units, taking as the four centers the atoms surrounding the alpha carbon atoms of each amino acid unit. To each tetrahedron is associated a triple of ξs, accounting for its volume (product $\xi_1\xi_2\xi_3$) and surface area $\sum_{i<j} \xi_i\xi_j$).

4 Tetrahedral Networks for Protein Structures

In previous works [43, 48, 61, 62] we considered applications to protein structures for which the shape coordinates and derived the deformation indexes, properly defined, where calculated single amino acids (GLY, PRO, ALA) or globally for all the amino acids.

Here, given certain molecular structures, namely the sets of Cartesian coordinates defining its geometry, the procedure illustrated in previous Sects. 3.1

and 3.2 provides a recipe to build up a tetrahedral molecular network, by identifying the C_α atoms and the surrounding four centers defining deformed tetrahedra. To each of such tetrahedra a triple of ξs can be associated.

To obtain numerically the ξ values we use the following relationship coming
from Eq. 3:

$$ZZ^t = R\Xi\Xi^t R^t \tag{8}$$

where the product $\Xi\Xi^t$ is a 3×3 square diagonal matrix, whose entries are
the squares of the ξ's. The diagonal entries are just the eigenvalues of the product matrix ZZ^t, obtained from the position matrix. Once the ZZ^t matrix is
built from the Cartesian components of the mass scaled atomic position vectors
(see Sect. 3.1), this can be diagonalized by a numerical procedure or analiti-
cally through the Cardano's formula applied to the third degree characteristic
equation [40].

As and example of application we consider here two different proteins, whose
structures are available from the Protein Data Bank [63] and are shown in Fig. 2.
They have different secondary structures, one being made up by β-sheets only,
the other characterized by prevalent α-helix motifs. For each structure the Cartesian coordinates have been extracted, the coordinates of the four atoms surrounding the C_α atoms of each amino acid have been identified and used to build up
the product matrix of Eq. 8, so calculating the values of the ξs. The shape coordinates account for the local structure of the tetrahedra in the network, as they
occur in the protein chain (also repeatedly). In particular we consider the prod-
ucts $\xi_1\xi_2\xi_3$ and $\sum_{i<j}^{3} \xi_i\xi_j$, as obtained from the network, representative of the
tetrahedron volume and surface area, respectively. In Fig. 3 the two above quan-

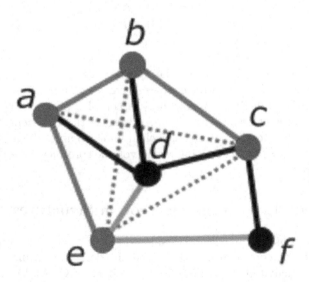

Fig. 1. Representation of a molecular network, the vertices represent atoms and the
link connection between them, as established by a measurable neighbourhood notion.

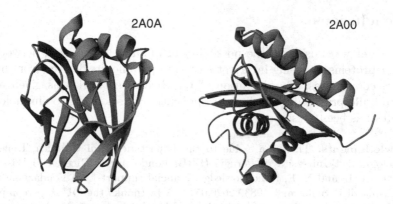

Fig. 2. Schematic representation of the two proteins 2A00 and 2A0A (Protein Data Bank classification name). The 2A0A structure accounts for a β-protein, since in β-sheets prevail, while 2A00 is mixed with a strong α-helix presence.

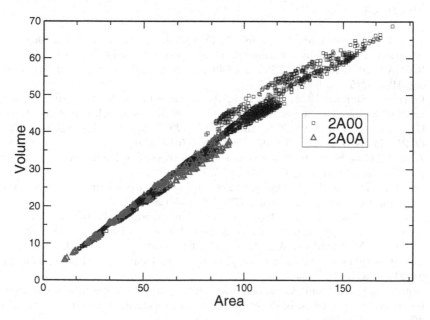

Fig. 3. Two-dimensional plot of the shape coordinate volume and area for the 2A0A and 2A00 protein structure obtained from the database [63]

tities are represented in a 2-dimensional plot. It can be seen that the shape coordinate volume/area plots, as expected, show apparently a linear correlation, but the range of the two quantities differ for the two proteins, probably due to their different secondary structures. Further analysis of such behaviour is beyond the scope of present work. However, this is a preliminary indication of the suitability of shape coordinates to identify structural properties.

5 Conclusions

In this paper we considered the possibility of building tetrahedral networks to represent proteins, by using invariant structure parameters derived from hyperspherical coordinates. The definition of tetrahedral network was given and a recipe to build provided. A preliminar application to selected protein molecular structures has been presented.

Acknowledgments. Thanks are due to the Dipartimento di Chimica, Biologia e Biotecnologie dell'Università di Perugia (FRB, Fondo per la Ricerca di Base 2019 and 2020). A. L. and N. F. L. acknowledge financial support from Fondazione Cassa di Risparmio di Perugia, n.# 19839.2020.0513. A.L. thanks the OU Supercomputing Center for Education & Research (OSCER) at the University of Oklahoma, and the Italian GARR for allocated computing time.

References

1. Perri, D., Simonetti, M., Lombardi, A., Faginas-Lago, N., Gervasi, O.: Binary classification of proteins by a machine learning approach. In: Gervasi, O., et al. (eds.) ICCSA 2020. LNCS, vol. 12255, pp. 549–558. Springer, Cham (2020). https://doi.org/10.1007/978-3-030-58820-5_41
2. Perri, D., Simonetti, M., Lombardi, A., Faginas-Lago, N., Gervasi, O.: A new method for binary classification of proteins with machine learning. In: Gervasi, O., et al. (eds.) ICCSA 2021. LNCS, vol. 12958, pp. 388–397. Springer, Cham (2021). https://doi.org/10.1007/978-3-030-87016-4_29
3. Zhao, B., Guo, H.: State-to-state quantum reactive scattering in four-atom systems. WIREs Comput Mol Sci **7**, e1301 (2017)
4. Skouteris, D., Castillo, J., Manolopoulos, D.E.: ABC: a quantum reactive scattering program. Comput. Phys. Comm. **133**, 128–135 (2000)
5. Lepetit, B., Launay, J.M.: Quantum-mechanical study of the reaction He+H_2^+ → HeH$^+$ + H with hyperspherical coordinates. J. Chem. Phys. **95**, 5159–5168 (1991)
6. Aquilanti, V., Beddoni, A., Cavalli, S., Lombardi, A., Littlejohn, R.: Collective hyperspherical coordinates for polyatomic molecules and clusters. Mol. Phys. **98**(21), 1763–1770 (2000)
7. Aquilanti, V., Beddoni, A., Lombardi, A., Littlejohn, R.: Hyperspherical harmonics for polyatomic systems: basis set for kinematic rotations. Int. J. Quantum Chem. **89**(4), 277–291 (2002)
8. Aquilanti, V., Lombardi, A., Littlejohn, R.: Hyperspherical harmonics for polyatomic systems: basis set for collective motions. Theoret. Chem. Acc. **111**(2–6), 400–406 (2004)
9. Kuppermann, A.: Quantum reaction dynamics and hyperspherical harmonics. Isr. J. Chem. **43**, 229 (2003)
10. De Fazio, D., Cavalli, S., Aquilanti, V.: Benchmark quantum mechanical calculations of vibrationally resolved cross sections and rate constants on ab initio potential energy surfaces for the F + HD reaction: comparisons with experiments. J. Phys. Chem. A **120**, 5288–5299 (2016)
11. Aquilanti, V., Cavalli, S.: The quantum-mechanical hamiltonian for tetraatomic systems insymmetric hyperspherical coordinates. **93**, 801–809 (1997)

12. Barreto, P.R.P., Vilela, A.F.A., Lombardi, A., Maciel, G.S., Palazzetti, F., Aquilanti, V.: The hydrogen peroxide-rare gas systems: quantum chemical calculations and hyperspherical harmonic representation of the potential energy surface for atom-floppy molecule interactions. J. Phys. Chemis. A **111**(49), 12754–12762 (2007)

13. Lombardi, A., Laganà, A., Pirani, F., Palazzetti, F., Lago, N.F.: Carbon oxides in gas flows and earth and planetary atmospheres: state-to-state simulations of energy transfer and dissociation reactions. In: Murgante, B., et al. (eds.) ICCSA 2013. LNCS, vol. 7972, pp. 17–31. Springer, Heidelberg (2013). https://doi.org/10.1007/978-3-642-39643-4_2

14. Lago, N.F., Albertí, M., Laganà, A., Lombardi, A.: Water $(H_2O)_m$ or benzene $(C_6H_6)_n$ aggregates to solvate the K^+. In: Murgante, B., et al. (eds.) ICCSA 2013. LNCS, vol. 7971, pp. 1–15. Springer, Heidelberg (2013). https://doi.org/10.1007/978-3-642-39637-3_1

15. Faginas-Lago, N., Albertí, M., Costantini, A., Laganá, A., Lombardi, A., Pacifici, L.: An innovative synergistic grid approach to the computational study of protein aggregation mechanisms. J. Mol. Model. **20**(7), 2226 (2014)

16. Faginas-Lago, N., Yeni, D., Huarte, F., Alcamì, M., Martin, F.: Adsorption of hydrogen molecules on carbon nanotubes using quantum chemistry and molecular dynamics. J. Phys. Chem. A **120**, 6451–6458 (2016)

17. Faginas-Lago, N., Lombardi, A., Albertí, M., Grossi, G.: Accurate analytic intermolecular potential for the simulation of Na^+ and K^+ ion hydration in liquid water. J. Mol. Liq. **204**, 192–197 (2015)

18. Albertí, M., Faginas Lago, N.: Competitive solvation of K^+ by C_6H_6 and H_2O in the K^+-$(C_6h_6)_n$-$(H_2O)_m$ (n = 1–4; m = 1–6) aggregates. Eur. Phys. J. D **67**, 73 (2013)

19. Albertí, M., Faginas Lago, N.: Ion size influence on the Ar solvation shells of M^+-C_6F_6 clusters (m = Na, K, Rb, Cs). J. Phys. Chem. A **116**, 3094–3102 (2012)

20. Albertí, M., Faginas Lago, N., Pirani, F.: Ar solvation shells in K^+-HFBz: From cluster rearrangement to solvation dynamics. J. Phys. Chem. A **115**, 10871–10879 (2011)

21. Lago, N.F., Albertí, M., Laganà, A., Lombardi, A., Pacifici, L., Costantini, A.: The molecular stirrer catalytic effect in methane ice formation. In: Murgante, B., et al. (eds.) ICCSA 2014. LNCS, vol. 8579, pp. 585–600. Springer, Cham (2014). https://doi.org/10.1007/978-3-319-09144-0_40

22. Faginas-Lago, N., Huarte Larrañaga, F., Albertí, M.: On the suitability of the ILJ function to match different formulations of the electrostatic potential for water-water interactions. Eur. Phys. J. D **55**(1), 75 (2009)

23. Bartolomei, M., Pirani, F., Laganà, A., Lombardi, A.: A full dimensional grid empowered simulation of the CO_2+ CO_2 processes. J. Comp. Chem. **33**, 1806 (2012)

24. Lombardi, A., Lago, N.F., Laganà, A., Pirani, F., Falcinelli, S.: A bond-bond portable approach to intermolecular interactions: simulations for n-methylacetamide and carbon dioxide dimers. In: Murgante, B., et al. (eds.) ICCSA 2012. LNCS, vol. 7333, pp. 387–400. Springer, Heidelberg (2012). https://doi.org/10.1007/978-3-642-31125-3_30

25. Albertí, M., Faginas-Lago, N., Laganà, A., Pirani, F.: A portable intermolecular potential for molecular dynamics studies of NMA-NMA and NMA-H_2O aggregates. Phys. Chem. Chem. Phys. **13**(18), 8422–8432 (2011)

26. Albertí, M., Faginas-Lago, N., Pirani, F.: Benzene water interaction: From gaseous dimers to solvated aggregates. Chem. Phys. **399**, 232 (2012)

27. Falcinelli, S., et al.: Modeling the intermolecular interactions and characterization of the dynamics of collisional autoionization processes. In: Murgante, B., et al. (eds.) ICCSA 2013. LNCS, vol. 7971, pp. 69–83. Springer, Heidelberg (2013). https://doi.org/10.1007/978-3-642-39637-3_6

28. Lombardi, A., Faginas-Lago, N., Pacifici, L., Costantini, A.: Modeling of energy transfer from vibrationally excited CO_2 molecules: Cross sections and probabilities for kinetic modeling of atmospheres, flows, and plasmas. J. Phys. Chem. A **117**(45), 11430–11440 (2013)

29. Lombardi, A., Pirani, F., Laganà, A., Bartolomei, M.: Energy transfer dynamics and kinetics of elementary processes (promoted) by gas-phase CO_2-N_2 collisions: Selectivity control by the anisotropy of the interaction. J. Comp. Chem. **37**, 1463–1475 (2016)

30. Pacifici, L., Verdicchio, M., Faginas-Lago, N., Lombardi, A., Costantini, A.: A high-level ab initio study of the n2 + n2 reaction channel. J. Comput. Chem. **34**(31), 2668–2676 (2013)

31. Lombardi, A., Faginas-Lago, N., Pacifici, L., Grossi, G.: Energy transfer upon collision of selectively excited CO_2 molecules: State-to-state cross sections and probabilities for modeling of atmospheres and gaseous flows. J. Chem. Phys. **143**, 034307 (2015)

32. Celiberto, R., Armenise, I., Cacciatore, M., Capitelli, M., Esposito, F., Gamallo, P., Janev, R., Lagana, A., Laporta, V., Laricchiuta, A., et al.: Atomic and molecular data for spacecraft re-entry plasmas. Plasma Sources Sci. Technol. **25**(3), 033004 (2016)

33. Faginas-Lago, N., Lombardi, A., Albertí, M.: Aqueous n-methylacetamide: New analytic potentials and a molecular dynamics study. J. Mol. Liq. **224**, 792–800 (2016)

34. Palazzetti, F., Munusamy, E., Lombardi, A., Grossi, G., Aquilanti, V.: Spherical and hyperspherical representation of potential energy surfaces for intermolecular interactions. Int. J. Quantum Chem. **111**(2), 318–332 (2011)

35. Lombardi, A., Palazzetti, F.: A comparison of interatomic potentials for rare gas nanoaggregates. J. Mol. Struct. (Thoechem) **852**(1–3), 22–29 (2008)

36. Barreto, P.R., Albernaz, A.F., Palazzetti, F., Lombardi, A., Grossi, G., Aquilanti, V.: Hyperspherical representation of potential energy surfaces: intermolecular interactions in tetra-atomic and penta-atomic systems. Phys. Scr. **84**(2), 028111 (2011)

37. Barreto, P.R., et al.: Potential energy surfaces for interactions of H_2O with H_2, N_2 and O_2: a hyperspherical harmonics representation, and a minimal model for the H_2O-rare-gas-atom systems. Comput. Theor. Chem. **990**, 53–61 (2012)

38. Lombardi, A., Pirani, F., Bartolomei, M., Coletti, C., Laganà, A.: A full dimensional potential energy function and the calculation of the state-specific properties of the CO+ N_2 inelastic processes within an Open Molecular Science Cloud perspective. Front. Chem. **7**, 309 (2019)

39. Faginas Lago, N., Lombardi, A., Vekeman, J., Rosi, M., et al.: Molecular dynamics of CH_4/N_2 mixtures on a flexible graphene layer: adsorption and selectivity case study. Front. Chem. **7**, 386 (2019)

40. Aquilanti, V., Lombardi, A., Yurtsever, E.: Global view of classical clusters: the hyperspherical approach to structure and dynamics. Phys. Chem. Chem. Phys. **4**(20), 5040–5051 (2002)

41. Sevryuk, M.B., Lombardi, A., Aquilanti, V.: Hyperangular momenta and energy partitions in multidimensional many-particle classical mechanics: The invariance approach to cluster dynamics. Phys. Rev. A **72**(3), 033201 (2005)

42. Castro Palacio, J., Velazquez Abad, L., Lombardi, A., Aquilanti, V., Rubayo Soneira, J.: Normal and hyperspherical mode analysis of NO-doped Kr crystals upon Rydberg excitation of the impurity. J. Chem. Phys. **126**(17), 174701 (2007)
43. Lombardi, A., Palazzetti, F., Aquilanti, V.: Molecular dynamics of chiral molecules in hyperspherical coordinates. In: Misra, S., et al. (eds.) ICCSA 2019. LNCS, vol. 11624, pp. 413–427. Springer, Cham (2019). https://doi.org/10.1007/978-3-030-24311-1_30
44. Lombardi, A., Palazzetti, F., Sevryuk, M.B.: Hyperspherical coordinates and energy partitions for reactive processes and clusters. AIP Conf. Proceed. **2186**, 030014 (2019). AIP Publishing LLC (2019)
45. Lombardi, A., Palazzetti, F.: Chirality in molecular collision dynamics. J. Phys.: Condens. Matter **30**(6), 063003 (2018)
46. Lombardi, A., Palazzetti, F., Peroncelli, L., Grossi, G., Aquilanti, V., Sevryuk, M.: Few-body quantum and many-body classical hyperspherical approaches to reactions and to cluster dynamics. Theoret. Chem. Acc. **117**(5–6), 709–721 (2007)
47. Aquilanti, V., Grossi, G., Lombardi, A., Maciel, G.S., Palazzetti, F.: Aligned molecular collisions and a stereodynamical mechanism for selective chirality. Rend. Fis. Acc. Lincei **22**, 125–135 (2011)
48. Lombardi, A., Faginas-Lago, N., Aquilanti, V.: The invariance approach to structure and dynamics: classical hyperspherical coordinates. In: Misra, S., et al. (eds.) ICCSA 2019. LNCS, vol. 11624, pp. 428–438. Springer, Cham (2019). https://doi.org/10.1007/978-3-030-24311-1_31
49. Caglioti, C., Dos Santos, R.F., Lombardi, A., Palazzetti, F., Aquilanti, V.: Screens Displaying Structural Properties of Aminoacids in Polypeptide Chains: Alanine as a Case Study. In: Misra, S., et al. (eds.) ICCSA 2019. LNCS, vol. 11624, pp. 439–449. Springer, Cham (2019). https://doi.org/10.1007/978-3-030-24311-1_32
50. Caglioti, C., Ferreira, R.d.S., Palazzetti, F., Lombardi, A., Aquilanti, V.: Screen representation of structural properties of alanine in polypeptide chains. AIP Conf. Proceed. **2186**, 030015 (2019). AIP Publishing LLC (2019)
51. Horn, R.A., Johnson, C.R.: Matrix Analysis, 2nd edn. University Press, Cambridge (1990)
52. Gatti, F., Lung, C.: Vector parametrization of the n-atom problem in quantum mechanics. i. jacobi vectors. J. Chem. Phys. **108**, 8804–8820 (1998)
53. Aquilanti, V., Lombardi, A., Sevryuk, M.B.: Phase-space invariants for aggregates of particles: hyperangular momenta and partitions of the classical kinetic energy. J. Chem. Phys. **121**, 5579 (2004)
54. Aquilanti, V., Carmona Novillo, E., Garcia, E., Lombardi, A., Sevryuk, M.B., Yurtsever, E.: Invariant energy partitions in chemical reactions and cluster dynamics simulations. Comput. Mat. Sci. **35**, 187–191 (2006)
55. Aquilanti, V., Lombardi, A., Sevryuk, M.B., Yurtsever, E.: Phase-space invariants as indicators of the critical behavior of nanoaggregates. Phys. Rev. Lett. **93**, 113402 (2004)
56. Calvo, F., Gadea, X., Lombardi, A., Aquilanti, V.: Isomerization dynamics and thermodynamics of ionic argon clusters. J. Chem. Phys. **125**, 114307 (2006)
57. Lombardi, A., Aquilanti, V., Yurtsever, E., Sevryuk, M.B.: Specific heats of clusters near a phase transition: Energy partitions among internal modes. Chem. Phys. Lett. **30**, 424–428 (2006)
58. Lombardi, A., Maciel, G.S., Palazzetti, F., Grossi, G., Aquilanti, V.: Alignment and chirality in gaseous flows. J. Vacuum Soc. Japan **53**(11), 645–653 (2010)
59. Palazzetti, F., et al.: Aligned molecules: chirality discrimination in photodissociation and in molecular dynamics. Rendiconti Lincei **24**(3), 299–308 (2013)

60. Littlejohn, R.G., Mitchell, A., Aquilanti, V.: Quantum dynamics of kinematic invariants in tetra-and polyatomic systems. Phys. Chem. Chem. Phys. **1**, 1259–1264 (1999)
61. Lombardi, A.: Symmetry and deformations of cluster and biomolecules by invariant shape coordinates. AIP Conf. Proceed. **2343**, 020004 (2021). AIP Publishing LLC (2021)
62. Andrea, L., Faginas-Lago, N., Pacifici, L.: Protein networks by invariant shape coordinates and deformation indexes. In Gervasi, O., Murgante, B., Misra, S., Rocha, A.M.A.C., Garau, C., eds.: Computational Science and Its Applications - ICCSA 2022 Workshops. ICCSA 2022. Lecture Notes in Computer Science, vol. 13382, pp. 348–359. Springer, Cham (2022). https://doi.org/10.1007/978-3-031-10592-0_26
63. Berman, H., et al.: The protein data bank. Nucleic Acid Res. **28**, 235–242 (2000)

Guided Clustering for Selecting Representatives Samples in Chemical Databases

Felipe V. Calderan[1] , João Paulo A. de Mendonça[2] ,
Juarez L. F. Da Silva[2] , and Marcos G. Quiles[1](✉)

[1] Institute of Science and Technology, Federal University of São Paulo,
São José dos Campos, SP, Brazil
{fvcalderan,quiles}@unifesp.br
[2] São Carlos Institute of Chemistry, University of São Paulo, PO Box 780, 13560-970
São Carlos, SP, Brazil
jpalastus@gmail.com, juarez_dasilva@iqsc.usp.br

Abstract. Machine Learning (ML) methods, from unsupervised to supervised algorithms, have been applied to solve several tasks in the Materials Science domain, such as property prediction, design of new chemical compounds, and surrogate models in molecular dynamics simulations. ML methods can also play a fundamental role in screening materials by reducing the number of compounds under scrutiny. This reduction assumes that compounds similarly represented by a given descriptor might have similar properties; thus, an unsupervised ML method, such as the K-Means algorithm, can cluster the data set and deliver a set of representative samples. However, this selection depends on the molecular representation that might not directly relate to the target property. Here, we propose a framework that lets the specialist select a set of representative samples in a guided fashion. In particular, a loop between a clustering algorithm (k-means) and an optimization method (Basin-Hopping) is implemented, which allows the system to learn feature weights to form more homogeneous clusters given the target property. The framework also offers other visual and textual functionalities to support the expert. We evaluate the proposed framework in two scenarios, and the results show that the guidance enhances clustering formations, both in coarse (few and big clusters) and fine (many small clusters) analyses.

Keywords: Guided Data Clustering · Data Visualization · Representative Chemical Sample Selection

1 Introduction

Materials Science research has a direct impact on human civilization development, from the building of tools of iron to the creation of the semiconductors we use on every electronic device today. In order to achieve these advancements, Material Science requires its own set of technological leaps, and one of the most

O. Gervasi et al. (Eds.): ICCSA 2023 Workshops, LNCS 14111, pp. 133–149, 2023.
https://doi.org/10.1007/978-3-031-37126-4_10

promising techniques today is the use of Machine Learning. This branch of Artificial Intelligence has provided sophisticated algorithms for regression analyses [16], classification [41], clustering [3], dimensionality reduction [7] and other useful tools to support the study of existing materials and the discovery of new ones [9, 22, 26].

A particularly interesting application of machine learning to Materials Science arise from the challenge of grouping similar items together (i.e., data clustering [17]) and electing one sample of each group to represent everyone else in that group. This problem is known as representative selection, and many examples of this type of algorithm to solve it exist in the literature, as they are flagship methods of filtering massive amounts of data in order to acquire insights. Bayada, Hamersma, and van Geerestein [5] studied different methods such as Ward agglomerative clustering [39], Kohonen maps [20] and partitioning methods to select representative samples of compounds for more specialized testing. Likewise, Engels et al. [13] utilized Ward to obtain homogeneous subsets (and closely related candidates) of Janssen's corporate database. McGregor and Pallai [24] used the Jarvis-Patrick algorithm to get representative samples from the centroids computed to make compound acquisition more efficient. Brockherde et al. [8] extracted 2000 representative conformers selected from classical MD trajectories by K-Means sampling. Batista et al. [3, 4] used the same clustering algorithm to choose representative samples for the Ab-initio investigation of CO_2 adsorption on Transition Metals 13-atom 4d clusters and to study the energy decomposition to access the stability changes induced by CO adsorption on Transition Metals 13-atom clusters. Finally, Zibordi-Besse et al. [42] applied the Euclidean Similarity Distance (EDS) [11] to get a representative set of structures for the $(MO_2)_n$ cluster for different metals M and values n in order to calculate the properties of those chemical clusters.

Clustering algorithms are typically unsupervised Machine Learning methods, which can lead to a significant limitation when trying to examine specific properties of a chemical system. The feature vector describes how they see the universe in which the items reside, and since clustering formations are directly tied to the chosen representation, they might not reveal the best structure according to the property under research, causing a suboptimal representative selection. We propose that guidance be introduced into the clustering process, in order to gradually change the weights to optimize the clusters formed concerning a given property. This guidance consists of a loop with two main blocks: a clustering algorithm and an optimization one. When the clustering algorithm produces a configuration, it is directed to the optimization algorithm to compute the sum of the desired property intracluster variance of all clusters. After that, new weights for the features are selected in an attempt to feed them to the clustering algorithm to generate clusters that reduce the variance. This approach has the potential to create more cohesive groups that will emphasize the particular property under study.

To make guided representative selection accessible to the community, we developed a user-friendly tool called GuidedClustering where the user fill in the input data and essential parameters, and the software does the rest. In summary, the user provides a data set with the features and properties of interest, then a property is specified as a target and not used as a feature during clustering. The tool can automatically cluster the data into K groups, where K is a suggested value based on clustering quality measures (like the Silhouette score [33] or the Calinski-Harabasz index [10]). Later on, the clustering-optimization loop starts, and when it is finished, the software reports the results as textual and graphical information. The space-representing scatter plots are projected in two dimensions using PCA [1] and t-SNE [23].

The approach was tested with the use of two sets of molecular structures (nanoclusters). These data sets differ not only in their chemical systems, but also in how they were built. One of them was generated through Molecular Dynamics and the other through Density Functional Theory. Our results demonstrate that the strategy is versatile to different types of chemical data and is promising in enhancing the qualitative analyses of the clustering process in both cases. This allowed interesting thermodynamic insights on the structure-property relation in our test cases.

2   Theoretical Approach for Data Clustering in Quantum-Chemistry Problems

2.1   Clustering Algorithms

Clustering algorithms seek to group entries from a data set based on a similarity measure, bringing forth a final result where items belonging to one cluster (group of items) are more similar between themselves than to items from external clusters [19]. There are many of these algorithms [18] and they can be very different, but at the same time, share many common characteristics.

A simple mathematical representation for a generic clustering method is:

$$K(\mathbb{X}) = \overrightarrow{\mathbb{L}} \tag{1}$$

where K is the clustering method, $\mathbb{X} \in (\mathbb{R}^n \times \mathbb{R}^m)$ is the input data set with n entries and m features, and $\overrightarrow{\mathbb{L}} \in \mathbb{Z}_+^n$ is the label vector, which contains the cluster assigned for each one of the n items.

There must be a way of calculating the similarity between entries in the feature space. This can be done by measuring the distance between the values of each of the items features. A method that has predominated for millennia [11] to execute this measurement is the *Euclidean distance*, but other methods, like the *Manhattan Distance* [12] can also be used. It all depends on the data set being clustered and the expected results.

K-Means typically uses the *Euclidean Distance* and is the clustering algorithm of choice for GuidedClustering, specifically scikit-learn's implementation due to good results obtained by the QTNano group using it in past researches

---

Algorithm 1. K-Means Clustering

1: *Centroids* ← *K* random items ∈ X
2: **while** STOP CRITERION not satisfied **do**
3:     **for each** x ∈ X **do**
4:         ASSIGN(x, closest c ∈ *Centroids*)
5:     **end for**
6:     **for each** c ∈ *Centroids* **do**
7:         c ← AVERAGE(x's assigned to c)
8:     **end for**
9: **end while**

---

[4]. It is a partitional method and is very simple and commonly used in the literature, due to its simplicity and swiftness. Algorithm 1 describes how K-Means operates.

One of the most notable K-Means limitation is that it needs to know beforehand the amount *K* of clusters to be generated. The proposed toolbox suggests a sensible amount by applying a simple brute-force optimization. It calculates the *Silhouette Score* [33] for a range of possible number of clusters informed by the user, then returns the best one.

2.2 Optimization Algorithms

Mathematical optimization tries to find the best available values for a function, given certain constraints and objectives. Problems with explicit objectives can be expressed as:

$$\min_{x \in \mathbb{R}^n} / \max f(x), \ x = \begin{bmatrix} x_1 \ x_2 \cdots x_n \end{bmatrix}^T \in \mathbb{R}^n,$$

$$\text{subject to } \phi_j(x) = 0, \ j \in [1..M], \tag{2}$$

$$\psi_k(x) \geq 0, \ k \in [1..N][40]$$

where $f(x)$ is the cost function, x is the decision vector (and $x_1, \cdots, x_n$ is a state), $\phi_j(x)$ are constraints in terms of M equalities and $\psi_k(x)$ are constraints in terms of N inequalities.

After the amount K has been defined, GuidedClustering uses a global-search optimization algorithm to minimize the total intracluster variance. Global optimization tries to escape local optima by adding an item of randomness to the search and/or an acceptance criterion. These keep the algorithm from being so easily convinced that a current best-found solution is the global optimum [21].

We chose Basin-Hopping [38] as the global optimizer. It not only does local search, but also perturbs the current search position in a randomized, but controlled manner. Algorithm 2 shows Basin-Hopping in its simplest form, which always store the best found value up to the current point and reject anything that is not as good (therefore, being a monotonic optimizer). Generally, operation 7 is replaced by the Metropolis criterion of the Monte Carlo algorithms.

Algorithm 2. Monotonic Basin-Hopping [29]

1: $i \leftarrow 0$
2: $X_i \leftarrow$ random initial point in variable space
3: $Y_i \leftarrow$ LOCALSEARCH(X_i)
4: **while** STOP CRITERION not satisfied **do**
5:     $X_{i+1} \leftarrow$ PERTURB(Y_i)
6:     $Y_{i+1} \leftarrow$ LOCALSEARCH(X_{i+1})
7:     **if** $f(Y_{i+1}) < f(Y_i)$ **then**
8:         $i \leftarrow i + 1$
9:     **end if**
10: **end while**

2.3 Guided Clustering

What we call Guided Clustering are clustering algorithms that use additional background knowledge information about the data to produce better clusters. In the literature, it is common to see explicit definitions of *Must-link* vs *Cannot-link* constraints [37] or *Positive label* and *Negative label* constraints (of course, there are algorithms that support both [2]). GuidedClustering does not use explicit constraints, rather, it implicitly generates the constraints as a side effect of the optimization, which tries to minimize the sum of intracluster variances.

Let $\mathbb{X} \in (\mathbb{R}^n \times \mathbb{R}^m)$ be the input data set and $\overrightarrow{\mathbb{B}} \in \mathbb{R}^n$ the bias property vector, with n values (one for each entry in the input matrix). Also, let $\overrightarrow{\mathbb{W}} \in \mathbb{R}^m$ be the weights vector. The first step to generate a guided clustering is to apply the weights to $\mathbb{X}$. This is done by multiplying the values of each column j of the data set by the value of the index j in the weights vector. To write this procedure mathematically, let's define an operator $\bullet$:

$$A \bullet \overrightarrow{B} = A \cdot diag(\overrightarrow{B}),$$

$$diag(\overrightarrow{B}) = \sum_{i=1}^{m} (e_i e_i^T)(e_i^T \overrightarrow{B}) \in (\mathbb{R}^m \times \mathbb{R}^m), \tag{3}$$

$$A \in (\mathbb{R}^n \times \mathbb{R}^m),\ \overrightarrow{B} \in \mathbb{R}^m,\ e_i \text{ is the } i\text{th basis}$$

Therefore:

$$\mathbb{X} \bullet \overrightarrow{\mathbb{W}} = \begin{bmatrix} x_{11} & \cdots & x_{1m} \\ \vdots & \ddots & \vdots \\ x_{n1} & \cdots & x_{nm} \end{bmatrix} \bullet \begin{bmatrix} w_1 \\ \vdots \\ w_m \end{bmatrix} = \begin{bmatrix} x_{11}w_1 & \cdots & x_{1m}w_m \\ \vdots & \ddots & \vdots \\ x_{n1}w_1 & \cdots & x_{nm}w_m \end{bmatrix} \tag{4}$$

The next step is to feed the clustering method with the newly generated weighted features matrix to obtain the labels vector. Thus, according to Eq. 1: $K(\mathbb{X} \bullet \overrightarrow{\mathbb{W}}) = \overrightarrow{\mathbb{L}} \in \mathbb{Z}_+^n$. With this, the labels vector $\overrightarrow{\mathbb{L}}$ and the bias property vector $\overrightarrow{\mathbb{B}}$ are known, so it is possible to get the sum of the intracluster variance

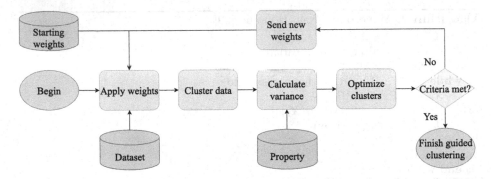

Fig. 1. Guided clustering flowchart. The first step is to apply the starting weights (normally 1) in each column of the data set. The next step is to cluster the data and then use the property data to calculate the property intracluster variance. Having the variance value, the next part of the program tries to reduce the variance by rerunning the previous steps with different weights. Finally, when a criteria is met (maximum iterations number, for instance), the program is finished.

of $\overrightarrow{\mathbb{B}}$:

$$V(\overrightarrow{\mathbb{L}}, \overrightarrow{\mathbb{B}}) = \sum_{j=1}^{k} \sigma^2 \left(\left[c_1 \cdots c_n \right]^T \right),$$

$$c_i = \begin{cases} \overrightarrow{\mathbb{B}}_i, & \text{if } \overrightarrow{\mathbb{L}}_i = j \\ 0, & otherwise \end{cases} , \ i \in [1..n], \tag{5}$$

k is the number of clusters

Then, all the pieces are ready to run the global optimization algorithm. Following the Set of Eq. 2, it is obtained that:

$$\min/\max_{\overrightarrow{\mathbb{W}} \in \mathbb{R}^m} f(\overrightarrow{\mathbb{W}}) = V(\overrightarrow{\mathbb{L}}, \overrightarrow{\mathbb{B}}) \in \mathbb{R}_+, \tag{6}$$

subject to the algorithm's parameters

Finally, the optimization algorithm is run until the maximum number of iterations is reached or the acceptance criteria is met. Figure 1 shows a diagram that summarizes the entire process. Although the implementation used to generate the results for this work uses K-Means as the clustering algorithm and Basin-Hopping as the global optimization one, they could be replaced.

3 Quantum-Chemistry Databases

3.1 Cu$_{55}$ Nanoclusters

This database was built to expand the knowledge about morphology on metallic nanoclusters. The geometries obtained via Revised Basin-Hopping Monte Carlo (rBHMC) in-house tool [31] for Cu$_{55}$ nanoclusters, where interactions are described via ReaxFF [34] with parameters from Nielson *et al.* [27]. In ten runs of rBHMC, a total of 1048 Cu_{55} geometries were generated, all corresponding to local minima on the potential energy surface of those systems. The focus of the clustering application in the original paper was to generate samples for additional analysis, but here we will look directly at the guided clustering process as a way to extract physico-chemical insights and strengthen the specialist's understanding of the data set itself.

3.2 $CeZrO_4$

This database was previously used to investigate the energetic, structural and electronic properties of mixed cerium and zirconium nanoclusters, which are very important in nanocatalysis [14]. In this original context, the data was used as it is, for direct analysis of the phisico-chemical quantities and the relation between them. Our idea here is to exploit the fact that the data can be labeled by composition (i.e., we already know that the data can be clustered using the Ce/Zr ratio as label) to see how the guidance can show new clusters that are different from this trivial one and bring up new facts about the stability of these mixed oxide nanoclusters.

The set contains mixed oxides from $Ce_{15}ZrO_{30}$ to $CeZr_{15}O_{30}$ with 1646 structures generated from the variation in the amount of Ce and Zr atoms, exploring different patterns of substitution of Ce and Zr, but also different geometrical arrangements and nanocluster shapes for each concentration.

4 Technical Details of the Computational Framework

4.1 Number of Clusters by Visualization Approach

It is possible to visually approximate the amount of clusters in the system by looking at a two-dimensional projection of the data. Take Fig. 5 as an example: looking at the chart **d**, even if there were no distinct colors, it is easy to visually reach the conclusion that there are around 16 clusters of data.

In this particular example, the number of true clusters (defined by the specialist) coincides with the projection. This does not mean that this is always the case, because projections are not perfect representations of the distances between the items in higher dimensions, they just provide an idea on how the entries are distributed.

To better meet the needs of the specialist, GuidedClustering provides two different projection solutions: the tested and trusted PCA (Principal Component Analysis) and the state-of-the-art t-SNE (t-distributed Stochastic Neighbor Embedding). Both implementations are from the scikit-learn library.

PCA receives the multidimensional table as input, then find a new set of orthogonal variables (the *principal components*) which explain most of the variance in the data, by removing inter-correlated columns and performing other mathematical procedures. Since it is possible to obtain an arbitrary number (up to the amount of dimensions that originally exists) of principal components, selecting the two most important allows the construction of more meaningful 2D charts [1].

The other method, t-SNE [23], is the actual state-of-the-art in projections. It differs from PCA in two main points: it is a non-linear method (which lets it understand more complex underlying patterns) and it cares about the local neighbors (since it tries its best to keep similar items close together).

There are two different measures to evaluate a PCA projection: Explained Variance Ratio and Trustworthiness. The explained variance ratio is a metric that reflects the percentage of the variance that is attributed to each component. Trustworthiness expresses the preservation of local structures and is given by the Eq. 7:

$$T(k) = 1 - \alpha(k)\beta(k), \text{ such that}$$
$$\alpha(k) = \frac{2}{nk(2n - 3k - 1)},$$
$$\beta(k) = \sum_{i=1}^{n} \sum_{j \in U_i^{(k)}} (r(i,j) - k) \tag{7}$$

where $r(i, j)$ represents the rank of the output space item j according to the pairwise relation with the other output space items. The set of k-nearest neighbors in the output space but not in the input space [36] is given by $U_i^{(k)}$.

The Trustworthiness metric is also able to evaluate t-SNE's projection performance, while the Explained Variance Ratio is something more attached to the way PCA creates the projection.

Thus, having ran GuidedClustering for a given k, it is possible to verify if k is a satisfactory value by visual inspection, calculation of the evaluation measures or by deep inspecting which entries belong to which cluster (looking into their features).

4.2 The Importance of the Silhouette to Obtain the Number of Clusters

K-Means will always divide the data set into the specified number K of clusters, given that there are enough entries to cluster, but the problem is to identify if the division is meaningful (of high quality). Over the years, some methods were developed to address this issue, silhouette being one of them.

Silhouette uses the mean intracluster distance a and the mean distance b of the closest group for each item (note that b refers to the group closest to the item under analysis, other than the group it belongs to). The result of this measure for an item i is inside the range $[-1, 1]$, where, -1 indicates that the item has been incorrectly assigned and 1 is the best possible value. Given a data set $\mathbb{X}$, the silhouette score over all samples is given by Eq. 8.

$$\mathbb{S} = \frac{\sum_{i=1}^{|\mathbb{X}|} \frac{b_i - a_i}{max(a_i, b_i)}}{|\mathbb{X}|}, \ 2 \leq K \leq |\mathbb{X}| - 1 \tag{8}$$

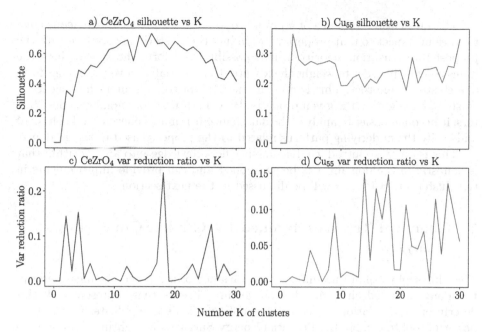

Fig. 2. In **a** and **b**, it is demonstrated the silhouette score, as K increases, for the initial unguided clustering of the data sets $CeZrO_4$ and Cu_{55}, respectively. The charts **c** and **d** show the percentage of overall intracluster variance reduction, as K increases, for the data sets $CeZrO_4$ and Cu_{55}, respectively.

The silhouette coefficient depends solely on the partition of the data and not on the clustering algorithm used, and is a powerful tool to help the interpretation and validation of cluster formations [33]. Since it can quantitatively express the clustering quality, GuidedClustering can use it to automatically choose a value K of clusters, if the user wishes to. The provided value is only a suggestion and should be further analyzed by the specialist, since there is no right answer to the correct amount of clusters (it depends on the context and what are the expected results). Figures 2(a) and (b) show the silhouette scores for 2 different chemical data sets.

4.3   The Role of the Variance Minimization in the Clustering

It is typical for clustering algorithms to minimize the distance between the entries within a cluster (consequently reducing the within-cluster variance), in fact, that is precisely what K-Means tries to do. Unfortunately, K-Means does not have any explicit physical-chemical knowledge, so its procedure does not attribute weights to the different features, which can result in suboptimal results in the point-of-view of the specialist.

The intracluster variance of a given property shows how heterogeneous clusters are in respect to that property. By guiding the clustering procedure with the proposed optimization algorithm, it is possible to deform the space where the items co-exist in order to weight the features to potentially move the entries from one cluster to another. This is done in an attempt to form more homogeneous clusters, highlighting the given property. By generating more homogeneous clusters, it becomes easier to analyze the data (since it is more coherent and cohesive) and verify the underlying patterns related to the property used in the guidance.

This is a way to introduce domain-specific knowledge into an algorithm that is agnostic to the domain it is being applied and can provide improvements in the cluster structures, as will be discussed in the next section.

5   Chemical Trends Obtained by Guided Clustering Analysis

The philosophy behind minimizing the variance of a physico-chemical descriptor along a guided clustering lies on getting clusters that represent well this descriptor accumulation points on the configuration space. Clustering can be a powerful tool to explore the Potential Energy Surface, highlighting local minima and basins that are better labeled by a single energy value. In this section, we present two test cases where we explore this feature to perform clustering in sets of nanoclusters.

5.1 Cu_{55} Nanoclusters

The structures on this data set were used in a previous work from Mendonça et al. [25], where a default clustering strategy, without any guidance, was used. The structures on the data set were originally obtained via Revised Basin-Hopping Monte Carlo Algorithm (rBHMC) [31] using previously parameterized ReaxFF potential energy [27,34]. A total of 1048 nanocluster structures were obtained with respective energies also reported.

Here, the structural data was processed to obtain the eigenvalues of the Coulomb matrix for each structure. In the Basin-Hopping approach, we try to explore the configuration space, jumping between different local minima and trying to explore different basins of the potential energy surface. These basins are regions of concentration around local minima points on the potential energy, and we expect a concentration of structures with similar energy value inside the same basin. Based on that, we propose the use of the potential energy to guide the clustering towards those minima, aiming to identify them. Visualization of the distribution of the potential energy, as well as clustering results, can be seen in Fig. 3.

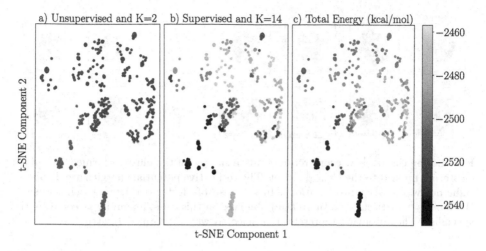

Fig. 3. All the charts show the 2D projection of the 55D data using the t-SNE method. Chart **a** has 2 colors, representing the label of each item given by the unguided clustering procedure for K=2. Chart **b** has 14 colors, each one representing a label attributed by the guided clustering procedure for K=14. Finally, chart **c** is colored by the value of total energy property. t-SNE perplexity was set as 30.0.

Observing the unguided clustering, we diagnosed that two clusters is the best configuration, in respect of silhouette metric, for this data set. The structures were separated in sets, one with higher energy and bigger variance and another with lower energy and lower variance. Those sets describe the difference between structures with high ordering (associated with the solid phase) and low ordering (associated with amorphous or liquid nanoclusters). Not by coincidence, those two clusters showcased potential energy variance of 102.86 and 86.45 kcal/mol, the equivalent (via $3/2Nk_bT$) to 627 and 527 K, in the range of the phase transition temperatures the authors listed on the original work. This can be seen as the clustering algorithm is grouping structures that are in basins accessible at these temperatures. We also highlight that for $k = 2$, the guided and unguided clusterings are very similar (Normalized Mutual Information (NMI) evaluated as 0.986), showing that this is a very natural configuration that does not demand a strong distortion of the descriptors space to be captured.

In another hand, this analysis was not enough to identify the different basins inside the solid phase structures, that we know exist and are explored via additional molecular dynamics on the original publication. A completely different scenario is seen in the case where we select k based on the optimal guidance performance. Here, we identified that $k = 14$ minimizes the potential energy variance per cluster, which indicates that this configuration is far more adapted to the detection of small local minima on the PES explored by the rBHMC. In fact, three of the four clusters with lower average energies can be directly associated to the isometric I_h, pseudo-tetragonal (C_2, but close to T_d) and the capped decahedron (D_{5h}) shapes of nanoclusters, already known as highly stable

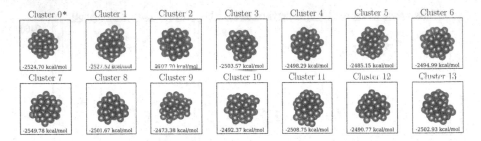

Fig. 4. The charts show every representative sample of the clusters formed by guided clustering applied to the Cu_{55} data set. The respective potential energies are displayed right below the 3D representations. In the case of cluster 0 (*), we to choose show the more symmetrical structure (D_{5h}) observed in this class, manually selected by the specialist. The automatic representative selected was a deformed I_h structure.

for Cu_{55}. The latter was not automatically selected as the representative of its cluster but has been included in Fig. 4, for ease of viewing. Here, we also saw that the weights on the coordinates of the configuration space greatly impacted the clustering process, having NMI= 0.730. Additionally, we observed that the highly symmetrical I_h and D_{5h} nanoclusters are present in very specialized clusters, with variance inferior to 0.15 kcal/mol, which can be understood as those structures being located in a very narrow basin and reinforces the stability associated to those geometries. Another structure was identified in a very narrow group (Cluster 3 in Fig. 4, variance of 0.16 eV), composed of a I_h Cu_13 core and a disorganized surface with [555] and [666] CNA signatures. This was not reported yet, and since this structure can be a solid liquid intermediate, further investigations are necessary to understand it in depth.

5.2 $CeZrO_4$

The set we are calling $CeZrO_4$ is actually a set of nanoclusters of ceria-zirconia with chemical formula $(CeO_2)_n(ZnO_2)_{15-n}$. This set was originally build by Felicio-Sousa et al. [14] to explore the stability and electronic properties of those systems. The quantum chemistry simulations were performed using numerical atom-centered orbitals [6,15] (NAOs) in the Fritz-Haber Institute Ab-initio molecular simulations [6,28] (FHI-aims) package. Perdew-Burke-Ernzenhof functional [30] (PBE) with Zeroth-order relativistic approximation [35] (ZORA) was used. Since the data was already refined in a quantum calculation, the clustering here is exploited to improve our understanding of the structure-property relation.

As the nuclei charge plays an important part in the Coulomb matrix definition, we visually observed that the proportion of each nucleus in the nanocluster (or even n itself) is a good candidate for clustering label for the data, since it looks well clustered in this representation space. We expect as a consequence that both methods will be able to cluster the data similarly. In fact, the natural

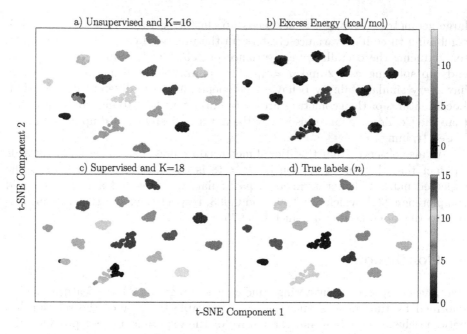

Fig. 5. All the charts show the 2D projection of the 45D data (Coulomb matrices eigenvalues) using the t-SNE method. Chart **a** has 16 colors, which represent the final configuration obtained by the unguided clustering procedure with $k = 16$. Chart **b** is colored by the value of excess energy property. Chart **c** has 18 colors (clusters) and was clustered by the guided procedure with $k = 18$. Finally, Chart **d** also has 16 colors, but this time they represent the true labels given by the amount of Ce and Zr on each entry. t-SNE perplexity was set as 30.0.

clustering in 16 groups was the one to minimize the silhouette metric, and the weighting on the features reduced the average variance per cluster by only 1% (NMI= 0.953).

In Figure 5(a), we show the t-SNE projection of the data for the unguided clustering when $k = 16$. We see that the clusters (gray and lime in Figure 5(a)) share together two visually distinct clusters on the unguided clustering. Those visual clusters correspond to $n = 12$ and $n = 11$, and were correctly separated by the guidance process. In the other hand, we see that both the guided and unguided labeling case clusters together two other visual clusters, associated to $n = 3$ and $n = 4$, that are the most stable systems reported by Felicio-Sousa et al. [14].

The guidance was done with the variance on the excess energy, and we observed that the number of clusters that minimized this metric (reducing it by 24%) was 18. Again, we see that most of the cluster labeling was similar between the guided and unguided case, with NMI= 0.940. The guided version ends up associating five representatives for $n = 15$, which can be explained by the natural lower variance on excess energies on those nanoclusters even with large geometrical changes. It also ends up clustering together $n = 1$, 2, and 3, combining three high variance clusters (in the unguided case) in the same cluster, reducing the overall average variance per cluster. The unguided clustering ends up splitting $n = 2$ and $n = 15$. This points to the fact that the clusters have very similar stability behavior, independent of the different composition. Local features of the geometries are more important here to determine stability than the Ce/Zr ratio, and this is why the natural clusters ended up mixed in the biased training.

We also observed that traditional metrics on guided clustering point towards the fact that the guided version for $k = 18$ is the one that better depicts the expected natural clustering in n. In particular, we measured homogeneity and completeness [32], which are 0.967 and 0.983, respectively, and the NMI in relation to the labeling with n, which is 0.975.

6   Conclusion

Here, we proposed a clustering guidance strategy based on feature scaling informed by the value of an auxiliary observable to enhance the relationship between clustering labels and the nature of the experiments that provided the data. In this approach, the k-means clustering is guided in two ways: (i) Global silhouette metric is used to suggest the number of clusters. (ii) Basin-Hopping optimization is used to find weights for each feature that minimize the average intracluster variance on the informed observable. It is also worth mentioning that projections are valuable tools for obtaining insights into how high-dimensional data is structured.

The proposed framework was evaluated on two sets of molecular structures represented by their respective Coulomb matrix eigenvalues. The combination of the suggested k and the guided variance strategy was shown to be a path to both explore clustering with a more broad thermodynamic sense (like in solid-liquid-like clusters for Cu_55, when $k = 2$) and detailed explorations on more complex structure-property relations (like the clustering relation to the number of Ce atoms per nanocluster in the $CeZrO_4$ case). Finally, our results with this procedure might inspire future automated sample selection and configuration space exploration strategies.

7   Data and Software Availability

Data can be obtained directly with the authors under request.

Acknowledgements. The authors gratefully acknowledge support from FAPESP (São Paulo Research Foundation) and Shell, projects No. $2017/11631-2$, $2018/21401-7$ and $2022/09285-7$, and the strategic importance of the support given by ANP (Brazil's National Oil, Natural Gas and Biofuels Agency) through the R&D levy regulation. The authors also thank for the infrastructure provided to our computer cluster by the Department of Information Technology - Campus São Carlos.

References

1. Abdi, H., Williams, L.J.: Principal component analysis. WIREs. Comput. Statist. **2**(4), 433–459 (2010). https://doi.org/10.1002/wics.101. https://onlinelibrary.wiley.com/doi/abs/10.1002/wics.101
2. Bai, L., Liang, J., Cao, F.: Semi-supervised clustering with constraints of different types from multiple information sources. IEEE Transactions on Pattern Analysis and Machine Intelligence, p. 1 (2020). https://doi.org/10.1109/TPAMI.2020.2979699
3. Batista, K.E.A., Ocampo-Restrepo, V.K., Soares, M.D., Quiles, M.G., Piotrowski, M.J., Da Silva, J.L.F.: Ab Initio investigation of co_2 adsorption on 13-atom $4d$ clusters. J. Chem. Inf. Model. **60**(2), 537–545 (2020). https://doi.org/10.1021/acs.jcim.9b00792. https://doi.org/10.1021/acs.jcim.9b00792
4. Batista, K.E.A., Soares, M.D., Quiles, M.G., Piotrowski, M.J., Da Silva, J.L.F.: Energy decomposition to access the stability changes induced by co adsorption on transition-metal 13-atom clusters. J. Chem. Inf. Model. **61**(5), 2294–2301 (2021). https://doi.org/10.1021/acs.jcim.1c00097. https://doi.org/10.1021/acs.jcim.1c00097. pMID: 33939914
5. Bayada, D.M., Hamersma, H., van Geerestein, V.J.: Molecular diversity and representativity in chemical databases. J. Chem. Inf. Comput. Sci. **39**(1), 1–10 (1999)
6. Blum, V., et al.: Ab initio molecular simulations with numeric atom-centered orbitals. Comput. Phys. Commun. **180**(11), 2175–2196 (2009). https://doi.org/10.1016/j.cpc.2009.06.022. https://doi.org/10.1016/j.cpc.2009.06.022
7. Boubchir, M., Boubchir, R., Aourag, H.: The principal component analysis as a tool for predicting the mechanical properties of perovskites and inverse perovskites. Chem. Phys. Lett. **798**, 139615 (2022)
8. Brockherde, F., Vogt, L., Li, L., Tuckerman, M.E., Burke, K., Müller, K.R.: Bypassing the Kohn-sham equations with machine learning. Nat. Commun. **8**(1), 1–10 (2017)
9. Butler, K.T., Davies, D.W., Cartwright, H., Isayev, O., Walsh, A.: Machine learning for molecular and materials science. Nature **559**(7715), 547 (2018)
10. Caliński, T., Harabasz, J.: A dendrite method for cluster analysis. Commun. Statist. **3**(1), 1–27 (1974). https://doi.org/10.1080/03610927408827101. https://www.tandfonline.com/doi/abs/10.1080/03610927408827101
11. Cha, S.H.: Comprehensive survey on distance/similarity measures between probability density functions. City **1**(2), 1 (2007)
12. Craw, S.: Manhattan Distance, p. 639. Springer, US, Boston, MA (2010). https://doi.org/10.1007/978-0-387-30164-8_506
13. Engels, M.F., Thielemans, T., Verbinnen, D., Tollenaere, J.P., Verbeeck, R.: Cerberus: a system supporting the sequential screening process. J. Chem. Inf. Comput. Sci. **40**(2), 241–245 (2000)
14. Felício-Sousa, P., et al.: Ab initio insights into the structural, energetic, electronic, and stability properties of mixed $ce_n zr_{15-n} o_{30}$ nanoclusters. Phys. Chem. Chem. Phys. **21**(48), 26637–26646 (2019). https://doi.org/10.1039/c9cp04762j. https://doi.org/10.1039/c9cp04762j
15. Havu, V., Blum, V., Havu, P., Scheffler, M.: Efficient integration for all-electron electronic structure calculation using numeric basis functions. J. Comput. Phys. **228**(22), 8367–8379 (2009). https://doi.org/10.1016/j.jcp.2009.08.008. https://doi.org/10.1016/j.jcp.2009.08.008
16. Hkdh, B.: Neural networks in materials science. ISIJ Int. **39**(10), 966–979 (1999)

17. Jain, A.K., Murty, M.N., Flynn, P.J.: Data clustering: a review. ACM Comput. Surv. **31**(3), 264–323 (1999). https://doi.org/10.1145/331499.331504. https://dx. doi.org/10.1145/331499.331504

18. Jain, A.K., Murty, M.N., Flynn, P.J.: Data clustering: A review. ACM Comput. Surv. **31**(3), 264–323 (Sep1999) 10.1145/331499.331504, https://doi.org/10.1145/ 331499.331504

19. Jain, A.K.: Data clustering: 50 years beyond k-means. Pattern Recogn. Lett. **31**(8), 651–666 (2010). https://doi.org/10.1016/j.patrec.2009.09.011. https:// www.sciencedirect.com/science/article/pii/S0167865509002323. Award winning papers from the 19th International Conference on Pattern Recognition (ICPR)

20. Kohonen, T.: Self-organized formation of topologically correct feature maps. Biol. Cybern. **43**(1), 59–69 (1982)

21. van Laarhoven P.J.M., A.E.: Simulated annealing. In: Simulated Annealing: Theory and Applications, vol. 37, pp. 7–15. Springer, Dordrecht (1987). https://doi.org/ 10.1007/978-94-015-7744-1_2

22. Lo, Y.C., Rensi, S.E., Torng, W., Altman, R.B.: Machine learning in chemoinformatics and drug discovery. Drug Discov. Today **23**(8), 1538–1546 (2018)

23. van der Maaten, L., Hinton, G.: Visualizing data using t-SNE. J. Mach. Learn. Res. **9**, 2579–2605 (2008). https://www.jmlr.org/papers/v9/vandermaaten08a.html

24. McGregor, M.J., Pallai, P.V.: Clustering of large databases of compounds: using the mdl "keys" as structural descriptors. J. Chem. Inf. Comput. Sci. **37**(3), 443–448 (1997)

25. de Mendonça, J.P.A., Calderan, F.V., Lourenço, T.C., Quiles, M.G., Da Silva, J.L.F.: Theoretical framework based on molecular dynamics and data mining analyses for the study of potential energy surfaces of finite-size particles. J. Chem. Inf. Model. **62**(22), 5503–5512 (2022). https://doi.org/10.1021/acs.jcim.2c00957. https://doi.org/10.1021/acs.jcim.2c00957. pMID: 36302503

26. Morgan, D., Jacobs, R.: Opportunities and challenges for machine learning in materials science. Annu. Rev. Mater. Res. **50**(1), 71–103 (2020). https://doi.org/10. 1146/annurev-matsci-070218-010015

27. Nielson, K.D., van Duin, A.C.T., Oxgaard, J., Deng, W.Q., Goddard, W.A.: Development of the ReaxFF reactive force field for describing transition metal catalyzed reactions, with application to the initial stages of the catalytic formation of carbon nanotubes. J. Phys. Chem. A **109**, 493–499 (2005)

28. Nocedal, J., Wright, S.J.: Numerical Optimization. Springer, New York (2006). https://doi.org/10.1007/978-0-387-40065-5

29. Olson, B., Hashmi, I., Molloy, K., Shehu, A.: Basin hopping as a general and versatile optimization framework for the characterization of biological macromolecules. Advances in Artificial Intelligence 2012 (2012). https://doi.org/10.1155/ 2012/674832

30. Perdew, J.P., Ernzerhof, M., Burke, K.: Rationale for mixing exact exchange with density functional approximations. J. Chem. Phys. **105**(22), 9982–9985 (1996). https://doi.org/10.1063/1.472933

31. Rondina, G.G., Da Silva, J.L.F.: Revised basin-hopping Monte Carlo algorithm for structure optimization of clusters and nanoparticles. J. Chem. Inf. Model. **53**(9), 2282–2298 (2013). https://doi.org/10.1021/ci400224z

32. Rosenberg, A., Hirschberg, J.: V-measure: A conditional entropy-based external cluster evaluation measure. In: Proceedings of the 2007 Joint Conference on Empirical Methods in Natural Language Processing and Computational Natural Language Learning (EMNLP-CoNLL), pp. 410–420 (2007)

33. Rousseeuw, P.J.: Silhouettes: A graphical aid to the interpretation and validation of cluster analysis. J. Comput. Appl. Math. **20**, 53–65 (1987). https://doi.org/10.1016/0377-0427(87)90125-7. https://www.sciencedirect.com/science/article/pii/0377042787901257

34. van Duin, A.C.T., Dasgupta, S., Lorant, F., Goddard, W.A.: ReaxFF: a reactive force field for hydrocarbons. J. Phys. Chem. A **105**, 9396–9409 (2001)

35. van Lenthe, E., Snijders, J.G., Baerends, E.J.: The zero-order regular approximation for relativistic effects: the effect of spin-orbit coupling in closed shell molecules. J. Chem. Phys. **105**(15), 6505–6516 (1996). https://doi.org/10.1063/1.472460

36. Venna, J., Kaski, S.: Local multidimensional scaling. Neural Netw. **19**(6), 889–899 (2006). https://doi.org/10.1016/j.neunet.2006.05.014. https://www.sciencedirect.com/science/article/pii/S0893608006000724. Advances in Self Organising Maps - WSOM2005

37. Wagstaff, K., Cardie, C., Rogers, S., Schrödl, S., et al.: Constrained k-means clustering with background knowledge. In: ICML, vol. 1, pp. 577–584 (2001)

38. Wales, D.J., Doye, J.P.K.: Global optimization by basin-hopping and the lowest energy structures of Lennard-jones clusters containing up to 110 atoms. J. Phys. Chemis. A **101**(28), 5111–5116 (1997). https://doi.org/10.1021/jp970984n

39. Ward, J.H., Jr.: Hierarchical grouping to optimize an objective function. J. Am. Stat. Assoc. **58**(301), 236–244 (1963)

40. Yang, X.S.: Introduction to Mathematical Optimization: From Linear Programming to Metaheuristics. Cambridge International2 Science Publishing (2008)

41. Zheng, J., Lu, T., Lian, Z., Li, M., Lu, W.: Machine learning assisted classification of post-treatment amines for increasing the stability of organic-inorganic hybrid perovskites. Mater. Today Commun. **35**, 105902 (2023)

42. Zibordi-Besse, L., Seminovski, Y., Rosalino, I., Guedes-Sobrinho, D., Da Silva, J.L.F.: Physical and chemical properties of unsupported $(mo_2)_n$ clusters for $m = ti, zr$, or ce and $n = 1--15$: A density functional theory study combined with the tree-growth scheme and euclidean similarity distance algorithm. J. Phys. Chem. C **122**(48), 27702–27712 (2018). https://doi.org/10.1021/acs.jpcc.8b08299

Thermodynamic Analysis of Digestate Pyrolysis Coupled with CO_2 Sorption

Antonella Dimotta[1]($\boxtimes$) (iD) and Cesare Freda[2] (iD)

[1] Earth- and Eco-Systems Expertise for Environmental Modelling and Restoration Company - EESEEMR, Synergy Centre ITT Dublin, TU Dublin-Tallaght Campus, Dublin 24, Dublin 24 A386, Ireland
a.dimotta.eeseemr@gmail.com

[2] Laboratory of Thermochemical Processes for Waste and Biomass Valorization National, ENEA Research Centre, SS Jonica 106 km 419+500, 75026 Rotondella, Trisaia (MT), Italy
cesare.freda@enea.it

Abstract. To date the management of digestate is a crucial task for anaerobic digestion process. In the present work a strategy for digestate management is thermodynamically analyzed by a commercial software for process simulation called CHEMCAD®. Pyrolysis of digestate is simulated by a minimization of the free Gibbs energy. The sequestration of the carbon dioxide (CO_2) released by the pyrolysis is investigated by the addition of calcium oxide, in order to reduce CO_2 emissions. The effect of the pyrolysis temperature between 400–900 °C and of the CaO/digestate mass ratio between 0–0.5 was discussed, as well. The CHEMCAD application allowed to investigate the chemisorption behaviour by focusing on the temperature-dependent CO_2 sorption trends in relation to different values of the CaO mass ratio. Temperature below 650 °C should be considered for CO_2 sorption by CaO. CO_2 molar fraction below 10% was obtained for temperature below 450 °C and CaO/digestate mass ratio higher than 0.4.

Keywords: Pyrolysis · Digestate · CO_2 Sorption · Gas

1 Introduction

Anaerobic digestion (AD) consists of a sequence of processes through which microorganisms break down the biodegradable compounds in anaerobic environment through the following four key steps, such as hydrolysis, acidification, acetogenesis, and the final conversion of acetic and hydrogen gas into methane (CH_4) and carbon dioxide (CO_2) [1, 2]. This process is used for industrial or domestic purposes to manage waste or to produce biogas for heat and power production. Digestate is the solid by-product remaining after the anaerobic digestion of a biodegradable feedstock. Digestate comprises of the solid fibrous material fraction emanating from the AD bio-reactor, and the liquid portion. It usually contains macro-elements such as nitrogen (N), phosphorous (P), potassium (K), calcium (Ca), sulphur (S), magnesium (Mg); recalcitrant organic molecules such as lignin, cutin, humic acids, complex proteins which allow to consider it as valuable

O. Gervasi et al. (Eds.): ICCSA 2023 Workshops, LNCS 14111, pp. 150–161, 2023.
https://doi.org/10.1007/978-3-031-37126-4_11

substitute, with lower environmental impact, of synthetic fertilizers. Digestate is often widespread in agricultural fields near the site where it is produced, unfortunately this is not always the optimal strategy as it could cause soil and water pollution, namely eutrophication, under specific condition. Therefore, planning how to manage the digestate is a crucial task when a biogas plant needs to be realized [3].

Since the present paper focuses on a pyrolysis digestate, it is relevant to shortly deal with how this process works. As reported by Stauffer et al. [4], pyrolysis is a thermal degradation process, an endothermic one, aimed at reducing a solid (or a liquid) into smaller volatile molecules, without interacting with oxygen or any other oxidants. It is a necessary process for the combustion of most solid fuels. Such process can produce a very complicated pattern of products depending on the substance being pyrolyzed as well as the environment (temperature, pressure, presence of extra reactants, etc.) in which it takes place [5].

Also, as argued by Al-Haj Ibrahim [6], the pyrolysis process is a proven and energetically efficient chemical technology that is used in the chemical industry. Moreover, pyrolysis may be used in biorefineries for making a wide range of products and materials aimed at making society more sustainable across time, including many forms of carbon, fuels and other potentially valuable chemicals and chemical feedstocks. In terms of air emissions, comparing this process with other treatment processes, such as gasification, pyrolysis produces, in general, fewer air emissions, lower emission of nitrogen and sulphur oxides, less CO_2 generation, less dust emission and no emission of dioxin inside the pyrolyzer due to the pyrolysis with deoxidized hydrocarbon gas [6]. Thermochemical treatment processes are generally classified according to their equivalence ratio (ER), which is defined as the amount of air added relative to the amount of air required for stoichiometric combustion. The equivalence ratio for pyrolysis is 0 (ER = 0). In terms of reactions, they typically occur at temperatures between 400 and 800 °C. The distribution of the products may be changed as a function of temperature, with lower pyrolysis temperatures often producing more liquid and solid products and higher temperatures capable of generating more gases as a result of more potent thermal cracking events. The characteristics of the pyrolysis products are significantly impacted by the pyrolysis temperature as well. Solid residual coproducts and ash, non-condensable gases, and condensable liquids, also referred to as pyrolysis oil, pyrolytic oil, bio-oil, or tar, are the end products of pyrolysis [6]. The type of material treated largely determines the type and yields of the pyrolysis products. By regulating pyrolysis variables like temperature, heating rate, residence duration, pressure, input particle size, and reactor type, the end products of pyrolysis may also be controlled. Specifically, the pyrolysis products can be classified into three typologies, such as biochar, syngas and bio-oil [7].

The generated biogas can be used as a renewable fuel for a variety of operations, such as the direct combustion generation of heat and/or power. When properly stored and applied to avoid nitrate leaching, the digestate produced can be utilized as a fertilizer [8]. Since the anaerobic digestion industry's sustainability is inextricably linked to proper digestate management and disposal, the aim of the present research work consisting of studying an alternative strategy able to efficiently and effectively manage digestate.

Particularly, the digestate pyrolysis is proposed coupled with the CO_2 sorption by calcium oxide (CaO). Calcium oxide (CaO, well-known as quicklime) is one of the most suitable heterogeneous base catalysts due to their comparatively high basic sites, nontoxic, low solubility in methanol and can be manufactured from cheap materials like lime stone and calcium hydroxide [9].

As reported by Zhang [10], CaO is industrially produced by calcining $CaCO_3$ at temperatures ranging from 810 °C to 1100 °C, according to the following solid-gas phase heterogeneous reaction:

$$CaCO_3 \rightarrow CaO + CO_2$$

The use of CaO-based adsorbents is characterized by a great potential for capturing CO_2 in a variety of systems due to their high reactivity for CO_2 high capacity and low cost of naturally occurring CaO. Such carbon dioxide removal is based on a reversible reaction between CaO and CO_2 [11]. The use of high-temperature adsorbents, including CaO, has a high potential to capture CO_2 from various systems [12], both in pre-combustion and post-combustion capture [13].

As demonstrated by Chen et al. [14], from the thermodynamic equilibrium point of pyrolysis process, if the CO_2 formed during pyrolysis can be absorbed, then it may promote the decarboxylation of carboxyl compounds, ultimately promoting the deoxygenation of bio-oil in the form of CO_2. Based on the specific observations and the favou-rable CO_2 adsorption performance of CaO in biomass gasification [15–19], it was proposed that CaO could represent a superior additive for deoxygenation in the fast pyrolysis process.

Wiśniewski et al. [20] pyrolyzed dried digestate in an electrically heated batch reactor. At pyrolysis temperature of 500 °C the composition of pyrolysis gas was checked (24 vol% CO_2, 10 vol % CO, 8 vol% CH_4, and 2 vol% H_2, and the calorific value was assessed (3.7 MJ/Nm^3). Doukeh et al. [21] pyrolyzed conditioned digestate over WO3/γ-Al2O3 catalyst in a continuous laboratory system using a quartz tubular reactor at atmospheric pressure, temperature 425 °C and feeding rate of 0.33 mL/min. They analyzed by GC–MS the bio-oil and they detected that it is composed by a large number of linear and branched aliphatic hydrocarbon components, alcohols, phenols and alkyl aromatic hydrocarbons with two or three methyl-type substituents. The major components present in the cracking gas are methane (CH_4) and carbon oxide (CO). Petrovic et al. [22] carried out a kinetic and thermodynamic study about digestate pyrolysis by thermogravimetric analysis data recorded up to 800 °C. Bio char was characterized, as well. Kinetic and thermodynamic parameters revealed a complex degradation mechanism of digestates, as they showed higher activation energies than undigested materials. Liu et al. [23] evaluated the digestate generated in AD of food wastes as a potential feedstock for the preparation of biochars by pyrolysis. They executed thermogravimetric analyses with different heating rates, and they calculated apparent activation energy. The TG–FTIR–MS gas analysis showed that dehydration and CO_2 emission were the main reasons for mass loss, and light hydro-carbons were released in step II of the pyrolysis.

The pyrolysis temperature significantly influenced the physicochemical properties and surface properties of the biochars.

From this literature review it can be argued that there is a recent and crescent interest of the scientific community towards the investigation of the pyrolysis as method to manage the digestate from biogas plants.

At the best of our knowledge and bibliographic search, all the works were carried out at laboratory scale and with the help of theoretical model. Therefore, in this strategic and interesting field, the authors of the present work paid their efforts to an unexplored topic that is the pyrolysis of digestate with negative CO_2 emissions by the addition to the thermal process of calcium oxide.

2 Materials and Methods

In the present work a thermodynamic approach was set. Thermodynamic equilibrium model is a smart tool to calculate the output streams of a pyrolyser. As already observed by Freda et al. in a previous research work, it is relevant to highlight that the model calculation is independent of reactor design. It is also described as zero-dimensional and unaffected by residence periods of the reactants and their hydrodynamics. Thence, it is extremely helpful for studying the influence of the process parameters, such as temperature, pressure, moisture of feedstock, secondary reaction with sorbents [24].

In relation to reaction with sorbents and related chemical adsorption processes, it is relevant to highlight that, in this case, two species have been considered, such as CaO as adsorbent and CO_2 as adsorbate. A chemical adsorption process is a chemical reaction and the development of a covalent bond between the molecule and one or more surface atoms are both necessary components of such adsorption process known as chemisorption.

Usually, thermodynamic equilibrium models are stoichiometric or non-stoichiometric. The stoichiometric model requires a definition of chemical species and of the equilibrium constants of pyrolysis reactions [25]. In the non-stoichiometric model, Gibbs free energy of the system is minimized without specifying any chemical reaction [26]. The two models (stoichiometric and non-stoichiometric) are essentially equivalent, when in the stoichiometric approach all possible chemical reactions are consi-dered. In this work the non-stoichiometric approach was applied. The Gibbs free energy of the chemical species involved in the process is minimized.

In order to find the equilibrium composition for a given feed to the pyrolyser at fixed temperature and pressure, the phases chemical reaction equilibrium criterion can be applied that is expressed as follows:

$$\left(dG_{\text{gasifier}}\right)_{T,P} = 0 \tag{1}$$

The Gibbs free energy is:

$$nG = \sum n_i \Delta G_{\text{fi}}^0 + RT \ln P \sum n_i + RT \sum n_i \ln y_i + RT \sum n_i \ln \phi_i \tag{2}$$

where:

n_i is number of moles of ith species in the system;

ΔG^0_{fi} is standard Gibbs free energy of formation of compound i;

y_i is the molar fraction of the compound i;

ϕ_i is the fugacity coefficient;

P is the pressure;

T is temperature;

R is universal gas constant.

As reported by Freda et al. [27], the minimization of this function occurs under restraints imposed by the atomic mass balances of each elements of the system and by the method of Lagrangian undetermined multipliers. A system of n-linear equation is obtained in as many unknown (chemical species involved in gasification).

An iterative solution method provided by the commercial freeware software CHEM-CAD® gives the composition corresponding to the minimum Gibbs free energy [28]. The chemical species considered for the chemical equilibrium calculation were: $C_6H_{10}O_4$ (ethylidene diacetate), H_2O (water), C (carbon), H_2 (hydrogen), CO (carbon monoxide), CO_2 (carbon dioxide), CH_4 (methane), C_2H_6O (ethanol). Digestate was simulated by ethylidene diacetate, because its elemental composition and heating value (LHV, low heating value) are remarkably close to digestate, as Table 1 clearly shows [29].

Table 1. Elemental composition and low heating value (LHV) of digestate and $C_6H_{10}O_4$.

	Digestate dry ash free	$C_6H_{10}O_4$
C, wt %	51	49
H, wt %	6	7
O, wt %	43	44
LHV, MJ/kg	19.5	19.6

Char was simulated by pure carbon. In the sensitivity analyses, CaO was co-fed with the biomass in mass ratio variable from 0 to 0.5. More in detail, CaO/digestate mass ratio was set at 0, 0.2, 0.4 and 0.5. Pyrolysis temperature was varied from 400 up to 900 °C, in eleven temperature steps. The dependent variables detected were dry gas yield (m^3/kg $_{biomass}$) and gas volumetric composition (H_2, CO, CO_2, CH_4). Therefore, for each dependent variable a total of 44 output values were calculated.

The calculation of the simulated process was performed by the abovementioned software, CHEMCAD®.

In Fig. 1 a layout of process simulation is shown. The stream 1 is composed of the biomass (digestate) and the adsorbent CaO. The unit 1 is a Gibbs reactor, where the minimization of Gibbs free energy occurs. The stream 2 gives the thermodynamic equilibrium composition of the mixture at the set temperature. The unit 2 is a phase separator, where the solids are removed.

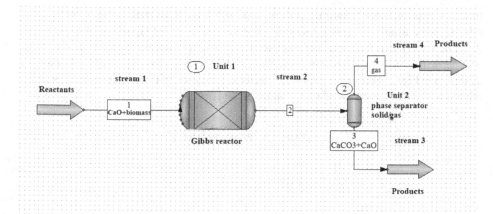

Fig. 1. CHEMCAD software application: pyrolysis process scheme in relation to the streams and reactors set.

3 Results and Discussion

In Fig. 2 the equilibrium composition of a mixture equimolar of CaO (1 mol/h) and CO_2 (1 mol/h) that gets at 20 °C and 1 bar into a thermodynamic Gibbs unit is plotted as function of the reactor temperature. At temperature below the 500 °C the formation of $CaCO_3$ is clearly favoured with heat loss; on the contrary, at temperatures above 800 °C, the $CaCO_3$ decomposition with formation of CaO and CO_2 occurs with heat duty (Fig. 2).

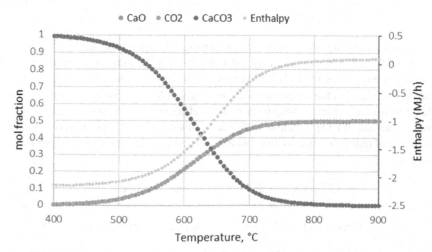

Fig. 2. CHEMCAD software application: carbonatation of the carbon dioxide as a function of the temperature.

Focusing on the results of sensitivity analyses, chemisorption mechanisms were observed and evaluated through CHEMCAD® process simulation software. Specifically, the CO_2 sorption *vs* temperature trends related to the CaO mass ratio values ranging from 0 to 0.5 were evaluated. It is relevant to observe that the most significant temperature-dependent CO_2 sorption capacity is registered into a temperatures ranging from 400 °C to 650 °C, with a strongly decreasing behaviour of CO_2 adsorption at higher temperatures, as shown in Fig. 2. Thus, CO_2 capture capacity is increased with the CaO content strictly related to the abovementioned temperature range (Fig. 3).

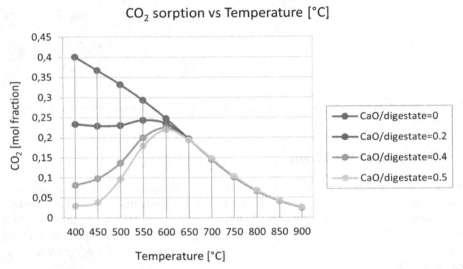

Fig. 3. CO_2 sorption vs Temperature [°C] trend in relation to an increasing CaO/digestate mass ratio.

Despite the CaO/digestate mass ratio increases, at temperatures higher than 650 °C, the CO_2 behaviour is not affected by the CaO content. In fact, as emerged from the plot results coming from the CHEMCAD® software application, CO_2 sorption by CaO should be performed at the temperature below of about 646 °C. Such thermal conditions would allow to reach a greater adsorption process efficiency. At temperature above 750 °C the molar fraction of CO_2 is below 10%, but in this case the low content is reached by other chemical reactions such as Boudouard reaction and dry reforming of methane, as follows:

$$C + CO_2 = 2CO \quad \text{(Boudouard reaction)}$$

$$CH_4 + CO_2 = 2CO + 2H_2 \quad \text{(Methane dry reforing)}$$

In Fig. 4 the molar fration of H_2 of the dry gas is plotted versus temperature at fixed parametric values of CaO/digestate mass ratio. Figure 4 shows that at temperatures higher than 650 °C the concentration of H_2 is independent of CaO/digestate. This indirectly means that the chemisorption of CO_2 by CaO is inefficient at temperatures above 650 °C.

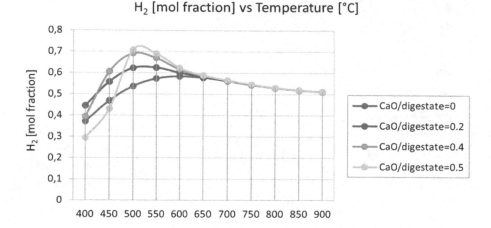

Fig. 4. H_2 [mol fraction] vs Temperature [°C] trends in relation to an increasing CaO/digestate mass ratio.

Above 650 °C the H_2 molar fraction in the dry gas has a slight decreasing trend that can be probably justified by the exothermicity of the following water gas shift reaction:

$$H_2O + CO = CO_2 + H_2$$

Below 650 °C the hydrogen molar fraction ranges from 0.3 to 0.7. The highest variability is observed at the highest CaO/digestate mass ratio (0.5), that gives the maximum CO_2 chemisorption with the higher fluctuations of the relative composition of the other permament gas.

Regarding the behaviour of CO [mol fraction] in relation to the temperature (ranging from 400 °C to 900 °C), as shown in Fig. 5, it is possible to observe that at temperatures ranging from 400 °C to 550 °C the CO trend decreases in relation to the CaO/digestate content (ratio) in a range from 0.008 to 0.06 mol fraction, highlighting that CO reaches the minimum value of 0.0008 with the higher CaO/digestate content (0.5) at temperature of 400 °C. A faster and more evident growth is observed at temperatures higher than 550 °C with a more evident growing trend up to 900 °C, where it reaches 0.46 ($\approx$ 0.5) mol fraction.

Figure 6 shows that CH_4 [mol fraction] trend is affected by the CaO/digestate content, since its behaviour describes a systematic and directly proportional growth from 0 to 0.5 Ca/digestate ratio at temperature of 400 °C. At temperature of 450 °C, an evident growth of CH_4 trend is observed in relation to the maximum content of CaO/digestate (0.5). Such an evident growing trend is observed from 400 °C to 550 °C. It is probably linked to the higher CO_2 adsorption at the lower temperature and higher CaO/digestate and to the less advancement of the dry reforming of methane. At temperatures higher than 600 °C it is possible to notice that the CH_4 trends tend to reach a plateau, reporting values ranging from 0.01 to 0.0006 mol fraction.

CO [mol fraction] vs Temperature [°C]

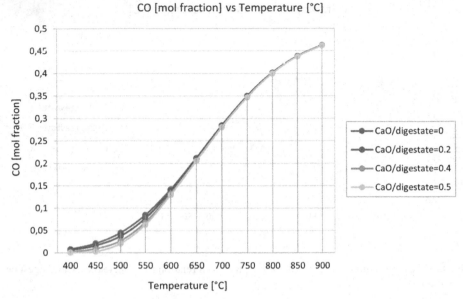

Fig. 5. CO [mol fraction] vs Temperature [°C] trends in relation to an increasing CaO/digestate mass ratio.

CH$_4$ [mol fraction] vs Temperature [°C]

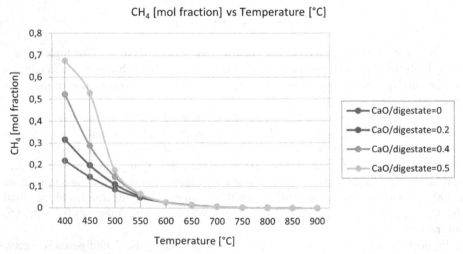

Fig. 6. CH$_4$ [mol fraction] vs Temperature [°C] trends in relation to an increasing CaO / digestate mass ratio.

Gas yield [m³/kg digestate]

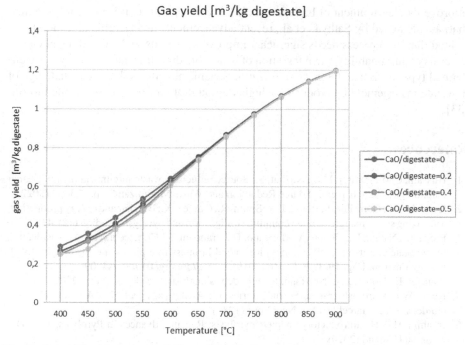

Fig. 7. Gas yield vs Temperature [°C] trends in relation to an increasing CaO/digestate mass ratio.

As expected, Fig. 7 shows that the gas yield is temperature-dependent: it tends to increase. At temperature lower than 600 °C, it is possible to observe an inversely proportional behaviour between the gas yield value and the CaO/digestate mass ratio. Such behaviour is consistent with the sorption of CO_2 by the CaO.

4   Conclusions and Final Remarks

The resulting framework of the present modelling application has allowed to high-light that CO_2 chemisorption capacity of CaO is a temperature-dependent process and CaO/biomass ratio-dependent up to about 646 °C, along with the gases (H_2, CO, CH_4) behaviour temperature- and CaO/digestate-related, included in the simulated process.

Since it has been widely demonstrated that anaerobic digestion can lead several environmental benefits, such as reduction in greenhouse gas emission, reduction in organic waste and production of methane gas [30], carrying out thermodynamic analyses of digestate can synergically contribute to give qualitative and quantitative responses on the ever-increasing energy requirements as well as environmental pollution management.

As a long-term response in sustainability scope, anaerobic digestion is a process able to act as a full circular economy technology in bioproduction, since it plays a key role in residual waste valorization and energy production, and can be incorporated into the biorefinery context [31]. Such specific aspect derives from the utilization of biomass for generating *value-added* products as chemicals or energy, in order to ever-extend and improve the development of biorefineries [2]. For this purpose, it is relevant to remind that, as mentioned by Sathyan et al., recent advancements in anaerobic digestion highlighted that this process needs significant improvement in its yield and efficiency [32]. In terms of sustainability, the integration of anaerobic digestion and pyrolysis is a well-defined type of cascade biomass valorization scheme aimed at solving the challenge of digestate management by producing a higher amount of biofuels (pyro-gas and bio-oil) [33].

References

1. Hussain, C.M., Paulraj, M.S., Nuzhat, S.: Source reduction, waste minimization, and cleaner technologies. In: Chapter 2: Source Reduction and Waste Minimization, pp. 23–59 (2022)
2. González, R., González, J., Rosas, J.G., Smith, R., Gómez, X.: Biochar and energy production: Valorizing swine manure through coupling co-digestion and pyrolysis. Carbon 6(2), 43 (2020)
3. Freda, C., Nanna, F., Villone, A., Barisano, D., Brandani, S., Cornacchia, G.: Air gasification of digestate and its co-gasification with residual biomass in a pilot scale rotary kiln. Int. J. Energy Environ. Eng. 10(3), 335–346 (2019). https://doi.org/10.1007/s40095-019-0310-3
4. Stauffer, E., Dolan, J.A., Newman, R.: Fire debris analysis. Academic Press (2007)
5. Irwin, W.J.: Chromatographic Science Series. In: Analytical Pyrolysis - A Comprehensive Guide, vol. 22. Marcel Dekker, New York (1982)
6. Ibrahim, H.A.H.: Introductory chapter: pyrolysis. Recent Advances in Pyrolysis, 1. BoD – Book on Demand (2020)
7. Zaman, C.Z., et al.: Pyrolysis: a sustainable way to generate energy from waste. vol. 1, p. 316806. Rijeka, Croatia: IntechOpen (2017)
8. Roddy, D.J., Manson-Whitton, C.: Biomass gasification and pyrolysis. Comprehensive Renewable Energy-Biomass & Biofuels (2013)
9. Lam, M.K., Lee, K.T.: Production of biodiesel using Palm oil. Biofuels: alternative feedstocks and conversation process, pp. 353–374 (2011)
10. Zhang, D.: Ash fouling, deposition and slagging in ultra-supercritical coal power plants. In: Ultra-Supercritical Coal Power Plants, pp. 133–183 (2013)
11. Konopacka-Łyskawa, D., Czaplicka, N., Szefer, A.: CaO-based high temperature CO2 sorbents–Literature review. In: Chemical and Process Engineering-Inżynieria Chemiczna i Procesowa 42, pp. 411–438 (2021)
12. Sreenivasulu, B., Sreedhar, I., Suresh, P., Raghavan, K.V.: Development trends in porous adsorbents for carbon capture. Environ. Sci. Technol. 49(21), 12641–12661 (2015)
13. Perejon, A., Romeo, L.M., Lara, Y., Lisbona, P., Martinez, A., Valverde, J.M.: The Calcium-Looping technology for CO2 capture: On the important roles of energy integration and sorbent behavior. Appl. Energy 162, 787–807 (2016)
14. Chen, D., Cen, K., Cao, X., Li, Y., Zhang, Y., Ma, H.: Restudy on torrefaction of corn stalk from the point of view of deoxygenation and decarbonization. J. Anal. Appl. Pyrol. 135, 85–93 (2018)
15. Acharya, B., Dutta, A., Basu, P.: Chemical-looping gasification of biomass for hydrogen-enriched gas production with in-process carbon dioxide capture. Energy Fuels 23(10), 5077–5083 (2009)
16. Acharya, B., Dutta, A., Basu, P.: An investigation into steam gasification of biomass for hydrogen enriched gas production in presence of CaO. Int. J. Hydrogen Energy 35(4), 1582–1589 (2010)
17. Guoxin, H., Hao, H.: Hydrogen rich fuel gas production by gasification of wet biomass using a CO2 sorbent. Biomass Bioenerg. 33(5), 899–906 (2009)

18. Han, L., Wang, Q., Yang, Y., Yu, C., Fang, M., Luo, Z.: Hydrogen production via CaO sorption enhanced anaerobic gasification of sawdust in a bubbling fluidized bed. Int. J. Hydrogen Energy **36**(8), 4820–4829 (2011)

19. Wei, L., Xu, S., Liu, J., Liu, C., Liu, S.: Hydrogen production in steam gasification of biomass with CaO as a CO2 absorbent. Energy Fuels **22**(3), 1997–2004 (2008)

20. Wisniewski, D., Gołaszcwski, J., Białowiec, A.: The pyrolysis and gasification of digestate from agricultural biogas plant. Archives of Environmental Protection **41**(3), 70–75 (2015)

21. Doukeh, R., Bombos, M., Bombos, D., Vasilievici, G., Radu, E., Oprescu, E.-E.: Pyrolysis of digestate from anaerobic digestion on tungsten oxide catalyst. React. Kinet. Mech. Catal. **132**(2), 829–838 (2021). https://doi.org/10.1007/s11144-021-01952-7

22. Petrovič, A., et al.: Pyrolysis of solid digestate from sewage sludge and lignocellulosic biomass: Kinetic and thermodynamic analysis, characterization of biochar. Sustainability **13**(17), 9642 (2021)

23. Liu, J., Huang, S., Chen, K., Wang, T., Mei, M., Li, J.: Preparation of biochar from food waste digestate: pyrolysis behavior and product properties. Biores. Technol. **302**, 122841 (2020)

24. Freda, C., Tarquini, P., Sharma, V.K., Braccio, G.: Thermodynamic improvement of solar driven gasification compared to conventional one. Energy **261**, 124953 (2022)

25. Mendiburu, A.Z., Carvalho, J.A., Jr., Coronado, C.J.: Thermochemical equilibrium modeling of biomass downdraft gasifier: Stoichiometric models. Energy **66**, 189–201 (2014)

26. Mendiburu, A.Z., Carvalho, J.A., Jr., Zanzi, R., Coronado, C.R., Silveira, J.L.: Thermochemical equilibrium modeling of a biomass downdraft gasifier: Constrained and unconstrained non-stoichiometric models. Energy **71**, 624–637 (2014)

27. Freda, C., Della Vittoria, U., Fanelli, E., Cornacchia, G., Braccio, G.: Thermodynamic analysis of biomass gasification by different agents. Italian J. Eng. Sci. (2020)

28. Gartman, T.N., Sovetin, F.S., Novikova, D.K.: Experience in the application of the CHEMCAD program to the modeling of reactor processes. Theor. Found. Chem. Eng. **43**, 944–954 (2009)

29. ECN Phyllis Classification: Database for the physicochemical composition of (treated) lignocellulosic biomass, micro- and macroalgae, various feedstocks for biogas production and biochar, https://phyllis.nl/Browse/Standard/ECN-Phyllis#digestate, last accessed 07 May 2023

30. Čater, M., Fanedl, L., Malovrh, Š, Logar, R.M.: Biogas production from brewery spent grain enhanced by bioaugmentation with hydrolytic anaerobic bacteria. Biores. Technol. **186**, 261–269 (2015)

31. Szymanska, M., et al.: A bio-refinery concept for n and p recovery – a chance for biogas plant development. Energies **12**, 155 (2019)

32. Sathyan, A., Haq, I., Kalamdhad, A. S., Khwaraikpam, M.: Recent advancements in anaerobic digestion: A Novel approches for waste to energy. In: Advanced Organic Waste Management, pp. 233–246. Elsevier (2022)

33. Fabbri, D., Torri, C.: Linking pyrolysis and anaerobic digestion (Py-AD) for the conversion of lignocellulosic biomass. Curr. Opin. Biotechnol. **38**, 167–173 (2016)

Coding Cross Sections of an Electron Charge Transfer Process: Analysis of Different Cuts for the Entrance and Exit Potentials

Noelia Faginas-Lago[1]($^{(\boxtimes)}$) (iD), Emília Valença Ferreira de Aragão[1,2] (iD),
Luca Mancini[1] (iD), Marzio Rosi[4] (iD), Daniela Ascenzi[3] (iD),
and Fernando Pirani[1,4] (iD)

[1] Dipartimento di Chimica, Biologia e Biotecnologie, Università degli Studi di
Perugia, 06123 Perugia, Italy
{emilia.dearagao,luca.mancini2}@studenti.unipg.it,
{noelia.faginaslago,fernando.pirani}@unipg.it
[2] Master-tec srl, Via Sicilia 41, 06128 Perugia, Italy
emilia.dearagao@master-tec.it
[3] Dipartimento di Fisica, Università di Trento, Trento, Italy
daniela.ascenzi@unitn.it
[4] Dipartimento di Ingegneria Civile ed Ambientale, Università degli Studi di Perugia,
06125 Perugia, Italy
marzio.rosi@unipg.it

Abstract. The paper presents the algorithm of a code written for exploring the collision dynamics of an electron transfer process between a neutral species and helium cation. Cuts of the entrance and exit potential energy surfaces are calculated in function of the radial distance to the center of mass of the neutral molecule, inclination angle and azimuth. Entrance and exit potential are calculated accounting for the electrostatic contribution and for non-electrostatic forces by employing the Improved Lennard-Jones function.

The code implemented has been employed in systems involving helium cation and a small organic molecule, such as methanol, dimethyl ether and methyl formate.

Keywords: Astrochemistry · Semiempirical potential · Improved Lennard-Jones · Charge exchange process

1 Introduction

Among more than 289 molecular species detected in the interstellar and circumstellar medium [1–4], particular interest is directed to the so called interstellar Complex Organic Molecules (iCOMS), namely organic molecules containing at least six atoms, including heavier element such as nitrogen and/or oxygen [5,6]. The detection of relatively complex and prebiotic molecules in the harsh regions of the interstellar medium (where the temperature can go down to 10 K and the particle density can be as low as 10^4 particles cm^{-3} [7]), led to an increased interest in our understanding of interstellar chemistry. In order to properly describe the chemical complexity of the interstellar medium (ISM), different astrochemical models have been developed [8–13]. In particular, a multidisciplinary approach appears to be pivotal, combining data coming from astronomical observations as well as chemical and physical investigations. At the present stage, in order to explain the abundances of interstellar molecules, a synergy between two main reaction mechanism, namely grain surface processes and gas-phase reactions, must be invoked. The only use of grain surface chemistry (according to which iCOMs are initially formed through hydrogenation and radical recombination processes on the surface of the grains and subsequently ejected in the gas phase [7]) does not allow to reproduce the detected abundances. Therefore, a combined approach including gas-phase reactions is crucial for a correct implementation of astrochemical models, as pointed out by recent works [14–16]. Considering the prohibitive conditions of the interstellar medium, only barrierless and exothermic process appears to be feasible chemical routes in the gas phase, namely reaction between ions and/or radicals with closed-shell species. An accurate characterization of chemical reactions (both with theoretical calculation and experimental investigations) is indeed pivotal to derive the parameters used in the astrochemical models. An example of the aforementioned models is represented by the two KIDA [17] and UMIST [18] databases, in which the abundances of detected species are accounted for by considering their formation and destruction routes. Unfortunately, among the 8000 reactions considered, only a small fraction is derived through accurate chemical analysis, while the remaining part is included with estimated parameters considered on the basis of chemical analogies. As already mentioned, together with the possible formation mechanisms, also destruction routes play an extremely important role for the global astrochemical modeling. The main destruction processes for iCOMs in the gas phase are driven by ions, namely He^+ or H_3^+ and HCO^+. Among this species, He^+ represents one of the best candidate [19,20], due to its high value of ionisation energy [21], leading to a charge transfer process followed by the dissociation of the new-formed ion. The dynamics of the charge transfer processes is driven by the probability of the transition between different intermolecular Potential Energy Surfaces (PESs), which depends on the orientation of the interacting fragments. In the present contribution, we describe a code developed by our group in order to calculate the cross sections for the global electron transfer process, to be compared with results measured as a function of the collision energy with the molecular beam technique, and, subsequently, to evaluate related reaction rate constants as a function of the temperature.

2   Program Implementation

The code has been developed to compute cuts of entrance and exit potential energy surfaces for the charge exchange process. The cuts are calculated in function of the spherical coordinates of He^+ and He for the entrance and exit PESs, respectively. The goal is to identify the configurations where an exothermic crossing between the two PESs can be observed. The code was written in C language, and has the following structure:

1. Inclusion of useful libraries as stdio.h, math.h, stdlib.h and string.h;
2. Definition of assorted functions;
3. Main program section, defined inside *"int main{...}"*.

In the next sections, a detailed description of the contents of each piece of code is given.

2.1   Definition of Assorted Functions

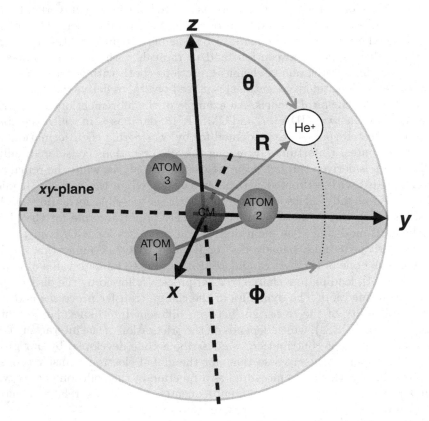

Fig. 1. Scheme representing a system in a three-dimensional space. The molecule is represented by its effective atoms, in blue, and by its center of mass (CM), in red, which is used as the origin of the Cartesian reference system. In the code, the position of He$^+$ is declared in terms of spherical coordinates, with R being the distance between the molecule's CM and the ion, θ being the angle made by the R vector with the z-axis and ϕ defined as the azimuthal angle.

The functions implemented here are similar to what was described in a previous work by our group [22]. They involve the definition of the frame of reference and the definition of the entrance and exit potentials functions. As in our previous work, what we call "configuration" here is an individual relative spatial orientation between the neutral molecule (e.g. dimethyl ether, methyl formate, methanol) and He^+.

Before using the code, the user must obtain the optimized geometry of the molecule and the partial atomic charges via quantum chemistry calculations employing *ab initio* methods. In case of molecules containing many atoms, it is recommended to replace functional groups with effective atoms, for instance C_{eff} instead of a methyl group. Here, C_{eff} has the mass and the polarizability of a methyl group. The partition of the molecular polarizability in functional group components has been successfully adopted to build up the force field useful in several molecular dynamics simulations (see, for instance, [23,24]) Moreover, for the molecules of interest in this study, the partial charge of the effective atom will be the sum of the partial charges of all the atoms it is representing. The center of mass (CM) of the molecule, shown in red in 1, is defined via the equations:

$$x_{CM} = \frac{\sum_{i=1}^{N} x_i m_i}{M}; \quad y_{CM} = \frac{\sum_{i=1}^{N} y_i m_i}{M}; \quad z_{CM} = \frac{\sum_{i=1}^{N} z_i m_i}{M} \qquad (1)$$

where x_i, y_i and z_i are the coordinates of each effective atom, m_i its mass, N the total number of effective atoms and M the total mass of the molecule. A new Cartesian frame of reference must be defined, with CM placed at its origin, in order to make the declaration of the position of the ion easier later. The coordinates of the effective atoms in this new frame of reference, are obtained by extracting the CM coordinates from the original atomic coordinates:

$$x_i' = x_i - x_{CM}; \quad y_i' = y_i - y_{CM}; \quad z_i' = z_i - z_{CM} \qquad (2)$$

As for He^+, the user must give the value of the spherical coordinates and the program will compute the Cartesian coordinates (denoted by j) using the following formulae:

$$x_j = R sin(\theta) cos(\phi) \qquad (3)$$

$$y_j = R sin(\theta) sin(\phi) \qquad (4)$$

$$z_j = R cos(\theta) \qquad (5)$$

where R is the distance between the ion and the CM, θ the angle in relation with the z-axis and ϕ is the azimuth angle. R values can range from 0 to infinite, θ values range from $0°$ to $180°$ and ϕ ranges from $0°$ to $360°$. For a molecule with a certain degree of symmetry, the user can choose to explore a reduced range of values for θ and ϕ.

As shown in Fig. 2, the potential functions are dependent of the distance between each effective atom of the molecule and the ion, r_{ij}, which can be calculated as follows:

$$r_{ij} = \sqrt{(x_i - x_j)^2 + (y_i - y_j)^2 + (z_i - z_j)^2} \qquad (6)$$

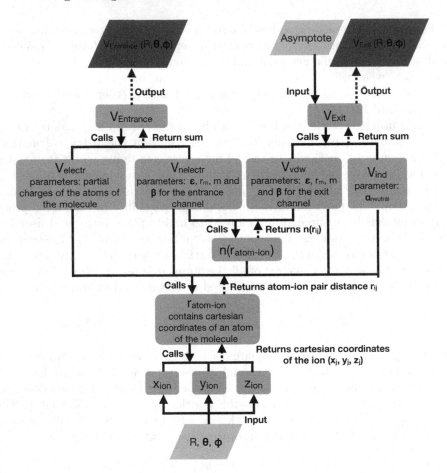

Fig. 2. An overall view of the algorithm in *pes.c* code. In green, the input information, in grey the output. Blue blocks refer to functions that have been defined outside the main section of the program.

The potential functions must also be adapted to each system, and so the definition of some parameters are necessary before using the program. For instance, the partial charges on the neutral species obtained through *ab initio* calculations are used to estimate the electrostatic contribution for the entrance PES, $V_{electr}(R)$. In the case of the non-electrostatic contribution, represented by the sum of individual V_{ij} (again, i represents an atom of the molecule and j denotes He$^+$), a handful of parameters must be adopted. These parameters are the potential well ε_{ij} and the related equilibrium distance $r_{m_{ij}}$, whose values are used to evaluate V_{ij} through the Improved Lennard-Jones model [25]:

$$V_{ij}(r_{ij}) = \varepsilon_{ij} \left[\frac{m}{n(r_{ij}) - m} \left(\frac{r_{m_{ij}}}{r_{ij}} \right)^{n(r_{ij})} - \frac{n(r_{ij})}{n(r_{ij}) - m} \left(\frac{r_{m_{ij}}}{r_{ij}} \right)^{m} \right] \quad (7)$$

where m, as explained in [25,26], is parameter depending on the nature of the system: it assumes the value of 1 for ion-ion interaction, 2 for ion-permanent dipole, 4 for ion-induced dipole, and 6 for neutral-neutral pairs. In the present case, since the entrance channel involves a small ion and a neutral molecule, the induction attraction dominates over the dispersion, and so $m = 4$ is assumed. After the charge transfer process, we have a molecular ion interacting with an atom with low polarizability, so the dispersion plays a more important role and m assumes the value of 6. The modulation in the decline of the repulsion and the enhancement of the attraction in Eq. 7, $n(r_{ij})$ takes the following form:

$$n(r_{ij}) = \beta + 4\left(\frac{r_{ij}}{r_{m_{ij}}}\right)^2 \qquad (8)$$

where β is a parameter related to the nature and the hardness of the interacting particles [26–29] and the $\frac{r_{ij}}{r_{m_{ij}}}$ ratio is introduced as a reduced distance. The total non-electrostatic contribution, which is the sum of all V_{ij} of a given configuration, is called $V_{nelectr}$ in the entrance channel and V_{vdw} in the exit channel (see Fig. 2).

In the entrance channel, the electrostatic component $V_{electr}(R)$ is defined by the Coulomb's law:

$$V_{\mathrm{electr}}(R) = \frac{1}{4\pi\varepsilon_0}\sum_{i}^{N}\frac{q_i}{r_{ij}} \qquad (9)$$

where R is again the distance between the ion and CM, r_{ij} is again the distance between an atom of the molecule and the ion, obtained deconvolving R into partial components, ε_0 is the vacuum permittivity, and q_i corresponds to the partial charge on each atom of the molecule.

In the exit channel, an induction term is inserted to represent the ion-induced dipole contribution as a pertubative approach. The induction term, $V_{ind}(R')$, describes the interaction between the newly formed molecular cation and He. Considering the polarizability $\alpha_{neutral}$ of the He, $V_{ind}(R')$ is expressed adopting the following formalism:

$$V_{ind}(R') = -7200\frac{\alpha_{neutral}}{R'^4} \qquad (10)$$

By analogy to R, R' is the distance between the neutralized species and the center-of-mass of the newly formed cation. In our code, we assume $R = R'$ whenever we want to explore a crossing between the entrance and the exit channels.

Our code requires one parameter for the exit channel, the so called asymptote. The asymptote is calculated by taking the first ionization energy value of Helium and subtracting the ionization energy of the molecular orbital from which the electron is being extracted. This allows the user to estimate from which orbital(s) of the molecule the electron might be removed during the charge transfer process. The difference between the two energies must be taken into account when defining the exit PES in order to see if the cuts of the entrance and exit PESs are crossing each other at some point. Figure 2 shows the algorithm of the *pes.c* code. In green are represented the input information, such as the spherical coordinates of the ion and the asymptote. In blue are reported the functions code in the program, implemented with the equations previously reported. The outputs, represented in grey, contain the values of the entrance and exit potentials for a given configuration. With this program, it is possible to have different cuts of the entrance and exit PESs, and so it is possible to visualise in which configurations the crossing might happen. In the next sections, we will briefly talk about the options of routine in the code that produce different outputs.

2.2   Calculating the PESs Curves in Function of R

The previous section described all the functions that have been implemented in the code. This section provides an explanation on how the program calculates the entrance and exit potential in function of R, as depicted in Fig. 3.

First, in the user must declare the value of the inclination (θ), azimuth (ϕ), frozen distance (d) and asymptote inside the program. θ, ϕ must be declared in radians, d in angstroms and the asymptote must be in eV. Then the program will open two empty output files, one for the entrance potential and one for the exit potential. A loop will start by setting the value of R to 1.0 (in angstroms) and it will run until R = 12.0 Å by increasing the value of R with 0.001 Å at each step. Of course, these values may be modified according to the user needs. Inside the loop, the code will call for the function $V_{Entrance}$, which will in turn call a succession of other functions (see Fig. 2). Then the code will write a line in the output file 1 the values of R, $V_{Entrance}(R)$ ($= V_{Entrance}(R, \theta, \phi)$) and the respective electrostatic and non-electrostatic components of $V_{Entrance}(R)$. Output file 1 should have 4 columns is total. Next, the code calls for the function V_{Exit}, which like $V_{Entrance}$ will call for many other functions. It will write in output file 2 a line with the values of R, $V_{Exit}(R)$ ($= V_{Exit}(R, \theta, \phi)$) and the respective non-electrostatic contribution and induction contribution.

Once the loop ends, the program will open a third output file in .xyz format. It will also open and read a file called "molecule.xyz", which should contain the total number of atoms in the molecule and their respective Cartesian coordinates. Next, the program will attribute a value to the frozen distance d, for instance 3.5 Å. The Cartesian coordinates of He^+ will then be computed for a configuration where He^+ is 3.5 Å away from the center of mass of the molecule. The program will write in output file 3 in .xyz and write the total number of atoms of the complex, the Cartesian coordinates of the atoms of the molecule and the Cartesian coordinates of He^+. Finally, the program will close the output files and stop.

The purpose of output file 3 is to help the user visualize the relative orientation of He^+ and the molecule for a specific pair of θ and ϕ. This file can be open with a molecular visualization software such as Avogadro [30]. Output files 1 and 2, on the other hand, can be read by any software for data analysis. The user can ask the software, for instance, to plot the entrance and exit PESs curves together in order to observe the presence of an exothermic crossing or to

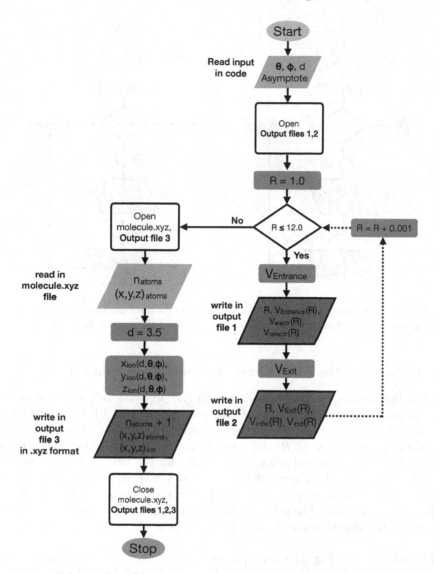

Fig. 3. Flowchart showing how the program operates for the calculation of the entrance and exit potential in function of the distance R. R is assumed as the distance between He^+ and the center of mass of the molecule as well as the distance between He and the center of mass of the molecular cation.

analyse the effects of the electrostatic and non-electrostatic contributions in the total potential.

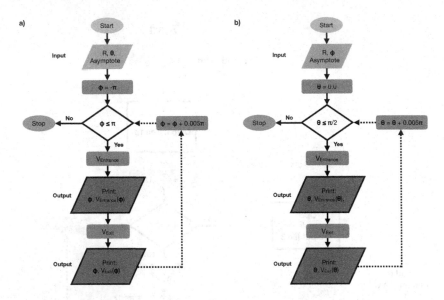

Fig. 4. Flowchart showing how the program operates for the calculation of the entrance and exit potential in function of the azimuth ϕ (a) and the inclination angle θ (b).

2.3   Calculating the PESs Curves in Function of θ and ϕ

The routines in this program are similar to the previous one, but instead the user can use it to explore the cuts of the entrance and exit PESs in function of the azimuth ϕ (Fig. 4a) and the inclination angle θ (Fig. 4b). The routine starts by reading a fixed value of R, the asymptote and θ (or ϕ). Then the value of ϕ (or θ) is set to a minimal value. In principle, for the loop in Fig. 4a, one can calculate the potential for any value of $-\pi \leq \phi \leq \pi$. If the molecule presents a certain degree of symmetry, the values of the loop can be reduced to $0 \leq \phi \leq \pi$ at the user's discretion. The same can be done in Fig. 4b in respect to the values of θ, which in principle range from $-\frac{\pi}{2}$ to $\frac{\pi}{2}$, but in the image is shown from 0 to $\frac{\pi}{2}$.

Inside the loop in Fig. 4a, the output files should contain two columns, one for ϕ and another for the $V_{Entrance}$ (or the V_{Exit}) in function of (R,θ,ϕ). As input values, the user can add columns in the previous file to be able to calculate the potential at different values of R (2 Å, 10 Å, 15 Å, etc.), in order to have an idea of the long range behaviour of the potential observed at different values of the azimuth. Again, this also applies to the routine in Fig. 4b.

The user can open the output files with any software that plots graphs. The plot will show the behaviour of the entrance and exit potentials at a given distance R between the two chemical species for many angles of attack.

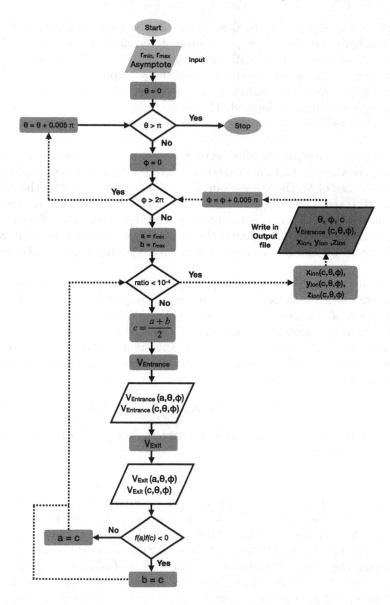

Fig. 5. Flowchart showing the process of finding the crossing point for several configurations.

2.4 Mapping the Crossing Points

In this section we present a new feature of our code. In fact, one of the goals of the analysis of the entrance and exit PESs cuts is to find the configurations in which an exothermic crossing is possible. We found it could be interesting to have a way to visualize the regions surrounding the molecule where the crossing can happen. For that, we created a routine in the code that will go through several configurations (θ and ϕ pairs) around the molecule and try to find if crossing is possible and at what distance from the CM it will happen.

First, the user must declare the value of the asymptote and r_{min} and r_{max} which are, respectively, the minimum and maximum values of the distance where the crossing point might be located. They have to be adapted by the user for the system of interest. From this point on, the program will enter a series of three loops.

The outermost loop starts after setting the value of θ to 0 and it will run by increasing the value of theta θ by 0.005 π until $\theta > \pi$. This corresponds to 201 individual values of θ. The second outermost loop is entered after the value of the azimuth is set to 0 as well and it runs until $\theta > 2\pi$, with the increment of 0.005 π at each turn. Therefore, the program runs for about 401 different values of ϕ. In total, the program evaluates the possibility of crossing points in 80.601 different configurations and for a molecule with 3 effective atoms it takes around 28 s.

Inside that second loop, $i.e$ for a given configuration, two variables called a and b are set with the values of r_{min} and r_{max}, respectively. At this point the program starts a routine to find the value of the distance where the entrance and exit potential curves intersect. This is done by means of the well known bisection method, an iterative method that consists in updating the value of the distance (here c), until the root of the function of interest is found. Lets call the function of interest $f(x)$, defined as:

$$f(x) = V_{Entrance}(x, \theta, \phi) - V_{Exit}(x, \theta, \phi) \tag{11}$$

By entering the innermost loop of our program, the value of c is set as the midpoint of $[a;b]$ interval:

$$c = \frac{a+b}{2} \tag{12}$$

The program calls the function $V_{Entrance}$ to compute $V_{Entrance}(a, \theta, \phi)$ and $V_{Entrance}(c, \theta, \phi)$ and then it calls the function V_{Exit} to compute $V_{Exit}(a, \theta, \phi)$ and $V_{Exit}(c, \theta, \phi)$. With this information, $f(a)$ and $f(c)$ are calculated using the formula in Eq. 11. The need to readjust either the value of a or b is then evaluated by observing the sign of the product of $f(a)f(c)$. If $f(a)f(c) < 0$, that means that the function $f(x)$ went through a sign change between a and c. In other words, the root of $f(x)$ is somewhere between a and c, but not between c and b. So b value is updated to take the value of c. On the contrary, if $f(a)f(c) < 0$, then a takes the value of c instead. The program stays in the innermost loop until it fulfils the following condition:

$$\left| \frac{a-b}{a+b} \right| < 10^{-4} \tag{13}$$

In Fig 5, $\frac{a-b}{a+b}$ is represented by "ratio". At this point, the value of c should give the location of the crossing point. The Cartesian coordinates of He+ are computed and then a line in the output file is printed with θ, ϕ, c, the value of the entrance potential at this configuration, and the Cartesian coordinates of He^+. The program stops when it fulfils the condition $\theta > \pi$.

The generated output file should have more than 80.000 lines, each corresponding to a configuration. In some of them, the value of c is close to r_{max}, and in this case it is probable that there is not a crossing point for that configuration. In other cases, the value of c will be somewhere between the r_{min} and r_{max}, but the value of the potential will be positive, which means that the crossing point is endothermic. Alternatively, the user might chose to ask the code to write in the output only the configurations where the crossing is exothermic. Then, the user can use a program to make a 3D scattering plot containing the Cartesian coordinates of Helium. In the same graph, the user can plot the Cartesian coordinates of the molecule. This will give the user an overall view of the configurations around the molecule where the exothermic crossing is possible.

3   Conclusions

The piece of code described has been used in four systems so far, all of them involving He^+ colliding with dimethyl ether [31], methyl formate [32], methanol [33] and acetonitrile (under study) . The results of these codes are very important as they are the preliminary step before calculating the total cross section, as detailed in [22]. Compared to [22], more time has been dedicated to explore the PESs cuts as a function of the angle θ and azimuth ϕ. In addition, a new routine was implemented to generate a file where the user can see in 3D the regions surrounding the molecule where the crossing can happen. This will be helpful when the user later defines the set of preferential orientations to compute the cross section, as done in [33].

Acknowledgements. The authors thank Andrea Cernuto who originally developed the code. This project has received funding from the European Union's Horizon 2020 research and innovation programme under the Marie Skłodowska Curie grant agreement No 811312 for the project "Astro-Chemical Origins" (ACO).

The authors thank the Herla Project(http://www.hpc.unipg.it/hosting/vherla/vherla.html)-Università degli Studi di Perugia for allocated computing time.

N.F-L acknowledges also Fondazione Cassa di Risparmio di Perugia n 19839_2020_0513 to C.E.

D.A. and M.R. acknowledge funding from MUR PRIN 2020 project n. 2020AF B3FX.

References

1. McGuire, B.A.: 2021 census of interstellar, circumstellar, extragalactic, protoplanetary disk, and exoplanetary molecules. Astrophys. J. Suppl. Ser. **259**(2), 30 (2022). https://doi.org/10.3847/1538-4365/ac2a48
2. Müller, H.S.P., Thorwirth, S., Roth, D.A., Winnewisser, G.: The cologne database for molecular spectroscopy, CDMS. A& A **370**(3), L49–L52 (2001). https://doi.org/10.1051/0004-6361:20010367.   https://cdms.astro.uni-koeln.de/classic/molecules. Accessed 13 April 2022

3. Müller, H.S., Schlöder, F., Stutzki, J., Winnewisser, G.: The cologne database for molecular spectroscopy, CDMS: a useful tool for astronomers and spectroscopists. J. Mol. Struct. **742**(1), 215–227 (2005). https://doi.org/10.1016/j.molstruc.2005.01.027

4. Endres, C.P., Schlemmer, S., Schilke, P., Stutzki, J., Müller, H.S.. The cologne database for molecular spectroscopy, CDMS, In the virtual atomic and molecular data centre, VAMDC. J. Molecular Spectroscopy **327**, 95–104 (2016). https://doi.org/10.1016/j.jms.2016.03.005. New Visions of Spectroscopic Databases, Volume II

5. Herbst, E., Van Dishoeck, E.F.: Complex organic interstellar molecules. Ann. Rev. Astron. Astrophys. **47**, 427–480 (2009)

6. Ceccarelli, C., et al.: Seeds of life in space (SOLIS): the organic composition diversity at 300–1000 au scale in solar-type star-forming regions. Astrophys. J. **850**(2), 176 (2017)

7. Caselli, P., Ceccarelli, C.: Our astrochemical heritage. Astron. Astrophys. Rev. **20**(1), 1–68 (2012). https://doi.org/10.1007/s00159-012-0056-x

8. Herbst, E.: The synthesis of large interstellar molecules. Int. Rev. Phys. Chem. **36**(2), 287–331 (2017)

9. Agúndez, M., Wakelam, V.: Chemistry of dark clouds: databases, networks, and models. Chem. Rev. **113**(12), 8710–8737 (2013)

10. Taquet, V., Ceccarelli, C., Kahane, C.: Multilayer modeling of porous grain surface chemistry-I. GRAINOBLE Model. Astron. Astrophys. **538**, A42 (2012)

11. Garrod, R., Herbst, E.: Formation of methyl formate and other organic species in the warm-up phase of hot molecular cores. Astron. Astrophys. **457**(3), 927–936 (2006)

12. Vasyunin, A.I., Caselli, P., Dulieu, F., Jiménez-Serra, I.: Formation of complex molecules in prestellar cores: a multilayer approach. Astrophys. J. **842**(1), 33 (2017)

13. Garrod, R.T., Weaver, S.L.W., Herbst, E.: Complex chemistry in star-forming regions: an expanded gas-grain warm-up chemical model. Astrophys. J. **682**(1), 283 (2008)

14. Balucani, N., Ceccarelli, C., Taquet, V.: Formation of complex organic molecules in cold objects: the role of gas-phase reactions. Monthly Notices Royal Astron. Soc.: Lett. **449**(1), L16–L20 (2015)

15. Skouteris, D., et al.: The genealogical tree of ethanol: gas-phase formation of glycolaldehyde, acetic acid, and formic acid. Astrophys. J. **854**(2), 135 (2018)

16. Rosi, M., et al.: Possible scenarios for SiS formation in the interstellar medium: Electronic structure calculations of the potential energy surfaces for the reactions of the SiH radical with atomic sulphur and S_2. Chem. Phys. Lett. **695**, 87–93 (2018). https://doi.org/10.1016/j.cplett.2018.01.053

17. Wakelam, V., et al.: A kinetic database for astrochemistry (KIDA). ApJS **199**(1), 21 (2012). https://doi.org/10.1088/0067-0049/199/1/21

18. Woodall, J., Agúndez, M., Markwick-Kemper, A.J., Millar, T.J.: The UMIST database for astrochemistry 2006*. A&A **466**(3), 1197–1204 (2007). https://doi.org/10.1051/0004-6361:20064981

19. Lepp, S., Stancil, P., Dalgarno, A.: Atomic and molecular processes in the early Universe. J. Phys. B: At. Mol. Opt. Phys. **35**(10), R57 (2002)

20. De Fazio, D.: The $H + HeH^+ \rightarrow He^+ H_2^+$ reaction from the ultra-cold regime to the three-body breakup: exact quantum mechanical integral cross sections and rate constants. Phys. Chem. Chem. Phys. **16**(23), 11662–11672 (2014). https://doi.org/10.1039/C4CP00502C

21. Mallard, W., Linstrom, P.: NIST Chemistry WebBook, NIST Standard Reference Database Number 69. Gaithersburg, MD 20899 (2000). https://doi.org/10.18434/T4D303

22. de Aragão, E.V.F., et al.: Coding cross sections of an electron charge transfer process. In: Gervasi, O., Murgante, B., Misra, S., Rocha, A.M.A.C., Garau, C. (eds.) Computational Science and Its Applications - ICCSA 2022 Workshops. ICCSA 2022. Lecture Notes in Computer Science, vol. 13382, pp. 319–333. Springer, Cham (2022). https://doi.org/10.1007/978-3-031-10592-0_24

23. Albertí, M., Faginas-Lago, N., Laganà, A., Pirani, F.: Phys. Chem. Chem. Phys. 13(18), 8422 (2011)

24. Faginas Lago, N., Albertí, M., Lombardi, A., Pirani, F.: A force field for acetone: the transition from small clusters to liquid phase investigated by molecular dynamics simulations. Theoret. Chem. Acc. 135(7), 1–9 (2016). https://doi.org/10.1007/s00214-016-1914-9

25. Pirani, F., Brizi, S., Roncaratti, L.F., Casavecchia, P., Cappelletti, D., Vecchiocattivi, F.: Beyond the Lennard-Jones model: a simple and accurate potential function probed by high resolution scattering data useful for molecular dynamics simulations. Phys. Chem. Chem. Phys. 10(36), 5489–5503 (2008)

26. Pirani, F., Albertí, M., Castro, A., Moix Teixidor, M., Cappelletti, D.: Atombond pairwise additive representation for intermolecular potential energy surfaces. Chem. Phys. Lett. 394(1–3), 37–44 (2004). https://doi.org/10.1016/j.cplett.2004.06.100

27. Bartolomei, M., et al.: The intermolecular potential in NO-N$_2$ and (NO-N$_2$)$^+$ systems: implications for the neutralization of ionic molecular aggregates. Phys. Chem. Chem. Phys. 10, 5993–6001 (2008). https://doi.org/10.1039/B808200F

28. Cappelletti, D., Pirani, F., Bussery-Honvault, B., Gomez, L., Bartolomei, M.: A bond-bond description of the intermolecular interaction energy: the case of weakly bound N$_2$-H$_2$ and N$_2$-N$_2$ complexes. Phys. Chem. Chem. Phys. 10, 4281–4293 (2008). https://doi.org/10.1039/B803961E

29. Pacifici, L., Verdicchio, M., Faginas-Lago, N., Lombardi, A., Costantini, A.: A highlevel ab initio study of the N$_2$ + N$_2$ reaction channel. J. Comput. Chem. 34(31), 2668–2676 (2013). https://doi.org/10.1002/jcc.23415

30. Hanwell, M.D., Curtis, D.E., Lonie, D.C., Vandermeersch, T., Zurek, E., Hutchison, G.R.: Avogadro: an advanced semantic chemical editor, visualization, and analysis platform. J. Cheminform. 4(1), 1–17 (2012)

31. Cernuto, A., Tosi, P., Martini, L.M., Pirani, F., Ascenzi, D.: Experimental investigation of the reaction of helium ions with dimethyl ether: stereodynamics of the dissociative charge exchange process. Phys. Chem. Chem. Phys. 19(30), 19554–19565 (2017). https://doi.org/10.1039/C7CP00827A

32. Cernuto, A., Pirani, F., Martini, L.M., Tosi, P., Ascenzi, D.: The Selective Role of Long-Range Forces in the Stereodynamics of Ion-Molecule Reactions: the He$^+$ + Methyl Formate Case From Guided-Ion-Beam Experiments. Chem. Phys. Chem. 19(1), 51–59 (2018). https://doi.org/10.1002/cphc.201701096

33. Richardson, V., et al.: Fragmentation of interstellar methanol by collisions with he+: an experimental and computational study. Phys. Chem. Chem. Phys. 24(37), 22437–22452 (2022)

Transport Infrastructures for Smart Cities (TISC 2023)

Sustainable Retrofitting of Urban Streets for Mitigation of Traffic Vibration by Means of Anti-vibrating Trenches

Mauro D'Apuzzo[1](✉) [iD], Azzurra Evangelisti[1] [iD], Giuseppe Cappelli[1], and Vittorio Nicolosi[2] [iD]

[1] University of Cassino and Southern Lazio, Via G. Di Biasio 43, 03043 Cassino, Italy
`{dapuzzo,giuseppe.cappelli1}@unicas.it`
[2] University of Rome Tor Vergata, Via del Politecnico 1, 00133 Roma, Italy
`nicolosi@uniroma2.it`

Abstract. Vibrations induced by vehicular traffic are of increasing concern in urban areas, especially because of nuisance issues perceived by inhabitants and possible damage problems experienced by exposed heritage buildings. Among the several countermeasures aiming at reducing the level of vibration at source or at mitigating the propagation of ground-borne vibration through pavement layers and underlying soils, the use of anti-vibrating trenches may offer an interesting solution in mitigating the vibrations caused by heavy vehicle traffic. In this paper, an original vibration prediction numerical model is developed and proposed that may help in the design procedure of such countermeasures. Following an initial calibration of the numerical model and a validation with experimental results derived by technical literature, preliminary findings obtained by making use of different materials and complex trench layouts are briefly presented and reviewed. It is acknowledged that an evaluation in frequency domain may offer an effective tool to retrofit existing urban road exposed to this issue.

Keywords: Road traffic induced vibration · Ground-borne vibration · Anti-vibration trenches

1 Introduction

The environmental impact of transport infrastructures represents a critical issue, especially in urban areas [1–4, 31]. Among different vehicular impacts (noise, air pollution, etc.) vibrations induced by road traffic have recently gained wider attention. It is worth to notice that traffic vibrations may be divided into two main types: air-borne and ground-borne vibrations. These latter are characterized by lower frequency content (0–20 Hz) and are produced by dynamic overloads transmitted to the pavement surface by heavy vehicles. Therefore, ground-borne vibrations propagating through road superstructure and underlying soils up to the foundation level finally reach the structural elements of the buildings close to the street. These type of vibrations are often claimed to be responsible for severe nuisance to building occupants and for minor structural damage in historical buildings [1, 5].

© The Author(s), under exclusive license to Springer Nature Switzerland AG 2023
O. Gervasi et al. (Eds.): ICCSA 2023 Workshops, LNCS 14111, pp. 179–193, 2023.
https://doi.org/10.1007/978-3-031-37126-4_13

The problem is usually divided into three main phases: a generation phase due to the dynamic interaction between vehicle and the roughness of road profile, a propagation phase of vibrations through the road superstructure and, subsequently, through the underlying soils up to the foundations and to the structures of adjacent buildings and, finally, a reception phase regarding the sensitivity of building occupants and dynamic response of building elements.

The study of the problem seems to be extremely complex: the generation phase implies knowledge of mechanical engineering as far as the vehicle model is concerned, whereas the highway engineering expertise is required for road profile representation; furthermore, the propagation phase implies knowledge of geotechnical engineering, as far as dynamic behavior of soils is concerned, and, finally in the reception phase, structural dynamics is the main topic involved. For these reasons, there are few studies in the literature where the problem has been addressed as a whole. Up to now, the approach followed in order to tackle the problem has often been mainly experimental or theoretical.

An in-depth experimental study [6–9] on ground-borne traffic induced vibrations has been carried out at Transport and Road Research Laboratory, (now Transport Research Laboratory, TRL) in UK within the past thirty years. It has been observed that a strong link exists between heavy vehicle traffic, vehicle speed and height of localized surface irregularities (humps). In Italy, few experiments have been recently conducted on traffic induced vibrations and most of them were aimed at evaluating possible damaging effects for heritage buildings [1, 5, 10].

Prediction models for traffic vibration level, can be broadly divided into two groups: empirical and semi-empirical ones, on one hand, and analytical and numerical ones, on the other. Among the former ones, the most noticeable appears to be that developed by TRL, where an estimate of the vertical Peak Particle Velocity (PPV) vibration induced at the foundation level when an heavy vehicle is moving over a localized unevenness is proposed. The formula takes into account the maximum height or depth of a singular surface irregularity (hump) over which the heavy vehicle transits, the speed of the vehicle, the type of road surface, soil properties and the distance between the unevenness and the building foundation [11, 12]. This model has been modified in order to take into account longitudinally distributed road surface irregularity [1].

Empirical and semi-empirical models, due to their simplifying assumptions, cannot take into consideration all the factors involved in the phenomenon, therefore more refined analytical and numerical prediction models have been developed. An analytical model that allows to evaluate the vertical vibration level (vertical displacement, velocity or acceleration) in terms of Power Spectral Density (PSD) function, at an arbitrary distance from the road has proposed by H. M. Hunt [13]. Different authors have developed prediction models employing a Finite Element Method (FEM) approach in order to study the propagation through the road pavement and through underlying soils [14]. It is also worth to mention a recent analytical model developed by Lombaert et al. [15] that allows to evaluate the vibration level, expressed in terms of PSD or frequency spectrum, produced by an half-car model that is interacting with a stochastic (PSD) or a deterministic road profile, and is moving on a visco-elastic layered medium.

1.1 Vibration Mitigation Countermeasures

Basing on the previous phenomenological description, several countermeasures aimed at mitigating the vibration can be employed and accordingly grouped:

- *generation related countermeasures* where factors affecting the dynamic interaction between vehicle and pavement are addressed; typical example of such measures are traffic restrictions (as far as heavy vehicles and limit travel speed are concerned) or pavement surface smoothing (by improving maintenance by means of frequent resurfacing and re-shaping interventions);
- *propagation related countermeasures* where vibration waves are usually intercepted at pavement level or in the underlying soils or finally at building foundation level; in this case feasible solutions may be anti-vibrating pavement, anti-vibrating trenches or building base isolation respectively.

As regards this latter family of measures, anti-vibrating pavements may represent an effective solution to mitigate the vibration level [16] but, on the other hand, they appear more invasive and time-consuming if traffic disruptions related to roadworks are concerned. Building base isolation is a well-known solution derived from earthquake engineering but it is rather expensive and therefore cannot be systematically implemented along a continuous building façade facing the road. In this connection, the use of anti-vibrating trenches may offer a more feasible and somehow affordable solution to tackle the problem.

As a matter of fact, the use of trenches for vibration screening has been the subject of several research efforts in the past fifty years. Most relevant pioneering work has been presented by Barkan and by Woods that evaluated the effectiveness of some trench layout by means of an experimental campaign with surface harmonic vibration source [17, 18]. Later on, Haupt presented major contributions by means of an extensive numerical sensitivity analysis by a FEM approach thus providing a more comprehensive theoretical background for the operational aspects of these kind of trenches [19, 20]. More recently, several remarkable works employing a combined 2D FEM-BEM (Boundary Element Method) approach [21–23] has provided more insight in the behavior of open or filled trenches whereas the recent use of geofoam polyurethane based products as filling material has been investigated and appears promising [24–27].

However, it seems that till now no enough effort has been devoted in analyzing the performance of finite trenches or in evaluating the effectiveness of more complex geometric layouts other than a continuous plane screen or pile walls.

To this purpose, following a preliminary calibration and experimental validation an innovative 3D FEM model has been developed in order to evaluate mitigation performance of this latter trench layout in near-field conditions typically encountered in a urban environment.

The novelty of the proposed approach lies in:

- the use of a simple FEM model to simulate the vibration propagation in the near field conditions instead of an hybrid BEM-FEM approach that is not so widespread diffused in the technical community;
- the numerical validation of the FEM model with closed-form analytical solutions that can guarantee a better mathematical reliability of the proposed modeling approach

- the experimental validation of the FEM model with field data collected on different soils and derived from scientific literature;
- the ability to implement complex trench layout that could be designed in a tailoring way for the specific intervention site.

2 Modelling Vibration Propagation

2.1 Basic Assumptions

As far as the modeling of traffic induced vibrations is concerned, an important assumption that has been widely accepted is that the dynamic coupling between vehicle and road superstructures can be neglected, since mass and stiffness of pavement involved in the vibration phenomenon are much larger than those pertaining the heavy vehicles. Therefore, the problem can be split into two steps: 1) evaluation of dynamic overloads and 2) application of dynamic forces to the pavement surface. Accordingly, the prediction model is divided into two sub-models described in the followings.

Vibrations originated by dynamics loads propagate through the various pavement layers and to subgrade soils and finally reach the foundations of the sensitive structures close to the road. In order to mathematically simulate the phenomenon, the dynamic response (in terms of displacement, velocity or acceleration) for a point located at a defined distance from a vertical pulsating force acting on the surface of a medium (within which the phenomenon can still be considered relevant) has to be evaluated.

When the geometrical layout of this medium is not complex, such as for simple or multi-layered half-space, approximated analytical solutions are available [13, 28]. When finite pavement cross-sections or trenches are present, the geometrical layout is more complex, and a Finite Element Method (FEM) approach has to be used.

2.2 FEM Propagation Model Description and Calibration

The development of a FEM model aimed at simulating vibration wave propagation, implies a major drawback that is related to the correct modeling of boundary conditions. Since the medium modeled is inherently finite, vibration waves impacting to boundary surfaces may be reflected and propagate back to the source. This may dramatically alter the dynamic response evaluated at a defined point, since in the real conditions, vibration waves are not reflected but propagate to the infinite and, moreover, they undergo to an attenuation due to the well-known "radiation damping" effect. In order to correctly simulate this aspect, very complex boundary conditions have been developed by several authors [14, 29] or Finite Element Method combined with Boundary Element Method approaches have been used [21–23].

In this study, the propagation phenomenon has been simulated by a transmission sub-model, that employs a FEM technique. The novel feature of this approach is that nor particular boundary conditions neither BEM elements have been used. This allows to virtually implement the propagation simulation on every commercially available general purpose FEM code. As a matter of fact, the vibration waves directed to the external surfaces of the finite medium are progressively attenuated within a damping zone [16, 30] that envelopes the whole finite medium. Material properties of the damping zone are equal to those of the adjoining medium, except the damping coefficient. This latter varies according to a quadratic law with initial null tangent when going far away from the vibrating source.

In FEM models, the simulation of wave propagation in viscoelastic solids is usually tackled through a a step by step dynamic analysis. This procedure has proven to reproduce transient phenomena in the dynamic response more effectively than a natural frequency analysis performed by means of an Eigenvalue extraction. The equilibrium equations of a discretized model can be written in matrix form. In order to obtain the time history response of each node in the model a step by step integration in the time domain has to be performed. By assuming that equations of motion describing the problem are satisfied at discrete time points within the solution time interval and by postulating the variation of displacement, velocity and acceleration within the time increment, Δt, several direct integration schemes possessing different accuracy and stability properties have been proposed. Within the numerical simulation performed, an implicit direct integration scheme has been adopted since it can be demonstrated that this computational procedure is unconditionally stable with respect to the time increment value, Δt.

In order to verify the effectiveness of the FEM model in describing wave propagation phenomenon, a comparison has been made with results provided by an equivalent analytical solution. According to [13], within the frequency domain, the dynamic vertical displacement in far field conditions, at a defined distance from a vertical pulsating force acting on the surface of a viscoelastic half-space, can be synthetically expressed through the following expression:

$$H_z(r, \omega) = \left(\frac{\omega K}{2\rho \, c_R^3} \right) \cdot e^{\left(-\frac{D\omega^2 r}{2c_R} \right)} \cdot H_0^{(2)} \left(\frac{\omega r}{c_R} \right) \tag{1}$$

where r is the distance from the pulsating point force, ω is the circular frequency, K is a function that depends on Poisson's Ratio of the material, ρ is the material density, c_R is the velocity of Rayleigh surface waves, D is the damping coefficient, $H_0^{(2)}$ is the second type Hankel function of zero order.

As far as the FEM model by means of a General Purpose FEM Simulation Tool (LUSAS™) is concerned, an axisymmetric model has been developed and characteristic element dimension and therefore optimal mesh discretization can be derived when material properties (density and Young modulus) and maximum frequency of interest are known. As a matter of fact, if the relationship:

$$v = \lambda \cdot f \tag{2}$$

that ties wave velocity, v (that, for viscoelastic solids, depends only on material properties), with wavelength, λ, and frequency, f, is taken into account, by fixing the wave speed and the maximum frequency of interest, the minimum wavelength and thus the minimum element dimension (at least, equal to $\lambda/4$) is determined, in order to correctly simulate the wave propagation phenomenon. In the following figure, a comparison between the dynamic vertical displacement in the frequency domain provided by the expression (1) and those derived from numerical FEM model (the first one with uniform, not optimized, discretization and the second one with an optimized mesh) is presented. As it can be easily observed, there seems to be a reasonable agreement between the analytical and the numerical FEM frequency response functions, even with a very low number of elements provided that a suitable mesh transition bands have been conveniently placed in the model in order to reduce the overall amount of elements (Fig. 1).

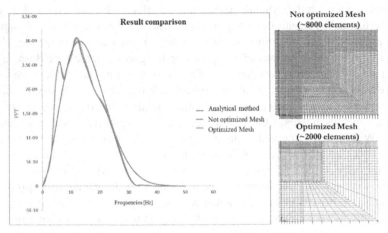

Fig. 1. Comparison in the frequency domain between the analytical and the numerical FEM dynamic response.

2.3   Experimental Validation of the Vibration Propagation Numerical Prediction Model

Following these results, an attempt to experimentally validate the simulation model with field data reported in an experimental study on traffic induced vibration carried out in UK [11, 12] has been performed. To this purpose, data on soil properties, on road superstructure and pulse loads by means of a Falling Weight Deflectometer (FWD, namely a Dyntest 8000 model with a peak loading of 60–70 KN and a sampling window of about 60 ms), have been collected and implemented in the simulation model.

Experimental frequency response functions (FRF) have been derived at various distance from the vertical pulse force. FRF Modulus of surface vertical vibration velocity measured at 12 Hz for increasing distance has been compared with that provided by FEM model where a visco-elastic material behaviour has been assumed. In detail, elastic behaviour is described by the Young Modulus and Poisson Ratio. Viscous behaviour has been taken into account by means of a Rayleigh damping parameters (stiffness and mass proportional) that have been calibrated in order to approximate the real damping properties (viscous, hysteretic or mixed) of the specific material examined [16, 30].

A sample of the results of comparison are conveniently reported in the following figure. As it can be seen, agreement between experimental and numerical dynamic response seems acceptable thus demonstrating the soundness of the FEM modelling developed (Fig. 2).

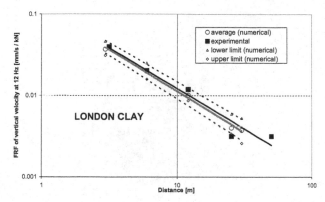

Fig. 2. Comparison between experimental and theoretical 12 Hz FRF for a FWD test performed on a London Clay soil in [11, 12] and compared in [30].

3 Analysis of Results

Basing on the aforementioned results, a new 3D numerical model has been developed in order to study the screening effectiveness of several type of trenches' layouts filled with geofoam.

The use of 3D modelling is related to the need of investigating different layouts (such as finite and infinite trenches or trenches with specific and complex shapes) and different relative positions for vibration source and for the receiver that cannot be accurately captured by a 2D modeling approach. However, it has to be acknowledged that a 3D propagation numerical model requires a dramatically higher computational effort.

Basing on these premises, an overall 20 x 20 x 20 m long study area was chosen to evaluate the trench mitigation effectiveness. As previously highlighted, the size of the study area is consistent with near-field behavior that it is intended to be investigated since in urban areas distance between the vibration source and the receiver is often very low.

Similarly to what carried out in the 2D modelling, a surrounding damping volume that is wrapping the study area has been conveniently considered in order to simulate far field restraining conditions. Furthermore, dual orthogonal symmetry conditions were exploited to represent a much wider area (as a matter of fact, the actual size of the FEM model corresponds to one fourth of the real investigated area). By making use of the calibration results obtained from the aforementioned axisymmetric propagation model, it was possible to reduce the overall amount of solid elements from nearly 180000 to about 55000, thus yielding a substantial reduction of computational time. In the following figures a general view of the 3D model and a plan view where the position of the vibration source and of several receiver points for a infinite (continuous) and finite trenches are reported (Figs. 3 and 4).

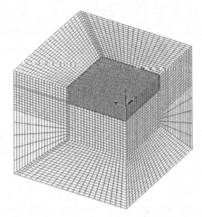

Fig. 3. A general view of the 3D FEM propagation model developed (nearly 55000 solids elements).

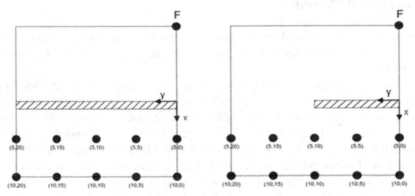

Fig. 4. A schematic plan view of the position of vibration source (point F), position and layout of trench and receiver's position for an infinite (on the left) and finite (on the right) trench.

3.1 Results from Numerical Simulations

By applying a pulse load, it was possible to obtain the frequency response function for a specific receiver located behind the trench. This information appears to be more useful if the screening effectiveness of a specific trench layout placed on a defined terrain throughout the frequency domain has to be investigated, especially if vehicular traffic ground-borne vibrations can be regarded as a narrow band frequency phenomenon.

In this regard, an attenuation parameter expressing the trench performance can be defined as:

$$Attenuation = \frac{Response\ in\ the\ frequency\ domain\ with\ trench}{Response\ in\ the\ frequency\ domain\ without\ trench} \quad (3)$$

As far as the numerical simulation are concerned, particle vibration vertical velocity was assumed as reference frequency response parameter. Geofoam material (two-component Polyurethane lightweight material) properties were derived from [24–27] whereas a common sand soil was considered with a Young Modulus of about 300 MPa, Poisson Ratio of 0,35 and Density of 1800 kg/m^3.

Attenuation has been evaluated throughout the frequency domain for a receiver located behind the trench at 5 and 10 m far away from the trench itself. The vibration source is positioned at 10 m far away from the trench. A continuous layout has been considered and two different trenches depth (namely H = 10 and 20 m) have been examined. Results have been summarized in the following figure (Fig. 5).

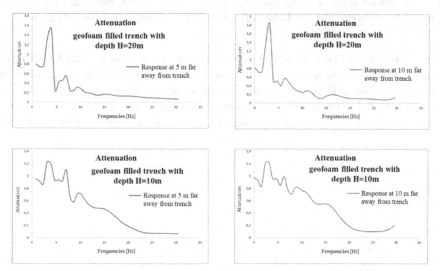

Fig. 5. Influence on attenuation in frequency domain of trenches with different depth and receiver's position behind the trench.

As it can be observed, deeper trench may offer a more effective mitigation of vibration with respect to shallow ones as also reported in scientific literature [17–23]. It is also worth to be noticed that attenuation is not always effective within the investigated frequency range. As a matter of fact, even for trenches filled with geofoam (soft) materials a clear resonance peak can be detected in the 2–3 Hz range thus arising some cautions on the design of this countermeasure as far as the predominant frequency content of the vibration source is concerned.

Another interesting aspect that can be tackled by means of a numerical FEM 3D modelling is the evaluation of vibration mitigation in case of complex geometric trench layout. In this connection, the effectiveness in attenuation has been investigated by comparing the performance provided by a conventional (infinite) trench and variable (depth-dependent) porosity trench that are depicted below (Fig. 6).

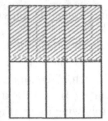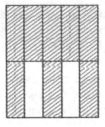

Fig. 6. Schematics of the examined different trench geometric layout. Front view for a conventional trench (on the left) and a variable (depth-dependent) porosity trench (on the right).

In the following figure the attenuation is reported for receivers located at different distance from the trench. As it can be observed for the specific investigated scenario, the performance of variable porosity trench is even somehow better in the first resonance peak only to slightly worsen at higher frequencies thus suggesting that the trench complex layouts may offer more "tailored" solutions apart from trivial economic benefits (Fig. 7).

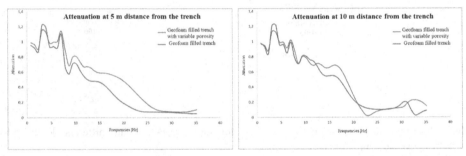

Fig. 7. Performance comparison between conventional geofoam filled trench and variable porosity geofoam filled trench.

Basing on the evaluation of the *Average Attenuation* within a defined frequency range, *Trench Efficiency, TE,* may be defined as:

$$Trench\,Efficiency = 1 - Average\,Attenuation \tag{4}$$

In the following figure the comparison between an infinite and a finite trench is conveniently reported in terms of *Trench Efficiency* for different receiver positions that progressively move away from the vibration source. As it can be easily highlighted, efficiency generally decreases going far away from the trench and from the vibration source. However, 3D modelling seems able to capture the typical "*shadow zone effect*" provided by finite (in terms of plan view layout) trenches with respect to the continuous (infinite) ones (Fig. 8).

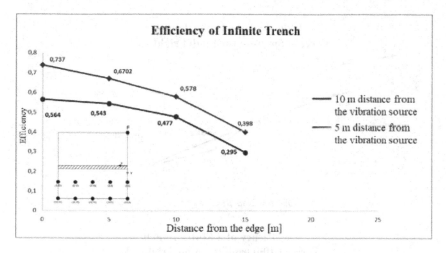

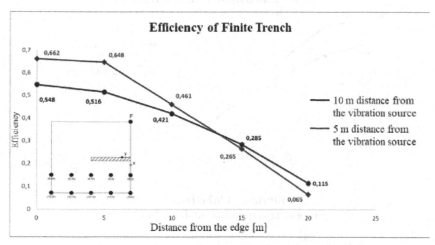

Fig. 8. Trench efficiency comparison between infinite (above) and finite (below) trench. A plan view of the investigated schemes is also reported for sake of clarity.

4 Discussions

It seems to be worth to mention that the 3D modelling approach employed may allow a more realistic modelling of the phenomenology related to vehicular traffic induced vibrations.

As a matter of fact, as far as ground-borne vibration induced by vehicular traffic is concerned, it has to be acknowledged that the vibration source is inherently moving with respect to the receiver position.

Furthermore, it has to be highlighted that as far as road traffic vibration is concerned, because of the low vehicle speed compared with relevant vibration wave speed (in such case Rayleigh waves are predominant [6]), the system can be regarded as dynamically

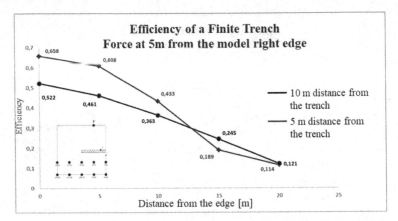

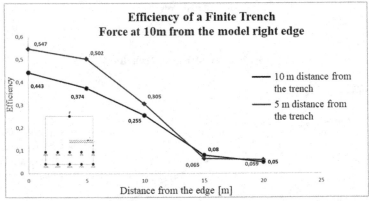

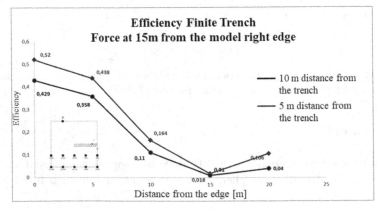

Fig. 9. Trench efficiency comparison of finite trench for different relative vibration source position. A plan view of the investigated schemes is also reported for sake of clarity.

uncoupled and therefore the moving vibration source can be modelled as nearly quasi-static.

It can be therefore relevant to study the performance of a finite trench with respect to different vibration source position. This task can be easily accomplished by making use of a typical hemi-symmetric scheme and of the effect superposition principle because of the linear mechanical behavior of involved materials. Basing on these premises, it has been possible to study the efficiency of finite trenches for different position of vibration source travelling along the road alignment. Results are conveniently depicted in the following figure where again the "*shadow zone effect*" can again be found i.e. the efficiency of the Finite Trench drops when the receiver is directly exposed to the vibration source whereas significantly increased when the receiver point is located just behind the anti-vibrating screen.

These results that seem consistent with those provided by main scientific literature [17–27] may offer an interesting starting point to develop more simplified phenomenological-based predictions tools to evaluate efficiency of specific finite trench in terms of filling material geometrical layouts and on site soil conditions (Fig. 9).

5   Conclusions

In this paper, following a review of scientific literature on ground-borne vibration induced by road traffic, a new 3D numerical model has been developed in order to study the vibration screening effectiveness of several type of trenches layouts filled with geofoam to be employed in an urban environment.

The use of 3D modelling is related to the need of investigating different layouts (such as finite and infinite trenches or trenches with specific and complex geometries) and different relative positions for vibration source and for the receiver that cannot be accurately captured by a 2D modeling approach. Due to the required higher computational effort, a preliminary mesh optimization has been performed. Preliminary results obtained with a sand soil seem to highlight that:

- geofoam filled trenches may offer a valid solution in mitigating traffic vibrations;
- theoretical numerical model should be carefully developed and calibrated in order to help designer in evaluating the effectiveness of specific solutions;
- although deeper trenches are more effective than shallow ones, the attenuation is not uniform within the investigated frequency range due to trench material and soil resonance/impedance phenomena;
- variable depth porosity trenches appear more beneficial at lower frequencies;
- for finite (in plan) trenches, the developed model seems to adequately capture the "*shadow zone effect*" in attenuation for different position receivers behind the trench or by moving vibration sources.

The novelty of the proposed approach may be of interest for future research because of:

- the use of a simple FEM model to simulate the vibration propagation in the near field conditions instead of a hybrid BEM-FEM approach that is not so widespread diffused in the technical community;

- the numerical validation of the FEM model with closed-form analytical solutions that can guarantee a better mathematical reliability of the proposed modeling approach
- the experimental validation of the FEM model with field data collected on different soils and derived from scientific literature;
- the ability to implement complex trench layout that could be designed in a tailoring way for the specific intervention site.

However, additional simulations have to be undertaken in order to highlight the performance with soils other than that specifically examined (both in terms of material properties and in terms of geometrical layout such as *layered* soils). Furthermore, it is worth to observe that an experimental validation with test trials would be beneficial in assessing the effectiveness of such mitigation solutions.

Acknowledgements. This study was carried out within the MOST – Sustainable Mobility Center and received funding from the European Union Next-GenerationEU (PIANO NAZIONALE DI RIPRESA E RESILIENZA (PNRR) – MISSIONE 4 COMPONENTE 2, INVESTIMENTO 1.4 – D.D. 1033 17/06/2022, CN00000023). The research leading to these results has also received funding by Project "Ecosistema dell'innovazione Rome Technopole" financed by EU in NextGenerationEU plan through MUR Decree n. 1051 23.06.2022 - CUP H33C22000420001.

This manuscript reflects only the authors' views and opinions, neither the European Union nor the European Commission can be considered responsible for them.

References

1. Crispino, M., D'Apuzzo, M.: Measurement and prediction of traffic induced vibrations on a heritage building. J. Sound Vib. **246**(2), 319–335 (2001)
2. D'Apuzzo, M., Aiello, V., Boiero, D., Socco, L.V., Silvestri, F.: Experimental and numerical analysis of vibrations induced by underground trains in urban environment. Structural Control & Health Monitoring **15**(3), 315–348. Elsevier (2008)
3. D'Apuzzo, M., Nicolosi, V., Bogazzi, E.: A Unified Approach for the Prediction of Vibration Induced by Underground Metro. In: D'Andrea, A. (ed.) PROCEEDINGS OF SIIV 2012, in PROCEDIA: SOCIAL & BEHAVIORAL SCIENCES **53**, 62–71. Elsevier (2012)
4. D'Apuzzo, M., Esposito, M., Festa, B., Nicolosi, V.: Modelling Vibrations Induced By Underground Railways in Urban Areas. In: International Conference on Traffic and Transport Engineering, pp. 290–296. City Net Scientific Research Center Ltd. Belgrade, Serbia (2014)
5. D'Apuzzo, M., Antonucci, G., Costanzo, R., Crispino, M., Lamberti, R.: Road traffic induced vibration: a field investigation in the city of naples. In: Pereira, P., Miranda, V. (eds.) Proceedings Of International Symposium On Environmental Impact of Road Pavement Uneven-Ness, pp. 177–192. Porto (1999)
6. Whiffin, A.C., Leonard, D.R.: A survey of traffic-induced vibrations, Transport and Road Research Laboratory, LR 418, Crowthorne, pp. 1–53 (1971)
7. Watts, G.R.: Traffic-induced ground-borne vibrations in dwellings, Transport and Road Research Laboratory, RR102, Crowthorne, pp. 1–17 (1987)
8. Watts, G.R.: Case studies of the effects of traffic induced vibrations on heritage buildings, Transport and Road Research Laboratory, RR 156, Crowthorne, pp. 1–22 (1988)
9. Watts, G.R.: The effects of traffic induced vibrations on heritage buildings –further case studies, Transport and Road Research Laboratory, RR 207, Crowthorne, pp. 1–45 (1989)

10. Clemente, P., Rinaldis, D.: Protection of monumental buiding against traffic-induced vibrations. Soil Dynamics and Earthquake Engineering, Elsevier Science **17**, 289–296 (1998)
11. Watts, G.R.: Traffic induced vibrations in buildings, Transport and Road Research Laboratory, RR 246, Crowthorne, pp. 1–31 (1990)
12. Watts, G.R.: The generation and propagation of vibration in various soils, produced by the dynamic loading of road pavements. J. Sound Vib. **156**(2), 191–206 (1992)
13. Hunt, H.E.M.: Stochastic modelling of traffic-induced ground vibration. Journal of Sound and Vibration 144, 53–70. Academic Press (1991)
14. Hanazato, T., Ugai, K., Mori, M., Sakaguchi, R.: Three dimensional analysis of induced traffic vibrations. Journal of Geotechnical Engineering 117(8), ASCE, 1133–1151 (1991)
15. Lombaert, G., Degrande, G., Clouteau, D.: Numerical modelling of free field traffic-induced vibrations. Soil Dyn. Earthq. Eng. **19**, 473–488 (1998)
16. D'Apuzzo, M., Nicolosi, V.: Evaluation of pavement-oriented countermeasures to mitigate traffic induced vibrations in urban areas. In: Ianniello, C. (ed.) Proceedings of 5th European Conference on Noise Control, Euronoise 2003, 19–21 May, Naples, 1–7 (2003)
17. Barkan, D.: Dynamics of bases and foundations. McGraw Hill Book, New York (1962)
18. Woods, R.D.: Screening of surface waves in soil. Journal of Soil Mechanics and Foundation Engineering ASCE **94**(SM4), 951–979 (1968)
19. Haupt, W.A.: Surface-waves in non-homogeneus halfspace, Proceedings of DMSR 77/5 Vol. 1, 16 (1977)
20. Haupt, W.A.: Model tests on screening of surface waves. In: Proceedings of the Tenth International Conference on Soil Mechanics and Foundation Engineering, vol. 3, pp. 215–22. Stockholm (1981)
21. Beskos, D.E., Dasgupta, B., Vardoulakis, I.G.: Vibration isolation using open or filled trenches, part 1: 2-D homogeneous soil. Comput. Mech. **1**(1), 43–63 (1986)
22. Beskos, D.E., Dasgupta, B., Vardoulakis, I.G.: Vibration isolation using open or filled trenches, part 2: 3-D homogeneous soil. Comput. Mech. **6**(2), 129–142 (1990)
23. Ahmad, S., Al-Hussaini, T.M.: Simplified design for vibration screening by open and in-filled trenches. ASCE Journal of Geotechnical Engineering **117**(1), 67–88 (1991)
24. Wang, Z.L., Li, Y.C., Wang, J.G.: Numerical analysis of attenuation effect of EPS geofoam on stress-waves in civil defense engineering. Geotext. Geomembr. **24**, 265–273 (2006)
25. Murillo, C., Thorel, L., Caicedo, B.: Ground vibration isolation with geofoam barriers: Centrifuge modeling. Geotext. Geomembr. **27**, 423–434 (2009)
26. Alzawi, A., Hesham El Naggar, M.: Full scale experimental study on vibration scattering using open and in-filled (GeoFoam) wave barriers. Soil Dynamics and Earthquake Engineering **31**, 306–317 (2011)
27. Bose, T., Choudhury, D., Sprengel, J., Ziegler, M.: Efficiency of Open and Infill Trenches in Mitigating Ground-Borne Vibrations. Journal of Geotechnical and Geo-environmental Engineering **144**(8), 1–11 (2018)
28. Auersh, L.: Wave propagation in layered soils: theoretical solution in wavenumber domain and experimental results of hammer and railway traffic excitation. Journal of Sound and Vibrations **173**(2), 233–264 (1994)
29. Wolf, J.P., Song, C.: Some cornerstones of dynamic soil–structure interaction. Eng. Struct. **24**, 13–281 (2002)
30. D'Apuzzo, M.: Some remarks on the prediction of road traffic induced ground-borne vibrations. In: Proceedings of International SIIV Congress SIIV 2007, 1, pp. 1–13, Grafill S.r.l., Palermo, Italy (2007)
31. Coni, M., Murgia, R., Rassu, N., Maltinti, F.: Study on Vibrations Produced by New City Rail of Cagliari. In: Gervasi, O., et al. (eds.) ICCSA 2021. LNCS, vol. 12956, pp. 580–594. Springer, Cham (2021). https://doi.org/10.1007/978-3-030-87010-2_43

Some Remarks on Automatic Braking System Related to Pedestrian Safety

Mauro D'Apuzzo[1]([✉]) [iD], Azzurra Evangelisti[1] [iD], Giuseppe Cappelli[1,2],
Sofia Nardoianni[1], and Vittorio Nicolosi[3]

[1] University of Cassino and Southern Lazio, Via G. Di Biasio 43, 03043 Cassino, Italy
{dapuzzo,giuseppe.cappelli1,sofia.nardoianni}@unicas.it
[2] University School for Advanced Studies, IUSS, Piazza della Vittoria n.15, 27100 Pavia, Italy
giuseppe.cappelli@iusspavia.it
[3] University of Rome "Tor Vergata" Via del Politecnico, 1, 00133 Rome, Italy

Abstract. Collision avoidance systems (CAS) have greatly increased in automotive market since they have proven to be effective in reducing head-on crashes. An interesting application of these system has been used in pedestrian safety by means of automatic braking systems. The key operating parameter for these advanced emergency braking system is based on the Time-To-Collision (TTC) concept that, in turn, it is strongly affected by the actuated overall mean deceleration that on dry pavement surface is about 8 to 10 m/s2. However, since the corresponding stopping distance is mainly influenced by tire-road friction level, on wet pavement surfaces much lower deceleration values can be reached thus implying a dramatic recalibration of decision rules governing the operating conditions of the system. In this paper a methodology to evaluate the mean deceleration useful to estimate optimal TTC values on wet pavement surface is presented as far as an advanced emergency braking system designed to reduce the risk in pedestrian vehicle crashes is concerned. By making use of a correlation model between pavement surface characteristics and tire performance, this latter expressed by means of a conventional tire labeling value, according to current EU legislations, stopping distance and corresponding mean deceleration value can be derived on a stochastic basis. An example application is finally presented to illustrate the methodology developed.

Keywords: CAS · TTC · friction coefficient · braking · tire labeling

1 Introduction

Nowadays there is a great demand for intelligent transport systems (ITS) by car companies. ITS systems include driver assistance systems (ADAS) [1] that aim to increase safety and facilitate driving. These systems have allowed a marked decrease in accidents and injuries as they help drivers to distinguish between safe and unsafe driving situations. ITS on-board systems, most of which are mandatory on newly approved vehicles (from city cars to the most luxurious sedans, trucks and buses), are impacting a wide range of operating driving scenarios.

© The Author(s), under exclusive license to Springer Nature Switzerland AG 2023
O. Gervasi et al. (Eds.): ICCSA 2023 Workshops, LNCS 14111, pp. 194–209, 2023.
https://doi.org/10.1007/978-3-031-37126-4_14

Indeed, modern cars are equipped with different vehicle dynamics stability control systems. These systems regulate the forces transmitted to the tire that depend on the tire-road slip ratio. Among the numerous control systems for driving dynamics and driving safety are tire slip control systems such as Anti-Braking System (ABS) and Traction Control System (TCS) or Anti-Skid Control (ASC).

Anti-lock systems (ABS) aim to reduce the loss of friction caused by sliding; therefore, they prevent the locking of the wheels in case of sudden stop on slippery surfaces, thanks to the presence of sensors positioned on the single wheels that "interact" with an electronic control unit. This calculates the rotation speed of each wheel and, if the control unit detects the locking of one or more wheels during braking, it intervenes on the hydraulic pump to decrease the braking force. In a sudden braking, therefore, the driver will only have to worry about pressing the brake pedal without having to think about the possible locking of the wheels.

On the other hand, as far as Traction Control System (TCS) is concerned, this system intervenes on engine power and on the ignition system to reduce power if a drive wheel starts to spinning significantly faster than another.

The Anti-Skid Control (ASC), on the other hand, maintains the rotation of the drive wheel within the optimum range during acceleration, even on slippery surfaces. Regardless of the strength with which the driver presses the accelerator pedal, the ASC system intervenes on the power of the engine and on the brakes controls the acceleration of the car as efficiently as possible, ensuring that none of the drive wheels travel too far.

Other systems help to avoid accidents by alerting drivers of a potential collision and sometimes initiating a braking response. For example, these technologies include Forward Collision Warning (FCW), also known as "Safe Braking", "Collision Warning with Automatic Braking", "Pre-crash Warning Systems", "Collision Mitigation Braking System", "Predictive Warning "collision"", etc. These systems combine sensors and brake controls and warn the driver in the event of an imminent collision with a visual/audible signal. The operation varies depending on the method used to detect collisions and how the vehicle is ready to stop or for a collision after an alarm is activated Alarm systems use radar, a laser, or a camera to detect previous vehicles. Braking assistance usually works in conjunction with *Anti-Lock Braking Systems (ABS)* to make braking more effective by avoiding the locking of the wheels. These are classified into two categories: electronic and mechanical, the difference is due to the method used to distinguish the "failure of panic" from normal braking, in fact, electronic brake assistance systems use an *Electronic Control Unit (ECU)* that compares the braking cases with pre-established thresholds. For example, if a driver pushes the brake hard enough and fast enough to cross the threshold, the ECU will determine that there is an emergency and increase braking power. While mechanical systems are found in older vehicles and use, as in the previous case, pre-established thresholds, but are not adaptable to individual drivers. That is, locking occurs when the valve stroke, which is related to the brake pedal push, passes to a critical point and exceeds the threshold, so the locking mechanism then provides braking assistance.

A key factor in the design of such systems is *Time-To-Collision* (TTC) [3]. Hayward (1972) [4] defined it as: *"The time required for two vehicles to collide if they continue at their speed and on the same path"*.

An analysis of the literature shows that the TTC has a maximum value of 4 s [5] and allows to distinguish situations of safety and discomfort. The most recurrent formulation of the TTC is the following:

$$TTC = t_s - \frac{d \cdot t_s^2}{2V} \tag{1}$$

where t_s is the perception and reaction time, d is the deceleration and V is the initial vehicle speed.

The theory behind the determination of the TTC has been suggested by Burgett et al. (1998) [6] who believes that the alarm criteria can be summarized by considering:

- the leading vehicle that continues to decelerate at the current speed until it stops;
- the following vehicle maintains the same constant speed until the driver responds to the warning by applying the brake.
- the time required for a careless driver to respond to a warning by applying the brake pedal is 1.5 s.
- the following vehicle where the warned driver operates, must brake at a constant deceleration of 0.75 g.
- the minimum distance between vehicles during or after braking is two meters.

Given these premises, it can be observed that the TTC is a function of the vehicle deceleration, d, that, in turn, can be expressed by the following well-known kinematic relationship (according to the assumptions of uniformly accelerated motion) as a function of the Braking Distance, D_b:

$$D_b = \frac{V^2}{2 \cdot d} \tag{2}$$

If the vehicle is physically modelled as a point mass, the Braking Distance, D_b, can be evaluated (by assuming a flat road and neglecting both the vehicle aerodynamic and rolling resistances) by the following expression:

$$D_b = \frac{V^2}{2 \cdot g \cdot f_{long}} \tag{3}$$

where g is the acceleration of gravity and f_{long} is the tire-road friction longitudinal coefficient.

In such hypotheses, by equaling the formulations (2) and (3) the tie between the constant deceleration in braking, d, and tire-road friction longitudinal coefficient, f_{long}, can be easily derived thus providing the evidence that the previously assumed constant deceleration of 0.75 g implies a 0.75 for the tire-road friction longitudinal coefficient that represents a realistic (and perhaps conservative) value for most of dry road surfaces.

However, it can be observed that tire-road friction plays a key role in the evaluation of TTC and therefore some additional remarks are needed on this issue.

The tire/road friction is a complex phenomenon, and it is affected by several factors as: the tire type, pressure, load and operating conditions, tread design, air and road temperature, vehicle velocity, road surface texture, interposed material between tire and ground, etc. It means that the variation of even only one of these factors produces a modification of the friction force.

Meyer and Kummer [7] defined mainly two physical mechanisms responsible for tire/road friction: surface adhesion and bulk hysteresis mechanism. The first one is primarily due to intermolecular bonds between the rubber and the aggregate in the road surface; and the last one can be defined as the energy loss in the rubber deformation when sliding over the aggregate in the road.

The tire/road friction coefficient can be conventionally defined as the ratio between the friction force (longitudinal or transversal) and the normal force which occur within the tire/road contact area.

The most common tire/road friction model used in literature, takes into account that, within the tire-road contact area, during braking or traction operations, the tire deformation and slip occurs. Because of this physical phenomenon, longitudinal friction force and slip coexist, and it is possible to find a relationship between longitudinal friction coefficient μ, and the longitudinal slip rate s, defined as a percentage of the linear speed (v):

$$s = \left(1 - \frac{\omega \cdot r}{V}\right) 100 \tag{4}$$

Where:

   s = longitudinal slip rate (%);
   r = rolling radius of the wheel (m);
   ω = angular velocity of the wheel (rad/s);
   v = linear velocity of the vehicle (m/s).

Following this definition, the absolute value of the slip rate belong to the interval [0, 100]: s = 0 means pure rolling (no sliding) and |s| = 100 indicates full sliding/skidding (see Fig. 1).

The evaluation of the friction coefficient assumes a crucial role for both road managers and tire producers which use different approaches to measure and estimate it. In particular, on the road agency side, a critical issue reflects the fact that in the world, several different measuring devices have been developed to evaluate tire/pavement friction and within the same country, different road management authorities use indifferently one or more of them.

To harmonize different skid measuring devices and methods, since the early 90's an international experiment [8] has been performed by the Permanent International Association of Road Congresses (PIARC). The result of this massive effort has been to identify a common scale, called *International Friction Index (IFI)* useful to convert measured of skid and macrotexture of different devices into the IFI parameter.

Further efforts have been needed to improve and update the harmonization: the standard CEN/TS 13036-2 [9] introduces the *Skid Resistance Index* (SRI) to convert the friction measured by some fixed dynamic devices into a common scale and the Standard ASTM E 1960 [10] disciplines the IFI calculation including new devices.

In particular, according to the Standard ASTM E 1960 [10], the IFI consists of two parameters; F60, which is the harmonized friction value at 60 km/h and Sp, the speed gradient coefficient related to the macrotexture of the tested surface. The IFI parameters are calibrated using the following procedure:

$$IFI = (F60, Sp) \tag{5}$$

Where:

$$Sp = k_a + k_b \cdot TX \tag{6}$$

$$F60 = K_A + K_B \cdot FRS \ \exp\left(\frac{S - 60}{Sp}\right) + K_C \cdot TX \tag{7}$$

Sp = Speed costant (km/h) related to the tested surface characteristics and given in ASTM E 1960 Appendix;

k_a and k_b = constants depending upon the method used to determine the macrotexture;

TX = Macrotexture value (mm).

$F60$ = Friction Number (dimensionless),

K_A, K_B and K_C = calibration constants for a particular device and given in ASTM E 1960 Appendix;

FRS = measure v.ed friction value at slip speed S,

S = slip speed between tire and road surface (km/h).

Instead, on the tire industry side, the friction estimation becomes significant within the tire performance evaluation. For this reason, a different *Wet Grip Index* (*WGI*) has been defined within *Tire Labeling* procedures. In fact, with the aim to harmonize information about wet grip, external rolling noise and fuel consumption, and to assist end-users in tire choice, several regulations have been issued and now are mandatory throughout Europe.

In particular, according to the Regulations (EC) No 1222/2009 [11] and No 228/2011 [12], the *Wet Grip Index* (or *G* as titled in the Regulations), can be evaluated as:

$$WGI(T) = \frac{\left[125 \cdot \frac{\mu_p(T)}{\mu_p(R)} + k_1 \cdot (t - t_0) + k_2 \cdot \left(\frac{\mu_p(R)}{\mu_p(R_0)} - 1\right)\right]}{100} \tag{8}$$

Where:

$\mu_{p(T)}$ = peak braking force coefficients for the candidate tire;

$\mu_{p(R)}$ = the peak braking force coefficients for the reference tire;

t = wet surface temperature (°C);

t_0 = wet surface reference temperature condition (20 °C for normal tires, 10 °C for snow tires).

$\mu_{p(R0)}$ = peak braking force coefficient for the reference tire and surface (= 0.85);

k_1 and k_2 = coefficients for temperature and surface adjustments given in Regulation No 228/2011.

It is important to observe that, according to the regulation and in the ASTM standards [11–13], the most important conditions of the test are: the Standard Reference Test Tyre (SRTT) as reference tire; 180kPa as tire inflation pressure; 547 dN (± 5%) as test static wheel load; 65 ± 2 km/h as test operating speed and 1 mm ± 0,5 mm as water film thickness.

Table 1. Wet Grip Classes [11].

WGIndex	WG class C1 tires
1.55 ≤ WGI	*A*
1,40 ≤ WGI ≤ 1.54	*B*
1,25 ≤ WGI ≤ 1.39	*C*
Empty	*D*
1,10 ≤ WGI ≤ 1.24	*E*
WGI ≤ 1.09	*F*

According to the Regulation [11], a wet grip classification of tires, based on the WGI, has been proposed and summarized in the Table 1.

Previous efforts have be done to define friction prediction models [14, 15] and, in particular, the European project FRICTION was sponsored for developing an on-board system to measure and evaluate tire/road friction [1]. The FRICTION system was based on three parameters as defined:

Friction used = tire/road friction currently used and it is mainly evaluated using standard vehicle based driving dynamics sensors;

Friction Potential = maximum tire/road friction available which is not directly measured.

Friction available = friction gap between potential and used.

These definitions are represented in the Fig. 1.

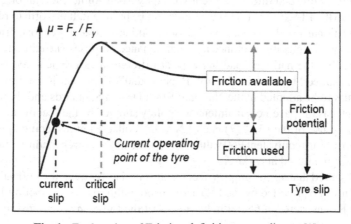

Fig. 1. Explanation of Friction definitions according to [1].

Usually, due to the impossibility of measuring the Potential Friction, the active safety systems contains proprietary algorithms for its estimation, which use indirect methods based on on-board vehicle information (as longitudinal and lateral motions, wheel speed and steering angle, environmental sensors and vehicle to vehicle communication).

Nowadays, different algorithms to estimate the road friction have been proposed, but the knowledge of the maximum available friction value (Potential) and of its reliability is still lacking and however this parameter is of paramount importance for TTC devices design. In this paper a novel methodology to tackle this problem is proposed.

2 Objective

The main aim of this work is to propose a methodology for the estimation of the potential friction value and therefore the corresponding deceleration rate and, at the same time, its variability range, which can be used by the automobile industries for the design of more efficient and safer TTC systems. Relevant novel features of the proposed method are the following:

- the evaluation of the maximum friction value is carried out for road wet condition.
- the corresponding probability density function is derived in order to allow the identification of plausible threshold design;
- the estimation of friction epitomizes the combined actual knowledge level on tire-road friction of the road agencies and tire industries.

3 Methodology

The general framework of the proposed methodology that can be easily decomposed in several calculation step is described in the followings.

The starting point of the methodology is represented by the probability density function of the Friction Number, FN measured by national Road Agencies. FN is intended to be the wet road-tire friction value collected by a friction measuring device (under specific tire and test operating conditions), currently used by Road Authorities, among those that participated to the PIARC Friction Harmonization Experiment. It is worth to remind that almost all National Road Agencies worldwide routinely collect wet road friction data for pavement works quality assurance and maintenance purpose. The amount of friction data collected on the national road network at different measurement speeds helps to define the so called "Friction Evaluation Background", FEB, that is used to define the friction values to be adopted in the National Road Design Standards and therefore each FEB, also reflects the pavement maintenance policy adopted by the specific country [16].

By making use of the (5) – (7) each FN value collected at a specific speed can be easily converted into equivalent F60 value that represents the corresponding International Friction Index measured at 60 km/h.

It has observed that a good empirical correlation exists between the F60 value and the peak friction value provided by the SRTT tire used within the Tire Labeling Procedure, namely $\mu_P(R)$, measured at 65 km/h, by means of the following relationship [17]:

$$\mu_P(R) = 1.3683 \cdot F60^{0.5967} \tag{9}$$

By rearranging (8), once that a specific tire grip class has been specified, it is possible to estimate the peak friction value for a conventional tire of i-class, $\mu_P(Ti)$, by the following formulation:

$$\mu_{p(Ti)} = \frac{\mu_{p(R)}}{125}\left[WGI_i \cdot 100 - k_2\left(\frac{\mu_{p(R)}}{0.85} - 1\right)\right] \tag{10}$$

where WGIi is the Wet Grip Index of i-class, according to Regulations (EC) No 1222/2009 [11] and No 228/2011 [12] and therefore it represents an information that is clearly available for the owner of the vehicle, once that the new tire set has been purchased and mounted on the vehicle itself.

Recalling the (2), the equivalent constant deceleration rate, d, that can be employed in the previous reported TTC formulation can be evaluated as:

$$d = \frac{V^2}{2 \cdot D_b}$$ (11)

where, D_b is the braking distance and V is the initial vehicle speed. However, if the D_b has to be estimated on wet pavement surfaces by means of a point-mass vehicle model, motion resistance forces other than friction cannot be neglected and have to be taken into account. Basing on these premises, it can be easily demonstrated that the *Braking Distance*, D_b, can be calculated by the following relationship:

$$D_b = \int_{V_{ini}}^{0} \frac{V \cdot dV}{g \left[r_r(V) \pm i + \mu_{p(Ti)}(V) + \frac{\rho \cdot C_x \cdot A_f \cdot V^2}{2 \cdot W_v} \right]}$$ (12)

where:
V is the vehicle velocity i.e. the integration variable (m/s),
V_{ini} is the initial vehicle speed (m/s),
g is the acceleration of gravity (m/s^2),
$r_r(V)$ is rolling resistance coefficient (dimensionless) that in most of analytical formulations can be expressed as a function of tire and road surface properties and of vehicle speed itself, V,
i is the road longitudinal slope (dimensionless),
ρ is the air density (kg/m^3),
C_x is the aerodynamic drag coefficient (dimensionless),
A_f is the vehicle frontal area (m^2),
W_v is the weight of the vehicle (kg m/s^2), i.e. the vehicle mass, M, multiplied by the acceleration of gravity, g,
$\mu_{p(Ti)}(V)$, is the peak friction value for a conventional tire of i-class on wet surfaces (dimensionless), according to the tire labeling procedure that is a function of vehicle speed itself, V.

On this latter term, some additional observations are needed.

In the evaluation of Braking Distance, D_b, according to (12), the peak friction values has been employed. The choice of selecting the higher peak friction value that is reached for a critical slip (see Fig. 1) instead of the lower terminal value that is reached in full sliding/skidding condition, is justified by the worldwide diffusion of the anti-lock braking systems (ABS) in nowadays circulating vehicles.

Indeed, it has to be reminded that tire-road friction on wet surface is strongly affected by vehicle speed, V, if all the other influencing factors are keep constant. With vehicle velocity increasing, hydrodynamic pressure at the tire road interface builds up and therefore the detachment between the tire and road surface gradually affects the entire tire footprint area, till tire hydroplaning is reached. This implies a marked diminution of tire-road friction as the vehicle speed increases as evidenced by all previous studies on this matter.

Among the several empirical and analytical models proposed to capture the velocity dependence of sliding friction values on wet road surfaces, the exponential Penn-State model (that also provided the theoretical background for the International PIARC Friction Harmonization Experiment) [8], is the most reliable. Recently this model has also proved to be effective in capturing the velocity dependence of peak friction values on wet surface and therefore the friction term appearing in the (12) can be easily expressed as [18]:

$$\mu_{p(Ti)}(V) = \mu_{p(Ti)0} \cdot e^{-K \cdot V} \tag{13}$$

where

$\mu_{p(Ti)0}$, is the peak friction value at null velocity i.e. when the wheel is stopped ($V = 0$) that is similar to the maximum dry friction value since there is a full contact in the tire footprint area [20],

K is a calibration constant that can be easily derived, once that the peak friction value for a specific vehicle speed is known.

It is worth to be noticed that, basing on these premises, the evaluation of the Braking Distance, D_b, by means of (12) can be tackled only by a numerical approach. However, once that the D_b has been calculated for a specific tire set and vehicle and according to different values of the initial vehicle speed, V_{ini}, in order to speed-up the evaluation of *Braking Distance* an *Equivalent Longitudinal Friction Coefficient*, f_e, can be derived as a function of the initial vehicle speed only, V_{ini}:

$$D_b = \frac{V_{ini}^2}{2g\,(f_e(V_{ini}) \pm i)} \tag{14}$$

where

V_{ini} is the initial vehicle speed (m/s),

g is the acceleration of gravity (m/s^2),

i is the road longitudinal slope (dimensionless),

$f_e(V_{ini})$ is the *Equivalent Longitudinal Friction Coefficient* (dimensionless) that is a function of initial vehicle speed only, V_{ini}, and can be evaluated by means of the following expression:

$$f_e(V_{ini}) = \frac{V_{ini}^2}{2g \cdot D_b} \mp i \tag{15}$$

V_{ini} is the initial vehicle speed, g is the acceleration of gravity, i is the road longitudinal slope and D_b is the *Braking Distance* numerically calculated by the (12).

By equaling (2) and (14), it can be easily observed that a more rigorous estimation of the constant deceleration rate, d, useful for the *TTC* evaluation, can be obtained by the following expression:

$$d = g\,(f_e \pm i) \tag{16}$$

where

   g is the acceleration of gravity (m/s²),

   i is the road longitudinal slope (dimensionless),

   f_e is the *Equivalent Longitudinal Friction Coefficient* (dimensionless) that, recalling all the previously described procedure, is, in turn, dependent on:

- the initial vehicle speed, V_{ini},
- the *Friction Number, FN*, measured on the road surface by national Road Agencies,
- *Wet Grip Index* of i-class, WGI_i, for the tire set mounted on the vehicle,
- the features of the specific vehicle examined, expressed in terms of, weight, rolling resistance, aerodynamic resistance properties.

Therefore, once that a specific vehicle characteristics and *Tire Wet Grip Class* have been defined, a parametric analysis can be performed in order to obtain an f_e estimation according to different values of initial vehicle speed, V_{ini}, and *Friction Number, FN*.

If a reliable regression model can be fitted following the parametric analysis, the probability density function of f_e can be easily derived by a transformation of stochastic variables from the probability distributions of *FN* values, for each specific value of initial vehicle speed, V_{ini}.

In order to demonstrate the effectiveness of the proposed methodology, an application study is reported in the following section.

4 Case Study

To represent a realistic case study, the values used to describe the pavement road features has been chosen as follows: the Texture value (TX) has been supposed constant and equal to MPD = 0.5 mm (which can be considered a plausible and average value for most

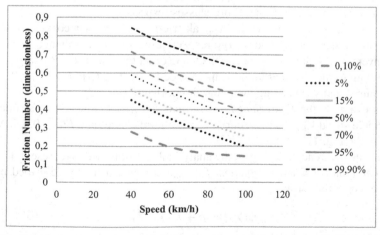

Fig. 2. Friction Evaluation Background, FEB, for Germand Road Network. Skid-resistance vs vehicle speed curves have been depicted according to the several percentiles derived by the statistical analysis of the overall tire-road friction data collected by Road Agencies throught standard tire-road friciton measuring devices [16].

of road pavement) and the Friction Number (FN) has been derived from the probability density curve of real pavement at different speed [16]. A typical FEB representation is depicted in the Fig. 2 for German road network.

For example, by choosing a speed of 60 km/h, and referring to the values indicated in Fig. 2, it is possible to obtain the probability density curve represented in Fig. 3.

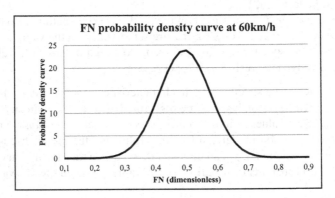

Fig. 3. Probability density curve of FN at 60 km/h extracted by the German FEB.

A set of eleven *FN* has been selected from the curve (from 0.2 to 0.7 with a step of 0.05), by means of the (6) and (7) the relative eleven IFI values have been evaluated and, for each one, the peak friction value μp(R) provided by the SRTT tire, measured at 65 km/h, has been calculated by (9).

Two different tire classes has been chosen among the values presented in the Table 1. The class C and the class E have been selected and the mean value of WGI for each class has been evaluated and used in the application. In particular, 1.32 and 1.17 have been selected as WGI values, for C and E tire classes respectively.

Then, by using the (10), the eleven peak friction values for a conventional tire of both classes, namely, $\mu_{p(TC)}$ and $\mu_{p(TE)}$, respectively have been evaluated.

A conventional sedan car has been selected in order to evaluate the *Braking Distance*, D_b, according to the different initial vehicle speed V_{ini}, Tire Grip Class, *WGI*, and *FN* value by numerically evaluating the integral reported in Eq. (12).

As an example, the *Equivalent Longitudinal Friction Coefficient* as a function of initial vehicle speed $V_{ini}, f_e(V_{ini})$, curves for both tire classes and $FN = 0.5$, have been reported in the Fig. 4.

Observing the trend in the Fig. 4, the analytical function used to represent the *Equivalent Longitudinal Friction Coefficient*, $f_e(V_{ini})$ can be effectively described by a the negative exponential form:

$$f_e(V_{ini} = a + b \cdot e^{cV_{ini}}) \tag{17}$$

Where a, b and c are function of the FN.

In particular two different calibrations, for both tire classes, have been performed and the results have been summarized in the Tables 2 and 3.

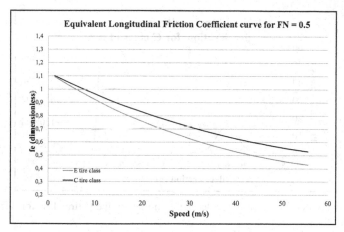

Fig. 4. Equivalent Longitudinal Friction Coefficient vs Initial Vehicle Speed curves for C and E tire classes and FN = 0.5.

Table 2. Calibration Values for C tire class.

Function	Coeff.	Value
$a = A\,FN + B$	A	0,571
	B	0,0045
$b = C\,FN + D$	C	−0,5926
	D	1,1371
$C = cost$	cost	−0,025

Table 3. Calibration Values for E tire class.

Function	Coeff.	Value
$a = A\,FN + B$	A	0,3216
	B	0,059
$b = C\,FN + D$	C	−0,3463
	D	1,0864
$C = cost$	cost	−0,028

Once that f_e formulations have been derived as a function of *FN*, *Tire Grip Class*, *WGI*; and initial vehicle speed, V_{ini}, if the probability density function of *FN* is known, it is possible to perform a transformation of random variables to evaluate the probability density curve of the constant deceleration rate, *d*, (see (16)). Results obtained for a flat road (longitudinal slope, *i,* = 0), at four different initial vehicle speed values have been summarized in the following figures.

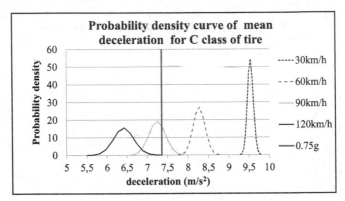

Fig. 5. Probability density curve of the deceleration rate for the C tire class for different initial vehicle speed values.

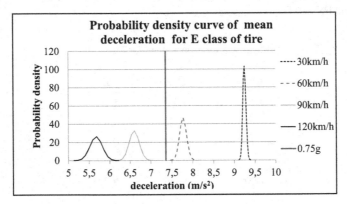

Fig. 6. Probability density curve of the deceleration rate for the E tire class. for different initial vehicle speed values.

It is worth to underline by observing these results that the constant deceleration of 0.75 g, usually adopted for the TTC evaluation (red line in the Figs. 5 and 6), appears a rather non-conservative values in case of high vehicle speed and wet road pavement.

The evaluation of the corresponding cumulated probability i.e., the probability to have a constant deceleration rate lower than 0.75 g, is expressed according to different initial vehicle speed and Tire Grip Class values in the Table 4:

Table 4. Probability to have a constant deceleration rate lower than 0.75 g for both tire classes.

30 km/h	60 km/h	90 km/h	120 km/h
Class tire C			
1,553E-201	*1,260E-10*	*7,070E-01*	*9,999E-01*
Class tire E			
0,000E + 00	*4,614E-07*	*1,000E + 00*	*1,000E + 00*

5   Conclusion

An innovative methodology for the estimation of the potential friction value and therefore the corresponding deceleration rate, useful for TTC evaluation, has been presented.

Starting from a probability density function of the *Friction Number* for wet road pavement, collected at different operating speed, the probability density function of the equivalent friction coefficient (directly related to the deceleration rate) has been calculated for different initial vehicle velocities and tire grip classes.

The proposed methodology has been applied at two tire class (C and E) and to four different vehicle initial speed values (30 km/h, 60 km/h, 90 km/h and 120 km/h). As it is possible see from Figs. 5 and 6, the conventional fixed deceleration rate value for the TTC evaluation, equal to 0.75 g, is fairly non- conservative in case of high vehicle speed and wet road pavement.

The proposed methodology shows several improved aspects:

- may take into account actual operating conditions (in some cases stricter than the standard ones, as the wet road pavement);
- the real variability of the road friction, achieved from conventional tire, has been considered;
- the system can be useful in case of on-board vehicle friction measurement device failure.

The preliminary results obtained have been encouraging, and future research developments will focus on the study of the influence of: water thickness, effects of braking distribution systems on the variability of friction and braking performance of the vehicle.

Acknowledgements. This study was carried out within the MOST – Sustainable Mobility Center and received funding from the European Union Next-GenerationEU (PIANO NAZIONALE DI RIPRESA E RESILIENZA (PNRR) – MISSIONE 4 COMPONENTE 2, INVESTIMENTO 1.4 – D.D. 1033 17/06/2022, CN00000023). The research leading to these results has also received funding by Project "Ecosistema dell'innovazione Rome Technopole" financed by EU in NextGenerationEU plan through MUR Decree n. 1051 23.06.2022 - CUP H33C22000420001.

This manuscript reflects only the authors' views and opinions, neither the European Union nor the European Commission can be considered responsible for them.

References

1. Sami, K. Pertti, P.: FRICTI@N, 2009, Final Report, WP1 Project Management. available online http://friction.vtt.fi/presentation.html. 31 Aug 2009
2. Koskinen,S.: Determination of tyre-road friction using sensor fusion. Congress to scientific and technical papers, Stockholm (2009)
3. Sultan, B., McDonald, M.: Assessing the safety benefit of automatic collision avoidance systems (during emergency braking situations). In: Proceedings of the 18th International Conference on the Enhanced Safety of Vehicles, Nagoya, Japan (2003)
4. Hayward, J.Ch.: Near miss determination through use of a scale of danger. Report no.TTSC 7115, The Pennsylvania State University, Pennsylvania (1972)
5. Van der Horst, R., Hogema, J.: Time-To-Collision And Collision Avoidance Systems. TNO Institute for Human Factors Soesterberg, The Netherlands (1994)
6. Burgett, A.L., Carter, A., Miller, R.J., Naim, W.G., Smith, D.L.: A Collision Warning Algorithm For Rear-End Collisions. National Highway Traffic Safety Administration United States (1998)
7. Meyer, W.E., Kummer, H.W.: Mechanism of Force Transmission between Tire and Road. Society of Automotive Engineers, Paper No. 620407 (490A) 18 p. (1962)
8. Wambold, J.C., et al.: International PIARC Experiment to Compare and Harmonize Skid Resistance and Texture Measurements. PIARC Publication n° 01.04.T, Paris (1995)
9. Standard CEN/TS 13036–2: Road and airfield surface characteristics – Test methods – Part 2: Assessment of the skid resistance of a road pavement surface by the use of dynamic measuring systems (2010)
10. American Society for Testing and Materials ASTM E1960–07: Standard Practice for Calculating International Friction Index of a Pavement Surface. ASTM International, West Conshohocken, PA (2015). www.astm.org
11. Regulation (EC) No 1222/2009 of the European Parliament and of the Council of 25 November 2009 on the labelling of tyres with respect to fuel efficiency and other essential parameters, Official Journal of the European Union 22.12.2009, L 342/46. http://eurlex.europa.eu/legal-content/EN/ALL/?uri=CELEX%3A32009R1222. Accessed 17 Jul 2017
12. Regulation (EU) No 228/2011 of 7 March 2011 amending Regulation (EU) No 1222/2009 of the European Parliament and of the Council with regard to the wet grip testing method for C1 tyres. http://eur-lex.europa.eu/legalcontent/EN/TXT/PDF/?uri = CELEX:32011R0228&from=EN Accessed 17 Jul 2017. https://eur-lex.europa.eu/legal-con tent/EN/TXT/?qid=1542150818726&uri =CELEX:32011R0228
13. American Society for Testing and Materials ASTM F 2493–18. Standard Specification for P225/60R16 97S Radial Standard Reference Test Tire. ASTM International, West Conshohocken, PA (2018). www.astm.org
14. Andrieux, A., Vandanjon, P.O., Lengelle, R., Chabanon, C.: New results on the relation between tyre-road longitudinal stiffness and maximum available grip for motor car. Veh. Syst. Dyn. 48(12), 1511–1533 (2010). https://doi.org/10.1080/00423111003770421
15. Singh, K.B., Taheri, S.: Estimation of tire–road friction coefficient and its application in chassis control systems. Published online: 08 Dec 2014. https://doi.org/10.1080/21642583. 2014.985804
16. Lamm, R., Psarianos, B., Mailaender, T.: Highway Design and Traffic Safety Engineering Handbook. McGraw-Hill handbooks (1999) ISBN 0070382956, 9780070382954
17. D'Apuzzo, M., Evangelisti, A., Nicolosi, V.: An exploratory step for a general unified approach to labelling of road surface and tire wet friction. In: Accident Analysis and Prevention, vol. 138 ISSUE 105462, 2020, pp.1–11 (2020). https://doi.org/10.1016/j.aap.2020.105462

18. Leandri, P., Losa, M.: Peak Friction Prediction Model Based on Surface Texture Characteristics, In: Transportation Research Record: Journal of the Transportation Research Board, vol 2525, pp. 91–99. Issue published: January 1 (2015)
19. MacIsaac, J.D., Riley Garrott, W.: Preliminary Findings of the Effect of Tire Inflation Pressure on the Peak and Slide Coefficients of Friction, Report No. DOT 809428, Washington D.C. National Highway Traffic Safety Administration. June (2002)

Potential Application of Marble and Crushed Mussel Shells By-products to be Used as Aggregates in Plain Concrete Mixes

James Rombi$^{(\boxtimes)}$ ⓘ, Marta Salis ⓘ, Marco Olianas ⓘ, Francesca Maltinti ⓘ, and Mauro Coni ⓘ

Department of Civil Environmental Engineering and Architecture, University of Cagliari, 09042 Cagliari, Italy
james.rombi@unica.it

Abstract. The main objective of the following paper is to verify the possible applications of marble by-products obtained from the ornamental stone industry and mussel shells deriving from aquaculture farming to be used as alternative aggregates in plain concrete mixes. Both marble and mussel shells came from Sardinia Island (Italy), very active in the commercialization of marble for ornamental purposes and mussels from aquaculture farming. Italy is the third producer in Europe of mussel and one of the leaders worldwide together with China and Turkey for the production of marble. Marble by-products were used to replace coarse natural aggregates while the crushed mussel shells partially replaced fine aggregates. The mixes were studied to obtain non-structural concrete. Various mix designs were studied, in which marble and mussel shells, in different percentages, replaced natural aggregates (sand and gravel). The research aimed to identify the characteristics of the materials through laboratory tests and to create the optimal mix design. From the test conducted it was possible to evaluate that marble and mussel shells by-products can be considered valid alternatives to natural aggregates. From the preliminary results, encouraging mechanical performances were obtained when replacing 50% of coarse aggregates fraction 8–16 mm with marble by-products and 8% of fine aggregates 0–4 mm with crushed mussels shells. The reuse of these materials is essential in a sustainable and environmentally friendly circular economy approach, which focuses on reducing waste and reusing materials within production cycles. The resulting advantages are less exploitation of natural aggregates and less production of waste.

Keywords: By-products · Marble · Mussels shells · Concrete · Circular Economy

1 Introduction

The European Union is increasingly focused on the reuse of waste materials, that must have good mechanical and physical performance to be reused in civil engineering, but also produced with low CO_2 emissions. Based on these considerations, this work evaluated the potential applications of marble and mussel shells by-products as a valid alternative replacing natural aggregates in plain concrete mixes. The marble used in the research derives from the region of Orosei located on Sardinia Island and is purely characteristic of the eastern coastal area of the island [1]. Since the 1970s, Orosei marble has been extracted from quarries located on the slopes of Monte Tuttavista. The Monte Tuttavista deposit extends for about 300 hectares and it is currently exploited for 6% of proven reserves. In the quarrying of ornamental stones, the percentage of commercial blocks produced with respect to the volume of deposit demolished averages around 30% of the total. The remaining 70% represents scrap which, in the absence of incisive valorization activities, is partially abandoned within the site or disposed of in landfills. In the landfill area, around 3000,000 m^3 have now fallen over an area of 15.5 hectares, with evident piles of debris whose height and irregularity have created a significant impact on the landscape and compromised the functionality of the site. The mining activity has generated a significant quantity of scraps of different natures and characteristics, the arrangement of which represents a problem of considerable importance for the quarrying activities, for the environment, and for the community.

Considering bivalve molluscs they represent almost 10% of the world's total fishery production, 26% of the entire volume, and 14% of the entire value of the world's total aquaculture production [2]. Global bivalve mollusc production has increased substantially in the last fifty years, going from nearly 1 million tonnes in 1950 to about 14.6 million tonnes in 2010. China is by far the leading producer of bivalve molluscs, with 10.35 million tonnes in 2010, representing 70.8% of global molluscan shellfish production and 80% of global bivalve mollusk aquaculture production. Considering only mussel shells production China, Chile, and Spain were the top three producers considering the period 2011–2020 (see Fig. 1), providing 74% of the global production. Italy in 2020 was the third producer in Europe of mussel (12%), behind Spain (47%) and France (14%) [3]. Analyzing the different regions of Italy in which mussels shells are produced (see Fig. 2), Sardinian Island is 5th in terms of production after the region of Emilia-Romagna, Veneto, Puglia, and Friuli Venezia Giulia [3, 4]. The mussel shells used in this research came from the aquaculture forming in the Gulf of Oristano, positioned on the west coast of the Island of Sardinia (see Fig. 2). As it is well known, the shell is about 33% of the entire weight of mussel shell waste. Thus, it can be confirmed that the canning industry generates over 1 million tonnes worldwide. This implies a significant waste problem on a global scale. For this reason, potential applications to use such by-products are vital to limit the disposal in landfills. In this paper potential application of marble and mussel shells by-products are studied to partially replace natural aggregates in non-structural concrete.

In recent years the construction industry has become increasingly aware of the need to change towards sustainability methods, studying and introducing new materials. Few researchers have studied the use of mussel shell waste as construction material, using it as an aggregate or filler to be incorporated into concretes or mortars [5, 6]. Mussel shells have been studied as a substitute for coarse and fine natural aggregates in concrete mixes. There is no trace of such research topics for the Italian mussel shell industry. In the following work, preliminary laboratory tests were carried out on both Orosei marble and mussel shells to determine the characteristics of these materials. Various cement mixtures were made, replacing Orosei marble and mussel shells in various percentages.

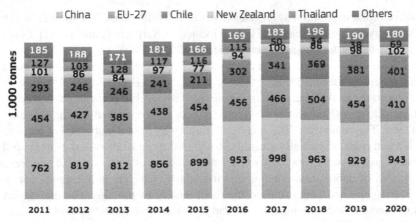

Fig. 1. Global mussel production 2011–2022 source FAO (Food and Agriculture Organization).

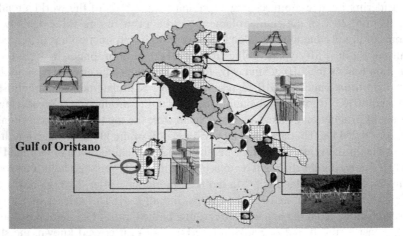

Fig. 2. Main mussel shells aquaculture production in Italy (Source ISPRA, Institute for Environmental Protection and Research).

Obtaining the correct mix design using high percentages of marble and mussel shells by-products by understanding the best substitution rate of each size fraction and maintaining good mechanical and physical performances is the main goal of the research.

The paper is structured as follows. Section 2 describes the materials and methods followed in this research. Section 3 presents the tests carried out in the laboratory on marble by-products and mussels shells. The mixes with the alternative materials prepared in the laboratory were reported in Sect. 4. Section 5 illustrates the potential applications, limits of this research, and future studies. Finally, Sect. 6 provides the conclusions of this research.

2 Materials and Methods

The Orosei marble used in this research comes from a carbonate formation that develops in correspondence with Tuttavista Mount (see Fig. 3), a region of Orosei, located on the east coast of Sardinia. The sedimentary rock that makes up the carbonate formation is classified as biopelsparite, i.e. a limestone with a prevalent structure of very fine-grained calcium carbonate (calcite, dolomite, micro and cryptocrystalline minerals) within which they are distributed, in different ways from area to area, particles such as fossils, shells and remains of organisms and fragments of other carbonate minerals. It is classified as a colorful non-crystalline marble, with a high percentage of calcium carbonate. The production of Orosei marble has produced around 3 million cubic meters of scraps in Sardinia with characteristics of excellent mineralogical and technological quality and different granulometry (0.001 mm – 2000 mm). The marble by-products were used to replace the coarse natural aggregate fraction. In this work, the following tests were performed on marble scraps: Particle Size Distribution (PSD) analysis, Atterberg Limits (AL), and Los Angeles Abrasion (LAA) test.

Fig. 3. View of Orosei marble district.

The other by-products used in this research are mussel shells that are considered waste materials of the maritime industry and a large part ends up in landfills, generating millions of tons of waste every year. They are mainly composed of calcium carbonate (90–95%) [5–7].

The shells are inorganic and of calcareous composition, incompatible with the accelerated composting process. They mainly end up in landfills or at the bottom of the sea, thus producing an important environmental impact. This work investigated the performance of mussel shells as an aggregate in concrete as a partial replacement of natural fine aggregates.

To prepare the mixes, Portland Cement (PC) was used, type CEM II 42.5R, 12% by weight of the aggregates and water 9% by weight of aggregates. The mussel's by-products before any utilization were treated at 135 °C for 30 min [2], using the treatment required by European regulations for poultry, feeding as a reference [7]. This procedure ensures the disinfection of the aggregates and warrants their safe handling and storage. After the treatment, the mussel by-products were crushed and screened obtaining a fraction 0–4 mm. Finally, the mixes were studied for non-structural concrete (NSC) for a total of n°6 mix designs. For the first n.5 mixes six cubic samples (150 × 150 × 150 mm) were prepared and cured at 14 days, while for the mix n.6 specimens were cured and tested at 14 and 28 days before undergoing compressive strength.

3 Laboratory Test

The first material tested was the Orosei marble by-product. The aggregates were collected from stockpiles according to UNI EN 932–1 [8] (Italian organization for standardization and specifications and methods of testing). In the laboratory, they were reduced (see Fig. 4) according to UNI EN 932–2 [9] specifications to perform physical and mechanical tests. Preliminary tests carried out consisted of the determination of PSD according to UNI-EN 933–1 [10], AL according to CNR UNI 10014 [11], and the LAA test according to UNI EN 1097 2 [12]. To perform the tests the Orosei marble was dried in hoven at 105 °C as shown in Fig. 5 and, once cooled, they were quartered. A quarter of the material was used for the PSD and a quarter for the AL. For the AL, a quantity of material passing through 0.42 mm was used. The plastic limit is determined by measuring the minimum water content at which the material can be shaped into sticks with a 3 mm diameter until it starts to crack. It has been found that the material is not plastic. In Fig. 6 is

Fig. 4. Laboratory sample of marble by-product.

reported the PSD of the marble by-products that passes the 16 mm sieve. According to the classification UNI EN 10006 [13] the material resulted in class A1-a.

Fig. 5. Sample of marble by-products in the oven to be dried.

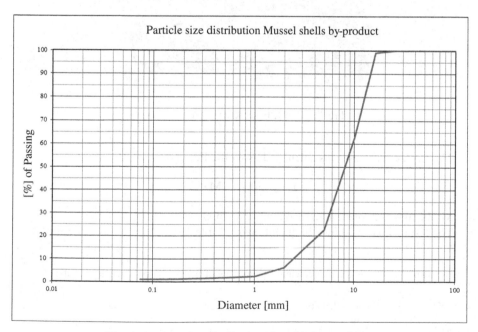

Fig. 6. Particle size distribution of marble by-products.

The other test conducted on Orosei marble was the LAA test. The LAA test measures the weight loss due to the fragmentation of a stone aggregate subjected to rolling action with metal spheres in a special cylinder. The sample was prepared for the test according to the indications in the UNI EN 1097-2 technical standard (see Fig. 7). The sample was initially screened, washed, and dried in the oven. The test portion used weights of 5000 g. The sample and the spheres were introduced inside the cylinder. The machine was made to complete 500 revolutions at a constant speed between 31 and 33 rpm. At the end of the test, the material was washed and passed through a 1.6 mm sieve, and the portion retained on the 1.6 mm sieve was dried.

Fig. 7. Marble by-products being washed.

The LAA coefficient was calculated using the Eq. (1):

$$LA = 5000 - M/50 \qquad (1)$$

M: the mass retained on the 1.6 mm sieve, in grams.
The test results are shown in the following Table 1.

Table 1. Physical and mechanical properties of marble by-products aggregates.

Sample n.	Particle density (g/cm^3)	Los Angeles Abrasion (%)	Atteberg Limit
1	2.62	24.47	Non-plastic
2	2.63	24.50	Non-plastic
3	2.63	24.48	Non-plastic

From this preliminary data, the material is non-plastic and with a low value of LAA, all characteristics good to be used in the road industry.

Based on the chemical analysis that has been conducted it can be said that the composition of the Orosei marble has a 97% of calcium carbonate ($CaCO_3$) [14].

The other tested material was the mussel shells (see Fig. 8). The main component of mussel shells is calcium carbonate, approximately at a percentage of 95% [2].

Fig. 8. Mussel shells before any treatment.

The mussel shells before any testing procedure were placed in a hoven and treated at 135 °C for 30 min. This procedure is necessary to ensure the disinfection of the aggregates and warrants their safe handling and storage. Subsequently, the mussels shells were crushed and during crushing separated from the byssus (see Fig. 9). The byssus is the bundle of filaments secreted by mollusc that function to attach the mollusc to a solid surface. To perform the crushing a LAA machine was used with n. 11 steel spheres and a time of rotation of 30 min. This type of procedure ensured the possibility of obtaining a good fine fraction of the shells and also the possibility of removing the byssus attached to the mussels. On the obtain fine fraction of crushed mussels PSD tests were performed. In Fig. 10, is reported the chart of the PSD, in which more than 90% passes the 5 mm sieve. For the research only the fraction 0–4 mm was used for the mixes, for this reason, sieving was performed to eliminate the fraction above the 5 mm sieve. Also, an AL test was performed and as expected the aggregates resulted in non-plastic. According to the classification UNI EN 10006 [13] the material resulted in class A1-b and so, a good material for road construction purposes.

From this preliminary characterization of the marble and mussel shells by-products, the research focused the attention on the potential application of using such materials in plain concrete mixes. For this reason, n.6 mixes were prepared, cured, and tested to evaluate mechanical performances. More specifically, the marble by-products partially replaced the coarse natural aggregates. The crushed and sieved mussel shells totally or partially replaced the fine natural aggregates.

Fig. 9. Mussel shells crushed and separated from the byssus.

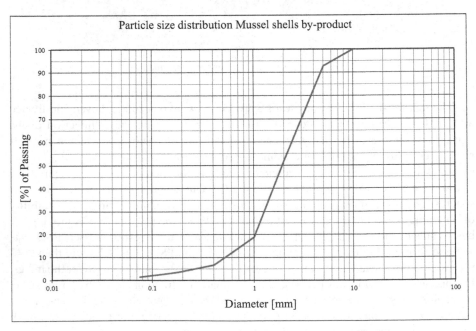

Fig. 10. Particle size distribution of mussel shells by-product.

4   Materials and Plain Concrete Mixes

In the first phase, a total of n.5 mixes were prepared, varying the substation rates of each natural aggregate size fraction (fine or coarse) using marble and mussel shells by-products. The cement used was a CEM II 42.5R, and no type of additive was introduced. A natural gravel coarse aggregate of 2–10 mm fraction was used. The water-cement (w/c) ratio used was 0.75, corresponding to 9% of water by weight of the aggregates and 12% cement by weight of the aggregates. The lowest w/c recorded in the literature was 0.3 [15] whereas the highest recorded w/c ratio was 0.8 [16] (see Fig. 11).

Fig. 11. Preparation of one of the mixes.

In this first series, no fine natural aggregates were used. Natural coarse gravel was partially replaced by Orosei marble by-products using 3 substitution rates 80%, 70%, and 50% (by weight), while mussel shells were used as fine aggregates. In Fig. 12 are shown different plain concrete mix samples, ready to be tested.

The following mixes were prepared as shown in Table 2.

The compressive strength test of the concrete specimens was carried out according to the UNI EN 12390–3:2003. The test was performed on each sample at 14 days of curing. The average results obtained are shown in the Table 3.

From the preliminary tests conducted, it can be seen that the concrete obtained from mix n.1 can be qualified as structural concrete. It must be said that structural concrete must have a value of compressive strength ≥ 20 MPa, while NSC must have a value of at least 10 MPa.

In this preliminary set of tests, segregation appeared during the granular aggregate mixture, especially in mix n.1 and mix n.2 attributed to the lack of fine aggregates in the mix design.

On the basis of these preliminary results, a n.6 mix was studied and tested. It consisted of cement type CEM II 42.5R, additive was used a super-plasticizer based on polycarboxylate, to give fluidity to the mix and also increase workability.

Fig. 12. Different mixes of plain concrete cubic samples ready for testing.

Table 2. Plain concrete mixes design.

Mixes n.	Orosei Marble (%)	Natural Gravel Coarse Aggregates (%)	Mussel Shells (%)
1	80	20	0
2	80	15	5
3	70	10	20
4	70	0	30
5	50	0	50

Table 3. Average Compressive strength results.

Mixes n.	Orosei Marble (%)	Natural Aggregates (%)	Mussel Shells (%)	Compressive Strenght (MPa)
1	80	20	0	20.92
2	80	15	5	15.93
3	70	10	20	11.77
4	70	0	30	10,67
5	50	0	50	7,47

The w/c ratio used was 0.50.

Regarding the aggregates used, natural gravel coarse aggregate fraction of 8–16 mm and 4–8 mm fraction was introduced in the mix, while a silica sand fraction of 0–4 mm was also used. In this mix, the marble by-products were used to partially replace 50% by weight of the fraction 8–16 mm coarse natural aggregate, while the crushed mussel shells were used to partially replace 19.5% of the fraction of silica sand fraction 0–4 mm. In Table 4 is reported the mix design composition for mix n.6.

Table 4. Plain concrete mixes.

Mix n.	Orosei Marble By-product 8–16 mm (%)	Natural Gravel Coarse Aggregates 8–16 mm (%)	Natural Gravel Coarse Aggregates 4–8 mm (%)	Natural Silica Sand Aggregates 0–4 mm (%)	Fine Mussel Shells by-product 0–4 mm (%)
6	14.3	14.3	29.55	33.81	8.1

For the mix n.6 compressive tests were performed at 14 and 28 days of curing. Two sets of specimens were cast and cured at 14 days consisting of n.3 specimens and n.3 specimens were cured at 28 days and tested. In Table 5 are reported the average compressive strength results at 14 and 28 days of curing.

Table 5. Average Compressive strength results.

Mixes n.	14 days curing Comprresive Strenght (MPa)	28 days curing Comprresive Strenght (MPa)
6	6.2	10.2

It can be seen from the results that mix design n.6 reaches the minimum value of compressive strength resistance to be considered NSC. It was seen from the test conducted and during the preparation of the mixes that the presence of fine mussel shells in concrete mixes: workability, density, and compressive strength of concrete decrease as the percentage of seashells increases, this is known in literature [2].

5 Potential Applications and Future Studies

The potential application of mussel shells by-products as substitute aggregate in concrete can be considered a valid alternative to improve various properties of concrete. The use of mussel shells by-products in concrete could provide environmental benefits in different ways: introduce a circular economy approach to the waste management of mussel shells, and reduce the exploitation of natural aggregate leading to a reduction of CO_2 emissions.

Also, the use of mussel seashells aggregates could provide an economic advantage in the construction industry since seashell by-products are generated in large quantities and have lower commercial value than natural aggregates. Possible implications of seashell aggregate concrete in construction are illustrated below.

Reduction in the density of concrete due to the incorporation of mussel seashells aggregates could be beneficial in special applications where lower self-weight of concrete is needed and not great strength is required. The possible application of seashell aggregate concrete in road pavements subjected to light traffic volume will depend on the mechanical properties (especially hardness) of the seashells, as well as the skid resistance and abrasion resistance of seashell aggregate concrete.

Current research shows that seashell aggregate has restricted potential in high-performance applications such as structural concrete and concrete exposed to aggressive environments. This is due to the presence of salts and organic impurities in seashells as well as reduced workability and lower strength of seashell aggregate concrete. In future applications, proper cleaning is needed by washing the shells and also to improve workability superplasticizers are essential. At present there are no studies on using mussel shells aggregate in reinforced concrete for this reason there is a need to study the structural behavior of reinforced concrete slabs, beams, and columns manufactured with treated seashells as partial replacement aggregate at different substitution levels and mix ratios is needed.

6 Conclusions

In this work, the potential use of Orosei marble scraps and mussel shells by-products was examined. The physical and mechanical properties of the material were analyzed and various concrete mixtures were prepared, with different percentages of substitution. Finally, the mechanical performances of each mixture were evaluated. Initially, five mixes were prepared in which coarse aggregates were replaced by marble by-products, and mussel shells totally replaced fine aggregates. In these mixtures with higher percentages of mussel shells, workability decreases, this behavior is known in the literature. In fact, the decrease in workability is owing to the irregular shape of the particle, which promotes particle friction, and the increased surface area, which increases the demand for water, as well as water absorption due to internal voids in seashell debris [17]. Also, it must be said that no super-plasticizer was used in the preliminary tests, which could have helped the fluidity and workability of the mixes. In all the compressive tests conducted in which mussels shells by-products were introduced in the mixes, all values were under 20 MPa. While mix n.2, n.3 and n.4 had compressive strength values that could be suitable for NSC.

In mix design n.6 marble by-products were used to partially replace 50% by weight of the fraction 8–16 mm coarse natural aggregate, while the crushed mussel shells were used to partially replace 19.5% of the fraction of silica sand fraction 0–4 mm. An increase in the fluidity of the mix was obtained by introducing a super-plasticizer. Also, no segregation appeared in this mixed design. The compressive strength value obtained at 28 days achieved the value of 10.2 MPa suitable to be considered a NSC.

From the preliminary tests conducted, it can be said that by-products of marble and mussel shells can be considered a valid alternative to partially replace natural aggregates. Further studies are needed to better understand such materials especially evaluate the more suitable percentage of mussel shells by-products in substitution of natural aggregates. Considering the data from the literature review and the data obtained in this research optimum percentage replacement of fine natural aggregates must not exceed 20%.

The reuse of these materials is essential in a sustainable and environmentally friendly circular economy approach. The resulting advantages are less exploitation of natural resources, less waste production, and less CO_2 consumption.

Acknowledgements. This study is supported by the projects "WEAKI TRANSIT: WEAK-demand areas Innovative TRANsport Shared services for Italian Towns (Project protocol: 20174ARRHT_004; CUP Code: F74I19001290001), financed with the PRIN 2017 (Research Projects of National Relevance) program and e.INS Ecosystem of Innovation for Next Generation Sardinia - SPOKE 8 - (CUP F53C22000430001 –MUR Code: ECS00000038) financed with PNRR (National Recovery and Resilience Plan). We authorize the MIUR to reproduce and distribute reprints for Governmental purposes, notwithstanding any copyright notations thereon. Any opinions, findings and conclusions or recommendations expressed in this material are those of the authors, and do not necessarily reflect the views of the MIUR.

Author Contributions. Concept and methodology, Rombi, J., Salis M. and Coni, M.; experimental campaign and validation, Rombi, J., Salis M. and Olianas M., analysis, Rombi, J., Salis M., and Maltinti F., writing, review and editing, Rombi, J., Salis M. and Maltinti F., project administration, Coni, M.. All authors have read and agreed to the published version of the manuscript.

References

1. Careddu, N., Siotto, G.: Promoting ecological sustainable planning for natural stone quarrying. The case of the Orosei marble producing area in eastern sardinia. Resour. Policy **36**(4), 304–314 (2011)
2. Martínez-García, C., González-Fonteboa, B., Martínez-Abella, F., Carro-López, D.: Performance of mussel shell as aggregate in plain concrete. Constr. Build. Mater. **139**, 570–583 (2017)
3. EUMOFA, European Market Observatory for Fisheries and Aquaculture Products, Mussels Shells in EU, European Commision, pp. 1–91 (2022)
4. ISPRA, Institute for Environmental Protection and Research. https://www.isprambiente.gov.it/files2018/eventi/cadeau/Giovanardi_ISPRA_MolluschicolturainItalia. Report (2018)
5. Martínez-García, C., González-Fonteboa, B., Carro-López, D., Martínez-Abella, F., Juan Luis Pérez, O.: Characterization of mussel shells as a bio-based building insulation material. In: The 3rd International Conference on Bio-Based Building Materials, Proceedings, pp. 526–531. Belfast (2019)
6. Uchechi, G.E., John, C.E., Bennett, I.E.: Properties of seashell aggregate concrete: a review. Constr. Build. Mater. **192**, 291–299 (2018)
7. Parliament, European. Regulation (EC) No 1069/2009 of the European parliament and of the council. 21 October 2009. Laying down healt rules as regards animal by-products ande derived products not intended for human consumption and repealing Regulation (EC) No 1774/2002 (Animal by products Regulation)

8. UNI EN 932–1. Tests for general properties of aggregates - Methods for sampling. Italian Organization for Standardization (U.N.I.)
9. UNI EN 932–2. Tests for general properties of aggregates - Methods for reducing laboratory samples. Italian Organization for Standardization (U.N.I.)
10. UNI EN 933–1. Tests for geometrical properties of aggregates - Determination of particle size distribution - Sieving method. Italian Organization for Standardization (U.N.I.)
11. CNR-UNI 10014. Determination of the Consistency (Atterberg) of a Soil. Italian National Research Council (C.N.R.) and Italian Organization for Standardization (U.N.I.)
12. UNI EN 1097 2. Tests for mechanical and physical properties of aggregates. Methods for the determination of resistance to fragmentation (2010)
13. UNI 10006. Road construction and maintenance - Technical provisions for use of soils (2002)
14. file:///C:/Users/james/Downloads/Materiali%20lapidei.pdf (2011)
15. Nguyen, D.H., Boutouil, M., Sebaibi, N., Leleyter, L., Baraud, F.: Valorization of seashell by-products in pervious concrete pavers. Constr. Build. Mater. **49**, 151–160 (2013)
16. Falade, F., Ikponmwosa, E.E., Ojediran, N.I.: Behavior of lightweight concrete containing periwinkle shells at elevated temperature. J. Eng. Sci. Technol. **5**(4), 379–390 (2010)
17. Mo, K.H., Alengaram, U.J., Jumaat, M.Z., Lee, S.C., Goh, W.I., Yuen, C.W.: Recycling of seashell waste in concrete: a review. Constr. Build. Mater. **162**, 751–764 (2018)

Impact Indexes Comparison Study Using Environmental Product Declarations (EPDs) on Innovative Cement Bound Granular Material Pavement Layers

Andrea Serpi[(✉)] [iD], James Rombi [iD], Francesca Maltinti [iD], and Mauro Coni [iD]

Department of Civil Environmental Engineering and Architecture,
University of Cagliari, Via Marengo 2, 09123 Cagliari, Italy
andrea.serpi93@unica.it

Abstract. In the last decades, the need to perform experiments with innovative new materials to be used in civil engineering and replace Portland Cement (PC) by embracing the concept of circular economy and environmentally sustainable engineering. PC production is responsible each year of 8% of the total CO_2 emitted into the atmosphere, for this reason, it is vital to find valid alternatives to PC. Such innovative materials must not only have good mechanical and physical performances if compared with PC but also be obtained with very low CO_2 emissions. In this research innovative mix designs for road Cement Bound Granular Material (CBGM) layers were analyzed to evaluate the environmental impact, in which PC was partially replaced with Anhydrous Calcium Sulphate (ACS), a by-product of the hydrofluoric acid industrial production process. This paper analyzes the Environmental Product Declarations (EPD) of two main mixes, one with 3% of ACS and 2% of cement and the other one with 4% ACS and only 1% of cement. The selected mixes had already been studied from a mechanical and physical point of view. Laboratory and in situ tests ensured good mechanical and physical performances. This paper wanted to analyze the environmental impacts of such mixes using the EPD of each material forming the CBGM layers. For comparison, two reference mixes one with only 5% of PC and the other with 5% of Green Cement (GC) were also analyzed. The research aims to compare the blends and evaluate the mix design with less environmental impacts. Twelve mix designs were considered, varying the type of hydraulic binders, that is PC, GC, and ACS and also the type of aggregates divided into Natural Aggregate (NA) and Recycled Aggregate (RA). The best design solution for the Global Warming Potential (GWP), which is one of the EPD parameters, was the mix incorporating 1% GC, 4% ACS and only RA.

Keywords: Environmental Product Declarations · Pavement Layers · By-Product

O. Gervasi et al. (Eds.): ICCSA 2023 Workshops, LNCS 14111, pp. 225–243, 2023.
https://doi.org/10.1007/978-3-031-37126-4_16

1 Introduction

This study aims to demonstrate the feasibility of using Anhydrous Calcium Sulphate (ACS) as a viable alternative to Portland Cement (PC). To this end, twelve different mix designs were compared by varying the type and quantity of the hydraulic binder PC, Green Cement (GC), ACS, and the type of Natural Aggregate (NA) and Recycled Aggregate (RA). The purpose of the research is to evaluate the environmental impact indices of the various design solutions with the aim of highlighting their positive and critical aspects, shedding light on the strengths of innovative solutions and those of traditional solutions. The current paper aims to demonstrate the feasibility of the use of ACS as a valid alternative to PC. PC production has an elevated impact on abiotic depletion, global warming potential, ozone depletion, human toxicity, freshwater aquatic ecotoxicity and other impacts [1]. The International Energy Agency [2] states that the amount of energy spent on cement production is currently 105 kWh/t for a material production of 4300 Mt per year. Cement production is responsible of about 7–8% of the CO_2 emissions released globally, which is the construction material with the highest CO_2 emissions, but an industrial product essential for the economic growth of a country [3]. The PC preheating and calcination process generates on average 0.85 kg of CO_2 per 1 kg of cement [4]. Furthermore, the use of cement involves serious risk factors for humans, such as hexavalent chromium, exposure to allergens or crystalline-free silica, which can cause damaging consequences as chemically hazardous substances [5]. For this reason, new approaches have been developed that limit the negative environmental impacts related to cement production aiming at developing advanced methodologies in the processes of raw material processing and clinker manufacture, improving energy efficiency and decreasing emissions to the atmosphere [6, 7]. The use of energy-efficient materials that can moderately replace PC in binders can be considered one of the possible methods to mitigate environmental risks [8]. Also various types of supplementary cementitious materials were used in the past to partially replace PC and other pozzolanic materials are tested with the same aim [9, 10]. In recent decades, European policy has increasingly aimed to support environmental policies and environmental protection, first with the Treaty of Amsterdam (1999), then with the Treaty of Lisbon (2009) and finally with the Paris Agreement 2015. In Italy, the new Public Procurement Code [11] came into force in 2016, which transposes Directives 2014/23/EU [12], 2014/24/EU [13], 2014/25/EU [14] of the European Parliament, providing guidelines and specifications for the three levels of infrastructure design. In June 2022, Decree No. 256 [15] emphasized the minimum environmental criteria for construction, which are based on circular economy and eco-sustainable architecture, enabling contracting authorities to reduce the impacts related to works for the maintenance, renovation and construction of public buildings and the management of related construction sites. The Action Plan for Environmental Sustainability of Consumption in the Public Administration Sector, the National Action Plan on Green Public Procurement (PANGPP) [16] contains the Minimum Environmental Criteria (MEC) to be included in public tenders. These criteria include new approaches to the design and use of materials such as Life Cycle Assessment (LCA) and include EPD (Environmental Product Declaration) certification of the material used in the construction works. This last document describes the environmental impact generated by the product taken into consideration, analyzing different impact categories, resources use, and waste production. The PANGPP [16] inserts a correlation for awards on a tender basis for projects with LCAs with improvements in environmental indicators. Significantly linking the monetary and environmental aspects, implying a preference for environmentally sustainable solutions over those that cost less but care less for the environment. Is discussed how investments made for the beauty and health of landscape and nature are repaid in terms of social consensus and have a strong return from the business community [17]. As far as the road sector in Europe is concerned, the GPP for road design, construction and maintenance emphasizes the possibility for administrations to take into account design experience and competence in relation to environmental aspects relevant to the subject matter of the contract, excluding operators who violate environmental laws. In Italy, the PANGPP criteria for design and works services for new road construction and maintenance are currently being defined. The work covered in this paper fits into this context, attempting to analyze the best solution in terms of lower environmental impact and performance. Some recent studies highlighted how ACS can partially replace PC in Cement Bound Granular Pavement (CBGM) layers and also in cementitious mortars. On the bases of laboratory tests [18, 19] which demonstrated good mechanical and physical performances and in situ tests performed on a trial embankment [20]. This paper studies the EPD of two main mixes, one with 3% of ACS and 2% of PC and the other one with 4% ACS and only 1% of PC, and for comparison two reference mixes were also analyzed one with 5% of PC and the other with 5% of Green Cement (GC). GC is an innovative type of cement, that uses less amount of non-renewable resources and emits less CO_2. LCAs and EPDs present themselves as a functional tool in precisely and objectively defining the environmental impacts of a product or process [21] to be used in compliance with environmental policies as a parameter in tenders according to the documents mentioned above [15]. In the road sector, the LCA study involved comparative material analyses, studying, as in the case of [22], the impacts on climate and the depletion of fossil resources resulting from the reduction of asphalt production temperatures, not only focusing on the carbon footprint. The research [23] carrying out studies on modified bitumen states that the use of 15% recycled pavement decreases impacts, climate change, fossil depletion, and total cumulative energy demand by 13–14%. While [5] addresses a comparison of four different types of cement by comparing them using criteria that fall into the three macro areas of environmental impact, worker health and socio-economic impact. The study [24] compares the impacts of recycled aggregates versus natural aggregates by analyzing the entire process and demonstrating that recycling one ton of material ensures fewer CO_2 emissions and fewer impacts regarding eutrophication and acidification. Other topics [25] propose an analysis of the environmental, construction and maintenance costs of various design alternatives using virgin materials, stabilized materials, and recycled materials. This study shows that it is possible to obtain the 34% reduction in energy and the 30% reduction in CO_2 with the use of RA if compared to NA, and to reduce the environmental impact with stabilization using lime, and the reduction in total costs with the use of RAP. In the study [26] with the help of the ECOCER tool and its database assesses how impacts vary with the consumption of materials. The current paper analyses twelve different mix designs using traditional and innovative materials such as PC, low carbon emissions cement GC, ACS, NA and RA. For all the mixes the total binder percentage was 5% by weight of the aggregates. The analyses were conducted by re-weighting the environmental impact indices in the EPDs of the products used according to the quantities of each individual material used for the mix design taken into consideration, in order to be able to conduct a comparative analysis of the strengths and weaknesses of the mixtures analyzed.

2 Methodology

The paper presents comparative analyses of various mix designs that can be used for the road base course layer. The environmental impacts of the composite product were analyzed by studying the EPDs issued by the manufacturers of the materials used in the mixes. The various mixes that were chosen for the analysis, were derived from previous studies in which good mechanical and physical performances were demonstrated [18–20].

Following the standard EN 15804 2019 [27], ten impact categories were considered, and it was evaluated which mix design was more impactful to the environment. The binder materials used for the various cement mixes are PC (European Cement Association Cembureau, owner of EPD), GC (produced by the company Italcementi), and ACS (produced by the company Fluorsid), which were combined in various percentages. The aggregates used are NA and RA (produced by the company Nuova Demi).

3 Case Study

Starting from the need to reduce emissions from cement production, it was decided to design mixes for road layers in which cement was partially replaced with ACS. ACS can be considered chemical gypsum, a by-product of the chemical industry obtained from the production of hydrofluoric acid. The material is obtained by the chemical reaction of sulphuric acid and fluorspar without additional energy expenditure, by mass of 80 percent vs. 20 percent hydrofluoric acid [28]. Its use in roads meets the concept of circular economy and environmentally sustainable engineering.

As a by-product it is on the market as a material with low production costs [28] and low emissions [29] as all emissions from the chemical process are attributed to the core product of the production process. Mix designs using in a total of 5% of hydraulic binders were analyzed, and two reference mix one with 5% of PC and the other with 5% of GC were compared with innovative mixes respectively 3% of ACS and 2% of cement that could be PC or GC, and 4% ACS and 1% of cement that could be once PC and then GC. Ensuring the specifications of standard EN 15804 2019 [27], the following environmental impact indices were taken into consideration.

- GWP: Global Warming Potential.
- ADPE: Abiotic depletion potential of non-fossil resources.
- ADPF: Abiotic depletion potential of fossil resources.
- AP: Soil and water acidification potential.
- ODP: Stratospheric ozone depletion potential
- EP-FRESHWATER. Freshwater eutrophication potential
- EP-TERRESTRIAL: Terrestrial eutrophication potential

- EP-MARINE: Seawater eutrophication potential
- POCP: Tropospheric ozone formation potential
- WDP: Water Deprivation Potential

Each index was taken from the following EPDs:

- Portland Cement EPD (Cembureau) [30]
- Green Cement EPD (Italcementi) [31]
- Anhydrous Calcium Sulphate EPD (Fluorsid) [29]
- Aggregate EPDs [32]

Combinations were made:

- PC mix (5% cement by weight of the aggregates), in two combinations, respectively with only NA, and only RA. Total number of mixes two.
- GC mix (5% cement by weight of the aggregates), in which Italcementi's green cement (Italcementi EPD Termocem green Type CEM III-A 42.5 N) was used and also combined first with NA aggregates, and then with RA. Total number of mixes two.
- Innovative cement mixes (3% ACS and 2% cement) with, respectively: NA-PC, NA-GC, RA-PC and RA-GC. Total number of mixes four.
- Innovative cement mixes (4% ACS and 1% cement) with, respectively: NA-PC, NA-GC, RA-PC and RA-GC. Total number of mixes four.

The analyses of the various mix designs were charted for both the 3% ACS and 2% cement and 4% ACS and 1% cement quantities and compared accordingly. The mix designs are numbered from 1 to 12, each mix proportion was named in terms of hydraulic binder percentage, followed respectively by the type of binder (PC, GC and ACS) and then the type of aggregate NA or RA.

In the first group of mixes only NA are used:

- 1) CBGM with 5% PC and only NA (Labelled 5PC_NA)
- 2) CBGM with only 5% GC and only NA (Labelled 5GC_NA)
- 3) CBGM with 3% ACS and 2% PC and only NA (Labelled 3ACS_2PC_NA)
- 4) CBGM with 4% ACS and 1% PC and only NA (Labelled 4ACS_1PC_NA)
- 5) CBGM with 3% ACS and 2% GC and only NA (Labelled 3ACS_2GC_NA)
- 6) CBGM with 4% ACS and 1% GC and only NA (Labelled 4ACS_1GC_NA)

In the Second group of mixes only RA are used:

- 7) CBGM with 5% PC and RA (Labelled 5PC_RA)
- 8) CBGM with 5% GC and RA (Labelled 5GC_RA)
- 9) CBGM with 3% ACS and 2% PC and only RA (Labelled 3ACS_2PC_RA)
- 10) CBGM with 4% ACS and 1% PC and only RA (Labelled 4ACS_1PC_RA).
- 11) CBGM with 3% ACS and 2% GC and only RA (Labelled 3ACS_2GC_RA)
- 12) CBGM with 4% ACS and 1% GC and only RA (Labelled 4ACS_1GC_RA).

As a result, graphs were analyzed for each index according to the 12 mixes.

It follows that: to Global Warming Potential Index (GWP) (Fig. 1):

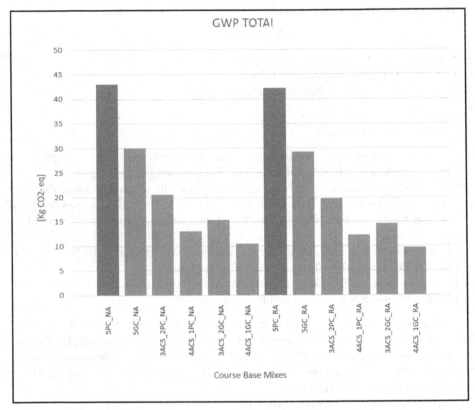

Fig. 1. This figure shows the different mix design impacts for the GWP (Global Warming Potential) Total Index.

- Traditional PC solutions are the most impactful (5PC_NA and 5PC_RA), there is no big difference if NA or RA are used in the mix.
- GC solutions (5GC_NA and 5GC_RA) are less impactful than those using PC (5PC_NA and 5PC_RA). In mix designs where part of the cement is replaced with ACS (3ACS_2PC_NA, 3ACS_2GC_NA, 4ACS_1PC_NA, 4ACS_1GC_NA), impacts are lower than in mixes where cement is the only binder. Solutions using recycled aggregates (3ACS_2PC_RA, 3ACS_2GC_RA, 4ACS_1PC_RA, 4ACS_1GC_RA) are slightly less impactful than those using natural aggregates (3ACS_2PC_NA, 3ACS_2GC_NA, 4ACS_1PC_NA, 4ACS_1GC_NA).
- For innovative mix designs (mixes with ACS percentage) lower impacts are found for the 4% and 1% mix than for the 3% and 2% mix. This evidence stems from the fact that ACS is less impactful than cement, and that the first design solution uses one point more of ACS at the expense of cement.
- It follows that the least impactful solution turns out to be the solution 4ACS_1GC_RA.

Abiotic Depletion Potential of non-Fossil Resources (ADPE) (Fig. 2):

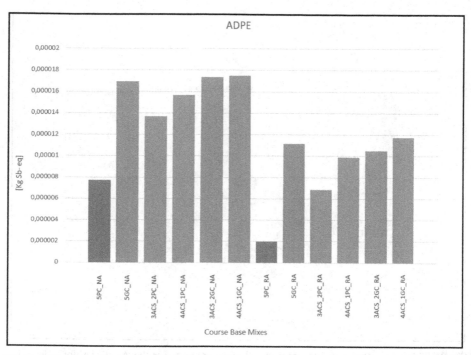

Fig. 2. This figure shows the different mix designs impacts for the ADPE (Abiotic depletion potential of non-fossil resources) Index.

- Again, solutions using RA are less impactful than those using NA.
- In this case, mix designs with GC and ACS have a greater impact than those with PC alone. In fact, the ADPE index of GC and ACS is an order of magnitude higher than that of conventional PC.
- RA also prove to be less impactful than NA.
- The best solution is 5PC_RA, which involves the use of PC and RA, but without the use of ACS.
- The most impactful solutions are the ones using GC and ACS (4ACS_1GC_NA), which have higher ADPE values than the other alternatives.

Abiotic Depletion Potential of Fossil Resources (ADPF) (Fig. 3):

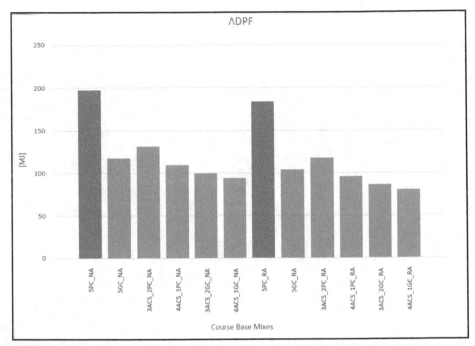

Fig. 3. This figure shows the different mix designs impacts for the ADPF (Abiotic depletion potential of fossil resources) Index.

- Mix designs using PC alone are the most impactful (5PC_NA and 5PC_RA), while options with GC alone are significantly less (5GC_NA and 5GC_RA).
- Using RA slightly lowers the impacts of cement mixes if compared with mixes with NA.
- A similar argument can be made regarding the use of ACS instead of cement in fact where is used 4% ACS and 1% PC rather than 3% ACS and 2% PC impact are lowest.
- It follows that the least impactful solution is 4ACS_1GC_RA.

Soil and Water Acidification Potential (AP) (Fig. 4):

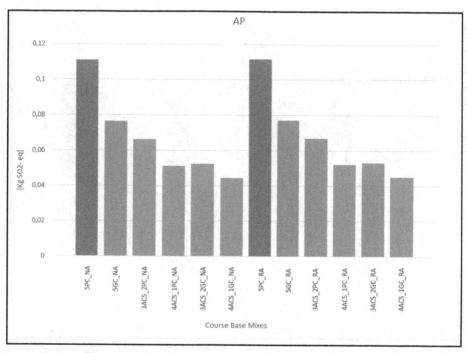

Fig. 4. This figure shows the different mix design impacts for the AP (Soil and water acidification potential) Index.

- The design solution using PC (5PC_NA and 5PC_RA) is always more impactful than the innovative ones using GC and ACS (3ACS_2GC_NA, 4ACS_1GC_NA, 3ACS_2GC_RA, 4ACS_1GC_RA).
- The difference between 3% ACS and 2% cement and 4% ACS and 1%, proves that the mix incorporating less percentage of cement is the best solution. In fact, although green solutions (5GC_NA and 5GC_RA) are preferable to the traditional cement mix (5PC_NA and 5PC_RA), the use of ACS reduces impacts compared to non-innovative solutions and obviously reaches the optimum when using GC and ACS (4ACS_1GC_NA, 4ACS_1GC_RA).
- RA have no visible influence compared to NA, in fact, the AP index for the two categories is almost the same.

Stratospheric Ozone Depletion Potential (ODP) (Fig. 5):

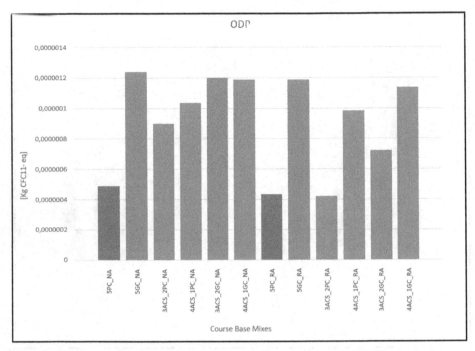

Fig. 5. This figure shows the different mix designs impacts for the ODP (Stratospheric ozone depletion potential) Index.

- In the case of this index, there is an opposite trend to the investigations of the other indices considered.
- RA bring a present but insignificant improvement. (RA mixes versus NA mixes)
- The mixes with PC (5PC_NA and 5PC_RA) are less impactful than GC mix without ACS (5GC_NA and 5GC_RA), which are the most impactful.
- Analyzing the ODP indices of ACS and GC shows that they are two orders of magnitude higher than those of PC. Therefore, in this case, the innovative solutions with ACS are more impactful than the reference mix with PC (5PC_NA and 5PC_RA), among which a slight improvement can be seen with the use of recycled aggregates (RA group).

Freshwater Eutrophication Potential (EP-FRESHWATER) (Fig. 6):

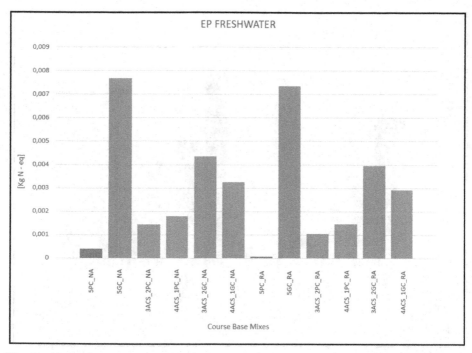

Fig. 6. This figure shows the different mix design impacts for the EP FreshWater (Freshwater eutrophication potential) Index.

- Options using RA (RA group) were found to be less impactful than those using NA (NA group).
- The most impactful solutions are those in which GC is used (5GC_NA and 5GC_RA). ACS has a higher EP FW index than PC but lower than GC, so its use offsets the impact of GC in innovative solutions (3ACS_2GC_NA,4ACS_1GC_NA, 3ACS_2GC_RA, 4ACS_1GC_RA).
- GC has four orders of magnitude more than PC and one more than ACS. This means that when using PC, the 3% and 2% solution is less impactful than the 4% and 1%, while when using GC, in this case, the most impactful, a greater amount of ACS lowers the impacts of the 4% and 1% compared to the 3% and 2%.

Terrestrial Eutrophication Potential (EP TERRESTRIAL) (Fig. 7):

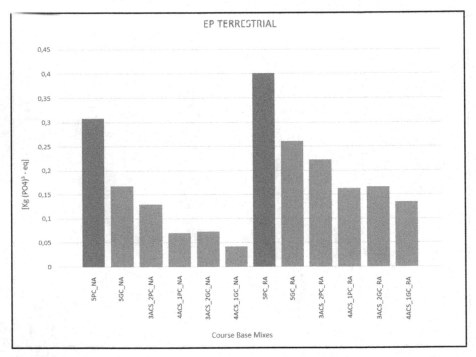

Fig. 7. This figure shows the different mix design impacts for the EP T (Terrestrial eutrophication potential) Index.

- RA have a large impact on the EP index of various mix designs compared to when NA are used.
- The use of ACS goes towards reducing impacts (mixes with ACS).
- The solution with PC and RA is very impactful 5PC_RA.
- By using more ACS at the expense of cement, 4% - 1% solutions are better than 3% -2%.
- Solutions with GC (5GC_NA and 5GC_RA) are less impactful than those with only PC (5PC_NA and 5PC_RA).
- The best solution is with GC, NA and ACS (4ACS_1GC_NA).

Seawater Eutrophication Potential (EP MARINE) (Fig. 8):

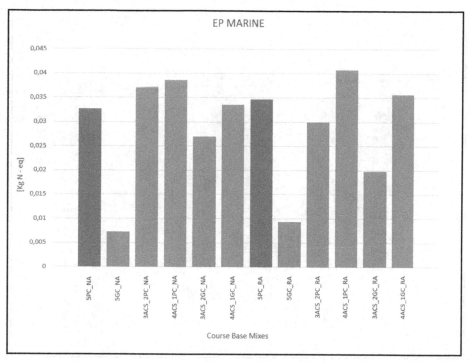

Fig. 8. This figure shows the different mix design impacts for the EP Marine (Seawater eutrophication potential) Index.

- The greatest impacts occur with the use of ACS in the innovative solutions, it follows that the 4% and 1% solution is more impactful than 3% and 2%.
- Higher relative impacts are seen with the use of only PC (5PC_NA and 5PC_RA) compared to only GC (5GC_NA and 5GC_RA).
- RA group is more impactful than the NA group.
- The best solution turns out to be 5GC_NA, with GC and NA. Looking at the indices, it can be seen that GC has 100 times less impact than PC and ACS.

Tropospheric Ozone Formation Potential (POCP) (Fig. 9):

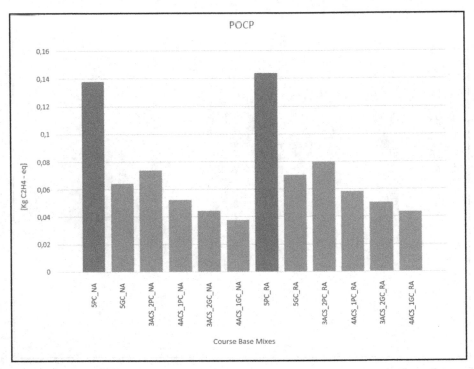

Fig. 9. This figure shows the different mix design impacts for the POCP (Tropospheric ozone formation potential) Index.

- The most impactful solutions are those with PC (5PC_NA and 5PC_RA).
- RA group is slightly more impactful than the NA group.
- The lowest impacts occur with the use of GC and ACS, particularly on the 4% and 1% ratio (4ACS_1GC_NA, 4ACS_1GC_RA). This result is associated with GC being less impactful than PC and ACS.

Water Deprivation Potential (WDP) (Fig. 10):

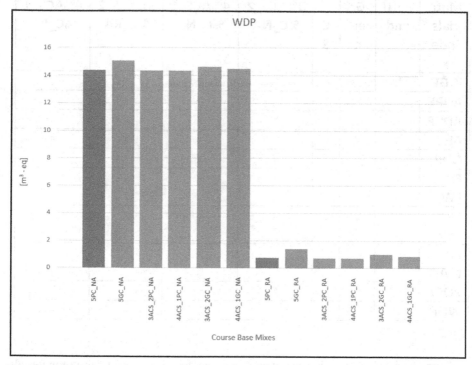

Fig. 10. This figure shows the different mix design impacts for the WDP (Water Deprivation Potential) Index.

- Solutions using NA have much heavier impacts than options using RA. The reason lies in the size of their water consumption index, which is 100 times higher for NA. It follows that all solutions with RA are preferable.
- PC and ACS have almost the same impacts. Solutions with GC are slightly more impactful (5GC_RA, 3ACS_2GC_RA, 4ACS_1GC_RA).
- There is a slightly higher level of impact for 4% and 1% solutions than for 3% and 2%.

4 Discussion

The results of the analysis on each individual index are summarized in the following table, the best solution contains the binder and the mix percentage indicated with the green tick "√", (where the percentage is not indicated the best solution provides only single 5% binder use), while options to be inconvenient are indicated with a red cross "X". The equal sign "=" indicates that there is no difference between the options (Table 1).

Table 1. Positive and negative contribution of materials for each Index.

Materials Index	Portland	Green	ACS	3%ACS_2%C_NA	4%ACS_1%C_NA	3%ACS_2%C_RA	4%ACS_1%C_RA
WGP	X	√	√	X	X	X	√
ADPE	√	X	X	X	X	X	X
ADPF	X	√	√	X	X	X	√
AP	X	√	√	X	=	X	=
ODP	√	X	X	X	X	√	X
EP FW	√	X	X	X	X	X	X
EP TER	X	√	√	X	√	X	X
EP MAR	X	√	X	X	X	X	X
POCP	X	√	√	X	√	X	X
WDP	√	X	√	X	X	=	=

From the analysis of each index, it emerged that there is no specific use of materials preferable to another, the impacts vary according to the material used, but in almost all the indices it appears that recycled aggregates are less impacting than the natural ones, even if slightly. While between the two innovative formulations, the mix with 4% ACS and 1% (GC or PC) is preferable to alternative 3% ACS and 2% (GC or PC) in a greater number of cases. Only in the case of ADPE and EP FW indexes, the solution that provides for the only use of PC is less impacting than the innovative solutions, while in the case of EP MAR, the solution with the GC is less impacting than the other alternatives.

5 Conclusion

Analyzing the various mix designs, it emerged from the environmental impact index analyses that there is no mix that is preferable over the others. From the study conducted, it emerged that considering the two alternatives mix design where ACS is used to replace partially PC and GC is possible to see that the mix design with 4% ACS and 1% (PC or GC) is less impactful than 3% ACS and 2% (PC or GC) except for ODP (Stratospheric ozone depletion potential) and EP MARINE (Seawater eutrophication potential) indexes. While to ADPE (Abiotic depletion potential of non-fossil resources) and EP FW (Freshwater eutrophication potential) the use of only PC binder is the better solution. The study shows that RA are less impactful than NA except to AP (Soil and water acidification potential) index, where both solutions are equal, and to EP TER (Terrestrial eutrophication potential), EP MAR (Seawater eutrophication potential) and POCP (Tropospheric ozone formation potential) index, where RA have a greater impact than NA. To WDP index RA are clearly the better choice. The use of ACS is a good design choice when considering indices GWP (Global Warming Potential) –ADPF (Abiotic depletion potential of fossil resources) -AP (Soil and water acidification potential) -EP TER (Terrestrial eutrophication potential) -POCP (Tropospheric ozone formation potential)-WDP (Water Deprivation Potential). Consequently, for such indices, it will be convenient to use the 4%ACS - 1%PC mix design as more of the same material is expected. Analysis shows that GC is preferred over PC in 60 percent of the cases, except for the indices ADPE (Abiotic depletion potential of non-fossil resources) -ODP (Stratospheric ozone depletion potential)-EP FW (Freshwater eutrophication potential) and WDP (Water Deprivation Potential). In conclusion, it must be said that the analyses of EPDs indices are a valid tool to better understand environmental impacts when analyzing the introduction of by-products as potential alternative materials in the construction sector. The suggested methodology and the reliable sources from which the data were taken allowed a detailed view of the strengths and weaknesses of innovative and traditional mix designs with regard to environmental implications related to the use of various binders and the use of aggregates. Proposing further parameters on which to base design choices useful in identifying the most suitable materials from an environmental point of view.

Acknowledgements. This study is supported by the projects "WEAKI TRANSIT: WEAK-demand areas Innovative TRANsport Shared services for Italian Towns (Project protocol: 20174ARRHT_004; CUP Code: F74I19001290001), financed with the PRIN 2017 (Research Projects of National Relevance) program and e.INS Ecosystem of Innovation for Next Generation Sardinia - SPOKE 8 - (CUP F53C22000430001 –MUR Code: ECS00000038) financed with PNRR (National Recovery and Resilience Plan). We authorize the MIUR to reproduce and distribute reprints for Governmental purposes, notwithstanding any copyright notations thereon. Any opinions, findings and conclusions or recommendations expressed in this material are those of the authors, and do not necessarily reflect the views of the MIUR.

Author Contributions. Concept and methodology, Rombi, J., Serpi A. and Coni, M.; experimental campaign and validation, Rombi, J.and Serpi A., analysis, Rombi, J.,Serpi A. and Maltinti F., writing, review and editing, Rombi, J., Serpi, A. and Maltinti F., project administration, Coni, M.. All authors have read and agreed to the published version of the manuscript.

References

1. Ige, O. E.: Environmental impact analysis of portland cement (CEM1) using the midpoint method energies. **15**(7), 2708 (2022). https://doi.org/10.3390/en15072708
2. International Energy Agency Homepage. https://www.iea.org/reports/cement
3. Uwasu, M.: World cement production and environmental. Environ. Dev. **10**, 36–47 (2014). https://doi.org/10.1016/j.envdev.2014.02.005

4. World Business Council for Sustainable Development (WBCSD); Cement Sustainability Initiative's (CSI). Cement Industry Energy and CO2 Performance. Getting the Numbers Right (GNR) Project, 1st ed.; World Business Council for Sustainable Development: Geneva (2016). (s.d.)

5. Moretti, L.: Environmental, human health and socio-economic effects of cement powders: the multicriteria. Int. J. Environ. Res. Public Health 14(6), 645 (2017). https://doi.org/10.3390/ijerph14060645

6. Valderrama, C.: Implementation of best available techniques in cement manufacturing: a life-cycle assessment study. J. Clean. Prod. 25, 60–67 (2012)

7. Summerbell, D.L.: Potential reduction of carbon emissions by performance improvement: a cement industry case study. J. Clean. Prod. 135, 1327–1339 (2016). https://doi.org/10.1016/j.jclepro.2016.06.155

8. Turk, J.: Environmental evaluation of green concretes versus conventional concrete by means of LCA. Waste Manag. 45, 194–205 (2015). https://doi.org/10.1016/j.wasman.2015.06.035

9. Bajare, D.: Coal combustion bottom ash as microfiller with pozzolanic properties for traditional concrete. Procedia Eng. 57, 149–158 (2013)

10. Bumanis, G.: Evaluation of Industrial by-products as pozzolans: a road map for use in concrete production. Case Stud. Constr. Mater. 13, e00424 (2020)

11. Dlgs 50/2016,(s.d.). Public Procurement Code

12. Directive 2014/23/EU of the European Parliament and of the Council of 26 February 2014 on the award of concession contracts

13. Directive 2014/24/EU of the European Parliament and of the Council of 26 February 2014 on public procurement

14. Directive 2014/25/EU of the European Parliament and of the Council of 26 February 2014 on procurement by entities operating in the water, energy, transport and postal services sectors

15. Decree MITE N.256, 23 June 2022

16. PAN GPP: National Action Plan on Green Public Procurement

17. Miccoli, S.: Social evaluation approaches in landscape projects. Sustainability 6(11), 7906–7920 (2014). https://doi.org/10.3390/su6117906

18. Rombi, J., Coni, M., Olianas, M., Salis, M., Portas, S., Scanu, A.: Application of anhydrous calcium sulphate in cement bound granular pavement layers: towards a circular economy approach. In: Gervasi, O., et al. (eds.) ICCSA 2021. LNCS, vol. 12958, pp. 91–99. Springer, Cham (2021). https://doi.org/10.1007/978-3-030-87016-4_7

19. Francesconi, L., Pala, L., Pani, L., Rombi, J., Salis, M.: Influence on mechanical performance of cementitious mortar incorporating anhydrous calcium sulphate. In: 18th Fib Symposium Concrete Structure: New Trends for Eco-Efficiency and Performance, Proceedings, Lisbon, pp. 302–311 (2021)

20. Rombi, J., Olianas, M., Salis, M., Serpi, A., Coni, M.: Performance evaluation of in situ application of anhydrous calcium sulphate in pavement layers. In: Gervasi, O., Murgante, B., Misra, S., Ana, M.A., Rocha, C., Garau, C. (eds.) Computational Science and Its Applications – ICCSA 2022 Workshops: Malaga, Spain, July 4–7, 2022, Proceedings, Part VI, pp. 640–649. Springer, Cham (2022). https://doi.org/10.1007/978-3-031-10592-0_46

21. Rebitzer, G.: Life cycle assessment part 1: framework, goal and scope definition, inventory analysis, and applications. Environ. Int. 30(5), 701–720 (2004). https://doi.org/10.1016/j.envint.2003.11.005

22. Anthonissen, J.: Life cycle assessment of bituminous pavements produced at various temperatures in the Belgium context. Transp. Res. Part D 41, 306–317 (2015). https://doi.org/10.1016/j.trd.2015.10.011

23. Vidal, R.: Life cycle assessment of hot mix asphalt and zeolite-based warm mix asphalt with reclaimed asphalt pavement. Resour. Conserv. Recycl. 74, 101–114 (2013)

24. Simion, I.M.: Comparing environmental impacts of natural inerts and recycled construction and demolition waste processing using LCA. J. Environ. Eng. Lands. Manag. **21**(4), 273–287 (2013)
25. Celauro, C.: Environmental analysis of different construction techniques and maintenance activities for a typical local road. J. Clean. Prod. **142**(4), 3482–3489 (2017). https://doi.org/10.1016/j.jclepro.2016.10.119
26. Jullien, A.: Environmental assessment of road construction and maintenance policies using LCA. Transp. Res. Part D **29**, 56–65 (2014)
27. UNI EN 15804:2019 Sustainability of construction works - Environmental product declarations - Core rules for the product category of construction products
28. Fluorsid. (s.d.): Anhydrous Calcium Sulphate Life Cycle Assessment
29. Fluorsid. (s.d.): Anhydrous Calcium Sulphate Environmental Product Declaration. 29. Cembureau. (s.d.). Portland Cement (CEMI) Environmental Product Declaration
30. Cembureau. (s.d.): Portland Cement (CEM I) Environmental Product Declaration
31. Italcementi. (s.d.): Termocem Green CEM III-A 42,5 N Environmental Product Declaration
32. Findo. (s.d.): Dichiarazione Ambientale di Prodotto Aggregati Naturali

The Effect of Subgrade Cavity on Pavement.
A Case Study

Mauro Coni[✉], Silvia Portas, James Rombi, and Francesca Maltinti

DICAAR, Department of Civil Engineering, Environment and Architecture,
Faculty of Engineering, University of Cagliari, Via Marengo 2, 09123 Cagliari, Italy
{mconi,sportas,maltinti}@unica.it, james.14@tiscali.it

Abstract. The paper reports the finite element analysis of the effect of subgrade cavities on urban pavements. The study starts after a critical collapse event in 2008 in Cagliari (Italy), where a 110 m^3 sinkhole suddenly opened up, swallowing one car on an urban street. The cavity, originated by water network failure, occurred in the urban area built in a zone of abandoned limestone quarries. Pressured water erodes the subsurface and effortlessly flows through rock debris voids. The cavity grows until the weight of the above materials and traffic load trigger a collapse of the pavement. In order to evaluate the effect on the dimensions' stress field and the cavity's location below the pavement, a parametric study of the finite elements was carried out with ANSYS® software. In a section of 25 x 10 m, which comprises the road pavement and the adjacent buildings, the FEM mesh includes not linear materials and the presence in the subgrade of a circular cavity with a variable radius (0.30 ÷ 1.80 m), depth (0.50 ÷ 3.00 m) and loads (0 t, 4 t, and 8 t). The F.E. simulations' results define the pavement's bearing capacity and the developed plastic yielding of the subgrade for each condition analyzed. No trivial cavity collapse conditions and mechanisms have been discussed in detail. The results show how the effects of the dimension and position of the cavity are not linear. Small and deep cavities collapse immediately with depth increases but with progressively smaller effects on the surface. Larger and superficial cavities are critical, and the vehicular load significantly affects the superficial cavities. Future research may address how these events may affect the road network.

Keywords: Asphalt pavement · Sinkhole · FEM simulation · Stress-strain effects · Underground · Bearing capacity

1 Introduction

A rising number of failures have been reported in the last decade on the urban streets in Italy related to underground cavities and sinkholes. To ensure safety conditions and avoid pavement collapses, the evaluation of the underground cavities became a priority [1–4].

Tomita et al. (1995) developed a detection method and surveyed Japan to identify and understand the nature of subsurface voids. The Authors report more than 2.000 pavement failures per year caused by voids in Tokyo. About 200 detected voids (through GPR and

O. Gervasi et al. (Eds.): ICCSA 2023 Workshops, LNCS 14111, pp. 244–259, 2023.
https://doi.org/10.1007/978-3-031-37126-4_17

borehole camera) were classified based on the volume ($1.0 \div 4.0 \text{ m}^3$) and thickness ($0.2 \div 1.0 \text{ m}$) under the pavement.

The underground cavities may be natural or artificial and generated from different phenomena such as water-soluble materials, mining activity, digging of the subsurface utility networks, and related actions of soil excavation [5–8]. Moreover, the urban development concern mainly regions of previous excavation human activities [9].

The potential presence of cavities must be considered in the pavement to design safe roads [10].

Several studies [5–9], and many others have been carried out on the identification and characterization of cavities, but few studies are available in the literature regarding design and evaluation criteria in pavement design. In recent years, Lee (2018) [10] has reported a 3D finite element parametric study varying cavity dimension, deep pavement thickness, and HMA stiffness, assuming the critical conditions regarding surface deflections and tensile strains.

Choi et. Al (2018) [11] extends the research developing procedures on the risk assessment in Japan for asphalt pavements due to the subsurface cavity. This relevant study considers a rectangular cavity and materials characterized by the modulus of the asphalt, subbase, and subgrade subject on a 40 kN load applied on one circular loading plate. The research pointed out how tensile strain depends primarily on the cavity depth and A.C. modulus. However, different cavity shapes, cohesive elastic-plastic subgrade, or visco-elastic A.C. proprieties can be significant in different situations. The superimposed effect of the two wheels of the axle load and the location concerning cavity position can affect the critical pavement response. Moreover, failure can also occur when the pavements have no load or with only cars loaded [12].

An important aspect concerns the evolution of the process before they evolve into dangerous pavement failures. The migration of loose material begins with an air pocket that moves upwards, increasing dimension due to the additional material being washed away. The air void moves upwards because the ceiling of the cavity falls on the floor, leaving the new ceiling uncovered. The process continues until the resisting layers of the pavement are encountered. In cold climatic conditions, the asphalt pavement could maintain enough bearing capacity to support the vehicles, while during hot weather, the stiffness of HMA drops drastically, and the pavement capability is significantly lowered [4]. The collapses remain latent in winter and reach a critical state during the summer, as Tomita et al. survey [6] pointed out.

Some relevant studies concern the cavity effect on the bearing capacity of footing [13–17].

Wang and Badie (1985) [18, 19] investigated the bearing capacity of shallow foundations on the underground cavity by 3D finite element model (FEM). The simulations point out a critical condition only for the void above the critical depth, which is not a constant. It depends on the shapes of the cavity, orientation and size, soil type, and footing dimensions. In this condition, the bearing capacity of the footing decreases the closer the cavity becomes.

Azam et al. (1997) [20] studied the bearing capacity of strip footing in two-layer soils by elastoplastic 2D FEM. The analysis provides the progress of plastic yielding and the ultimate bearing capacity for a wide range of cavity conditions and soil layers type,

Some theoretical and experimental studies investigated the mitigation methods to improve spread footing capacity above the voids. Das and Khing (1994) [21] built and tested a two layers laboratory model with a rectangular void below the foundation. The bearing capacity is reduced and can significantly increase with a geogrid layer.

In 2009 analogous study in the laboratory, developed by Sireesh et al. [22], investigated a circular footing over a circular void. They report considerable bearing enhancements providing a geo-cells reinforcement between the footing and the void.

Fang and Li (2011) [23] use elastic-plastic dynamic FEM to evaluate the differential settlement of the half-filled and half-dug embankment under the traffic load. The deformations of the asphalt layers under different conditions have been considered to identify the critical condition and settlement of the pavement.

Several Authors pointed out how nonlinear FEM analysis affects asphalt pavement stress-strain response.

Deng et al. (2004) developed an elastic-plastic dynamic F.E. model to evaluate the differential settlement of the half-filled and half-dug embankment under automobile load and subsoil consolidation.

Al-Qadi, Wang, and Coni (2010, 2013) [25, 26] studied the response of an instrumented runway asphalt pavement and developed 3D finite element simulations considering A.C. layers with viscoelastic proprieties and introducing elastoplastic characteristics in the subgrade and subbase materials. The pavement layers were equipped with 149 instruments (LVDT for displacement, pressure cells, TDR for moisture content, T-thermocouples, and strain gauges), monitoring in real-time the effects of landing and take-off in the pavement. The data collected from over 48000 movements during 2009–2011 have been used to validate the advanced pavement model. Good agreements were achieved at various locations, comparing measured responses from field instrumentation and calculated pavement responses.

Based on the results and remarks of these researchers, the papers summarize the case of the study and describe the FEM modeling and results.

Future research may investigate how these events may affect the road network. Some Authors pointed out how developing the model architecture of traffic control and microsimulation modeling is a valuable tool to analyze the road urban transport network and its capacity through a dynamic assignment model [32–35]. In addition, early simulation can address and minimize road network vulnerability in areas with sinkhole risk.

2   Case Study

The research started when a critical collapse occurred in August 2008 in Cagliari (Italy), where a 110 m^3 sinkhole suddenly opened up, swallowing one car on an urban street (Fig. 1). The cavity, originated by water network failure, occurred in the urban area built in a zone of abandoned limestone quarries. Pressured water erodes the subsurface and effortlessly flows through rock debris's voids. The cavity grows until the weight of the above materials and traffic load trigger a collapse of the pavement.

Similar events in the area have occurred in the last decades, involving buildings and urban streets (Fig. 2). The presence of cavities below the road level in the area is well known, and their evolution caused detachments and collapses.

In 2007, a large mass of about 8 tons detached from the roof of a cavity determining the permanent limitation to road traffic. In 1993, a large cavity (4.0 × 13.0 × 3.0) suddenly opened on the roadside, causing building flood, structural failures and traffic restrictions. A critical collapse occurred on May 12, 1987.

Fig. 1. The collapse occurred on August 11, 2008

A chasm of similar size dragged the facade of a building and part of the roadway. In August 1961, a cavity collapse caused severe structural failure, an entire building was demolished, and a large roadside was closed to traffic. A more significant number of events caused minor damage but manifested a widespread and high-risk problem.

The geology of the area presents several outcrops of Cenozoic and Neozoic formations. It consists mainly of well-cemented arenaceous benches, alternating with incoherent sand and layers of conglomerates with Paleozoic rock clusters and limestone and marly sandstones that emerge in the urban landscape.

Marly - yellowish arenaceous limestone, badly stratified with thicknesses up to 50 m, is also present, sometimes overlaid by biocalcarenites. The basal part is characterized by slumping, faults, erosion surfaces, and different intrusions with variable thicknesses of 0 and 40 m.

The geotechnics problems of the area affect the building's stability and road regularity, often resulting from inadequate foundations and construction methods, considering the substrate's heterogeneous and poor geotechnical characteristics.

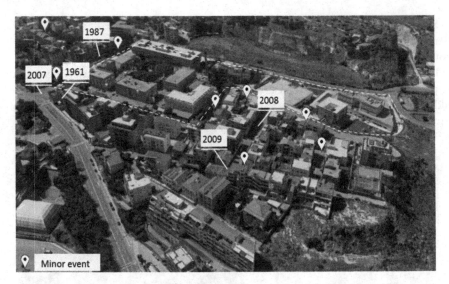

Fig. 2. The area affected by the landslide hazard and the event location.

During the post-war reconstruction and urban expansion, the area was affected by widespread construction without considering the plane-altimetric remodeling that occurred to fill and regularize the artificial morphological irregularities.

In the first half of the 20th century, the area underwent intense activity to extract rocks destined for the cement industry. The closure of the mining activity was gradual until the complete disposal in 1977 (Fig. 3).

In the last 20 years, the surveys highlighted a high geomechanical anisotropy, manifested by several subsidence and settlements of buildings foundations and investigated by an extensive survey campaign conducted between 2008 and 2011.

These included gravimetric geophysical tests, seismic tomographies, deep prospecting and superficial trenches surveys, penetrometer tests, exploration wells, and building inspections, laboratory tests (humidity, monoaxial compression, limits, Atterberg, particle sizes, classifications, cutting tests, etc.), carried out first on a large scale and then concentrated in the areas identified at greater risk.

The surveys, carried out at depths between 10 and 45 m, show the quarry debris overlay with thicknesses ranging between 1.80 to 25.0 m. These materials represent the greatest geostatic criticality of the area, with non-stabilized, non-densified soils predisposed to further settling, locally soft and porous, with primary voids generated by the laying technique.

These materials are susceptible to the action of groundwater, especially those under pressure resulting from water losses.

The traces and slopes of the quarry processing planes, built to facilitate the transport of the extracted material, are essential for understanding the underground water flow of the infiltration waters.

The geotechnical plane-altimetry variability makes complex the modeling of the subsoil. Therefore, it is fundamental to know the thicknesses of the debris and their

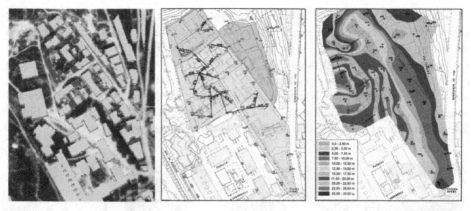

Fig. 3. On the left: aerial photo in 1946 shows the sign of quarry activity and the later building's construction (yellow). In red are the damaged buildings. In the middle: the survey and seismic topographies locations. On the right: the reconstructed thickness of the quarry debris. (Color figure online)

syngeneic porosity, which is often crossed by underground water flows due to percolation or to the losses water network.

The solution identified in order to mitigate the risk involved the construction of a technological tunnel below the roads, waterproof and easy inspection, within which to house all the utilities (white water, sewage, telecommunications, electricity, gas, public lighting, rainwater network, etc.) equipped with sensors to immediately detect leaks and activate specific maintenance. Moreover, the realization of rigid road pavement maintains the integrity of the road pavement even in case of sinking. At the same time, the Cagliari Municipality, up to the implementation of the technological tunnel, has ordered building and urban transformation restrictions (Fig. 4).

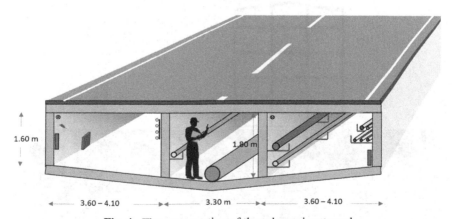

Fig. 4. The cross-section of the sub-services tunnel

Between 2013 and 2014, Cagliari Municipality planned, designed, and financed four sub-service tunnels under the roads. The construction of the first tunnel, concerned with securing the road affected by the collapse of 2008, started in 2015. After excavating the whole road section up to a depth of 2.50 m, the bottom and sides of the dugout have been consolidated with injections of cement grouting. The reinforced concrete foundations, walls, and roof define three compartments that house all the underground services and safely manage any water leaks. The tunnel was completed in 2017, as shown in Fig. 5. The second tunnel work began in 2018, and it is under construction.

Fig. 5. The construction site and works for the first subservice tunnel.

3   Research Methodology

During the study for a proper consolidation method, an important aspect has been to evaluate the level of risk connected to the presence of a cavity. In order to calculate the effect on the stress and strain of the dimensions, the shape, and the location of the cavity below the pavement, a parametric study of the finite elements was carried out with ANSYS® software, considering the influence of asphalt and granular materials nonlinearity [24].

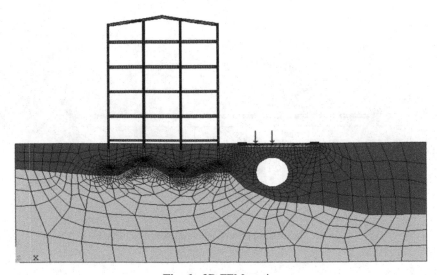

Fig. 6. 2D FEM section

Several Authors investigate the sinkhole phenomena with the finite element method [28–30].

In a section of 25×10 m, which comprises the road pavement and the adjacent buildings, the 2D FEM mesh (Fig. 6) includes not-linear materials and the presence in the subgrade of different shapes of a cavity (triangular, square, rectangular, and circular) with variable dimension ($0.10 \div 1.80$ m), depth ($0.40 \div 4.00$ m) and loads (0 t, 4 t, and 8 t).

Each combination generates different conditions in the subgrade and the pavement layers in terms of a) superficial deflections, b) stresses, and c) strains.

a) The cumulated plastic deformation determines a superficial permanent deflection as a function of traffic load spectra. In the study, the total permanent deflection δ_p of 10 mm, under wheel axis and standard traffic, was assumed as the limit to define a critical condition for superficial planarity. The value of 10 mm is the same limit assumed for rutting in road management.

b) The magnitude of shear stress compared to shear strength has been adopted to estimate if the soil can sustain the stress. The shear resistance of soil is a result of friction (ϕ) and cohesion (c), according to Navier–Coulomb criterion:

$$\tau_{cr} = c + \sigma \tan \phi \tag{1}$$

The normal stress has a stabilizing consequence, increasing the shear stress strength. Mohr theory defines, in the shear surface, the relationship between shear and normal stresses. The following equations can express them:

$$\sigma = \frac{\sigma_1 + \sigma_3}{2} + \frac{\sigma_1 - \sigma_3}{2}\cos2\theta \tag{2}$$

$$\tau = \frac{\sigma_1 - \sigma_3}{2}\sin2\theta \tag{3}$$

where σ_1 and σ_3 are the major and minor principal stress and θ the angle between major principal stress and shear plane direction. Applying trigonometric functions, they can be expressed by:

$$\left(\sigma - \frac{\sigma_1 + \sigma_3}{2}\right)^2 + \tau^2 = \left(\frac{\sigma_1 - \sigma_3}{2}\right)^2 \tag{4}$$

It is possible to define the state of limit failure, combining Mohr theory and Navier–Coulomb criterion (Figure 7), when the strength line is tangent to the Mohr circle. Solving the system of equations (1) and (4) allow us to determine τ_{cr}.

Many factors affect the value of c and ϕ, such as the kind of material, the morphology of the grains, and water [27]. In particular, moisture content decreases cohesion, increasing weight and pore water pressure in granular media.

Among the geotechnical data, dozens of friction and cohesion value are available in different locations and depths of the area, ranging from 23° to 29° and 4 kPa and 11 KPa for the fill materials. Also, a mean value of density (18.2 kN/m^3) and stiffness modulus (31 MPa) are available to perform F.E. simulation.

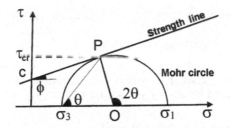

Fig. 7. Strength line and Mohr circle in σ-τ plane.

A mean value of 26° and 7.5 KPa have been introduced in Navier–Coulomb equation as well σ_1 and σ_3 values derived from F.E. simulation to estimate the shear strength. Finally, for each condition considered in a parametric analysis and for each position, τ_{cr} was compared with τ evaluated from the F.E. model at the same point.

c) The tensile strain at failure depends on the moisture content and the level of compaction. In undrained tests, well-compacted soils (100% γ_s, the maximum density of AASHTO T180 at w_{opt}, the optimum moisture content) have a typical maximum tensile strain ε_{tmax} around 0.2 ÷ 0.3%. Increasing moisture content, the ε_{tmax} grows until the maximum value of 0.7 ÷ 0.8% for $w = w_{opt} + 6\%$ [31]. The values of the ε_{tmax} are in the range of 0.2–0.6 % and growth with the plasticity index value. The drained triaxial test exhibit very different behavior, and the ε_{tmax} is about 10 times higher. The landfill soils in the area have been mainly classified as A2-4 HRB classification, with plasticity index Ip = 4 and liquid limit L.L. = 38. According to the mean value of the soils tested in the area, it has been assumed $\varepsilon_{tmax} = 0.6\%$.

4   F.E. Results

Equivalent strains ε_t vary considerably with load, cavity depth, and size and range from 2136 to 8287 μstrain (Fig. 8).

It is relevant to note that critical conditions of εt also occur in the absence of vehicular load for small cavities and at depths of 4.0 m. However, this condition does not create

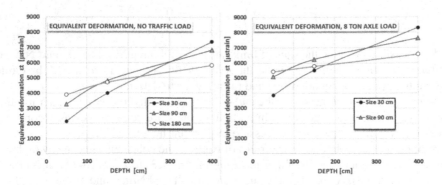

Fig. 8. Equivalent deformation with and without traffic load

critical conditions at the pavement surface because the material plastically collapsing fills the small cavity with negligible effects at the surface.

In the 30 cm cavities, as depth increases, the ε_t grows from 2150 μstrain to over 7400 μstrain, while for sizes between 90 ÷ 150 cm, the deformations are smaller, between 3200 ÷ 6990 μstrain. The following graph shows a nontrivial trend. Larger cavities are more critical but still within tolerable values of $\varepsilon_t < 4000$ μstrain, compared to cavities of smaller size but placed at greater depths. With no load, ε_t is greater for cavities of large diameters near the surface and grows less rapidly than for smaller cavity sizes. Similar behavior is observed when a vehicular load is present but with ε_t values 32% greater for 4 t axles and 25% greater for 8 t axles.

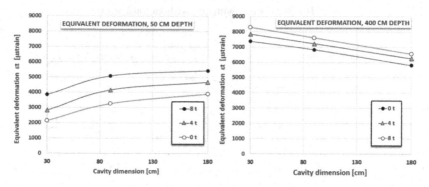

Fig. 9. Equivalent deformation for different depth cavity

The ε_t shows a monotonic decreasing behavior for surface cavities (−50 cm) and increasing diameters, while the trend is decreasing for deep cavities (400 cm) (Fig. 9). In the first case, the values are, under all conditions considered, less than 5500 μstrain. In the absence of vehicular load and only self-weight, they assume a fly of 3900 μstrain and increase by about 760 μstrain with a 4 t axle and 1520 μstrain with an 8 t axle.

The stresses also show a nontrivial trend. Without traffic loads, the maximum τ occurs with large-diameter cavities (180 cm) at small depths with 10.3 kPa values above τ_{cr}. As depth increases, the values decrease rapidly (2.3 kPa). Smaller cavities have the opposite behavior. For cavities of 90 cm, the τ grow as depth increases linearly, while small cavities of 30 cm are progressively less significant. For small depths, as load increases, the curves translate toward values of τ greater than 7.0 kPa for each 4 t increase in vehicular load. At depths greater than 150 cm, the curves tend to overlap, remaining less than τ_{cr} in each case (Fig. 10.)

For small diameters (30 cm), a critical depth of around 150 cm is highlighted by the bell curves in Fig. 11. It is observed that the maximum τ peaks at 12.0 kPa for loads of 8 t. Lower loads result in reduced peaks that are absent when only the fill's weight acts on the cavity. This particular behavior is not found in larger cavities. Whereas depth increases, the curves progressively decrease (Fig. 12).

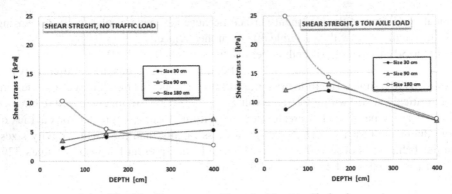

Fig. 10. Shear stress with and without traffic load

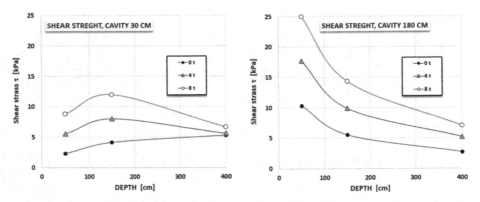

Fig. 11. Shear stress for small and large cavities

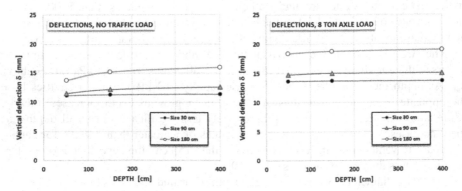

Fig. 12. Deflection with and without traffic load

In the following graphs (Figs. 13, 14, and 15), the complexity can be better represented in 3D by setting for the 3 axes the values of load, depth, and cavity size.

The vertical deflections δv have more local minimum conditions for both small and large depths. For a depth of about 150 cm, the deflections are almost indifferent to load and depth, presenting very similar values between 1.30 and 1.40 cm. The minimum values occur for depths of 150 cm, dimensions of 70 cm, and the load of 4 t.

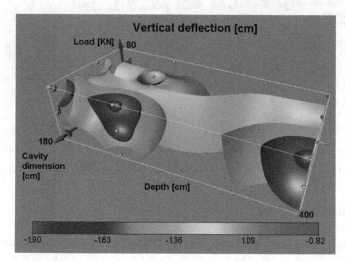

Fig. 13. Vertical deflection in 3D vs. loads, cavity dimension, and depth

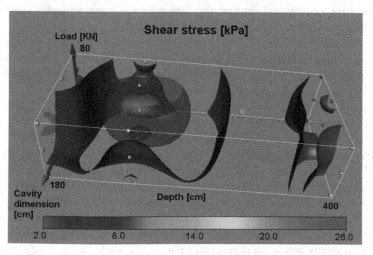

Fig. 14. Shear stress in 3D vs. loads, cavity dimension, and depth

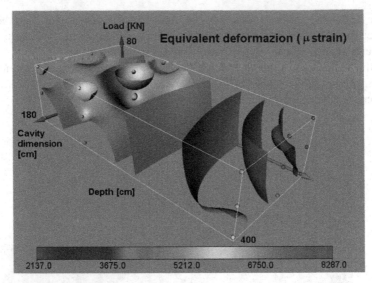

Fig. 15. Equivalent deformations in 3D vs. loads, cavity dimension, and depth

5   Conclusion

The paper reports the finite element analysis of the effect of subgrade cavities on urban pavements.

The detailed numerical investigation showed how an underground cavity under the road pavements could induce the failure event in no trivial. A numerical model based on finite element analysis and elastoplastic materials was implemented to determine the failure mechanism and the critical cavity characteristics.

The results show that underground cavities under urban roads play an essential role in the collapse and deformation phenomena of the road surface. It is predicted that gravity may damage lead to crises for cavities greater than 1.50 m, thus destabilizing the roadway's surface and, in extreme cases leading to its collapse.

This study can provide predictive analysis methods for hidden cavities and as a case study to prevent similar geological hazards in the study area.

The study starts after a critical collapse event in 2008 in Cagliari (Italy), where a $110\,\mathrm{m}^3$ sinkhole suddenly opened up, swallowing one car on an urban street. The cavity, originated by water network failure, occurred in the urban area built in a zone of abandoned limestone quarries. Pressured water erodes the subsurface and effortlessly flows through rock debris's voids. The cavity grows until the weight of the above materials and traffic load trigger a collapse of the pavement.

In order to evaluate the effect on the stress and strain field of the dimensions and the location of the cavity below the pavement, a parametric study of the finite elements was carried out with ANSYS® software. In a section of 25×10 m, which comprises the road pavement and the adjacent buildings, the FEM mesh includes not linear materials and the presence in the subgrade of a circular cavity with a variable radius ($0.30 \div 1.80$ m), depth ($0.50 \div 4.00$ m) and loads (0 t, 4 t, and 8t).

No trivial cavity collapse conditions and mechanism have been discussed in detail. The results show how the effects of the dimension and position of the cavity are not linear. Small and deep cavities collapse immediately with depth increases but with progressively smaller effects on the surface. Larger and superficial cavities are more critical, and the vehicular load has more significant effects on the superficial cavities.

Equivalent deformation ε_t varies with load, cavity depth, and size and ranges from 2136 to 8287 µstrain. Critical values of ε_t also occur in the absence of vehicular load for small cavities and at depths of 4.0 m. However, this condition does not create critical conditions at the pavement surface because the material plastically collapsing fills the small cavity with negligible effects at the surface.

In the 30 cm cavities, as depth increases, the ε_t grows from 2150 µstrain to over 7400 µstrain, while for sizes between $90 \div 150$ cm, the deformations are smaller, between $3200 \div 6990$ µstrain. With no load, ε_t is greater for cavities of large diameters near the surface and grows less rapidly than for smaller cavity sizes. Similar behavior is observed when a vehicular load is present but with ε_t values about 30% greater.

The ε_t shows a monotonic decreasing behavior for surface cavities (-50 cm) and increasing diameters, while the trend is decreasing for deep cavities. The stresses also show a nontrivial trend. Without traffic loads, the maximum τ occurs with large-diameter cavities at small depths. As depth increases, the values decrease rapidly. Smaller cavities have the opposite behavior. For average cavities the τ grow as depth increases linearly, while small cavities are progressively less significant.

For small diameters, a critical depth of around 150 cm is highlighted by Fem simulation. This particular behavior is not found in larger cavities. Whereas depth increases, the curves progressively decrease. The 3D maps δ_v, τ and ε_v versus depth and size of cavity and load can better represent the behavior complexity.

Acknowledgments. The Road Department of the Cagliari Municipality in Italy supports the research. The authors want to acknowledge Dr. D. Olla and Dr. A. Masala for their technical support during the in situ investigations.

References

1. Zhao, Y., Shi, Y., Wua, F., Sun, R., Feng, H.: Characterization of the sinkhole failure mechanism induced by concealed cave: a case study. Eng. Fail. Anal. **119**, 105017 (2021)
2. Debasis, D., Choi, S.O., Shin, H.S.: Analysis of sinkhole formation over abandoned mine using active-passive finite elements. Tunnel Undergr. Space 14(6), 441–422 (2004). Journal of Korean Society for Rock Mechanics
3. Tao, X., Ye, M., Wang, X., Wang, D., Castro, R.P., Zhao, J.: Experimental and numerical investigation of sinkhole development and collapse in Central Florida (2015).
4. Shalev, E., Lyakhovsky, V., Yechieli, Y.: Salt dissolution and sinkhole formation along the Dead Sea shore. J. Geophys. Res. Solid Earth 111(B3), B03102 (2006)
5. Zam, G., Jao, M., Wang, M.C.: Cavity effect on the stability of strip footing in two-layer soils. Geotech. Eng. **28**(2), Southeast Asian Geotechnical Society, ISSN: 0046-5828 (1997)
6. Al-Jazaairry, A.A., Sabbagh, T.T.: Effect of cavities on the behaviour of strip footing subjected to inclined load. Int. J. Civ. Environ. Struct. Constr. Archit. Eng. 11(3), 292–298 (2017)

7. Baryakh, A.A., Fedoseev, A.K.: Sinkhole formation mechanism. J. Min. Sci. **47**(4), 404–412 (2011)
8. Tharp, T.: Cover-collapse sinkhole formation and soil plasticity. In: Beck, B.F. (ed.) Sinkholes and The Engineering and Environmental Impacts of Karst; 6–10 Sept 2003; Huntsville, Alabama, pp. 110–123 . ASCE Publishing (2003)
9. Badie, M.C., Wang: Stability of spread footing above void in clay. J. Geotech. Eng.-ASCE **110**(11), 1591–1605 (1984)
10. Crapps, D.K.: The effects of cavities upon foundation design & construction. In: Art of Foundation Engineering Practice. ASCE (2010)
11. Kawana, F., Kubo, K., Ueda, N., Takeuchi, Y., Matsui, K.: Study of the cavity problem under the pavement caused by the earthquake. In: Richard Kim, Y. (ed.) Asphalt Pavements, 1st edn. (2014)
12. Tomita, H., Tada, H., Nanbu, T., Chou, K., Nakamura, T., McGregor, T.: Nature and Detection of Void-Induced Pavement Failures, Transportation Research Record 1505, Pavement Design, Management, and Performance. National Academy Press, Washington D.C. (1995)
13. Kovacs, A., Morey, R.M.: Detection of cavities under concrete pavement, U.S. Army Corps of Engineers CRREL, Cold Regions Research Engineering Laboratory, REPORT 8/18 (1983). https://apps.dtic.mil/dtic/tr/fulltext/u2/a131851.pdf
14. Gucunski, N., Shokouhi, P.: Detection and characterization of cavities under the airfield pavements by wavelet analysis of surface wave. In: 2004 FAA Worldwide Airport Technology Transfer Conference, Atlantic City, USA (2004). https://www.researchgate.net/publication/228563347_Detection_and_characterization_of_cavities_under_the_airfield_pavements_by_wavelet_analysis_of_surface_waves
15. Abbasghorbani, M., Bamdad, A.: Nondestructive detection of voids under airfield pavement. In: Proceedings of the 10th International Conference on the Bearing Capacity of Roads, Railways and Airfields (BCRRA 2017), 28–30 June 2017, Athens, Greece (2017)
16. Lee, W.S., Woo Choi, Y., Jong Lee, H., Mun Park, H.: Sensitivity analysis on the effect of cavity in structural capacity of asphalt pavement using finite element analysis. In: Proceedings of the Korean Society of Road Engineers Conference, Spring Conference (2018). http://db.koreascholar.com/article?code=348335
17. Choi, Y.W., Park, H.M., Kim, Y.T., Lee, W.S., Lee, H.J.: A risk assessment of asphalt pavement for depression and cave-in caused by a subsurface cavity. Int. J. Pavement Eng. **21**, 1092–1102 (2018). https://doi.org/10.1080/10298436.2018.1520231
18. Wang, M.C., Badie, A.: Effect of underground void on foundation stability. J. Geotech. Eng. **111**(8), 1008–1019 (1985)
19. Badie, A., Wang, M.C.: Stability of spread footings above void in clay. J. Geotech. Eng. ASCE **110**(11), 1591–1605 (1984)
20. Azam, G., Jao, M., Wang, M.C.: Cavity effect on stability of strip footing in two-layer soils. Geotech. Eng. J. SEAGS **28**(2) (1997). Ed. Southeast Asian Geotechnical Society, ISSN 0046–5828 (1997)
21. Das, B.M., Khing, K.H.: Foundation on layered soil with geogrid reinforcement effect of a void. Geotext. Geomembr. **13**(8), 545–553 (1994)
22. Sireesh, S., Sitharam, T.G., Dash, S.K.: Bearing capacity of circular footing on geocell-sand mattress overlying clay bed with void. Geotext. Geomembr. **27**(2), 89–98 (2009)
23. Fang, S., Li, H.: Mechanical analysis of asphalt pavement structure affected by underground pipeline of urban road. J. Hefei Univ. Technol. 2011-04 (2011)
24. Deng, W., Zhang, X., Chen, B., Yan, S.: Nonlinear FEM analysis of influence of asphalt pavement under non-homogenous settlement of roadbed. China J. Highw. Transp. 2004-01 (2004)

25. Wang, H., Al-Qadi, I.L., Portas, S., Coni, M.: Three-dimensional finite element modeling of instrumented airport runway pavement responses. In: TRB Transportation Research Board, 92th Annual Meeting, Washington, 12–17 January 2013

26. Al-Qadi, I.L., Portas, S., Coni, M., Lahouar, S.: Runway pavement stress and strain experimental measurements, Transportation Research Record, No. 2153 (2010)

27. Vanicek, I.: The importance of tensile strength in geotechnical engineering. ACTA Geotechnica Slovenica (2013). http://www.fg.uni-mb.si/journal-ags/pdfs/AGS_2013-1_article_1.pdf

28. Ahmed, M.: Experimental and numerical modeling of sinkhole collapse. In: Proceedings of the Transportation Research Board 92nd Annual Meeting, 13–17 Jan 2013, Washington, D.C (2013)

29. Shalev, E., Lyakhovsky, V.: Viscoelastic damage modeling of sinkhole formation. J. Struct. Geol. **42**, 163–170 (2012)

30. Caudron, M., Emeriault, F., Kastner, R.: Collapses of underground cavities and soil-structure interactions: experimental and numerical models. In: Proceedings of the 1st Euro Mediterranean Symposium on Advances on Geomaterials and Structures, 3–5 May 2006, Hammamet, Tunisia (2006)

31. Jin, W., Wang, W., Wang, B., Pan, Z.: Shear failure criteria of soft soil under complex stress condition. In: Qi, L. (ed.) ISIA 2010. CCIS, vol. 86, pp. 17–23. Springer, Heidelberg (2011). https://doi.org/10.1007/978-3-642-19853-3_3

32. Torrisi, V., Ignaccolo, M., Inturri, G.: The microsimulation modeling as a tool for transport policies assessment: an application to a real case study. In: AIP Conference Proceedings, vol. 2611, no. 1, p. 060006. AIP Publishing LLC (2022)

33. Bourguignon, F., Spadaro, A.: Microsimulation as a tool for evaluating redistribution policies. J. Econ. Inequality **4**, 77–106 (2006). https://doi.org/10.1007/s10888-005-9012-6

34. Torrisi, V., Ignaccolo, M., Inturri, G.: Innovative transport systems to promote sustainable mobility: developing the model architecture of a traffic control and supervisor system. In: Gervasi, O., et al. (eds.) ICCSA 2018. LNCS, vol. 10962, pp. 622–638. Springer, Cham (2018). https://doi.org/10.1007/978-3-319-95168-3_42

35. Torrisi, V., Ignaccolo, M., Inturri, G.: Analysis of road urban transport network capacity through a dynamic assignment model: validation of different measurement methods. Transp. Res. Procedia **27**, 1026–1033, ISSN: 2352-1465 (2017). https://doi.org/10.1016/j.trpro.2017.12.135

Motorway Performance in Europe and Greece

Ioannis Karamanlis[1], Dimitrios Papaioannou[2], Alexandros Kokkalis[1],
George Botzoris[1] (ID), Efstathios Bouhouras[3](✉) (ID), and Socrates Basbas[3] (ID)

[1] Democritus University of Thrace, 67100 Xanthi, Greece
[2] Citymapper by Via, London, UK
[3] Aristotle University of Thessaloniki, 54124 Thessaloniki, Greece
stbouh@auth.gr

Abstract. In terms of road safety, motorways offer much better records as compared to other road types. In EU, motorways represent an approximately 10% of all paved road network. Greece had until recently a significantly lower percentage of motorways, but during the last 15 years this percentage has been sharply increased to approach the EU average. The present paper provides a comparative analysis of motorways' safety between Greece and EU, using certain safety indicators, mainly fatality rates. The analysis is particularly concentrated in similar to Greece EU countries. Overall, Greek road safety records are traditionally poor compared to other EU countries, due to drivers' aggressive driving as the main reason. However, safety records in Greek motorways are comparable to those of EU motorways, hence the many km of newly constructed motorways in Greece have been contributed to improve country's safety indices.

Keywords: Motorways · Road safety · Safety indicators · Road fatality index

1 Introduction

Road safety in motorways is considered systematically better than in other road types. Any accident rate on motorways is lower than on main trunk or other primary highways connecting urban areas or other major trip generators. This occurs, despite the significantly higher speeds in motorways, because access to them is controlled and traffic streams are separated. Although motorways are expensive to be constructed, they do offer less travel time, comfort and travel safety. It is in favor of traffic safety to upgrade trunk roads to motorways.

In most EU member states, motorways represent a small percentage of all primary and secondary roads of the national and regional network which varies between 1% and 27% (EU15). In Greece, this figure has been at the lower limit until 2004; since then it has been sharply increased, exceeding 5%. Road safety levels have been also improved because of that.

Traffic safety levels vary widely within countries and road types, the least variation met in motorways. However, even in motorways traffic safety levels depend on their geometric characteristics, traffic volumes and composition, vehicles', max permitted speed as well as the country's driving culture.

The aim of this paper is to compare motorways' safety performance among EU states emphasizing on Greek motorways and how they contributed to alter safety indices in the latest years. It also attempts to interpret relevant findings and to identify some of the possible causes for that. Although several statistics are published in Greece concerning road safety, no comparisons are made with had happen in European level.

Data have been obtained by OECD (Organization for Economic Co-operation and Development), international and European transport and safety websites, Hellenic Police, Hellenic Motorways (Egnatia Odos, Attica Odos etc.), Eurostat and Greece national statistical service. Statistical data have been homogenized and analyzed to serve the objective of the paper (compare motorways' level of safety between EU and Greece).

Many safety indicators could be used, both simple and combined, concerning accident types and severity. Fatality index has been selected as the most suitable. Indicators should be deduced to road type length and/or to millions of vehicle-kilometers travelled.

2   Road Safety in Europe Versus Greece

Road safety in the EU as a whole has definitely been improving during the last years. Ambitious objectives set by the EU respective policy have not yet been exactly met but in most member states have been approached. Figure 1 presents the actual versus the targeted road fatalities set by the White Paper for EU-27 member States during the period 1990–2020, (Papaioannou et al. [1], Eurostat [2]). Between 1990 and 2020, the applied measures and policies led to a reduction by 73.5% in fatalities by road accidents. Although for the time period 2000–2010 the objectives set by the White Paper were not achieved, the difference with the actual figures was about 10%.

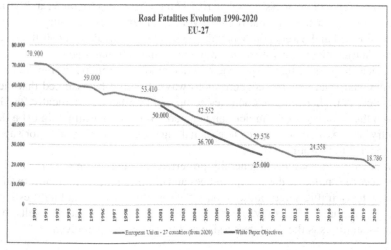

Fig. 1. A historic plot of 30-year reference EU-27 fatalities: recorded versus White Paper objectives (Own Process)

For the current decade (2020–2030) new fields will assist to improve further more levels of traffic safety, for example autonomous vehicles, artificial intelligence and vehicles' interconnection. Automotive industry has announced huge alliances and investments towards auto pilot level 5, a driver independent status of driving. There are estimations that autopilot and vehicle interconnection might decrease accident figures by as much as 90%. Since all these are still conjectures, no relevant references are available. On the other hand, the noiseless motion of electric vehicles could boost accident figures in urban areas.

Figure 2 presents the safety performance in Greece for the period 1990–2010. A gentler slope of accident reduction curve can be noticed. A worth noting peak is also detected during years 1998–2000. The peak is actually erroneous, because during that period the definition for a heavy injury road accident has been changed in Greece, as EU standards were adapted concerning both types of injuries and days of hospitalization. During 1998, a change in accident reporting and registering procedure also reduced underreporting. For a road, fatality the definition is that of a death within a 30-day period due to injuries received in the road crash. Overall, historically, accident safety performance in Greece was both worse and slower improving than in other EU countries. In an attempt to explain that slow improvement, the reference period 1990–2010 was a prosperous carefree period for the Greek society bucking against austere targets and transformations.

As above-mentioned, the length of motorways in several EU member States varies between 1% and 27%. Table 1 presents the length of motorways and all other primary and secondary rural roads in several EU member States as well as the ratio between motorways and rural roads. Greece lags in motorway length figures. However, during period 2000–2020, several motorways were constructed improving thus relevant figures. Figures and percentages of rural roads are fuzzy, because there are differences in the border between secondary rural roads (included) to lower-type rural roads (not included) among countries.

Table 1 presents motorways' length in EU-27 member states for the year 2019 as well their percentage over the national road network total length per country. Except from Denmark, Finland and Sweden in which the percentage is equal or higher than 1.0%, in all other countries motorways are a tiny fragment of the national road network. For these countries, it is impressive that despite the weather conditions mainly during winter, 1.0% of their national road network concern motorways. It could be assumed that the level of road safety is higher in these countries compared to others. Specifically for Greece, apart from the poor economic indices and an economic crisis lasting almost a decade, the country has a particularly ragged terrain making the construction of motorways more expensive (cost per kilometre).

Rounded figures have been generally preferred to accurate ones. It is the simplest way to reduce the 'noise' at the various indices and highlight the main trends. In addition, among the many traffic safety indices, only the one concerning the fatalities has been selected for emphasis. Generally, all safety indices provide consistent results, but that referring to fatalities is the most depressive and more readily perceived.

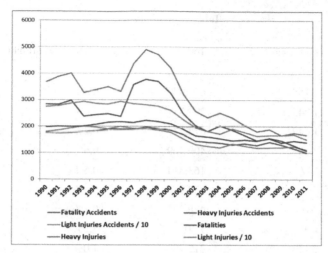

Fig. 2. Evolution of accidents, fatalities and injuries in Greece during period 1990–2010 (Own Process)

Table 1. Length (km) of Motorways in EU-27 for the year 2019 (Source: ERF, 2019 [3])

	Motorways	Total	Motorways /Total (%)
BE	1,763	2,075,018	0.1%
BG	740	969,583	0.1%
CZ	1,223	1,862,624	0.1%
DK	1,255	1,920,316	0.1%
DE	12,996	937,061	1.4%
EE	145	1,733,026	0.0%
IE	916	1,846,097	0.0%
GR	1,843	718,244	0.3%
ES	15,444	1,658,791	0.9%
FR	11,612	1,736,503	0.7%
HR	1,310	601,171	0.2%
IT	6,943	1,000,755	0.7%
CY	272	644,478	0.0%
LV	–	575,727	-
LT	314	748,368	0.0%
LU	161	634,719	0.0%
HU	1,924	505,761	0.4%

(continued)

Table 1. (*continued*)

	Motorways	Total	Motorways /Total (%)
MT	–	676,774	-
NL	2,758	630,070	0.4%
AT	1,743	299,357	0.6%
PL	1,640	672,279	0.2%
PT	3,065	490,469	0.6%
RO	747	163,314	0.5%
SI	773	252,910	0.3%
SK	463	478,758	0.1%
FI	890	77,091	1.2%
SE	2,118	212,787	1.0%

In Table 2, the average yearly motorway fatalities in European countries are displayed against relevant figures in Greece (2000 – 2019). Fatalities are presented in rounded 4-year periods. This is to reduce both the extent of the Table and the noise of a year-to-year variations, which may obscure the real trend. Comparably to countries of similar extent, bigger figures are acknowledged for Greece. In addition, the decline of the fatalities is not as sharp as in other States. Data for Tables 2 and 3 have been extracted and aggregated by different sources [4–7].

Table 2. Average yearly fatalities along European countries' motorways (Source: ERF, 2019 [3])

Country	2000–2003	2004–2007	2008–2011	2012–2015	2016–2019
GR	80	110	90	70	50
AT	180	110	80	50	35
BE	200	150	110	100	100
CZ	45	40	30	30	25
DE	800	690	440	400	400
DK	40	40	35	15	15
ES	360	160	90	70	80
FI	20	15	10	10	5
FR	560	330	270	240	280
HU	50	60	45	30	
IE	5	10	10	10	5

(*continued*)

Table 2. (*continued*)

Country	2000–2003	2004–2007	2008–2011	2012–2015	2016–2019
IT	770	700	380	220	280
LT			30	15	10
LU	100	85	60	75	70
NL	50	35	40	50	70
PL	130	110	110	65	50
PT	30	25	20	30	25
SE	25	25	25	20	20
SI	200	200	110	100	100
UK	950	800	600	350	210

The temporal motorway fatalities increase in Greece during the period 2004–2007 is attributed to the coincidental sharp increase in the length of trafficked motorways.

During the last four-year period, an increase at motorway accident fatalities can be spotted in few countries as well as a stagnancy in many more. Actually, advanced in traffic safety countries, have achieved the peaks at traffic safety indices beyond which any improvement would be very difficult and marginal by existing means. Hopes for impressive further safety improvement are put on the eminent electronic and artificial intelligence evolutions.

Fatalities across the rest rural road network are presented in Table 3(2000 – 2019). It is necessary to show these figures as a reference, because the length of motorways may vary considerably, whilst the length of the primary and secondary rural roads are almost constant and representative to the extent of each country. Empty slots means that relevant data could not be found.

Table 3. Average yearly fatalities along European countries' rural roads (Source: ERF, 2019 [3])

Country	2000–2003	2004–2007	2008–2011	2012–2015	2016–2019
GR	950	800	600	350	210
AT	550	460	340	170	170
BE	840	640	460	350	310
CZ	800	600	490	460	360
DE	300	200	140	120	110
DK	4500	3000	2400	2400	2200
ES	4500	3000	1900	1250	1350

(*continued*)

Table 3. (*continued*)

Country	2000–2003	2004–2007	2008–2011	2012–2015	2016–2019
FI	300	270	210	200	170
FR	5300	3300	2600	2200	2400
HU	750	750	460	360	
IE	300	290	150	130	120
IT	3000	3100	2100	1600	1900
LT			530	250	130
LU	70	50	40	30	10
NL	560	400	260		
PL	3000	3000	2400	1800	1600
PT	950	690	400	240	170
SE	400	300	220	190	240
SI	170	100	100	50	30
UK	2400	2200	1300	1200	1200

It should be mentioned that Table 3 does not present all the other fatalities along European countries road network. There are few fatalities in lower hierarchy rural roads, as well as quite strong figures in urban areas. Comparably to countries of similar population to Greece, bigger figures are again acknowledged for Greece. However, the improvement of road safety in terms of fatalities decline is quite noticeable as in other States. Greece having the most unfavourable starting point, achieves rival safety improvements. It worth mentioning that Greece lags analogue EU countries by almost twenty years.

However, the proper denominator should be neither country's extent nor population. The proper denominator over which all traffic accident figures should be reduced is the relevant number of the travelled vehicle-kilometres. This best measures the exposure to traffic incidents. Vehicle-kilometres per road type is a difficult figure to be obtained. Consequently, the second best ratio would be used, that of fatalities to the length of the relevant category road network. This is considered a better indicator than that of the number of registered vehicles, because the study is concentrated in motorways. Table 4 presents average yearly fatalities in 4-years sub periods per motorway kilometre along European countries.

Figures for travelled vehicle-kilometres along motorways are available for Greece. The ratio of motorway fatalities to travelled vehicle-kilometres are presented in Table 5.

The trend, as well as the rate of reduction is similar to that of Table 4. This secures the conclusion drawn by studying Table 4 only. During 2019–2021, EU's-27 average number of fatalities per million population were 51, 42 and 44, for Greece the respective numbers were 64, 54 and 57. Although in Greece in 2021 the number of fatalities per million population due to road accidents was decreased by 12% when compared to 2019, when compared to 2020 it was increased by 5% [8].

Table 4. Average yearly fatalities per motorway km along European countries (Source: ERF, 2019 [3])

Country	2000–2003	2004–2007	2008–2011	2012–2015	2016–2019
GR	0.12	0.11	0.07	0.05	0.04
AT	0.11	0.07	0.05	0.03	0.02
BE	0.05	0.05	0.04	0.03	0.02
CZ	0.05	0.05	0.04	0.03	0.02
DE			0.09	0.05	0.03
DK	0.09	0.06	0.05	0.03	0.02
ES	0.05	0.05	0.05	0.04	0.03
FI	0.12	0.07	0.05	0.03	0.02
FR	0.02	0.01	0.01	0.01	0.01
HU	0.05	0.04	0.03	0.03	0.02
IE	0.03	0.02	0.02	0.01	0.01
IT	0.04	0.04	0.03	0.03	0.02
LT	0.02	0.02	0.01	0.01	0.01
LU	0.07	0.06	0.04	0.03	0.03
NL	0.04	0.02	0.01	0.01	0.01
PL	0.06	0.04	0.03	0.02	0.02
PT	0.1	0.1	0.07	0.04	0.03
SE	0.08	0.05	0.05	0.05	0.05
SI	0.06	0.06	0.04	0.03	0.03
UK	0.12	0.08	0.04	0.03	0.03

Table 5. Average yearly fatalities per 10^9 vehicle-kilometre along Greek motorways

Country	2000–2003	2004–2007	2008–2011	2012–2015	2016–2019
GR	20	13	11	8.5	6.5

Generally, to compare traffic safety indices along motorways is the safest way to evaluate certain traffic safety issues. Motorways have the most consistent and of high quality characteristics in all countries, thus traffic safety indices along them reflect differences mainly in traffic monitoring and policing, speed limits and driver's behaviour. Delving into Table 4 figures, Greece has systematically the worst traffic fatalities ratios. However, these ratios are not as bad as the absolute figures presented in Tables 2 and 3, relatively to the rest EU countries. The sharp increase in Greek motorway network during the 20-year period of the study improved the traffic accidents' fatality ratio.

However, in 2019 Greek motorway fatality ratio remains one of the highest. First parameter to explain that is the poor policing applied along Greek motorways. The operation and utilization of Greek motorways belongs mostly to the private sector. Traffic monitoring is in a European average level, but traffic policing lags. In addition, vehicles' age is higher comparing to other European countries, but very few accidents (2%) are mainly attributed to vehicle failures [9]. Greek driver's behaviour is rather aggressive. They ignore Highway Codes suggestions mainly due to the poor policing. Driver's behaviour is generally the main cause of traffic accidents and the leading variable explaining the worse than average Greek motorway safety performance.

It is a principle that comparisons are more realistic under similar conditions. In Table 4, European countries independently their size, terrain type or traffic safety culture are presented. The ragged terrain of Greece has no match to many other EU countries. Thus, it would be interesting to constrain the comparison among same size countries to Greece. In Fig. 3 the average yearly fatalities in 4-years sub periods per motorway kilometre for similar to Greece EU countries is presented. As such, Czech, Hungary, Eire, Lithuania and Portugal have been selected. Greece has, historically, the poorest traffic safety records among EU countries, thus it would not be proper and realistic to be compared with other similar to population countries like the Netherlands, Belgium or Denmark, having excellent traffic safety performance for decades. The case of Austria is different, as Austria is the only EU country having a similar (actually more) ragged terrain to Greece. The comparison of Austria versus Greece is independently presented in Fig. 4.

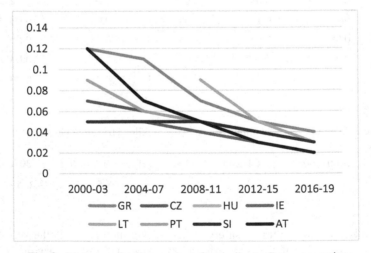

Fig. 3. Motorway fatality numbers for similar to Greece countries

Again, among somehow similar European countries, Greece has the poorest motorway safety records. Lithuania, a country recently entered the European Union, with poorer entry relevant records has outperformed Greece in 2016–2019 period. However, the differences are not prominent, motorway safety records for Greece (as already

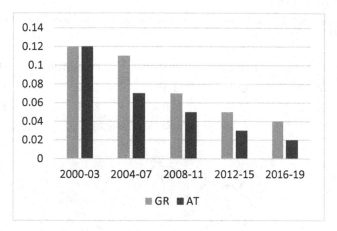

Fig. 4. Motorway fatality numbers for Greece and Austria (Own Process)

mentioned) are quite near to other similar European countries. According to firstly published statistics by the European Commission and republished by other sources, more than 22.500 people were killed in road accidents on motorways in the European Union countries between 2007 and 2016 [10]. Moreover, during this period (2007–2016) the annual fatalities per 1,000km of motorways were significant. The worst performance was reported in Bulgaria (83.1 fatalities per year and per 1,000km of motorways) while in Greece the respective number was 28.3, in Germany 30.2 and in Italy 39.5 [10]. Overall, Greece was ranked 11th among 22 European countries [10].

The same is valid for Austria as well, a country with better-established traffic safety culture (figures by Table 2) and a comparable to Greece ragged terrain. Actually, Austria and Greece have a similar motorway safety starting point (year 2000), but Austria achieved a better improvement during that 20-year period, being a more discipline and better-policed society.

A final aspect of European motorways' safety is presented in Table 6, which presents a comparison of an average percentage distribution of motorway fatalities per mode of transport for the EU-21 member states and Greece. The only figure that clearly differentiates between Greece and EU-21 countries are those of the contribution of lorries and 2-wheelers. Greece, lying at the edge of Europe, has the lowest percentage of lorries in her motorways. In addition, the mild climate of Greece encourages more kilometers to be travelled by 2-wheelers; therefore, the higher participation in traffic accidents of this mode of transport is considered as a surprise. It should be mentioned, however, that a typical motorway accident involving a 2-wheeler has higher death rates than one without a 2-wheeler. This observation may partly explain the higher fatality rates met along Greek motorways.

Greece's motorway network in Greece is presented in Fig. 5. In the framework of EN.I.R.I.S.S.T. project [11], a GIS map was developed, presenting the number of fatalities due to road accidents per a million of residents, clustered in four clusters and using as s geographical unit NUTS 3 regions (see Fig. 6).

Table 6. Comparison of % distribution of motorway fatalities per mode of transport (EU-21 versus Greece)

	Cars	Lorries	2weelers	Pedestrians	Others
EU-21	65.2%	13.5%	11.3%	8.2%	1.8%
GR	64.2%	6.7%	20.0%	8.2%	1.0%

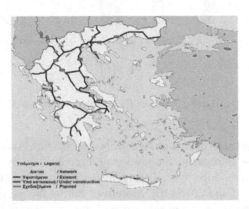

Fig. 5. Motorway's network in Greece for the year 2022 (Source: [12])

It can be easily derived when comparing Figs. 5 and 6 that in NUTS 3 regions in which motorways are passing through, the number of fatalities is less than the rest, except from regions in Peloponnesus and Central Greece. It seems that motorways contribute to improve road safety levels for inter-regional movements.

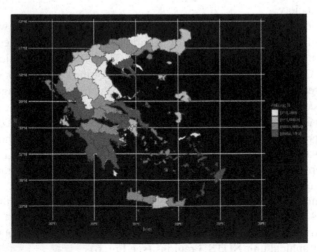

Fig. 6. Map of fatalities by road accidents per million of residents in NUTS 3 regions (2012–2019) (Source: [11])

3 Discussion and Conclusions

The design standards of motorways enhance by default higher levels of road safety. Along motorways, based on the above-mentioned statistical analysis, traffic accidents are not so often comparing to other road types. In this respect, the higher the percentage of motorways in the total road network the better the road safety in the country. During recent years (2000 – 2020), motorway construction plans in Greece flourish and the relevant figures have been noticeably improved and approach EU's averages. The most representative and impressive road safety indicator is the one concerning fatalities per kilometer of motorway network, which was reduced.

Greek motorways' safety, as expressed by fatalities per motorway length is worse than the EU's averages. Even for similar to Greece countries by size or by type of terrain, Greek motorways' safety performance lag by 20 to 50%. This lower performance may be attributed to deficient policing, more aggressive driving behavior and higher percentage of 2-wheelers. An in-depth examination of accidents along Greek motorways, as well as along the whole road network, is necessary in order to determine the most important causal factors.

The full application of a recently introduced safety audit methodology is expected to contribute towards this goal [13, 14]. Relevant projects have started to be undertaken during recent years along both motorways as well as the rest primary road network.

References

1. Papaioannou, D., Kokkalis, A.: Motorway safety in Europe and Greece: a comparative analysis. Elsevier Procedia – Soc. Behav. Sci. Transp. Res. Arena **48**, 3428–3440 (2012)
2. Eurostat, European Commission Statistics Database (2022). https://ec.europa.eu/eurostat/dat abrowser/view/sdg_11_40/default/line?lang=en
3. European Union Road Federation (2022). https://erf.be/statistics/road-network-2019/
4. Traffic Safety Basic Facts 2007, 2010, Motorways, DaCoTA Project, co-financed by the European Commission, Directorate-General for Mobility and Transport. http://www.dacota-project.eu/index.html
5. Eurostat, European Commission, Statistics Database. http://epp.eurostat.ec.europa.eu/
6. ERSO (the European Road Safety Observatory), Road Safety, CARE database – reports and graphics, European Commission
7. International Transport Forum, Statistics Briefs. http://internationaltransportforum.org/statis tics
8. Assocation Europeene des Concessionnaires d' Autoroutes et d' Ouvrages a Peage (ASE-CAP). http://www.asecap.com
9. Road Safety in the EU: fatalities in 2021 remain well below pre-pandemic level. Directorate-General for Mobility and Transport, European Commission, Online article. https://transport. ec.europa.eu/news/preliminary-2021-eu-road-safety-statistics-2022-03-28_en
10. Mungnimit, S., Jierranaitanakit, K., Chayanan, S.: Sequential data analysis for black spot identification. In: 4th IRTAD Conference, 16–17 September, Korea (2009)
11. How many people die on European motorways? Statista (2021). Online article. https://www. statista.com/chart/25098/fatality-rate-and-speed-limit-on-european-motorways/
12. EN.I.R.I.S.S.T. Project, Deliverable 5.3.5.1, Implemented under the action "Reinforcement of the Research and Innovation infrastructure", funded by the Operational Programme "Competitiveness, Entrepreneurship and Innovation", co-financed by Greece and the European Union (European Regional Development Fund) (2022)

13. Wikipedia, National Roads and Motorways in Greece (2022). [File:Greekmotorways2017 2.jpg|Greekmotorways2017 2], CC BY-SA 4.0
14. PIARC Road Safety Manual, PIARC (2015)
15. Quantifying safety in the road safety audit process, US Dpt of Transportation (2015). https://safety.fhwa.dot.gov/tools/crf/resources/cmfs/

Execution Time Experiments to Solve Capacitated Vehicle Routing Problem

Adriano S. Silva[1,2,3,4,5(✉)] [ID], José Lima[1,3] [ID], Ana I. Pereira[1,3] [ID], Adrián M. T. Silva[3,4] [ID], and Helder T. Gomes[2,3] [ID]

[1] Research Centre in Digitalization and Intelligent Robotics (CeDRI), Instituto Politécnico de Bragança, 5300-253 Bragança, Portugal
{adriano.santossilva,jllima,apereira}@ipb.pt
[2] Centro de Investigação de Montanha (CIMO), Instituto Politécnico de Bragança, 5300-253 Bragança, Portugal
htgomes@ipb.pt
[3] Laboratório Associado para a Sustentabilidade e Tecnologia em Regiões de Montanha (SusTEC), Instituto Politécnico de Bragança, 5300-253 Bragança, Portugal
adrian@fe.up.pt
[4] Laboratory of Separation and Reaction Engineering - Laboratory of Catalysis and Materials (LSRE-LCM), Faculty of Engineering, University of Porto, Porto, Portugal
[5] ALiCE - Associate Laboratory in Chemical Engineering, Faculty of Engineering, University of Porto, Porto, Portugal

Abstract. Studies dealing with route optimization have received considerable attention in recent years due to the increased demand for transportation services. For decades, scholars have developed robust algorithms designed to solve various Vehicle Routing Problems (VRP). In most cases, the focus is to present an algorithm that can overcome the shortest distances reported in other studies. On the other hand, execution time is also an important parameter that may limit the feasibility of the utilization in real scenarios for some applications. For this reason, in this work, a Guided Local Search (GLS) metaheuristic available in open-source OR-Tools will be tested to solve the Augerat instances of Capacitated Vehicle Routing Problems (CVRP). The stop criterion used here is the execution time, going from 1 s (standard) to 10 s, with a last run of 360 s. The numerical results demonstrate that increasing the execution time returns significant improvement in distance optimization. However, the optimization found considering high execution times can be expensive in terms of time, and not feasible for situations demanding faster algorithms, such as in Dynamic Vehicle Routing Problems (DVRP). Nonetheless, the GLS has proven to be a versatile algorithm for use where distance optimization is the main priority (high execution times) and in cases where faster algorithms are required (low execution times).

This work has been supported by FCT - Fundação para a Ciência e Tecnologia within the R&D Units Project Scope: UIDB/05757/2020, UIDP/05757/2020, UIDB/00690/2020, UIDB/50 020/2020, and UIDB/00319/2020. Adriano Silva was supported by Doctoral Grant SFRH/BD/151346/2021 financed by the Portuguese Foundation for Science and Technology (FCT), and with funds from NORTE 2020, under MIT Portugal Program.

O. Gervasi et al. (Eds.): ICCSA 2023 Workshops, LNCS 14111, pp. 273–289, 2023.
https://doi.org/10.1007/978-3-031-37126-4_19

Keywords: Route planning · Open-source · Versatile algorithm

1 Introduction

In the current scenario, companies and manufacturing services are constantly facing logistics challenges, one of them associated with delivery time [14]. In this regard, research on Vehicle Routing Problems (VRP) is gaining attention [16,17]. VRP is a fundamental combinatorial problem in distribution, logistics, and transportation. The first problem in this strand reported in the literature dates from 1959 when Dantzig and Ramser solved a truck disposing of problem [5]. Since then, several formulations and solutions have been reported in the literature, considering various scenarios [3]. Since the first formulation, the objective of these problems was always focused on cost reduction via finding the shortest path to execute a determined service [13]. In brief, the problem is used in cases where an agent needs to find the best way to serve different customers with more than one vehicle available to perform the task [26]. To increase the compatibility of the problem with a determined real scenario, constraints are considered.

In this regard, modifications in the original formulation of VRP were made along time, with new formulations arising. The most known formulation considers the capacity of the trucks and customer's demands as constraints to find the shortest path, the Capacitated Vehicle Routing Problem (CVRP) [19]. Another well-studied formulation is the Vehicle Routing Problem with Time Windows (VRPTW), which considers time windows the main constraint for route planning [6]. The Capacitated Vehicle Routing Problem with Time Windows (CVRPTW) is another formulation example, considering capacity and time constraints. Other formulations besides the above-mentioned can be found in this work [18]. All the formulations shown so far have one thing in common apart from the objective of reducing traveled distances: they are static. In other words, the data required to execute the algorithm is known before the decision-making procedure, and the route will not change once planned [10]. In recent years, the Dynamic Vehicle Routing Problem (DVRP) has received attention due to the more realistic nature of algorithms operation [17]. In this approach, the customers' set is not completely known once the truck leaves the central depot to execute the task, and the next stop is dynamically planned based on demands. For this application, the execution time of algorithms is precious since the stop times of trucks can range from seconds to minutes. Despite the difference regarding decision-making for route planning, algorithms developed for static approach can easily be adapted to execute the task in a dynamic environment.

Therefore, this work will assess the Guided Local Search (GLS) metaheuristic's performance in OR-Tools, considering different execution times as stop criteria. To perform this evaluation, Augerat dataset [2], available in the literature and used by other authors, was considered. Most authors dealing with algorithm development are only focused on optimization performance without considering the feasibility of their algorithm in terms of execution time. In light of the necessity to develop faster solvers, the performance evaluation will consider not only the algorithm's ability to find the optimal and shortest distance. Still, it will consider the execution time as well. The rest of the paper will bring relevant literature on algorithms development to solve CVRP considering execution times in Sect. 2, along with the applications of this problem for real life. Section 3 shows the method adopted to perform the study, Sect. 4 presents the numerical results and discussions, and Sect. 5 brings the conclusions and future work.

2 Related Literature and Applications

The relevant literature was gathered upon searching in Web of Science and Scopus for works dealing with "Capacitated Vehicle Routing Problem" and "Execution Time". The word cloud with the most relevant author's keywords is shown in Fig. 1 for both databases.

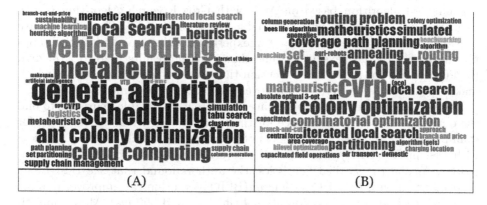

| (A) | (B) |

Fig. 1. 50 most relevant keywords in (A) Web of Science and (B) Scopus database.

The word clouds obtained with literature analysis using data gathered from the databases shows similar tendencies for studies in this field. In this case, metaheuristic algorithms have a significant presence in both clouds, which is comprehensible due to the fast response achieved using this class of algorithms to solve CVRP. In the next sections, the strategies used by works in this strand will be reviewed, along with real-case applications of CVRP.

2.1 Algorithm's Execution Time in Capacitated Vehicle Routing Problems

The VRP is the most important problem encountered at the operational level for transportation systems. The family of problems in this strand is classified as NP-hard problems, meaning the solution by exact methods can take a long time depending on the size of the problem considered. Since the first formulation in

1959, the family of VRP problems has increased through time, with the emergence of more formulations approaching different aspects of real transportation systems [15]. Improving the algorithm's performance through execution time has been recognized as an important task in recent years. Authors exploring this particular path often explore the hybridization of a particular algorithm as a strategy, considering the assembly of a new algorithm changing the time-consuming step for another mechanism available in other algorithms. This strategy is based on the identification of time-consuming steps during the execution of the algorithm and modification of this stage with the aid of other mechanisms used by other algorithms. It is important to highlight that this is the only possible way to solve the problem. There are other solutions as well, such as using parallel computation technologies.

For instance, Ant Colony Optimization (ACO) has stagnation property, which reduces the exploration of new routes and increases the processing time to return the solution. To tackle this issue, a study has considered developing a hybrid algorithm based on ACO with Crowd Search Algorithm (CSA) to achieve better solutions with reasonable execution time [7]. The authors have considered the Augerat database to run experimental tests to validate their approach. Despite the fast execution time shown by the results (828 to 2374 ms), the authors did not report the execution time obtained with their ACO, which makes it difficult to observe the improvement in execution time.

Some works are devoted to exploring the currently available heuristics to find the one with the best performance for their case of study. Dubois *et al.* [9], for example, have assembled a new model of VRP named Vehicle Routing Problem with Deadlines (VRPD), which includes several constraints from typical formulations. Among the studied heuristics, the authors found that the Best Flowtime Insertion with Order Questioning (BFIOQ) routine can improve by more than 55% with affordable computational time (around 600 ms). More sophisticated heuristics were also used to evaluate the resource dispatch criteria to solve the VRP. The comparison between Greedy Resource Dispatch 1 (GRD1) and Constant Objective Detection Resources Dispatch (CODRD) revealed a better performance of GRD1 compared to CODRD. However, despite the improved performance, GRD1 can result in infeasible situations for real scenarios, raising questions regarding the usage of this algorithm in a final tool.

Most solutions for time improvement in execution times are related to algorithm modification to increase the feasibility. However, other strategies must be explored to utilize the current hardware to run algorithms. Abdelatti *et al.* [1] employed parallel computation to solve a large instance CVRP taking advantage of the special CUDA GPU architecture on an NVIDIA GPU grid. In brief, the authors distributed the array elements over the GPU grid and used the GPU kernel functions to find high-quality solutions with acceptable execution times. To validate their strategy to speed up the execution of the algorithm, the authors have compared the solutions obtained in GPU with the ones achieved via CPU. The numerical results obtained by the authors show that the execution time of the GPU is 52.7, 162.6, 368.6, 321.5, 339, 454.4 times faster than the CPU for problems comprised of 21, 31, 40, 50, 60, and 76 nodes. The gap increase observed for the comparison between the two processing agents is related to the capacity of the GPU to handle problems with a higher number of nodes, which is not observed for the CPU. In other words, execution times are not affected similarly according to the number of nodes in the CPU and GPU.

2.2   Applications of CVRP

Over the last decades, the utilization of optimization packages based on mathematical programming for the logistics sector has increased significantly. The increased number of publications has proven the ability of computerized processes to save resources up to 20% in the transportation sector. For instance, most works dealing with optimization in this context often refer to a real-case situation to explain the motivations behind the study. The applications of CVRP extend to any situation in which it is possible to identify a set of customers with associated demands requiring service and a set of vehicles that needs to serve the customers.

Silva *et al.* [22] have studied route optimization in municipal solid waste collection. In their work, three metaheuristics available in open-source OR-Tools were studied to optimize waste collection tasks, considering execution time as an important parameter. For instance, several works are devoted to this variant of CVRP, which has enabled the emergence of a new class of VRPs named Capacitated Waste Collection Problems (CWCP). The formulations, in this case, are similar to CVRP ones, with the addition of new constraints related to the service addressed. The obnoxious effect of organic waste, heterogeneous fleets collecting different types of waste, and multi-compartment trucks collecting more than one type of waste are examples of considerations taken into account. Additionally, works focus on collecting and transporting other residues, mostly from industrial sites.

Another class of real problems emerging in recent years is the Capacitated Electric Vehicle Routing Problem. The increase in electric vehicles fleet and the viability of using those vehicles in cargo transportation systems, especially deliveries, has created this new variant of CVRP. The problem is based on the premise that electric vehicle consumption is directly connected with the weight they are carrying. Several works have been reported on route planning, considering the best delivery path using electric vehicles. The main considerations in this formulation are related to the necessity of those vehicles to recharge during the path and the consideration of a dynamic consumption based on the cargo. For instance, Jia *et al.* [12] proposed a confidence-based bilevel ACO algorithm to solve the problem of delivery service and vehicle charging. The ACO was adapted to solve the delivery problem at the upper level, and a new metaheuristic was used to determine the need to recharge the vehicle (simple enumeration).

Other real-world applications for CVRP are less frequently found in the literature, such as relief systems. Despite fewer studies in this field, the relevance is not diminished. These works are fundamental to studying new strategies that could save lives. The principal difficulty in studying the systems is associated with the lack of information regarding disasters to model new formulations and explore solutions in simulated environments. Data gathering is not the priority in these situations. Regardless, the study by Dubois *et al.* [9] evaluates the execution time and efficiency of different algorithms in the context of flooding crises.

3   Methodology

This work aims to analyze the influence of execution time in the performance of GLS, available in OR-Tools, to solve the Augerat instances of CVRP. Previous works demonstrated that Guided Local Search (GLS) is the best heuristic for solving CVRP [20,22]. For this reason, we used GLS to solve the Augerat instances of CVRP, defining the execution time as stop criteria. In these instances, $(n-1)$ represents the number of nodes, and k is the number of trucks considered to find the optimized path. In most real-life cases where VRP emerges as problem seeking solution, execution time is a key tool to present feasible solutions. In this context, the execution times considered in this work were chosen in the time interval $t = [1, 10]$; with $\Delta t = 1$. By solving the instances, a comparison of the gap between execution times and solution improvement was made to demonstrate the applicability of this algorithm in cases that require faster solutions and also for cases demanding high performance. The solutions for each instance were further gathered in a single file with the aid of the pandas' package, and the complete algorithm was written in python. Figure 2 brings an overview of the complete work.

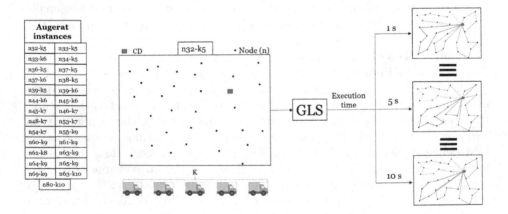

Fig. 2. Representation of the study performed.

3.1   Capacitated Vehicle Routing Problem

The formulation presented here is based on the literature [21]. In this problem, the customers have requested services of pick-up or deliveries, and the demands are deterministic and known in advance. The fleet of vehicles ascribed for the task can be homogenous or heterogeneous, directly impacting vehicles' capacity and route planning. The objective is to find the shortest routes and distances to serve all the customers. The problem can be described formally as a graph theoretic problem. Let $G = (V, A)$ be a complete graph, for which $V = \{0, 1, 2, \ldots, n\}$ is the vertice set, and $A = \{(i, j) : i \neq j$ for $i, j = 0, \ldots, n\}$ represents the set of arcs. Each arc $(i, j) \in A$ is associated with a non-negative cost $c_{i,j}$ that expresses the travel cost spent from vertex i to j. In this representation, node 0 represents where vehicles depart and return at the end of the routes (central depot). Correlated to a location l, there is a demand d_l, defined as null to the central depot. The problem will be solved assuming that the set of trucks k is homogeneous and trucks have the same capacity Q. Therefore, the assumptions summarizing the problem are:

- The number of trucks is supposed to be limited (K) and homogeneous.
- Every location is visited once by exactly one truck.
- Trucks have limited capacity Q.
- Trucks must empty their load in the central depot once full capacity is reached and remain there.
- Full demand cannot exceed the total capacity of the fleet.
- Each route begins and ends at the central depot.
- The routes are calculated with all information available in a static approach.
- Demands from customers cannot be split.

The mathematical formulation that was considered to solve the CVRP described above was written based on the general formulation in the literature [25]. The visit sequence for the routes for each truck was found based on the definition of decision variables as shown next:

$$\text{Minimize} \sum_{l \in N} \sum_{i \in N} c_{lj} \sum_{k \in K} x_{ljk} \tag{1}$$

subject to:

$$\sum_{l \in N} d_l y_{lk} \leq Q, \quad \forall k \in K \tag{2}$$

$$\sum_{k \in K} y_{0k} \leq K \tag{3}$$

$$\sum_{j \in N} x_{ljk} = \sum_{j \in N} x_{jlk} = y_{lk}, \quad \forall l \in N, \forall k \in K \tag{4}$$

$$\sum_{k \in K} y_{lk} = 1, \quad \forall l \in N \setminus \{0\} \tag{5}$$

$$u_{jk} \geq u_{lk} + Q(x_{ljk} - 1) + d_j, \quad \forall l, j \in N \setminus \{0\}, l \neq j, \tag{6}$$
$$\text{such that } d_l + d_j \leq Q, \forall k \in K$$

$$d_l \leq u_{lk} \leq Q, \quad \forall l \in N \setminus \{0\}, \forall k \in K \tag{7}$$
$$x_{ljk} \in \{0,1\}, \quad \forall l, j \in N, \forall k \in K \tag{8}$$
$$y_{lk} \in \{0,1\}, \quad \forall l \in N, \forall k \in K \tag{9}$$

The decision variables are defined as follows:

$$x_{ljk} = \begin{cases} 1, \text{ if truck } k \text{ visits location } j \text{ after location } l \\ 0, \text{ otherwise.} \end{cases}$$

$$y_{lk} = \begin{cases} 1, \text{ if truck } k \text{ visits location } l \\ 0, \text{ otherwise.} \end{cases}$$

The objective function represented in (1) enables minimizing the total cost to serve all the customers, respecting the stated constraints. Constraint (2) is the main constraint in this problem, stating that the sum of demands of vertices visited in a route is equal or smaller to the truck's capacity. Constraints (3) and (4) are related to vehicle circulation, ensuring that every truck leaves the depot only once and keeps performing the service as long as the capacity constraint is not violated (continuity of the route). Constraint (5) guarantees that every location is visited exactly once by only one truck, illustrating that demands are not split in this formulation. The constraint in (6) ensures all routes are connected to the central depot. The next constraint, (7), is connected to the previous and represents the truckload k after visiting the location l (u_{lk}). At last, constraints (8) and (9) are responsible to specify the domain of decision variables x_{ljk} and y_{lk}.

3.2   Guided Local Search

Guided Local search is a successful metaheuristic algorithm for solving many problems since the latest '90s. The algorithm is a penalty-based implementation whose efficiency is penalizing some solution features along the iterations.

The mathematical formulation presented here was based on the literature [27]. Denoting by I_i the following indicator function and assuming minimization:

$$I_i(x) = \begin{cases} 1, \text{ if solution } x \text{ has feature } i \\ 0, \text{ otherwise.} \end{cases}$$

Let p_i be a penalty function associated with a feature i of the solution, denoting as f the original objective function. The GLS will use the following augmented objective function g:

$$g(x) = f(x) + \lambda \sum_i I_i(x) \times p_i \qquad (10)$$

The GLS will use the function shown in (10) to find new solutions. The penalty factor (λ) can be used to tune the search to find completely different solutions (high λ value, diversification) or similar solutions (low λ value, intensification). Penalties start with a null value and are incremented by 1 with each local optimum found. The mechanism behind penalties in GLS is defined upon the assessment of the utility of a feature, being the penalization attributed in the case of large utilities. The utility function is calculated as follows for a feature i in a solution x:

$$u_i(x) = I_i(x) \times \frac{c_i(x)}{1 + p_i} \qquad (11)$$

In Eq. 11, the value $c_i(x)$ is the cost associated with a feature i in a solution x. If the feature i does not apply to a solution x, its utility will be defined as 0 ($I_i(x) = 0$). On the other hand, the utility $u_i(x)$ is proportional to the cost $c_i(x)$ of the feature i in solution x. However, the utility tends to disappear if a determined feature is often penalized because a feature that appears with frequency in a local optimum might be part of a good solution. Based on the general formulation of GLS introduced here, the algorithm used to solve the CVRP in this work is based on the following description. Denoting by $d_{i,j}$ the cost for traveling the arc (i, j), this will be considered as the cost of the objective function for that arc, and then $c_{ij} = d_{i,j}$. With this in mind and considering the general definition presented above, the augmented objective function of the GLS here used will be:

$$g(x) = \sum_{(i,j)} d_{i,j}(x) + \lambda \sum_{(i,j)} c_{ij}(x) \times p_{i,j} \times I_{ij}(x) \qquad (12)$$

Penalty factor λ starts with value 0.1 by default.

4   Numerical Results

This section will discuss the results obtained for route optimization using GLS available in OR-Tools to solve the Augerat CVRP dataset. The main goal is to determine the best-case execution time feasible in the context of dynamic scenarios of CVRP and also evaluate the algorithm performance for cases demanding for higher performance regarding distance shortening. In this regard, the execution time should be as low as possible. For this reason, here we tested the performance of GLS to solve the Augerat instances considering as criteria stop execution times between 1 and 10 s.

4.1   Optimal Distances

The Augerat instance considered for this work comprises 27 datasets, each exploring a different scenario. The most important difference between each dataset is the number of customers and trucks since the truck's capacity is the same for all datasets ($Q = 100$). For all sets, increasing the execution time from 1 to 360 s returned the best improvement in distance optimization. Comparing the results obtained using GLS with the literature revealed that GLS can overcome the literature in 62.96% of the datasets. Figure 3 brings the comparison between optimal values and the results obtained by GLS in the maximum execution time considered here.

The sets for which the distance obtained was worse than the optimal had a ratio of nodes/truck above 7, which reveals that the algorithm would need more execution time to achieve better results. Although a good result was observed in increasing the execution time from 1 to 360 s, it is important to consider the need to study the execution times as well. For instance, the maximum execution time considered in this study would not be feasible for applications in real and dynamic scenarios.

4.2   Execution Time and Optimal Distances

The best result observed for all tests was obtained with the maximum execution time. This can be explained due to the higher time available for the algorithm to process the information and search for the optimal solution, escaping local minima. On the other hand, it is important to evaluate the improvement in the solution according to the execution time. Figure 4 brings the sum of optimal distances found for each set considering execution times from 1 to 10 s and the execution time of 360 s.

The summary of the optimal distances found according to the execution time shows how powerful this parameter can be in tuning the algorithm's performance. However, the distance shortening by increasing the execution time is clearly not linear, as reported in other works that utilize metaheuristic algorithms for route optimization. For this reason, it is important to consider the algorithm's future application to choose the proper execution time better. For instance, if one considers it more important to achieve better solutions no matter the execution time, a higher execution time would return better solutions. On the other hand, considering dynamic scenarios (i.e. dynamic route planning in waste collection) would demand faster algorithms since time is also precious in these activities. For instance, a deeper evaluation of how execution time impacts the algorithm's

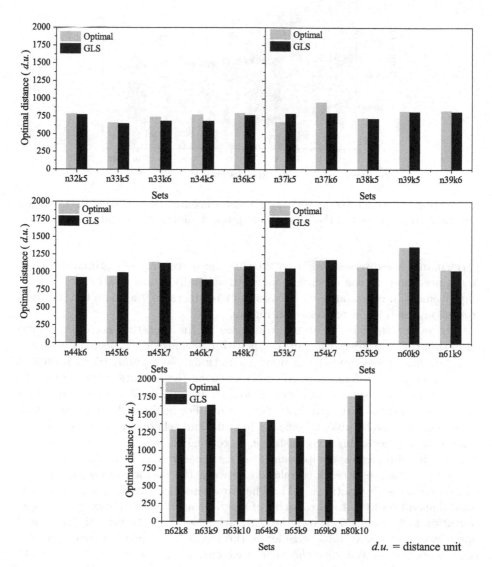

Fig. 3. Best results obtained with GLS compared to optimal reported on the literature

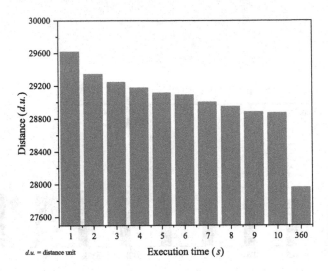

Fig. 4. Sum of optimal distance found for Augerat instances according to the execution time used (time interval in the X-axis is not proportional to the actual time interval).

performance is expressed in Fig. 5a showing the percentage of optimal distances found according to the execution time. Additionally, an evaluation of distance improvement in consonance with execution time increase, based on the standard execution time (1s), is expressed in Fig. 5b.

The evolution of better results compared to the literature according to the execution time considered to run the algorithm was already expected due to the observed differences reported in previous sections. Both summarized results in Figs. 4 and 5a have demonstrated that increasing the execution time from 1 to 360 s returns more significant optimization. However, Fig. 5b demonstrates that this improvement is expensive in execution time. For instance, the high execution time would not be feasible nor efficient in situations where time is more valuable than distance shortenings. For instance, increasing the execution time from 1 to 360 s returned an average improvement of less than a unit (0.11 d.u./s).

Some studies reported a correlation between the performance of their algorithm and the set's tightness [8, 11]. The parameter is a correlation between the total demand and the total capacity of the fleet ascribed to perform the transportation task. Figure 6a shows the correlation between the set's tightness and optimization achieved upon considering the maximum execution time. The distance savings achieved with the highest execution time were also compared to the systems' size, and the result is shown in Fig. 6b. The result demonstrates that GLS optimization results achieved with increased execution time correlate poorly with the set's tightness. However, it is important to highlight that the tightness interval in Augerat instances is low (0.82-0.94), which can explain the low correlation between the parameters. On the other hand, improvement in distance optimization seems more related to the size of the system considered.

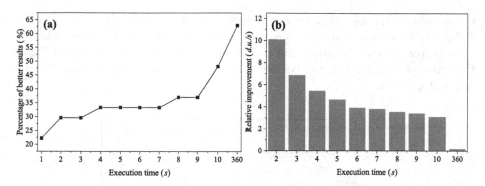

Fig. 5. (a) Percentage of better results achieved with GLS according to the execution time and (b)optimization performance by increasing execution time from standard value (1 s). Time interval in the X-axis is not proportional to the actual time interval.

For instance, GLS algorithms can achieve higher distance savings increasing the execution time in bigger systems.

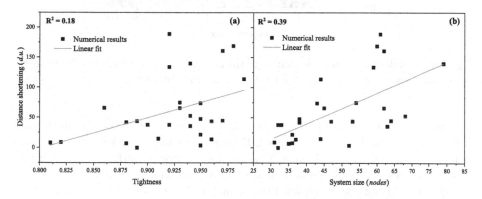

Fig. 6. Correlation between distance shortening and (a) tightness, (b) system size

4.3   Environmental Analysis in Distance Savings

Most trucks and vehicles used in the fleets are moved by petroleum-based fuels responsible for emitting gaseous fractions of environmentally harmful compounds, such as SO_x, CO_x, and NO_x. In Europe, the fleet of trucks represents around 4% of the total number of vehicles on roads, but they are responsible for 25% of the total CO_2 emission. Several studies have been devoted to analyzing the investments required to reduce emissions by trucks [4,23,24]. One alternative is route optimization since traveling shorter distances will emit fewer gases into the atmosphere. Recent studies and reports have also demonstrated that urban delivery trucks with a 4×2 axle configuration (4-UD) emitted, on average, $307\,gCO_2/t$-km. For instance, considering the distance optimization achieved upon increasing the execution time would return CO_2 emissions shown in Fig. 7. For this calculation, km was considered as distance unit, kg as capacity and demand units.

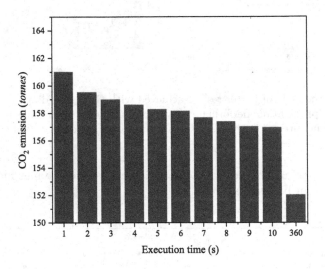

Fig. 7. CO_2 emission estimate according to the algorithm's execution time. Time interval in the X-axis is not proportional to the actual time interval.

The result shown in Fig. 7 has the same tendency observed for optimized distances shown in Fig. 4, as expected. Representing the results in terms of CO_2 emission is fundamental to increasing awareness of how powerful route optimization can be to spare the environment from more pollution. For instance, in a real scenario, increasing the execution time from 1 to 10 s could result in up to 29.91 tonnes less CO_2 being thrown into the atmosphere. The value increases even more, considering the highest execution time used here (66.45 tonnes). On the other hand, it is also important to remember that the optimal execution time must be defined to meet the application scenario of the algorithm.

5   Conclusions and Future Work

In this work, GLS available in open-source OR-Tools have demonstrated the capacity to solve the Augerat instances considering different execution times. The algorithm has demonstrated a significant increase in distance savings upon increasing the execution time. Most importantly, the results shown here regarding the algorithm's performance in solving the Augerat instances have proven the versatility of the algorithm. For instance, increasing the execution time from 1 to 10 s would not affect the viability of employing the tool in a real scenario of dynamic route planning. One example could be the dynamic route planning in waste collection, for which the route can be planned during truck stops to perform the collection service. In this regard, the execution time of 10 s would not delay the collection task and could significantly improve the result considering the standard execution time. Furthermore, if the main purpose is distance shortening, the algorithm can also be tuned by increasing the execution time to return more improvements in distance shortening. We anticipate the tool being studied for a diverse range of services in the transportation sector.

References

1. Abdelatti, M.F., Sodhi, M.S.: An improved GPU-accelerated heuristic technique applied to the capacitated vehicle routing problem. In: Proceedings of the 2020 Genetic and Evolutionary Computation Conference, pp. 663–671 (2020). https://doi.org/10.1145/3377930.3390159
2. Augerat, P., Naddef, D., Belenguer, J., Benavent, E., Corberan, A., Rinaldi, G.: Computational results with a branch and cut code for the capacitated vehicle routing problem (1995)
3. Braekers, K., Ramaekers, K., Van Nieuwenhuyse, I.: The vehicle routing problem: state of the art classification and review. Comput. Indust. Eng. **99**, 300–313 (2016). https://doi.org/10.1016/j.cie.2015.12.007
4. Breed, A.K., Speth, D., Plötz, P.: CO_2 fleet regulation and the future market diffusion of zero-emission trucks in Europe. Energy Policy **159**, 112640 (2021). https://doi.org/10.1016/j.enpol.2021.112640
5. Dantzig, G.B., Ramser, J.H.: The truck dispatching problem. Manage. Sci. **6**(1), 80–91 (1959). https://doi.org/10.1287/mnsc.6.1.80
6. Desaulniers, G., Errico, F., Irnich, S., Schneider, M.: Exact algorithms for electric vehicle-routing problems with time windows. Oper. Res. **64**(6), 1388–1405 (2016). https://doi.org/10.1287/opre.2016.1535
7. Dhanya, K.M., Kanmani, S., Hanitha, G., Abirami, S.: Hybrid crow search-ant colony optimization algorithm for capacitated vehicle routing problem. In: Zelinka, I., Senkerik, R., Panda, G., Lekshmi Kanthan, P.S. (eds.) ICSCS 2018. CCIS, vol. 837, pp. 46–52. Springer, Singapore (2018). https://doi.org/10.1007/978-981-13-1936-5_5
8. Dohn, A., Rasmussen, M.S., Larsen, J.: The vehicle routing problem with time windows and temporal dependencies. Networks **58**(4), 273–289 (2011). https://doi.org/10.1002/net.20472
9. Dubois, F., Renaud-Goud, P., Stolf, P.: Capacitated vehicle routing problem under deadlines: an application to flooding crisis. IEEE Access **10**, 45629–45642 (2022). https://doi.org/10.1109/ACCESS.2022.3170446
10. Haghani, A., Jung, S.: A dynamic vehicle routing problem with time-dependent travel times. Comput. Oper. Res. **32**(11), 2959–2986 (2005). https://doi.org/10.1016/j.cor.2004.04.013
11. Hannan, M., Akhtar, M., Begum, R., Basri, H., Hussain, A., Scavino, E.: Capacitated vehicle-routing problem model for scheduled solid waste collection and route optimization using PSO algorithm. Waste Manag. **71**, 31–41 (2018). https://doi.org/10.1016/j.wasman.2017.10.019. https://www.sciencedirect.com/science/article/pii/S0956053X17307675

12. Jia, Y.H., Mei, Y., Zhang, M.: Confidence-based ant colony optimization for capacitated electric vehicle routing problem with comparison of different encoding schemes. IEEE Trans. Evol. Comput. **26**(6), 1394–1408 (2022). https://doi.org/10.1109/TEVC.2022.3144142

13. Jozefowiez, N., Semet, F., Talbi, E.G.: Multi-objective vehicle routing problems. Eur. J. Oper. Res. **189**(2), 293–309 (2008). https://doi.org/10.1016/j.ejor.2007.05.055

14. Mehmood, T.: Does information technology competencies and fleet management practices lead to effective service delivery? Empirical evidence from e-commerce industry. Int. J. Technol. Innov. Manag. (IJTIM) **1**(2), 14–41 (2021). https://doi.org/10.54489/ijtim.v1i2.26

15. Mohammed, M.A., et al.: Solving vehicle routing problem by using improved k-nearest neighbor algorithm for best solution. J. Comput. Sci. **21**, 232–240 (2017). https://doi.org/10.1016/j.jocs.2017.04.012

16. Montoya, A., Guéret, C., Mendoza, J.E., Villegas, J.G.: The electric vehicle routing problem with nonlinear charging function. Transport. Res. Part B: Methodol. **103**, 87–110 (2017). https://doi.org/10.1016/j.trb.2017.02.004

17. Pillac, V., Gendreau, M., Guéret, C., Medaglia, A.L.: A review of dynamic vehicle routing problems. Eur. J. Oper. Res. **225**(1), 1–11 (2013). https://doi.org/10.1016/j.ejor.2012.08.015

18. Pisinger, D., Ropke, S.: A general heuristic for vehicle routing problems. Comput. Oper. Res. **34**(8), 2403–2435 (2007). https://doi.org/10.1016/j.cor.2005.09.012

19. Praveen, V., Keerthika, P., Sivapriya, G., Sarankumar, A., Bhasker, B.: Vehicle routing optimization problem: a study on capacitated vehicle routing problem. Mater. Today: Proceed. **64**, 670–674 (2022). https://doi.org/10.1016/j.matpr.2022.05.185

20. Silva, A.S., et al.: Solving a capacitated waste collection problem using an open-source tool. In: Gervasi, O., Murgante, B., Misra, S., Rocha, A.M.A.C., Garau, C. (eds.) Computational Science and Its Applications - ICCSA 2022 Workshops. ICCSA 2022. Lecture Notes in Computer Science, vol. 13378, pp. 140–156. Springer, Cham (2022). https://doi.org/10.1007/978-3-031-10562-3_11

21. Silva, A.S., et al.: Dynamic urban solid waste management system for smart cities. In: Simos, D.E., Rasskazova, V.A., Archetti, F., Kotsireas, I.S., Pardalos, P.M. (eds.) Learning and Intelligent Optimization. LION 2022. Lecture Notes in Computer Science, vol. 13621, pp. 178–190. Springer, Cham (2023). https://doi.org/10.1007/978-3-031-24866-5_14

22. Silva, A.S., et al.: Capacitated waste collection problem solution using an open-source tool. Computers **12**(1), 15 (2023). https://doi.org/10.3390/computers12010015. https://www.mdpi.com/2073-431X/12/1/15

23. Siskos, P., Moysoglou, Y.: Assessing the impacts of setting CO_2 emission targets on truck manufacturers: a model implementation and application for the EU. Transport. Res. Part A: Policy Pract. **125**, 123–138 (2019). https://doi.org/10.1016/j.tra.2019.05.010

24. Tian, J., Yang, D., Zhang, H., Liu, L.: Classification method of energy efficiency and CO_2 emission intensity of commercial trucks in china's road transport. Procedia Eng. **137**, 75–84 (2016). https://doi.org/10.1016/j.proeng.2016.01.236. Green Intelligent Transportation System and Safety

25. Toth, P., Vigo, D.: The vehicle routing problem. SIAM (2002). https://doi.org/10.1137/1.9780898718515

26. Vidal, T., Laporte, G., Matl, P.: A concise guide to existing and emerging vehicle routing problem variants. Eur. J. Oper. Res. **286**(2), 401–416 (2020). https://doi.org/10.1016/j.ejor.2019.10.010
27. Voudouris, C., Tsang, E.P., Alsheddy, A.: Guided local search. In: Gendreau, M., Potvin, JY. (eds.) Handbook of Metaheuristics. International Series in Operations Research & Management Science, vol. 146, pp. 321–361. Springer, MA (2010). https://doi.org/10.1007/978-1-4419-1665-5_11

Analysis of the Impact on the Safety and Sustainability of Vehicular Traffic in the Landside Area of Olbia - Costa Smeralda-Airport

Nicoletta Rassu(✉) ⓘ, Mauro Coni ⓘ, and Francesca Maltinti ⓘ

Department of Civil and Environmental Engineering and Architecture, University of Cagliari, 09129 Cagliari, Italy
{nicoletta.rassu,maltinti}@unica.it

Abstract. The quality and efficiency of the landside area of an airport are strongly conditioned by the circulation of the internal mobility that must be efficient and safe at the same time. Key elements in this regard are: (1) the curbisde highway, (2) the roads that wind around the terminal area and (3) the parking areas.

The traffic on the roads serving the airport area is clearly distinguished from that on ordinary roads (urban and suburban) both because of the geometry, strongly conditioned by limited space, both for the different traffic composition and the expectations of their drivers. The concentration of a multitude of structures with different functionalities, located in relatively small areas, means that the signage are abundant and complex to code quickly, especially for those users who are unfamiliar with the infrastructure and who represent the dominant share of users. In addition, the latter live with regular users (mainly private transport operators) who have a casual drive.

This is the scenario that is the background to the study whose concrete case concerned the Airport of Olbia Costa Smeralda. In the Sardinian airport, in July 2019, some rental operators/ remote parking won the appeal to the Regional Administrative Court (TAR) for the annulment of the ENAC Order and in this case the section concerning the limitation of the free admission to only three entrances to the parking area in front of the terminal and called Short term parking.

The aim of the study is to analyze the traffic flows resulting from the application of this amendment and to assess its effects in terms of traffic efficiency and the safety of users.

Keywords: Airport terminal · landside areas · curbside highway · parking areas · pick-up areas · drop-off areas · safety

1 Introduction

Airports are strategic infrastructures of modern life and play a crucial role for transportation of passengers with different purposes, such as tourism and businesses. They become even more important in complex contexts such as islands where they are part of a complex transport system whose efficiency is vital for economic, social and territorial development [1–4].

O. Gervasi et al. (Eds.): ICCSA 2023 Workshops, LNCS 14111, pp. 290–307, 2023.
https://doi.org/10.1007/978-3-031-37126-4_20

Airport planning is a complex process because an airport involves a wide variety of activities, with different and often contradictory requirements [5], which must be analyzed and solved separately but need integrated policies choices.

The overall level of service (LOS) of a terminal system depends on the LOS of individual components, such as check-in, departure lounges, landside, ect., as well as socio-economic variables [6, 7]. Parking is a integral part of the landside and its operation affects the level of service of an airport [8]. Anderson et. al. [9] show that curbside operations is one of the most significant factors affecting of the overall LOS of the airport terminal system.

So, the curb-side and the access roadway are two important segments of the terminal that needs in depth analysis in order to identify their operational characteristics [10]. The operational characteristics of the curbside terminal significantly differ from those of most other roads due to several reasons such as different traffic composition, passenger expectations and driver behavior, vehicle downtime and etc.. Moreover, the planning of future expansions of the terminal will have to be based on the analysis of the vehicular traffic, the choice of the mode of travel, the queues of the vehicles along the parking lanes, the times of permanence of the vehicles and the level of occupation of the passengers [11].

The regulation of accessibility to the airports landside areas arises from the need to guarantee a multiplicity of aspects. The most important is to organize and regulate, according to a hierarchy of priorities, the access of vehicles to the area in an orderly, safe and controlled manner.

It is quite clear that emergency vehicles, law enforcement and public security vehicles, airport inspection and maintenance vehicles as well as public vehicles should have absolute priority over other vehicles. The latter mainly include private vehicles, rental cars, on-demand and pre- reserved taxicabs, prearranged and on-demand limousines or Town Cars, door-to-door vans, courtesy vehicles, charter buses, scheduled buses, and service and delivery vehicles.

The Ordinance issued by the Italian Civil Aviation Authority (ENAC) [12], which governs the management of spaces (road network and parking) and regulates access, establishes that access to the "Short term parking" is free of charge for 15 min and for a maximum of 3 consecutive daily accesses. Beyond these, parking must be charged according to the airport's tariff scheme.

At Olbia "Costa Smeralda" airport, some operators appealed to the Regional Administrative Tribunal (TAR) to remove the limitation of the free allowance to only three accesses, winning the appeal. Hence, this study on the evaluation of the effects of this decision and the resulting set up on landside area traffic and security on operators and users was born.

Section 2 reports issues that specifically concern airport operations with particular reference to the definition of the internal road system and the physiological differences with the ordinary road system in urban and suburban areas. In Sect. 3 the case study will be presented and in Sect. 4 the conclusions.

2   Management Criteria for Airport Landside Operations

The quality and efficiency of the landside area of an airport are conditioned by the circulation of the internal road system, which must be both efficient and safe.

In literature there are two guidelines which analyze and evaluate the performance of the curbside and roadway operations of landside, 1. International Air Transport Association (IATA) Manual [13], which gives standard figures can be used in planning and design and 2. The methodology proposed in Airport Cooperative Research Program (ACRP) Report 40 [14].

Report 40 emphasizes that key elements are the lanes and curbside highway, where travelers with their luggage enter and leave the terminal, the roads in the terminal area travelled by private and commercial vehicles accessing the arrivals and departures area, and the parking area.

The maintenance of safety and efficiency standards must be ensured even with increasing traffic volumes (seasonal or annual growth), but often, the geometry of the lanes is constrained by the presence of terminal buildings and the proximity of other infrastructures serving the airport. So, their size, and therefore capacity, cannot always be modulated and aligned with traffic increases.

Traffic on airport roads differs significantly from that on ordinary roads (urban and rural) due to the highly restricted geometry, the different traffic composition, and the travelers' expectations. Unaccustomed drivers - unfamiliar with the area - mingle with a significant number of airport service operators and professionals who, driving vans, buses, and shuttles, due to their natural knowledge of the routes drive at operating speeds far above those of unaccustomed users.

Furthermore, there is a difference between traffic conditions within the same landside. The access and transit road network is characterized by traffic flows with driving styles typical of rural areas, while the road network of the landside areas is more akin to that of urban areas, both in terms of low travel speeds and the mix of traffic composition (private cars/pedestrians/buses and shuttles) and the multitude of manoeuvres permitted.

Figure 1 describes airport road network and its hierarchy by type.

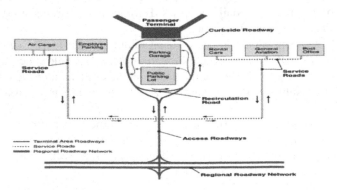

Fig. 1. Landside Hierarchy [14]

Roads are divided into:

Access Roadway: are roads that connect the regional road and motorway network with the terminal and other areas of the airport. They attract large volumes of traffic and generally have a limited number of decision points (i.e. entrances or exits).

Curbside Roadways: are one-way roadways which are placed directly in front of the terminal buildings where vehicles stop to pick up and drop off airline/non-airline passengers and their bags. Generally, curb side roadways consist of following road categories. (1) Inner lanes where vehicles stop or stand in a nose-to- tail manner while passengers loading and unloading. (2) Adjacent manoeuvring lane which is used to approach the inner lane. (3) Through or bypass lanes, which are used to move the vehicles through the facility without stopping. [11]. Depending on the configuration of the terminals, these roadways may be on staggered levels. In airports with a two-level Curbside Roadway, the area on the upper level serves the Departures area (i.e. ticketing and check-in). Those on the lower level are on the same level as the Arrivals (baggage claim and passengers).

Recirculation Roads: provide a variety of routes for the movement of vehicles between terminals, car parks and rental car facilities. Compared to access roads, Recirculation Roads generally serve a smaller volume of traffic, are less direct, operate at a lower speed and have more singular points (intersections with other roads, intersections between vehicle streams, etc.).

2.1 Aspects that Make Operating on Airport Roads Unique

The operational characteristics of airport roads and in particular of Curbside Roadways differ from other types of roads due to the peculiarities of the traffic and users they serve [15]. They can be summarized as follows:

1. Numerous and complex directional signs;
2. High percentage of large vehicles;
3. High percentage of unfamiliar drivers;
4. Mix of familiar and unfamiliar drivers;
5. Traffic circulation;
6. Presence of pedestrian flows;
7. Drivers often under stress.

Numerous and Complex Directional Signs. Airport directional signs often provide more information, that is more lines of text in the same sign, than the one on public roads, because of multiple and concentrated areas and services to reach. Signals often include colors, characters, symbols and messages not used on other public road signs. Due to the number, size and complexity of the signals, motorists may in some cases not notice regulatory signals and/or restrictions, thus contravening one regulation rather than another or due to information overload, slow down the gear to acquire all the necessary information causing slowdowns. Research suggests that drivers take at least 0.5s to read every word on signage and 1s to symbols [16].

High Percentage of Large Vehicles. More than 10 types of ground transport services operate on airport roads. The characteristics of each service, the needs of customers who use them and the operational characteristics of the vehicles used must be considered when drawing up operational plans for the roads located within the airport area and, in particular, the terminal area.

Courtesy vehicles, door-to-door vans, buses and other large vehicles may account for 10 to 20% of the traffic volume. On public roads, the presence of these types of vehicles is less than 10%. The consequence of this, and at the same time a critical issue, is that the presence of large vehicles can obstruct drivers' view of signs and interfere with the movement of passing vehicles.

High Percentage of Unfamiliar Drivers. Most airport passengers are not frequent users and likewise the accompanying persons are often unfamiliar with the airport and consequently with the access roads. The mental workload of the occasional driver is higher as there are multiple facilities to be reached, arrival/departure terminal areas, time differentiated parking areas, transport service areas etc. Simplifying maneuvers, he often must find the correct entrance to the desired terminal road, a place to stop to accompany or pick up a passenger, he must pay attention to the maneuvers of other vehicles and pedestrian crossings. Finally, in these areas confusion and thus discomfort can be fuelled given the short distances available, the complexity of maneuvers, the limited lines of sight and the large amount of signage that must be coded in a reasonably short time [15].

All of these elements make travelling within the terminal area challenging, stressful and characterized by low speeds that for this category of users.

Mix of Familiar and Unfamiliar Drivers. Although most drivers of private vehicles rarely use an airport, 20% to 30% of the vehicles on airport roads (taxis, courtesy vehicles and limousines) are driven by professionals. These, like commuters and regular users, are familiar with airport roads and therefore have a more casual driving style than unfamiliar users since they know how to get to the various areas and therefore do not need to dwell on reading directional signs, which is required for the other category of users.

Traffic circulation. Entering and exiting the innermost lanes of the Curbside Roadway generate potentially dangerous conflict points due to sudden lane changes. In addition, it often happens that motorists, if they cannot find a space to stop and are waiting for an oncoming passenger, are forced to exit the terminal area. These recirculating vehicles contribute to road congestion and represent unnecessary traffic volumes (passive traffic).

Presence of Pedestrian Flows. The presence of large numbers of pedestrians, crossing either at zebra crossings or without rules and/or attention to traffic, constitutes an additional element of risk for traffic safety on this type of infrastructure.

Drivers Often Under Stress. The mental workload faced by a motorist travelling on airport roads, by the very nature of the facility, is a risk factor. It is further aggravated by the presence of conflict points, i.e. intersections between vehicle flows that perform constant lane-change manoeuvres, and by the presence of heavy pedestrian traffic, characterized by a higher crossing density than that normally found on urban roads.

The stressful condition stems from the knowledge that small delays or wrong turns can cause delays that can affect the rest of the travel chain up to the loss of the flight in extreme cases.

Airport travel includes intermodal actions and/or connections: car - plane, car - bus, car - train, searching for a rest area or parking space; in addition, there is the action of finding a passenger, the correct place to drop off or pick up a passenger, locating a taxi, courtesy vehicle or city bus stop, and so on. Each action is therefore part of a chain of events, so it is clear that if just one element goes wrong, it can interrupt or delay a holiday, business meeting or other important event.

2.2 Airport Policies to Improve the Functionality of Roads Adjacent to Terminals

The airport management companies regulate the airport grounds by requiring commercial vehicle operators interacting with passengers to comply with the rules and regulations they prescribe:

1. The roads that each operator may use;
2. The parking areas where they may drop off or pick up passengers;
3. The maximum permitted parking times;
4. The speed limits and other restrictions with which they must comply;
5. The fees they must pay to operate at the airport.

Airport operators may charge commercial ground transport operators fees to recover costs or manage demand. These fees include those charged per company or per vehicle and cost recovery charges generally calculated based on the transport operator's vehicle trip volume or the volume of airport-related business.

Demand management fees may also include penalties for operators who fail to comply with airport regulations such as, for example, staying in the parking area beyond a set maximum time, exceeding the daily or monthly limit on the number of allowed passages, and violating the minimum time intervals established between successive courtesy vehicles. Airport operators can use these charges to improve traffic operations along curbside roadways, discourage unnecessary trips, reduce vehicle emissions, and improve air quality by incentivizing the use of alternative fuel vehicles or consolidated shuttle vehicles using concessionary charges.

Among the airports examined in Report 40 [14], the best airport with best Curbside Roadways arrangements are those airports that (a) physically separate private vehicles from commercial vehicles through the use of multi-level infrastructure or dedicated zones or areas, (b) provide good signage, and (c) provide a traffic direction that is easily readable by drivers.

The curbside roadway and the designated parking area are important components of the airport facilities on the ground [10]. As mentioned in the previous section, the operational characteristics of Curbside Roadways differ significantly from those of most other ordinary roads in terms of: vehicle dwell time, continuous lane changes and demand fluctuation. Therefore, operation and intervention plans must take into account in addition to the analysis of vehicular traffic, travel mode choices and vehicle queues along the Curbside Roadways, vehicle dwell times, passenger occupancy time at the platforms, etc.

Therefore, airport terminal curbsides are critical infrastructures, and their correct design is a crucial step for achieving positive passenger experiences avoiding long pedestrian paths, lack of information or long waiting time for transportation [17].

As airport passenger traffic increases, curbside roadway congestion is a growing problem. The capacity of a curbside is influenced by long dwell times of pickup vehicles at the curb, double parking, excessive queue lengths for taxi and limousines, and shortages of taxis and limousines. Congestion can be prevented through efficient curbside design and effective curbside management policies. Many airports accommodate the increase in passenger traffic by relying on policy and design measures to alleviate congestion and optimize operations [18].

Report 40 [14] provides a comprehensive summary of measures for improving curbside operations. The measures can be physical improvements and operational measures. Physical improvements, such as widening or lengthening the roadway, providing alternative pickup/drop-off areas, and constructing additional curbside levels, require substantial financial investment and space. Operational measures manage demand at the curbside by improving the public transit mode share, developing offsite facilities and rearranging curbside spaces. Wong and Baker [19] focus on rail transportation as a means to reduce curbside congestion and emissions and consider policies of US airports which promote the public transportation mode share.

3   Real Work – Aeroporto di Olbia Costa Smeralda

Olbia Costa Smeralda Airport is the second largest in Sardinia in terms of importance and number of passengers handled (3.2 mln in 2022 [20]).

As a result of the Ordinance issued by Enac [12] that regulates for each airport the management of spaces and regulates access, access to the parking area intended for short stay, enjoys a 15' free allowance valid for three daily entries. In the face of this, some operators appealed to the Regional Administrative Tribunal (TAR) for the removal of the free allowance limitation to only three accesses, winning the appeal. Hence the analysis of the effects of the measure.

3.1   ENAC Ordinance

Enac Ordinance [12] of March 2019 regulates vehicular movement on the state-owned area of Olbia Airport open to public use. It contains 20 articles of which the ones of interest and concerning the regulation of parking areas and the management of spaces for NCCs are Art.ii 8 and 13, respectively, which are given below.

As regulated by ENAC [12], parking spaces for NCCs, as just anticipated, are regulated by Art.13 which in summary:

- It identifies two areas where passenger loading and unloading can take place depending on the size of the buses:

  o NCC1: vehicles with capacity over 7 seats, within the BUS area;
  o NCC2: vehicles with capacity up to 7 seats, within the short-term parking area.

Both *"may only stay within the parking areas for the period of time necessary to drop off/pick up customers. Stops in excess of 30 min are not permitted."*

According to the regulations of the ENAC ordinance in Art. 8, *"In consideration of the safety needs of vehicular and pedestrian transit and the characteristics of vehicular flows in the vicinity of the air terminal, entrance with free allowance is permitted up to a cumulative maximum of 3 (three) accesses per day by the same vehicle. Accesses after the third will be charged according to the rules for the area concerned without any allowance."*

In the face of this, a remote parking company filed an appeal against ENAC and the Airport Management Company for the annulment of the ENAC order [12] and in this case on the daily limitation of the free allowance to only 3 daily passes per car. On the face of this, the TAR for Sardinia ruled that the appeal was well-founded.

The grounds for the merits of the appeal, as justified by the TAR are: on the unlawfulness of the measure because the safety protection justifications were not found to be objective, as it concludes that: *"[...] Collective transportation, whether public or private, abates traffic and does not increase it."* The statement that logically *"Collective transportation, breaks down traffic"* recalled in the judgment deserves further study.

In some cases, it is evident that collective transport can reduce the vehicular traffic circulating on ordinary roads, but - on the other hand - it significantly increases pedestrian flows and conflicts between pedestrians and vehicles. Moreover, the peculiarity of this type of transportation (remote parking buses/shuttles) does not reduce the flow of cars at all but rather increases it. In fact, they themselves generate a continuous flow in the short-term parching area to accompany their customers/passengers who if they had gone independently to the airport would certainly not have transited in the short-term parching but at the long-term parching.

The critical issues of the Olbia airport are common to most airports and depend on the operations that characterize the road system in front of the terminal, which, it is worth reiterating, is characterized by vehicles that often stop in areas not allowed, maneuver and transit in a disorderly and unregulated manner in areas of limited size, which is precisely the part in front of the terminal. During the seasonal peak of the summer months, the promiscuity and number of vehicles in this area means that transit times, maneuvering spaces, and accessibility are severely affected.

In addition, the conspicuous presence of large vehicles limits visibility and all maneuvers are longer, uncertain, and unsafe. Still the presence of large flows of pedestrians, which in the peak season period reaches 20,000 passengers/day, pouring into the area in front of the air terminal, has important repercussions on the safety and service level of landside crossing operations.

3.2 Analysis of Passenger Traffic and Vehicular Transits

Olbia Costa Smeralda Airport serves a commercial passenger traffic of about 2.9 million (pre-pandemic data (2019)), of which 47% belongs to the Domestic segment and 53% to the International segment. Looking at the data for the first 6 months of 2022 (green), it can be seen that the traffic trend follows that prior to the downturn due to the pandemic years (2019 - blue), which suggests that the alignment will continue for the following months as well.

However, the aspect to be highlighted is the airport's tourist vocation, which serves traffic purely belonging to the leisure segment, which characterizes its marked seasonality. In fact, 78% of traffic (about 2.3 million) is handled in the 5 months between May

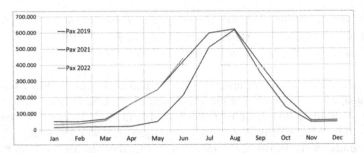

Fig. 2. Commercial passenger traffic (2019/2021/2022) (Data processing [20])

and September, months in which traffic exceeds the average monthly value (about 245 thousand pax) (Fig. 3).

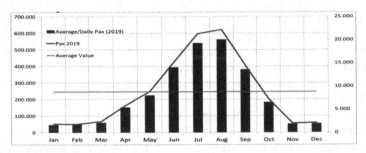

Fig. 3. Monthly passenger traffic trends (total and average daily), Year 2019

Staying on average values, an average of about 15,000 passengers pass through each day in the peak months with peaks of 20,000 passengers/day in August.

Such fluctuations inevitably spill over to the landside as well. In this regard, going into the specifics of the study, see the data on vehicular transit in the short-term parking area (Table 1).

Table 1. Number of transits with short stop tickets - historical series 2018–2022–

Year	Jan	Feb	Mar	Apr	May	Jun	Jul	Aug	Sep	Oct	Nov	Dic	Tot
2018	21.851	20.082	27.932	34.973	44.917	67.176	104.338	116.209	65.169	39.837	23.888	27.897	**594.269**
2019	21.407	20.201	24.283	39.470	42.197	63.607	99.987	109.994	59.847	36.769	22.001	26.260	**566.023**
2020	21.637	1.576	0	0	1	15.475	65.471	101.897	41.791	17.806	6.821	9.882	**282.357**
2021	8.040	8.498	10.103	10.710	19.055	51.656	112.234	145.055	65.978	26.745	18.267	21.178	**497.519**
2022	14.608	14.261	20.131	40.010	49.130	81.086							**219.226**

Until the date of the issuance of the Ordinance [12], a number of operators specialized in the business of remote parking and remote car rental operated within the airport grounds, and they managed their operations by benefiting from the time allowance within the short-stay to carry out loading and unloading operations. Some of them, as a result of the Ordinance [12], which let us recall limits the maximum number of free daily passes to three and obliges commercial operators entering the short stop to agree with the Manager on the time and manner of their operations, have:

- Negotiated and found an agreement, signing an ad hoc sub-concession contract (3 operators). A specific area has been dedicated to them for this purpose to serve the loading/unloading activities, inside the main park that guarantees full security of operations;
- Relocated their headquarters within the rent-a-car area (1 operator);
- Stopped operating (2 operators).

Ultimately, remote parking and car rental operators agreed to two important conditions:

1. To be subject to a fee, recognizing that their business is related to and in absolute interdependence with the airport development activities of the operator,
2. To carry out service not at the short-term parking, but within the main park/rent-a-car area, safeguarding congestion and ensuring proper usability of the thoroughfares in the short-term parking area often subjected to slowdowns and blockages of both vehicular and pedestrian traffic.

The effects of the aforementioned ordinance can be seen by comparing the data of accesses to the short-term parking area in the pre-ordinance period: May - September (2018) with the same period in 2019 (Fig. 4).

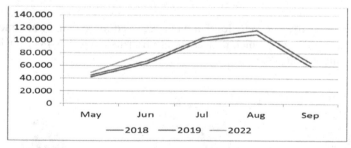

Fig. 4. Short-term parking area access comparison - Period May - September 2018/2019 - May - June 2022

The average seasonal change recorded between 2019 and 2018 is worth about - 6%. Contributing to this decline is undoubtedly the transfer of 4 of the 6 remote rental operators from the short-term parking area to the long-term parking area and the discontinuation of 2 operators. Inserting the data for May-June 2022 (in green) into the analysis, on the other hand, shows a clear reversal of the trend compared to 2019, with an average increase in the two months of reference of about 7%, a value that is not supported by the traffic trend, which grows by an average of 1% during the same period (Fig. 2).

Downstream of the analysis just conducted and with regard to the passages recorded in the short-term parking area, it can certainly be concluded that the opposite trends recorded at the turn of the pandemic period, i.e., the 2019/2018 traffic inflection (-6%) and the 2022/2019 increase (+7%) are the direct consequences, the former of the ENAC regulation of the airport's road system and airport grounds spaces, the latter of the decay of the same following the Sardinia TAR ruling.

Delving deeper into the issue of multiple passages, the following graphs show the processing of data referring to the transits in the short-term parking area and extracted on the day of 24/07/2022. Since the license plate of the car is recorded at each passage, the data processing made it possible to identify the number of passages made by each vehicle.

A total of 4.272 vehicles passed through the area for a total number of passages of 5.232. Of these 3.710 transited only once while 562 cars (13%) transited several times, from 2 to 14 times, generating 1.522 (29%) additional transits (Fig. 5).

Fig. 5. Distribution of access time on the day of July 22, 2022

Limiting the analysis to vehicles that have accessed more than three times, they in absolute value are 84 (2%) which translated into transits are worth 484 transits or 12% of the total daily transits (Fig. 6).

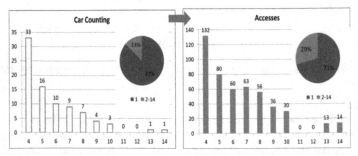

Fig. 6. Distribution of the number of vehicles with access greater than 4 and their number of transits

These multiple passes ranging from 4 (for 33 vehicles) up to a maximum of 13 and 14 for two individual operators respectively, are made throughout the day which confirms the operation of private collective transport services.

3.3 Parking Areas

The parking lots at Olbia Costa Smeralda Airport are located frontally and at a maximum distance from the Terminal entrance of about 140m. There are over 1.100 parking spaces available and they are divided into 3 sectors (Fig. 7).

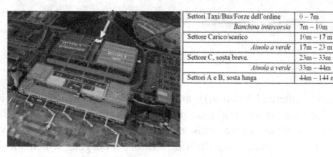

Settori Taxi/Bus/Forze dell'ordine	0 – 7m
Banchina intercorsia	7m – 10m
Settore Carico/scarico	10m – 17 m
Aiuola a verde	17m – 23 m
Settore C, sosta breve.	23m – 33m
Aiuola a verde	33m – 44m
Settori A e B, sosta lunga	44m – 144 m

Fig. 7. Aero photogrammetry landside Parking Area Olbia Airport

The small distances mean that they are absolutely walkable to such an extent that the airport, among the domestic ones, is the one with the greatest proximity of the parking area from the air terminal (Table 2).

Table 2. Distances parking areas at major national airports

National Airports	short-term parking Distance	Long-term parking Distance
Pisa	50 m ÷ 100 m	110 m ÷ 300 m
Bologna	40 m ÷ 125 m	250 m ÷ 460 m
Cagliari	28 m ÷ 45 m	80 m ÷ 210 m
Olbia	23 m ÷ 33 m	44 m ÷ 144 m
Milano - Linate	200 m ÷ 320 m	360 m ÷ 660 m
Alghero	60 m ÷ 170 m	120 m ÷ 330 m
Genova	45 m ÷ 85 m	85 m ÷ 220 m
Trieste	145 m ÷ 250 m	145 m ÷ 250 m
Bergamo	45 m ÷ 200 m	190 m ÷ 710 m
Bari	45 m ÷ 130 m	170 m ÷ 300 m
Palermo	28 m ÷ 110 m	300 m ÷ 700 m

Access to Sector C is through the gate located in the west area, in which there are 4 lanes (Fig. 8).

Starting from the right, the First is intended for access for the parking of State and relief agencies, vehicles for unloading goods for the air terminal, cabs and for the transit of vehicles designed to the bus parking lot previously authorized [12].

Fig. 8. Sector C gate

The Second (Commercial Aviation) is an access lane in which no stopping is allowed. In this lane, as indicated in the road markings, only the loading and unloading of passengers is allowed, a maneuver that must be carried out without the car driver getting out of the car. Access is allowed by collecting a ticket at the gate, which allows to cross the area for a time equal to 10', after which the short-term parking tariff will be applied [12].

Finally, the last two lanes provide access to the short-term parking area where incoming vehicles can stop for a time of 15' free of charge.

Once through the gate, the lane reserved for State Bodies/Taxi/Buses is protected and no longer accessible from the others (Fig. 9).

Fig. 9. Sector C gate - Lane division.

The distance between the air terminal and the Short Stop and Long Stop areas is 23 m and 44 m, respectively. The inconvenience generated to passengers in reaching the Long Stop compared to the Short Stop is insignificant, i.e. 21 m more, compared to the aggravation of traffic and safety conditions in the area in front of the air terminal. Wanting to quantify numerically the time loss of a passenger, assuming an average walking speed of 1 m/s [21] it is about 21 s. Conversely, the times for the parking maneuver are about 18 s (entry/exit), so a total of 36 s[22]. However, the times given are standard average values for passenger cars, under average traffic conditions and road sections. In the reference context, which is characterized by mixed vehicular currents (pedestrians - NCC - BUS) and operations different from ordinary roads, as described in Sect. 2.1, the times are longer. From a survey conducted by the Manager, the average times to make a parking space within the short stop area were found to be no less than 90 s.

However, if the benefit of 21 s saved per passenger are for the benefit of the individual, the 90s are for the benefit of all vehicles passing during that period. Referring to the data on transits at the short-term parking on July 22, reviewed in the previous section, there were 5.232 vehicle transits on that day, of which 381 were in the rush hour and in minutes 6,35 vehicles per minute. Translating the figure into time loss to vehicular traffic, for each individual passage, both have a cumulative time loss of 572 s. In summary, the advantage of a single passenger in saving 21 s translates into overall collective time loss of 572 s.

Regarding safety conditions, a rigorous and timely analysis on pedestrian and vehicular flows would be necessary, however, the current unavailability of data postpones the analysis to future research developments. Nevertheless, it is sufficient to observe that the conflict points between pedestrian (P) and vehicular (V) flow is proportional to the product of the two flows (P x V) resulting from the 4 areas: Long-term parking, short-term parking, Loading/Unloading, Bus/Taxi.

Each vehicle operating in the long-term parking will see its passengers crossing vehicular flows V_1, V_b, $V_{c/s}$ and $V_{b/t}$, vehicles transiting in the long-term parking, short-term parking, Loading/Unloading, and Bus/Taxi, respectively, with $V = V_1 + V_b + V_{c/s} + V_{b/t}$. Conflict points with pedestrians transiting in the Long Stop area (P_1) should be added to these conflict points.

In this case, the total conflict points for each passenger will be:

$$V_1 + V_b + V_{c/s} + V_{b/t} + P_1 \tag{1}$$

Similarly, each vehicle operating in the short-term parking will see its passengers crossing the V_b, $V_{c/s}$ and $V_{b/t}$ vehicular flows. To these conflict points should be added the pedestrian flow conflict points of the two areas: Long Stop (P_1) and Short Stop (P_b).

In this case total conflict points for each passenger will be:

$$V_b + V_{c/s} + V_{b/t} + P_1 + P_b \tag{2}$$

Whence the difference between (1) and (2):

$$V_1 - P_b \tag{3}$$

Substituting the symbols for the numbers gives: (i) the vehicular flows at the long-term parking (V_1) gate are of the same order of magnitude as those transited in the short-term parking (about 5.000/day); (ii) the pedestrian flow was calculated assuming a certain rate of use of the area by passengers. In this regard, considering the average daily passenger figure for the month of July (19.000), conservatively assuming a utilization coefficient of the short-term parking area of 15%, the (3) returns 2.150 additional conflict points. This value certainly constitutes a high risk factor such that encouraging the presence of vehicles in the short-term parking area, without any restrictions, generates an increased probability of risks on pedestrians.

The following images show the irregular use of the parking area by remote parking/rental operators and or by unauthorized operators.

The images highlight the incompatibility of this service with the area under consideration, both in terms of the size of the vehicles, for which those over 9 seats, exceeding

Fig. 10. Use of the short-term parking by remote parking and rental operators

the size of the regulatory stalls, encroach on the traffic lanes, limiting transit and traffic capacity, and the way passenger loading and unloading operations are carried out, often inside the lanes and/or in areas that are not allowed, with what follows in terms of safety and traffic fluidity of private users.

The additional 21 m route to the long-term parking is indicated by a pedestrian segment protected by canopies (Fig. 11). It not only provides protection to pedestrians in case of rain and sunshine in warmer months, but also ensures excellent visibility of the pedestrian route to guarantee their safety, unlike the random crossing of the individual pedestrian.

Fig. 11. Covered shelters connecting the long-term and short-term parking and Sector C - short-term parking and Loading/Unloading Stalls

In fact, passengers of NCCs, remote parking shuttles, i.e., the authorized and non-authorized operators who benefit from the multiple accesses, if they went to the airport independently, would at most use the long-term parking and not the short-term parking. It emerged from the data analysis reported in the previous section, that there were 562 multiple passes on the sample day. Of these, 84 vehicles accessed the short-term parking area more than 3 times, generating 484 transits. It is reasonable to assume that these transits were made by commercial operators and not private individuals.

Hence the consideration that the annulment of the [12] ordinance has in fact transferred a collective benefit i.e. safety, good organization of the areas and thus their orderliness in favor of only the users of the commercial operators (private parties).

Added to this is the irregular activity of those who, in order to evade the payment of parking fees, wait for incoming flights in unregulated outdoor areas (e.g., at the traffic circle, traffic island divider beds, and at prohibited parking), creating situations of disorder, danger, and not least congestion. It is common and observed practice for passengers arriving and leaving the terminal to contact their pickups who move in platoons accessing the loading/unloading area and/or Short Stopover (Ref. Fig. 10) creating de facto congestion.

4 Conclusions

The study highlighted how the operation of roads within the airport grounds differ from ordinary roads. They are characterized by: (1) complex traffic flow with rapid lane changes, (2) a high percentage of buses/shuttles whose size may interfere with the lines of visibility of signs (articulated and complex) by motorists, (3) high percentage of unaccustomed drivers who perceive the complexity of the system and therefore have a mental workload that causes stress resulting in uncertain and unsafe driving different from users/operators who are familiar with the infrastructure and therefore adopt agile driving, and finally (4) high percentage of pedestrians with luggage in tow. It is evident from the above that although the road system in general, at whatever level one reasons, must be appropriately regulated in the pursuit of high standards of operation and safety, this applies even more so within the airport grounds.

Hence the analysis of Olbia airport, which in 2019 saw the cancellation of the ENAC Order [12] and in this case the daily limitation of the free allowance to only 3 daily passes per car. The analysis conducted in Sect. 3 highlighted how remote parking/rental operators and passenger shuttles are the only ones to benefit from this measure, allowing them free access to the Stopover/Breakdown area to carry out loading and unloading of their passengers. On a typical day in July, 4.272 vehicles passed through. Of these, 3.710 passed only once while 562 cars (13%) passed several times, from 2 to 14 times, generating 1.522 (29%) additional transits. It is evident how this results in worsening traffic conditions (queues, waits, congestion) and safety (significant increase in conflict points). At the same time, phenomena of irregular parking, the presence of unauthorized parties, conflicts and disorder not compatible with the orderly processing and routing of passengers are encouraged in a sensitive area facing the terminal.

At the conclusion of the study, it was found that the annulment of Article 8 of the [12] actually created a worsening of the situation, primarily by causing multiple passages with inevitable repercussions on security. In summary, it was observed:

- Creation of parasitic traffic in the landside road system;
- Continuous rotation of parking payment evaders creates additional use of the infrastructure by accelerating wear and tear on the roadway and the automated access system;
- There is objective confusion between licensed and unlicensed operators, with diversion of road space and capacity to the detriment of licensed operators;

- The management company loses control and the ability to regulate the most sensitive areas of the part facing the air terminal;
- The management company has a commercial detriment from the transit of squatter business operators without the necessary agreement with the Managing Company.

Hence the need for a more effective and efficient regulation that would remark the destination areas of operators' flows by reintroducing the limitation of multiple accesses to three. This regulation, benefiting from a reduction of transits in a parking area adjacent to the terminal and as such characterized by the different components of traffic, vehicular and pedestrian, deserves and needs to be regulated more effectively.

This does not mean taking away operating space from remote parking and rental operators, who would operate in areas dedicated to them, with the consequent benefit of harmonizing the entire landside area.

Acknowledgements. This study is supported by the projects WEAKI TRANSIT: WEAK-demand areas Innovative TRANsport Shared services for Italian Towns (Project protocol: 20174ARRHT_004; CUP Code: F74I19001290001), financed with the PRIN 2017 (Research Projects of National Relevance) program and e.INS Ecosystem of Innovation for Next Generation Sardinia - SPOKE 8 - (CUP F53C22000430001 –MUR Code: ECS00000038) financed with PNRR (National Recovery and Resilience Plan). We authorize the MIUR to reproduce and distribute reprints for Governmental purposes, notwithstanding any copyright notations thereon. Any opinions, findings and conclusions or recommendations expressed in this material are those of the authors, and do not necessarily reflect the views of the MIUR.

Author Contributions. Conceptualization, Nicoletta Rassu, Francesca Maltinti, Mauro Coni; methodology and formal analysis, Nicoletta Rassu, Francesca Maltinti; Mauro Coni; introduction and literature review Nicoletta Rassu, Francesca Maltinti; t; writing-original draft preparation Nicoletta Rassu, Francesca Maltinti, Mauro Coni; writing review and editing, Nicoletta Rassu and Francesca Maltinti; visualization, all. All authors have read and agreed to the published version of the manuscript.

References

1. Garau, C., Desogus, G., Barabino, B., Coni, M.: Accessibility and public transport mobility for a Smart(er) Island: evidence from Sardinia (Italy). Sustain. Cities Soc. **87**, 104145 (2022)
2. Garau, C., Desogus, G., Stratigea, A.: Territorial cohesion in insular contexts: assessing external attractiveness and internal strength of major Mediterranean islands. Eur. Plan. Stud. 1–20 (2020)
3. Coni, M., Garau, C., Maltinti, F., Pinna, F.: Accessibility improvements and placebased organization in the Island of Sardinia (Italy). In: Coni, M., Garau, C., Maltinti, F., Pinna, F. (eds.) Computational Science and Its Applications. Lecture Notes in Computer Science, vol. 12255, pp. 337–352. Springer, Heidelberg (2020). https://doi.org/10.1007/978-3-030-58820-5_26
4. Garau, C., Desogus, G., Coni, M.: Fostering and planning a smart governance strategy for evaluating the urban polarities of the Sardinian Island (Italy). Sustainability **11**(18), 4962 (2019)
5. De Neufville, R.: Airport Systems Planning. MacMillan Press, London (1976)
6. Correia, A.R., Wirasinghe, S.: Development of level of service standards for airport facilities: application to Sao Paulo International Airport. J. Air Transp. Manag. **13**(2), 97–103 (2006)

7. Churchill, A., Dada, E., De Barros, A.G., Wirasinghe, S.C.: Quantifying and validating measures of airport terminal wayfinding. J. Air Transp. Manag. **14**(3), 151–158 (2008)
8. Psaraki, V., Abacoumkin, C.: Access mode choice for relocated airports: the new Athens International Airport. J. Air Transp. Manag. **8**(2), 89–98 (2002)
9. Correia, A.R., Wirasinghe, S.C., De Barros, A.G.: A global index for level of service evaluation at airport passenger terminals. Transp. Res. Part E: Logist. Transp. Rev. **44**(4), 607–620 (2008)
10. Galagedera, S.B.D., Pasindu, H.R., Bandara, J.M.S.J.: Airport curbside and parking area operations at BIA–analysis of user behavior. J. Inst. Eng. Sri Lanka (2014)
11. Udayanga, P.A.S., Pasindu, H.R.: Incorporating user characteristics for level of service improvement at airport curbside and roadside operations at BIA. In: Annual Sessions of IESL (2015)
12. Ordinanza n. 1/2019/OLB - ENAC - Protocol of 28/03/2019 0036002/ESR
13. IATA, Airport Development Reference Manual, Chapter 1, Section 11, 12, 13, 9th edition (2014)
14. Transportation Research Board Commission, Report ACRP 40, Washington DC (2010)
15. Lo, J.: A discussion of road safety issues at airport terminal pick-up and drop-off areas. In: TAC (2015)
16. Houghton, J., Eng, P., Philp, C.: Highway signing for drivers' needs. In: Annual Conference of the Transportation Association of Canada (2004)
17. Passos, L.S., Kokkinogenis, Z., Rossetti, R.J.F., Joaquim, G.: Multi-resolution simulation of taxi services on airport terminal's curbside. In: 16th International IEEE Conference on Intelligent Transportation Systems (ITSC 2013), pp. 2361–2366. IEEE (2013)
18. Harris, T.M., Nourinejad, M., Roorda, M.J.: A mesoscopic simulation model for airport curbside management. J. Adv. Transp. (2017)
19. Wong, D., Douglas, B.: Airport ground transportation policies and the future of rail connections at US airports. In: Proceedings of the Transportation Research Board 92nd Annual Meeting, Washington, DC, USA, January 2013
20. https://assaeroporti.com/statistiche/
21. Decreto Legislativo 30 aprile 1992, n.285
22. Engineering National Academies of Sciences (and Medicine), and Transportation Research Board. Highway Capacity Manual 7th Edition: A Guide for Multimodal Mobility Analysis. National Academies Press (2022)

International Design Practices for Roundabouts

Angelos Nikiforiadis[1], Andreas Nikiforiadis[2(✉)] ⓘ, Lambros Mitropoulos[3] ⓘ, Socrates Basbas[2] ⓘ, and Tiziana Campisi[4] ⓘ

[1] Region of Central Macedonia, Thessaloniki, Greece
anikiforiadis@topo.auth.gr
[2] School of Rural and Surveying Engineering, Aristotle University of Thessaloniki, Thessaloniki, Greece
anikiforiadis@topo.auth.gr
[3] School of Rural, Surveying and Geoinformatics Engineering, National Technical University of Athens, Athens, Greece
[4] Faculty of Engineering and Architecture, University of Enna Kore, Enna, Italy

Abstract. Roundabouts are a special form of junction, which has been widely implemented during the last years, since for specific cases they are considered a suitable solution, in terms of safety and capacity, compared to conventional intersection types. Different types of roundabouts exist, and the design of each type follows specific principles, for reaching their design potential and avoiding negative implications. Although the roundabout types are common among several countries, the design principles and guidelines vary. This paper reviews the guidelines of six major countries (i.e., the United Kingdom, France, Germany, the Netherlands, the United States and Australia), which are considered front-runners in the design of roundabouts. For each national guideline, the main goal, the field of application and the estimation of basic roundabout geometric elements are identified. Through the comparison of national guidelines, points of convergence and divergence are identified and discussed. Recognizing these points can be a useful guidance for the development of guidelines for other countries, by identifying and transferring elements that best fit their road conditions.

Keywords: Roundabout · Geometric characteristics · Guidelines · Design elements

1 Introduction

The roundabout is an intersection type that is mainly used in urban areas. Its application in modern road design dates back to the 20th century; however, in the 1950s, it was abandoned due to increased traffic and congestion, use of traffic signals, and increased number of road accidents. Traffic congestion was radically addressed in the UK in 1966 with the provision of right-of way to circulating vehicles. This regulation resulted in the systematic study for implementing roundabouts, which showed that without the use of traffic signals a sufficient degree of road safety and capacity could be achieved.

O. Gervasi et al. (Eds.): ICCSA 2023 Workshops, LNCS 14111, pp. 308–326, 2023.
https://doi.org/10.1007/978-3-031-37126-4_21

The type of intersection that will be selected and applied is evaluated by weighting criteria, including road safety, capacity (level of service), environment, economy, and social acceptance (Tollazzi et al. 2015). However, the roundabout design is not a standard process that is followed by all countries, since roundabout involves choosing between trade-offs of safety and capacity criteria. Smooth traffic flow conditions are achieved when the traffic volumes all evenly distributed to all converging roads. Increasing the number of entry, exit and circulatory lanes to improve capacity results to increases vehicle speeds and lower safety levels.

The roundabouts provide better safety compared to conventional intersections, where traffic is regulated by traffic signals, as the number of possible vehicle conflict points is significantly lower (Wu and Brilon 2017; Giuffre et al. 2018). Conflict points are locations in or on the approaches to an intersection where vehicles paths merge, diverge, or cross. Pedestrian and bicycle crossings are also facilitated, because shorter crossing lengths are required, while at the same time vehicle speeds are lower (Campisi et al. 2020; Gruden et al. 2022). Although their advantages, the design elements of the roundabouts may limit their application in a road network. The circular movement of heavy vehicles usually becomes a challenge for transportation engineers, especially on urban roads with a significant number of buses.

Following the selection of a roundabout as the optimal intersection type, the geometric elements are designed. The approaching leg axes are laid and the entry/exit lanes, the circulatory roadway and the central island are calculated. The roundabout design usually requires three performance checks: 1) The examination of the design vehicle swept path, 2) the fastest path analysis, and 3) the visibility checks. If these checks do not agree with the design guidelines, the geometry of the elements is modified (Ahac et al. 2021). Several countries at global level have developed technical guidelines for the design, dimensioning and operation of roundabouts, which evolved over time. To review and compare existing practices on roundabout design, six countries are selected among different continents, in Europe (i.e., United Kingdom, France, Germany, the Netherlands), in North America (the United States of America) and in Australia/Oceania (Australia). These countries are selected because they use similar design elements for roundabouts (i.e., the inscribed circle diameter, the circulatory roadway, the apron, the splitter island, and the entry and exit leg design) and also because they are considered front-runners in roundabout design.

The technical guidelines that are reviewed in this study aim to determine the scope of roundabout application in the road network and then provide the optimum design for road safety and capacity. The identified differences between the various national guidelines mainly concern the way these problems are approached.

2 Roundabout Design

The first technical guideline for roundabouts was introduced in the UK in 1993, whereas the second one was released by Australia the same year. In European countries, the formation of technical instructions for roundabouts started in France in 1998, and in Germany and Switzerland in 1999. In 2000, a manual with instructions for designing and evaluating the performance of roundabouts was published in the US, based largely on the experience of Australia, the United Kingdom, France, and Germany. The roundabout design requires a considerable amount of iteration among geometric layout, operational analysis, and safety evaluation (Federal Highway Administration 2011). Therefore, variations in the design guidelines for roundabouts and emphasis on the estimation of geometric elements' values are presented in the following sections for six major countries: the UK, France, Germany, the Netherlands, the US and Australia.

2.1 United Kingdom

Design Principles

In the UK, the design guideline (The Highways Agency 2007; Highways England 2020) aims to minimize vehicle delays while maintaining safety for all intersection users. Therefore, attributes such as the traffic flow, speed, and the intersection site, are considered for the estimation of geometric elements. Two important elements are: the deflection of the route in the entry lane of the roundabout to ensure safety, and the width of the entry lane and its angle relative to the roundabout to ensure traffic performance. Nevertheless, the guideline recommends that a maximum number of three lanes could be used for the entry legs and the circulatory roadway. Finally, it is allowed to design roundabouts without a circular central island and a stable number of traffic lanes in the circulatory roadway.

Roundabout Types

According to the UK road and bridge design instruction manual (The Highways Agency 2007; Highways England 2020), roundabouts are classified into the following five types: a) Regular roundabouts, b) Single-lane roundabouts, c) Mini roundabouts, d) Roundabouts with traffic lights, e) Double roundabouts.

It is pointed out that in continental European countries the roundabouts with traffic lights are not considered as roundabouts, because priority is determined by traffic lights. Table 1 summarizes the basic geometric elements for the design of roundabouts in UK.

Regular Roundabouts. They are applied in the following cases:

- On roads with a permitted speed of more than 50 mph and an average daily traffic of more than 8,000 vehicles/day per converging road.
- On roads with a permitted speed of less than 40 mph and an average daily traffic of more than 12,000 vehicles/day per converging road.

The number of lanes in the entry/exit routes varies; however, it is intended to provide 2 or even 3 entry/exit lanes to increase the roundabout capacity. Regular roundabouts are designed with a maximum number of 4 legs, since more legs result to increased inscribed circle diameter and higher vehicle speeds. The following guideline applies for designing the basic geometric elements of regular roundabouts:

- The inscribed circle diameter has a value of at least 28 m, and max 100 m.
- The width of the circulatory roadway is estimated as 1.0 to 1.2 times the wider entry width, but it is recommended not to exceed 15 m. This width does not include the width of the mountable apron around the central island.

- The central island has a diameter of at least 4 m.
- The width of a single-lane entry ranges between 3.0 and 4.5 m.; for multiple lanes entries the width ranges between 3.0 and 3.5 m. for each lane. The entry radius ranges between 10 and 100 m.
- The exit width for single-lane roundabout ranges between 7.0 and 7.5 m. For two-lanes exits the width ranges between 10.0 and 11.0 m. The exit radius ranges between 20 and 100 m., but a radius of 40 m. is recommended.

Single-Lane Roundabout. Single-lane roundabouts are applied for single-lane converging roads, with:

- A permitted speed of more than 50 mph and a maximum average daily traffic of 8,000 vehicles/day per converging road.
- A permitted speed of less than 40 mph and a maximum average daily traffic of 8,000 vehicles/day per converging road.

The size of the central island for single-lane roundabouts is similar to the one applied for regular roundabouts. However, due to single lane entries and exits, the single-lane roundabouts allow the application of lower entry/exit radius; thus, resulting in greater route deflection for incoming vehicles and safer pedestrian and bicycle crossings. The following applies to the basic geometric elements for single-lane roundabouts:

- The inscribed circle diameter ranges from 28 to 36 m.
- The width of the circulatory roadway is estimated as 1.0–1.2 times the wider entry width, but it is recommended not to exceed 6.0 m.
- The circular island has a diameter of at least 4.0 m.
- The width of the island apron (if required) depends on the inscribed circle diameter and the central island diameter.
- The entry radius ranges between 10 and 100 m., but a minimum radius of 20 m. is recommended if heavy vehicles use the roundabout.
- The exit width is similar to the entry width; a value of 4.5 m. is recommended while the exit radius ranges between 15 and 20 m.

Mini Roundabouts. They operate similar to a regular roundabout; however, their central island (the diameter ranges between 1.0–4.0 m.) is completely mountable. They are not used if more than four roads converge in urban areas and all entry/exit routes have only one lane. The permitted speed limit for all legs is set to 30 mph. They are primarily used to achieve speed reduction for passenger vehicles; however, due to their geometric elements, they are not recommended for:

- Separated roads
- Roads serving buses and heavy vehicles
- Roads serving U-turns

- Intersections, with converging roads with: 1) a maximum average traffic volume of 500 vehicles/day, or 2) a total peak load of less than 500 vehicles/hour.

Roundabouts with Traffic Signals. For roundabouts with high traffic volumes, it is possible to install traffic signals in one or more legs, or/and at the respective intersecting points of the circulatory roadway. Such conditions may allow the implementation of different types of intersection, which depends on the width of the roads, traffic volumes and the coordination of traffic lights.

Double Roundabouts. The design of each roundabout in a double roundabout layout, may be regular, single-lane or mini. The two roundabouts are connected by a road section, with a width that depends on the traffic volume between them. Double roundabouts are mainly applied:

- When more than four roads converge
- When all roads do not converge at the same location
- To connect two parallel roads, separated by an obstacle (e.g., highway, river).

Table 1. Roundabout types and basic geometric elements in the UK.

Geometric element	Roundabout type		
	Regular	Single-lane	Mini
Inscribed circle diameter [m]	28.00–100.0	28.00–36.00	$\leq$28.00
Circulatory roadway width [m][1]	$\leq$15.00	$\leq$6.00	n.a
Diameter of central island [m]	$\geq$4.00	$\geq$4.00	1.00–4.00 (mountable)
Entry width [m]	3.00–4.50	3.00–4.50	n.a
	3.00–3.50 per lane		
Entry radius [m]	10.00–100.00	n.a	3.00–4.00
Exit width [m]	7.00–7.50	4.50	n.a
	10.00–11.00[2]		
Exit radius [m]	20.00–100.0	15.00–20.00	n.a

[1]The width is estimated as 1.00–1.20 times the wider entry width. [2] Refers to two-lanes exits

2.2 France

Design principles

The design of roundabouts in France started in 1984 and the national guideline is divided into urban and rural design (Service d'Études Techniques des Routes et Autoroutes 1998; CERTU 2010). The basic principles governing the roundabouts' design according to the French guidelines are:

- A maximum number of 6 routes are allowed to converge to the intersection. The angles between the entry/ exit legs on the perimeter of the circulatory roadway should be evenly distributed.
- For a single-lane roundabout an inscribed circle diameter of 15 m. is considered satisfactory, as it ensures a smooth traffic flow and facilitates the pedestrians and bicycles crossings. In areas with negligible traffic volumes, the diameter may be reduced up to 12 m. For two-lanes a diameter of 25 m. is acceptable.
- The central island of the roundabout has a circular shape. The axes of the legs should go through, as close as possible, the center of the island. The value of radius for entry, circular routing, exit routes depends on the radius of the inscribed circle, and should not exceed 100 m.
- The exits have only one lane; using a second lane is justified only in case of high traffic volumes.
- The entry and exit legs are separated by splitter islands. Replacement of islands with road markings is only allowed at minor roundabouts.

According to the French guidelines three types of urban roundabouts are recommended:

Mini Roundabout. They have been implemented since late 1980s. The central island is completely mountable with a diameter ranging between 3.0 and 5.0 m.

Single-Lane Roundabout. It is the typical form of roundabout that is used on urban roads with increased traffic volume. All entries and exits are designed as a single-lane routes. The central island is surrounded by a mountable road strip 1.0–2.0 m. wide, while the splitter islands are 2.0 m. wide, to provide safe pedestrian crossings.

Medium and Large Roundabouts. They are used when at least one of the converging roads has more than one lane or when more than four roads converge. Two lanes are used for the exit route, if the peak traffic volume exceeds 1,200 vehicles/hour. Table 2 provides the basic geometric features of urban roundabouts.

Roundabouts that are located on rural roads vary according to the value of the inscribed circle radius. The following recommendations apply for selecting the appropriate radius:

- National and provincial roads without median: On the main interurban road the value of the inscribed circle radius ranges between 15 and 25 m., to facilitate trespassing of heavy vehicles. A radius of 20 m. is preferred for three-lanes roads, whereas a radius between 20 and 25 m. is used for intersections with more than four legs.

Table 2. Types and basic geometric characteristics for urban roundabouts in France.

Geometric element	Roundabout type		
	Mini	Single-lane	Medium and large
Inscribed circle diameter [m]	7.50–12.00	12.00–15.00	>15.00
Circulatory roadway width [m]	6.00–9.50	≥6.00	7.20–8.40
Width of mountable island [m]	n.a	1.00–2.00	n.a
Central island radius [m]	1.50–2.50 (mountable)	n.a	n.a
Entry width [m]	2.50–3.50	3.00–3.50	6.00–7.00
Entry radius [m]	n.a	8.00–15.00	n.a
Exit width [m]	2.75–3.50	≥3.50	≥7.00
Exit radius [m]	n.a	15.00–20.00	n.a

- National and provincial divided roads: As a general rule, a radius of 25 m. is selected.
- Local interurban roads: If traffic of heavy vehicles is negligible, a radius between 12–15 m. is applied.

The value of the inscribed circle radius defines the rest of the design elements as shown in Table 3.

Table 3. Types and basic geometric characteristics for rural roundabouts in France.

Geometric element	Thresholds	Usual values [m]			
Inscribed circle radius Rg	12 m–25 m	Rg = 12	Rg = 15	Rg = 20	Rg = 25
Circulatory roadway width la	6.00 m–9.00 m	7.00	7.00	7.00	8.00
Width of mountable island slf	1.50 m–2.00 m	1.50	1.50	n.a	n.a
Central island radius Ri	Rgxlaxslf	3.50	6.50	13.00	18.00
Entry width le	4.00 m	4.00	4.00	4.00	4.00
	2 × 3.50 m	2 × 3.50	2 × 3.50	2 × 3.50	2 × 3.50
Entry radius Re	10.00 m–15.00 m και Re≤Rg	12.00	15.00	15.00	15.00
Exit width ls	4.00 m–5.00 m	4.00	4.00	4.50	5.00
	2 × 3.50 m	2 × 3.50	2 × 3.50	2 × 3.50	2 × 3.50
Exit radius Rs	15.00 m–30.00 m και Rs>Ri	15.00	20.00	20.00	20.00
Route diverging radius Rr	Rr = 4 × 0Rg	48	60	80	100
Median width	≥2.00 m	≥2.00	≥2.00	≥2.00	≥2.00

2.3 Germany

Design Principles

The German guidelines places particular emphasis on road safety compared to capacity. Thus, the roundabout design is governed by the following basic principles (Forschungsgesellschaft für Straßen- und Verkehrswesen 1998; Forschungsgesellschaft für Straßen- und Verkehrswesen 2006):

- The circular island should achieve speed reduction due to its configuration.
- The entry and exit legs are designed as perpendicular as possible to the central island (i.e., their axes pass as close as possible to the center of the circle). Sharp angled legs are not allowed to converge with the roundabout as they would enable high vehicle speeds.
- All entries and exits are designed as single-lane routes. Two-lanes entries/exits are allowed for larger diameter roundabouts.
- Road pavement markings are avoided as they encourage the parallel movement of vehicles in the roundabout (even for roundabouts with a large circulatory roadway width).

Roundabouts are implemented in urban and interurban areas, at intersections with high number of road accidents and at intersections that are controlled by traffic signals and long waiting time are recorded on the main arterial road. On the contrary, roundabouts are avoided on roads with high traffic volumes, increased pedestrian and bicycle traffic and on city bus-routes.

Roundabout Types

Mini Roundabouts. They are implemented exclusively on urban roads for a maximum traffic volume of up to 12,000 vehicles/day. In special cases the capacity may reach 18,000 vehicles/day; in such cases the traffic volumes are uniformly distributed on entry legs and the number of left movements is low. Experiments with rural mini-roundabouts have also been performed. Results showed that mini-roundabouts are not recommended outside built-up areas due to safety concerns (Brilon 2011).

Roundabouts with Small Diameter – Urban Roads. They are applied on urban roads with a maximum traffic volume of 25,000 vehicles/day. However, when traffic exceeds 15,000 vehicles/day, the level of service depends on the distribution of traffic on individual legs. A mountable central island is used to facilitate the movement of heavy vehicles. A splitter island is used between entry/exit legs to ensure the safe crossing of pedestrians and bicycles. For pedestrians and cars this type of roundabout seems to be the safest type among all types of intersections (Meewes 2003).

Roundabouts with Small Diameter – Interurban Roads. They are applied on interurban roads without using a mountable central island. Their capacity is similar to urban roundabouts. A splitter island is used between entry/exit legs to ensure the safe crossing of pedestrians and bicycles.

Large Roundabouts. They are rarely used on urban and interurban roads, due to their lower road safety level compared to other types. Their capacity reaches 32,000 vehicles/day regardless of the distribution of the traffic volume on individual legs. The design of entries as two-lane routes is allowed.

Special Types of Roundabouts. The German guidelines also provide directions for designing exclusive lanes for the direct connection of two adjacent legs (i.e., right turns). In such cases, and if the required area is available, the additional right-hand lanes are considered particularly beneficial, as they prevent the design of a second lane in the entry leg. In special cases the central island may be also designed as a spiral node (i.e., turbo roundabouts), which were developed and implemented mainly in the Netherlands. Table 4 summarizes the basic geometric characteristics for roundabouts in Germany.

Table 4. Types and basic geometric characteristics for roundabouts in Germany.

Geometric element	Roundabout type				
	Mini roundabout	Small diameter – Urban roads	Small diameter – Interurban roads	Large roundabouts	
				Urban roads	Interurban roads
Maximum daily traffic [vehicles/day]	12,000 (18,000)[*]	25,000	25,000	32,000	32,000
Inscribed circle radius D [m]	13.00–22.00	26.00–40.00	30.00–50.00	40.00–60.00	45.00–60.00
Circulatory roadway width B_K (with mountable central island) [m]	4.00–6.00	6.50–8.00	6.50–7.50	8.00–10.00	8.00–10.00
Ratio roadway to mountable central island	Mountable central island	3:1	Without mountable central island		
Entry width B_Z [m]	3.25–3.75	3.25–3.75	3.50–4.00	3.25–3.75	3.50–4.00
				2 x 3.25	2 x (3.25–3.50)
Exit width B_A [m]	3.50–4.00	3.50–4.00	3.75–4.50	3.50–4.00	3.75–4.50

(continued)

Table 4. (*continued*)

Geometric element	Roundabout type				
	Mini roundabout	Small diameter – Urban roads	Small diameter – Interurban roads	Large roundabouts	
				Urban roads	Interurban roads
Entry radius R_Z [m]	8.00–10.00	10.00–14.00	14.00–16.00	12.00–16.00	16.00–20.00
Exit radius R_A [m]	8.00–10.00	12.00–16.00	16.00–18.00	14.00–16.00	16.00–20.00
Width of island between entry and exit legs B_F [m]	n.a	1.60–2.50	1.60–2.50	1.60–2.50	1.60–2.50

*The values in brackets refer to conditions that traffic flow is uniformly distributed.

2.4 The Netherlands

For selecting the optimum intersection type in the Netherlands, three criteria are considered important, the intersecting roads' classification, capacity, and road safety. The most important criterion is the roads' functional classification. Roundabouts are designed when collector roads converge or when a collector and an access road intersect (in such case the conventional priority intersection is preferred, followed by the roundabout) (Royal Haskoning 2009). A single-lane roundabout may serve an average daily traffic volume of 25,000 vehicles/day. For higher traffic volumes, the following recommendations are provided (Royal Haskoning 2009):

- Integration of an additional lane that provides exclusive right-turns for adjacent legs.
- Widening of the circulatory roadway width (i.e., two traffic-lanes), while the entry and exit lanes maintain a single lane, (capacity up to 30,000 vehicles/day).
- Widening of the circulatory roadway width (i.e., two traffic-lanes) and use of two-lanes for entry and exit legs (capacity up to 40,000 vehicles/day).
- Development of a spiral circular intersection (turbo).

The Netherlands applies mostly the first and the last recommendation. On the contrary, the implementation of two-lane roundabouts has been abolished, because performance in terms of safety and capacity have been disappointing. Existing nodes of this shape are gradually transformed into spiral circular nodes. Tables 5 and 6 summarize the basic geometric characteristics for single-lane and two-lane roundabouts, respectively, in the Netherlands.

Table 5. Types and basic geometric characteristics for single-lane roundabouts in the Netherlands.

Geometric element	Design vehicle		
	Typical vehicle (Length 15.50m)	Vehicle length 22.00m	vehicle length 27.00m
Inscribed circle radius R_{bu} [m]	18.00	18.00	18.00
Central island radius R_{bi} [m]	12.75	12.75	12.75
Circulatory roadway width B [m]	5.25	5.25	5.25
Width of mountable central island [m]	1.50	3.00	4.00
Entry width B_t [m]	3.50–4.00	4.00	4.00
Exit width B_a [m]	4.00- 4.50	4.50	4.50
Entry radius R_t [m]	8.00–12.00	12.00	12.00
Exit radius R_a [m]	12.00–15.00	15.00	15.00
Width of island between entry and exit legs B_m [m]	3.00	3.00	3.00
Length of island between entry and exit legs L_m [m]	10.00–15.00	10.00–15.00	10.00–15.00

Table 6. Types and basic geometric characteristics for two lanes roundabouts the Netherlands.

Geometric element	Values				
Inscribed circle radius R_{bu} [m]	20.00	25.00	29.00	33.50	38.00
Central island radius R_{bi} [m]	10.00	16.00	20.00	25.00	30.00
Circulatory roadway width B [m]	10.00	9.00	9.00	8.50	8.00
Entry width [m]	3.50–4.00	3.50–4.00	3.50–4.00	3.50–4.00	3.50–4.00
Entry width 2-lanes [m]	Width varies				
Exit width [m]	4.00–4.50	4.00–4.50	4.00–4.50	4.00–4.50	4.00–4.50
Exit width 2-lanes[m]	Width varies				
Entry radius R_t [m]	12.00	12.00	12.00	12.00	12.00
Exit radius R_a [m]	15.00	15.00	15.00	15.00	15.00

2.5 United States of America

Design Principles

Emphasis is placed on the geometric elements that aim to achieve speed reduction to vehicles entering a roundabout. This is achieved by using route diversions and providing narrow cross-sections, which in turn negatively affect the roundabout's capacity.

It is advisable that the axis of the approaching legs should be aligned as close as possible to the center of the roundabout circle. Crossing the center, to the left of the center is acceptable. However, crossing to the right of the center should be avoided as it encourages higher entry speeds.

At roundabouts all converging roads are treated equally; vehicles entering the roundabout must give priority to those moving on the roundabout. For this reason, the US guideline recommends that the design of the roundabouts should take into account the roads' functional classification, but it does not provide specific directions for selecting a roundabout (Federal Highway Administration 2000; Federal Highway Administration 2011; Transportation Research Board 2016).

Roundabout Types

Mini Roundabout. They are implemented at urban intersections with a maximum traffic volume of 10,000 vehicles/day and a maximum vehicle speed of 25 km/h. The design is mainly based on the German experience.

Urban Compact Roundabouts. They are implemented at urban intersections with a maximum traffic volume of 15,000 vehicles/day and a maximum vehicle speed of 25 km/h. Their design is based mainly on the German experience. The main features include a mountable circular apron around the central island, the splitter island between entry/exit legs, and a single-lane entry/exit.

Urban Single-Lane Roundabouts. They are implemented in urban intersections with significant traffic of up to 20,000 vehicles/day. The desired maximum entry speed is 35 km/h. They differ from the urban compact roundabouts, as their diameter is larger. The main features are the mountable circular apron around the central island and the splitter island between entry/exit legs. Their design has been influenced by the respective guidelines of Australia, France and the United Kingdom.

Urban 2-Lanes Roundabouts. At urban intersections, where at least one entry road occupies two lanes, the diameter is widened to allow two vehicles to move simultaneously. The entry speed should not exceed 40 km/h. This type is similar to the urban single-lane roundabout; however, a mountable apron is not used. Their design has been primarily influenced by the respective guidelines of the United Kingdom, and secondarily by Australia and France.

Interurban Single-Lane Roundabouts. They are similar to urban single-lane roundabouts. They are selected for a maximum traffic volume of 20,000 vehicles/day. However, they differ from the urban single-lane roundabout, as they may have a larger diameter, they lack a mountable central apron and their exits are more tangential to the roundabout circle. The desired maximum entry speed is 40 km/h. Their design is based on the respective guidelines of Australia, France and the United Kingdom.

Interurban 2-Lanes Roundabouts. At interurban intersections, where at least one entry occupies two lanes, the diameter is widened to allow two vehicles to move simultaneously. They are designed similarly to urban two-lanes roundabouts. Differences include: the exits are designed more tangential to the circle to increase the exit speed of vehicles due to the reduced pedestrian and bicycle volumes; the entry speed should not exceed 50 km/h. Their design is based on the methods used mainly in the United Kingdom and secondarily in Australia and France.

Table 7 summarizes the geometric elements for various types of roundabouts in the United States.

Table 7. Roundabout types and basic geometric characteristics in the US.

Geometric element	Roundabout type					
	Mini	Urban compact	Urban single lane	Urban 2-lanes	Interurban single lane	Interurban 2-lanes
Maximum daily traffic [vehicles/day]	10,000	15,000	20,000	45,000 (estimation is required)	20,000	45,000 (estimation is required)
Inscribed circle radius [m]	13.00–25.00	25.00–30.00	30.00–40.00	45.00–55.00	35.00–40.00	55.00–60.00
Circulatory roadway width (without mountable island)[a] [m]	≥5.00	≥5.00	≥5.00	≥9.10	≥5.00	≥9.10
Width of mountable central island	Mountable central island	1.00–4.00	1.00–4.00	n.a	(1.00–4.00)	n.a
Entry width [m]	n.a	4.30–4.90	4.30–4.90	≥6.00	4.30–4.90	≥6.00
Entry radius[2] [m]	n.a	10.00–30.00	10.00–30.00	uniform 30–60	10.00–30.00	uniform 40–80
				Two consecutives		Two consecutives
Exit radius[2] [m]	10.00–12.00	10.00–12.00	>15.00	n.a	>15.00	n.a
Width of island between entry and exit legs [m]	n.a	>1.80	>1.80	>1.80	>1.80	>1.80

[a]The circulatory roadway width varies between 100% and 120% of the width of the wider entry leg. 2 The estimated entry and exit radius are affected by the transition curves of the internal boundaries of entry legs to the circular island.

2.6 Australia

Design Principles

Instructions for the design of roundabouts in Australia and New Zealand have been incorporated into road design manuals issued by Austroads as well as the Queensland State Road Service (Austroads 2009; Department of Main Roads 2006). The general principles governing the design of roundabouts in Australia are:

- The roundabout must be visible and recognizable to drivers prior reaching it; the estimated sight distance depends on the operating speed of the road.
- The number of roundabout legs should not be more than four. However, if all legs have an entry lane, the maximum number of legs could be six.
- Speed reduction is achieved by adjusting the horizontal curvature design of entry legs.
- The width of the circulatory roadway depends on the dimensions of the largest vehicle that uses the roundabout (design vehicle).
- The number of lanes in the entry/exit legs, and the circulatory roadway are designed based on the desired level of service.

The Australian guidelines contain directions for the implementation of roundabouts that depend on the road functional classification as shown in Table 8.

Table 8. Directions for selecting a roundabout in Australia.

Road classification	Interstate – Primary arterial	Interurban road – Secondary arterial	Collector road	Local road
Freeway	D	E	E	E
Interstate – Primary arterial	B	B	C	C
Interurban road – Secondary arterial	n.a	B	B	C
Collector road	n.a	n.a	A	B
Local road	n.a	n.a	n.a	A

A: Suitable selection; B: Possibly suitable selection; C: Not suitable selection; D: Unsuitable selection for the main road, possibly suitable for level junctions on converging legs; E: Unacceptable.

Roundabout Types

The Australian guidelines do not categorize roundabouts; however, different design approach is envisaged depending on the number of lanes for the entry/exit legs and the circulatory roadway. The guidelines provide the possibility to add an exclusive left-turn lane for connecting adjacent legs with high traffic volumes (note: Australians drive on the left side of the road). These left-turn lanes merge into the exit leg by using an acceleration lane. Additionally:

- The number of entry lanes is estimated based on the estimated level of service. However, if any of the converging roads has two lanes per direction, these will be maintained.
- The number of lanes on the circulatory roadway after each entry, is equal to or higher than the number of lanes of the entry leg; a lane on the circulatory roadway may be dropped after an exit.
- The number of exit lanes must not exceed the number of lanes on the circular roadway.
- The diameter of the central island is determined by the speed limit of converging roads (i.e., the higher speed limit affects the design). It also depends on the largest vehicle to be served (design vehicle). The minimum diameter values for the central island without a mountable part are presented in Table 9.
- The width of the circulatory roadway depends on the diameter of the central island, the number of lanes and the length of the larger vehicle that will use the roundabout. Recommendations for selecting an appropriate width are presented in Table 10.
- The operating speed V85 when entering a roundabout should not exceed 60 km/h. The radius of the successive opposite curves of the entry leg, the circular trajectory, and the exit leg should not exceed 100 m.

Table 9. Recommendations for selecting a diameter value for the central island in Australia.

Entry lane speed [km/h]	Minimum diameter of the central island [m]		Required measures for speed reduction in the entry lane
	Single-lane roundabout	Two-lanes roundabout	
≤40	10–20	16–24	No
50	16–22	16–24	No
60	20–24	28–32	No
70	24–36	36–40	No
80	28–44	40–48	Desired
≥90	28–44	40–48	Mandatory

Table 10. Recommendations for selecting a width for the circulatory roadway in Australia.

Central island diameter [m]	Circulatory roadway [m]	
	Single-lane roundabout	Two-lanes roundabout
10	9.20	n.a
12	8.90–9.90	n.a

(*continued*)

Table 10. (*continued*)

Central island diameter [m]	Circulatory roadway [m]	
	Single-lane roundabout	Two-lanes roundabout
16	6.70–10.90	9.70
20	6.30–12.40	9.30–11.00
24	5.90–11.90	9.00–11.50
28	5.80–11.40	8.80–12.50
32	5.60–10.90	8.60–13.90
36	5.40–10.50	8.40–13.50
40	5.20–10.10	8.20–13.10
46	5.10–9.60	8.10–12.60
52	4.90–9.20	7.90–12.20
60	4.80–8.60	7.70–11.60
70	4.80–8.00	7.60–11.00
80	4.80–7.60	7.50–10.60
90	4.80–7.20	7.40–10.20
100	4.80–6.90	7.30–9.90
120	4.80–6.30	7.20–9.30
140	4.80–6.00	7.10–9.00
160	4.80–5.70	7.0–8.70

3 Comparison Analysis

The analysis of the design guidelines for roundabouts in six countries of different continents has shown that in general the design follows similar fundamental principles, that may be summarized as follows:

- The roundabouts are applied on both urban and interurban roads. In urban areas, the central island is usually surrounded by a mountable strip to facilitate the movement of heavy vehicles. Especially for urban roads, the design of mini roundabouts foresees a completely mountable central island.
- The roundabouts are categorized based on their inscribed circle radius; increasing the radius improves the level of service. The feasibility of applying a roundabout on an intersection depends on the traffic volumes of the converging roads.
- On highways and expressways, the application of roundabouts is prohibited.
- The application of roundabouts is preferred when policy-makers aim to change the drivers' behavior prior reaching an intersection, such as when a road changes from interurban to urban or when the road's cross-section changes.

Roundabouts have become particularly attractive for existing intersections, partially due to their simplicity for providing right-of way to vehicles moving in the roundabout over incoming vehicles. Their application offers advantages over other types of intersections because they are characterized by a high degree of safety and a satisfactory level of service without using traffic signals. Roundabouts are safer compared to other types of intersections, since they are designed to reduce vehicles' speed and engage a low number of possible collision points. The provided level of service depends on the distribution of the total traffic volumes to respective roundabout legs. The roundabout design aims to combine two principles, which are often in conflict with each other, namely the achievement of a high level of road safety and the ability to provide a satisfactory level of service for high traffic volumes. The differences among the examined national roundabout guidelines mainly concern the way in which these two criteria are approached within the design process. The need to serve high traffic volumes when designing a roundabout, results to increased speeds and the additional lanes that permit the parallel movement of vehicles. More specifically:

- The entry legs are occasionally designed tangentially to the circulatory roadway, in order to increase the entry, circular and exit speed. However, this configuration, deteriorates the level of safety since the vehicle speed increases and the drivers' visibility range decreases.
- The entry/exit legs and the circulatory roadway are widened with more than one traffic lane. However, the vehicles' parallel movement along these segments increases the number of conflict points, which deprives the roundabouts' advantage of having a low number of possible conflict points.

The UK and the Australian roundabout guidelines promote the application of roundabouts by using more than one lane on entry/exit legs and in the circulatory roadway. In contrast, continental European countries emphasize on road safety by limiting the application of roundabouts to non-divided roadways and low road functional classes. For example, in Germany, the technical Directive RAL 2012 recommends the application of roundabouts on single-lane roads that are classified as inter-county roads or lower functional class (Forschungsgesellschaft für Straßen- und Verkehrswesen 2012). In the Netherlands, the technical directive for the design of interurban roads does not consider the application of roundabouts for roads on the principal road network (i.e., classified as national or provincial) (CROW 2013).

4 Conclusions

In the 1950s with the increase of motorized traffic and the widespread use of traffic lights, roundabouts were abandoned. However, in the late 1990s, with the introduction of a simple and uniform rule of priority, according to which, the vehicles entering the junction (i.e., roundabout) must give priority to the vehicles already moving inside the junction, the problem of traffic congestion was radically addressed. As a result, a systematic study for the implementation of roundabouts begun, for providing a sufficient degree of road safety and a satisfactory level of service, without the use of traffic lights. Many countries then proceeded to the formation of technical guidelines for the design, scope, dimensioning and operation of roundabouts. Over time and with the acquisition of experience the technical guidelines evolved significantly. This paper aims to briefly present the guidelines of the most advanced/ experienced countries in roundabout design in order to guide public administrators and engineers that implement relevant studies.

All national technical guidelines are governed by the same basic design principles and determine the traffic volume service possibilities according to the geometric characteristics of the roundabouts. The main differences concern the exact scope and dimensioning of the individual geometric elements, as any attempt to increase the level of service is to the detriment of the degree of road safety provided. Given that in modern times road transport, but also the transport sector, has acquired an international character, it is appropriate, at least at European level, to apply roundabouts at roads of similar functional classification and to design them based on uniform rules.

References

Ahac, S., Dragcevic, V.: Geometric design of suburban roundabouts. Encyclopedia **1**, 720–743 (2021). https://doi.org/10.3390/encyclopedia1030056

Austroads: Guide to Road Design – Part 4B: Roundabouts (2009)

Brilon, W.: Studies on roundabouts in Germany: lessons learned. In: Proceedings of the 3rd International TRB-Roundabout Conference, Carmel, Indiana, May 2011

Campisi, T., Deluka-Tibljaš, A., Tesoriere, G., Canale, A., Rencelj, M., Šurdonja, S.: Cycling traffic at turbo roundabouts: some considerations related to cyclist mobility and safety. Transp. Res. Procedia **45**, 627–634 (2020)

CERTU: Carrefours urbains: Guide (2010)

CROW: Handboek Wegontwerp (2013)

Department of Main Roads: Road Planning and Design Manual, Chapter 14: Roundabouts. Queensland (2006)

Federal Highway Administration: Roundabouts: An Informational Guide, Publication No. FHWA-RD-00-067. U.S Department of Transportation (2000)

Federal Highway Administration: Roundabouts: An Informational Guide. NCHRP Report 672. U.S Department of Transportation (2011)

Forschungsgesellschaft für Straßen- und Verkehrswesen: Merkblatt für die Anlage von kleinen Kreisverkehrsplätzen (1998)

Forschungsgesellschaft für Straßen- und Verkehrswesen: Merkblatt für die Anlage von Kreisverkehren (2006)

Forschungsgesellschaft für Straßen- und Verkehrswesen: Richtlinien für die Anlage von Landstraßen (RAL) (2012)

Giuffrè, O., et al.: Evaluation of roundabout safety performance through surrogate safety measures from microsimulation. J. Adv. Transp. **2018**, 1–14 (2018)

Gruden, C., Otković, I.I., Šraml, M.: Pedestrian safety at roundabouts: a comparison of the behavior in Italy and Slovenia. Transp. Res. Procedia **60**, 528–535 (2022)

Highways England: Design Manual for Road and Bridges – CD 116: Geometric Design of Roundabouts (2020)

Meewes, V., Sicherheit von Landstrassen-Knotenpunkten: Safety of rural intersections, part 1 to 3, Strassenverkehrstechnik, vol. 47, no. 4-6 (2003)

Royal Haskoning: Roundabouts – Application and design – A practical manual. Ministry of Transport, Public Works and Water Management (2009)

Service d'Études Techniques des Routes et Autoroutes: Aménagement des Carrefours Interurbains sur les Routes Principales – Carrefours plans (1998)

The Highways Agency: Design Manual for Road and Bridges, Volume 6: Road Geometry, Section 2: Junctions - Part 3: Geometric Design of Roundabouts (2007)

Tollazzi, T., Tesoriere, G., Guerrieri, M., Campisi, T.: Environmental, functional and economic criteria for comparing "target roundabouts" with one-or two-level roundabout intersections. Transp. Res. Part D: Transp. Environ. **34**, 330–344 (2015)

Transportation Research Board: NCHRP Synthesis 488 – Roundabout Practices, A Synthesis of Highway Practice (2016)

Wu, N., Brilon, W.: Roundabout capacity analysis based on conflict technique. In: 5th International Conference on Roundabouts, Green Bay, Wisconsin, 8–10 May 2017

Urban Regeneration: Innovative Tools and Evaluation Model (URITEM 2023)

Decision Support System for the Management of Interventions on Buildings in the Historic Centre of Florence: From Conservation to Regeneration

Giovanna Acampa[1] ⓘ, Fabrizio Battisti[1] ⓘ, and Mariolina Grasso[2]([✉]) ⓘ

[1] University of Florence, 50121 Firenze, FI, Italy
[2] University of Enna "Kore", 94100 Enna, EN, Italy
mariolina.grasso@unikore.it

Abstract. The goal of this paper is defining a methodology for assessing priorities among interventions in the historic center of Florence, going from the conservation to the regeneration of its heritage. The possibility to re-use a building with new characterizations depends on binding and administrative issues while the optimization of resources depends on the planning and organization of the construction sites. The proposed methodology falls within the so called "mixed methods", as it integrates within a multi-criteria model, specific degradation analysis methods and parameters for construction cost optimization. This research proposes a model that interfaces and integrates projects already running in the area already included in the. This, data will be included in the Geographic Information System with the aim of carrying out comprehensive analysis, monitoring, and management of the building heritage in the historic center of Florence that is under development. The methodology can be considered as a contribution to the Management Plan of the site of the Historic Center of Florence. In addition, the defined method, besides being is in accordance with some action projects of the second macro-area of the management plan is also in keeping with the provisions of the Municipal Operational Plan, which in Sect. 4.3 calls for a reinterpretation of the existing building stock. With the aim to preserve them, we will start from individual building monitoring, moving on to study the condition promoting the creation of joint construction sites, thus optimizing costs. Hence the methodology selects areas suitable for regeneration, whose different transformation alternatives are evaluated (HIA) and hierarchized (MCDA).

Keywords: Management · Cultural Heritage · DSS

1 Introduction

The old city center of Florence has been on the World Heritage List since 1982 [1]. To make its safeguard more incisive and the heritage better protected and monitored, UNESCO, since 2004, has recommended the adoption of a Management Plan to all the sites on its List. The Management Plan follows an embedded strategies combining cultural heritage protection and conservation with the development needs (referring to socio-economics aspects) of the area in order to guarantee choices sustainability.

To meet the needs related to the drafting, implementation and monitoring of the Management Plan, the UNESCO Office was set up within the municipal organizational structure in 2005.

In 2016 the Municipality of Florence approved the second Management Plan [2] after the first version released in 2006. In 2018 it was also presented a monitoring plan. The lattes signed a fundamental phase both for the management of the World Heritage site and for the implementation of UNESCO requirements. These objectives were achieved as result of the collaboration between the Region of Tuscany and the University of Florence. In fact, it was born Here Lab - Heritage Research Lab [3] within the Department of Architecture (DIDA) which was involved both in the research applied to the Management Plan and in defining the monitoring plan.

Indeed, a monitoring plan is fundamental to guarantee the implementation of a Management Plan providing all the needed information to review, adapt and update it.

The monitoring process of the Management Plan for the Historic Centre of Florence is structured into:

1. checking projects consistency in terms of both respecting to the Mission of the site and the maintenance of its Outstanding Universal Value;
2. checking projects breakthroughs, establishing monitoring indicators and verifying whether the project objectives are being achieved on time.
3. The monitoring plan drawn up in 2018 was updated in 2022 with Preliminary Document to the 2022 Management Plan, monitoring 33 projects, divided into 5 macro-areas (Fig. 1).

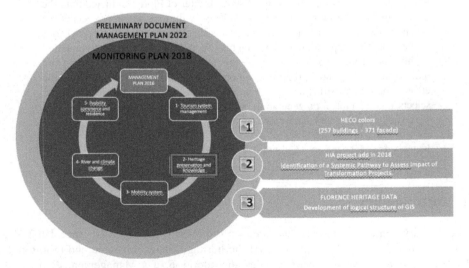

Fig. 1. Management Plan outline

Basically, the methodology presented here aims at implementing and linking the results achieved in 3 projects (HECO Colors, HIA and Florence Heritage Data) belonging to macro area no. 2 (Heritage Conservation and Knowledge) through a new approach based on 4 main steps:

1. Creation of a degradation index, referred to a single building as if it was stand-alone;
2. Definition of an opportunity matrix, relating possible interventions on the different buildings of a block;
3. Outline of possible regeneration interventions and evaluation of their impacts.
4. Multi-criteria analysis, for the choice of the best regeneration hypothesis aimed at achieving the objectives of the Management Plan.

The proposed methodology belongs to the so-called "mixed methods" as it integrates within a multi-criteria model, specific methods of degradation analysis and definition of intervention opportunities. It is applied to buildings in the historic center of Florence and its buffer zone. In particular, the degradation study focuses on vertical and horizontal opaque structures (elevations and roofs). Although constructed and applied according to the UNESCO context of the Historic Centre of Florence, the methodology lends itself to being adaptable also to other contexts and in this sense to be applied in the management plans of historic centers or sites.

2 State of the Art

2.1 Evaluation Tool for Cultural Heritage

While urban context has evolved and changed steadily with population growth, cultural heritage has continued expressing the historical evolution of cities. Indeed, Cultural Heritage and its safeguard and sustainable development plays a fundamental role in maintaining the link between the past and the future. Due to rapid urbanization of historical city, heritage properties can be threatened by the development of urban areas. This discrepancy between heritage preservation and urban development has led to several challenges in the historic urban environment.

Recognizing this challenge, the Heritage Impact Assessment is an assessment tool to identify and analyze the potential impacts of new projects on World Heritage cultural properties. The HIA is a version of the Environmental Impact Assessment (EIA) tailored for cultural heritage properties, specifically focusing on its preservation.

Environmental Impact Assessment (EIA)
Since 1970, EIA has been the official tool "to identify the environmental, social and economic impacts of a project prior to decision-making. It aims to predict environmental impacts at an early stage of planning and design, to find ways and means to reduce negative impacts, to shape projects to fit the local environment and to present predictions and options to decision-makers".

To achieve its objectives, EIA should be incorporated into the management system at urban and regional levels. In this regard, the International Association for Impact Assessment (IAIA) and the UK's IEA have indicated as a primary goal for EIA implementation to "address and incorporate development decision-making" and to "promote development that is sustainable and optimizes resource use and management opportunities".

EIA results has an useful assessment tool providing an integrated methodology reviewing projects drafts, assessing their impacts and facilitate decision-making process thus defining mitigation strategies. Furthermore, EIA has become a legally binding tool in several countries around the world to prevent adverse effects of development proposals before important decisions are taken [4].

In 1999, the IAIA published the principles of EIA as an interdisciplinary process [5]. In this document, the IAIA presents culture, traditions and the value of communities as characteristics that should be respected and taken into account in Environmental Impact Assessment. Subsequently, in many EIA guidelines, cultural heritage is considered as a separate and sensitive element that must be taken into account in order to protect its qualitative characteristics.

As indicated by UNESCO, heritage assets are 'non-renewable resources' of any community extremely linked to its identity and sense of belonging. The World Heritage Convention of 1972 recognized Outstanding Universal Values (OUV) as a central concept in reference to World Cultural and Natural Heritage, which deserves to be protected and passed on to subsequent generations. Safeguarding heritage values is a key factor in the management and protection of World Cultural Heritage [6].

Therefore, identification and mitigation of potential threats to values must be an integral part of heritage conservation.

"Value has always been the basis of heritage conservation. It is evident that no society strives to preserve what it does not value". In this regard, Member States have a responsibility to safeguard the OUV and its associated attributes, taking into account the integrity and authenticity of World Heritage properties from significant negative impacts imposed by change and development. As a result, EIAs do not explicitly address OUV: "If the cultural heritage sections of EIAs do not clearly focus on OUV attributes, they do not meet the desired standards in managing changes in World Heritage properties".

Heritage Impact Assessment
To meet this challenge, in the context of the 'Environmental Impact Assessment' (EIA), the Cultural Heritage Impact Assessment (HIA) has been developed in recent years which considers the specific characteristics and qualitative values of World Heritage properties as a key factor in the management and protection of cultural heritage [7]. Heritage Impact Assessment is a procedure to identify and analyze the potential impacts of human-induced threats on cultural heritage and, therefore, supports better protection and management of cultural heritage. The need for development and change and heritage conservation may cause conflicts between stakeholders dealing with new development in historic urban areas. Heritage Impact Assessment is a tool that can bridge the gap between urban development and heritage conservation needs. In addition, the HIA provides a new assessment tool to facilitate heritage conservation within broader sustainable development policies [8].

HIA is an assessment methodology based on the indications contained in the Guidance on Heritage Impact Assessments for Cultural World Heritage Properties of ICOMOS International (2011, hereafter ICOMOS Guidelines) [9]. It aims to assess, through a systematic and consistent process, the positive/negative impact of one or more transformation projects affecting the values, attributes, authenticity, and integrity of World Heritage sites. The assessment is useful to indicate recommendations and possible mitigation measures to reduce or avoid possible negative effects on heritage and should be used to monitor the rehabilitation of large complexes and new infrastructure projects located both in the World Heritage site and its Buffer Zone.

HIA is currently only recommended for large-scale heritage, such as historic centers instead it is a widespread tool (and in some cases mandatory) for archaeological areas [10].

An effective approach to large-scale HIA is to proceed step by step, introducing the assessment into studies at different levels (e.g. constraint studies, environmental impact assessments, etc.).

The key to a successful HIA is the production of an adequate inventory of the attributes that give the site an Outstanding Universal Value; this inventory, organised in a database, must be linked to a GIS (GIS-linked database) and must contain basic information on the location of the property and its components, information on the regulatory constraint and information on the value of the property [11].

The Guidance on Heritage Impact Assessments for Cultural World Heritage Properties (ICOMOS, 2011) provides a methodology enabling heritage impact assessment by considering the attributes making up the OUV as separate entities. Also, it allows assessing them in a systematic and consistent manner.

2.2 Project for the Safeguarding of Florence Historical City Center

The Historic Centre of Florence was inscribed on the World Heritage List after the Sixth Session of the UNESCO World Heritage Committee, held in Paris at the headquarters of the United Nations Educational, Scientific and Cultural Organisation (December 1982). Based on the data provided each State is responsible for disseminating a list of World Heritage properties considered to be of outstanding universal value. Also, it is mandatory indicating the Cultural Heritage Properties in danger that need to be protected as well as the restoration work and eventually the assistance required. After a strong call by UNESCO in 2000, each Member State is responsible for providing even old cultural heritage sites with a management plan. In Italy in 2005 there was an abrupt acceleration about this topic when a the Ministry of Cultural Heritage and Activities and the managers of World Heritage sites was implemented. Regarding Florence and its historical center, among the peripheral state administrations and the municipality there was only a minimal awareness that was inscribed on the World Heritage List. As evidence, this unique feature was mentioned in any official document, regulation or spatial planning instrument.

In order to assess the need of drawing up a document for the preservation and enhancement of the site the Municipality of Florence, the body responsible for the site, set up the "UNESCO office" specifically dedicated to the drafting and monitoring of the Management Plan. The Office also deal with the following tasks:

- Promoting the conservation, enhancement and sustainable management of the Historic Centre of Florence by drafting and monitoring the Management Plan envisaged by the World Heritage Convention.

- Coordinate public and private actors as well as the stakeholders operating in the Historic Centre of Florence.
- Co-ordination and management of the funding allocated to the Management Plan and the related Action Plan.
- Create periodical reports about the state of conservation of the Historic Centre and on modifications to the Management Plan and the Action Plan.
- Implementation and monitoring of projects financed by Law no. 77 of 20 February 2006 "Special measures for the protection and enjoyment of Italian sites of cultural, landscape and environmental interest included in the "World Heritage List", under the protection of UNESCO.

The 2022 management plan was recently drafted, updating the previous 2016 version. With the aim to track the progress of this plan, a monitoring plan is carried out every two years. It involves public and private actors of the projects selected within the management plan and monitors 33 projects subdivided into 5 macro areas: 1) management of the tourist system; 2) conservation and knowledge of the monumental heritage; 3) mobility system; 4) Arno River and climate change; 5) livability, commerce and residence in the historic center.

The methodology proposed in this work focuses on "Conservation and knowledge of the monumental heritage" and aims to link three action projects:

1. HECO _[12] financed by the MiBACT funds of Law 77/2006 "Special measures for the protection and enjoyment of Italian sites of cultural, landscape and environmental interest, included in the 'world heritage list', under the protection of UNESCO"- is an open data system of the architecture of the Historic Centre and is based on the recognition of the color language of architecture and aims to develop guidelines to be used in urban prevention and maintenance.
2. HIA_ [13] Implementation of a Heritage Impact Assessment (HIA) protocol for the assets of the Historic Centre of Florence and experimentation of possible applications of the model on concrete cases of ongoing transformations. The HIA project - financed with the MiBACT funds of Law 77/2006 "Special measures for the protection and enjoyment of Italian sites of cultural, landscape and environmental interest, included in the 'World Heritage List', under the protection of UNESCO" - was born from the synergy between Heritage_CITYlab, a joint laboratory between the University of Florence and UNESCO that makes a multidisciplinary approach possible. The experimentation, in accordance with the Guidelines issued by ICOMOS (2011), aims at assessing, through a systematic and coherent path, the positive/negative impact of transformation projects that affect the values, attributes, authenticity and integrity of the World Heritage Site, the Historic Centre of Florence.
3. Florence Heritage Data [14]_ the project proposes to define and develop the logical and physical structure of a Geographic Information System intended for the analysis, monitoring and integrated management of the transformations of the building heritage and open spaces of the Historic Centre of Florence. This system will consist of an information infrastructure potentially open to interaction with databases in use by different entities, applied to different sectors, which share the objective of promoting the enhancement of the city's excellence, its active protection and the valorization of its cultural heritage. The Information System that constitutes the objective of the

project can be considered as a fundamental 'spatial index' able to allow the connection of databases available or being implemented, pertaining to public and private entities, engaged in institutional or economic valorization activities, having as their object the consistency, state of preservation and conditions of use of the building heritage of the Historic Centre.

3 About the Method

The proposed method belongs to the so called mixed-methods which systematically combines and integrates different methods in an evaluation process where both quantitative and qualitative data are collected and analyses. These are mainly adopted when:

- Each question has more than one answer, so that several evaluation methods are required.
- Accuracy and consistency of the results need to be increased.
- Several steps are involved in the evaluation process. Also, the results obtained by one method are useful for subsequent steps.

It is evident that more methods are able to capture a wider range of perspectives. Specifically in this paper, an experimental evaluation based on four steps is used:

1. Definition of a degradation index, referring to each building as stand-alone.
2. Creation of an opportunity matrix, which relates possible interventions on the different buildings of a block.
3. Outline of possible regeneration interventions and evaluation of their impacts.
4. Multi-criteria analysis, for the choice of the best hypothesis to comply with the objectives of the Management Plan.

3.1 Definition of a Degradation Index, Referring to Each Building as Stand-Alone

Following a careful and thorough analysis, a synthetic index is defined for each building indicating its level of degradation (id1, id2, id3,..., idn). The index is calculated as the ratio of the damaged areas of the facade and roof to the total area of the facade and roof multiplied by factors related to the type and severity of degradation. In this way, specific evaluation criteria and indicators of degradation (limited to facades and roofs) define the conservation status of the envelope of each building. This phase can be carried out independently or as an extension of the HECO (Heritage Colors) project. HECO is an integrated open data system to monitor the state of deterioration of public and private buildings, suggesting methods of execution for the management of planned interventions.

3.2 Creation of an Opportunity Matrix, Which Relates Possible Interventions on the Different Buildings of a Block

By relating buildings to each other costs are optimized and restoration and reuse activities are concentrated according to economies of site and scale. The rows and columns of the matrix refer to the buildings in a block. Each quadrant resulting from the intersection is filled according to the degradation index, proximity of buildings, continuity of building site areas, and homogeneity of the technological envelope. In this way, the matrices provide a clear view of the blocks where the need for joint interventions is greatest. All the information can be collected and integrated into Florence Heritage Data, a Geographic Information System designed for the joint analysis, monitoring and management of the transformations of the built heritage and open spaces of the Historic Center of Florence.

3.3 Outline of Possible Regeneration Interventions and Evaluation of Their Impacts

Once suitable blocks for regeneration have been selected, urban planning constraints and regulations are analyzed and various solutions are designed taking into account different scenarios. The goal of this phase is to outline multiple project alternatives. For each project, a HIA (Heritage Impact Assessment) is conducted to strategically assess the corresponding potential impacts (both direct and consequential) on the cultural heritage, particularly on the OUV.

Basically, HIA is a process of identifying, predicting, evaluating, and communicating impacts that integrates results during the development of each phase of the project. Stakeholders (municipality, ministry, region, citizens) are involved to minimize impacts and identify possible mitigation. In the assessment process, we used the standard classifications for assessing heritage attributes (very high, high, medium, low, negligible) and standard criteria for assessing the weight of changes brought by each project We relied on the model created by HeRe Lab in collaboration with the UNESCO City Center Office.

3.4 Multi-criteria Analysis, for the Choice of the Best Hypothesis to Comply with the Objectives of the Management Plan

Once the eligible interventions have been identified, the last step is to specify the criteria for selecting the best alternative or at least the best compromise to achieve the objectives of the Management Plan. At this stage, it is essential to clearly state the needs and strategic objectives of regeneration. In general, these goals should aim to address issues such as the impact of mass tourism on city life, the effect of which has been a decrease in the number of residents in urban centers.

Useful tools for achieving these goals are provided in a number of documents already issued. Among them, the "Urban Regulations," one of the projects included in the Management Plan of the Municipality of Florence, defines the discomfort/disturbance factors affecting the livability conditions of the historic center and the factors impoverishing the urban image, while the "Regulations for the Protection and Enhancement of Historic and Traditional Florentine Economic Activities" deals with the protection of small commercial activities that were traditionally carried out in the city. In general, in the field of decision-making, multi-criteria analyses have become a widespread tool that can address problems involving more than one objective.

These, in addition to the possibility of considering data of different natures (quantitative and qualitative) offer the opportunity to assign different weights to identified criteria, manage conflicts between objectives, and infer priorities among alternatives.

Analysis of the main scientific literature with applications of multi-criteria analysis to decision-making problems concerning cultural heritage reveals the importance of using combined methodologies, which are particularly useful for dealing with complex situations and capable of structuring more inclusive decision-making processes aimed at greater sharing of choices [15].

Generally speaking multi-criteria analyses can be classified as follows:

• Outranking methods
• Full aggregation methods
• Target, aspiration, or reference level methods

As previously illustrated, multicriteria analysis techniques are various, and the choice of which method to adopt is rarely trivial. The steps that follow propose an investigation of some specific techniques that, based on the literature review, have been proved to be most effective in the context of cultural heritage evaluation. This is to identify the analysis best suited to solve the decision-making problem at hand.

The in-depth study starts with outranking methods and in particular ELECTRE (Elimination Et Choix Tradusiant la Realité) methods, which consist of the so-called outranking relationship..

The two principal processes featuring ELECTRE are: a) multiple-criteria aggregation procedure that constructs one or more outranking relations to compare each pair of alternatives comprehensively; b) exploitation procedure that can provide results depending on how the problem is approached, choosing, ranking or ordering.

ELECTRE methods make it easy to skip inter-criteria compensation and any normalization process, which distorts the original data. The disadvantage is that they require various technical parameters, which are not always easy to read. Also in the field of outranking methods is PROMETHEE "Preference Ranking Organization METHods for Enrichment Evaluations," which is based on pairwise comparisons between alternatives in which the decision maker's preference is de-ranked according to the distance between two hypothetical alternatives for each individual criterion.

The PROMETHEE method allows one to operate directly on the variables included in the decision matrix without requiring any normalization and is applicable even when there is insufficient information. Nevertheless, when there are many criteria involved, method development becomes complex, making it difficult for decision makers to get a good picture of the problem.

Regarding the "Technique for Order Preferences by Similarity to an Ideal Solution" (TOPSIS), the idea behind this method is to choose the best alternative between the one closest to the optimal solution and the one furthest from the worst solution. Every alternative is represented by a vector whose elements describe the performance of the alternative for each decision criterion.

Thus, the best solution turns out to be the one that maximizes performance for the criteria associated with a benefit (output) and minimizes performance for the criteria associated with a cost (input). The advantage of this method is that it requires only little input from the decision maker and its result is easy to understand. However, in the case of multidimensional problems, vector normalization must be used, making the decision-making process particularly complex (Fig. 2).

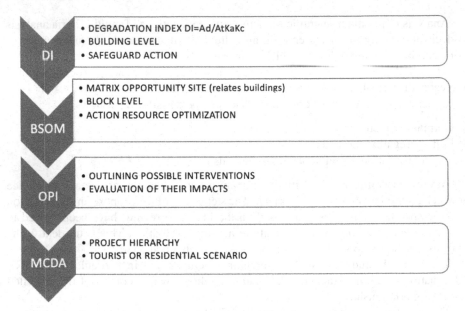

Fig. 2. Summarizing scheme of methodological steps

4 Conclusions

The research conducted so far aims to coordinate and aggregate outputs from three action projects contained within the Management Plan for the Historic Center of Florence in order to optimize their results:

- HECO_financed by MiBACT funds of Law 77/2006 "Special measures for the protection and enjoyment of Italian sites of cultural, landscape and environmental interest, included in the 'world heritage list', placed under the protection of UNESCO"-is an integrated open data system of the architecture of the Historic Center.
- HIA_Realization of a Heritage Impact Assessment (HIA) protocol for the assets of the Historic Center of Florence and testing of possible applications of the model on concrete cases of ongoing transformations.
- Florence Heritage Data_the project aims to define and develop the logical and physical structure of a Geographic Information System intended for the analysis, monitoring and integrated management of the transformations of the built heritage and open spaces of the Historic Center of Florence.

The defined mixed method makes use of a series of assessments involving the calculation of a degradation index, the definition of a matrix of opportunities for intervention, the definition of different types of intervention and the choice of the best alternative (among the types of intervention) using multi-criteria analysis. Thus, methodologies based on both quantitative (e.g., degradation index calculation) and qualitative (e.g., definition of intervention opportunity matrix) data are alternated.

Generally, heritage regeneration interventions concern single portions of buildings (e.g., their envelope); through the application of the proposed methodology, the aim is instead to consider a broader perspective, which does not only take into account the external envelope of buildings but also the set of infrastructures serving them, so as to ensure a deep regeneration action.

Although still in the experimental stage, the method is easily exportable to other systems (e.g., different technical elements that make up the building) given the flexibility and generality of the individual methods that comprise it.

The natural development of the research is based on the experimentation/application of the method to the reference context, after the selection of buildings falling within the historic center of Florence and its buffer zone. Following this experimentation, eventually, it will be possible to define any points or phases of the method that need further implementation.

References

1. Unesco World Heritage List [Internet]. [citato 25 marzo 2022]. https://whc.unesco.org/en/sta tesparties/it/
2. Piano di Gestione Firenze [Internet]. Firenze Patrimonio Mondiale. [citato 25 marzo 2023]. https://www.firenzepatrimoniomondiale.it/il-piano-di-gestione-2021-2022-e-piani-di-gestione-precedenti/
3. Here Lab Florence [Internet]. Firenze Patrimonio Mondiale. [citato 25 marzo 2023]. https://www.firenzepatrimoniomondiale.it/here_lab-heritage-research/
4. Morgan, R.K.: Environmental impact assessment: the state of the art. Impact Assess. Proj. Apprais. **30**(1), 5–14 (2012)
5. IAIA - International Association for Impact Assessment [Internet]. IAIA - Environmental Impact Assessment. [citato 25 marzo 2022]. https://www.iaia.org/best-practice.php
6. UNESCO - World Heritage Convention [Internet]. WHC. [citato 25 marzo 2022]. https://whc.unesco.org/en/conventiontext/
7. Silva, A., Roders, A.: Cultural heritage management and heritage (impact) assessments. Proc. Jt. CIB W **70**, W092 (2012)
8. Ashrafi, B., Kloos, M., Neugebauer, C.: Heritage impact assessment, beyond an assessment tool: a comparative analysis of urban development impact on visual integrity in four UNESCO world heritage properties. J. Cult. Herit. **47**, 199–207 (2021)
9. ICOMOS 2011 [Internet]. ICOMOS 2011 Guidelines on Heritage Impact Assessment. [citato 25 marzo 2023]. https://www.icomos.org/en/charters-and-texts/179-articles-en-francais/res sources/charters-and-standards/187-guidelines-for-education-and-training-in-the-conservat ion-of-monuments-ensembles-and-sites
10. Acampa, G., Battisti, F., Grasso, M.: An evaluation system to optimize the management of interventions in the historic center of florence world heritage site: from building preservation to block refurbishment. Land **12**(4), 726 (2023)
11. Noszczyk, T., Gawronek, P.: Remote sensing and GIS for environmental analysis and cultural heritage. Remote Sens. **12**(23), 3960 (2020)
12. HECO (HEritage COlors) [Internet]. Firenze Patrimonio Mondiale. [citato 25 marzo 2023]. https://www.firenzepatrimoniomondiale.it/progetti/heco-heritage-colours/

13. Valutazione di Impatto sul Patrimonio - Heritage Impact Assessment [Internet]. Firenze Patrimonio Mondiale. [citato 25 marzo 2023]. https://www.firenzepatrimoniomondiale.it/progetti/heritage-impact-assessment-hia/

14. Florence Heritage Data System [Internet]. Firenze Patrimonio Mondiale. https://www.firenzepatrimoniomondiale.it/progetti/florence-heritage-data-system/

15. Wang, J.J., Jing, Y.Y., Zhang, C.F., Zhao, J.H.: Review on multi-criteria decision analysis aid in sustainable energy decision-making. Renew. Sustain. Energy Rev. **13**(9), 2263–2278 (2009)

Knowledge as a Prodromal Action for Urban Regeneration and Sustainable Development: The Case Study of Municipality of Fondi

Fabrizio Battisti[1]([⊠]) [iD], Carlo Pisano[2] [iD], and Saverio Torzoni[2]

[1] Department of Architecture, University of Florence, Via di San Niccolò, 93, 50125 Florence, Italy
fabrizio.battisti@unifi.it
[2] Department of Architecture, University of Florence, Via P.A. Micheli, 2, 50121 Florence, Italy
{carlo.pisano,saverio.torzoni}@unifi.it

Abstract. Retracing the process of forming the Knowledge Framework (KF) of the Italian Municipality of Fondi, this research aims to describe the methodology used to cope with the necessity to recount all those disturbances that, in dynamic modern times, animate spaces and relationships, giving the territory multiple identities, interdependent and with uncertain edges. Combined with analyses of structures that are by nature more defined, the text deals with comparisons with other planning processes in force in Italy, reinterpreting some parts of them and transposing them to the study area, through the filter provided by the analysis tools of Regional Design. This reading aims to stimulate new reflections and ideas, not only within the governing bodies, but also to the community, providing a framework capable of innovating the KF by recognizing it, not only as an analytical process, but also as a fundamental urban planning tool.

Keywords: Municipally Planning · Knowledge Framework · Regional Design

1 Introduction

1.1 Knowledge Framework as an Urbanistic Tool

The Knowledge Framework (KF) is the integrated system of information and data necessary to understand the intrinsec issues of land-use and urban planning tools. It constitutes the amount of information necessary for an organic and comprehensive representation together with an evaluation of the state of the territory and its evolutionary processes, as well as the indispensable reference for the definition of the objectives and contents of the plan for sustainability assessment.

The importance of the knowledge dimension in planning was reinforced in the early 20th century by the Modern Movement, marking the establishment of deterministic and reductionist functionalism. During the 4th CIAM in 1933, under the leadership of Cornelius van Eesteren, the principles of 'The Functional City' were defined [1, 2]. During this fundamental event for the subsequent scientific approach to the plan, the

O. Gervasi et al. (Eds.): ICCSA 2023 Workshops, LNCS 14111, pp. 341–354, 2023.
https://doi.org/10.1007/978-3-031-37126-4_23

complex analytical work and early design findings of van Eesteren's plan for the city of Amsterdam was examined and discussed along with other examples [3]. Such a work is now identified as one of the most significant examples, particularly for the methodology adopted in the construction of the KF.

In the Italian context, Giovanni Astengo [4] represents an important figure related to the role of knowledge apparatus in the urban planning process. He emphasized the importance of recognizing a scientific role to urban planning throughout his career. The Plan, in its interpretation, is understood as a tool for knowing, designing and transforming a complex reality. Therefore, the articulation of the process that is produced is fundamental produces and must initially go through a phase of quantitative analytical reading, followed by as clear an understanding of reality as possible, and then define the objectives within which the choice is oriented (example: Assisi Plan) [5].

This brief historical excursus highlights how during the twentieth century, knowledge data represent an essential material in the study of urban phenomena-both as components or aspects taken individually and in their reciprocal interrelationships-because they are capable of directing the many political, legislative, administrative and technical actions that continually modify the reality of a territory [6].

1.2 Knowledge Framework of Fondi's Territory

In this perspective, the collaboration between the Municipality of Fondi and the Department of Architecture of the University of Florence, formalized in June 2022, for the drafting of the KF of the municipal territory has begun. The research agreement, which was created with the intention of analyzing and experimenting with a new approach to the territorial study, is proposed as the first step for the presentation of the general variant that will affect the General Regulatory Plan (PRG) of the municipality, in force since 1973.

The balance to be found between these two purposes is assured by the decision to lay on a renew language, freed from the deterministic language of the last century's urbanism. Therefore, laying the foundation for the insights that will determine future land governance and that which sees the KF as the moment in which the territory is discovered, manifesting its subjects, scenarios and processes, is ensured by the decision to rely on a renewed language, which, although it follows the normative demands on planning documents, breaks free from the deterministic language of last century's urbanism [7] and which contributed to the critical issues described above. Therefore, the KF appears as the organic set of knowledge referring to the territory and landscape, on which to base future plan forecasts and assessments [8, 9].

Analyzing the blurred edges that, however, are based on clear boundaries [10]: the certainty of an artifact's location is matched by the uncertainty of its use, amalgamating these two levels of analysis with themes such as vocation and potential.

In this twofold analytical front, the present research proposes its own innovative role, that is, guaranteeing to the future planning phase of the general variant, in addition to a rich and homogeneous database, also the identification of a network of guidelines and nodes to be systematized and enhanced within a vision that accomunizes all levels of the territory [11–13]. This tool also aims to act as a link between administrations and the population, proposing itself as an opportunity to get to know the Municipality of Fondi and to promote it, so as to give future policies of renovatio urbis the best degree of sense and coherence [14].

2 Background and References

2.1 Plans and Laws

This research takes place into the procedural mechanism of the formation of a planning instrument and, as such, according to Italian regulations, it responds to the directives of the regional urban planning law in force, which in Lazio is Law 38 of 1999, "Norms on the government of the territory" [15]; on the basis of this norm, it was therefore possible to know the elaborates of which the KF, by law, must be composed.

Willing to provide a critical analysis to the territory through specific cartographies, but also thanks to a process of research and restitution as organized and communicative as possible, the normative and methodological references have also been grasped in the rest of the national panorama, where the different regional norms condition the structures. In this context, made up of a multifaceted and varied regulatory patchwork, Emilia-Romagna's Piani Urbani Comunali (PUC) and Tuscany's Piani Strutturali (PS) [16, 17], the instruments corresponding to Lazio's PRGs, with their proposals and methodologies helped define the direction to be given to the research. From the Emilian Plans, the division into Systems that these tools propose was extrapolated and reinterpreted, considered as a key piece for the communicative effectiveness of the study, but also, and above all, for the clear framing of the territory's emergencies. Tuscany's Structural Plans are connoted for their adherence to the concept of a Territorial Statute, born out of the need to re-address the growing need to manage and transform the territory by virtue of the principles of sustainable development. It is an instrument that gathers within it the entire territorial heritage, proposed as a constituent common good of the regional collective identity by which is meant the set of long-lasting structures produced by the coevolution between the natural environment and human settlements, whose value for present and future generations is recognized.

The aforementioned tools have been interpreted and appropriately transposed on the regulatory and territorial reality of this area of Latium, which, however, needs to be studied according to a specific urban and territorial context and the logics implied by it.

2.2 Regional Design Approach

In order to succeed in understanding and hinging together the different shapes that make up the territory, the principles of study and representation proposed by Regional Design (RD) has been proved fundamental. This discipline, born as a reaction to the now manifest inability of large-scale Plans to respond to the new and increasingly pressing needs of the population and of the different territorial areas, bases its processes on the awareness that the administrative limits (within which, as a rule, the Plans, of classical setting, impose and define their directives) poorly dialogue with all those flows that animate the territory within them (transportation systems, water, energy, commerce, information infrastructure, but also local identities, associations, traditions) [18].

To witness the complexity of a place becoming a feature slot, the RD relies on a new mode of representation with abstract features, now more than ever in line with that dissolution of roles and forms, increasingly evident, in our cities and countryside. The functional dissolution and hybridization, the extinction of the form follows function paradigm, and the disjunction of the relationship between the two terms have helped generate new research on space [19]. It is based on a dynamic mode of depiction, capable of capturing future developments through a visioning process [20, 21], enlivened by debates with stakeholders [22, 23] about shared territory [24] and suggestions, thus finding a strong link with the activity of planning, seen as a tool for persuasive storytelling [25, 26]. Thus, the concepts of percolation, density and porosity take over, moving out of the principles of hierarchy, seen before as the only possible form of organization, and into a field of horizontal and diffuse relationships, stimulating different ideas of modernity. The descriptive form chosen to narrate the territory, therefore, adapts to the transformations taking place on the territory, which, insofar as they are undefinable and purely concrete, find correspondence in the tool of concept and diagram [27].

An excellent example of the application of these principles can be found in Florence's 2017 Metropolitan Strategic Plan (MSP) [28], which puts the bases of the future ambitions of the Tuscan Metropolitan City on a much more qualitative than quantitative reading. Within this plan, the different parts of the territory no longer come to be unpacked on the basis of political boundaries but through rhythms [29], figures with uncertain boundaries and changing meanings, with the specific purpose of not dogmatically fixing the (unattainable) intrinsic characteristics of the areas but, exclusively, of interpreting their trends and transformations.

A mode of research is thus proposed that, with a holistic approach [30], allows as much study material as possible, in the certainty that every factor or action that influences a small part of the territory, as it unfolds and repeats itself over time, also influences all other factors and actions.

3 Research Methods

As introduced before, the research followed the RD approach, which gives the design the dual role of descriptor of the present and prefigurator of possible futures. This dual role is particularly relevant from a scientific/operational point of view in the construction of a KF, capable in fact of overcoming the analytical question, normally understood as the only component of this document, by providing for an interpretative and synthetic restitution that aims to shape the various parts of the territory, analyzing them in their singularities and in their mutual inseparability. Through this kind of reading, the different scales and components on which a territory is structured are interconnected by multiple levels of analysis and suggestions, but nevertheless brought back to a system of their own, thus ensuring effective communicability of the results of the study.

Starting from the documents required by Departmental Circular No. 11302 of 09/25/2000, the regulatory reference of the Lazio Region regarding the new implementation of PRG and listing the minimum contents of the new KF, the research reorganized the required information into five systems: Environmental System; Settlement System; Socio-economic System; System of Vigorous Planning; Landscape System.

Finally, each system is summarized in a concluding paper that is entrusted with the task of gathering the outcomes of the previous analysis on the territory, in order to grasp its main peculiarities.

The structuring of the KF in the five systems, the list of documents falling under each system and the summary papers constitute the operational framework described in detail in the following.

4 Results

4.1 The Contents of the Knowledge Framework

The construction of the KF, as anticipated, followed the need to meet the requirements of Departmental Circular No. 11302 of 09/25/2000. In the case of KF construction, it was possible to learn the need for the composition of a report and the following graphic drawings:

- Territorial Framework;
- Main geomorphological features of the territory;
- Areas under hydrogeological instability;
- Areas under hydrogeological constraint;
- Framework of the PRG forecasts on the graphic elaborations of the Territorial Landscape Plan (PTPR);
- Framing of PRG forecasts with superordinate planning instruments;
- Aerophotogrammetry;
- Land cover;
- Areas and properties of state property;
- Areas of special naturalistic importance;
- Relationship between land, infrastructure network and the settlement structure;
- Agropedological map;
- Identification of homogeneous territorial zones "A" and "B";
- Equipment;
- Elements that appear likely to be safeguarded;
- Identification of squatter cores;
- Planimetry of the municipal territory showing the existing state of affairs;
- Road network and other communication and relationship systems;
- Focus on built-up areas.

4.2 Data Sources

To enrich the already vast database provided by the municipality, it was useful to consult the info-geographical portal of the Lazio Region (geoportale.regione.lazio.it), from which decisive information was drawn for the systemic organization of territorial planning [31], particularly in the definition of the regulatory context and the environmental and landscape contexts, combined also with the study of the provincial plans of Latina and sector studies.

Among the materials collected from these sources, the Regional Territorial Landscape Plan (PTPR), approved in 2021, most determined the direction and reliability of the research. This document gathers a wide range of information useful for the under-standing, first, and management, later, of the regional territory, reporting in a single and homogeneous language the protections and ambitions of the whole of Lazio.

To complete the framework of data collection, the research relied on an extensive bibliographic apparatus, consisting of texts by different authors and with different pur-poses. This sampling of publications, in which one finds ancient essays [32], historical [33, 34] and thematic insights [35–37], collections of postcards [38] and hiking guides [39, 40], ensured, during the phase of defining the overall ambitions of the study, an even greater understanding of the identities that intertwine and amalgamate in this place (Fig. 1).

Fig. 1. Potential and criticality map. Produced in the research area as a study analysis

4.3 Five Systems

The first observation made in response to the list of required elaborates concerns the strong homologation of different themes, which are found to be described sometimes broad and generic and at other times very specific containers, resulting in elaborates that have little dialogue with each other and, above all, of complicated interpretation by non-technical readers.

Therefore, the required elaborates were collected into four thematic groups, which take the role of the backbone of the Fondi KF, proposing themselves as the Systems [41] of the Fondi territory. Thus, the 19 papers are redistributed in such a way to facilitate their consultation, both during the process of composition and approval of the general variant to the PRG and in other fora.

Once the Systems were composed, they were evaluated on the basis of the level of depth guaranteed by the 19 elaborates and, consequently, aspects worthy of further study and research were identified; the need thus arises to add further analyses that can thus ensure a more authentic and ramified restitution of the current state of the Municipality of Fondi.

The papers, from the initial 19, increase up to 41, which create a new additional System, that of Landscape. The framework of the KF is thus being defined into a recognizable graphic design has been attributed, capable of better guiding and orienting both the technician and the casual reader.

The work is completed by the KF Report, which is also structured according to the outline and graphic palettes proposed by the five Systems, of which it serves as a summation.

Each of the five is defined by an almost consequential order of content (from national to local, from the vast area to the single point) or by a sectorial order (natural-anthropic, places-activities) so as to help, those who will interface with the study, in the search for the single topic, without, however, ever losing sight of the complexity in which that one fits in and with which it relates (Fig. 2).

Fig. 2. Faceplates used for the works belonging to the five Systems

At the end of each System, which are proposed as coherent binders of data in each case objective and deducible, a further elaboration is included, defined as the System Synthesis [42], and of which it is proposed to tell, in an outline design, its peculiarities and trends.

4.4 Synthesis of the Systems

In order to bring together and organize the results of the analysis of each System, as anticipated, each of them concludes with a synthetic elaboration that has been given the task of capturing the emergencies and anomalies that have emerged.

Each summary paper presents its own language and goes beyond the analytical value in order to highlight the subtext behind each information layer, identifying therein a crucial value for the future design phases of the General Variant to the PRG.

Environment Structures of Territory
The map, at the conclusion of the Environmental System, aims to define the load-bearing characteristics of the municipal territory, that is, those that are to be accumulated [43] and highlighted over the course of the previous analyses belonging to the system. Through the delimitation of these compartments and networks, future operations on the territory can be conducted with the critical awareness that realities insist on the municipality that can only escape the rigid administrative perimeter and that, therefore, will necessarily have to be studied in dialogue with other neighboring municipal realities, thus also providing the basis for the stipulation of future pacts, collective and concerted, of management and transformation, such as River Contracts [44] and forms of associationism [45].

Settlement Centralities
This paper aims to close the Settlement System through an identification of the different identities present in the area. Fondi, as can be deduced from the Historicization of building sites, is a municipality that has historically seen its population, and consequently its built-up area, traceable exclusively around its main town. With the completion of the reclamation works on the Plain then, which took place in the years immediately following World War II, the municipality was provided with new and extensive land to devote to agriculture. It is thus that, in the midst of these large crops, new nuclei began to spring up and expand, which today define small agglomerations and hamlets, with their own and perceived identity and substantial autonomy, but all bearing the vice of unplanned and previously studied building, and witness the unbalanced distribution of services and sub-services, the ineffective connections offered by the road network and the very numerous scattered houses.

The elaborate Settlement Centralities, using a unique language and scale appropriate to each case, brings out, through excerpts from previous cartographies and interpretive readings, those identities that are latent today, giving the settlements a renewed recognizability and value [46]. The ultimate intention is to make people reflect on the many micro-identities formed spontaneously, through unconventional fabrics and building, by employing a conceptual shift [47] that pushes to reevaluate and integrate them into the overall identity of the municipality (Fig. 3).

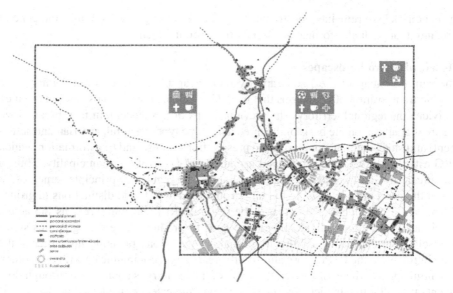

Fig. 3. Morphological-interpretative analysis, Settlement Centralities, extract

Relations Between Territory, Settlements and Infrastructures

As a synthesis of the Socio-Economic System, this map brings together the relational subplots between the spheres of inhabitants and workers, and how these are interwoven in the network proposed by the local road system and the distribution of services and work areas. What emerges is a map indicating the gaps and potentialities of specific areas, their degree of reachability and traversability, according to the concentration of areas on which different interests gravitate.

Map of Transformability

Going to close one of the most crucial systems in the facilitation of the strategic phase and transformations, this map intends to convey, more than the others, the possible directions that future spatial decision-makers can take [48].

By carefully analyzing the current Plan, with its variants realized or only planned in the last 50 years, and the standards indicated by superordinate plans, among which the PTPR stands out in importance, the map gives each area its own gradient of transformability. The reflections from which the specific gradient is generated take the forecasts of the PRG as a reference base, focusing in particular on those that have not yet been realized and that, today, must necessarily be confronted with the new indications on the use of landscapes, with the presence of new constrained areas or areas that are now built up illegally. Thanks to these parameters, it has also been possible to locate some areas that, although outside the original forecasts of the Plan, lend themselves to possible transformations, both in terms of regulatory compliance but also by virtue of a possible future process of redevelopment of the territory, through acupunctural and strategic designs [49, 50]. The map, in contrast to the areas of great transformability, also inserts the element of enduring structures [51], interpreted as those parts of the territory that over the centuries have remained mostly unchanged determining, thanks to this, the general structure that gradually formed and transformed around them.

Mosaic of Micro-landscapes

The summary map of the Landscape System encapsulates, in an overall image, the graphic transposition of the Norms that the PTPR defines for the landscapes into which it divides the regional territory. The previous maps of this system, in fact, break down the areas analyzed on the basis of the three landscape types (natural, agrarian and settlement) and study them by comparing the prescriptions for use and transformation, which PRG establishes, with the actual land use and land cover of the municipality. Thus, a classification of areas based on their compliance with regulatory principles emerges, in which the new coloring given to the lots -from green to red- and distinctions in groups -Elements to be safeguarded, Areas to be restored, Risk elements- returns the actual adherence to the superordinate plans. The need to produce these cartographies stems precisely from the manifest difficulty in making two urban planning instruments, the PRG in force and the PTPR, born almost fifty years apart, communicate with each other, in a municipality where, moreover, the study of the territory is approached through documents that, although meticulous, are poorly communicated with each other. The PTPR itself, because of the limits imposed by the vast scale in which it necessarily sets its studies, cannot count itself the claim to have studied the individual peculiarities of each area within the municipality, which has meanwhile addressed and absorbed the natural flows that traverse and transform every landscape. Intangible flows, bundles of tensions through which the landscape, including the anthropogenic landscape, is shaped and interrelated;

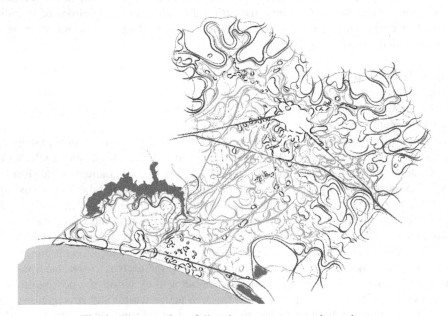

Fig. 4. Interpretation of disturbances present on the territory

though intangible, they establish margins, with which human and ecological processes relate continuously.

Given the previous considerations, the Mosaic of Micro-Landscapes intends to shape, together with the Regional Norms regarding area management, also those flows that, with uncertain margins and continuous overlaps, form the overall picture of the relationships that exist between landscapes, thus seeking to bring out and give dignity to each individual ecosystem (Fig. 4).

5 Discussion and Conclusions

The research that produced the KF of Funds, in its first graphic results, traces the complexity of the territory and the different souls intertwined in it as the keystones on which to hinge future decisions. These, in their branching and entangling, define, more than any decision dropped from above, the actions that shape spaces and activities, and this is why new territorial policies will have to take them into account and to be able to visualize them.

The visualization of the multifaceted identities of places thus becomes, through this research lens, the ultimate goal to which an instrument that undertakes to manage the life of a community, such as the PRG, will have to aim at; detaching itself, therefore, from the static forms of representation of the old instruments, it will have to try to embrace and identify that dynamism proper to each environment.

Based on the historical evolution of places and activities, but also on ambitions for the future, the analyses that the Authority will have at its disposal at the end of the research will represent an important and coherent set of vocations and insights, never fixed, but always open to new considerations and insights [52].

In this peculiarity of non-determination of the narrative, the research faces the necessary limitation of non-completeness, since, in order to effectively read the whole palimpsest of places and actors of which a territory is composed, further - and potentially infinite - analyses would have to be con-ducted. In its representing a criticality, this aspect of the research also plays, in a parallel way, a role of great potential, which, given the popularizing value of the work, can serve as a stimulus to enrichment, through new comparisons and insights.

The tool of the interview is proposed in conclusion, aware that only the interpretation of the multiple specificities that regulate the interactions between humans and the environment will be able to adapt to the infinite weave of actions and reactions that animate and structure a territory, for desirable future phases of analysis. Through social surveys that focus on the inhabitability of spaces but also give ample value to the individual perceptions of citizens [53, 54], it will in fact be possible to visualize even more of those relational substructures and thus be able to channel and exploit them, if possible, or to rest on them so as not to come into conflict; in either case, to the benefit of the overall integrity and identity of the territory.

Moreover, taking advantage of the information base provided by the research, it would also be useful to verify the reactions and insights of third parties, chosen for their extraneousness with the territory and for this reason able to read it without educations or filters given by self-interest. Along these lines, we therefore propose the activation of laboratories and workshops, in which university students or simple enthusiasts could be involved, and during which some specific aspects would be deepened and rethought, by virtue of an already established vision.

References

1. Gold, J.R.: Creating the charter of athens: CIAM and the functional city, 1933–43. Town Plan. Rev. **69**, 225–247 (1998)
2. Harbusch, G., Pérez, M., Somer, K.; Weiss, D., van Es, E. (eds.): Atlas of the functional city: CIAM 4 and comparative urban analysis. gta Verlag/eth Zürich, Bussum, The Netherlands (2014)
3. van der Cammen, H., de Klerk, L.A., Dekker, G., Witsen, P.P.: The Selfmade Land: Culture and Evolution of Urban and Regional Planning in the Netherlands. Spectrum, Amsterdam (2012)
4. Di Biagi, P., Gabellini, P.: Urbanisti italiani: Piccinato, Marconi, Samonà, Quaroni, De Carlo, Astengo, Campos Venuti/Di Biagi, P., Gabellini, P. (eds.) : Postcript Secchi, B.. Editori Laterza, Roma (1992)
5. Astengo, G.: Assisi: Piano Generale e Piani Particolareggiati Di Primo Intervento. Edizioni di Urbanistica, Torino (1958)
6. Portoghesi, P.: Dizionario enciclopedico di architettura e urbanistica. Ediz. illustrata. Siracusa-Zwirner. Gangemi Editore, Roma (2007)
7. Zagari, F.: La convezione verso una politica di progetti sperimentali. Urbanistica Informazioni **266**, 25–27 (2016)
8. Biagi, M., Sargolini, M.: Governo delle tensioni tra città e campagna. Urbanistica Informazioni **237**, 32–34 (2011)
9. Rossi, F.: Atelier internazionale per l'applicazione della Convenzione Europea del Paesaggio n Calabria. Urbanistica Informazioni **265**, 4–6 (2016)
10. Leone, N.G.: Possibilismo e determinismo nel rapporto tra analisi e piano. In: Terrana, A. (eds.) Piano Territoriale Urbanistico Paesaggistico, Tematiche Paesaggistiche, pp. 21–24, Assessorato Regionale BB.CC.AA. e P.I., Caltanissetta (2009)
11. Magnaghi, A.: Scenari strategici: visioni identitarie per il progetto di territorio. Alinea, Firenze (2007)
12. Guida, G.: Immaginare città. Metafore e immagini per la dispersione insediativa. Franco Angeli, Milano (2011)
13. Pisano, C., Lingua, V.: The impact of regional design on river agreements: the case of the Ombrone River in Tuscany. Planning Practice & Research, Taylor & Francis Online (2021)
14. Secchi, B.: Diario 10: progetti, visions, scenari, Planum Magazine, Diario 10 I Progetti, visions, scenari - Planum - The journal of Urbanism
15. Consiglio Regionale Del Lazio - Leggi Regionali (Testo Coordinato) - Legge Num. 38 Del 22 Dicembre 1999. https://www.consiglio.regione.lazio.it/consiglio-regionale/?vw=leggiregi onalidettaglio&id=7647&sv=vigente. (accessed on 5 April 2023)
16. Ventura, F.: Paesaggio e sviluppo sostenibile. il. Ponte **10**, 35–52 (1994)
17. Maggio, M.: Invarianti strutturali nel governo del territorio. Firenze University Press, Firenze (2014)
18. Neuman, M., Zonneveld, W.: The Routledge Handbook of Regional Design. Taylor & Francis, New York (2021)
19. Ellin, N.: Postmodern Urbanism. Princeton Architectural Press, New Yotk (1996)
20. Thierstein, A., Forster, A.: The image and the region-making. Mega-city region visible!. Lars Muller Publishers, Balden (2008)

21. Balz, V., Zonneveld, W.: Regional design in the context of fragmented territorial governance. South Wing Studio. Regional Design 6 (2019). https://doi.org/10.7480/abe.2019.8.3900
22. Lingua, V.: From tactics to strategies and back: regional design practices of contamination. Urbanistica **157**, 55–60 (2017)
23. Helling, A.: Collaborative visioning: proceed with caution! results from evaluating Atlanta's Vision 2020 project. J. Am. Plann. Assoc. **64**, 335–349 (1998)
24. Nam, T.: Citizen participation in visioning a progressive city: a case study of Albany 2030. Int. Rev. Public Adm. **18**, 139–161 (2014)
25. Throgmorton, J.A.: Planning as persuasive storytelling in a global-scale web of relationships. Plan. Theory **2**, 125–151 (2003)
26. Kempenaar, A., Brinkhuijsen, M., Van der Brink, A.: The impact of regional designing: new perspectives for the Maastricht/Heerlen, Hasselt/Genk, Aachen and Liège (MHAL) Region. Environ. Plann. B Urban Analytics City Sci. **46**, 359–376 (2017)
27. Viganò, P.: Territorio dell'urbanistica. Il progetto come produttore di conoscenza. Officine Editori, Modena (2010)
28. Città Metropolitana di Firenze: Rinascimento Metropolitano. Piano Strategico 2030. Firenze (2017)
29. Lingua, V.: Regional design for strategic planning: a vision for the metropolitan city of Florenze. In: Velo, L., Pace, M. (eds.) Utopia and the Project for the City and Territory, pp. 158–164. Officina, Roma (2018)
30. Neuman, M., Zonneveld, W.: The resurgence of regional design. Eur. Plan. Stud. **26**, 1297–1311 (2018)
31. De Luca, G.: A che punto siamo con la pianificazione territoriale regionale e paesaggistica? Urbanistica Informazioni **258**, 7 (2014)
32. Amante, B., Bianchi, R.: Memorie storiche e statutarie del Ducato, della Contea e dell'Episcopato di Fondi in Campania. Dalle origini fino a' tempi più recenti. Ermanno Loescher & Co., Roma (1903)
33. De Bonis, A., Casale, C., Russo, C.R.: Sviluppi storici nelle terre del basso Lazio. Dalla preistoria all'avvento dei Longobardi. Tre Bit Edizioni, Roma (2018)
34. Piscitelli Carpino, T. (eds.): Fondi tra antichità e medioevo. Atti del Convegno 31 Marzo-1 Aprile 2000, Fondi (2002)
35. Serao, G.: L'arancio nella Piana di Fondi. Società Anonima Arte della Stampa, Roma (1934)
36. Attanasio, A.: La macchina vecchia di Pantano. La bonifica della Piana di Fondi e l'idrovora di AKFuachiara. Carte Pontine 5, Latina (2006)
37. Cassieri, N., Nicolai Fiocchi, V. (eds.): Il Monastero di San Magno a Fondi. Edizioni Tored, Roma (2013)
38. Carnevale, G.: Retrospettiva fondana. Grafiche PD, Fondi (1998)
39. Ente Parco Naturale dei Monti Aurunci: Carta dei sentieri, Latina (2010)
40. De Bonis, A., De Bonis, B., Catena, V.: Il percorso della Via Francigena del sud nel Parco Naturale Regionale dei Monti Ausoni e Lago di Fondi: censimento e catalogazione dei beni. Editore Coordinamento CREIA Regione Lazio, Stampa Hornet Multimedia (2013)
41. Morelli Di Popolo, C.: La rilettura della città come sistema organico verso nuove interpretazioni. Urbanistica Informazioni ISSN 2239–4222 (2013)
42. Moccia, F.D., Sepe, M. (eds.): Beessere e salute delle città contemporanee. INU Edizioni, Roma (2021)
43. Corboz, A.: Le territoire comme palimpseste. Diogène **121**, 14–35 (1983)
44. Voghera, A.: Contratti di fiume. Un metodo per il progetto resiliente di territorio e paesaggio. In: Angrilli, M. (eds.), BikeFlu. Atlante dei Contratti di Fiume in Abruzzo. Gangemi Editore, Roma (2020)
45. Palazzo, A.L.: Il caso francese tra innovazione e tradizione. Urbanistica Informazioni **237**, 19–20 (2011)

46. Lanzani, A.: Il territorio al plurale. Interpretazioni geografiche e temi di progettazione territoriale in alcuni contesti locali. Franco Angeli, Milano (1991)
47. Viganò, P.: Territori della nuova modernità. Piano Territoriale di Coordinamento Provinciale di Lecce. Electa Napoli, Salerno (2001)
48. Occhiuto, R.: Il progetto come condizione del paesaggio sostenibile. In: Palazzo, A.L. (ed.) Prove di territorializzazione della sostenibilità, Urbanistica Informazioni vol. 241, pp. 23–25 (2012)
49. Pisano, C., Cocco, G.B.: Una lettura critica del Bando Periferie. Sei strategie di modificazione urbana e metropolitana. Urbanistica **161**, 1–17 (2018)
50. Battisti, F., Campo, O.: The assessment of density bonus in building renovation interventions. The case of the city of Florence in Italy. Land **10**, 1391 (2021). https://doi.org/10.3390/land10121391
51. De Luca, G.: Interviste sul concetto (di Invariante Strutturale) e le sue applicazioni. In: Maggio, M. (ed.) Invarianti strutturali nel governo del territorio. Firenze University Press, Firenze (2014)
52. Acampa, G., Battisti, F., Di Pietro, G., Parisi, C.M.: City information model for the optimization of urban maintenance cost. Paper presented at the AIP Conference Proceedings, p. 2343 (2021). https://doi.org/10.1063/5.0047779
53. Battisti, F., Pisano, C.: Common property in Italy. Unresolved issues and an appraisal approach: towards a definition of environmental-economic civic value. Land **11**, 1927 (2022). https://doi.org/10.3390/land11111927
54. Campo, O., Battisti, F., Acampa, G.: Integrated multi-criteria assessments in support of the verifying the feasibility of recovering archaeological sites: the case of Portus-Ostia Antica. In: Bevilacqua, C., Calabrò, F., Della Spina, L. (eds.) NMP 2020. SIST, vol. 178, pp. 1952–1961. Springer, Cham (2021). https://doi.org/10.1007/978-3-030-48279-4_184

Metabolic Approaches to Regeneration of the Historic Mondeggi Villa Estate

Fabrizio Battisti[1]([✉]) [iD], Carlo Pisano[2] [iD], and Giuseppe De Luca[2]

[1] Department of Architecture, University of Florence, Via di S. Niccolò, 93, 50125 Florence, Italy
fabrizio.battisti@unifi.it

[2] Department of Architecture, University of Florence, Via P.A. Micheli, 2, 50121 Florence, Italy
{carlo.pisano,giuseppe.deluca}@unifi.it

Abstract. The social and economic crisis that accompanied the Covid-19 pandemic has emphasized the need to rethink consumption, production and collective life in the peri-urban areas surrounding large cities. With this in mind it seems important that studies of urban spaces should include an interpretation of the different needs and sensitivities of the local communities involved. New behaviour models, both individual and collective, in line with the principles of environmental and social responsibility, have been used as the basis for developing new design approaches.

The Metropolitan City of Florence (CMF) seized the opportunity to adopt Integrated Urban Plans as a tool for sustainable urban regeneration and used funds provided by the National Recovery and Resilience Plan (PNRR) to develop a project for the Monteggi Villa Estate, a vast tract of land in a state of semi-abandonment, owned by the CMF, and located on the south-eastern outskirts of Florence.

This paper outlines the regeneration project for the Monteggi estate, developed by the CMF with the support of the Department of Architecture of Florence University, highlighting its ethical and cultural premises; it also describes the steps taken for obtaining the approval of the Technical Economic Feasibility Project.

Keywords: Integrated Urban Plans · Urban planning · PNRR · Metabolism

1 Introduction

The Metropolitan City of Florence (CMF) seized the opportunity to adopt Integrated Urban Plans as a tool for sustainable urban regeneration. Using funds provided by the National Recovery and Resilience Plan (PNRR) the CMF developed a project for Mondeggi Villa Estate, a valuable 170 hectares historical-agricultural heritage, unique in Tuscany for the breadth and richness of its territorial, architectural and rural assets, and promoted it as a metropolitan project par excellence. To date, very few historic Tuscan estates can boast such large tracts of land with architectural assets and artifacts as valuable as those belonging to Mondeggi.

O. Gervasi et al. (Eds.): ICCSA 2023 Workshops, LNCS 14111, pp. 355–368, 2023.
https://doi.org/10.1007/978-3-031-37126-4_24

The 52 million euro loan offered to the CMF for the «Integrated Plans-M5C2-Investment 2.2» project was a precious opportunity for ensuring a unified, integrated approach to both programmatic and spatial solutions, through which to create the conditions for implementing environmental quality and social cohesion at the metropolitan level and for ensuring the Estate's long-term economic self-sustainability. It is essential to grasp the metropolitan value of the Mondeggi project, given its spatial dimensions and its strong relationship with other projects envisaged in the Florentine area, all of which are linked to issues promoted by the National Recovery and Resilience Plan (PNRR) [1].

Mondeggi can be seen as the principal island in a newly created archipelago of regenerated spaces which has the potential to enhance large portions of the peri-urban metropolitan area; the projects and goals developed by the CMF will play a vital role in ensuring transformability and resilience throughout the metropolitan area and will tackle the main critical issues of our era: the fight against poverty, food security, health, education and training, gender equality, management of water resources, clean energy, work, industry and innovation, equality, sustainable cities, circular economy, climate change, environmental protection, peace and institutions [2, 3]. Modeggi also has the peculiar characteristic of having only one owner, of a public nature, the CMF. Unfractionated property of wide extension, barycentric position within the metropolitan territory, combination of environmental, historical-cultural and landscape emergencies make this asset of great interest to be able to configure itself as a flywheel of regeneration of a large quadrant of metropolitan territory.

On the basis of these premises an institutional agreement was drawn up between the CMF and the Department of Architecture of Florence University and a working group from the Department of Architecture was set up (De Luca G., Pisano C., Battisti F., Collotti F., Carta M., Matteini T.) to carry out research with the goal of establishing a preliminary cognitive framework for defining a project for redeveloping and enhancing the Mondeggi Villa Estate; a project that would be aligned with the principles of sustainable development, as laid down in the 2030 Metropolitan Agenda as well as being inclusive, fair, sustainable and metabolic.

The experience of redeveloping and re-purposing the Mondeggi Villa Estate estate is configured as a case study in which the term "redevelopment" is given a broader meaning than that traditionally adopted in the urban-building sphere; here it involves redeveloping and re-purposing a historic asset with valuable environmental and landscape qualities, in order to enable profound, long-lasting actions and processes of renewal of places and spaces whose use and fruition make them critically important, and these actions and processes will increase citizen well-being in an entire metropolitan peri-urban quadrant.

2 Context Analysis: Intervening in Peri-Urban Areas

In recent decades, concepts such as regeneration and redevelopment have gradually expanded, and now include measures in different parts of cities (historic centres, industrial areas, established urban fabrics) as well as involving partially urbanised areas (peri-urban or sprawl).

Peri-urban space is a border space that can be defined as a buffer area between urban and rural contexts; in recent decades it has been characterised by fringe areas increasingly subject to transformation and change brought about by the exchange and mutual contamination between physical dimensions and living practices [4]. In recent times, it has been recognized that this spatial typology offers an alternative interpretation of contemporary territories as autonomous spaces [5]: a new form of city, whose built environment, landscape, lifestyles, social relationships and economy have all been studied [6].

These spaces thus lend themselves to being studied as places of practices, flows, economies and ways of inhabiting unprecedented, and as yet not fully explored, contemporary territories. These places can strongly influence the quality of the territory [7], where, albeit indirectly, public operators have used the paradigm of dividing and separating [8], using the parametric and quantitative zoning introduced by DM 1444/68 to establish clear borders between functions, materials and people, without however attributing and recognizing a public role at the fringes of urbanisation. Present-day interventions in peri-urban spaces should avoid redefining or identifying new perimeters of separation between city and countryside, and should recognize the role of peri-urban fringes as spaces for engagement or conflict where new rules for contemporary living and new metropolitan landscapes are defined [9].

The highly fragmented morphology and the composition of a territorial mosaic made up of numerous different land-use categories configure areas with a strong, but often uncontrolled and poorly planned, evolutionary dynamism which results in the progressive dispersion of the urban system within the rural one. This gives rise to numerous problems of an agronomic nature, defined as urban sprawl, in addition to the ongoing phenomenon of sealed soul, the result of urban development that is unsustainable relative to the resources available in that land area.

These two phenomena cause most of the risks to which the inhabitants of peri-urban areas are subject [4].

Peri-urban spaces are created to satisfy primary needs, such as the need to have a place to live, work, spend free time and socialize. However, it is within these spaces that loss of neighbourhood relationships is experienced, with families who live outside the classic boundaries of the urbanised city often being confined by autonomous, closed and restricted lives with unvaried, self-limiting outlooks which become real impediments to experiencing the diversity that the city offers.

Despite this, peri-urban metropolitan spaces are configured as areas with high potential, fabrics where innovative models can be experimented against the background of the 2030 Agenda: a strategic vision for improving urban quality and livability in complex peri-urban territories, by tackling productive, landscape, environmental and sociocultural issues. It is also important to consider that the progressive urban expansion of cities, even beyond their administrative boundaries, cannot fail to refer to the theme of urban regeneration, as seen at an international and national level, inspired by the goals and targets of the 2030 Agenda for sustainable development.

In this context, the importance of redeveloping a significant historical asset such as the Mondeggi Villa Estate does not primarily lie in the conservation of an asset of historical architectural value, but in the role this asset can play in enhancing a large metropolitan peri-urban area. Redeveloping and repurposing the Mondeggi Villa Estate can be configured as grafting functions and activities capable of re-activating production chains, recreational activities, inclusion and energy conservation onto a metropolitan peri-urban area.

3 Mondeggi Villa Estate

3.1 General Description

The Estate consists of about 170 hectares mostly situated within the Municipality of Bagno a Ripoli but with some land in the Municipalities of Figline and Incisa Valdarno. It is a complex area in which architectural and land assets sometimes overlap. The values, textures and conservation of the architectural assets vary greatly; the land assets are mainly composed of wooded areas, cultivated land, olive groves and vineyards, connected by a network of paths. The original relationship of spatial and functional continuity between the villa - of over 4,000 square metres - the system of outbuildings, rural houses and the agricultural areas has remained intact.

The original nucleus of the villa dates to the late Middle Ages. The most important additions and modifications were carried out by the della Gherardesca family who owned the estate for four centuries. They acquired further land, both woods and farms, expanding the estate beyond its present size, built new service artifacts for agricultural activities and expanded the system of gardens, paths and roads. In 1964 the entire property was purchased by the Province of Florence, (the Province has since been replaced by the CMF), with the intention of using it as an extension of the San Salvi psychiatric hospital in Florence but this never happened. Between 1988 and 1989, the Province carried out works of modernization and partial functional adaptation of portions of the villa building with the intention of using the upper floors as managerial offices. The land and the ground floor of the villa were leased to the Mondeggi Lappeggi company, which provided agricultural machinery and equipment for the production and sale of wine and oil. In the same period some plots of land were entrusted to the Faculty of Agriculture. Productive activity ceased in 2009: the villa was closed and most of the land and crops were abandoned. In 2012, some of the farmhouses were illegally occupied: the occupants, however, did recuperate and clean up some of the olive groves and vineyards [10]. In 2013 an association, "Towards the Common Good of Mondeggi - A Farm without Masters" was set up with the goal of reutilizing the land for farming. The following year those living on the Mondeggi Estate and farming the land made a commitment to not abandon the land or the farmhouses and to not sell the estate thereby realising the goal set the previous year. In 2019, the "Friends of Mondeggi - A Common Good" committee was set up as a supervisory entity, with the goal of preserving the Mondeggi area as a common good [11]: eight local associations and individual citizens are members.

3.2 The Project

The exploratory approach used in the definition of the general project is inserted in phase 1 of the Technical-Economic Feasibility Plan - the technical "container" which provided a framework for the scientific assignment given to the University of Florence - and coherent with the goal of developing a unitary project, it considered the separate, fragmented or autonomous management of the land assets and architectural heritage to be unfeasible. This approach has led to the creation of a general proposal, characterized by some insights and design alternatives, inserted into a structure made up of invariants which are identified as a system of choices structuring the estate and around which the various alternatives are organized and articulated.

The general project therefore took the form of a masterplan (Fig. 1) whose goal is to coordinate the spatial and programmatic structuring choices set out below; these choices constitute the basis for creating a common governance system capable of managing the Mondeggi Villa Estate in a uniform manner.

The first objective of the master plan was to establish those characteristics that define the genius loci [12] of the estate, which in Mondeggi have been maintained despite land acquisitions, transformation of architectural heritage, modification of production systems and access networks and changes of ownership and use. This attribute, characteristic of many historical and patrimonial assets [13], cannot be taken for granted: the risk lies in proposing a generic project which robs the assets of their exceptionality and identity. The general project is therefore based on the relationship between the topography of the area, which defines the typical Florentine hilly agricultural landscape dominated by olive groves, vineyards and arable land with the presence of rows of trees and wooded areas, and the settlement system, made up of of the villa, with its gardens and outbuildings, and six farmhouses: the dialectic between productive land and architectural assets, framed in an open landscape without fences except those required for protecting the crops, represents the genius loci of Mondeggi and the starting point of the design proposal.

The social component, understood as an engine for experimenting with new ways of vivre ensemble [14] and for seeking the coexistence of different rhythms of life within collective configurations of space, plays a decisive role in the proposal. Indeed, in this specific historical period, the search for the relationship between individuals and community, between autonomy and sharing [15] and for the right distance [16] for social relations, appears to be an absolutely relevant theme, especially in an area like that of the Mondeggi Estate which exists outside the interpretative schemes of the well-established city.

In the project this research is expressed through some specific programmatic choices that have characterized the detailed designs. For example, the six farmhouses have been designed as "association houses". Each farmhouse will be managed by one or more associations and will be characterized by a specific social and cultural focus. On the basis of their individual typological, constructive and heritage restraint characteristics, each farmhouse has specificities related to the activities to be established, but all of them have areas dedicated to producing and transforming agricultural products, spaces for associative activities and rooms for housing, both permanent and temporary.

The program for the villa is different, but complementary. Functions of a metropolitan and institutional nature will be housed in the villa: these will include, managerial and didactic spaces associated with agri-tech, a guesthouse and ethical restaurant, and the cellar, with its wine shop and wine making area. All this will lead to the co-presence of workers, visitors and citizens, and will generate innovative spaces for cohabiting which will be further explored once a management and governance system has been defined in the subsequent co-planning phase.

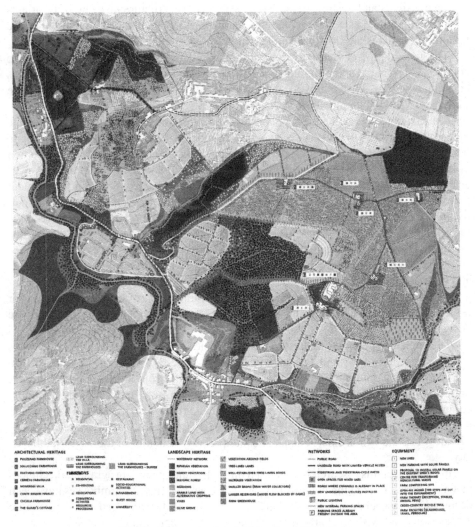

Fig. 1. Masterplan for the Mondeggi Villa Estate

The current proposal intends to maintain a high degree of flexibility so it will be remain relevant to the requirements of the estate for another century and will be able to adapt to any social, economic and cultural changes that may occur. The layout of the buildings will be in line with the various existing levels of protection, but will seek maximum adaptability; plant engineering will be designed so it can be easily modified and adapted; the creation of new reservoirs is aimed at facilitating crop diversification. In general, every choice has the goal of generating opportunities for future developments, program, uses and users.

The project is implemented with a strong emphasis on environmental and economic sustainability, using a metabolic approach [17–19] (Fig. 2). The transition from linear production consumption approaches towards circular systems now seems imperative in order to reduce the impacts of urban and peri-urban environments and to comply with both the general environmental goals laid down in the European agenda and the specific goals indicated in the «Integrated PlansM5C2- Investment 2.2″ Project. This project, therefore, considers the Estate and its immediate context as a metabolic ecosystem within which it is possible to carefully analyse water, energy and production cycles, and the use and recycling of raw materials. This type of approach requires the preparation of an energy community, the creation of a system of reservoirs, the design of constructed wetlands and the valorisation of agricultural waste and forest cuttings.

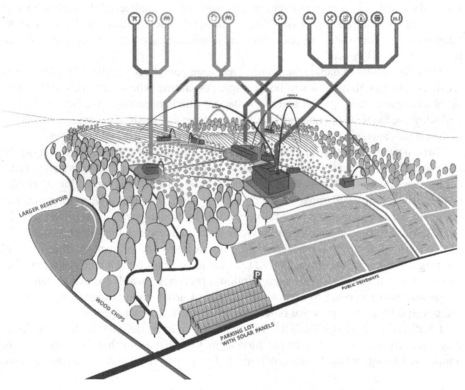

Fig. 2. Diagram showing Mondeggi's metabolic processes

3.3 Project Sustainability and Metabolism

In developing the project for eco-sustainably restructuring and rendering operational the Villa Mondeggi Estate, the goal was to define the conditions required for achieving complete sustainability - environmental, social and economic - of the complex systems envisaged for the estate and their implementation. Sustainability is, therefore, simultaneously characterised by different dimensions that pursue heterogeneous and often conflicting goals; in order to adequately respond to all the complex, heterogeneous and potentially energy-intensive project requirements, it is essential to identify which elements should be transformed into design strategies.

In this case, the objective of the project was to combine economic sustainability, often the only parameter used for evaluating complex projects, with social sustainability and environmental sustainability, which in this project depends on energy efficiency, use of water resources and waste generation.

Economic sustainability depends entirely on the ability to generate income consistently over time in order to maintain the efficiency of the complex system of assets that make up the Mondeggi Villa Estate.

Environmental sustainability depends on the ability to safeguard and maintain natural and ecosystemic resources over time, without producing irreversible alterations; in other words, it is a question of verifying the project's "metabolism", understood as the relationship between the resource flows (energy, water resources) absorbed and produced by the "Mondeggi system".

Once the eco-sustainable restructuring has been completed and the Villa Mondeggi Estate is fully functioning, it will be a complex organism, whose activities will require the absorption of energy, water and raw materials which, once they have "metabolized", will allow the Estate to operate until they become slag and waste. This applies especially to the estate's agricultural activities and its restored and re-purposed buildings.

This methodology was first devised by Abel Wolman in 1965 [20] to analyse the directions of energy, water, nutrient, material and waste flow in urban systems, in order to quantify the inputs, outputs and parts stored in the system. This methodology is used to assess the stability and impact of a production system. Nowadays the concept of urban and territorial metabolism has been fully embraced by contemporary urban planning [17–19, 21]. Many European administrations have promoted research that adopts a metabolic and ecosystem perspective when preparing urban plans and projects both at national (Foresight Future of Cities Project, UK) [22] and local levels (eg. Genoa, Antwerp). The transition from linear production-consumption approaches towards circular systems now seems imperative in order to reduce the impacts of urban and periurban environments and to respect the environmental objectives set by the European agenda.

Finally, the social sustainability of this project can be defined as the capacity to guarantee fair access and use of the Mondeggi Villa Estate so that the conditions of human well-being that the Estate generates are fairly distributed and create employment.

3.4 Preliminary Evaluations on Sustainability

On the basis of this brief premise, the assessments that follow are intend to provide some initial elements for verifying the sustainability of the eco-sustainable redevelopment and re-purposing project for the Mondeggi Villa Estate.

The three components of sustainability were studied separately as follows:

- assessment of economic sustainability, identifying sustainable lease/concession fees for the various real estate assets, with appropriate deductions in the light of the exclusively public function envisaged in the project;
- assess environmental sustainability, deducing the project's metabolism with reference to its energy, water and waste components;
- assess social sustainability, here defined as access to the assets/public amenities and other amenities available to the public which generate benefits as envisaged in the project.

The range of sustainability assessment methods currently available ranges from highly technical tools to very simplistic methods [23, 24]. Most of the methods adopted for assessing sustainability are based on a qualitative rather than a quantitative approach. According to Brown et al. [25], this is because the analysis required to address the wide range of issues surrounding these assessments is extremely complex. This raises another critical question, namely how to integrate qualitative and quantitative information into a single assessment.

In the present case, since these assessments are associated with a project, a quantitative approach is proposed for evaluating economic and environmental sustainability, with the goal of the latter being to evaluate the complex cycles (water, energy and waste) associated with the Estate's architectural assets and the land to define the metabolism of the project. A quantitative approach is proposed for assessing the project's social sustainability. The evaluations are conducted using available data where possible; where there is none then data inferable from similar case studies will be used.

Although this study is general and characterised by the three components of sustainability, the initial results suggest that the conditions exist for integrated sustainability; subsequent design phases will therefore have to develop the topics set out below in greater detail.

Economic Sustainability: Guarantee the Operation and Maintenance of the Estate
The economic sustainability of the eco-sustainable restructuring and repurposing project of the real estate compendium that makes up the for the Mondeggi Villa Estate was determined by assessing whether or not the activities envisaged in the project would be capable of generating sufficient income.

Once the Villa Mondeggi Estate has been repurposed, there will be some areas completely or partially given over to public use which will not generate any income, and other areas that will generate an income. All agricultural land intended for production will generate income.

All assets capable of generating income have been identified.

The following architectural assets will generate income:

1. residential assets: residences and co-housing;
2. commercial assets: trade, restaurant, cellar and warehouse;
3. tertiary   assets: associations,   multi-purpose,   managerial/start-up   and social/educational;

4. hospitality assets: guesthouse.

The following land assets will generate income:

5. agricultural assets: i) vineyards; ii) olive groves; iii) arable land; iv) orchards; v) greenhouses for growing vegetables

Studies of the potential real estate income to be generated from the assets, which will take the form of sustainable rental fees/concessions, have revealed that: i) category 1 assets can be leased at controlled rental fees; this means that management and ordinary maintenance can be delegated to the tenants, thereby reducing CMF management-maintenance costs; ii) assets in categories 2, 3 and 4 will generate "corporate" income, i.e. cash flows for each activity established; in other words, the conditions exist for establishing productive activities whose profitability will be in line with market trends. These productive activities once established on the Estate will not only generate a lease/concession fee, but will also reduce the management maintenance burden for the CMF. The capability of the category 5 land assets to generate a net yield from wine and oil production has already been verified; this production generates income which makes it possible to delegate the task of maintaining the lands destined for agriculture - a substantial part of the 170 hectare estate - to the producers rather than the CMF assuming this burden.

Although the project cannot provide precise estimates, most of the functions to be established on the Estate will be able to generate income. The prerequisites required for the successful implementation of these functions exist right from the design phase, to be more fully researched in future design phases, and this creates favourable conditions for ensuring the project is economically sustainable. It follows that project development should privilege functions and intended uses that generate income while safeguarding the project's social and environmental values. In any case, even considering that the PNRR provides loan, albeit without interest, to be repaid, the individual activities that can be implemented in the estate capable of generating income will have to be subjected to a concession or lease fee with income in favor of CMF; based on this, a management scenario can be outlined where CMF retains the management of the estate in its entirety and identifies, for the various inse-diable activities, suitable entities to which to concession or lease certain spaces.

Environmental Sustainability: The Project's Metabolism

The metabolic processes at work on the Villa Mondeggi Estate were studied in order to evaluate the complex cycles (water, energy and waste) associated with the estate's land and architectural assets.

The architectural assets, as defined in the project, are listed in the previous paragraph. Land assets are divided into:

– agricultural assets: i) vineyards; ii) olive groves; iii) arable land; iv) orchards; v) greenhouses for growing vegetables
– forestry assets: i) forest; ii) historical forest; iii) deforestation areas.

The research focused on studying the metabolic processes related to the architectural and agricultural component of the estate, comparing the volume of water required for performing the functions to be established using project assets and the areas destined for agriculture with the rainwater collection capacity of the new collection and conservation reservoir envisaged in the project.

Using synthetic evaluation methods to research data relating to the specific water requirements for each type of agricultural activity envisaged for the estate, it was possible to estimate an annual water requirement of approximately 60,000 m^3 for agriculture on the estate. The estimated annual requirement of the other activities envisaged for the estate (those in categories 2, 3, 4) is approximately 30,000 cubic meters (of which approximately 50% can be considered "clean" water which would be supplied via the aqueduct). So there is a hydro-requirement for approximately 75,000 m^3 of recyclable water (which would have to undergo a purification process). As these are rough assessments carried out without any precise information regarding the business activities to be established on the estate, a precautionary 10% incremental coefficient was added to the estimated parameters, and the maximum annual overall recyclable water requirements on the Villa Mondeggi Estate is considered to be approximately 82,500 m^3. These water requirements would seem to be met by the collection and reservoir system envisaged in the project which has a capacity of about 40,000 m^3: this would guarantee the supply of as much as 50% of the Estate's annual hydro-need.

The self-regulatory capacity of wooded areas is such that it was considered that rainwater alone was sufficient for the forestry assets.

As regards energy needs, the in-depth study carried out for the CMF revealed the possibility of creating an "energy community" within the Estate which would make it practically autonomous, and capable of generating a positive Current Net Value and a positive Internal Rate of Return.

With regard to the production of waste associated with agricultural activities, the agricultural waste generated each year on the estate amounts to about 200 tons. It can be used as fuel to generate about 500 mWh/year of energy (or transformed into bio-pellets or chips that can be sold on the market: this production could be increased if the wood waste deriving from forest maintenance were also utilised).

An estimation of the amount of urban solid waste generated by the activities involving the estate's architectural assets, used the European person equivalent (PE) figures to ascertain that the waste generated was equivalent to that of 544 people. This certainly represents a significant increase in urban solid waste production but it can be absorbed by the separate collection system that has been established in the Municipality of Bagno a Ripoli for some time.

The above summarizes a series of studies and evaluations which, although only approximate, suggest that careful circular planning, to be developed in the future phases of definitive and executive planning, can guarantee robust environmental sustainability for the Estate.

Social Sustainability: Collective and Inclusive Use of the Mondeggi Villa Estate
Social sustainability can be defined as the ability to guarantee conditions of well-being (i.e. health, safety, education) to every individual in an equitable measure, without distinction of class or gender. It was Khan [26] who defined the principles of the social dimension of "sustainability", recognizing that equity, legitimacy, accessibility, participation, cultural identity and institutional stability were the indispensable foundations

for a socially-just distribution of the benefits (and costs) deriving from way in which humans manage the natural and man-made environment.

In the case of the Villa Mondeggi Estate, social sustainability very much depends on the benefits that the property can generate, i.e. job creation and social and cultural growth.

The planning set-up hypothesized for the Mondeggi Villa Estate guarantees direct employment for about 35–40 people mostly in primary and tertiary production activities (staff hired to carry out the various functions of the Estate) as well as some indirect employment (collateral activities required to ensure the continued efficiency of these activities, for example building maintenance).

Although the land assets that remain in public use (woods, open appurtenant areas with or without equipment/facilities) are not considered to have production cycles they do still generate employment, closely associated with their use and maintenance. From a social point of view, these assets are extremely important because, despite not having a "real" market that would allow them to generate an income, they have a high non-monetary value, for which specific estimates need to be implemented [27, 28].

The social sustainability associated with the use of the public (land) assets of the Estate is also associated with social sustainability as a byproduct of social and cultural growth. It is closely linked to the activities that will be carried out in the context of tertiary assets such as multi-purpose and social/educational associations as well as management/start-up activities.

It is thought that the planned sustainable re-purposing of the Mondeggi Villa Estate, which will greatly increases its accessibility and usefulness, will bring about widespread social benefits. A Cost-Benefit Analysis can be added to the subsequent design phases to assess the social outcome of the project for eco-sustainably redeveloping and re-purposing the Estate.

4 Conclusions

The strong point of the Mondeggi project, given its complexity and long-term strategy, lies in the preparation of a complex, open system that defines a stable framework within which activities, functions and programs can change over time. The project responds to the stimuli and possibilities of different forms of living together [29], it embodies the principles of territorial porosity and it constitutes a democratic space [30] where new paradigms of citizenship can emerge. Mondeggi provides an opportunity to activate a process of enhancing metropolitan peri-urban spaces through redeveloping and increasing the accessibility of an important public and historical asset.

Given this framework, when the project is implemented, it is essential that a governance path be put into place to ensure that the management and transformation of the individual buildings and plots are harmoniously articulated with the needs of the place, the activities and agricultural production as well as with the community that these attract: changing and sometimes unexpected communities.

Further research developments will be oriented to the in-depth study of the sustainability-related component of the project, in its environmental, social and economic aspects. When the project is at an advanced stage Mondeggi will be included in a social and metabolic circuit, designed so it absorbs and internalizes future dynamics of transformation - social, environmental, economic - thereby guaranteeing a continuous dialogue between the history that has passed through the estate and the events that are destined to pass through it in the future.

References

1. Italian Government. Piano Nazionale di Ripresa e Resilienza (PNRR). Roma, Palazzo Chigi (2021)
2. Biggeri, M.: A "Decade for Action" on SDG localisation. J. Hum. Dev. Capabilities **22**(4), 706–712 (2021)
3. Biggeri, M., Clark, D.A., Ferrannini, A., Mauro, V.: Tracking the SDGs in an 'integrated' manner: a proposal for a new index to capture synergies and trade-offs between and within goals. World Dev. **122**, 628–647 (2019)
4. Micelli, E.: La riqualificazione ora è anche sociale: la Puglia lancia i programmi di Rigenerazione. Edilizia e Territorio **34**, 6–8 (2008)
5. Mininni, M.: Territori di frontiera e l'infinito attraversare. In: E. Marchigiani e S. Prestamburgo, Strategie e progetti per la valorizzazione delle risorse territoriali. Milano, Franco Angeli. 2012 Approssimazioni alla città. Roma, Donzelli (2010)
6. SECCHI, Bernardo. Le forme della città. In: testo della conferenza inaugurale del Festival della città e del territorio (2009)
7. Quinn, J., Blandon, C., Batson, A.: Living beyond words: post-human reflections on making music with post-verbal people. Arts & Health **13**(1), 73–86 (2021)
8. Mininni, M. (a cura di), Donadieu, P.: Campagne urbane. Una nuova proposta di paesaggio della città. Roma, Donzelli (2006)
9. Valentini, A.: Progettare i paesaggi del limite. In: Treu, M., Palazzo, D. (a cura di) Margini descrizioni, strategie, progetti. Firenze, Alinea (2006)
10. Angiolini, C.S.A.: About the commons. The case study of mondeggi. Ricerche Giuridiche **4**(1), 137–143 (2015)
11. Poli, D.: Campagne insorgenti. Agricoltura contadina e "bene comunitario" nella fattoria di Mondeggi a Firenze. In: Archivio di Studi Urbani e Regionali, no. 24, pp. 49–72 (2017)
12. Norberg-Schulz, C.: Genius loci. Electa (1981)
13. Magnaghi, A.: Il progetto locale. Verso la coscienza di luogo. Bollati Boringhieri, Torino (2010)
14. Barthes, R.: Traces écrites. Seuil, Paris (2002)
15. Pellegrini, P., Viganò, P. (a cura di): Comment Vivre Ensemble. Officina Edizioni, Venezia (2020)
16. Schopenhauer, A., Colli, G.: Parerga e paralipomena, 2 ed. Adelphi (1998, orig.1851)
17. Kennedy, C., Pincetl, S., Bunje, P.: The study of urban metabolism and its applications to urban planning and design. Environ. Pollut. **159**, 1965–1973 (2011)
18. van Bueren, E., Bohemen, H., Itard, L., Visscher, H.: Sustainable Urban Environments: An Ecosystem Approach. Springer, Dordrecht (2012)
19. Ibañez, D., Katsikis, N. (a cura di): New Geographies 6: 'Grounding Metabolism'. Harvard University Press (2014)
20. Wolman, A.: The metabolism of cities. Sci. Am. **213**, 178–190 (1965). https://doi.org/10.1038/scientificamerican0965-178
21. Sijmons, D.F., Hugtenburg, J., Feddes, F.M., Hoorn, A.: Landschap en energie: ontwerpen voor transitie. Nai010 uitgevers/publishers (2014)

22. GOfS 2017b Future of Cities: Foresight for Cities See. http://www.gov.uk/government/pub lications/future-of-cities-foresight-for-cities. (accessed: 14/02/2023)
23. Battisti, F.: ELECTRE III for strategic environmental assessment: a "Phantom" approach. Sustainability 14(10), 6221 (2022). https://doi.org/10.3390/su14106221(2022)
24. Battisti, F., Campo, O.: The assessment of density bonus in building renovation interventions. The case of the city of Florence in Italy. Land 10(12), 1391 (2021). https://doi.org/10.3390/ land10121391
25. Brown, J., Soderbaum, P., Dereniowska, M.: Positional Analysis for Sustainable Development: Reconsidering Policy, Economics and Accounting. Taylor & Francis (2017)
26. Khan, M.A.: Sustainable development: the key concepts, issues and implications. Keynote paper given at the international sustainable development research conference, 27–29 March 1995, Manchester UK. Sustain. Dev. 3, 63–69 (1995)
27. Battisti, F., Pisano, C.: Common property in Italy. Unresolved issues and an appraisal approach: towards a definition of environmental-economic civic value. Land 11(11), 1927 (2022). https://doi.org/10.3390/land11111927
28. Guarini, M.R., Battisti, F., Buccarini, C.: Rome: re-qualification program for the street markets in public-private partnership. A further proposal Flaminio II street market.https://doi.org/10. 4028/www.scientific.net/AMR.838-841.2928
29. Viganò, P., Pellegrini, P.: Comment Vivre Ensemble. Officina, Roma (2006)
30. Sennet, R.: La società civile. In: Sendra, P., Sennet, R., Progettare il disordine. Treccani, Roma (2022)

Environmental and Landscape Constraints and Legislative Provisions in Territorial/Urban Planning and Building Constructions: Impacts in Urban Regeneration

Fabrizio Battisti[1](✉) , Giovanna Acampa[1] , and Mariolina Grasso[2]

[1] Department of Architecture, University of Florence, Via di S. Niccolò, 93,
50125 Florence, Italy
{fabrizio.battisti,giovanna.acampa}@unifi.it
[2] Faculty of Engineering and Architecture, University of Enna "Kore", University Square,
94100 Enna, Italy
mariolina.grasso@unikore.it

Abstract. Legislative framework on territorial and urban planning has become more and more rich and complex in the European Union and in particular in Italy. The structured – and often hindering – system of division of responsibilities between the central State, Regions, local institutions, and organisms, generates different levels of administrative verification. The several environmental and landscape constraints by which each public administration with jurisdiction over the territory exercises its powers have a strong impact on the territorial management and negative effects on investments. Over years, this has been one of the main reasons behind the significant dilation of the risk and the time required to obtain the authorizations required to start construction, hence producing "business risk". Based on this premise, the present work investigates, on a methodological point of view, the relationships between environmental and landscape constraints, the regulatory framework to which a building is subjected, and its impacts in urban regeneration processes. This is finally aimed at finding suitable methods and procedures to formulate an opportune discount rate considering the constraints and the related regulations that operate on an asset. A mixed method that integrates Capital Asset Pricing Model, Analytic Hierarchy Process and Delphi Method is proposed to assess the discount rate component related to urban risk.

Keywords: landscape · environmental · constraints

1 Introduction

The complexity that characterizes the tools for territorial governance has a relevant role in interventions connected to development of urban plans and programs, and in new constructions or building renovations, especially with changes in in-use destinations and/or building extensions [1], actions that characterize urban regeneration interventions.

O. Gervasi et al. (Eds.): ICCSA 2023 Workshops, LNCS 14111, pp. 369–380, 2023.
https://doi.org/10.1007/978-3-031-37126-4_25

In the last years, the legislative framework on territorial and urban planning – including all laws on zoning, landscape, environment, and building constructions that affect building transformations – has become more and more rich and complex [2].

This is compounded by the frequent changes in constraints: when these affect already-started authorization processes, they mutate the context of the building production intervention.

This complexity is diffusely present throughout the European Union; in Italy, it is combined with a structured – and often hindering – system of division of responsibilities between the central State, Regions, local institutions, and organisms, with a strong impact on the territorial management and negative effects on investments.

In Italy, in addition to Municipality-level legislative frameworks (General Regulatory Plan and its Regulations, implementation tools, and Building Regulations), building transformation also depends on a complex system of national and regional laws, and on the framework of constraints. This is the result of different sectorial plans with a conjunct efficiency, which impose different levels of administrative verification since as a rule, specific responsibilities are attributed to respective Public institutions according to the typology of the field regarded by the constraints.

Indeed, it must be considered that tendentially (not always) there is a dynamic relationship between the constraints and the territory: the legislative framework on constraints constantly changes and gets updated, modifying the intervention possibilities on an asset (this occurs and produces effects also after the start of authorization processes).

Over years, this has been one of the main reasons behind the significant dilation of the time required to obtain the authorizations required to start construction, hence producing "business risk" [3–5]: the complex administrative process for the approval of plans/projects can lead to significant variations from the starting hypotheses. This is compounded by the issues related to the insufficient service personnel of the Public Administration, with respect to the present workload, which often leads to a delay in administrative times; the juridical periods established by the laws, which usually represent the foundation for intervention plans and financial and economic assessments, end up being significantly exceeded [6].

The resulting uncertainty, which characterizes every single action of building transformation – yet in different entities according to the specific cases and territorial contexts – must be taken into account when assessing a building, for urban regeneration purposes, associated with an expected transformation intervention (real estate development, new construction, or refurbishment), and consequently with an investment opportunity, also in light of the financialization of the real estate sector. The latter requires transparency on the investment risks, as the profitability of these operations depends on them [7–9].

The complex system of planning constraints has a significant impact on the assessment of the Market Value of the asset to be regenerated, as it requires estimating an adequate discount rate to relate the return on industrial capital to the risks and times of real estate development initiatives [10].

In the evaluations of buildings and projects based on the capability to generate financial/economic flows both in the private and public sectors, the discount rate is a key parameter to understand the profitability of investments; however, its definition is certainly problematic.

Indeed, the discount rate must incorporate all the factors that influence the investment risk (inflation, condition of financial markets, monetary policy, and possibility of alternative investments). Unlike financial investments, real estate investments are characterized by high inhomogeneity and by a fixed position, which makes each of them unique and unrepeatable, and requires a specific risk/return evaluation in the choice of the rate [11–13].

The complex legislative framework on building transformations has specific effects on the component of the discount rate that is defined by the literature as "regulatory/administrative risk" [14, 15]. The relationship between the administrative system and the framework of constraints in a given territory, and their corresponding effects on the expected profitability, has been the object of a renovated interest in recent times.

Based on this premise, the present work investigates the relationships between constraints, the regulatory framework to which a building is subjected, and its Market Value. This is finally aimed at finding suitable methods and procedures to formulate an opportune discount rate considering the constraints and the related regulations that operate on an asset.

More in detail, the article shows the first methodological results of an (in progress) research work whose (primary) goals are: i) the recognition of constraints (landscape, environmental) on the territory; ii) the construction of an evaluation procedure within the so-called "mixed methods", integrating the Analytic Hierarchy Process (AHP) [16, 17], the Delphi Method (DM) to gain experts opinion about constraints [18, 19], and the still applicable Capital Asset Pricing Method (CAPM) [20–23], to ponder the capacity of the various typologies of constraints to consider specific risk levels for the legitimation of programs/projects of building transformations. From an operational standpoint, the implementation of the AHP through DM allows the construction of regulatory/administrative risk indexes. Following an opportune elaboration process, these could generate a "fictitious Beta" to implement the CAPM for the determination of a discount rate that considers the suitable return on the equity capital needed for the start of the building transformation/real estate development, which will be transformed/valorized with certainty only after a complex administrative authorization process.

Through this clarification on the administrative conditions of the asset, the estimation can significantly contribute to the definition of the basket of investments, given the transparency of real estate players in relation to the risks of the action.

The paper fits in the theme of internationally codified mixed methods. In particular, the definition of the method is a contribution to the implementation of the Highest and Best Use [24] as a methodological approach, recognized by the Royal Institution of Chartered Surveyors (RICS) for the Market Value appraisal of assets that: need to undergo a transformation, have not obtained yet the authorizations for the intervention, and are subjected to the establishment of constraints and/or limitations by the regulatory framework. In this sense, the model can be also applied in extra-national contexts, following an opportune operational articulation.

In the rest of the paper: paragraph 2 proposed a literary review of the materials and methods in the theme of the research work: a synthesis of the European references for the environmental and landscape constraints and a synthesis of AHP, DM and CAPM; paragraph 3 illustrates the proposed method, which integrates AHP, DM, and CAPM; paragraph 4 includes the discussions on the expected results of the proposed method and the conclusions of the present work.

2 Materials and Methods

A constraint - in detail environmental, landscape and zoning constraints - is a tool of protection, which can completely prohibit, limit, or regulate in detail the transformations of an area and/or a building. Hence, only some constraints lead to the total inhibition of any territorial and/or building transformation. In most cases, a constraint creates pre-conditions for a territorial transformation (both at an urban and building scale).

In general, territorial constraints, which regulate territorial management/transformation, fall into 3 categories: "environmental" constraints, "landscape" constraints, and "zoning" constraints. The latter derive from specific territorial plans and are aimed at the functional protection of specific territorial infrastructures/equipment.

The individuation of the constraint can occur through delimitations on the maps of the respective competent authorities. Constraints can be established or placed through specific provisions, such as national/regional decrees and laws, or through landscape plans, aimed at regulating this complex theme [25]. Delimitations can be: i) punctual: localized on a single building or a portion of a single building; ii) linear: a buffer zone, traced in parallel to the route of a linear element (rivers, power lines); iii) areal: a wide perimeter of any shape, defined according to the specific needs (landscape-related).

The European Union considers natural resources as a key contribution to ecosystemic balance, but also to the attractiveness of regions, their recreational value, and life quality: this is the basic motivation behind the need for protection and valorization [26–29].

Environmental preservation and protection are performed through the safeguarding of ecological diversity, hydric resources, reconstitution, and protection of ecosystems, including ecological networks, all vulnerable areas with high ecological value, and wetlands, which are part of those networks. To achieve this goal, several ecological elements must be individuated: these include proximal natural areas, hydric resources, therapeutic climates, and abandoned industrial areas to be redeveloped. Their care requires adequate protective measures, which result in direct constraints or prescriptions of constraints by the Member States.

Concerning the environment, the legislator framework currently includes several hundred Directives, regulations, and decisions. However, the effectiveness of the environmental policy in the European Union largely depends on its national, regional, and local implementation.

At the same time, in some areas, the European Union has directly established regulations in the Member States. Among these, the ones with the greatest (territorial) impact are below: Natura 2000 network, Sites of Community Importance (SCI), Special Protection Areas (SPAs), Important Bird and Biodiversity Area (IBA), Wetlands of International Importance, Landscape Protection.

2.1 Analytic Hierarchy Process, Delphi Method, and Capital Asset Pricing Model

This section is aimed at a synthetic outline of the structure of AHP, DM, and CAPM (Fig. 1).

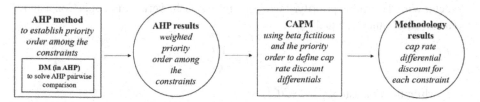

Fig. 1. Summary diagram on the integration of the methods used

These methods are already widely tested in the scientific literature and commonly used.

AHP is a multi-criteria decision support system, which allows comparing several alternatives according to multiple criteria, both quantitative and qualitative, based on pairwise comparisons. It has been considered to use, within the diversification of multi-criteria analysis methods available in the scientific literature, AHP as it allows, also thanks to Saaty's semantic scale, an easy pairwise comparison between the elements that constitute the evaluation. It is precisely from such a comparison that, through the proposed method, one can arrive at defining an order of importance to the various constraints that may intervene in a settlement transformation initiative.

The AHP process is broken down as follows:

- it starts with the definition of different alternatives to be ranked, and decision criteria, that is the factors to consider in the decision;
- the "evaluation problem" must be structured according to a hierarchy: first is the general goal, from which specific goals derive, then criteria are defined from specific goals, and indicators are associated with them. It is possible to attribute specific importance to each criterion through weight. Through a pairwise comparison related to the importance of each factor at every level (performance of the alternatives with respect to a single criterion, criteria with respect to specific goals, specific goals with respect to the general goal), it is possible to insert dominance coefficients in the pairwise comparison matrix, using Saaty's semantic scale. Saaty's semantic scale allows one to make a "weighted" judgment based on one's co-knowledge and experience regarding the comparison of evaluation items;
- after defining the problem and establishing criteria and alternatives, it is necessary to set the A matrix, that is an n x n matrix with the pairwise comparisons between the selected criteria, to attribute to each of them a preference degree (weight) with respect to the others. As mentioned above, preference degrees are attributed according to Saaty's scale;
- to guarantee an objective attribution judgment for the criteria preference degree, the decision-maker's opinion might result inadequate. For this reason, AHP is often supported by ad-hoc methods or tools for the evaluation of the preference degree.

These include the analysis of experts point of view, carried out by Delphi Method, described in the following section;

- after acquiring the experts' opinions, it is possible to attribute a weight to each criterion and hence proceed with the calculation of the vector with the criteria priorities. The latter, too, are hierarchized according to the preference degree. After calculating the vector with the criteria priority, the following step is the verification of is Consistency Ratio (CR), which is equal to:

$$CR = \frac{CI}{RI}$$

while the Consistency Index (CI) is:

$$CI = \frac{\lambda max - n}{n - 1}$$

where:

λmax represents the maximum eigenvector of the A matrix of criteria, while n is its dimension.

RI is the Random Index, a tabulated value associated with the size of the A matrix of criteria. The A matrix is considered to be consistent if CR <0,1 (10%);

- after verifying the Consistency Ratio, the final step is the hierarchization of alternatives (and the resolution of the evaluation problem). n B matrices with m x m size are defined, assigning a preference degree between alternatives with respect to the selected criteria. In this case, too, for each of the n matrices, a priority vector is calculated. At the end of this process, it is always possible to obtain the hierarchy between alternatives.

As mentioned above, within AHP, the attribution of a preference degree between the criteria is fundamental for the correct resolution of the evaluation problem. For this purpose, experts are consulted: this refers to subjects with a recognized experience and knowledge in the field of investigation/object of the problem. In the literature, the process of expert individuation is not methodologically standardized, but there are some best practices to follow:

- definition of the scope of the investigation in which the judgment is required;
- definition of the skills to seek in the experts: the expert must have proven knowledge in the field of investigation/object of the problem;
- choice of the criteria for the verification of their knowledge, such as: i) criterion 1: publications in the subjects in which the experience is required (monographs, contributions to collective volumes, articles in national and international journals, etc.); ii) criterion 2: degrees (PhD, specialization courses, masters concerning the subjects under evaluation); iii) criterion 3: professional skills and experiences.

After individuating the experts, it is only fundamental to define the most suitable consultation technique. Consultation techniques refer to the critical listening of the subjects' (experts') opinions, to expand the knowledge base related to the problem under evaluation.

There are several techniques to achieve consensus which have a specific role and are applied to support the decision-making process if the research context is characterized by a lack of scientific evidence, or if they are not demonstrated or fully shared, or even in the case of contradictions between the pieces of evidence or the sources that generated them, resulting in a misaligned picture, within which a reference point or shared guidelines must be sought. These techniques can include experts, stakeholders or both of them. Can be mentioned:

- Delphi Method is a typical methodology of social research, whereby a selected group (also known as a panel) of experts are interviewed anonymously to express their views and opinions on a given topic, with the aim of validating some of them through mutual comparison and progressive sharing [30];
- Focus Group: a discussion among a limited number of experts with the presence of the decision-maker, often supported by a tutor, to describe the nature and the main characteristics of a problem [31];
- Interviews: qualitative interviews are "extended" conversations between the researcher and interviewed people, during which the researcher tries to obtain as detailed and in-depth information as possible on the research theme [31];
- Questionnaire: an observation tool to quantify and compare the data collected on a population sample, chosen according to the characteristics of the evaluation [31].

The CAPM is a model that explains the capital market price formation mechanism. The CAPM allows determining the suitable expected return or discount rate considering the characteristics of the (generally financial) activity under evaluation (discounted cash flows generated by the activity), in relation to its risk.

The most common formula of the CAPM is [20]:

$$r_a = r_f + \beta_a * \left(r_m - r_f \right)$$

where:

ra = expected return on investment (in this case, asset);
rm = expected return of the market or its segment (in this case, real estate market);
rf = risk-free rate;
βa = beta coefficient of the investment (in this case, asset), that is the sensitivity coefficient of the stock in relation to the market [32].

In the CAPM, a particularly interesting element is the Beta coefficient, which synthetizes the relationship between the average market return rate and a specific return rate through the risk that can be associated with an asset [33].

In this sense, by expressing the covariance between a single stock and the whole market, it provides the simplest measurement of systematic risk, and hence information on the volatility and liquidity of the market. It is a simple risk index of a coefficient with practical use. Within the use of the CAPM in the field of finance, there is wide literature on the estimation of the Beta coefficient. The following proposal of a mixed method starts from the idea of considering a fictitious Beta to use for the estimation of the discount rate in real estate development actions; AHP and DM are conjunctly used for its estimation.

3 Articulation of Proposed Method

The structure of the proposed mixed method is based on AHP, DM, and CAPM, and is aimed at the determination of a discount rate that takes into account constraints and the regulatory framework that can affect urban transformation; the discount rate can hence be used for the appraisal of the Market Value of buildings that can be subjected to real estate development (pre-transformation or Transformation Value).

In detail, the proposed method is aimed at evaluating the so-called "regulatory/administrative risk" within the specific discount rate of an asset that will be subjected to a transformation intervention (that is, it will be transformed only at the end of a complex administrative authorization process). This component of the discount rate is a key element for the estimation of the pre-transformation Market Value and it also provides a parameter for the profitability of the initial capital that will be immobilized for the acquisition of the asset to transform.

The determination of the discount rate in relation to the real estate development risk can contribute to the definition of the basket of investments of real estate players.

The proposed method is articulated into 2 macro-phases:

1. the first, general, phase is aimed at the transformation of the constraints of a given context into a range of discount rate differentials depending on the same framework of constraints that affect the "regulatory/administrative risk" component;
2. the second, specific, phase is aimed at the definition of a specific discount rate for the building, in relation to the regulatory/administrative risk that can be envisaged in the valorization action.

Phase 1 is divided into the following actions:

1. recognition of the constraints within a specific territorial context, affecting territorial transformations (excluding not-buildability constraints);
2. application of the AHP, conjunctly with the DM, for the hierarchization of constraints (according to their importance) to attribute an importance index to (national) constraints. The AHP, carried out using Delphi Method results obtained with the support of experts in regulatory/administrative subjects (public officials of Regional Direction of the Urban Planning sector), will perform the pairwise comparison of each territorial constraint within the area, based on the elements that characterize the constraint itself, inferred from regulations. Two criteria are used: i) capacity to inhibit the transformation; ii) administrative-procedural time for the verification of the compatibility/conformity with the constraint. The capacity to inhibit the transformation is intended as the complexity of the constraint (so-called "vestizione", specification) and the verification process to which it is subjected (compatibility/conformity, or both). The administrative-procedural times for the verification of the compatibility/conformity with the constraint are related to the average time needed by the competent Authorities of the given constraint to elaborate the authorization/nihil obstat request and issue the related provision. The objective of this phase is to obtain weights/coefficients (as a result of the AHP) that, after opportune elaboration, can provide useful indications on the specific discount rate of a real estate development initiative in a constrained area. Each potential constraint in a given territorial area is

associated with a score, resulting from the AHP; these scores represent the "base" dataset to elaborate or normalize to proceed to the estimation of the fictitious Beta of the CAPM.

Phase 2 is articulated into the following actions:

1. identification of the fringe parameters related to the financial Beta coefficient of the CAPM. The proposed procedure considers numerical fringe values that, in the market, express the Beta coefficient that can be considered related to a riskless invest-ment (minimum parameter) or a high-risk investment (maximum acceptability by an investor). Fringe values are related to the context where an asset has to be transformed or built, hence expressing the risk components connected to the context, hence the market, inflation, etc.;

2. conversion of AHP results (scores representing hierarchical ratios) into coefficients between the minimum and maximum Beta. In brief, the point is to interpolate AHP results within a value scale between the minimum and the maximum Beta. The inter-polation leads to transforming "real Beta" coefficients related to the financial market into fictitious Beta coefficients related to the real estate market, and in the specific seg-ment of real estate development. In particular, each constraint (within the taxonomy of a specific territorial context) is associated with a variation of the fictitious Beta. To implement the AHP, a DM has to be carried out considering the point of views of Experts regarding the relation between constraints (environmental and landscape); in other words, Experts solve the AHP pairwise comparison;

3. the obtained fictitious Beta coefficients can be used in the Capital Asset Pricing Model (CAPM); in particular, they contribute to the determination of the "overall fictitious Beta" coefficient referred to a given asset to be transformed. Beta values above 1 imply a higher risk, compared to the average market (constraint condition above the average, associated with an expected lower "reactivity" in the conclusion of the authorization procedure, which remains under risk); instead, beta values below 1 correspond to a lower risk. It is evident that the overall dummy beta, whose estimation is based on the increase in the risk of the transformation of the asset due to the constraints, embeds the risk that is generally defined in the scientific literature as "regulatory/administrative", but it does not include all the multiple variables underlying the return rate, which also depend from other factors (generally: sector, location, typology, technical and financial aspects); in this case, these additional elements can be overlooked if the considered market return rm has no time and location inhomogeneity (with respect to the asset under evaluation). Considering the above, considering results from AHP implementation (phase 2.2), this phase is implemented through the summation of the variables of fictitious Beta associated with constraints, only in relation to the constraints that are present on the asset to transform, according to the formula:

$$\beta_a = f(v_1 + v_2 + v_3 + \cdots + v_n)$$

4. Implementation of the CAPM in its traditional formulation: the result of the imple-mentation of the CAPM is a discount rate that is calibrated on the specific constraint condition of the asset (deriving from the elaboration of the regulatory/administrative risk in one coefficient through AHP and EA), but also related to its historical-temporal-geographic context (deriving from the adoption of fringe parameters related to specific

contexts and periods). After determining the expected return through the CAPM, the future cashflows of the analyzed financial activity can be discounted, determining their current value. The discount operation allows determining the correct price of the financial activity. Hence, a riskier real estate development will have a higher beta value and will be discounted at a higher rate; less risky financial activities will have lower beta values and will be discounted at lower rates.

4 Discussion and Conclusions

This article has presented the methodological proposal for the investigation of the relationship between constraint frameworks and the Market Value of assets that suit real estate development initiatives, despite not having yet received the authorization for their transformation.

The financialization of the real estate market, that is considering real estate development interventions on assets as investments, led to the plausibility of the use of a method – the CAPM – that is typically used to determine the relationship between the return of a stock and its risk, measured through a single risk factor, called Beta.

This proposition of the CAPM provides the expected return through a fictitious Beta, which represents the object of the proposed method, configured as a suitable discount rate for the characteristics of the financial activity underlying the real estate development intervention. The premium will strongly depend on the fictitious Beta coefficient, which will measure the reactivity of the expected return in relation to the constraint conditions of the building, which determines whether an intervention is authorizable.

As in financial markets, the higher the Beta coefficient, the higher the expected return of the activity, as it has a greater degree of undiversifiable risk. Hence, an investor will require a higher return to carry out a riskier financial activity [34, 35].

With reference to the return range expressed by the financial market in a given geographic context and historical moment, the proposed procedure implicitly associates return with success risk (regardless of the specific industrial sector); the procedure, developed on a theoretical level, will have to be operatively verified by applying it on a set of buildings within a specific administrative context, for example within a Municipality.

Hence, the following developments of the research reside in its experimentation, which is aimed to achieve the results of mapping the municipal territory, which is associated with a given risk level in relation to the development of an initiative (and, consequently, a risk parameter) [36].

After mapping an administrative context, it will be possible to verify the results by comparing the discount rates and expected returns with the parameters of qualified investors within the sector.

In this sense, the proposed method aims at reducing the margins of error in the estimation of real estate with complex administrative and regulatory conditions and constraint frameworks, increasing the transparency on investment risks, which determine profitability.

References

1. Oppio, A., et al.: Urban rent at risk: the point of view of private investors. Valori e Valutazioni n. 27 (2020)
2. Battisti, F., Campo, O., Forte, F.: A methodological approach for the assessment of potentially buildable land for tax purposes: the Italian case study. Land **9**(1), 8 (2020)
3. Ribeiro, M.I., Ferreira, F.A., Jalali, M.S., Meidutė-Kavaliauskienė, I.: A fuzzy knowledge-based framework for risk assessment of residential real estate investments. Technol. Econ. Dev. Econ. **23**(1), 140–156 (2017)
4. Chong, J., Miffre, J., Stevenson, S.: Conditional correlations and real estate investment trusts. J. Real Estate Portfolio Manage. **15**, 173–184 (2009)
5. Chun, G., Sa-Aadu, J., Shilling, J.: The role of real estate in an institutional investor's portfolio revisited. J. Real Estate Finance Econ. **29**, 295–320 (2004)
6. Martinelli, N., Mininni, M.: Città Sostenibilità Resilienza: L'urbanistica italiana di fronte all'Agenda 2030. Donzelli Editore (2021)
7. Sun, C., Abbas, H.S.M., Xu, X., Gillani, S., Ullah, S., & Raza, M.A.A.: Role of capital investment, investment risks, and globalization in economic growth. Int. J. Finance Econ. (2021)
8. Chambers, D., Spaenjers C., Steiner E.: The rate of return on real estate: Long-run micro-level evidence. In: HEC Paris Research Paper. No. FIN-2019–1342 (2019). https://papers.ssrn.com/sol3/papers.cfm?abstract_id=3407236. Accessed 15 Feb 2023
9. Domian, D., Wolf, R., Hsiao, F.Y.: An assessment of the risk and return of residential real estate. Manag. Financ. **41**, 591–599 (2015)
10. Battisti, F., Campo, O.: The assessment of density bonus in building renovation interventions. the case of the city of florence in italy. Land **10**(12) (2021). https://doi.org/10.3390/land10 121391
11. Brueggeman, W., Chen, A., Thibodeau, T.: Real estate investment funds: performance and portfolio considerations. Real Estate Econ. **12**, 333–354 (1984)
12. Peng, L.: The risk and return of commercial real estate: a property level analysis. Real Estate Econ. **44**, 555–583 (2016)
13. Ross, S., Zisler R.: Risk and return in real estate. J. Real Estate Finance and Econ. **4**, 175–90 (1991)
14. Cannon, S., Miller N., Pandher G.: Risk and return in the U.S. housing market: a cross-sectional asset-pricing approach. Real Estate Econ. **34**, 519–552 (2006)
15. Case, K., Cotter J., Stuart G.: Housing risk and return: evidence from a housing asset-pricing model. J. Portfolio Manage. **37**(5), 89–109 (2011)
16. Saaty, T.L.: Decision making—the analytic hierarchy and network processes (AHP/ANP). J. Syst. Sci. Syst. Eng. **13**, 1–35 (2004)
17. Saaty, T.L.: Fundamentals of the analytic hierarchy process. the analytic hierarchy process in natural resource and environmental decision making, pp. 15–35 (2001)
18. Linstone, H. A., Turoff, M. (Eds.): The Delphi Method. Addison-Wesley, Reading, MA (1975). 3–12 pages
19. Gordon, T.J.: The Delphi Method. Futures Research Methodology **2**(3), 1–30 (1994)
20. Sharpe, W.: Capital asset prices: a theory of market equilibrium under conditions of risk. J. Financ. **19**, 425–442 (1964)
21. Jagannathan, R., McGrattan, E.R.: The CAPM debate. Fed. Reserve Bank Minneap. Q. Rev. **19**(4), 2–17 (1995)
22. Bartholdy, J., Peare, P.: Estimation of expected return: CAPM vs. Fama and French. Int. Review Financial Analysis **14**(4), 407–427 (2005)

23. Alves, P.: The fama french model or the capital asset pricing model: international evidence. Int. J. Bus. Finance Res. **7**, 79–89 (2013)
24. Battisti F., Campo, O.: A model for determining a discount rate in market value assessment of buildable areas subject to restrictions. In: Morano, P., Oppio, A., Rosato, P. Sdino, L., Tajani, F. (eds.) Appraisal and Valuation. GET, pp. 303–314. Springer, Cham (2021). https://doi.org/10.1007/978-3-030-49579-4_20
25. Colavitti, A.N.N.A., Serra, S.: Regional landscape planning and local planning. Insights from the Italian context. J. Settlements Spatial Planning (7), 81–91 (2021)
26. Sustainable Use of Natural Resources. https://ec.europa.eu/environment/archives/natres/index.htm. Accessed 15 Feb 2023
27. Nature and biodiversity EU website. https://ec.europa.eu/environment/nature/info/pubs/docs/nat2000/factsheet_it.pdf. Accessed 15 Feb 2023
28. Convention on Wetlands of International Importance especially as Waterfowl Habitat. https://en.unesco.org/about-us/legal-affairs/convention-wetlands-international-importance-especially-waterfowl-habitat. Accessed 15 Feb 2023
29. The Council of Europe Landscape Convention website. https://www.coe.int/en/web/landscape. Accessed 15 Feb 2023
30. Pretty, J., Hine, R.: Participatory Appraisal for Community Assessment: Principles and Methods; Centre for Environment and Society. University of Essex, Colchester, UK (1999)
31. Mattia, S.: Costruzione e Valutazione Della Sostenibilità dei Progetti. Franco Angeli, Milano, Italy; **1** (2008)
32. Faiteh, A., Aasri, M.R.: Accounting beta as an indicator of risk measurement: the case of the casablanca stock exchange. Risks **10**, 149 (2022). https://doi.org/10.3390/risks10080149lastaccessed2023/02/15
33. Tang, G., Wai, S.: The conditional relationship between beta and returns: recent evidence from international stock markets. Int. Bus. Rev. **12**, 109–126 (2003)
34. Baum, A.: Tokenisation—The Future of Real Estate Investment? The University of Oxford Research (2020). https://www.sbs.ox.ac.uk/sites/default/files/2020-01/tokenisation.pdf. Accessed 15 Feb 2023
35. Jordà, Ò., Knoll, K., Kuvshinov, D., Schularick, M., Taylor, A.: The rate of return on everything, 1870–2015. Q. J. Econ. **134**, 1225–1298 (2019)
36. Wong, S.K., Shing, C.K.: Renewing a lease at a discount or premium? J. Real Estate Res. **39**, 215–234 (2017)

**Urban Space Accessibility
and Mobilities (USAM 2023)**

Accessibility and Polarities of Pedestrian Network in University Campuses. A Space Syntax Application

Lea Jeanne Marinelli[1] , Alfonso Annunziata[2] , Barbara Caselli[1](✉) ,
Giulia Desogus[2] , Vincenza Torrisi[3] , and Chiara Garau[2]

[1] Department of Engineering and Architecture, University of Parma, Parco Area delle Scienze,
181/A, 43124 Parma, Italy
barbara.caselli@unipr.it
[2] Department of Civil and Environmental Engineering and Architecture, University of Cagliari,
09123 Cagliari, Italy
[3] Department of Electrical, Electronic and Computer Engineering, University of Catania,
via S. Sofia 64, 95125 Catania, Italy

Abstract. This paper examines the multiple interactions between pedestrian mobility systems and land use planning within the framework of Agenda 2030's sustainability goals involving the integration of mobility networks with urban planning development (i.e., targets 11.2 and 11.3). The study focuses on suburban university campuses and science parks as significant cases. Specifically, two different campuses and science parks have been selected as case studies, i.e., Parma and Monserrato (metropolitan city of Cagliari), located in peripheral areas and built during the second half of the 20th century. The methodological approach is based on Space Syntax, to analyse the spatial configuration of the pedestrian infrastructure of each campus. First, a segment map reflecting all pedestrian routes on each campus has been created. Then, multiple measures have been calculated using the DepthmapX software, evaluating accessibility and identifying polarities. Subsequently, the strengths and weaknesses of each campus's pedestrian infrastructure network have been identified and a comparison analysis between the two case studies has been performed to identify common and efficient space conformation characteristics according to the Space Syntax analysis. The study concludes with an analysis of the limitations of the methodology and provides suggestions for further research.

Keywords: University Campuses · Accessibility · Walkability · Active mobility · Space Syntax

1 Introduction

Nowadays, sustainable land use and transport mobility are two of the foremost worldwide issues to be pursued [1]. Urban mobility, which accounts for more than 60% of the travels performed by users, is the greatest contributor to carbon dioxide emissions and

O. Gervasi et al. (Eds.): ICCSA 2023 Workshops, LNCS 14111, pp. 383–400, 2023.
https://doi.org/10.1007/978-3-031-37126-4_26

air pollution [2]. Since 2018, 55% of the world's population resided in urban areas, as highlighted by the 2019 U.N. report *World Urbanisation Prospects: The 2018 Revision* [3]. This report also forecasts that by 2050, this percentage will increase to 68%, having a significant impact on urban mobility.

In Italy, from 2010 to 2021, urban mobility has increased by more than 4%, accounting for 70.6% of the overall travel. In 2022, the average length and duration of urban trips have also increased, with 78% within a range of 10 kms and among those, 28% within a 2-km range. The modal shift shows a significant decrease towards active mobility, particularly walking, compared to the values of 2020, with a decline from 32.8% to 23.7% primarily due to the overcoming of Covid-19 restrictions. Moreover, private cars remaining the preferred mode of transport, with a percentage value of 64% [4]. It is common knowledge that spatial design, as well as changes in lifestyles and travel patterns, have had a substantial impact on the above outlined conditions. Indeed, several scholars have emphasised the integration of spatial planning and transport planning [5–10] and explored methodological approaches to evaluate accessibility, especially within active mobility [11]. Active mobility, together with the promotion of less polluting transport systems, constitute one of the key research concepts on sustainable mobility systems. These approaches can also provide valuable insight for planning tools aimed at urban regeneration [12, 13]. Numerous studies have been conducted to assess walkability, identifying drivers or barriers to walking [14–19] or elements in urban design and planning that positively influence pedestrian accessibility [19–22]. Several studies considered the impact of the spatial configuration of urban areas for pedestrian mobility by employing the Space Syntax approach [23–27]. The Space Syntax methodology encompasses a range of concepts and methods for defining the interrelation between the spatial configuration of urban environments and human behaviours concerning movement preferences. As a result, the Space Syntax approach has the potential to provide valuable instruments to improve planning strategies and urban regeneration initiatives.

Within this framework, limited investigations concentrate on examining walkability in suburban campuses using the Space Syntax approach. Thus, the paper investigates the level of accessibility and polarities of the pedestrian network on suburban university campuses, addressing the issue of sustainable active mobility. Case studies are conducted on university campuses as they represent an urban microcosm wherein footpaths play a critical role for students and other pedestrian users moving between different structures [28]. Therefore, it is key to examine the spatial configuration and pedestrian environments of university campuses. In particular, the research considers the campuses of Parma and Monserrato (in the metropolitan city of Cagliari), which were designed in the latter half of the 1900s in accordance with planning theories that prioritised private mobility. Thus, the aim of the research is to understand if the two analysed university campuses are able to provide a good degree of pedestrian accessibility according, to the Space Syntax methodology.

The following sections of the paper are organised as follows: Sect. 2 introduces the two case studies (Campus *Scienze e Tecnologie* of Parma's University and the *Cittadella Universitaria* of Monserrato); Sect. 3 describes the Space Syntax methodological approach; Sect. 4 presents the results of the analyses, including criticalities and potentialities; Sect. 5 compares the two case studies to identify common and efficient spatial conformation characteristics, as revealed by the Space Syntax analysis; the research concludes with a discussion of the limitations of the methodology and a brief overview of prospective future research paths, also provided in Sect. 5.

2 Case Studies

This research focuses on suburban university campuses as an outcome of municipal expansion planning and dependence on private vehicles. The establishment of such infrastructures is closely connected to the rapid growth of the university system during the 20th century. Specifically, after the Second World War, several European universities located in historic city centres chose to construct suburban campuses in emulation of the campus model prevalent in the United States. Several factors were pivotal in prompting the design of such centres in the suburban setting, including i) scarcity of available space in urban areas; ii) the need for spacious facilities to accommodate science labs and machinery rooms; iii) the affordability of land; and iv) the conformity with the urban planning practices of the time, particularly functionalisation/zoning as stated by the Athens Charter 1933 [29].

The research analyses the pedestrian network of two specific suburban campuses, located in Italy. The first site refers to the Campus *Scienze e Tecnologie* of Parma's University, within the Emilia-Romagna region, in the northern part of the Italian peninsula. The second campus, the *Cittadella Universitaria* of Monserrato, is in the northern portion of the metropolitan city of Cagliari, within the island of Sardinia, in the southern part of Italy.

The case studies are selected among the campuses built in Italy in suburban areas. Both of the campuses in analysis have the same historical period of construction between the 1970s and 1980s. Despite having comparable facilities, Parma's campus boasts a significantly greater expanse than Monserrato's one and a discrete presence of the transport infrastructures. Additionally, they exist within two differing urban contexts, with Parma representing a medium-sized municipality and Cagliari as regional capital and metropolitan city, thus representing two interesting case studies to be compared.

2.1 Parma's Campus *Scienze e Tecnologie*

Parma's University is spatially distributed across multiple sites throughout the city. These sites can be categorised into four main areas. The first one corresponds to the historical city centre and hosts the departments of humanities, economics, and law. The second area is located outside the historical city centre and hosts the departments of medicine and surgery within the *Ospedale Maggiore* hospital complex. The third one is in the northwest suburban area of the city, characterized by the department of veterinary medical sciences. Finally, the fourth area, considered for this study, accommodates the scientific departments. Due to its territorial scattering, the Parma's University can be classified as a "diffuse" university [30]. This characteristic is also applicable to the University of Cagliari, which will be discussed in more detail in the next sub-section.

Parma's Campus *Scienze e Tecnologie* is located on the southern suburban area of the city (Fig. 1) and is delimited on the north by the southern roadway of the city's ring road. On the north-east, the site is bordered by an urbanised area characterized predominantly by local facilities. To the north-west, on the other hand, the Campus is belted by the *Cinghio* stream, while to the south and east it borders a rural area.

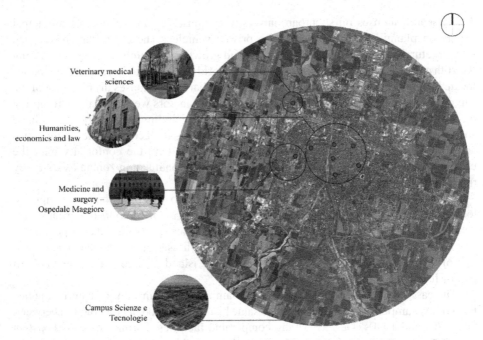

Fig. 1. Location of Parma's University main polarities. Circled in red is the Campus *Scienze e Tecnologie*. Source: elaboration from Esri Satellite. (Color figure online)

The Campus covers an area of about 77 hectares within which there are 114,000 m^2 consisting of built structures, 86,039 m^2 designated for parking and 103,328 m^2 dedicated to sports facilities. Specifically, Table 1 shows as the built facilities within Campus serve a variety of different functions.

According to the 2016 Urban Planning Implementation Plan (in Italian: Piano Urbanistico Attuativo) [31] for the Science and Technology Campus's 1997 master plan completion and functional reorganisation, it is estimated that the Campus daily users are between 6,000 and 10,000.

Table 1. Parma's campus facilities divided by functional class. Re-elaborated data from Parma's Urban Planning Implementation Plan [31].

Main functional class	N. of buildings	Usable area (m^2)
Research and teaching	17	83,772
Conference centre	2	3,055
Innovation and productive research	3	11,186
Administrative facilities	1	986
Catering facilities	3	2,520
Sports facilities	12	10,329
Other facilities	4	1,607

2.2 *Cittadella Universitaria* of Monserrato

The *Cittadella Universitaria* of Monserrato (in the metropolitan city of Cagliari) is a large university campus hosting numerous faculties of the University of Cagliari, including science, medicine, and biology. Founded at the end of the 1960s, the *Cittadella Universitaria* covers an area of approximately 48 ha (Fig. 2) between the national road SS 554 to the south, the provincial road SP8 communicating with Sestu to the west, and the Riu Saliu to the east.

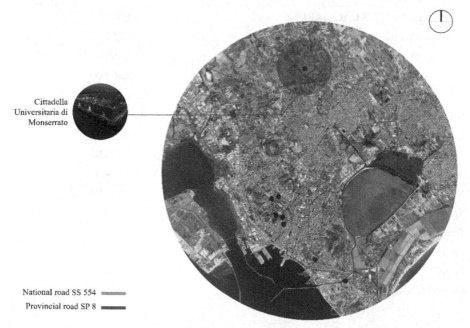

Cittadella Universitaria di Monserrato

National road SS 554
Provincial road SP 8

Fig. 2. Location of Cagliari's University main university buildings. The *Cittadella Universitaria* of Monserrato is encircled in red. Source: elaboration from Esri Satellite. (Color figure online)

The year of 1971 marked the beginning of the planning process for this area when the university conducted a national competition to collect proposals for an urban development plan. However, the construction plan was not drafted until 1984. The first General Variation for the Services Plan (In Italian: la prima Variante Generale per il Piano dei Servizi) was authorised between 1980 and 1983 by the Municipality of Cagliari and went into effect on April 20, 1983. After a lengthy authorization process, the foundation stone was laid on October 5, 1985, and the opening ceremony was held on August 8, 1996.

The *Cittadella Universitaria* of Monserrato is connected to the city of Cagliari by several public transport modes, including city buses (Consorzio Trasporti e Mobilità – CTM) and regional buses (Azienda Regionale Sarda Trasporti - ARST), as well as the light metro. Table 2 illustrates that, as in the case study of Parma's campus, the *Cittadella Universitaria*'s structures are distinct and serve various purposes. The project comprised the construction of a university centre with classrooms, laboratories, study areas, libraries, and service areas. In addition to university facilities, the campus hosts the Duilio Casula University Hospital (*Policlinico Universitario Duilio Casula*), which provides high-quality services in the medical and surgical fields and permits medical and surgical students to specialise in several fields.

Table 2. Monserrato's *Cittadella Universitaria* facilities divided by functional class. Re-elaborated data from Technical Implementation Standards [32].

Main functional class	Usable area (m^2)
Sports Facilities CUS CAGLIARI	1,869.00
Clinical departments	3,252.00
Building Q	2,165.00
Policlinico Universitario	9,867.00
National Research Council studies and lab and Parasitology	1,266.00
Student Secretariats	598.00
Chemistry and biology	4,925.00
Educational Axis 2 laboratory lot, classrooms, canteen	3,728.00
Animal enclosure	614.00
Neuroscience Department	907.00
Spina Departmental of Biology	4,010.00
Teaching Axis 1 lot	5,181.00
Spina Departmental Physics	6,788.00
Fourth Spina Departmental – CESAR	6,000.00
Central Library	1,839.00

3 Materials and Methods

In the proposed study, the accessibility and polarities of the pedestrian network of the two analysed case studies' pedestrian networks are determined using the Space Syntax methodology [33, 34]. The Space Syntax methodology has been originally developed in the late 1970's by Bill Hillier and his colleagues of the Bartlett School of Architecture of the College University of London. It consists of a set of theories and techniques to identify the correlation between the configuration of the street network and people's behaviour in relation to their choice of movement [35]. The set of these techniques for the configurational analysis of space, whether within structures or considering public spaces between buildings, enables the description of the relationship of a single spatial element and the system as a whole. Two software programmes are used to conduct the research: a Geographical Information System (GIS) program for generating the foundational maps and processing the data, and the DepthmapX software for performing the Space Syntax analyses. First, base maps are gathered, and employed as required within the GIS software, from the Territorial Information Systems of Cagliari and Parma municipalities incorporating topographical details about buildings location and street network. Then, a map of the footpath network (Fig. 3 and Fig. 4) is reconstructed, with each segment representing a portion of the network and is interrupted at every intersection with other paths. Upon the representation of the axial map, pedestrian pathways are not restricted to axes that have proper infrastructure, such as sidewalks or other areas specifically designated for pedestrian movement, but also include areas that are frequently used by pedestrians despite lacking supporting infrastructure. Second, the shapefile representing the footpath map is exported in dxf format and imported into the DepthmapX software, where it is converted into a segment map. In this research, the Normalised Angular Choice (NACH) and Normalised Angular Integration (NAIN) values are determined using the DepthmapX program. The NACH and NAIN indicators allow to identify within the route network the main routes for movement and the most vital and frequented spaces respectively.

The analyses are conducted for radii (r) of n, with respect to the whole system, and 400 m values, the latter corresponding to a travel distance of around 5 min for an average pedestrian [36].

Specifically, the formulas used to calculate the NACH (Eq. 1) and NAIN (Eq. 2) indicators correspond to the formulas proposed by Yamu and van Nes [37] and shown by the following equations:

$$NACH = \log(Choice(r) + 2) \tag{1}$$

$$NAIN = \log(Integration(r) + 2) \tag{2}$$

The NAIN indicator is often used to identify potential service sites in urban areas. In the cases studied, no buildings are assigned for housing, only for facilities. Thus, the NAIN indicator can be used to conduct preliminary evaluations to identify ideal locations for services with greater user flow or facilities with greater student numbers, as well as for the purpose of urban regeneration interventions.

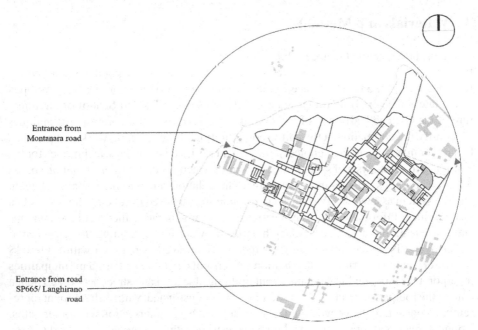

Entrance from
Montanara road

Entrance from road
SP665/ Langhirano
road

Fig. 3. Segment map representation of the Campus *Scienze e Tecnologie* of Parma. Grey dashed line indicates the perimeter of the study areas.

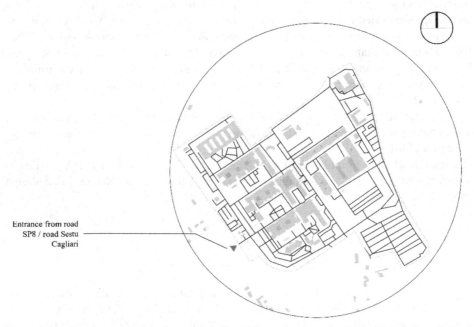

Entrance from road
SP8 / road Sestu
Cagliari

Fig. 4. Segment map representation of the *Cittadella Universitaria* of Monserrato. Grey dashed line indicates the perimeter of the study areas.

4 Results

The obtained results for the computed configurational indicators are graphically shown through axial maps, one for each performed analysis. The values are illustrated through a colour scale (from blue to red) to indicate the values. Specifically, the red and orange segments indicate high values of Integration and Choice, whereas blue segments indicate low values. The results are represented using an equal interval distribution and grouped in ten classes.

4.1 Accessibility and Polarities of Parma's Campus

Figures 5 and 6 visually display the outcomes acquired for Parma's Campus *Scienze e Tecnologie*. The evaluation of the NACH(n) indicator (Fig. 5a) indicates the sections with the highest potential of pedestrian through-movement for the entire system analysed. Even if the investigation is performed to study the pedestrian network, the analysis highlighted the primary foreground network of the infrastructure system for the conveyance of cyclists, pedestrians, and vehicles. By limiting the analysis radius to a 5-min travel time, the examination of the NACH (400) indicator (Fig. 5b) reveals that part of the sections with the highest potential of pedestrian through-movement are still included within the Campus foreground network. However, the analysis emphasizes the central and inner sections, not highlighting the perimeter network. Moreover, the remaining sections of the network with high through-movement potential, thus, high NACH (400) values, are network segments pertaining to the secondary paths, also located in the central area of the campus.

It is possible to recognise, for both examination radii, that the most critical portion of the path network is depicted by the zone situated towards the north/north-west of the examination area, which is primarily reserved for sport greenery. Moreover, concerning the NACH (400) indicator low pedestrian potential through-movement values are also depicted in the southern portion of the network. In addition to the NACH indicator, NAIN values are also represented, enabling the identification of the network segments more liable to pedestrian potential to-movement. This measure is employed to locate the most interlinked segments in the network.

The evaluation of the NAIN (N) indicator (Fig. 6a) across the whole network exposed a primary polarity located in the middle section of the campus. Moreover, the pathway originating from the Via Montanara access towards the campus is also included within this polarity. The values analysed for a 400 m radius (Fig. 6b), on the other hand, make it possible to identify a more diffuse centrality within the campus, which is however concentrated in its central portion and has slightly lower values concerning high potential to-movement rates. Nonetheless, it can be inferred that the pedestrian pathways throughout the Parma campus are effectively interconnected.

Table 3 displays the highest, lowest, and mean values determined for every indicator.

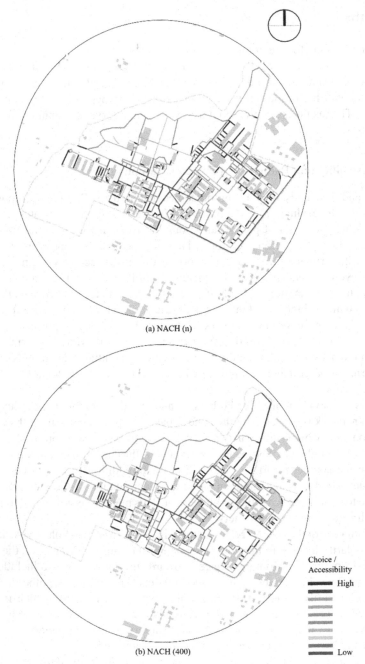

Fig. 5. Normalised values from the angular segment analysis: (a) NACH radius n, (b) NACH radius 400, (c) for Parma's Campus *Scienze e Tecnologie.*

(a) NAIN (n)

Integration /
Accessibility

High

Low

(b) NAIN (400)

Fig. 6. Normalised values from the angular segment analysis: (a) NAIN radius n, (b) NAIN radius 400, (c) for Parma's Campus *Scienze e Tecnologie*.

Table 3. Parma's campus main, average, and minimum values identified for the calculated indicators.

Indicator	Maximum value	Mean value	Minimum value
NACH (N)	5.277	2.908	0.301
NACH (400)	4.080	2.405	0.301
NAIN (N)	2.280	2.078	1.787
NAIN (400)	2.139	1.634	0.837

4.2 Accessibility and Polarities of Monserrato's Cittadella Universitaria

The visual representation presented in Figs. 7 and 8 illustrates the results obtained for the *Cittadella Universitaria* of Monserrato in the metropolitan city of Cagliari.

Similarly, to the campus of Parma, the NACH indicator values are computed first for the complete network and then for a radii of 400 m. Then, analysis of the normalised choice indicator for the entire network (Fig. 7a) identifies, also in this case, that the segments with the greatest pedestrian through-movement are the foreground network for vehicle and pedestrian transit. The arrangement of the grid representing the main mobility network of the campus is especially clear and easy to understand in this context. The outcomes of the NACH(400) indicator (Fig. 7b) underscore, much like before, the network that constitutes the campus foreground. Nonetheless, in this case the analysis emphasizes the horizontal components as opposed to the previous radii where the vertical ones where highlighted.

In relation to the analysis of Integration, the NAIN(N) indicator (Fig. 8a), similarly the NACH(N) analysis, emphasizes the vertical infrastructure axes of the network, also including the horizontal perimeter axis located south of the campus. Conversely, the NAIN indicator computed for a 400 m radius (Fig. 8b) reveals the significant inter-connectivity of the analysed path network, indicating a near absence of segments with exceedingly low movement potential values (dark blue).

Table 4 displays the highest, lowest, and mean values determined for each indicator evaluated.

Table 4. Monserrato's campus main, average, and minimum values identified for the calculated indicators.

Indicator	Maximum value	Mean value	Minimum value
NACH (N)	4.625	2.522	0.301
NACH (400)	3.709	2.182	0.301
NAIN (N)	2.192	1.998	1.761
NAIN (400)	2.010	1.721	1.183

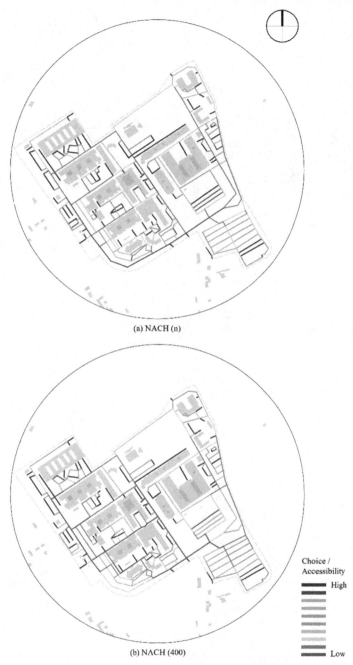

Fig. 7. Normalised values from the angular segment analysis: (a) NACH radius n, (b) NACH radius 400, (c) for the metropolitan city of Cagliari's *Cittadella Universitaria* of Monserrato.

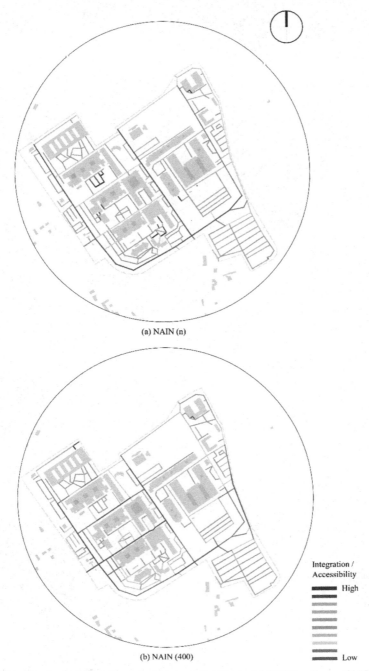

(a) NAIN (n)

(b) NAIN (400)

Integration /
Accessibility

High

Low

Fig. 8. Normalised values from the angular segment analysis: (a) NAIN radius n, (b) NAIN radius 400, (c) for Cagliari's *Cittadella Universitaria* of Monserrato.

5 Discussion and Conclusions

The achievement of climate change targets is strongly dependent on sustainable mobility, especially active mobility. To accomplish these objectives, it is crucial to plan infrastructures that are suitable and well-coordinated with appropriate land-use and transport planning. In specific urban enclaves, such as campuses and science parks, where pedestrian mobility ought to be the primary transport mode for users, this becomes even more important [28]. In this respect, the Space Syntax methodology can therefore provide useful tools for the configurational analysis of space to comprehend its impact on individuals' path choices, and thus as a tool to support planning tools and urban regeneration practices [34].

Within this context, the contribution proposed the study of two spatial configuration indicators, using the Space Syntax methodology, on two campuses (Parma and Monserrato), with the objective of assessing the degree of pedestrian accessibility. The performed analyses provided values demonstrating that the analysed campuses have a good degree of pedestrian accessibility, particularly as regards the *Cittadella Universitaria* of Monserrato. In fact, according to the NAIN indicator assessment, segments with very low values, and thus poorly integrated with the overall network of pedestrian routes, are almost absent.

Comparing the mean values of both case studies reveal that, with the exception of the NAIN(400) indicator, Parma's campus has slightly higher values than the *Cittadella Universitaria* of Monserrato. Therefore, it is possible to assume that this characteristic is mainly influenced by the campus' smaller size, as well as its higher building concentration. Additionally, the indicator could be affected by more systematic arrangement of footpaths and consequently, of structures / facilities. In both campuses, the analyses performed reveal that the parking areas are the most problematic zones for both campuses. These areas hold particular significance as they constitute a substantial portion of the total area of both campuses.

The evaluations conducted through the Space Syntax approach have certain constraints that impact the genuine pedestrian accessibility perceived by individuals. These include the impossibility of considering the quality of the analysed pedestrian routes and their urban context [38]. In fact, a portion of the segments of the pedestrian network analysed did not have sidewalks, especially regarding the Parma case study. Additionally, these analyses do not consider some key elements to be considered when assessing the degree of pedestrian accessibility to be evaluated through an inclusive design perspective such as the presence of elements to support vulnerable users (such as people with disabilities).

In conclusion, despite their limits, the analyses performed identify a considerable degree of pedestrian accessibility in the two case studies considered. To enhance the precision of these assessments, a prospective research advancement can merge spatial configurational analysis with the application of criteria to assess the standard of pedestrian walkways, such as the Synthetic Indicator of Perceived Road Quality or the Composite Indicator by Universal Design [39]. A subsequent phase instead involves scrutinizing the NACH indicator with the localisation of public transportation stations or other amenities (e.g., dining halls) to assess their appropriate placement.

Finally, an ultimate progression of the study involves theorising potential adaptations of the spaces designated for parking purposes to accommodate new uses in a perspective of urban regeneration and sustainable mobility, recurring once more to the Space Syntax methodology to assess optimal scenarios for pedestrian accessibility.

Attributions This paper is the result of the joint work of the authors. 'Abstract', and 'Discussion and Conclusions' were written jointly by the authors. BC wrote the 'Introduction'. LJM wrote the 'Introduction', 'Materials and Methods', 'Case studies' (Sect. 2 and 2.1) and 'Results' (Sect. 4 and 4.1). AA and GD wrote the 'Case studies' (Sect. 2.2) and 'Results' (Sect. 4.2). BC, CG and VT coordinated and supervised the paper.

Acknowledgements. This work is the result of a project proposal developed within the doctoral course Smart and Sustainable Cities (3rd edition) held at the University of Cagliari and coordinated by C. Garau (https://dottorati.unica.it/dotticar/smart-and-sustainable-cities-3-edizione/). The course was attended by LJM to refine theoretical and methodological tools with reference to the topics researched in the framework of the Sustainable Mobility Centre (CNMS) Spoke 9, WP3. Funder: Project funded under the National Recovery and Resilience Plan (NRRP), Mission 4 Component 2 Investment 1.4 - Call for tender No. 3138 of 16/12/2021 of Italian Ministry of University and Research funded by the European Union – NextGenerationEU. Award Number: Project code CN00000023, Concession Decree No. 1033 of 17/06/2022 adopted by the Italian Ministry of University and Research, CUP D93C22000400001, "Sustainable Mobility Center" (CNMS). The work of V. Torrisi was supported by European Union (NextGeneration EU), through the MUR-PNRR project SAMOTHRACE (ECS00000022).

References

1. United Nations, The 2030 Agenda for Sustainable Development, New York (2015)
2. Rode, P., et al.: Accessibility in Cities: Transport and Urban Form. NCE Cities Paper (03). LSE Cities. London School of Economics and Political Science (2014)
3. United Nations Department of Economic and Social Affairs (UN DESA), World Urbanization Prospects: The 2018 Revision, New York (2019)
4. Istituto Superiore di Formazione e Ricerca per i Trasporti (ISFORT), 19° Rapporto sulla mobilità degli italiani. https://www.isfort.it/wp-content/uploads/2022/12/19-Rapporto_mob ilita_italiani_Sintesi.pdf. Accessed 30 Mar 2023
5. Kenworthy, J.R., Laube, F.B.: Automobile dependence in cities: an international comparison of urban transport and land use patterns with implications for sustainability. Environ. Impact Assess. Rev. **16**(4–6), 279–308 (1996)
6. Newman, P., Kenworthy, J.: Sustainability and Cities: Overcoming Automobile Dependence. Island Press, Washington DC (1999)
7. Boarnet, M., Crane, R.: Travel by Design: The Influence of Urban Form on Travel. Oxford University Press, New York (2001)
8. Tira, M., Tiboni, M., Rossetti, S., De Robertis, M.: "Smart" planning to enhance nonmotorised and safe mobility in today's cities. In: Papa, R., Fistola, R., Gargiulo, C. (eds.) Smart Planning: Sustainability and Mobility in the Age of Change. GET, pp. 201–213. Springer, Cham (2018). https://doi.org/10.1007/978-3-319-77682-8_12
9. Tiboni, M., Rossetti, S., Vetturi, D., Torrisi, V., Botticini, F., Schaefer, M.D.: Urban policies and planning approaches for a safer and climate friendlier mobility in cities: strategies initiatives and some analysis. Sustainability **13**, 1778 (2021). https://doi.org/10.3390/su1304

10. Carpentieri, G., Guida, C., Chorus, P.: Land-Use and Transport integration polices and real estate values. the development of a GIS methodology and the application to Naples (Italy). TeMA – J. Land Use, Mobility Environ. **12**(3), pp. 313–330 (2019). https://doi.org/10.6092/1970-9870/6273

11. Pellicelli, G., Caselli, B., Garau, C., Torrisi, V., Rossetti, S.: Sustainable mobility and accessibility to essential services. an assessment of the san benedetto neighbourhood in Cagliari (Italy). In: Gervasi, O., Murgante, B., Misra, S., Rocha, A.M.A.C., Garau, C. (eds) Computational Science and Its Applications – ICCSA 2022 Workshops, ICCSA 2022, Lecture Notes in Computer Science (13382), Springer, Cham (2022). https://doi.org/10.1007/978-3-031-10592-0_31

12. Gallo, M., Marinelli, M.: Sustainable mobility: a review of possible actions and policies. Sustainability **12**(8) (2020). https://doi.org/10.3390/su12187499

13. Pellicelli, G., Rossetti, S., Caselli, B., Zazzi, M.: Urban regeneration to enhance sustainable mobility. TEMA – J. Land Use, Mobility and Environ., pp. 57–70 (2022). https://doi.org/10.6093/1970-9870/8646

14. Ewing, R., Handy, S.: Measuring the unmeasurable: urban design qualities related to walkability. J. Urban Des. **14**(1), 65–84 (2009). https://doi.org/10.1080/13574800802451155

15. Mrak, I., Campisi, T., Tesoriere, G., Canale, A., Cindrić, M.: The role of urban and social factors in the accessibility of urban areas for people with motor and visual disabilities, In: AIP Conference Proceedings, **2186**(1), p. 160008, AIP Publishing LLC (2019). https://doi.org/10.1063/1.5138076

16. Ignaccolo, M., Inturri, G., Giuffrida, N., Le Pira, M., Torrisi, V., Calabrò, G.: A step towards walkable environments: spatial analysis of pedestrian compatibility in an urban context. European Transport **76**(6) (2020)

17. Annunziata, A., Garau, C.: A literature review on walkability and its theoretical framework. emerging perspectives for research developments. In: Gervasi, O., et al. (eds.) ICCSA 2020. LNCS, vol. 12255, pp. 422–437. Springer, Cham (2020). https://doi.org/10.1007/978-3-030-58820-5_32

18. Caselli, B., Rossetti, S., Ignaccolo, M., Zazzi, M., Torrisi, V.: Towards the definition of a comprehensive walkability index for historical centres. In: Gervasi, O., et al. (eds.) ICCSA 2021. LNCS, vol. 12958, pp. 493–508. Springer, Cham (2021). https://doi.org/10.1007/978-3-030-87016-4_36

19. Blečić, I., Cecchini, A., Congiu, T., Fancello, G., Triunfo, G.A.: Evaluating walkability: a capability-wise planning and design support system. Int. J. Geogr. Inf. Sci. **29**(8), 1350–1374 (2015)

20. Talen, E.: Pedestrian access as a measure of urban quality. Plan. Pract. Res. **17**(3), 257–278 (2002). https://doi.org/10.1080/026974502200005634

21. Rossetti, S.: Planning for Accessibility and Safety: theoretical framework and research methodologies to address people friendly mobility. Maggioli Editore, Sant'Arcangelo di Romagna (2020)

22. Caselli, B., Carra, M., Rossetti, S., Zazzi, M.: Exploring the 15-minute neighbourhoods: an evaluation based on the walkability performance to public facilities. Transp. Res. Procedia **60**, 346–353 (2022)

23. Tsigdinos, S., Latinopoulou, M., Paraskevopoulos, Y.: Network configuration as tool for improving pedestrian accessibility: Implementing a street design methodology in an Athenian neighbourhood. In: Proceedings of the 12thSpace Syntax Symposium, SSS2019, (2019)

24. Lamíquiz, P.J., López-Domínguez, J.: Effects of built environment on walking at the neighbourhood scale. a new role for street networks by modelling their configurational accessibility?. Transportation Research Part A: Policy and Practice, **74**(2015), 148–163 (2015). https://doi.org/10.1016/j.tra.2015.02.003

25. Lerman, Y., Rofè, Y., Omer, I.: Using space syntax to model pedestrian movement in urban transportation planning. Geogr. Anal. **46**(4), 392–410 (2014). https://doi.org/10.1111/gean. 12063
26. Garau, C., Annunziata, A., Yamu, C.: A walkability assessment tool coupling multicriteria analysis and space syntax: the case study of Iglesias, Italy, European Planning Studies, pp. 1–23 (2020). https://doi.org/10.1080/09654313.2020.1761947
27. Soares, I., Yamu, C., Weitkamp, G.: The relationship between the spatial configuration and the fourth sustainable dimension creativity in university campuses: the case study of Zernike Campus, Groningen, The Netherlands, Sustainability **12**, 9263 (2020). https://doi.org/10. 3390/su12219263
28. Salingaros, N.: Planning, complexity, and welcoming spaces: the case of campus design, Chapter 18. In: Gert, R., Claudia, Y., Christian, Z. (eds.): Handbook on Planning and Complexity, pp. 353–372 (2020)
29. Bott, H.: City and university: an architect's notes on an intriguing spatial relationship. In: Meusburger, P., Heffernan, M., Suarsana, L.: Geographies of the University, Knowledge and Space 12, Springer International Publishing, pp. 375- 437 (2018)
30. Università degli Studi di Parma, Unipr sostenibile, Mobilità. https://ateneosostenibile.unipr. it/mobilita/. Accessed 30 Mar 2023
31. Università degli Studi di Parma, Piano Urbanistico Attuativo: completamento e riorganizzazione funzionale del piano particolareggiato 1997 per il Campus Scienze e Tecnologie, Relazione introduttiva: il progetto MASTERCAMPUS e relazione tecnica (2016)
32. SPA srl., Complesso Universitario di Monserrato. Proposta di riordino e assestamento del piano Italposte. Relazione paesaggistica ai sensi del DPCM 12/12/200 (2018)
33. Hillier, B., Hanson, J.: The Social Logic of Space. Cambridge University Press (1984). https:// doi.org/10.1017/CBO9780511597237
34. Hillier, B.: Space is the Machine: A Configurational Theory of Architecture. Cambridge University Press (1996)
35. Cutini, V.: La rivincita dello spazio urbano. L'approccio configurazionale all'analisi e allo studio dei centri abitati. Pisa University Press, Pisa (2010)
36. Yamu, C., van Nes, A., Garau, C.: Bill Hillier's legacy: space syntax—a synopsis of basic concepts, measures, and empirical application. Sustainability **13**(6), 3394 (2021). https://doi. org/10.3390/su13063394
37. Yamu, C., van Nes, A.: Analysing linear spatial relationships: the measures of connectivity, integration, and choice. In: Introduction to Space Syntax in Urban Studies **78** (2021)
38. Ratti, C.: Space syntax: some inconsistencies. Environ. Plann. B. Plann. Des. **31**(4), 487–499 (2004). https://doi.org/10.1068/b3019
39. Pinna, F., Garau, C., Maltinti, F., Coni, M.: Beyond architectural barriers: building a bridge between disability and universal design. In: Gervasi, O., et al. (eds.) ICCSA 2020. LNCS, vol. 12255, pp. 706–721. Springer, Cham (2020). https://doi.org/10.1007/978-3-030-58820-5_51

A Data-Driven Approach for a City-University Mobility Plan: The Case of the University of Pisa

Diego Altafini$^{(\boxtimes)}$, Federico Mara, and Valerio Cutini

Dipartimento di Ingegneria dell'Energia, dei Sistemi, del Territorio e delle Costruzioni,
Università di Pisa, Largo Lucio Lazzarino, 1, 56122 Pisa (PI), Italy
`diego.altafini@phd.unipi.it`

Abstract. University campuses concentrate people movement within a city, being places of study, work, research, and co-presence. In that aspect, the university community travel patterns must be addressed through Commute Management Plans (CMPs) which provide guidelines to policymakers' actions which envision a transition towards sustainable mobility alternatives. CMPs are accessories to Sustainable Urban Mobility Plans (SUMPs), focused on analysing supply and demand for transport, the university staff movement patterns, and the origin-destination dynamics between their households and workplaces. Moreover, besides the staff-oriented evaluation, universities must also consider the students' commute patterns, as those comprise a significative part of their community. While in most cases, university structures are placed in few campuses, with movement concentration towards those areas and within them, many Italian Universities, such as the University of Pisa, present a distinct spatial organization, as its various structures are parcellated and diffused within the city area; a paradigmatic case of a "city-university" where moving in-between and within the university sites is moving within the city itself. Such characteristics require a data-driven approach that integrates spatial, configurational, and transportation analyses. Considering this, the paper discusses computational methods used to elaborate the University of Pisa's CMP and how a data-driven approach that integrates multi-domain analyses can highlight the movement patterns in a "city-university" context. The discussions and findings can serve as examples to other CMPs for universities within similar contexts – important, given their requirement by law in several European countries – or even as approaches to be incorporated in urban mobility and city master plans.

Keywords: Mobility Plan · University Campuses · Urban Analysis

1 Introduction

Sustainable Urban Mobility Plans (SUMPs) are designed to outline the urban and regional policies that encourage the shift towards sustainable transportation modes and foster projects in line with the UN Sustainable Development Goal for Cities and Human Settlements (SDG 11) [1, 2]. In Europe, since the Urban Mobility Package of 2013

O. Gervasi et al. (Eds.): ICCSA 2023 Workshops, LNCS 14111, pp. 401–417, 2023.
https://doi.org/10.1007/978-3-031-37126-4_27

[3], SUMPs are established as the main guidelines for transportation systems' infrastructure development, being a central instrument to improve accessibility of urbanized areas and to provide to the population high-quality mobility solutions and transport options towards, throughout, and within the cities [1, 3]. Through the investigation of citizen and stakeholder demands regarding transport, those plans often propose to reshape the way that people move around urban spaces, which in turn affects the livability and economic vitality of the cities [4, 5]. By providing a comprehensive framework for transportation-oriented development, SUMPs can assure that mobility systems and solutions are designed to support the needs of all residents, above all: those without access to personal vehicles, those in low-income households, and those with disabilities. Additionally, SUMPs can aid in the environmental component of cities' sustainability, by reducing traffic congestion and improving air quality, as well as by promoting actions towards public health through the encouragement of pedestrian and cycling movement [2, 6, 7].

In recent years, certain demographics have been subject to detailed Commute Management Plans (CMPs) which address the transportation requirements and criticalities that are specific to these populational groups. In their principle, CMPs are accessories that are to be integrated to the SUMPs [8], being focused plans produced for the municipality or regional mobility manager by the mobility managers of public and private corporate entities with over a stipulated number of members in their community; therefore, that impact urban or regional movement in a significant manner [9]. CMPs focus in reducing the commute impact of these groups within the city, through the planning of better workplace routines, and the encouraging of the use of public transport or micromobility options where possible, instead of personal vehicles usage. In Italy, University CMPs' consist in one of these specific cases; moreover, as regulated by the ministerial decree of May 12, 2021, they are mandatory, as universities are public institutions [10]. CMPs become a rather particular mobility plan within the universities' context since, beyond an often-large personnel component (professors, researchers and technicians), they are structures that generate and receive movement from an even larger populational group, the students, which have a daily commute towards and within the campus [11].

Planning instruments such as the CMPs assume an even greater importance in a world still be marked by the consequences of the Covid-19 pandemic [12]. In the last three years, the restrictions on national and international travel, plus the shops, schools and universities closures have led to a significant decrease in the demand for mobility which has also contracted the public transport supply [13]. The City of Pisa, in Italy, where the case was developed, has suffered a dramatic impact in those terms, as its social and economic structure is rather dependent on activity and movement generated by tourism and, above all, by the university activities. In effect, the University of Pisa community has grown over the last decades to a much greater extent than the dynamics of the city's demographic trend, assuming a large size compared to that of the resident population: a community of about 53,000 people associated to the university in a city with less than 90,000 inhabitants [14]. Moreover, the specificity of the University of Pisa case resides in the manner in which its buildings (administrative, research and teaching) are spatially structured. The patterns follow a parceled and capillary distribution over the urban territory, so as to represent the most paradigmatic example of a "city-university" (Fig. 1).

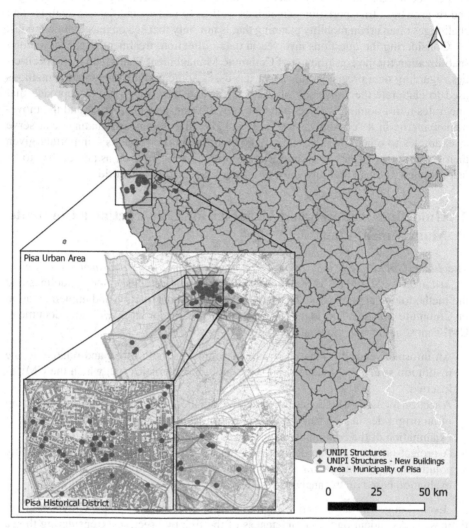

Fig. 1. The University of Pisa structures distribution: a "City-University".

In this sense, it is a university in which the spatial diffusion of its various buildings and campuses within the urban space materializes the integration that exists between its community and the city, as well as attest the interdependence between university issues and city-oriented issues.

While the pandemic brought economic challenges for the City of Pisa, it has also fueled some positive phenomena regarding urban mobility. The period verified a decrease in the use of public transport, yet it also shown an increase in pedestrian movements, in the use of bicycles, as well as verified a large increase in electric-based micromobility solutions [15], which all had an impact on the general traffic within the city. In that aspect, changes in the way urban planners structure SUMPs and CMPs in terms of data collection and analysis are needed to cope with the following period of changes and re-growth in transportation demand, as well as to understand the new realities and challenges of an urban mobility planning that is not only focused on mass public modes.

Considering the questions involved in data collection, treatment, organization and spatialization for the construction of Commute Management Plants, and their specificities regarding data precision, this paper discusses some computational-aided methods used to elaborate the University of Pisa's CMP and how a data-driven approach that integrates multi-domain analyses can highlight the transportation issues and the movement patterns in a "city-university" context. The discussions and findings can serve as examples to other CMPs for universities within similar contexts – important given their requirement by law in several European countries – or even as approaches to be incorporated in urban mobility and city master plans across the world.

2   Guidelines, Datasets and Variables for Constructing a Commute Management Plan

The *Linee Guida per la redazione e l'implementazione dei Piani degli Spostamenti Casa-Lavoro (PSCL)* [16] is the ministerial decree that establishes the guidelines and the methodological practices to be observed for to the construction and implementation of Commute Management Plans (CMPs) in Italy. In accordance with this document, CMPs must abide, at a minimal, to the following structure:

- An informative section, that describes the context – both urban and relative to the institution structures' location and personnel characteristics – in which the CMP is inserted.
- A section focused on assessing the criticalities in the community's mobility, consisting of an origin-destination study, a transportation supply and demand analysis, and an examination of the community's willingness to alter its commute habits.
- A project-oriented section dedicated to the design and implementation of mobility solutions, improvement strategies, plus the monitoring and ex-post-implementation evaluation based on the analyses results.

Even though the third section represents the main objective of a CMP, its effectiveness is dependent on the completeness of the first two sections. Considering this, a data-driven approach is important to assure up-to-date information regarding the community in question and its commute habits, as a manner to support the planning and sections of a mobility plan. Where possible, CMPs tend to employ internal-community surveys to collect metadata and construct the origin-destination datasets, to be used in conjunction with other – if available open-sourced – territorial and transportation supply datasets in the spatial analyses. In that aspect, University CMPs tend to differ from their corporate counterparts as they often deal with multiple destinations (structures, laboratories and campuses) and must accommodate the requirements of a larger and more heterogeneous community, as other than the university personnel, that itself comprehend several categories (professors, researchers, and technicians) all with different routines and demands, it also comprises the students, also with their different routines and demands [17]. Therefore, assuring the survey participation of the different communities within a community is also a challenge, that must be addressed through design. Moreover, there are several issues regarding data collection and aggregation that must be addressed. The next sections will provide an overview of the survey design and data collection procedures, as well as methods to spatialize the obtained datasets in a GIS environment, and the spatial databases and methods employed in the analysis [18].

2.1 Commute Behavior and Origin-Destination Survey Datasets – The Case of the University of Pisa

The University of Pisa Commute Management Plan survey was tailored to highlight the academic community's commute behavior and criticalities. The data collection period lasted for 40 days, from 6 June 2022 and ending on July 14, 2022. A website was created to redirect to, detail, and explain the survey, its objectives, and procedures [19].

Drafted and applied through the *Microsoft Forms* platform [20], the survey consisted of 25 individual questions, organized in ramifications that divided the paths for personnel and students-oriented questions, to understand particularities about these groups. Of these, 20 were structured as "multiple-choice" with two being "open multiple-choice" questions regarding critical aspects in the commute and the propension to change transportation modes, thus allowing more than one answer. The remaining 5 questions were proposed as "open-answer" questions, to allow respondents to express criticalities not foreseen in the survey. The time to complete the survey was predetermined to be between 3 and 10 min, with an observed average response time of 5:48 min [17].

The response rate was significant, as 11,812 people have completed the survey, corresponding to 22.4% of the University of Pisa community (52,669 individuals), a sample that allowed statistical significance and very high confidence levels to be reached (Fig. 2).

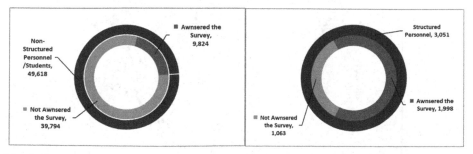

Fig. 2. Survey response rate, divided by group, in relation to the University of Pisa community total.

In accordance with demographics, this percentual is divided into 16.8%, associated to the structured personnel (professors, researchers, and technicians) – around 65.2% of the total of this group. The remainder 83.2%, correspond to the aggregate between non-structured personnel (post-graduate researchers and doctoral students) and undergraduate students. (Fig. 2). Despite included in the students' component, the non-structured personnel (mainly associated to research duties) have commute habits that are similar to the structured personnel, with designated departments and office spaces. Hence, for the analysis procedures, they were incorporated into the structured personnel group.

The construction of datasets based on the surveyed information was carried out under the binding requirement to ensure the anonymity of the respondents in accordance with the European legislation on data protection and privacy (GDPR - Regulation (EU) 2016/679, as amended on 23 May 2018) [21]. In effect, this presents an important issue regarding the spatial accuracy in the origin-destination analysis since precise origin addresses could not be collected, georeferenced, and spatialized.

To resolve this problem and attain a sufficient precision, while still in compliance with the GDPR, the survey used the Italian Postal Code *(Codice di Avviamento Postale – CAP)* as means to identify the respondents place of residence. From each CAP a set of

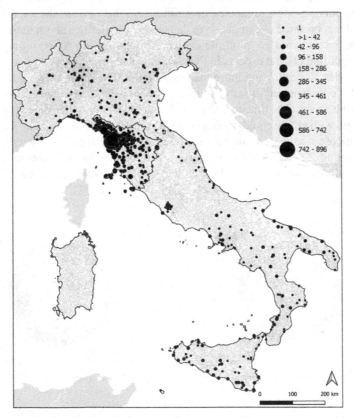

Fig. 3. Origin points distribution – information incorporates all survey answers without commute frequency distinctions.

coordinates was generated through the application GPS Visualizer [22] then aggregated according to their frequency and point-georeferenced on GIS (Fig. 3) [18].

Further on, the origin points dataset was incorporated with data regarding the commute frequency to differentiate regular from occasional commuters and to identify any respondents that do not commute at all – mostly students in distance learning.

The surveyed metadata is outlined in a diagram (Fig. 4). It describes the connections between the fields and highlights the general method/type of analysis used.

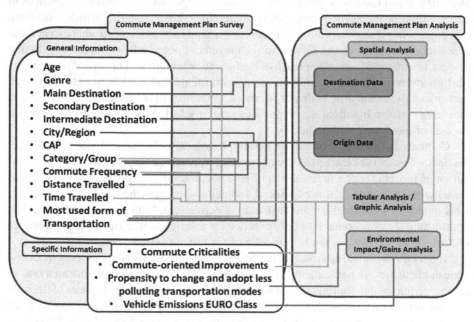

Fig. 4. CMP survey structure outline, contents, connections, and analysis diagram.

The results from the survey are divided in general information and specific information – this mainly collected from "open multiple-choice" and "open answers". From the general information data, origins and destinations datasets are aggregated, respectively, by "CAP" and by "Structure of Destination" (divided among main, secondary, and intermediate). This data is predominantly used to structure the base spatial analysis made in GIS [18] and is incorporated with variables such as the respondents' category/group, commute frequency, and most used form of transportation. Transportation related variables, when associated to the points of origin and destination allow to highlight specific dynamics related to the structures usage/accessibility to determined types of transport (Pedestrian, Bicycles, Public Transport and Automobiles) and to the movement towards and between the university structures.

Regarding identifying the inner-city movement patterns, several network models based on the Space Syntax methodology [22] were used to represent movement potentials within the City of Pisa. Those describe the relative accessibility and the *preferential routes* towards each university building. The use of *Space Syntax* is a rather innovative approach made in the University of Pisa CMP, and was intended to explain the urban dynamics given the university structures dispersion, a pattern that configures Pisa as a "city-university".

2.2 Spatial Datasets – University Within the City of Pisa Urban Context

The spatial structure of an urban aggregate has decisive effects on the settlement context and on the general conditions of accessibility towards its various spaces. Therefore, analyzing urban road-network morphology and configuration can reveal differences in accessibility, or the *relative accessibility* hierarchies. Understanding which spaces are more accessible than others allow to make comparisons and evaluate to what extent these characteristics influence the distribution of movement potentials within the city. In that respect, the methodological approach of configurational analysis known as *Space Syntax* [23] provides a suitable set of operational instruments and models to detect, through network analysis, the distribution of *relative accessibility* in urban spaces. Moreover, its measures can also highlight the *preferential routes*, selected by users in their presumed choices of movement within the city.

Compared to other approaches for the morphological and relational analysis of space, the *Space Syntax* is characterized by its capacity to combine tangible factors (the distribution of movement, the organization of land use, the internal geography of inhabited areas) with intangible factors of a social and cultural nature (the cognitive and behavioral modes of individuals, individual and collective social interaction relations), thus constituting the conceptual basis of reference for a series of non-discursive techniques of analysis of built space, and in particular of the urban environment.

The methodological approach of the Space Syntax draws its analysis tools from discrete mathematics, in particular from graph theory, in which road-graphs are analyzed to determine the spatial-configurational relations between the streets and spaces of the built environment, so as to attribute to each road-element their own characteristics of network centrality. Such an analysis can be conducted either on a general global scale (the entire network corresponding to the grid of a settlement), or by setting specific limits or radii corresponding to the size of the analysis area (whether metric or topological), demonstrating considerable flexibility of use. The existence of a proven correlation between pedestrian movement, vehicular movement and the configuration of urban space, following decades of theoretical and applicative experience [23–26], attests to the solid methodological foundation of Space Syntax, whose set of analysis tools lends itself to being used individually or in various forms of combination.

Space Syntax was used for the University of Pisa's CMP in order to model the movement structure in-between its several buildings. The analysis, carried out using road-graph data obtained from OpenStreetMap [27], focused on two indicators: the *Angular Integration index* and the *Angular Choice* index, in its normalized forms. The metrics were calculated through the software DepthMapX 0.8 [28] on a global scale (Rn) – the entire extension of Pisa's urban network – focused on estimating vehicular traffic, and using a radius limited to 1,200 m (R1200), equivalent to the average distance that can be covered in 15 min on foot [29]. *Angular Integration* and *Angular Choice* definitions, as well as the formulas used in the normalized measures [24] are summarized in Table 1.

Once completed, the *Space Syntax* models were exported to a GIS environment, where, combined with the University of Pisa's structures' location datasets, made available by the University and organized by the authors for the CMP (Fig. 1), a comparative analysis was made to highlight the movement patterns within the city global and local structures.

Table 1. Space Syntax ASA metrics – Angular Integration and Choice

Space Syntax	Graph Theory Equivalent	Formulas: Space Syntax	Concept
Integration (int.)	*Closeness Centrality*	$NAIN = \dfrac{n^{1.2}}{ATD_\alpha^\ell(x)}$ $NAIN_{RM\,1200} = \log(AInt + 2)$	Depicts *relative accessibility* (to-movement) – or the topological proximity of one road-element to all other road-elements
Choice (ch.)	*Betweenness centrality*	$NACH = \dfrac{Log(ACh_\alpha^\ell(x)+1)}{log(ATD_\alpha^\ell(x)+3)}$ $NACH - M_{RM\,1200} = \log(ACh + 2)$	Indicates the *preferential routes* – or the most travelled paths (through-movement) within the system, given the shortest path between a road-element and all other road-elements

Besides the configurational analysis, other kinds of spatial analysis were also part of the CMP. Another data-driven computational analysis was the isochrones-based approach to assess the correlation between the University of Pisa's structures' location and the micromobility stations (i.e. city bikes, e-bikes and electric scooters). Data on the station distribution was provided by the City of Pisa's Urban Mobility Agency – PISAMO [29] and covered the municipality designated spaces for the positioning of the mobility equipment. While these transportation modes function as "soft mobility" and have capillary availability within the city, meaning they are also available throughout the cities outside the designated parking spaces, the municipality designated spaces concentrate the locations with highest availability at any time.

The combined spatial datasets are used to evaluate the *accessibility* patterns from the university structures towards the micromobility stations given a set radius established by the isochrones' areas. The isochrones curves, constructed through the OpenRouteService (ORS) [30] and correspond to travel-times of 2 min and 5 min on foot from the university structures, considering the morphology of the area. Correlations are established when there is a designated parking space within the isochrones' radius.

3 A Data-Driven Approach for the Commute Management Plan – A Discussion of the Results Obtained for the University of Pisa CMP

Given the characteristics of the urban environment of Pisa, that has a rather small urbanized area, in comparison to the total municipality territory, the University of Pisa's Commute Management Plan objectives were structured in two main areas: promote an increase in micromobility usage in movements towards and between the structures; and reduce the usage of combustion-engine personal vehicles, through pedestrianization or mixed mobility solutions (train + pedestrian; bus + pedestrian; train + micromobility). In that aspect, the analysis of the movement dynamics within the urban area was important to define in which areas and structures the governance practices should be adopted.

The analysis of the global *relative accessibility* (Normalized Angular Integration index - NAIN) for the municipality of Pisa road-circulation network (Fig. 5, NAIN) reveals a rather particular urban movement concentration. This is characterized by the fact that the road-elements with the highest *relative accessibility* scores (here, represented in the red color) correspond to the extra urban roads, highways that extend around the medieval walls that encircle the historical centre – area where most of the university buildings are located.

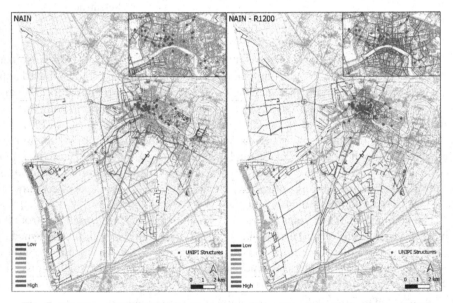

Fig. 5. NAIN and NAIN R1200 – University of Pisa Structures (Color figure online)

On the other hand, the innermost area of Pisa's historic centre presents intermediate values of integration (here, highlighted in the shades of yellow and green) (Fig. 5, NAIN), which attest a just modest *relative accessibility* and a lower potential of attractiveness of movement at a global scale (Fig. 5). From this standpoint, the analysis' results demon-strate that even if the historical centre was not already regulated as a Limited Traffic Zone (LTZ or ZTL), the area would only, marginally, attract vehicular traffic. This high-lights the vocation of Pisa's historical center as a pedestrian area, since its configuration naturally concentrate movements outside the innermost areas. Furthermore, the axes constituted by the two Arno River marginal roads represent the "load-bearing" elements of *relative accessibility* in the historic center. In that aspect, it is justified that they are excluded from the LTZ by the municipal authority. Due to the distance of the road axes that correspond to the spatial elements of greater centrality, the coastal area is consider-ably more segregated than the other urban spaces, presenting many areas characterised by a modest degree of relative accessibility (here, highlighted in blue) (Fig. 5, NAIN). Such a situation is also emphasised by the presence of individual connections to the historic centre area that lead to high values of the integration index on a limited number of street elements.

The movement potentials' distribution change considerably if a limited sphere of analysis – the 1,200 m radius – is considered (Fig. 5, NAIN R1200). The road-elements located within Pisa's historic centre are now assigned the highest values for *relative accessibility*, a pattern of increase that also observed in the centres of the coastal urban agglomerates. Since the metric radius of 1,200 m corresponds approximately to the distance that can be covered in 15 min on foot [28] or in 5 min by bicycle or scooter, it is conceivable that this pattern reproduces the distribution of accessibility levels for pedestrian movements or other forms of micromobility. In this respect, the measure highlights the historic centre of Pisa as its portion most suited to pedestrian use or with soft forms of mobility. Moreover, it can be stated that Pisa itself is a *15-min city*, since its *relative accessibility* core, at a metric radius advance into the residential areas positioned in the immediate vicinity of the historical centre, meaning that it is possible to walk towards the city centre, where most urban equipment – and university structures – are located, without a dependence on public transportation.

The global *choice* index (*Normalized Angular Choice* - NACH) provides a restitution of the hierarchy of *preferential vehicular routes* in the road system of Pisa (Fig. 6, NACH). The distribution of the *choice* index values confirms the patterns of movement potentials observed in the global *integration* index, where the most travelled routes (here, depicted in red) are those in the margins of the historical centre area, being the same as those with the highest *relative accessibility* roads. Furthermore, it can be observed that the innermost areas of the historical centre are – likewise with the *integration* – devoid of preferential routes at global scale, thus, vehicular movement would not tend to naturally pass through this area of the city. The *choice* index, once again, demonstrates the role of Arno River's marginal axes as "load-bearing" structures, as those road-elements concentrate through movement within central Pisa (Fig. 6, NACH).

The patterns of through-movement change considerably when *choice* modelling is restricted to a radius (Fig. 6, NACH – R1200). The innermost areas of the historical centre once again become the locus of through-movement in Pisa. In that aspect, the road-elements denote the sub-structure oriented to local pedestrian and bicycle movements.

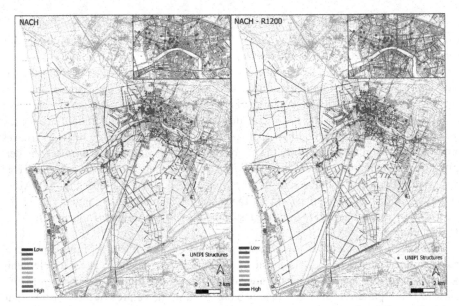

Fig. 6. NACH and NACH R1200 – University of Pisa Structures (Color figure online)

The local *choice* index (Fig. 6, NAIN R1200), when confronted with the distribution of the cycling roads and designated spaces for the micromobility stations (Fig. 7) reveal interesting patterns regarding the movement dynamics within Pisa's urban area, and the accessibility towards the University Structures. Moreover, it also describes how the historical centre is linked to the residential areas through soft mobility.

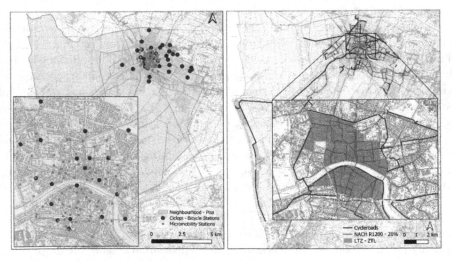

Fig. 7. Micromobility stations and NACH R1200 20% structure of movement

The cycleroads (Fig. 7) form a grid, together with the local through-movement structure – which is mostly located within the Limited Traffic Zone (LTZ – ZTL). This grid constitutes a continuity of spaces for micromobility and bicycle traffic, allowing access from the residential areas towards the centre and, by extent, towards the university structures.

In that regard, when considering the spatial correlation among the distribution of the micromobility stations (Fig. 7) in relation to the University of Pisa structures (Figs. 5, 6 and 8), it can be observed that the most of the buildings located in the central area are accessible in 2 min on foot and all within 5 min on foot. This coverage begins to rare near the outermost structures (Engineering building to the west and the University Hospital to the east), demonstrating some polarization in their immediate availability. In that aspect, potentializing the availability towards other areas not yet covered should be the main focus of the university actions towards incentivizing micromobility solutions.

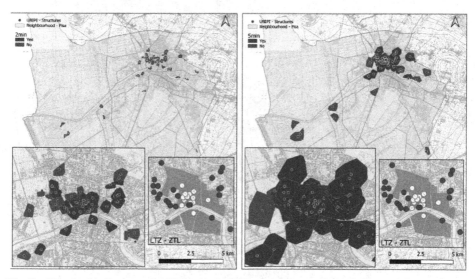

Fig. 8. Correlation between the University of Pisa structures and the designated spaces for the placement of micromobility structures. Isochrones calculated for 2 min and 5 min.

These proposals and conclusions regarding an improvement on micromobility conditions can be highlighted in Fig. 9, that spatializes the survey data regarding destinations in accordance with the most frequently utilized transportation mode. It is possible to see that, beyond pedestrian movement, bicycle movement correspond to the most frequently used transport modes towards the University of Pisa structures. However, the car component is still expressive on the outermost areas that are still accessible through pedestrian and bicycle movement – as seen on the previous analysis – but have a lower degree of *relative accessibility*. These results demonstrate that a data-driven approach can aid in the decision-making processes, and individuate actions based on movement estimation.

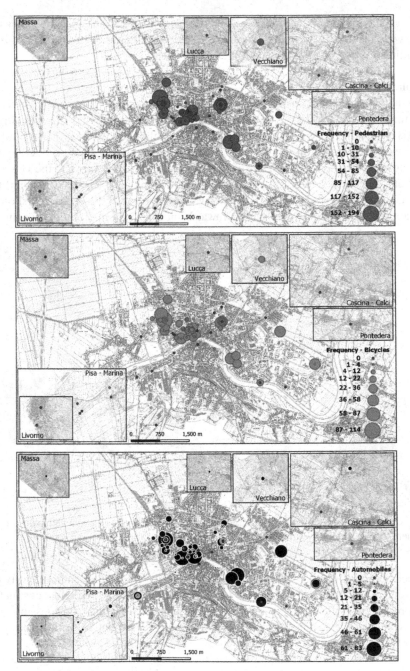

Fig. 9. Transport modes frequency towards the University of Pisa Structures – pedestrian movement, bicycle movement and automobiles movement

4   Concluding Remarks

Pisa proves to be an emblematic case as a city-university. With a large academic community, the University of Pisa's CMP becomes an essential instrument in the overall assessment and management of the mobility of the city and its interconnected surrounding areas. University of Pisa's uniqueness is also due to the diffuse location of its university facilities, which, given their spatial displacement and the functions contained in each one of the facilities, can be considered an almost as its own 15-min city. Nevertheless, the methodological approach thought and adopted to construct this CMP is independent of the uniqueness of the city and can be replicated in the most diverse urban contexts, for the realization of other CMPs. In this way, it would be possible to compare qualitatively and quantitatively structurally different contexts, deepening the fundamental relationships - which play a key role in university cities - between urban form, location of university facilities, infrastructure, and transport services.

In general, the conclusions made with the aid of the CMP, for the improvement of University's mobility can be summarized in 3 points: interventions to be promoted to improve urban sustainability, which are the direct results of the analysis discussed so far; methodological evaluation and efficacy; general considerations on CMPs.

The actions planned on the basis of the analyses carried out can be divided into two categories: actions that can be implemented directly by the university administration and larger-scale actions to be implemented in concert with external, public or private organizations. The former includes the following proposals: increasing parking spaces for bicycles and scooters, improving the usability of these areas and increasing their safety, implementing policies to encourage the use of sustainable means of transport and creating a permanent sustainability office. The latter, instead, include the following measures: stipulating students-specific conventions with lower prices, enhancing the regional and urban transport offer, strategical deploying of bike-sharing and scooter services, increasing the safety and recognizability of existing cycle routes and creating new strategic routes. It is this very second set of interventions that clearly demonstrates the need for close collaboration between universities and external organizations to make the city's mobility more efficient and sustainable. However, for the specific discussion of these interventions and the specific rationale behind them, please refer directly to the CMP [17].

From the methodological point of view, the effectiveness of Space Syntax theory in the reading of the urban fabric for the determination of preferential routes and the potential for movement – both from a vehicular as well as from a bicycle and pedestrian point of view – is confirmed. This, therefore, allowed multiscale analysis and, consequently, the determination of the criticalities of the existing network and services. In addition, the use of movement isochrones together with the configurational analysis described above made it possible to assess the actual use of mobility services by the university community. This made it possible to analyze the existing flows and assess the potential of the actual service without the need for modelling tools that include additional – unnecessary, for this type of analysis – complexity. Moreover, the importance of the movement data of specific classes of users emerges, as well as the difficulty in obtaining them –purposely designed and targeted surveys the only way. From an analytical standpoint, the need for sufficiently large samples with a significant composition (stratified sample) emerges.

This implies the need to raise the university community's awareness of the issue and promote a bottom-up approach, which is in fact part of the measures proposed by the CMP.

From a general point of view, it emerged that CMPs are an excellent instrument for assessing mobility and proposing guidelines to reduce pollution. In particular, they can contribute significantly – especially in university towns with large university communities – towards the goal of sustainable urban mobility.

According to this, it is illogical that CMPs could potentially not include the students, which represent the most consistent part of the community. It also emerged that the lack of integration of the CMP and SUMP in university cities - and in diffuse ones – represents a strong criticality considering that flows related to the university community represent a significant part of the city flows. In addition to causing a lack of comprehensive analyses, this lack of integration also means that it is impossible to implement effective and integrated project proposals that can effectively affect urban and suburban mobility. For this reason, it is highly recommended a greater integration between these plans and also between local, municipal and regional transport authorities, in order to fully include the CMP in city planning and promote sustainable urban mobility accordingly to the sustainability goals (SDGs) promoted by the UN.

References

1. United Nations (2022) The Sustainable Development Goals Report 2022. https://unstats.un. org/sdgs/report/2022/. Accessed 12 Jan 2022
2. European Commission (2007). *Sustainable Urban Transport Plans.* Preparatory Document in Relation to the Follow-Up of the Thematic Strategy on the Urban Environment, European Commission. https://ec.europa.eu/transport/sites/transport/files/themes/urban/studies/doc/2007_sutainable_urban_transport_plan.pdf. Accessed 12 Jan 2022
3. European Union. A Concept for Sustainable Urban Mobility Plan (2013). https://transport.ec.europa.eu/transport-themes/clean-transport-urban-transport/urban-mobility/urban-mobility-actions/sustainable-urban-mobility-plans_en. Accessed 12 Jan 2022
4. Kiba-Janiak, M., Witkowski, J.: Sustainable urban mobility plans: how do they work? Sustainability **11**(17), 4605 (2019)
5. Torrisi, V., Garau, C., Ignaccolo, M., Inturri, G.: Sustainable urban mobility plans": key concepts and a critical revision on SUMPs guidelines. In: , et al. Computational Science and Its Applications – ICCSA 2020. ICCSA 2020. Lecture Notes in Computer Science, **12255**. Springer, Cham (2020). https://doi.org/10.1007/978-3-030-58820-5_45
6. Garau, C., Pavan, V.M.: Evaluating urban quality: indicators and assessment tools for smart sustainable cities. Sustainability **10**(3), 575 (2018)
7. Louro, A., da Costa, N.M., da Costa, E.M.: Sustainable urban mobility policies as a path to healthy cities—the case study of LMA, Portugal. Sustainability **11**, 2929 (2019)
8. Rupprecht Consult (editor). Guidelines for Developing and Implementing a Sustainable Urban Mobility Plan. Second Edition (2019)
9. Repubblica Italina – Decreto ministeriale 27 marzo 1998, "Mobilità sostenibile delle aree urbane"
10. Repubblica Italiana - Decreto interministeriale 12 maggio 2021, "Modalità attuative delle disposizioni relative alla figura del Mobility Manager."

11. Ribeiro, P., Fonseca, F., Meireles, T.: Sustainable mobility patterns to university campuses: evaluation and constraints. Case Studies on Transport Policy **8**(2), 639–647, ISSN 2213–624X (2020)
12. Campisi, T., Basbas, S., Al-Rashid, M.A., Tesoriere, G., Georgiadis, G.: A regionwide survey on emotional and psychological impacts of COVID-19 on public transport choices in Sicily, Italy. Trans. Transp. Sci. **2**(2021), 1–10 (2021)
13. Cartenì, A., Di Francesco, L., Henke, I., Marino, T.V., Falanga, A.: The role of public transport during the second COVID-19 wave in Italy. Sustainability **13**(21), 11905 (2021)
14. ISTAT (2022) Popolazione Residente e Dinamica Demografica - Anno 2021 (2022). https://www.istat.it/it/files//2022/12/CENSIMENTO-E-DINAMICA-DEMOGRAFICA-2021.pdf. Accessed 12 Jan 2022
15. "Bilancio 2021 di Pisamo: ottimi risultati dal potenziamento della mobilità green", PisaToday (2022). https://www.pisatoday.it/cronaca/bilancio-2021-budget-2022-pisamo.html
16. Repubblica Italiana - Decreto dirigenziale 4 agosto 2021, n. 209
17. Altafini, D., Cutini, V.: Piano di Spostamento Casa-Lavoro/Studio - Università di Pisa (PSCL – 2022) (2023). https://mobility.unipi.it/p-s-c-l/. Accessed 20 Jan 2023
18. QGIS, version 3.22 (2022). http://www.qgis.org/en/site/index.html
19. Portale UniPi Sostenibile - https://sostenibile.UniPI.it/sondaggio/
20. Microsoft (2022). Microsoft Forms,
21. European Union (2018) Regolamento 2016/679 del Parlamento Europeo, rettificato il (2018). "Regolamento generale sulla protezione dei dati"
22. GPS Visualizer: Do-It-Yourself Mapping (2022). https://www.gpsvisualizer.com/
23. Hillier, B., Hanson, J.: The Social Logic of Space. Cambridge University Press, Cambridge (1984)
24. Hillier, B.: Space is the Machine: A Configurational Theory of Architecture. Cambridge University Press, Cambridge (2007)
25. Cutini, V.: La rivincita dello spazio urbano. L'approccio configurazionale all'analisi e allo studio dei centri abitati. Pisa University Press, Pisa (2010)
26. Van Nes, A., Yamu, C.: Introduction to Space Syntax in Urban Studies, p. 250. Springer Nature (2021). https://doi.org/10.1007/978-3-030-59140-3
27. OpenStreetMap Contributors (2022). https://planet.openstreetmap.org
28. depthmapX development team. (2018). depthmapX (Version 0.8.0) [Computer software]. https://github.com/SpaceGroupUCL/depthmapX/
29. Yamu, C., Garau, C. (2022). The 15-min city: a configurational approach for understanding the spatial, economic, and cognitive context of walkability in Vienna. In: International Conference on Computational Science and Its Applications, pp. 387–404. Springer, Cham. https://doi.org/10.1007/978-3-031-10536-4_26
30. OpenRouteService - ORS Tools – QGIS Plugin. https://github.com/GIScience/orstools-qgis-plugin/wiki/

Developing a Parsimonious Classification of Traffic Analysis Zones Using a Large Number of Accessibility Indicators and Transportation Level of Service

Konstadinos G. Goulias[✉]

University of California, Santa Barbara, CA 93106, USA
kgoulias@ucsb.edu

Abstract. Accessibility, the ease or difficulty with which activity opportunities can be reached from a given location, can be measured using the cumulative number of opportunities from an origin within a given amount of travel time and/or distance. Estimating accessibility indicators is used to show the level of service quality offered by a transportation system and as explanatory factors of travel behavior equations in transportation modeling and simulation. With the availability of large quantities of data, detailed representation of transportation networks (a set of nodes and links forming a graph), and level of service often measured in movement speed on network links, analysts can compute hundreds of accessibility indicators. Reporting of all these indicators is tedious, cumbersome, and too complicated. In this paper, the combination of principal component analysis to extract summaries of service quality from 190 indicators is demonstrated. Each of these indicators is computed for 1822 traffic analysis zones (TAZ - a convenient geographic subdivision used to model transportation systems) covering the entire country of Qatar in the Arabian Peninsula. Then, a small number of principal components (e.g., 27 components capturing 91.6% of the variance of 190 variables) are used to classify each TAZ in a group with clearly identifiable characteristics using hierarchical clustering. In this paper experiments with different subsets of the 190 indicators are also used to show how one can distinguish among different levels of service offered at each of the TAZs analyzed by time of day and means of travel.

Keywords: Accessibility · Opportunities · Principal Components · Clustering

1 Introduction

Accessibility is the ease (or difficulty) with which activity opportunities may be reached from a given location using one or more means of travel (transportation modes). Defined in this way, accessibility indicators (or measures) incorporate the spatial distribution of land-use activities and the performance of a transportation system within a given area. Accessibility indicators are needed for a variety of regional planning and modeling purposes, such as characterizing quality of life [1], describing transportation quality of

© The Author(s), under exclusive license to Springer Nature Switzerland AG 2023
O. Gervasi et al. (Eds.): ICCSA 2023 Workshops, LNCS 14111, pp. 418–436, 2023.
https://doi.org/10.1007/978-3-031-37126-4_28

service [2], measuring jobs and housing lack of balance [3], as a tool to assess inequity in spatial organization of activities and transportation [4], the dynamics of inequity evolution [5], and the study of reachable opportunities using non-motorized modes such as walking and bicycling [6]. A review of many different accessibility estimation methods employed in the past to serve a variety of purposes can be found in [7].

In this paper emphasis is given to accessibility indicators using the idea of "intervening opportunities." In the context of developing a large-scale activity-based microsimulation model for travel demand forecasting [8], accessibility indicators are computed by enumerating and cumulating the opportunities that are found within the area covered by a certain travel time from an origin point (in essence building buffers around points in space). This formulation is particularly intuitive, because it allows one to identify different travel time thresholds (e.g., 10 min, 20 min, and 50 min) and create geographic "buffers" within which activity opportunities that can be reached are counted. Travel time is measured using the speed of travel on the network by any mode of travel. This accessibility formulation is both a function of land use patterns and the performance of the transportation system [9]. The main application envisioned for the techniques presented here is functional classification of hierarchically classified zones to distinguish the center of a region or city from suburbs, exurbs, and rural geographies to then be used in simulation [10]. In this paper a new method is presented that first develops indicators similar to [9] that were developed for Southern California and expanded to include additional level of service data to achieve a more comprehensive representation of opportunities and level of service.

The geographic area of interest in this paper is the State of Qatar. However, the methods developed and illustrated use data that are often available from agencies that routinely provide information about the spatial distribution of employed persons by industry type and the transportation network that serves them. The unique aspect of our current method is that "static" sources of data are combined with secondary data on the temporal (within a day) availability of opportunities and the condition of the transportation network to develop accessibility indicators that vary by time of day. One outcome of the research here is a set of time-sequenced maps of activity opportunity availability and a classification of the TAZs by their access to these opportunities that are then used to create the final zonal classification. To achieve this, network and socioeconomic data at a fine level are prepared, and a methodology that integrates spatial/temporal factors reflecting the variation in available opportunities and travel time during the day is created. To the best of my knowledge this is the first time an analysis using this type of data and this type of zonal classification has ever been tested.

Section 2 describes the data used in the current research effort and outlines data processing and preparation details. Section 3 discusses the methodology for extracting the variance using principal components from accessibility indicators and then through hierarchical clustering classify geographical areas that are mapped for comparisons. Section 4 presents the analysis and results, and the last section provides a brief summary and next steps.

2 Data Used Here

The data used to develop traffic analysis zone classification are the accessibility indicators that are computed for each zone using a variety of databases available by different agencies in Qatar [11] aiming at the provision of accessibility indicators to be used in the models described in [12]. A first set of attributes are assigned to each of the 1822 zones and they are:

1. Employment by type from values in a land use database
2. Dwelling units by type from an inventory in parcel data
3. Lane kilometers by roadway type from a network database
4. Transit stops from an inventory in a shape file
5. Parking locations and size from an inventory with estimates from buildings and roadways
6. School types and capacity from an inventory of schools by type
7. TAZ area - computed from a GIS shape file

In this paper focus is on employment, travel time by roadway and public transportation, travel distance by roadway and public transportation, and the area of each TAZ. Travel times by car and public transportation are the outputs from a transportation simulation. The attributes are also divided into three groups depending on time of day corresponding to approximately morning peak travel period (AM peak from 6:00 to 8:59), midday (Midday 12:00 to 14:59), and after noon peak period (PM peak 17:00 to 19:59). Opportunities change by time of day due to opening and closing hours of stores and/or other restrictions of operations. In this application information was used from place-based diaries of households (attempting to interview every person in a household) and immigrant workers (called laborers in Qatar) of arrival at work and departure from work of respondents to build time of day profiles of workers in different industry sectors. Then, these profiles are converted into percentages of service availability offered by each TAZ and used to modify the availability of opportunities in each zone by each type of industry. This approach in essence attempts to capture the opening and closing hours of business establishments and the portion of the jobs capacity that is available to people for services throughout a day. A similar approach was used successfully in Southern California [9].

The basic process of accessibility calculation is as follows:

1. Start with a TAZ database that contains the attributes we want to convert to accessibilities as columns and the TAZs as rows.
2. Create a TAZ to TAZ database that contains the criteria for buffers (e.g., travel times from zone to zone or travel distances from zone to zone using the output of the transportation simulator.
3. Define a set of buffers to use (e.g., 0–10, 10–20, and 20–50 min travel time). These are "rings" around the centroid of each zone.
4. Select for each origin zone the zones that are within each of the set of buffers by creating a neighborhood matrix.
5. Sum the attributes of the zones that are within the neighborhoods defined in points 2 and 3.

6. Allocate these counts of attributes to each origin zone.

The process above allows any type of buffer and neighborhood decay functions of attractiveness or proximity and any type of zonal attributes that can be counted. This is also the portion of the accessibility computation that is designed to be eventually integrated in a transportation simulation system in Qatar called the Qatar Activity Based Model [12]. In this example of application, the accessibility computation is based on an aggregated type of jobs that are four categories: a) Construction; b) Leisure that includes accommodation, foodservice, arts, entertainment, and recreation; c) Service that includes finance and insurance, real estate, administrative and support services, public administration, health and social work, and other services; and d) All Other not included in the three groups above. These categories can be modified at will depending on the available data. In summary, we have 4 types of employment in 3 time of day periods within 3 buffers of travel time and travel distance from the centroid of each TAZ. Travel time buffers are 10 min, 10 to 20 min, and 20 to 50 min based on a distribution of trips observed in surveys. Similarly, the travel distance buffers are 2 km, 2 to 5 km, and 5 to 20 km. Table 1 shows a small sample of the 190 indicators that are used here reporting only indicators for the morning peak using travel time of 10 min buffer zones and buffer zones at the distance of 2 km.

3   Method

The method used here belongs in the cluster analysis family of methods that aim to divide observations into groups according to the values of variables these groups have in common. The ultimate objective is to partition the data in such a way that zones with high density and diversity of opportunities and a good roadway system and public transportation service end up in the same group because they are similar. We also know there is some degree of continuity in similarity in space for land use and for the transportation service provided. In this way zones that are adjacent to each other also have similar characteristics, but we also know we may have abrupt differences in space (see photos in Appendix A). The classification method used needs to be sensitive to both continuity and abrupt differences.

It is usual to differentiate between methods that are algorithmic, and they discern patterns in multidimensional data clouds (these are also labeled unsupervised methods) and methods that are model-based and require assumptions about the data generating mixing of distributions. The algorithmic approaches are the earliest clustering techniques and include the well-known K-means, K-medoids, and hierarchical clustering among many others [13]. Early concerns about important questions on deciding about the right number of clusters, treatment of outliers, and uncertainty about the right partition motivated the second family of methods that specify a probability model for the data (e.g., the likelihood function). To fill this void model-based cluster methods were developed that make assumptions about the probability distributions of the data analyzed (in reality a mixture of these distributions as in [14] and evolved into a major field of data that span the entire taxonomy of data types from simple continuous variables to text [15].

One of the thorniest problems in model-based clustering, however, is the specification of joint distributions of data that are fundamentally different such as binary variables

Table 1. A selection of the variables used to create principal components and clusters

Characteristic	N = 1,822 Mean [Median] (SD)
Number of persons employed in the construction sector that can be reached within 10 min by roadway in the AM morning peak	26,411.0 [18,638.3] (27,439.9)
Number of persons employed in the leisure sector that can be reached within 10 min by roadway in the AM morning peak	4,725.7 [816.6] (9,627.1)
Number of persons employed in the service sector that can be reached within 10 min by roadway in the AM morning peak	5,482.7 [1,350.2] (7,190.5)
Number of persons employed in all other sectors that can be reached within 10 min by roadway in the AM morning peak	6,875.7 [1,847.7] (21,500.1)
Total lane kilometers within 10 min by roadway in the AM morning peak	325.7 [311.9] (167.3)
Total number of public transport (transit) stops that can be reached in 10 min by roadway in the AM morning peak	60.4 [66.0] (36.7)
Number of persons employed in the construction sector that can be reached within 2 km by roadway in the AM morning peak	9,741.2 [4,280.8] (13,948.0)
Number of persons employed in the leisure sector that can be reached within 2 km by roadway in the AM morning peak	1,572.2 [122.6] (3,892.7)
Number of persons employed in the service sector that can be reached within 2 km by roadway in the AM morning peak	2,040.4 [133.8] (4,061.7)
Number of persons employed in all other sectors that can be reached within 2 km by roadway in the AM morning peak	1,457.1 [397.9] (7,485.4)
Total lane kilometers within 2 km by roadway in the AM morning peak	100.4 [102.6] (52.5)
Total number of public transport (transit) stops that can be reached within 2 km by roadway in the AM morning peak	23.5 [20.0] (20.0)

Note: Note: Travel time and distance buffers around a TAZ centroid are computed using time and distance measured along the network of roadways, area is the sum of the square kilometers of each TAZ reached, AM morning peak period is from 6:00 to 8:59

with multicategory variables and continuous variables and the restrictive assumptions needed to write the likelihood function that will be used to estimate model parameters [16, 17]. To avoid imposing restrictive assumptions on our data and to avoid issues with skewed distributions (see Table 1), a model-free algorithmic method in creating clusters is used here. This method takes advantage of more recent developments in data analysis of mixed types of variables (discrete and continuous) and a variety of diagnostics about cluster quality. The method used here is a distance-based clustering of mixed data [18]. The word "mixed" refers to quantitative (continuous numeric data of any distribution) and qualitative (categorical factor data). In this accessibility application we consider all indicators to be quantitative and continuous. Cluster analysis in this approach is the second step after a data combination and reduction step based on principal component analysis (PCA). The data are viewed as a table of rows representing the TAZs and columns representing the attributes standardized (subtract their mean and divide by their standard deviation). This decreases the possibility that one variable "dominates" all the other variables due to its size. The resulting matrix of rows of TAZs and columns of the transformed variables is then used to derive principal components projecting the observed data on an orthogonal coordinate system (axes that yield uncorrelated components) that captures variation in the data in a hierarchical way with the first component having the highest variation, the next component having the second highest variation and so forth until 100% of the observed variation is represented in the new coordinate system (in essence an eigenvalue/eigenvector computation). This allows to identify components that map the entire variation in the data from all the variables jointly. Then, retain for the subsequent step, which is cluster analysis, the desired number of components based for example on the percent of variance that is considered to be the signal (the variation we want to explore further) versus noise in the data.

The PCA in the way that is presented in [19] and implemented in FactoMineR [20] uses the matrix of the transformed variables described above. This is equivalent with the use of a pairwise distance (dissimilarity) between observations as the Euclidean distances [18, 19]. This technique produces principal components representing dimensions of the desired zonal characteristics (e.g., number of employees in construction that can be reached in the AM within 10 min, number of public transportation stops available within 10 min in the AM, and so forth). These are the examples of the variables presented in Table 1. After all the variables are transformed in the new coordinate system (the principal components) we retain the number of principal components that capture the desired variance. Then, these principal components are used in a hierarchical clustering routine to extract the clusters with systematic differences and similarities in their principal components and by reflection of the projection on the principal components of the original accessibility indicators. The principal components and their correlation with each of the accessibility indicators can be studied to assign role played by each component and to discern the most important variables in the indicators used. In this paper, I skip the presentation of these components favoring the clustering portion of the analysis.

Before presenting the findings it is worth mentioning that deciding on the number of clusters to retain in analyses of this type cannot be done exclusively based on indicators of "good" clusters. For example, one popular indicator is the total within cluster sum of squares. This tells us that we minimize the amount of variation of the spatial variables within each cluster by increasing the number of clusters. There are many types of indicators (statistical criteria) one can use to identify the "optimal" number of clusters and they are available in an R library NbClust [21]. As in most clustering methods to partition the observations here we aim to find groups (classes) with small within-class variability and large between-class variability. When we work with inertia we can achieve both aims contemporaneously because total inertia (which is a constant for the data we have) is the sum of within-class inertia and between-class inertia as shown in Eq. 1.

$$\sum_{k=1}^{K}\sum_{q=1}^{Q}\sum_{i=1}^{N} (x_{iqk} - \bar{x}_k)^2 = \sum_{k=1}^{K}\sum_{q=1}^{Q}\sum_{i=1}^{N} (x_{iqk} - \bar{x}_{qk})^2 + \sum_{k=1}^{K}\sum_{q=1}^{Q} (\bar{x}_{qk} - \bar{x}_k)^2 \quad (1)$$

i = 1,...,N observations
q = 1,...,Q classes
k = 1,...,K variables
x_{iqk} = value of variable k in class q for individual i
$\bar{x}_k$ = value of overall average for variable k
$\bar{x}_{qk}$ = value of average for variable k within class q

Hierarchical clustering when it is agglomerative starts will all the observations in one cluster (one class). This means the between inertia is equal to the total inertia. Then at a sequence of steps observations first and clusters afterward are combined to minimize the decrease in between-class inertia. In this way, observations are classed in the same cluster by minimizing the decrease in the between-class inertia. The difference between two cluster steps (one step with q clusters and the next with q + 1 clusters) is computed and if appearing to be a large difference the q + 1 number of clusters solution is accepted. This is shown in Fig. 1 left-hand side with an abrupt decrease from 1 to 2 clusters (the first bar in the graph) and then smaller changes in inertia as the number of clusters increases. This appears to be leveling off at 6 clusters (fifth dark bar on the figure). The right-hand side figure shows this 6-cluster solution in which the observations are classed in one of the six groups. Note that going from 6 clusters to 7 would not yield any major gain in maximizing between-cluster inertia. However, this is not a sufficient criterion to decide on the number of clusters as our final solution. Two additional criteria for deciding on the number of clusters are the relative balance of cluster membership and the interpretability of the solution [16, 17]. This is also demonstrated in [18] using the same method used here to illustrate its functionality.

At the end of this process the composition of these derived classes of zones can be presented in terms of the principal component scores and the original variables from Table 1 that are the zonal characteristics.

4 Analysis and Results

There are four examples in this section. The first analysis includes all 190 accessibility indicators to use as the baseline and retains 27 principal components capturing 91.6% of the variance in the 190 accessibility indicators. The second includes the public transportation (PT) accessibility indicators only to explore if higher access to public transportation

Fig. 1. Inertia gain by increasing number of clusters and dendrogram with six clusters highlighted by different colors and the height representing gain in difference of inertia (Color figure online)

is identified along corridors or areas in the center of Doha (the capital of Qatar and the most populous region). The third and fourth analyses are about the AM peak accessibility of which the first is clustering based on 23 principal components capturing 91.9% of the variance in the AM accessibility indicators and the second cluster analysis uses the rule of retaining principal components with eigenvalue > 1 yielding 13 components and capturing 80.4% of the variance in the AM accessibility indicators. Figures 2, 3, 4, and 5 show the Qatar maps and zoomed in the center of Doha. Tables 2, 3, and 4 contain a selection of accessibility indicators used to obtain the principal components and then clustering based on the components. There are many additional accessibility indicators used in each analysis but not shown in the paper and available upon request.

Figures 2 and 4 show the TAZs are classified in the typical core-periphery of a city (center of the city, suburbs, exurbs, and rural). Rural in Qatar is the dessert (mostly captured by the red color on the maps). Table 2 (all accessibility indicators) and Table 3 (AM retaining more than 90% of variance) have close similarity in the classification of zones and the number of employees that can be reached within the buffers used here. They have similarities in terms of the travel time by car in the AM peak period and travel distance by car in the AM peak period. This points out to the possibility of not needing to use all 190 different indicators to identify the area of a city that is well served by private transportation because the relative level of service by car does not change considerably between AM peak and PM peak. Major differences emerge in Figs. 2 and 4 and Tables 2 and 4, however, as we move away from the center of Doha to the zones of cluster 2 and cluster 4 that are very different in these two classifications.

Figure 3 and Table 3 show the maps of public transportation clusters and their characteristics respectively. This analysis shows clearly that there are public transportation corridors and an area that has the highest level of service by public transportation in the city center of Doha. This area includes the Souq al Wakif (an open-air market and the neighborhoods around this market to the South and East of the market – see also Figure A2). West of the market are zones with very low level of service by public transportation (yellow color) and those are parks, parking garages, a mosque, and other government buildings. The analysis here is also notable for its capability of identifying major points of interest that have a high level of accessibility within them but not around

Fig. 2. Maps of the 5 clusters (numbers 1,...,5) using all accessibility indicators and 27 principal components capturing 91.6% of the variance in accessibility indicators (Color figure online)

Fig. 3. Maps of 5 clusters (numbers 1,...,5) using only the public transportation accessibility indicators and 9 principal components capturing 90.2% of the variance in accessibility indicators (Color figure online)

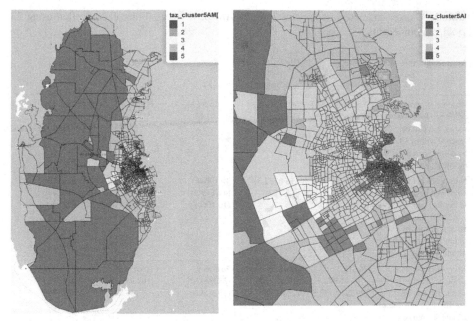

Fig. 4. Maps of the 5 clusters (numbers 1,…,5) using only the AM accessibility indicators and 23 principal components capturing 91.9% of the variance in accessibility indicators (Color figure online).

Fig. 5. Maps of the 5 clusters (numbers 1,…,5) using only the AM accessibility indicators and 13 principal components capturing 80.4% of the variance in accessibility indicators (Color figure online)

Table 2. Cluster characteristics selection of the AM peak accessibility classification using 23 principal components

Accessibility Indicator	Cluster 1 N = 79	Cluster 2 N = 285	Cluster 3 N = 41	Cluster 4 N = 894	Cluster 5 N = 523
Number of persons employed in the service sector that can be reached within 10 min by roadway in the AM morning peak	3,503.6 [195.6] (7,374.7)	560.2 [78.5] (1,118.4)	5,518.8 [334.7] (7,261.6)	6,524.1 [2,129.0] (8,236.2)	6,681.1 [5,190.3] (5,861.2)
Number of persons employed in the service sector that can be reached within a ring of 10 and 20 min by roadway in the AM morning peak	3,503.6 [275.1] (6,752.9)	496.6 [87.3] (1,470.3)	40,106.4 [44,119.9] (10,106.1)	19,456.1 [20,189.2] (12,814.4)	22,678.6 [22,484.4] (11,804.1)
Number of persons employed in the service sector that can be reached within a ring of 20 and 50 min by roadway in the AM morning peak	26,358.3 [26,111.9] (29,217.8)	22,484.6 [11,176.1] (23,875.5)	86,106.5 [88,899.8] (19,500.6)	105,493.2 [107,989.3] (18,289.7)	108,721.2 [109,779.4] (11,675.4)
Number of persons employed in the service sector that can be reached within 2 km minutes by roadway in the AM morning peak	735.6 [0.0] (3,310.6)	230.9 [0.1] (851.3)	622.8 [0.9] (3,207.2)	2,366.6 [83.9] (4,775.1)	2,777.1 [716.5] (3,576.9)
Number of persons employed in the service sector that can be reached within a ring of 2 and 5 km by roadway in the AM morning peak	756.7 [0.0] (3,262.3)	233.4 [13.8] (662.7)	10,137.9 [4,773.6] (11,487.5)	10,183.7 [9,331.0] (9,784.1)	13,639.2 [14,764.5] (7,408.9)
Number of persons employed in the service sector that can be reached within a ring of 5 and 20 km by roadway in the AM morning peak	9,853.9 [1,005.0] (15,486.3)	7,793.4 [1,549.9] (12,409.9)	102,385.1 [109,570.1] (25,328.1)	95,348.1 [101,470.2] (23,165.9)	108,816.4 [107,479.3] (8,679.9)
Total lane kilometers within 10 min by roadway in the AM morning peak	223.8 [210.3] (120.3)	168.4 [160.9] (96.2)	364.5 [407.5] (98.4)	376.3 [367.6] (189.2)	337.3 [329.5] (93.6)

(*continued*)

Table 2. (*continued*)

Accessibility Indicator	Cluster 1 N = 79	Cluster 2 N = 285	Cluster 3 N = 41	Cluster 4 N = 894	Cluster 5 N = 523
Total number of public transportation stops that can be reached within 10 min by roadway in the AM morning peak	9.5 [6.0] (9.4)	15.7 [14.0] (13.7)	54.3 [57.0] (25.8)	60.5 [63.0] (29.8)	92.9 [91.0] (21.9)
Total area in square km that can be reached within 10 min in the AM morning peak	442.4 [396.9] (302.8)	68.2 [44.5] (82.5)	75.4 [70.0] (39.2)	32.2 [28.2] (22.2)	18.6 [17.8] (6.6)

Note: Mean [Median] (SD); N is the number of TAZs in each cluster

them. In Table 3 this is the cluster 2 that has 80 zones and includes the harbor (right most side of Figure A1 and the Hamad International airport (right most side of Figure A2).

Table 3. Cluster characteristics selection of the public transportation (transit) accessibility classification

Accessibility Indicator	Cluster 1, N = 1[1]	Cluster 2, N = 80[1]	Cluster 3, N = 1,191[1]	Cluster 4, N = 336[1]	Cluster 5, N = 214[1]
Number of persons employed in the service sector that can be reached within 10 min by transit in the AM morning peak	0.0 [0.0] (NA)	1,900.9 [0.1] (3,897.5)	30.9 [0.0] (174.5)	26.5 [1.0] (85.2)	51.0 [25.6] (99.9)
Number of persons employed in the service sector that can be reached within a ring of 10 and 20 min by transit in the AM morning peak	0.0 [0.0] (NA)	2.1 [0.0] (13.3)	10.1 [0.0] (70.6)	656.5 [61.3] (1,953.8)	406.0 [310.8] (340.7)
Number of persons employed in the service sector that can be reached within a ring of 20 and 50 min by transit in the AM morning peak	0.0 [0.0] (NA)	246.8 [0.0] (1,265.0)	634.7 [0.0] (2,366.9)	9,543.7 [11,732.1] (5,969.7)	19,386.9 [23,385.6] (6,897.7)
Number of persons employed in the service sector that can be reached within 10 min by transit in the PM after noon peak	0.0 [0.0] (NA)	698.7 [0.1] (1,399.0)	16.8 [0.0] (101.7)	11.1 [0.3] (31.2)	18.6 [10.7] (31.9)

(*continued*)

Table 3. (*continued*)

Accessibility Indicator	Cluster 1, N = 1[1]	Cluster 2, N = 80[1]	Cluster 3, N = 1,191[1]	Cluster 4, N = 336[1]	Cluster 5, N = 214[1]
Number of persons employed in the service sector that can be reached within a ring of 10 and 20 min by transit in the PM after noon peak	0.0 [0.0] (NA)	0.7 [0.0] (4.3)	3.7 [0.0] (22.3)	254.4 [23.9] (816.7)	151.0 [116.3] (126.8)
Number of persons employed in the service sector that can be reached within a ring of 20 and 50 min by transit in the PM after noon peak	0.0 [0.0] (NA)	83.3 [0.0] (421.7)	260.8 [0.0] (998.7)	3,550.4 [4,036.4] (2,410.3)	8,027.3 [9,888.3] (3,232.5)
Total number of public transportation stops that can be reached within 10 min by transit in the AM morning peak	6.0 [6.0] (NA)	1.7 [1.0] (2.6)	0.9 [0.0] (1.5)	2.9 [2.0] (3.4)	4.8 [4.0] (3.2)
Total number of public transportation stops that can be reached within a ring of 10 to 20 min by transit in the AM morning peak	0.0 [0.0] (NA)	0.4 [0.0] (1.7)	1.7 [0.0] (4.1)	13.3 [12.0] (7.3)	30.9 [29.0] (12.7)
Total number of public transportation stops that can be reached within a ring to 20 to 50 min by transit in the AM morning peak	0.0 [0.0] (NA)	8.3 [0.0] (36.3)	19.0 [0.0] (37.5)	159.8 [161.0] (37.0)	248.2 [251.0] (45.9)

[1] Mean [Median] (SD); N is the number of TAZs in each cluster

In summary, the method used here classifying TAZs is able to pick up differences in zones based on low level of service (e.g., small number of bus stops in the zones but also surrounding zones through the distance and travel time buffers). It is important to note, however, that all this analysis is based on public transportation in the way it was a few years ago and before the opening of the Doha metro and Lusail tram (https://www. qr.com.qa/home). One should expect major differences in the accessibility of public transportation after their opening. Nevertheless, the analysis here provides important evidence about the method's capability of pinpointing places with low and high level of service and access to opportunities.

Figure 4 and Fig. 5 represent the same type of accessibility (AM peak by any mode) with the key difference that Fig. 4 shows the five clusters based on 23 principal components (capturing 91.9% of the accessibility indicator variance) and Fig. 5 shows the five clusters based on 13 principal components capturing only 80.4% of the variance. If one has evidence or suspicion the data are noisy Fig. 5 could be more appropriate. However, the number of clusters to use should have been based on Eq. 1 and not defined a priori

Table 4. Cluster characteristics selection of the AM peak accessibility classification using 13 principal components

Accessibility Indicator	Cluster 1, N = 71[1]	Cluster 2, N = 448[1]	Cluster 3, N = 46[1]	Cluster 4, N = 684[1]	Cluster 5, N = 573[1]
Number of persons employed in the service sector that can be reached within 10 min by roadway in the AM morning peak	4,446.3 [199.8] (8,276.0)	520.1 [78.5] (1,235.2)	8,025.2 [4,734.0] (8,856.7)	8,021.4 [6,574.1] (8,523.6)	6,256.6 [4,792.9] (5,818.7)
Number of persons employed in the service sector that can be reached within a ring of 10 and 20 min by roadway in the AM morning peak	4,999.9 [258.5] (9,583.5)	1,640.6 [212.0] (3,765.2)	41,497.1 [44,125.7] (7,336.4)	23,211.0 [23,505.9] (11,207.2)	21,714.0 [21,433.7] (11,839.5)
Number of persons employed in the service sector that can be reached within a ring of 20 and 50 min by roadway in the AM morning peak	24,659.6 [21,715.3] (28,902.4)	46,226.1 [39,270.6] (39,388.8)	92,115.9 [92,737.3] (7,687.1)	108,983.3 [110,940.4] (16,769.0)	108,116.6 [109,401.5] (12,414.3)
Number of persons employed in the service sector that can be reached within 2 km minutes by roadway in the AM morning peak	967.7 [0.0] (4,118.5)	171.8 [1.2] (715.8)	914.9 [6.0] (4,411.7)	3,074.6 [135.4] (5,238.6)	2,490.1 [666.8] (3,359.0)

(*continued*)

Table 4. (*continued*)

Accessibility Indicator	Cluster 1, N = 71[1]	Cluster 2, N = 448[1]	Cluster 3, N = 46[1]	Cluster 4, N – 684[1]	Cluster 5, N = 573[1]
Number of persons employed in the service sector that can be reached within a ring of 2 and 5 km by roadway in the AM morning peak	1,123.9 [0.0] (3,766.0)	257.3 [10.5] (954.4)	14,085.2 [13,539.5] (12,511.1)	12,229.8 [12,229.9] (9,609.8)	13,213.3 [14,051.7] (7,426.2)
Number of persons employed in the service sector that can be reached within a ring of 5 and 20 km by roadway in the AM morning peak	12,060.7 [843.9] (22,475.9)	25,134.4 [11,641.1] (29,854.8)	108,149.1 [109,005.7] (9,473.8)	103,192.3 [105,270.3] (13,983.8)	107,634.6 [107,305.3] (9,993.9)
Total lane kilometers within 10 min by roadway in the AM morning peak	231.6 [222.9] (123.2)	205.3 [201.9] (124.1)	393.5 [409.8] (83.8)	406.5 [396.9] (190.1)	329.7 [325.4] (104.3)
Total number of public transportation stops that can be reached within 10 min by roadway in the AM morning peak	10.8 [8.0] (10.4)	18.3 [16.0] (15.6)	64.1 [67.5] (25.2)	67.9 [69.0] (26.1)	90.3 [89.0] (23.7)

(*continued*)

Table 4. (*continued*)

Accessibility Indicator	Cluster 1, N = 71[1]	Cluster 2, N = 448[1]	Cluster 3, N = 46[1]	Cluster 4, N = 684[1]	Cluster 5, N = 573[1]
Total area in square km that can be reached within 10 min in the AM morning peak	477.5 [431.2] (302.0)	58.7 [38.8] (68.8)	60.7 [55.3] (20.1)	33.0 [28.4] (23.0)	18.3 [17.5] (6.5)

[1] Mean [Median] (SD); N is the number of TAZs in each cluster

as we did here for comparison with Fig. 4. The difference between the two AM analyses shows that this method is very sensitive to the number of components retained for the cluster analysis and one needs to be careful about the number of components to retain. In fact, using the rule of retaining eigenvalues that are larger than 1 would not work well here and this should be replaced by data verification with field surveys. In this analysis verification is facilitated by online mapping information and points of interest. Similar issues are found in other fields of inquiry too [22].

5 Summary and Conclusion

In this paper accessibility, the ease (or difficulty) with which activity opportunities can be reached from a given location, is used to classify the usual traffic analysis zones in transportation planning, modeling, and simulation. Many accessibility indicators used in a recent project in the State of Qatar are used here to illustrate a method that is able to extract zonal diversity in level of service and access to opportunities by two different transportation modes (private car and transit) using principal components analysis. Then, the scores of the principal components are used in a hierarchical clustering step to identify relatively homogeneous groups of zones. The analysis here uses 1822 zones and 190 indicators that reflect the differences in accessibility across different times of a day to distinguish travel times in the AM peak, midday, and PM peak periods. In addition, the illustration of the method here uses different subsets of these indicators to identify different facets and possibilities in this analysis and to identify recommendations for practice. For example, the number of principal components can be a small number (e.g., 27 components capture 91.6% of the 190 indicators variation) but practice should not use rules of thumb found often in PCA textbooks. Instead, makes more sense to perform sensitivity analysis based on the amount of variance captured by different sets of principal components retained for the subsequent cluster analysis. In the paper one example is the comparison for the AM peak period showing that selecting 23 components (capturing 91.9% of the accessibility variance) versus selecting 13 principal components (capturing 80.4% of the variance) yields significantly different classification. Moreover, using the public transportation accessibility indicators and their derived clusters a corridor and a central area of higher accessibility by public transportation is clearly identified. Overall, this method is precise enough to pinpoint specific areas where level of service can be improved, and accessibility increased substantially for the whole day or portions of it (AM as it is done in this paper).

There are however a few limitations in this method that point to possible next steps in research. The public transportation analysis is based on data before a major infrastructure component was added (the Doha Metro and Lusail tram). Moreover, walking and biking are absent as stand-alone modes (walking is implicit in the public transportation travel times and distances). Also, the use of large TAZs (outside the core of Doha) may decrease the accuracy of travel times and distances here. However, these are more prevalent in the desert where activity opportunities are scant.

Appendix A Additional Maps and Photos from Doha, Qatar

Fig. A1. Georeferenced photos showing the high differences in density among TAZs in the center of Doha, Qatar (photos by K.G. Goulias)

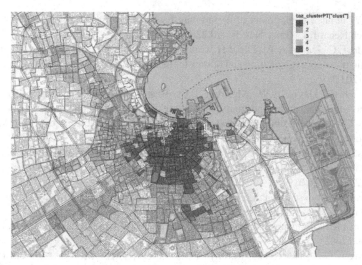

Fig. A2. Center of Doha and public transportation based zonal clusters – blue is highest level of service and green second highest (see also Table 3) (Color figure online).

References

1. Wachs, M., Kumagai, T.G.: Physical accessibility as a social indicator. Social –Econ. Planning Sci. **7**, 437–456 (1973)
2. Handy, S.L.: Regional Versus Local Accessibility: Variations in Suburban Form and the Effects on Non-Work Travel. Doctoral Dissertation, University of California, Berkeley (1993)
3. Blumenberg, E., Manville, M.: Beyond the spatial mismatch: welfare recipients and transportation policy. J. Plan. Lit. **19**(2), 182–205 (2004)
4. Pinna, F., Garau, C., Annunziata, A.: A literature review on urban usability and accessibility to investigate the related criteria for equality in the city. In: Gervasi, O., et al. (eds.) ICCSA 2021. LNCS, vol. 12958, pp. 525–541. Springer, Cham (2021). https://doi.org/10.1007/978-3-030-87016-4_38
5. Russo, A., Campisi, T., Tesoriere, G., Annunziata, A., Garau, C.: Accessibility and mobility in the small mountain municipality of Zafferana Etnea (sicily): coupling of walkability assessment and space syntax. In: Computational Science and Its Applications–ICCSA 2022 Workshops: Malaga, Spain, July 4–7, 2022, Proceedings, Part I, pp. 338-352. Springer International Publishing, Cham (2022). https://doi.org/10.1007/978-3-031-10536-4_23
6. Pellicelli, G., Caselli, B., Garau, C., Torrisi, V., Rossetti, S.: Sustainable mobility and accessibility to essential services. an assessment of the san benedetto neighbourhood in Cagliari (Italy). In: Computational Science and Its Applications–ICCSA 2022 Workshops: Malaga, Spain, July 4–7, 2022, Proceedings, Part VI, pp. 423-438. Springer International Publishing, Cham (2022). https://doi.org/10.1007/978-3-031-10592-0_31
7. Geurs, K.T., van Wee, B.: Accessibility evaluation of land-use and transport strategies:review and research directions. J. Transp. Geogr. **12**, 127–140 (2004)
8. Goulias, K.G., et al.: Simulator of activities, greenhouse emissions, networks, and travel (SimAGENT) in Southern California: design, implementation, preliminary findings, and integration plans. In: 2011 IEEE Forum on Integrated and Sustainable Transportation Systems, pp. 164–169. IEEE (2011)

9. Chen, Y., et al.: Development of opportunity-based accessibility indicators. Transportation Research Record: J. Trans. Res. Board **2255**, 58–68 (2011)

10. McBride, E.C., Davis, A.W., Lee, J.H., Goulias, K.G.: Incorporating land use into methods of synthetic population generation and of transfer of behavioral data Transp. Res. Rec. **2668**(1), 11–20 (2017)

11. Goulias, K.G., Davis, A.W., McBride, E.C., Bhat, C.R., Pendyala, R.M.: Traffic analysis zone attributes and opportunity-based accessibility indicators in qatar activity-based model – QABM accessibility. Final Report 3 Submitted to ItalConsult and Qatar Ministry of Transportation and Communication, March 31, p. 29 (2019)

12. Goulias, K.G,, Bhat, C.R., Pendyala, R.M.: Qatar Activity-Based Model - Overview Final Report 1 Submitted to ItalConsult and Qatar Ministry of Transportation and Communication, March 29, p. 19 (2019)

13. Kaufman, L., Rousseeuw, P.J.: Finding Groups in Data: An Introduction to Cluster Analysis. John Wiley & Sons (2009)

14. Vermunt, J.K., Magidson, J.: Latent class cluster analysis. Applied Latent Class Anal. **11**(89–106), 60 (2002)

15. Bouveyron, C., Celeux, G., Murphy, T.B., Raftery, A.E.: Model-based clustering and classification for data science: with applications in R, **50**. Cambridge University Press (2019)

16. Nylund-Gibson, K., Choi, A.Y.: Ten frequently asked questions about latent class analysis. Translational Issues in Psychological Sci. **4**(4), 440 (2018)

17. Weller, B.E., Bowen, N.K., Faubert, S.J.: Latent class analysis: a guide to best practice. J. Black Psychol. **46**(4), 287–311 (2020)

18. Van de Velden, M., Iodice D'Enza, A., Markos, A.: Distance-based clustering of mixed data. Wiley Interdisciplinary Rev.: Comput. Statistics **11**(3), e1456 (2019)

19. Pagès, J.: Analyse factorielle de donnees mixtes: principe et exemple d'application. Revue de Statistique Appliquée **52**(4), 93–111 (2004)

20. Lê, S., Josse, J., Husson, F.: FactoMineR: an R package for multivariate analysis. J. Stat. Softw. **25**, 1–18 (2008)

21. Charrad, M., Ghazzali, N., Boiteau, V., Niknafs, A.: NbClust: an R package for determining the relevant number of clusters in a data set. J. Stat. Softw. **61**, 1–36 (2014)

22. Björklund, M.: Be careful with your principal components. Evolution **73**(10), 2151–2158 (2019)

Research Trends in Tourism Participation: A Bibliometric Analysis Using the Scopus Database

Gagih Pradini[1,2], Tonny Hendratono[1], Azril Azahari[1], Ema Rahmawati[3], and Tutut Herawan[1,4(✉)]

[1] Sekolah Tinggi Pariwisata Ambarrukmo Yogyakarta, Jalan Ringroad Timur No. 52, 55281 Bantul, Daerah Istimewa Yogyakarta, Indonesia
{gagihpradini,tutut}@stipram.ac.id
[2] Universitas Nasional, Jl. Sawo Manila No.61, 12520 Jakarta Selatan, Daerah Khusus Ibukota Jakarta, Indonesia
[3] PT Gemilang Wisata Persada, Jl. Maninjau Barat No. 18 Sawojajar, 65139 Kota Malang, Jawa Timur, Indonesia
[4] AMCS Research Center, Jalan Griya Taman Asri 55512 Yogyakarta, Indonesia

Abstract. The study of tourism participation has been widely applied in the tourism sector. This tourism participation connects cultural villages with community-based tourism. In this paper, we present a bibliometric analysis of the tourism participation model. The novelty of our work is that unlike our previous work that using the Google Scholar database, this work has imported data from the Scopus database. The purpose of this study is to identify the evolution of tourism Participation researches, such as: source, document type, journal name, publisher name, topic trends, and author collaborations. Bibliometric analysis was used to analyze 1913 articles published from 2018 to 2023. Tourism participation is the main keyword used in article titles, abstracts, and keywords to obtain metadata retrieved from the Scopus database in March 2023, where most articles are written in English. We use Harzing's Publish or Perish to extract data from Scopus databases and further used for citation and metric analysis, finally VoS Viewer is employed for data visualization. Based on the network visualization, the most dominant terms are tourism, tourism development, sustainable tourism, local participation. When viewed from the overlay visualization more keywords are appeared i.e., community empowerment, sustainable tourism development, and destination management. Based on the findings displayed in network visualization and overlay visualization, it can be concluded that articles with the topic of tourism participation have been widely studied, so it can be further explored for research.

Keywords: Information visualization · Bibliometric analysis · Tourism participation · VoS Viewer · Scopus

O. Gervasi et al. (Eds.): ICCSA 2023 Workshops, LNCS 14111, pp. 437–454, 2023.
https://doi.org/10.1007/978-3-031-37126-4_29

1 Introduction

The rapid growth of tourism requires equitable distribution of benefits so that the beneficiaries of tourism activities are more comprehensive. Participation in tourism can be interpreted as active involvement in every development process of the tourism industry, starting from planning, determining design, development to supervision and evaluation, and enjoying the results.

In general, many studies on the participation of tourism activities that affect other sectors within or outside the tourism industry itself [1–11]. In the work of [1], it is said that the development of road and transportation infrastructure with community support to benefit the community. There is also a study that states that tourism helps the continuity of cultural heritage [2]. A review integrated indicators for tourism sustainability is presented in [3]. Review the application of customer relationships with within tourism and hospitality is given in [4]. Meanwhile, examining tourism governance and achieving sustainable development goals in Africa is available in [5].

This research discusses tourism participation in all activities in the world in terms of economically, socially, culturally, politically, and technological developments. We explored the Publish or Peris and VoS Viewer as our main vehicles for data analysis. We found that there are many interesting topics related to tourism participation. The objectives of conducting this research and research are:

a. To explain and explain all elements and elements that exist in tourism participation.
b. In addition, another purpose of this paper is to find out the development, community participation, social, political, economic, and so on that are considered as having something to do with tourism participation.
c. The goal of this paper is to determine the research mix related to tourism participation.

The scope of this research is focused on tourism participation that leads to the impact of tourism activities on certain sectors. One form of tourism participation is reflected in community-based tourism activities such as: Public participation in planning is considered a good and progressive exercise because it offers opportunities for various stakeholder interests to be combined, and is consistent with the right of communities to participate in decision-making that affects their lives [6]. Various models and typologies have been developed with their similar basic characteristics. It is generally agreed that a complete public participation process would not exist without elements of availability of informant, consultation, and empowerment. In general, tourism will have a valuable effect on other aspects such as the example above.

The rest of the papers are arranged as follows. In Sect. 2, we describe our proposed research method. Section 3 presents the results we obtained and is followed by a full discussion. Finally, we conclude our work and highlight future works in Sect. 4.

2 Proposed Method

In this paper, we adopt bibliometrics analysis method [12–20]. Our proposed method consists of five stages i.e.: Determining the keywords, initial searching and repair searching results; Compiling preliminary data statistics (before and after repairing) and saving in RIS format; Enter RIS data into Publish or Perish; Analysis of publications sources and citations; and finally visualize the results using VoS Viewer. Figure 1 below depicts the flow chart of our proposed method.

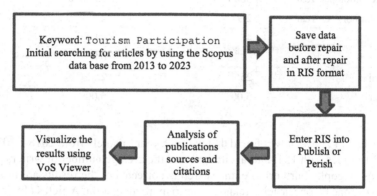

Fig. 1. Flow chart of the proposed method

3 Results and Discussion

This section explains the obtained results of this work, which includes publications and citations, visualizations, authors and networks, research locations and research domains.

3.1 Publications and Citations

For knowing comparison of the citation matrix on the data taken via Scopus, then researcher make the Table in which containing number arti cle, numbercitation, number citations per year, number authors per year, H index, G index, normal hI, and hI yearly at the beginning search and on results repair. Comparison data matrix in result search start and result search after repair could be seen in Table 1.

Table 1. Comparison Matrix

Data	Initial Search Results	Search Results Repair
Database	Scopus	Scopus
Year publishing	2018 – 2023	2018 – 2023
Year citation	5	5
Number of Articles	2430	1913
Number citation	15433	12773

(continued)

Table 1. (*continued*)

Data	Initial Search Results	Search Results Repair
Number Citation per Year	3086.60	2554.60
Number Authors per Year	2.97	2.89
H index	45	44
G index	67	64
hI Normal	25	25
hI Annual	5.00	5.00

From Table 1 above, it was found that within 5 years, namely from 2018 – 2023 there were 2430 articles with 15433 total citations and the average number of writers per year as many as 2 people. Furthermore, the search is corrected or the results are re-selected by observing one by one articles related to tourism participation. Articles obtained after improvement and selection were obtained as many as 1913 articles with a total of 12,773 citations obtained or an average of 2554 per year and an average of 2 authors per year. The index for measuring the productivity or impact of work published by scientists or academics (Hirsch's h-Index) is 44. Furthermore, based on the distribution of citations received by publications or research articles (Egghe's g-Index) obtained as many as 64. To find out the details of publication metric can be seen in Table 2 below which provides a more detailed picture of Table 1.

Table 2. The statistics descriptive of publication

Year	TP	% (N = 1913)	NCP	TC	C/P	C/CP
2018	305	0.16	264	4243	13,91	16,07
2019	349	0.18	284	3224	9,24	11,35
2020	364	0.19	272	2949	8,10	10.84
2021	453	0.24	315	1873	4,13	5,95
2022	382	0.20	198	646	1,69	3,26
2023	60	0.03	15	38	0.63	2,53
	1913	100%				

Note: TP = total number of publications; NCP = number cited publications; TC = total quotes; C/P = average citations per publication; C/CP = average citation per cited publication

From Table 2 above, it can be seen that in 2021 there were the most publications, namely 453 total publications and in 20 23 publications the least were 60 total publications. While the number of most cited articles was in 201 8 and the number of least cited articles was in 2023. For the total number of citations, the most was in 2018 and the fewest in 2023. Furthermore, to find out the description of the publication bar chart and citations can be seen in the graph presented in Fig. 2 below.

Documents by year

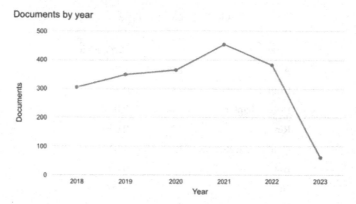

Fig. 2. Publication and citations form 2018–2023

It can be seen from Fig. 2 above that the publication and citation bar chart for a period of 5 years from 201 8–2023 experienced a fluctuating graph. The number of documents each year changes up and down. In 2018 to 2021 the publication and citation bar increased to reach the top position with the same number of documents. While in 20 22 the publication and citation bars decreased the number of documents in graph 11. In 2020 the publication and citation bars are in the same position and center. To see an overview of the document by its subject field can be seen more clearly in Fig. 6 below.

Documents by subject area

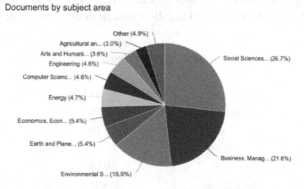

Fig. 3. Documents by subject area form 2018–2023

It can be explained from Fig. 3 above that the subject of Social Sciences is the subject that has the largest role in writing articles using the keyword tourism participation with a percentage of 26.7%. Furthermore, in second position followed by subject business, management, accounting with a percentage of 21.6% each. Then in third position is the environmental science project with 15.5%. Furthermore, to find out the type of document, it can be seen from the presentation of the citation matrix of scientific publications related to Tourism Participation from 2018–2023 in Table 3 below.

Table 3. Document Type

Type	Number	Percentage
Article	1453	0.76
Conference Paper	223	0.12
Book Chapter	154	0.08
Reviews	47	0.02
Conference Review	13	0.01
Book	9	0.00
Note	7	0.00
Letter	3	0.00
Erratum	2	0.00
Editorial	2	0.00
	1913	100%

From Table 3 above it can be seen that the types of documents we present are original documents derived from Articles, Conference Papers, Conference Reviews, and Book Chapters. We summarize in the description of Table 3 above, it can be seen that the article has domination in showing its role with a contribution of 1453 with a percentage of 76%, followed by conference paper 223 with 12% and the third position there is a book chapter of 154 with 8%. Table 4 as follow describes the type sources of publication.

Table 4: Type Source

Type	Number	Percentage
Journal	1512	0.79
Conference Proceedings	194	0.10
Book	107	0.06
Book Series	99	0.05
Trade Journal	1	0.00
	1913	100%

From Table 4 above, it can be observed that journals are the most important with a total contribution of 1512 or equivalent to 79%, followed by convention proceedings with a total of 194 or equivalent to 1o%, followed by books with a total of 107 or equivalent to 6%, and the last is a book Series as much as 99 or equivalent to 5%. For more details on article citations that make the top 20 list, see Table 5 below. Table 5 as follow describes the list of top 20 cited articles in the related field.

Table 5. Top 20 cited articles

Citation	Authors	Title	Year	Journal Name	Publisher
289	Z. Zeng, P.-J. Chen, A.A. Lew	From high-touch to high-tech: COVID-19 drives robotics adoption	2020	Tourism Geographies	Routledge
271	A.C. Campos, J. Mendes, P.O. do Valle, N. Scott	Co-creation of tourist experiences: A literature review	2018	Current Issues in Tourism	Routledge
149	A.G. Asmelash, S. Kumar	Assessing progress of tourism sustainability: Developing and validating sustainability indicators	2019	Tourism Management	Elsevier
141	W. Wei, R. Qi, L. Zhang	Effects of virtual reality on theme park visitors' experience and behaviors: A presence perspective	2019	Tourism Management	Elsevier
101	E. Agyeiwaah, F.E. Otoo, W. Injection, W.-J. Huang	Understanding culinary tourist motivation, experience, satisfaction, and loyalty using a structural approach	2019	Journal of Travel and Tourism Marketing	Routledge
97	N. Chen, L. Dwyer	Residents' Place Satisfaction and Place Attachment on Destination Brand-Building Behaviors: Conceptual and Empirical Differentiation	2018	Journal of Travel Research	SAGE
95	C. Antón, C. Camarero, M.-J. Garrido	Exploring the experience value of museum visitors as a co-creation process	2018	Current Issues in Tourism	Routledge

(continued)

Table 5. (*continued*)

Citation	Authors	Title	Year	Journal Name	Publisher
84	D. Huber, S. Milne, K.F. Hyde	Constraints and facilitators for senior tourism	2018	Tourism Management Perspectives	Elsevier
83	L. Grazzini, P. Rodrigo, G. Aiello, G. Viglia	Loss or gain? The role of message framing in hotel guests' recycling behaviour	2018	Journal of Sustainable Tourism	Routledge
81	G. Richards	Designing creative places: The role of creative tourism	2020	Annals of Tourism Research	Elsevier
81	S. Kanwal, M.I. Rasheed, A.H. Pitafi, A. Pitafi, M. Ren	Road and transport infrastructure development and community support for tourism: The role of perceived benefits, and community satisfaction	2020	Tourism Management	Elsevier
79	Ó. González-Mansilla, G. Berenguer-Contrí, A. Serra-Cantallops	The impact of value co-creation on hotel brand equity and customer satisfaction	2019	Tourism Management	Elsevier
79	S.-K. Tan, S.-H. Tan, Y.-S. Kok, S.-W. Choon	Sense of place and sustainability of intangible cultural heritage – The case of George Town and Melaka	2018	Tourism Management	Elsevier
78	M.C. tom Dieck, T.H. Jung, D. tom Dieck	Enhancing art gallery visitors' learning experience using wearable augmented reality: generic learning outcomes perspective	2018	Current Issues in Tourism	Routledge

(*continued*)

Table 5. (*continued*)

Citation	Authors	Title	Year	Journal Name	Publisher
71	A.K. Tripathy, P.K. Tripathy, N.K. Ray, S.P. Mohanty	ITour: The Future of Smart Tourism: An IoT Framework for the Independent Mobility of Tourists in Smart Cities	2018	IEEE Consumer Electronics Magazine	IEEE
70	C. Afonso, G.M. Silva, H.M. Gonçalves, M. Duarte	The role of motivations and involvement in wine tourists' intention to return: SEM and fsQCA findings	2018	Journal of Business Research	Elsevier
70	K.R. Kristjánsdóttir, R. Ólafsdóttir, K.V. Ragnarsdóttir	Reviewing integrated sustainability indicators for tourism	2018	Journal of Sustainable Tourism	Routledge
68	M. Sigala	Implementing social customer relationship management: A process framework and implications in tourism and hospitality	2018	International Journal of Contemporary Hospitality Management	Emerald
66	P. Siakwah, R. Musavengane, L. Leonard	Tourism Governance and Attainment of the Sustainable Development Goals in Africa	2020	Tourism Planning and Development	Routledge

From Table 5 above, in the first position is an article titled from high-touch to high-tech: COVID-19 drives robotics adoption in 2020 with author Zeng, *et al.* with 289 citations. Meanwhile in position 20 is an article titled Tourism Governance and Attainment of the Sustainable Development Goals in Africa with authors Siakwah, *et al.* in 2020 with a total of 66 citations. Table 6 as follow describes the top five publisher on the related field.

Table 6. Top five publishers on the related field

No	Publisher	Number of Articles	Percentage
1	Elsevier	208	0.28
2	MDPI	189	0.26
3	Springer	161	0.22
4	Emerald	98	0.13
5	Taylor and Francis	83	0.11
		739	100%

Based on Table 6 above, the top 5 publishers contributed the most, with a total of 739 articles published. Then we find 28% or some 208 articles published by Elsevier publishers occupy the top position, followed by MDPI publishers with 189 articles or equivalent to 2.6%. This was followed by publisher Springer who took third place with 161 articles, equivalent to 2.2%. The fourth positions occupied by Emerald publishing house with 98 articles, equivalent to 13%. Then the last position with the least number of articles as much as 83 or equivalent to 1.1% is occupied by Taylor and Francis publishers. Furthermore, to find out the results of the top five journals related to Tourism Participation, please refer to Table 7 below.

Table 7. Top five journals ranking

No	Journal Name	Number of Articles	Percentage
1	Sustainability (Switzerland)	139	52
2	Journal of Sustainable Tourism	53	20
3	Tourism Management	28	10
4	Journal of Env. Management and Tourism	25	9
5	Springer Proc. in Business and Economics	22	8
		267	100%

Based on Table 7 above, it can be presented that the names of the most influential journals in writing this journal and entered the top 5 with a total accumulation of 267 articles. It seems that International Sustainability (Switzerland) is the most active journal in publishing journals with 52% followed by the Journal of Sustainable Tourism 20%, then Tourism Management 10%, then Journal of Environmental Management and Tourism 9% and closed Springer Proceedings in Business and Economics 8%.

3.2 Visualization Topics Use VoS Viewer

Figure 4 below this show visualization of topic areas using network visualization from VoS Viewer.

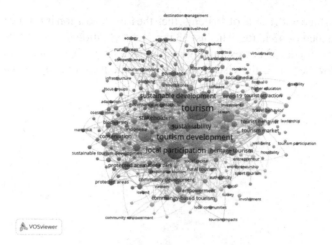

Fig. 4. Visualization topic area using network visualization

From Fig. 4 above, this study examines the title and abstract of documents collected based on the number of events using VoS Viewer software. This analysis uses the binary number method in entering data in VoS Viewer. The results of network visualization show that tourism participation is the main term that becomes the center of search results related to several other issues such as sustainable development, tourism, tourism development, local participation. To see which keywords, represent each cluster, we present them in detail in Table 8 below.

Table 8. Item number in clusters

Cluster	Color	Number of Items
1	Red	72
2	Green	67
3	Blue	46
4	Yellow	43
5	Purple	33
6	Light Blue	31

From Table 8 above, it can be said that the size at that point indicates the magnitude of occurrence of the item or term, while the line shows the strength of the relationship between items or terms. The color in the visualization indicates a cluster of items, in which there are 6 clusters. Items with cluster 1have connecting lines and red dots. Cluster 1 has 72 items, in cluster 2 there is green with a total of 67 items, followed by cluster 3 represented in blue with a total of 46 items, then the fourth position is forged by the yellow cluster with a total of 43 items. The last 33 items and position are represented by cluster 5 in purple which gets 33 corresponding items and cluster 6 light blue 31. Furthermore, Fig. 5 as follow describes the visualization topic area using overlay visualization from VoS Viewer.

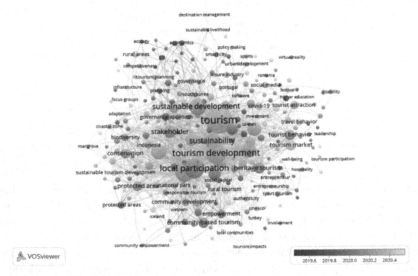

Fig. 5. Visualization topic area using overlay visualization

From Fig. 5 above, the topic of tourism participation shows an upward and bold trend. This overlay visualization figure is more indicative of the keyword with the study year being the base year of research, so it can also be seen that the keywords tourism, tourism development, sustainable tourism, and local participation appeared the current study. Figure 6 as follow describes the visualization topic area using density visualization from VoS Viewer.

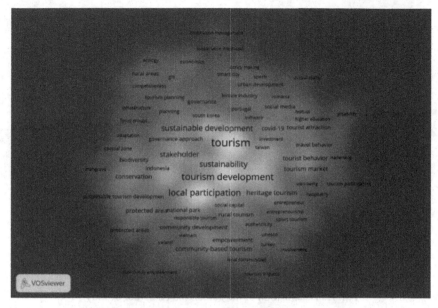

Fig. 6. Visualization topic area using density visualization

From Fig. 6 above, the lighter the color of keywords, the more articles published. Hence, it can be concluded that topics regarding community empowerment, sustainable tourism development, and destination management are the most dominant keywords appeared in the published articles.

3.3 Author and Relationship Between Writer

Figure 7 below depicts overlay visualization of the author and co-author using VoS Viewer. Since close to two thousand articles were found, then it can be seen that there are many authors who have many co-author links.

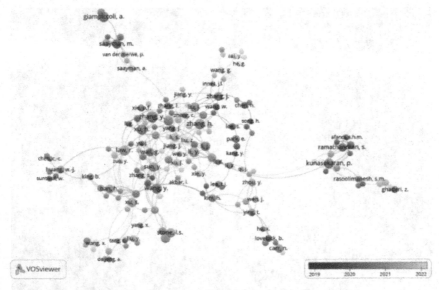

Fig. 7. Visualization of the author and co-author overlay

3.4 Research Locations and Research Domains

Figure 8 below depicts the author's country of origin.

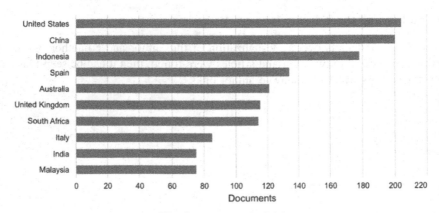

Fig. 8. Country of origin

Figure 9 below depicts the map of author's country of origin.

More details about Figs. 8 and 9 can be found in the following Table 9 which describes the number of documents along with the country of origin and with the research domain.

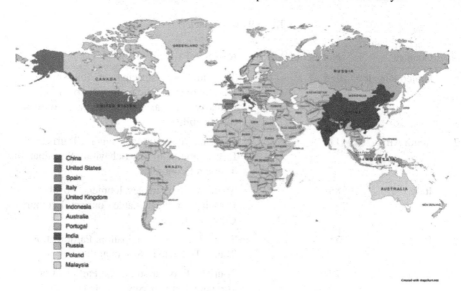

Fig. 9. Map of country of origin

Table 9. Country of location research and research domain

No	Country	Number of Articles	Research Domain
1	United States	204	Tourism, Local Participation, Tourism Development, Tourist Destination, Ecotourism, Tourism Management, United States, Tourist Behaviour
2	China	200	Tourism, Tourism Development, Sustainable Development, Local Participation, Ecotourism, Perception
3	Indonesian	178	Tourism, Tourism Management, Community Participation, Tourism Market, Rural Tourism, Tourist Behaviour, Rural Tourism
4	Spain	134	Tourism, Tourist Destination, Sustainability, Local Participation, Ecotourism, Tourism Development, Sustainable Development
5	Australia	121	Tourism, Community Based Tourism, Stakeholder, Participation, Tourism Development, Tourist Behaviour, Sustainable Tourism

(*continued*)

Table 9. (*continued*)

No	Country	Number of Articles	Research Domain
6	United Kingdom	115	Tourism, Local Participation, Tourism Development, Participation, Tourism Management Stakeholder, Heritage Tourism, Sustainability
7	South Africa	114	Tourism, Tourism Management, Tourism Development, Tourist Behaviour, Sustainability, Tourism Economics
8	Italy	85	Tourism, Tourism Development, Local Participation, Sustainable Tourism, Ecotourism, Cultural Heritage
9	India	75	Tourism, Local Participation, Participation, Tourist Behaviour, Sustainability
10	Malaysia	75	Tourism, Ecotourism, Local Participation, Heritage Tourism, Sustainable Development

Based on Table 9 above, the United States has the highest number of articles as many as 204 articles, the second position is China with 200 articles, the third position is Indonesia with 178 articles followed by Spain, Australia, UK, South Africa, Italy, and the bottom position is India and finally Malaysia with 75 articles.

4 Conclusion and Suggestions

Studies on tourism participation in the tourism sector have been studied extensively before. This paper has successfully presented a bibliometric analysis related to tourism participation. We found that most related articles were published in scientific journals, compared to other publication sources. Related articles published in scientific journals have received the highest citations. Based on the visualization of the network, the most dominant term is tourism participation, which is the main term that becomes the center of search results related to several other issues, such as tourism, tourism development, sustainable tourism, local participation. When viewed from the overlay visualization, it shows more about updating keywords and we found that the keywords community empowerment, sustainable tourism development, and destination management are the dominant themes for the recent years. Based on the findings displayed in network visualization and overlay visualization, it can be concluded that articles with the topic of tourism participation have been widely studied and hence they can be used for further research.

This paper also found several shortcomings that are expected to be extended in the future, so that more accurate data emerges and can be a benchmark for future source. The Scopus database [21, 22] sometimes provides searching results that do not match the keywords desired by researchers. Hence, it may take time to filter out article titles that do not match with research topic. The use of other scientific databases is encouraged to achieve better bibliometric data for further analysis. In future research, it is necessary also to study broader and in depth the combination of keywords lifestyle in tourism participation.

Acknowledgment. This research is fully supported by Sekolah Tinggi Pariwisata Ambarrukmo Yogyakarta.

References

1. Kanwal, S., Rasheed, M.I., Pitafi, A.H., Pitafi, A., Ren, M.: Road and transport infrastructure development and community support for tourism: the role of perceived benefits, and community satisfaction. Tour. Manage. **77**, 104014 (2020)
2. Tan, S.K., Tan, S.H., Kok, Y.S., Choon, S.W.: Sense of place and sustainability of intangible cultural heritage–the case of George Town and Melaka. Tour. Manage. **67**, 376-387 (2018)
3. Kristjánsdóttir, K.R., Ólafsdóttir, R., Ragnarsdóttir, K.V.: Reviewing integrated sustainability indicators for tourism. J. Sustainable Tour. **26**(4), 583-599 (2018)
4. Sigala, M.: Implementing social customer relationship management: a process framework and implications in tourism and hospitality. International J. Contemporary Hospitality Manage. (2018)
5. Siakwah, P., Musavengane, R., Leonard, L.: Tourism governance and attainment of the sustainable development goals in Africa. Tour. Planning Dev. **17**(4), 355-383 (2020)
6. Marzuki, A., Hay, I.: Towards a public participation framework in tourism planning. Tour. Planning Dev. **10**(4), 494-512 (2013)
7. Zhou, D., Yanagida, J.F., Chakravorty, U., Leung, P.: Estimating economic impacts from tourism. Ann. Tour. Res. **24**(1), 76–89 (1997)
8. Buckley, R.: Sustainable tourism: research and reality. Ann. Tour. Res. **39**(2), 528–546 (2012)
9. Wood, R.E.: Tourism, culture and the sociology of development. In: Tourism in South-East Asia, pp. 48–70. Routledge (2018)
10. Hailemariam, A., Ivanovski, K.: The impact of geopolitical risk on tourism. Current Issues Tour. **24**(22), 3134-3140 (2021)
11. Streimikiene, D., Svagzdiene, B., Jasinskas, E., Simanavicius, A.: Sustainable tourism development and competitiveness: the systematic literature review. Sustainable Dev. **29**(1), 259-271 (2021)
12. Donthu, N., Kumar, S., Mukherjee, D., Pandey, N., Lim, W.M.: How to perform a bibliometric analysis: overview and guidelines. J. Bus. Res. **133**, 285–296 (2021)
13. Resmi, P.C., Widodo, W.I., Ermawan, K.C., Anggraini, F.D., Ihalauw, J.J., Susanto, D.R.: A decade analysis communication model in tourism: a bibliometric approach. Int. J. Adv. Digital Library Inf. Sci. **3**(1) (2023)
14. Ellegaard, O., Wallin, J.A.: Bibliometric analysis of scientific production: how big is the impact? Scientometrics **105**(3), 1809–1831 (2015)
15. Moral-Muñoz, J.A., Herrera-Viedma, E., Santisteban-Espejo, A., Cobo, M.J.: Software tools for performing bibliometric analysis in science: a recent overview. Professional de la Información **29**(1) (2020)
16. Supriyadi, E.A., et al.: A decade analysis on rural tourism researches: a bibliometric approach. Int. J. Advanced Travel Dest. **2**(1) (2022)
17. Khanra, S., Dhir, A., Kaur, P., Mäntymäki, M.: Bibliometric analysis and literature review of ecotourism: towards sustainable development. Tour. Manage. Perspectives **37**, 100777 (2021)

18. Ermawati, K.C., Anggraini, F.D., Ihalauw, J.J., Damiasih, D.: A decade analysis of local wisdom in tourism: a bibliometric approach. Int. J. Adv. Psychology Human Sci. 4(4) (2023)
19. Xie, I., Chen, Z., Wang, H., Zheng, C., Jiang, J.: Bibliometric analysis and visualization from scientific publications on atlantoaxial spine surgery based on Web of Science and VOS Viewer. World Neurosurgery **137**, 435–442 (2020)
20. Pradini, G., et al.: A bibliometric analysis on community based tourism from 2018 to 2020. Int. J. .anced Sports Tour. Recreation **3**(1) (2023)
21. Boyle, F., Sherman, D.: Scopus™: products and their development. Serial Librarian **49**(3), 147–153 (2006)
22. Ballew, B.S.: Elsevier scopus® database. J. Electronic Res. Med. Libraries **6**(3), 245–252 (2009)

Describing and Understanding the Morphology of the Urban Landscape. The Case Study of Cagliari, Italy

Chiara Garau(✉) ⓘ and Alfonso Annunziata ⓘ

Department of Civil and Environmental Engineering and Architecture, University of Cagliari, Cagliari, Italy
cgarau@unica.it

Abstract. The development of a morphological analysis of the built environment emerges as a central issue for comprehending the structural properties of the urban layout and its generative processes and for establishing a knowledge framework for guiding planning decisions. The proposed study presents an analysis that combines space syntax and geo-spatial analysis tools to describe urban form quantitatively. The suggested analysis is structured as follows: i) definition of the case study and identification of available datasets; ii) definition of metrics for the description of the built environment; iii) discerning of distinct areas of the urbanised region, homogeneous in terms of configurational and functional properties. The proposed analysis is utilised to analyse the metropolitan area of Cagliari, in Sardinia, Italy. The case study underlines the relevance of developing a morphological understanding of urban form for addressing two issues: i) the definition of metrics for the description of the built environment, and ii) the discerning of distinct areas of the urbanised region. The proposed analysis contributes to applying the Geodesign paradigm to the urban realm by supporting the understanding of the spatial culture of a place.

Keywords: configuration · morphology · space syntax · urbanity · geo-design

1 Introduction

Urban morphology emerges as a privileged dimension for understanding the structural properties of the urban fabric and for developing the information base for urban policies.

Urban morphology is the study of urban form and of the processes responsible for its generation. More precisely, the term refers to a method of analysis used in urban design to investigate principles informing the transformation of the built environment [1]. An alternative conceptualisation, relative to the discipline of Geography, refers to

---

This paper is the result of the joint work of the authors. 'Abstract', and 'Datasets And Methods' were written jointly by the authors. Alfonso Annunziata wrote 'Theoretical Framework', and 'Results'. Chiara Garau wrote the 'Introduction' and 'Conclusions'. Chiara Garau coordinated and supervised the paper.

© The Author(s), under exclusive license to Springer Nature Switzerland AG 2023
O. Gervasi et al. (Eds.): ICCSA 2023 Workshops, LNCS 14111, pp. 455–469, 2023.
https://doi.org/10.1007/978-3-031-37126-4_30

urban morphology as the study of the topological, dimensional, geometrical relations that structure the urban fabric. Moreover, in the field of environmental psychology, urban morphology emerges as a central perspective for describing the impact of built environment components on perceptions, preferences, cognition, and social practices of urban populations [2–6]. This contribution presents the preliminary stage of a study aimed at defining an analysis that combines configurational and geo-spatial analysis to quantitatively describe the urban environment and measure the components of the urban fabric that influence users' perceptions and practices.

Consequently, the presented study addresses two questions: i) the definition of metrics for describing the built environment, and ii) the discerning of distinct areas of the urbanised region.

The development of a method analysis for quantitatively describing the built environment is instrumental in supporting informed decisions in urban policies by facilitating the identification of relations between urban form and social life, the identification of critical areas.

2 Theoretical Framework

Building on the Conzenian tradition, the urban form is conceptualised as the result of the geometrical and topological relations among building plots, land uses, spaces of mobility, and components of the ecological infrastructure.

The measurement of the components of urban form is instrumental to the recognition of portions of the built environment qualified by distinct levels of urbanity [7] and latent vitality [8–11]. Building on previous studies, specific factors related to urban form components, including spatial configuration, porosity, access to public transport, building density, density and diversity of uses, and access to urban green infrastructure (UGI), are identified as criteria for individuating distinct parts of an urbanised area. Empirical studies over time identify these urban form factors as variables influencing specific aspects of urbanity and of the use of spaces [6, 10, 12–15].

In particular, configurational properties are investigated as determinants of natural movement and co-presence across spaces. These spatial practices influence the distribution of economic activities and the formation of urban centralities. Configuration refers to spatial relations among elements interdependent in a global structure. In particular, the configurational properties of closeness and betweenness centrality determine the importance of space as a destination or as a movement space and, thus, its accessibility and intensity of use [12, 14–19]. Porosity is formalised in terms of the density of street segments, and it describes the availability of alternative routes. As a result, it is related to the distribution of pedestrian mobility, social interaction, and the availability of sites for commercial activities [20]. The organisation of the public transport infrastructure, described in terms of the distribution of stations and bus stops, influences the conditions of access to employment, services, and social and cultural activities [21]. Moreover, the distribution and quality of UGI components determine the conditions of access to ecosystem services. The density and diversity of points of interest are related to the vitality and vibrancy of the built environment; vitality and vibrancy, in turn, represent central objectives of sustainable urban development [10, 11, 14]. Lastly, the structure of the built fabric is described in terms of building density; Building density is related to the level of demand that, in turn, influences the density and diversity of uses and, consequently, the intensity of street life [20]. Therefore, the study focuses on defining metrics for describing properties of urban components to understand the distinct spatial conditions of an urbanised area. The formalisation of urban components' properties and the analytic analysis's structure are described in the subsequent sections.

3 Datasets and Methods

The proposed analysis combines geospatial and configurational analysis to describe in quantitative terms the urban form of the Metropolitan City of Cagliari (MCC) in Sardinia, Italy. The MCC consists of 17 municipalities (Cagliari, Assemini, Capoterra, Decimomannu, Elmas, Maracalagonis, Monserrato, Pula, Quartu Sant'Elena, Quartucciu, Sarroch, Selargius, Sestu, Settimo San Pietro, Sinnai, Uta, and Villa San Pietro), has approximately 420,000 inhabitants and an area of 1,248 square kilometres (Fig. 1). The MCC has many valued and unknown POIs (urban, public, commercial activities and recreational-cultural amenities), but all of them are part of an invaluable heritage [8, 22–27].

The study is articulated on four metrics: a ground-surface indicator (GSI), an ecological infrastructure indicator (ENV), a permeability indicator (PER), and a Land-Use indicator (USE). These indicators measure, respectively, the density of the built fabric, the distribution and quality of permeable surfaces, the centrality and density of street segments, the distribution of the nodes of the public transport infrastructure and the density and diversity of Points of Interest (POIs). The unit of analysis is the 150m * 150m cell of a regular square grid superimposed on the study area. The subdivision of the study area into regular square modules ensures the comparability of the units of analysis and the representation of the interdependence of public open spaces, building plots, and land uses [7, 8, 22]. The size of the modules ensures a detailed description of the area of study [7]. The individual and composite indicators are normalised in the 0–1 interval, to enable the aggregation of distinct metrics. The land use indicator is formalised as the mean of the density and diversity of POIs. The density of points of interest is formalised as the number of POIs contained in the i-th cell [9]. Points of interest are defined as point locations related to specific urban amenities. Four categories of points of interest are defined: residential buildings, public services (such as educational facilities, hospitals, public offices, banks, and post offices), commercial activities, and recreational-cultural amenities (such as sports facilities, restaurants, cultural sites).

Diversity is measured via Shannon's diversity index [9, 23]. The Ground-surface indicator is formalised as the ratio of the surface area of the projections of portions of buildings included in the i-th cell to the surface area of the i-th cell [7, 27, 28]. The permeability indicator is calculated as the mean of four metrics measuring the centrality and density of street segments and the distribution of bus stops and stations. These indicators are, respectively, the average Normalised angular integration (NAIN) and the average Normalised angular choice (NACH) of the segments intersecting the i-th cell, the total length of the portions of street segments contained in the i-th cell, and the density of the nodes of the public transport infrastructure.

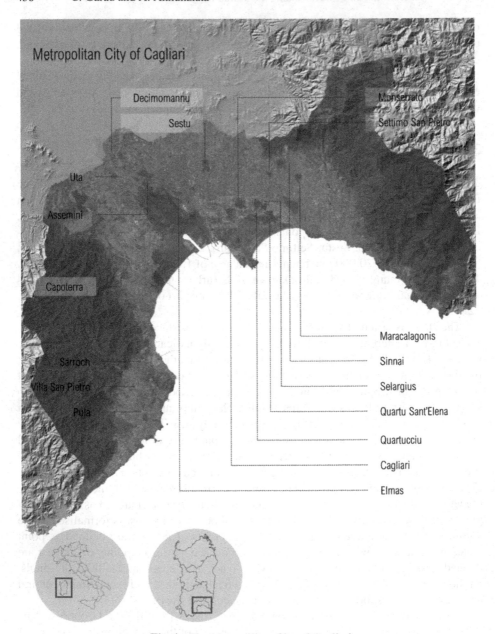

Fig. 1. The Metropolitan City of Cagliari

The latter is calculated as a function of the distance from the nearest node and of the number of nodes contained in the i-th cell. In particular, the NAIN and NACH metrics are utilised to measures the centrality of individual spaces, in order to understand the impact of the configuration of the built environment on patterns of movement. Indeed, configuration can be defined as the set of topological relations among spatial units that are interdependent within a larger structure. The distribution of movement within the urban environment and patterns of co-presence are influenced by topological relations because they determine the accessibility of spaces. Also, the location of economic activity and the development of urban centers are influenced by the simultaneous presence of people in the most important, integrated locations [29–34].

The indicators normalised angular segment Integration (NAIN) and normalised angular segment Choice (NACH) formalise the characteristics of closeness and betweenness centrality. The former refers to the distance – in terms of sum of angular deviations – of each space from any other space comprised in a spatial structure. The latter refers to the probability that a space is intersected by the shortest route between any pair of spaces comprised in a spatial layout. These properties of centrality result in the significance of a place as a destination and in its 'through-movement' potential, respectively. These metrics are measured via the software Depthmap X and are calculated for all spatial elements of the segment map of the metropolitan area, considering an 800 m radius around each element.

A segment map is a representation of the organisation of a spatial system. It is derived from an axial map or, in the case of complex metropolitan structures, from a database of road centrelines via a process of simplification of over-articulated geometries. The 800 m radius is selected in order to consider the most accessible areas in terms of pedestrian movement.

The ecological infrastructure indicator is calculated as the sum of surface areas of natural and semi-natural land cover parcels in the i-th cell, multiplied by a factor indicative of the environmental quality of the j-th land cover and divided by the surface area of the i-th cell.

The spatial elements are then categorised according to the values of the ground-surface indicator, the permeability indicator and of the ecological infrastructure indicator.

The categories identified represent specific spatial conditions; lastly, the land use indicator is calculated to measure the latent vitality of the distinct spatial needs of the area of study and identify critical areas. The subsequent sections describe the application of the proposed analysis and present the findings from the analysis of the MCC.

4   Results

The analysis of the MCC reveals nine distinct spatial conditions (Fig. 2).

Compact dense central areas, including the cores of ancient formation of the municipalities comprised in the MCC, are identified by values of GSI and permeability superior to 0.4, and environmental quality inferior to 0.1.

The Land Use indicator (Fig. 2) ranges from 0 to 0.95, presenting a significant variation (standard deviation equal to 0.22), representative of the concentration of points of interest in specific parts of the Metropolitan Area, particularly in the ancient core of the City of Cagliari.

This particular area emerges as the most integrated and vibrant portion of the MCC. The emergence of centres of ancient formation of the Municipalities constituting the MCC as compact integrated and vibrant cores reveals the potential polycentric structure of the MCC (Fig. 3, 4, 5, 6).

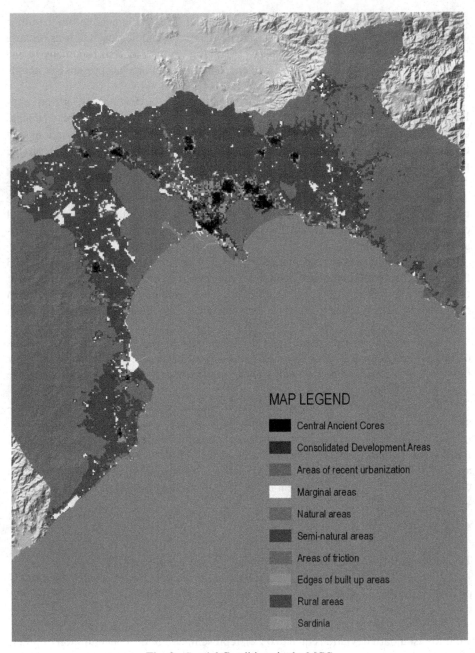

Fig. 2. Spatial Conditions in the MCC

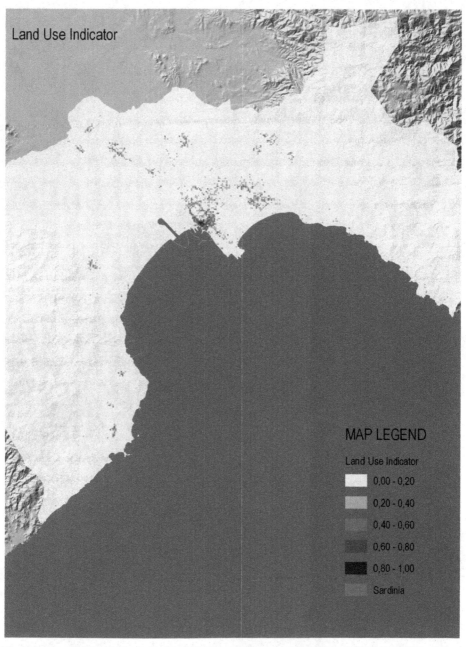

Fig. 3. Values of Land Use Indicator (USE) in the Metropolitan City of Cagliari (MCC). Values are grouped in 5 categories, based on equal intervals

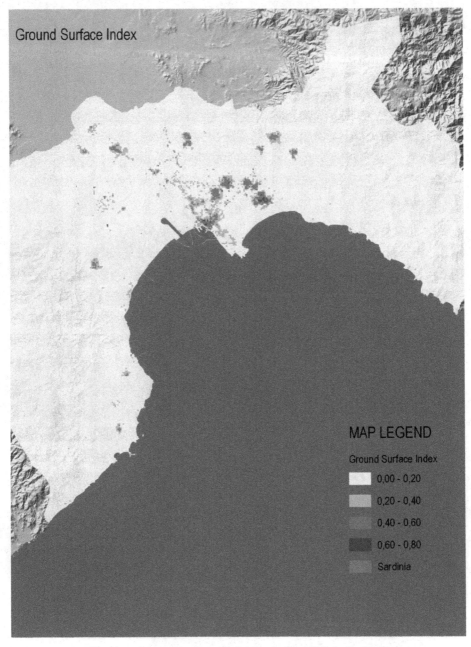

Fig. 4. Values of the Ground Surface Index (GSI) in the MCC

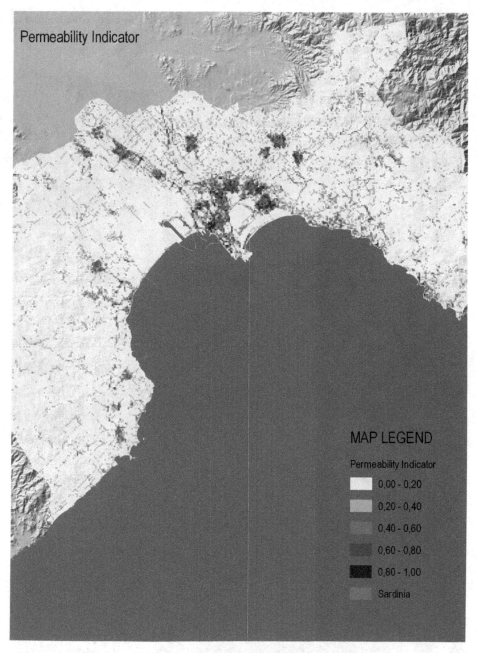

Fig. 5. Values of the Permeability Indicator

Consolidated development areas present a less dense urban fabric ($0.2 \leq$ GSI ≤ 0.4) and permeability superior to 0.4 and comprise compact modern districts contiguous to ancient cores. Density and diversity are inferior to central ancient cores (mean equal to 0.16) (Fig. 4 and 5).

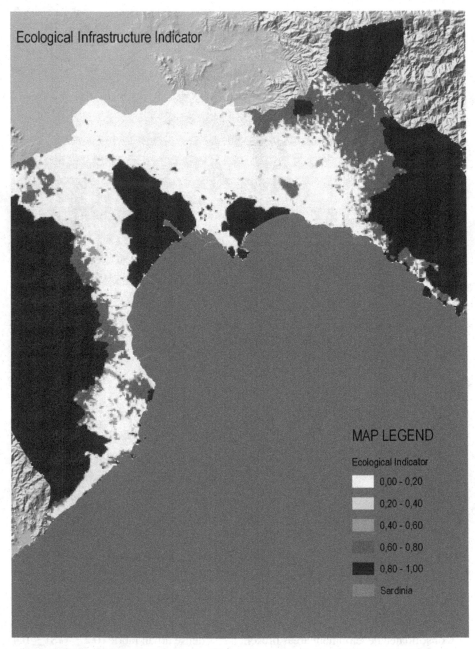

Fig. 6. Values of the Ecological Infrastructure Indicator (ENV) in the MCC

Significant values are observed in compact districts in the municipalities of Cagliari, Assemini, Decimomannu, Pula, Quartu and Quartucciu. Significant spatial conditions, presenting inadequate density and diversity of services, are represented by areas of recent urbanization ($0.0 < GSI \leq 0.4$; $0.2 \leq PER \leq 0.4$; $ENV < 0.1$), edges of built areas, identified as accessible areas ($PER \geq 0.4$) of dispersed urbanization ($0.0 < GSI \leq 0.2$), and areas of friction ($GSI > 0.1$; $ENV > 0.1$) separating built areas and components of the ecological infrastructure.

Moreover, a metropolitan ecological infrastructure emerges, articulated on distinct spatial conditions: Natural Core areas ($GSI < 0.1$; $ENV > 0.6$), transition areas ($GSI < 0.1$; $0.2 < ENV \leq 0.6$), rural areas ($GSI < 0.1$; $0.1 < ENV \leq 0.2$). Lastly, a critical condition is represented by marginal areas, including urbanised areas, presenting inadequate access conditions, and fringe spaces along with major transport infrastructures.

5 Conclusions

The distribution of centrality and integration conditions and built density reveal the polycentric structure of the MCC. Ancient compact areas and consolidated development areas emerge as vital cores, indicating the persistence, at distinct levels of scale, of a structural relation of dependence of the marginal areas on central, compact cores.

In particular, at the metropolitan scale, the compact ancient core and contiguous consolidated areas in the city of Cagliari emerge as the vibrant core of the MCC (Fig. 3). Natural core areas, transition areas, fragments of rural landscape and fringe areas along infrastructure emerge as components of regional ecological infrastructure. They can be conceptualised as metropolitan-scale amenities providing a diversified set of provisioning, cultural, and regulating ecosystem services – including production, recreation, and eco-tourism. The aim is to reinforce the ecological, economic, cultural, and symbolic role of areas of environmental quality. Lastly, the gradient of POIs density reveals the emergence of local centres along arterial metropolitan roads and inter-district distribution roads. As a result, the case study underlines that understanding the urban structure enables the recognition of distinct spatial conditions and the definition of requirements for urban strategies; in particular, four actions are central: i) the location of metropolitan scale amenities in built areas permeable edges and along with major infrastructures; ii) increasing density and diversity of land uses in areas of recent urbanisation, in particular in minor urbanised centres; iii) increasing conditions of access in urbanised marginal areas and of pedestrian access to local centres emerging in areas of dispersed urbanisation and along arterial roads, and iv) the project of a linear system of open spaces, functioning as ecological corridors, public spaces, and routes for soft mobility.

This analysis is the preliminary stage of a study that investigates the integration of spatial and configurational analysis into procedures and tools, enabling the quantitative description of urban form components determining the latent vitality of the urban environment. The objective is to structure an information base for supporting urban planning strategies based on criteria of sustainability, social inclusion, and spatial justice.

More precisely, the future development of this research will explore the influence of the structure of urbanised areas on three distinct topics. The first topic is related to individuals' emotional response to the built environment. The research will integrate the spatial and configurational analysis of the built environment with machine learning techniques for the analysis of micro-scale aspects of the design of urban spaces and deep learning techniques for facial emotion recognition [35, 36]. The aim is to explore the impact of macro-scale morphological factors of the built environment and micro scale aspects of the design of urban spaces – including the presence of vegetation, the presence of active street frontage, and the geometry of the urban space – on individuals' emotional response, formalised in terms of basic emotions – including joy, surprise, anger, sadness and disgust – and evaluated via deep learning techniques. The second topic is related to climate alterations and will focus on the analysis of the impact of the morphological features of the urban environment on micro-climate and on users' comfort. More precisely, this research will integrate spatial and configurational analysis of macro-scale morphological attributes of urban areas, machine learning techniques, based on street space images, for the analysis of micro-scale components of urban spaces – including presence of vegetation, morphology of the urban canyon, sky - view factor and building-view factor - and social media data on individuals' activity patterns. The objective is to measure the influence of macro-scale urban form factors, and of microclimatic conditions determined by the geometrical features of urban spaces on individual and social practices in the public spaces. Within this perspective, the future development of the proposed procedure will include the utilisation of clustering functions, based on machine learning and deep learning techniques [37–39], to improve the identification of distinct urban zones presenting analogous conditions in terms of configuration, density and diversity of functions, contiguity to natural and semi-natural areas, and access to public transit. Lastly, a third potential development concerns the use of the proposed set of metrics for the analysis of the pattern of urbanisation at the regional scale, by integrating different methods of analysis [25, 26, 40–42]. The objective is to understand the latent functional inter-dependencies between rural areas, peripheral centers, metropolitan and urban areas that constitute the framework for a trans-scalar, polycentric organisation of the settlement structure at the regional scale.

Acknowledgements. This study was supported by the MIUR through the project "WEAKI TRANSIT: WEAK"-demand areas Innovative TRANsport Shared services for Italian Towns (Project protocol: 20174ARRHT_004; CUP Code: F74I19001290001), financed with the PRIN 2017 (Research Projects of National Relevance) programme. We authorize the MIUR to reproduce and distribute reprints for Governmental purposes, notwithstanding any copyright notations thereon. Any opinions, findings, and conclusions, or recommendations expressed in this material are those of the authors and do not necessarily reflect the views of the MIUR. This study was developed within the Interdepartmental Center of the University of Cagliari "Cagliari Accessibility Lab". (Rector's Decree of 4 March 2020. https://www.unica.it/unica/it/cagliari_accessibility_lab.page). This study was also supported by the agreement "Evoluzione delle Condizioni di marginalità delle aree interne" stipulated between the School of Engineering of the University of Basilicata (SI-UNIBAS) and the Department of Civil and Environmental Engineering and Architecture of the University of Cagliari, (DICAAR_UNICA), scientific coordinators: Beniamino Murgante (UNIBAS) and Chiara Garau (UNICA). This study was also conducted within the "e.INS – Ecosystem of Innovation for Next Generation Sardinia" funded by the Italian Ministry of University and Research under the Next-Generation EU Programme (National Recovery and Resilience Plan – PNRR, M4C2, INVESTMENT 1.5 – DD 1056 of 23/06/2022, ECS00000038).

This manuscript reflects only the authors' views and opinions, neither the European Union nor the European Commission can be considered responsible for them.

References

1. Annunziata, A.: Spazi Urbani Praticabili. FrancoAngeli, Milan, Italy (2020)
2. Annunziata, A., Garau, C.: A literature review on the assessment of vitality and its theoretical framework. emerging perspectives for geodesign in the urban context. In: Gervasi, O., et al. (eds.) ICCSA 2021. LNCS, vol. 12958, pp. 305–322. Springer, Cham (2021). https://doi.org/10.1007/978-3-030-87016-4_23
3. Bielik, M., König, R., Schneider, S., Varoudis, T.: Measuring the impact of street network configuration on the accessibility to people and walking attractors. Networks and Spatial Econ. 18(3), 657–676 (2018). https://doi.org/10.1007/s11067-018-9426-x
4. Carmona, M.: Place value: place quality and its impact on health, social, economic and environmental outcomes. J. Urban Design 24, 1–48 (2019). 10.1080/13574809.2018.1472523
5. Conzen, M.R.G.: Alnwick, Northumberland: A Study in Town-Plan Analysis. Transactions and Papers (Institute of British Geographers), III–122 (1960). https://doi.org/10.2307/621094
6. Delclòs-Alió, X., Miralles-Guasch, C.: Looking at Barcelona through Jane Jacobs's eyes: mapping the basic conditions for urban vitality in a Mediterranean conurbation. Land Use Policy 75, 505-517 (2018). https://doi.org/10.1016/j.landusepol.2018.04.026
7. Erin, I., Fusco, G., Cubukcu, E., Araldi, A.: Quantitative methods of urban morphology in urban design and environmental psychology. In: Proceedings 24th ISUF 2017 - City and Territory in the Globalization Age (2018). https://doi.org/10.4995/ISUF2017.2017.5732
8. Garau, C., Annunziata, A.: A method for assessing the vitality potential of urban areas. the case study of the metropolitan city of Cagliari, Italy. City, Territory and Archit. 9(1), 1–23 (2022). https://doi.org/10.1186/s40410-022-00153-6
9. Garau, C., Annunziata, A.: Supporting children's independent activities in smart and playable public places. Sustainability 12(20), 8352 (2020). https://doi.org/10.3390/su12208352
10. Garau, C., Annunziata, A., Yamu, C.: The multi-method tool 'PAST' for evaluating cultural routes in historical cities: evidence from Cagliari, Italy. Sustainability 12(14), 5513 (2020). https://doi.org/10.3390/su12145513
11. Garau, C., Annunziata, A., Yamu, C.: A walkability assessment tool coupling multi-criteria analysis and space syntax: the case study of Iglesias, Italy. European Planning Studies, pp. 1–23 (2020). https://doi.org/10.1080/09654313.2020.1761947
12. Gebauer, M.A., Samuels, I.: Urban Morphology: An Introduction. Oxford Polytechnic Joint Centre for Urban Design, Oxford, United Kingdom (1981)
13. Gehl, J.: Life Between Buildings: Using Public Space. Island press, Washington DC, United States (2011)
14. Hillier, B.: Space is the Machine: A Configurational Theory of Architecture. University College of London, London, United Kingdom (2007)
15. Hillier, B., Hanson, J.: The Social Logic of Space. Cambridge University Press, Cambridge, United Kingdom (1984)
16. Jacobs, J.: The Death and Life of Great American Cities. Vintage, New York, United States (2016)
17. Jia, C., Liu, Y., Du, Y.: 'Evaluation of urban vibrancy and its relationship with the economic landscape: a case study of Beijing. ISPRS Int. J. Geo-Information 10(2), 72 (2021). https://doi.org/10.3390/ijgi10020072

18. Kim, S.: Urban vitality, urban form, and land use: their relations within a geographical boundary for walkers. Sustainability 12(24), 10633 (2020). https://doi.org/10.3390/su1224 10633

19. Liu, S., Zhang, L., Long, Y., Long, Y., Xu, M.: A new urban vitality analysis and evaluation framework based on human activity modeling using multi-source big data. ISPRS Int. J. Geo Inf. 9(11), 617 (2020). https://doi.org/10.3390/ijgi9110617

20. Lu, S., Huang, Y., Shi, C., Yang, X.: Exploring the associations between urban form and neighborhood vibrancy: a case study of Chengdu, China. ISPRS Int. J. Geo-Information 8(4), 165 (2019). https://doi.org/10.3390/ijgi8040165

21. Lynch, K.: The Image of the City. MIT Press, Cambridge, Massachusetts, United States (1960)

22. Pintus, S., Garau, C., Mistretta, P.: The paths of history for multicultural tourism: a smart real world in the metropolitan city of Cagliari (Italy). In: Schrenk, M., Popovich, V.V., Zeile, P., et al. (eds): Real Corp 2019-Is this the real world? Perfect smart cities vs. real emotional cities, pp 739–749. CORP Competence Center of Urban and Regional Planning, Vienna (2019)

23. Garau, C., Ilardi, E.: The "non-places" Meet the "places:" virtual tours on smartphones for the enhancement of cultural heritage. J. Urban Technol. 21, 79–91 (2014). https://doi.org/10.1080/10630732.2014.884384

24. Zamperlin, P., Garau, C.: Smart region: analisi e rappresentazione della smartness delle città metropolitane italiane. Bollettino dell'Associazione Italiana di Cartografia, 161, 59–71 (2017). https://doi.org/10.13137/2282-572X/21828

25. Garau, C., Desogus, G., Annunziata, A., Banchiero, F., Mistretta, P.: The monumental heritage in sardinia by historical eras: a research to evaluate the place-based connections. In: Innovation in Urban and Regional Planning: Proceedings of the 11th INPUT Conference, 2, pp. 168–174. Springer International Publishing (2022)

26. Garau, C., Desogus, G., Banchiero, F., Mistretta, P.: A multicultural tourism for evaluating the cultural heritage: the case study of the Region of Sardinia (Italy). In: La Rosa, D., Privitera, R. (eds.) INPUT 2021. LNCE, vol. 146, pp. 551–560. Springer, Cham (2021). https://doi.org/10.1007/978-3-030-68824-0_59

27. Mouratidis, K., Poortinga, W.: Built environment, urban vitality and social cohesion: do vibrant neighborhoods foster strong communities? Landsc. Urban Plan. 204, 103951 (2020). https://doi.org/10.1016/j.landurbplan.2020.103951

28. Ye, Y., Li, D., Liu, X.: How block density and typology affect urban vitality: an exploratory analysis in Shenzhen, China. Urban Geography 39(4), 631–652 (2018). https://doi.org/10.1080/02723638.2017.1381536

29. Pinna, F., Garau, C., Annunziata, A.: A literature review on urban usability and accessibility to investigate the related criteria for equality in the city. In: Gervasi, O., et al. (eds.) ICCSA 2021. LNCS, vol. 12958, pp. 525–541. Springer, Cham (2021). https://doi.org/10.1007/978-3-030-87016-4_38

30. van Nes, A., Yamu, C.: Introduction to Space Syntax in Urban Studies. Springer International Publishing, Cham, Switzerland (2021). https://doi.org/10.1007/978-3-030-59140-3

31. Vaughan, L.: The spatial syntax of urban segregation. Prog. Plan. 67, 205–294 (2007). https://doi.org/10.1016/j.progress.2007.03.001

32. Whyte, W.H.: The Social Life of Small Urban Spaces. Conservation Foundation, Washington, DC, United States (1980)

33. Yamu, C., van Nes, A., Garau, C.: Bill Hillier's legacy: space syntax—a synopsis of basic concepts, measures, and empirical application. Sustainability 13(6), 3394 (2021). https://doi.org/10.3390/su13063394

34. Ye, Y., Van Nes, A.: Quantitative tools in urban morphology: combining space syntax, spacematrix and mixed-use index in a GIS framework. Urban Morphology 18(2), 97–118 (2014)

35. Biondi, G., Franzoni, V., Gervasi, O., Perri, D.: An approach for improving automatic mouth emotion recognition. In: Misra, S., et al. (eds.) ICCSA 2019. LNCS, vol. 11619, pp. 649–664. Springer, Cham (2019). https://doi.org/10.1007/978-3-030-24289-3_48
36. Riganelli, M., Franzoni, V., Gervasi, O., Tasso, S.: EmEx, a tool for automated emotive face recognition using convolutional neural networks. In: Gervasi, O., et al. (eds.) ICCSA 2017. LNCS, vol. 10406, pp. 692–704. Springer, Cham (2017). https://doi.org/10.1007/978-3-319-62398-6_49
37. D'Apuzzo, M., Spacagna, R.-L., Evangelisti, A., Santilli, D., Nicolosi, V.: Sectioning procedure on geostatistical indices series of pavement road profiles. In: Balzano, S., Porzio, G.C., Salvatore, R., Vistocco, D., Vichi, M. (eds.) CLADAG 2019. SCDAKO, pp. 69–77. Springer, Cham (2021). https://doi.org/10.1007/978-3-030-69944-4_8
38. Anselin, L., Williams, S.: Digital neighborhoods. J. Urbanism: Int. Res. Placemaking and Urban Sustainability **9**, 305–328 (2016). https://doi.org/10.1080/17549175.2015.1080752
39. Mollick, T., Azam, M.G., Karim, S.: Geospatial-based machine learning techniques for land use and land cover mapping using a high-resolution unmanned aerial vehicle image. Remote Sensing Appl.: Society Environ. **29**, 100859 (2023). https://doi.org/10.1016/j.rsase.2022.100859
40. Annunziata, A., Desogus, G., Garau, C.: Smart tourism governance for urban bioregion: an evaluating approach to the relationship between coastal and inland areas of South Sardinia. Building the Urban Bioregion Governance Scenarios for Urban and Territorial Planning **290** (2022)
41. Garau, C., Desogus, G., Barabino, B., Coni, M.: Accessibility and public transport mobility for a smart (er) island: evidence from Sardinia (Italy). Sustain. Cities Soc. **87**, 104145 (2022)
42. Garau, C., Desogus, G., Stratigea, A.: Monitoring sustainability performance of insular territories against SDGs: the mediterranean case study region. J. Urban Planning Dev. **148**(1), 05021069 (2022)

The Emergence of Robotics in Tourism and Hospitality: A Bibliometric Analysis from 2017 to 2023

Tutut Herawan[1]([✉]), Sunyoto Sunyoto[2], Wahyu Indro Widodo[3],
Fatimatuz Zahra Disma[1], Lexi Pranata Budidharmanto[4], Damiasih Damiasih[1],
and Eka Novita Sari[5]

[1] Sekolah Tinggi Pariwisata Ambarrukmo Yogyakarta, Jalan Ringroad Timur No. 52, Bantul,
Daerah Istimewa, Yogyakarta 55198, Indonesia
{tutut,damiasih}@stipram.ac.id

[2] Dinas Pariwisata dan Kebudayaan Kabupaten Trenggalek, Jl. Brigjend Sutran No. 9,
Trenggalek, Jawa Timur 66315, Indonesia

[3] Lembaga Kajian Pariwisata Indonesia, Babadan, Sewon, Bantul, Daerah Istimewa,
Yogyakarta 55185, Indonesia

[4] School of Tourism, Universitas Ciputra CitraLand CBD Boulevard, Surabaya, Jawa
Timur 60219, Indonesia
llimbing@ciputra.ac.id

[5] AMCS Research Center, Jalan Griya Taman Asri, Yogyakarta 55512, Indonesia

Abstract. We present an analysis of the emergence of robotic technology researches in tourism and hospitality from 2017 to 2023. Bibliometric analysis was used to analyze 47 articles published from 2017 to 2023 based on source, document type, journal name, publisher name, topic trends, and author collaborations. We use the combination of Robotics+ Tourism+ Hospitality as our main keywords in searching related article titles, abstracts, and keywords to get metadata, where the Scopus database is the main source. The tools used in this bibliometric analysis are Harzing's Publish or Perish for importing source data from Scopus database. Furthermore, we employ VoS Viewer for data visualization and further used for citation and metrics analysis. The results indicate that most related articles to are published in scientific journals, compared to other publication outlets e.g., book chapter, conference proceedings and book. Related articles published in scientific journals have received the highest citations compared to others. Based on network and overlay visualization, the most dominant terms (often appearing) are "AI", "services robots", "human robot interaction", "autonomy".

Keywords: Bibliometric analysis · Robotics · Tourism · Hospitality · Publish or Perish · VoS Viewer

1 Introduction

Robotics technology has presently served tourism and hospitality sectors. Although the establishment of robot technology is already used in industries since long time ago, however the incorporation of robot technology came relatively late to the tourism and hospitality industries. Especially those involved in travel, food and beverage services, hotel service, entertainment, etc. Today, robotics has been used frequently since many of the tourism and hospitality services required sophisticated responses to the needs of the customers. While many automotive industries were largely employed by robots since 1990s, it was started by 2017 that tourism and hospitality researchers entered to the field i.e., added tourism and hospitality fields to robotics-based research. Joshi [1] initiated the used of robotics in Hospitality Industry. He took a case study at Henna Hotel, Huis Ten BoSch, Japan. Ivanov, *et al.* [2] adopted robots for service automation by tourism and hospitality companies. Ivanov & Webster [3] designed robot-base facilities for further friendly hospitality service. Bowen and Whalen [4] presented several trends that are changing travel and tourism, including robot technology. Ivanov & Webster [5] adopted AI, service automation and robots for travel, tourism and hospitality companies using a cost-benefit analysis. Kuo, *et al.* [6] investigated an innovative service with hospitality robots. Murphy, *et al.* [7]. Initiated a study of the age of robots in hospitality and tourism. Further they presented some challenges for teaching and research. Murphy, *et al.* [8] presented a research agenda involving robots in hospitality and tourism. Alexis [9] introduced the Potential Impact of Robotics and Service Automation in Tourism. Tung & Law [10] presented the potential for tourism and hospitality experience research in human-robot interactions.

In 2018, there are many researches in the filed done. Tussyadiah & Park [11] studied consumer evaluation of hotel service robots. Korstanje & Seraphin [12] presented a critical discussion of the role of robots in the rite of hospitality. Ukpabi, *et al.* [13] presented dual perspectives on the role of artificially intelligent robotic virtual agents in the tourism, travel and hospitality industries. Ivanov, *et al.* [14] studied consumers' attitudes towards the introduction of robots in accommodation establishments. Tung & Au [15] explored customer experiences with robotics in hospitality. Ivanov, *et al.* [16] presented a study on young Russian adults' attitudes towards the potential use of robots in hotels. Bowen & Morosan [17] studied the emergence of robot technology in hospitality industry. Primawati [18] studied the role of AI-based robot as an innovation in the hotel service.

In year 2019, Ivanov, *et al.* [19] reviewed the progress on robotics in hospitality and tourism. Gretzel & Murphy [20] studied consumer discourse on robots in tourism and hospitality service settings. Ivanov & Webster [21] proposed a conceptual framework of the use of AI, service automation, and robots in travel, tourism, and hospitality companies. Murphy, *et al.* [22] studied the role of anthropomorphism on marketing robot services in hospitality and tourism. Ivanov, [23] studied the ultimate transformation on how automation technologies disrupt the travel, tourism, and hospitality industries. Cain, *et al.* [24] presented the state of robotics and AI in the hospitality industry. Ivanov & Webster [25] compiled many studies on robots, artificial intelligence and service automation in travel, tourism, and hospitality. Popesku [26] presented current applications of artificial intelligence in tourism and hospitality. Ivanov & Webster [27] studied on perceived appropriateness and intention to use service robots in tourism.

In 2020, Christou, *et al.* [28] presented tourists' perceptions regarding the use of anthropomorphic robots in tourism and hospitality. Go, *et al.* [29] presented on machine learning of robots using interactive technology acceptance model in tourism and hospitality. McCartney & McCartney [30] proposed a conceptual service-robot research framework for the hospitality and tourism industry. Samala, *et al.* [31] presented a critical insight on the impact of AI and robotics in the tourism sector. Kilichan & Yilmaz [32] studied AI and robotic technologies in tourism and hospitality industry. de Kervenoael, *et al.* [33] presented a study on human-robot interaction in hospitality services. They incorporated the role of perceived value, empathy, and information sharing into visitors' intentions to use social robots. Reis, *et al.* [34] studied service robots in the hospitality industry, where the case study took place at Henn-na hotel, Japan.

In 2021, Belanche, *et al.* [35] presented both service enhancement or cost reduction studies involving robots in tourism and hospitality. Manthiou, *et al.* [36] examined the three themes of service robotics in tourism and hospitality. Abou-Shouk, *et al.* [37] explored customers' attitudes to the adoption of robots in tourism and hospitality. Fusté-Forné & Jamal [38] proposed new directions for service robots in hospitality and tourism. Koo, *et al.* [39] incorporated AI and robotics technologies in travel, hospitality, and leisure. Mingotto, *et al.* [40] presented several challenges in re-designing operations and jobs to embody AI and robotics in services. Findings from a case in the hospitality industry. Choi, *et al.* [41] Exploring the influence of culture on tourist experiences with robots in service delivery environment.

Since the starting interest in robotics in tourism and hospitality raises from above explanation, then the need for an analysis study on the development on the topic and an identification of future research avenues in the field is emerged. Therefore, this paper investigates the academic literature on robots and its relevance to the travel, tourism and hospitality industries, where a bibliometric analysis approach is used. I this work, we use the Scopus database from 2017 to 2023. We present both the publication source, document type, journal name and rank, publisher name and rank, topic trends, and author collaborations, and visualize them. Finally, we discuss some of the research highlights to be explore in future.

The rest of the paper is organized as follows. Section 2 describes the proposed stages of this work. Section 3 presents the results and following discussion. Finally, we draw conclusion and highlight future recommendations in Sect. 4.

2   Proposed Method

We present bibliometrics analysis which consists of five stages, namely: Determining the keywords, initial searching and repair searching results; Compiling preliminary data statistics (before and after repairing) and saving in RIS format; Enter RIS data into Publish or Perish; Analysis of publications sources and citations; and finally visualize the results using VoS Viewer. Figure 1 below depicts the flow chart of our proposed method.

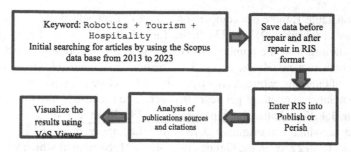

Fig. 1. Flow chart of the proposed method

3 Results and Discussion

This section explains the obtained results of this work, which includes publications and citations, visualizations, authors and networks, research locations and research domains.

3.1 Publications and Citations

For knowing comparison of the citation matrix on the data taken via Scopus, then researcher make the table in which containing number article, number citation, number citations per year, number authors per year, H index, G index, normal hI, and hI yearly at the beginning search and on results repair. Comparison data matrix in result search start and result search after repair could be seen in Table 1.

Table 1. Comparison Matrix

Data	Initial Search Results	Search Results Repair
Database	Scopus	Scopus
Year publishing	2017–2023	2017–2023
Year citation	6	6
Number of Articles	64	47
Number citation	2149	1719
Number Citation per Year	358.17	286.50
Number Authors per Year	3.13	3.11
H index	22	19
G index	46	41
hI Normal	14	13
hI Annual	2.33	2.17

Based on Table 1, there is a comparison matrix of data before and after comparison over a period of 6 years (2017–2023). In the Table 1, it can be seen several quantitative decreases, starting with the number of existing articles, it is presented that before the improvement there were 64 articles, but after the improvement to 47. The same is true of the number of citations, which were originally 2149 before the repair to 1719 after the repair. The number of citations per year also decreased because before the improvement amounted to 358.17 and after the improvement to 286.50. In relation to the author, there was a decrease, which was originally 3.13 before the improvement to 3.11. The H index also changed, from 22 to 19, the G index from 46 to 41. Normal hI which was originally 14 dropped to 13 and annual hI which was originally 2.33 to 2.17.

Table 2. The statistics descriptive of publication

Year	TP	% (N = 47)	NCP	TC	C/P	C/CP
2017	3	0.06	3	315	105.00	105.00
2018	3	0.06	3	285	95.00	95.00
2019	6	0.13	6	533	88.83	88.83
2020	5	0.11	5	243	48.60	48.60
2021	12	0.26	9	36	3.00	4.00
2022	14	0.30	12	107	7.64	8.92
2023	4	0.09	0	0	0.00	0.00
	47	100%				

Note: TP = total number of publications; NCP = number cited publications; TC = total quotes; C/P = average citations per publication; C/CP = average citation per cited publication.

From Table 2 above, in the first year, namely 2017, there were 3 publications where all three were cited 315 times. In 2018 with the publication of 3 journals and as many as 285 times citation from the three articles. In 2019, he succeeded in contributing 6 articles with 583 times the three articles were cited. In 2020 he succeeded in contributing to publishing 5 articles with 243 citations using the five articles. 2021 became the year with the most publications and was able to double the number from the previous few years with a total of 12 articles, of which 9 were cited 36 times in a percentage of 0.26%. Year 2022 is the year with the most publications, amounting to 14 publications with 12 of them quoted as many as 107 times and managed to contribute 0.30%. In 2023, so far it has succeeded in publishing as many as 4 articles and there is no data related to the number of publication citations and the number of citations. Figure 1 as follow depicts the bar chart of publication and citations.

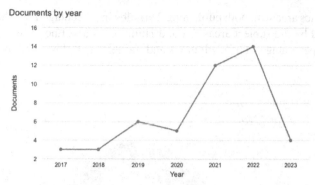

Fig. 2. Publication from 2017–2023

In Fig. 2 above, there is a graph that shows the number of documents in each year with the interval 2017 to 2023. It can be seen that 2021 is the year that outperforms the previous few years until 2022 becomes the peak point in journal publishing by publishing as many as 14 articles which is equivalent to a percentage of around 18%. 2017 and 2018 were the years with the least number of publications with 3 articles. Figure 3 as follow depicts the documents by subject area.

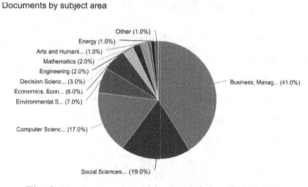

Fig. 3. Documents by subject area from 2017–2023

Figure 3 above displays data based on the subject area presented in the form of a pie diagram. Each portion and percentage on the chart are the search result on the Scopus page for further use in this article. The subject area of Business, Management, and Accounting became the most dominant with a contribution of 41 articles or in a percentage of 41% represented with a blue portion. Social Sciences occupies the second position with a contribution of 19 articles in a percentage of 19% represented by the portion of the red chart. The third largest portion is occupied by the subject of Computer Science with a contribution of 17 articles in a percentage of 17% represented by green. The next subject in a row is Environmental Science which succeeded in publishing 7 articles or 7%, Economics, Econometrics and Finance with 6 articles or 6%, next the subject of Decision Sciences with 3 articles or 3% followed by the subject of Engineering and Mathematics area with both publishing 2 articles in percentage 2%. Then the bottom 2 are occupied by the subject areas Art and Humanities and Energy who each publish 1 article in a percentage of 1%. Figure 4 and Table 3 as follow describes the type of documents.

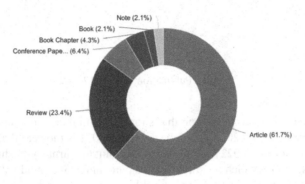

Fig. 4. The type of documents

Table 3. The type of documents

Type	Number	Percentage
Article	29	0.62
Review	11	0.23
Conference Paper	3	0.06
Book Chapter	2	0.04
Book	1	0.02
Note	1	0.02
	47	100%

Figure 4 and Table 3 above respectively depicts and describes document types that show the 6 types of documents used in the preparation of this article, namely Article, Review, Conference Paper, Book Chapter, Book and Note from Scopus datavase. The type of document with the type of Article is the most dominant with a total of 29 articles in a percentage of 62%, followed by the Review document type with 11 articles or in a percentage of 23%. Conference Paper ranked 3rd with 3 articles in a percentage of 6%, Book Chapters with 2 articles or 4%, and the last 2 types of documents occupied by Book and Note as much as 1 piece with a percentage of 2%. Figure 5 as follow depicts the documents per year by source.

Documents per year by source

Compare the document counts for up to 10 sources.   Compare sources and view CiteScore, SJR, and SNIP dat

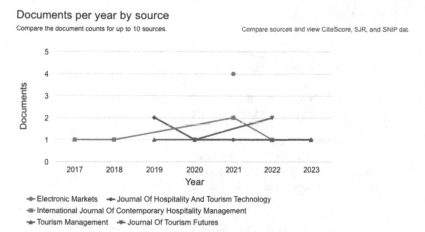

◆ Electronic Markets   ◆ Journal Of Hospitality And Tourism Technology
■ International Journal Of Contemporary Hospitality Management
▲ Tourism Management   ◆ Journal Of Tourism Futures

Fig. 5. Documents by source area from 2017–2023

From Fig. 7 above, sources from the International Journal of Contemporary Hospitality Management were published in 2014 and increased from 2018 to 2021 before declining in 2022. Sources from Tourism Management have successfully published from 2019 to 2023. Furthermore, the source of the Journal of Hospitality and Tourism Technology began publication in 2019 and experienced a decrease in 2020 in contrast to the source of the Journal of Tourism Features which increased from its inception in 2020 to 2022. Table 4 as follow describes the type sources of publication.

Table 4. Document source type

Type	Number	Percentage
Journal	41	0.87
Conference Proceeding	3	0.06
Book Series	2	0.04
Book	1	0.02
	47	100%

In Table 4 above, data is presented of document analysis or data based on the type of source. The data displayed is entirely derived from the Scopus database. In the first place comes from the Journal with a contribution of 41 articles which is equivalent to a percentage of 87%, which is then followed by Conference Proceedings which contributes 3 articles or equivalent to a percentage of 6%, then the third position is the Book Series with a contribution of 2 articles with a percentage of 4%. The last position is occupied by the Source Book type with a contribution of 1 book which is equivalent to a percentage of 2%. Figure 6 as follow depicts the documents by affiliation.

Documents by affiliation ⓘ

Compare the document counts for up to 15 affiliations.

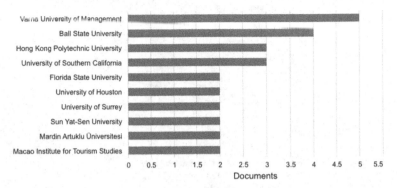

Fig. 6. Documents by affiliation area from 2017–2023

Figure 6 above displays documents based on their affiliation. Using the Scopus database, it was found that Vama University of Management was the most in contributing affiliates with a total of 5 articles. Bali State University occupies the second most positions with 4 articles, then followed by Hong Kong Polytechnic University and the University of Southern California as many as 3 articles. For other affiliates each donated 2 articles such as Florida State University, University of Houston, University of Surrey, Sun Yat-Sen University, Mardin Artuklu Universitesi, Macao Institute for Tourism Studies.

Table 5. Top 20 cited articles

Cites	Authors	Title	Year	Journal Name	Publisher
180	Tung & Au	Exploring customer experiences with robotics in hospitality	2018	International Journal of Contemporary Hospitality Management	Emerald
164	Li, *et al*	Hotel employee's artificial intelligence and robotics awareness and its impact on turnover intention: The moderating roles of perceived organizational support and competitive psychological climate	2019	Tourism Management	Elsevier

(*continued*)

Table 5. (*continued*)

Cites	Authors	Title	Year	Journal Name	Publisher
150	de Kervenoael, *et al*	Leveraging human-robot interaction in hospitality services: Incorporating the role of perceived value, empathy, and information sharing into visitorsâ€™ intentions to use social robots	2020	Tourism Management	Elsevier
149	Tung & Law	The potential for tourism and hospitality experience research in human-robot interactions	2017	International Journal of Contemporary Hospitality Management	Emerald
147	Murphy, *et al*	Marketing robot services in hospitality and tourism: the role of anthropomorphism	2019	Journal of Travel and Tourism Marketing	Routledge
146	Ivanov, *et al*	Progress on robotics in hospitality and tourism: a review of the literature	2019	Journal of Hospitality and Tourism Technology	Emerald
132	Murphy, *et al*	Dawning of the age of robots in hospitality and tourism: Challenges for teaching and research	2017	European Journal of Tourism Research	Varna University of Management
86	Bowen & Morosan	Beware hospitality industry: the robots are coming	2018	Worldwide Hospitality and Tourism Themes	Emerald
64	Belanche, *et al*	Frontline robots in tourism and hospitality: service enhancement or cost reduction?	2021	Electronic Markets	Springer
48	Ivanov & Webster	Robots in tourism: A research agenda for tourism economics	2020	Tourism Economics	SAGE
43	Samala, *et al*	Impact of AI and robotics in the tourism sector: a critical insight	2022	Journal of Tourism Futures	Emerald

(*continued*)

Table 5. (*continued*)

Cites	Authors	Title	Year	Journal Name	Publisher
41	Choi, *et al*	Exploring the influence of culture on tourist experiences with robots in service delivery environment	2021	Current Issues in Tourism	Routledge
38	Cain, *et al*	From sci-fi to sci-fact: the state of robotics and AI in the hospitality industry	2019	Journal of Hospitality and Tourism Technology	Emerald
34	Bowen & Whalen	Trends that are changing travel and tourism	2017	Worldwide Hospitality and Tourism Themes	Emerald
33	Nam, *et al*	The adoption of artificial intelligence and robotics in the hotel industry: prospects and challenges	2021	Electronic Markets	Springer
29	Ivanov & Webster	Robots, artificial intelligence and service automation in travel, tourism and hospitality	2019	Robots, Artificial Intelligence and Service Automation in Travel, Tourism and Hospitality	Emerald
26	Tuomi, *et al*	Spicing up hospitality service encounters: the case of Pepper™	2021	International Journal of Contemporary Hospitality Management	Emerald
24	Ivanov & Webster	Willingness-to-pay for robot-delivered tourism and hospitality services–an exploratory study	2021	International Journal of Contemporary Hospitality Management	Emerald
19	Blöcher & Alt	AI and robotics in the European restaurant sector: Assessing potentials for process innovation in a high-contact service industry	2021	Electronic Markets	Springer
19	Yu	Humanlike robot and human staff in service: Age and gender differences in perceiving smiling behaviors	2018	2018 7th International Conference on Industrial Technology and Management	IEEE

Table 5 above present 20 articles cited from various related fields. Based on the table above, an article by Tung & Au entitled "Exploring customer experiences with robotics in hospitality" in the International Journal of Contemporary Hospitality Management in 2018 occupies the first position that is most quoted, which is 180 times using the publisher Emerald The second position is occupied by a journal by Li, *et al.* in Tourism Management with the title "Hotel employee's artificial intelligence and robotics awareness and its impact on turnover intention: The moderating roles of perceived organizational support and competitive psychological climate" published by Elsevier. in 2019. In the last place occupied by the journal works Yu published in 2018 under the title "Humanlike robot and human staff in service: Age and gender differences in perceiving smiling behaviors" pada 2018 7th International Conference on Industrial Technology and Management published by oleh IEEE. Table 6 as follow describes the top five publisher on the related field.

Table 6. Top five publishers

No	Publisher	Number of Articles	Percentage
1	Emerald	19	0.46
2	Elsevier	11	0.27
3	Springer	6	0.15
4	Routledge	3	0.07
5	IEEE	2	0.05
		41	100%

Table 6 above displays the top 5 publishers used out of a total of 41 articles used. The first rank is occupied by Emerald publisher with 19 articles equivalent to a percentage of 46%, then followed by Elsevier with a contribution of 11 articles with a percentage of 27%. The third position is occupied by Springer publisher with a contribution of 6 articles with a percentage of 15%, followed by Routledge with a contribution of 3 articles with a percentage of 7% and the last position by the Institute of Electrical and Electronics Engineers Inc. With a contribution of 2 articles with a percentage of 5%. Table 7 as follow describes the top five journal on the related field.

Table 7. Top five journals ranking

No	Journal Name	Number of Articles	Percentage
1	Journal of Hospitality and Tourism Technology	5	0.28
2	Electronic Markets	4	0.22
3	International Journal of Contemporary Hospitality Management	4	0.22
4	Journal of Tourism Futures	3	0.17
5	Tourism Management	2	0.11
		18	100%

Table 7 displays a list of the top 5 journals that contributed to the publication of documents related to Smart Tourism from a total of 18 articles. Data shows that the Journal of Hospitality and Tourism Technology has a share of 5 articles in a percentage of 28%, then Electronic Markets and the International Journal of Contemporary Hospitality Management with a contribution of 4 articles in a percentage of 22%. The fourth position is occupied by the Journal of Tourism Futures with 3 articles equivalent to a percentage of 17% and closed by Tourism Management journal with a contribution of 2 articles in a percentage of 11%.

3.2 Visualization Topics Use VoS Viewer

Figure 7 below this show visualization of topic areas using network visualization from VoS Viewer.

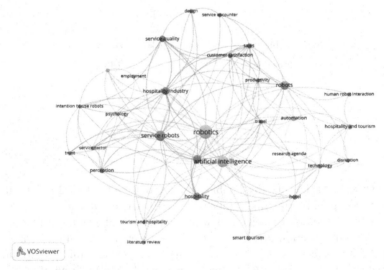

Fig. 7. Visualization topic area using network visualization

Table 8 as follow describes the item number in clusters obtained from VoS Viewer.

Table 8. Item number in clusters

Cluster	Color	Number of Items
1	Red	8
2	Green	6
3	Blue	6
4	Yellow	5
5	Purple	3
6	Light Blue	3

From Table 8 above, there are 6 clusters presented by 6 different colors. Several items obtained from mapping images with visualization of the Smart Tourism topic. Those colors are given follows by:

a. Red (8 items) consist of Hospitality Industry, Service Quality, Customer Satisfaction, Sales, Productivity, Service encounter, design and travel.
b. Green (6 items) consist of Robotics, Hospitality and Tourism, Technology, Disruption, Hotel, and Human robot interaction.
c. Blue (6 items) consist of Service robots, Artificial Intelligence, Hospitality, Perception, Service sector, and Trust.
d. Yellow (5 items) consist of Robotics, Artificial Intelligence, Smart Tourism, Automation, and Research Agenda.
e. Purple (3 items) consist of Service robots, tourism and hospitality, and Literature Review.
f. Light Blue (3 items) consist of Psychology, Intention to use robots, and employment.

Figure 8 as follow describes the visualization topic area using overlay visualization from VoS Viewer.

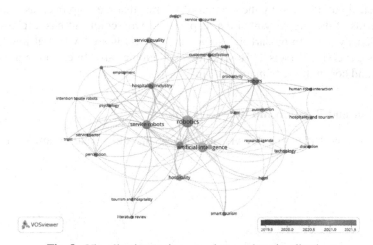

Fig. 8. Visualization topic area using overlay visualization

Figure 8 above shows the topic mapping with overlay visualization based on the color of the item. The color itself based on the longer a document produced which can be known that 2019 to 2020 is the darkest one than the other. That dark colors in 2019 include "Disruption", "Human robot interaction", "Customer satisfaction", "Service encounter". On 2020 there are "Robotics", "Psychology". Meanwhile, in 2021 there are "Service robots", "Artificial Intelligence", "Hospitality Industry", "Hospitality". Figure 9 as follow describes the visualization topic area using density visualization from VoS Viewer.

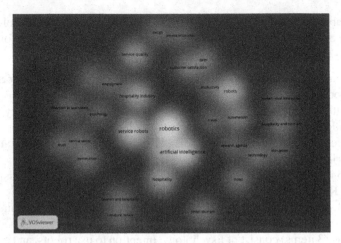

Fig. 9. Visualization topic area using density visualization

Figure 9 above depicts the density visualization. With this, the brighter color represents the presented the keywords. Brightly colored objects are meant to stand out and be more easily understood by the number of themes that are employed as study material. In terms of density, a symbol that is provided with color but has a relatively low level of density tends to be darker. The popular keywords are "Artificial Intelligence", "Robotics', "Service Robots", "Hospitality". Rare topics are "Intention to use robots", "tourism and hospitality", "Smart Tourism".

3.3 Author and Relationship Between Writer

Figure 10 below depicts overlay visualization of the author and co-author using VoS Viewer.

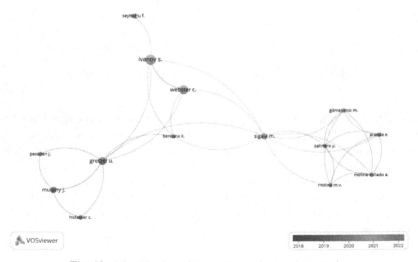

Fig. 10. Visualization of the author and co-author overlay

In Fig. 10 above, it is a mapping of the author visualization and co-author overlay which is analyzed using VoS viewer to get the relation between both author and co-author. Each author's nodes are colored according to the year they were published in the journal, and the number of nodes shows how many papers have been uploaded and how large the author network is. Based on the results, every author has share same connections on average. Gretzel who has connected to 6 authors and wrote article on average by 2018, secondly Webster, who has connections to 4 authors and wrote an article on average by 2020. Furthermore, Ivanov has connected to 4 authors who wrote on average year by 2021, likewise with Sigala. The last one Salinero who has 4 connections who wrote an article on the average year by 2022.

3.4 Research Locations and Research Domains

Table 9 below describes top 10 country of research location and research domain.

Table 9. Top 10 Country of research location and research domain

No	Country	Number of Articles	Research domain
1	United States	12	Robotics, robots, artificial intelligence, services robots, human robot interaction, AI awareness, autonomy, anthropomorphism
2	China	6	Robotics, service quality, service robots, AI awareness, ARMA model, acceptance of robots, air transportation
3	India	6	Artificial intelligence, automation, tourism, antecedent outcome framework, automation techniques
4	Turkey	5	Artificial intelligence, robotics, business process, collaborative spaces, contactless hosting, chatbots
5	United Kingdom	5	Artificial intelligence, hospitality industry, hospitality services, robotics, robots
6	Bulgaria	4	Robotics, robots, service robots, tourism, competitiveness, discrimination, hospitality
7	Hong Kong	4	Artificial intelligence, hospitality, perceived discrimination, robots
8	Australia	3	Robotics, autonomy, bibliometrics, hospitality, hotel, human robot interaction
9	Finland	3	Robotics, robots, artificial intelligence, hospitality, tourism,
10	France	3	Artificial intelligence, acceptance, biosensors, conceptual framework, contactless hosting

Table 9 above provides a more thorough explanation of the number of articles produced based on research domains from different nations. Similar to the preceding image, the United States has the -highest number of publications in the field of research, with 12 articles which include terms like "Robotics", "robots", "artificial intelligence", "services robots", "human robot interaction", "AI awareness", "autonomy", "anthropomorphism" as research domain keywords. Then came neighboring nations, like China and India with 6 shared articles, Turkey, United Kingdom, Bulgaria Hong Kong grouped by produced the similar amount which is 4 articles. Australia, Finland, and France all produced by 3 articles.

4 Conclusion and Suggestions

We have presented a bibliometric analysis on robotics technology researches in tourism and hospitality from 2017 to 2023. Our bibliometric study has shown in helping researchers to determine the characteristics of scientific production, including what, who, how, how, and where, it was published. Our bibliometric study contributes theoretically in determining the characteristics and evolution of scientific publication in the related field. Therefore, the results of this work can be a guideline for future researchers who are researching new topics in robotics technology in tourism and hospitality. Finally, the most found topics "AI", "services robots", "human robot interaction", "autonomy", and "anthropomorphism" can help the researchers to come up with alternative ideas of researches.

Since the coverage of Scopus database is smaller than that Google Scholar, thus it is recommended for future work to explore the Google Scholar which contain more published articles.

Acknowledgment. This research is fully supported by Sekolah Tinggi Pariwisata Ambarrukmo Yogyakarta.

References

1. Joshi, A.: Advances in hospitality & tourism robotics and hospitality industry at henna hotel, Huis Ten BoSch, Japan. KIMI Hosp. Res. J. **2**(1), 1 (2017)
2. Ivanov, S.H., Webster, C., Berezina, K.: Adoption of robots and service automation by tourism and hospitality companies. Revista Turismo & Desenvolvimento **27**(28), 1501–1517 (2017)
3. Ivanov, S.H., Webster, C.: Designing robot-friendly hospitality facilities. In: Proceedings of the Scientific Conference Tourism. Innovations. Strategies, pp. 13–14 (2017)
4. Bowen, J., Whalen, E.: Trends that are changing travel and tourism. Worldwide Hospitality and Tourism Themes (2017)
5. Ivanov, S.H., Webster, C.: Adoption of robots, artificial intelligence and service automation by travel, tourism and hospitality companies–a cost-benefit analysis. Artificial Intelligence and Service Automation by Travel, Tourism and Hospitality Companies–A Cost-Benefit Analysis (2017)
6. Kuo, C.-M., Chen, L.-C., Tseng, C.-Y.: Investigating an innovative service with hospitality robots. Int. J. Contemp. Hosp. Manage. **29**(5), 1305–1321 (2017). https://doi.org/10.1108/IJCHM-08-2015-0414

7. Murphy, J., Hofacker, C., Gretzel, U.: Dawning of the age of robots in hospitality and tourism: challenges for teaching and research. Eur. J. Tourism Res. **15**(2017), 104–111 (2017)
8. Murphy, J., Hofacker, C.F., Gretzel, U.: Robots in hospitality and tourism: a research agenda. eReview of Tourism Research, ENTER 8 (2017)
9. Alexis, P.: R-Tourism: introducing the potential impact of robotics and service automation in tourism. Ovidius University Annals, Series Economic Sciences **17**(1) (2017)
10. Tung, V.W.S., Law, R.: The potential for tourism and hospitality experience research in human-robot interactions. Int. J. Contemp. Hosp. Manag. **29**(10), 2498–2513 (2017)
11. Tussyadiah, I.P., Park, S.: Consumer evaluation of hotel service robots. In: Stangl, B., Pesonen, J. (eds.) Information and Communication Technologies in Tourism 2018, pp. 308–320. Springer, Cham (2018). https://doi.org/10.1007/978-3-319-72923-7_24
12. Korstanje, M.E., Seraphin, H.: Awakening: a critical discussion of the role of robots in the rite of hospitality. Tourism Hosp. Perspect. Opportunities and Challenges, 59–77 (2018)
13. Ukpabi, D., Karjaluoto, H., Olaleye, S.A., Mogaji, E.: Dual perspectives on the role of artificially intelligent robotic virtual agents in the tourism, travel and hospitality industries. In: EuroMed Academy of Business Conference Book of Proceedings. EuroMed Press (2018)
14. Ivanov, S., Webster, C., Seyyedi, P.: Consumers' attitudes towards the introduction of robots in accommodation establishments. Tourism: Int. Interdisc. J. **66**(3), 302–317 (2018)
15. Tung, V.W.S., Au, N.: Exploring customer experiences with robotics in hospitality. Int. J. Contemp. Hosp. Manag. (2018)
16. Ivanov, S., Webster, C., Garenko, A.: Young Russian adults' attitudes towards the potential use of robots in hotels. Technol. Soc. **55**, 24–32 (2018)
17. Bowen, J., Morosan, C.: Beware hospitality industry: the robots are coming. Worldwide Hospitality and Tourism Themes **10**(6), 726–733 (2018)
18. Primawati, S.: The role of artificially intelligent robot in the hotel industry as a service innovation. In: Proceedings of ENTER2018 PhD Workshop, vol. 42 (2018)
19. Ivanov, S., Gretzel, U., Berezina, K., Sigala, M., Webster, C.: Progress on robotics in hospitality and tourism: a review of the literature. J. Hosp. Tour. Technol. **10**(4), 489–521 (2019)
20. Gretzel, U., Murphy, J.: Making sense of robots: consumer discourse on robots in tourism and hospitality service settings. In: Robots, Artificial Intelligence, and Service Automation in Travel, Tourism and Hospitality. Emerald Publishing Limited (2019)
21. Ivanov, S., Webster, C.: Conceptual framework of the use of robots, artificial intelligence and service automation in travel, tourism, and hospitality companies. In: Robots, Artificial Intelligence, and Service Automation in Travel, Tourism and Hospitality (2019)
22. Murphy, J., Gretzel, U., Pesonen, J.: Marketing robot services in hospitality and tourism: the role of anthropomorphism. J. Travel Tour. Mark. **36**(7), 784–795 (2019)
23. Ivanov, S.: Ultimate transformation: how will automation technologies disrupt the travel, tourism and hospitality industries? Zeitschrift für Tourismuswissenschaft **11**(1), 25–43 (2019)
24. Cain, L.N., Thomas, J.H., Alonso, M., Jr.: From sci-fi to sci-fact: the state of robotics and AI in the hospitality industry. J. Hosp. Tour. Technol. **10**(4), 624–650 (2019)
25. Ivanov, S., Webster, C. (eds.): Robots, Artificial Intelligence and Service Automation in Travel, Tourism and Hospitality. Emerald Group Publishing (2019)
26. Popesku, J.: Current applications of artificial intelligence in tourism and hospitality. In: Sinteza 2019-International Scientific Conference on Information Technology and Data Related Research, pp. 84–90. Singidunum University (2019)
27. Ivanov, S., Webster, C.: Perceived appropriateness and intention to use service robots in tourism. In: Pesonen, J., Neidhardt, J. (eds.) Information and Communication Technologies in Tourism 2019, pp. 237–248. Springer, Cham (2019). https://doi.org/10.1007/978-3-030-05940-8_19

28. Christou, P., Simillidou, A., Stylianou, M.C.: Tourists' perceptions regarding the use of anthropomorphic robots in tourism and hospitality. Int. J. Contemp. Hosp. Manag. **32**(11), 3665–3683 (2020)
29. Go, H., Kang, M., Suh, S.C.: Machine learning of robots in tourism and hospitality; interactive technology acceptance model (iTAM) – cutting edge. Tourism Review **75**(4), 625–636 (2020). https://doi.org/10.1108/TR-02-2019-0062
30. McCartney, G., McCartney, A.: Rise of the machines: towards a conceptual service-robot research framework for the hospitality and tourism industry. Int. J. Contemp. Hosp. Manag. **32**(12), 3835–3851 (2020)
31. Samala, N., Katkam, B.S., Bellamkonda, R.S., Rodriguez, R.V.: Impact of AI and robotics in the tourism sector: a critical insight. J. Tourism Futures **8**(1), 73–87 (2020)
32. Kilichan, R., Yilmaz, M.: Artificial intelligence and robotic technologies in tourism and hospitality industry. Erciyes Üniversitesi Sosyal Bilimler Enstitüsü Dergisi **50**, 353–380 (2020)
33. de Kervenoael, R., Hasan, R., Schwob, A., Goh, E.: Leveraging human-robot interaction in hospitality services: incorporating the role of perceived value, empathy, and information sharing into visitors' intentions to use social robots. Tour. Manage. **78**, 104042 (2020)
34. Reis, J., Melão, N., Salvadorinho, J., Soares, B., Rosete, A.: Service robots in the hospitality industry: the case of Henn-na hotel, Japan. Technol. Soc. **63**, 101423 (2020)
35. Belanche, D., Casaló, L.V., Flavián, C.: Frontline robots in tourism and hospitality: service enhancement or cost reduction? Electron. Mark. **31**(3), 477–492 (2021). https://doi.org/10.1007/s12525-020-00432-5
36. Manthiou, A., Klaus, P., Kuppelwieser, V.G., Reeves, W.: Man vs machine: examining the three themes of service robotics in tourism and hospitality. Electron. Mark. **31**(3), 511–527 (2021). https://doi.org/10.1007/s12525-020-00434-3
37. Abou-Shouk, M., Gad, H.E., Abdelhakim, A.: Exploring customers' attitudes to the adoption of robots in tourism and hospitality. J. Hosp. Tour. Technol. **12**(4), 762–776 (2021)
38. Fusté-Forné, F., Jamal, T.: Co-creating new directions for service robots in hospitality and tourism. Tourism and Hospitality **2**(1), 43–61 (2021)
39. Koo, C., Xiang, Z., Gretzel, U., Sigala, M.: Artificial intelligence (AI) and robotics in travel, hospitality and leisure. Electron. Mark. **31**(3), 473–476 (2021). https://doi.org/10.1007/s12525-021-00494-z
40. Mingotto, E., Montaguti, F., Tamma, M.: Challenges in re-designing operations and jobs to embody AI and robotics in services. Findings from a case in the hospitality industry. Electron. Mark. **31**(3), 493–510 (2021). https://doi.org/10.1007/s12525-020-00439-y
41. Choi, Y., Oh, M., Choi, M., Kim, S.: Exploring the influence of culture on tourist experiences with robots in service delivery environment. Curr. Issue Tour. **24**(5), 717–733 (2021)

Sustainability Crossing the City: Developing a Sustainable Infrastructures System for Genoa Urban Center

Daniele Soraggi[1] (ID), Valentina Costa[1]([✉]) (ID), and Ilaria Delponte[2] (ID)

[1] Italian Excellence Center for Logistics, Infrastructures and Transport, University of Genoa, 16126 Genoa, Italy
valentina.costa@edu.unige.it
[2] Civil Chemical and Environmental Engineering Department, University of Genoa, 16145 Genoa, Italy

Abstract. Sustainable development of infrastructures is becoming more and more relevant within a European and International framework where effective connections are pivotal in terms of social and economic systems' growth.

Nevertheless, as far as urban historical, dense and concentrated areas are concerned, intervention on urban infrastructures network could represent a very challenging task. In this sense, a quite iconic case may be represented by Genoa urban center. Here, the viaduct connecting the Eastern and the Western part of the city -Sopraelevata- proves to be outdated and not able to cope efficiently with contemporary traffic flows and mobility needs. At the same time, it is perceived as a sort of urban landmark running along the former border between city and port areas, so that demolition is not welcomed by citizens; by the way, deep interventions would be needed to make it again an effective link suitable for vehicles connections.

The rationale of the Genoese project was to define a double system of sustainable infrastructures. The existing one (the Sopraelevata) was dedicated to pedestrian and bi-cycle mobility, thus creating a new panoramic view on the city and the seaside both for tourists and residents, while a new submarine tunnel crossing the gulf was to be built to support and ease vehicle flows passing city center.

Present work will focus on the methodological approach followed to define sustainability targets to be achieved in the project by the new infrastructural scheme, both for existing and new component.

Keywords: Sustainable Infrastructures · Sustainability Rating · Multi-dimensional Assessment

1 Introduction

Infrastructures' pivotal role in driving and leading territorial development strategies has been investigated for long [1]. Accessibility represent indeed one of the main competitive factors both for regions and stakeholders [2–6], and transport infrastructures represent somewhat the pre-condition making urban areas closer one to another, assuring efficient and effective relations, thus reducing real and perceived transport cost both for people and goods.

© The Author(s), under exclusive license to Springer Nature Switzerland AG 2023
O. Gervasi et al. (Eds.): ICCSA 2023 Workshops, LNCS 14111, pp. 489–507, 2023.
https://doi.org/10.1007/978-3-031-37126-4_32

Globalization, furthermore, making connections crucial for supply chain and individual lives which develop worldwide and going beyond traditional borders and boundaries, put transport infrastructures at the center of public debate and action [7]. Although this have already happened in the past, present boost to infrastructural development targets the need to ensure green, smart and inclusive transition towards a more sustainable transport and urban system [8].

The risk in investing in new transport infrastructures, especially when urban contexts are concerned, could be represented by the attraction of growing vehicles flows, thus hampering the need to reduce traffic and consequent polluting emissions. Nevertheless, according to the Avoid-Shift-Improve paradigm [9], being necessary to assure accessibility and effective mobility to urban areas, particular attention must be paid to the promotion of sustainability in all its three dimensions [10].

Dealing the avoiding part more with land-use planning -in this direction, boost to remote work and education due to Covid19 pandemic outbreak represented an essential tool [11], first component of this paradigm has been targeted with new approaches dealing with proximity and mixitè, 15-min city by Carlos Moreno above all [12–14].

Moreover, as far as the shift and improve part is concerned, focusing on transport and mobility planning, to balance both targets to shift urban mobility patterns to more sustainable modes that have less impact on society and environment, and to improve transport environmental performances where shift is still not possible, should be the aim of urban committed policy makers [15].

At the same time, when transport sustainability is concerned, main accent is put on reducing GHG emissions' through the use of greener technologies and the transition towards public transport and slow mobility (e.g. walking or cycling). It must be remembered as well that socio-economic aspects should be addressed.

Infrastructures' externalities proved indeed to be extremely relevant [16, 17] in terms of social inclusion, individual well-being, health and access to economic and personal growth opportunities [18]. These reasons together with the difficulties related to monetize qualitative impacts according to different users' interests and goals contributed to the strong request to assess infrastructural investments with multi-dimensional evaluation supporting and integrating traditional Cost-Benefits Analysis (CBA) [19, 20].

Present work aim is therefore to offer a potential way to approach infrastructures' sustainability referring to both existing and new interventions. This will be done through the application of two different methodologies: scenario design and learning by cases. In particular, Genoa case-study was investigated, as public debate and local administration re-cent attention and resources are focusing on the potential regeneration of an iconic urban infrastructure, the so-called Sopraelevata, which should be dedicated to pedestrian and cycle-mobility, and the simultaneous construction of a new submarine tunnel to cross more effectively the gulf.

In the next sections, the two methods that will be applied to the Genoa case study will be analyzed. The second section provides background knowledge useful for the subsequent methodological investigation. We focus on the sustainability of infrastructures following the analytical approach proposed by international systems for classifying the sustainability of new infrastructures and, finally, we highlight the link between the urban infrastructural heritage and certain declinations of green infrastructure that are of interest to future urban planning. Following the presentation of the Genoa Overpass case study (Sect. 3), the fourth part of this paper introduces the two methods adopted to investigate the future of the case study: scenario design and learning-by-case. Finally results on potential ways to face sustainable transition of present and future infrastructural heritage will be discussed (Sect. 4).

2 Background

Our research gravitates around the concept of sustainable infrastructure and how it affects urban planning and mobility. Two main issues emerge at this juncture: sustainability assessment and the green evolution of urban infrastructure assets.

For this reason, the next two subsections deal with these aspects, in order to apply the correct method to the case study of Genoa.

2.1 Measuring and Mainstreaming Infrastructures' Sustainability

Addressing sustainability in infrastructures design procedures, has been therefore one of the main challenges of the last decades. Due to their relevance both for their potential boost to local development and accessibility and their significant externalities, overlapping with most of the UNO's Sustainable Development Goals, infrastructural projects have been targeted has one the most eligible objects to implement sustainable policies [21–23].

Attention has been paid at embedding similar considerations from the very initial steps of spatial and strategic planning [24] as well as to the labelling of construction materials and processes [25].

Together with this growing sensitivity and commitment in implementing sustainable infrastructures planning and projects, the need to develop transparent, self-evident and measurable methodologies able to convey and prove to citizens this commitment and a responsible way to invest towards sustainability and resilience of urban systems [24] led to the affirmation of quantitative tools, such as the definition of several sets of indicators, checklist and scoring methodologies [26]. Following the approach already implemented for buildings [27], several assessing methodologies were defined indeed to support and standardize the evaluation of infrastructures' sustainability through checklists and rating systems [28]. Initially, this kind of initiatives was mainly boosted by private companies and associations providing certificates and labels, according to the sustainability level achieved (e.g. Envision Protocol, CEEQUAL, BCA Green Mark). Nevertheless, when sustainability become a legally-binding pre-requisite for public investment and projects, State and public bodies began to implement specifical assessing methodologies, as well. Italian Ministry for Infrastructures and Transport, for instance, developed the Scoring Model for Sustainable Mobility and Infrastructures-SIMS, in order to enhance a multi-dimensional approach to assess and identify priorities among public investments' alternatives targeting several kinds of infrastructures.

Implementing multi-dimensional assessment to develop sustainable infrastructural network represents nowadays one of the main challenges, so that several methodologies, proxies and protocols have been implemented (e.g. Envision, SIMS...). Usually, they offer checklist and scoring system, helping policy makers to identify priorities and more promising alternatives [29]. Most of them provide specific tools to include social, economic and environmental evaluation since the very first steps of designing process, in order to develop projects which integrate multiple dimensions intrinsically and not only to accomplish ex-post requirements.

Growing accent on quantitative and standardized approach was strongly supported as well not only to assure democratic control on public expenses of citizens, but to evidence the compliance to a more and more complex regulatory framework, as well, and for EU authorities and bodies to monitor public resources investments. This proved to represent a crucial element as far as Next Generation EU program dedicated unprecedented resources and efforts for green, smart and sustainable transition of European economy and system [30] to recover from Covid-19 pandemic related crisis.

Looking at rating systems criteria, nevertheless two issues emerge: they mainly deal with new infrastructures and they are implemented for individual project, which may be later compared through the score achieved.

Similar assumptions rarely reflect a real-life urban scenario.

As far as European cities are concerned, building new infrastructures is only one side of the green and sustainable mobility transition.

Existing infrastructural heritage needs to be innovated, when it is possible, or dedicated to alternative uses through regeneration processes, and finally demolished when other options are not available. In a circular perspective, even when new infrastructures need to be built, communities need to manage existing ones future perspective, trying to avoid unnecessary new soil consumption [31, 32].

Moreover, historical and consolidated urban areas often require integrated and complex intervention to act effectively on local transport and mobility system. Introducing new infrastructures or existing ones retrofitting and regeneration im-ply the development of multi-level and multi-dimensional scenarios [33].

Within this framework, checklist and rating systems need to be supported, enriched and implemented through the design of potential scenarios that may later be comprehensively assessed in terms of environmental, social and economic sustainability. Protocols and scoring methodologies may set the framework for the evaluation of urban infrastructure-based scenarios' sustainability as it will be shown regarding Genoa case-study.

2.2   Green Infrastructure in Urban Infrastructure Heritage

The circularity of the infrastructural heritage, the landscape value of urban infrastructures and the continuous grey-green of infrastructures are three themes that can dialogue in the sustainable redevelopment of infrastructures.

The urban landscape is the representation of the interaction between natural forces, technical and economic needs, the adaptation of space to use, cultural expressions and the needs of society. This knowledge and the symbolic bond that is generated over time represent opportunities for a more sustainable planning and management of the future urban landscape [34]. One of the prerequisites for starting a Heritage Conversion Project is that it also possesses an intrinsic value given by the link with the image of the city that its citizens have [35]. Furthermore, in a vision of green evolution of heritage, it cannot, by its very nature, disregard its origin as grey infrastructure.

In 2013, the European Commission published the report Building a Green Infrastructure for Europe [36]; an incipit for an increasingly intensive process of investigation, study and dissemination on the topic of Green Infrastructure (GI). In fact, it has emerged that the concept of GI is increasingly widespread and consolidated especially in the urban environment [37–39]; as they are seen as a tool to facilitate adaptation to climate change [38, 40] and to design a more resilient [41] and inclusive city [42].

How to make a Mediterranean City resilient is a complicated challenge since they are complex urban organisms that have grown up around the environmental, morphological limits that have characterized their history. The temporal continuity of the built heritage is relevant in interpreting an evolution towards a resilient city [43]. Furthermore, the literature shows that the topic of GI is shared and dealt with by numerous disciplines, including urban and landscape planning, environmental management, hydrology, ecology, mobility, engineering, and the real estate and commercial sector [44–49]. As we have just seen, the scope of GIs is very wide and varied, so they are mainly described through three fundamental and non-exclusive characteristics: all natural green areas, managed and unmanaged, both in urban and rural contexts; paths and connections between different green areas; GIs provide and continue to provide multiple benefits to people [50].

This subdivision, in relation to our research, is useful because it allows us to focus on the third aspect that characterizes a GI: providing environmental and social benefits to an (urban) environment. However, when considering existing and decommissioning infrastructure assets, it is complicated to give them a Green label. In this case, variables relating to use, economic investment and valorization of the element are involved [37, 51]. Indeed, the main challenge is to be able to encourage and stimulate the formulation of a new method or a new sustainable and green approach to the redevelopment of these artefacts [52]. GI is thus presented as complementary to various spatial planning approaches that can be effectively integrated with discussions on transport, health and urban growth.

GIs are attributed a chameleon-like characteristic [53], which derives from the combination of the multiple benefits to which it is required to respond and the disciplinary declinations that promote its use. There is a grey-green continuum of thought regarding the concepts of 'infrastructure', although 'green' can be used to indicate the function or structure provided by an element, even if it is not strictly 'green' in terms of land use [54]. Therefore, the distinction between grey and green is not entirely useful, but there is a range of nuances in between, such as cycle paths, elevated linear parks, and harbour waterfront reclamation. Elements that could be classified as 'grey', but contribute to the broader functioning of green infrastructure, should be treated as part of the Green Infrastructure Network [50].

In conclusion, the role of the built infrastructure heritage still remains insufficiently explored [35]; it is necessary to understand how it can become a resource for the urban ecosystem in terms of sustainability and green footprint or whether these are unreachable goals.

3 Genoa Case-Study

Considering the context of dense and consolidated urban areas, Genoa, located in North-Western Italy may represent a particularly relevant and iconic case-study. Globally, municipality population approximately counts 580.000 in-habitants and urban fabric develops over a thin land stripe running between the mountains and the coast, which measures a 30 km width at its maximum.

Coastline shapes a quite circular gulf facing the sea in the core of Genoese urban area, where population density reaches its highest level, going beyond 10 000 inhabitants/sq.km.

Space has historically been indeed a precious and critical issue for Genoese urban development, thus causing frequent territorial conflicts.

This critical balance was made even more precarious because of the co-existence of port and civil activities within the dense and complex historical center [55].

At the beginning of 1960s, when vehicles flows began to run across the city, a new viaduct -the so-called Sopraelevata- was built in order to provide drivers with an easier and more efficient way to cross the city [56]. To minimize its impact on urban and port uses and activities, its path was designed overlapping port-city border along the gulf.

This central and strategic location made the Sopraelevata a sort of landmark for Genoese residents and visitors, a panoramic balcony to look at the city skyline facing the city while crossing its historical center.

Despite its symbolic value, during the decades its transport and functional effectiveness decreased and nowadays it became self-evident its need to be updated and re-functionalized. Its strategic location, its pivotal role for urban mobility, as well as its iconic link with Genoese local community, sparked the debate on how dealing with its future.

During the decades several alternative scenarios were provided to design new routes to cross the city center. Most direct paths were identified crossing the gulf with submarine or over-sea solutions.

Final hypothesis was defined after Morandi Bridge collapse and subsequent de-cision to compensate Genoa municipality and community with a new strategic infrastructure as a way for the motorway network licensee to somewhat repay local society of the disaster and dramatic breakdown for the city [57] (Beltrametti et al., 2018): a submarine tunnel developing under Genoa Old Port basin, connecting the Eastern and the Western endpoints of the gulf was to be designed.

This decision is in continuity with the project for the infrastructural enhancement of medium-distance traffic on the sea side promoted by the municipality of Genoa [58] The central section of Strada a Mare Guido Rossi and Lungomare Canepa has already been realised, and the extension of the axis both to the west and to the east is planned (see Fig. 1). The issue of the San Benigno infrastructural node and the continuity of the Sopraelevata or the construction of the underwater tunnel is one of the challenges to which the municipality of Genoa is trying to find a solution. Once procedures for technical design of the submarine tunnel were started, questions about its relations and overlapping function with the Sopraelevata viaduct emerge.

Being necessary to assess new infrastructure project according to the sustainability rating system (SIMS) implemented by Italian Ministry for Infrastructure and Transport, the aim was to extend evaluation procedures from the individual project to a wider scenario including the Sopraelevata variable, as well.

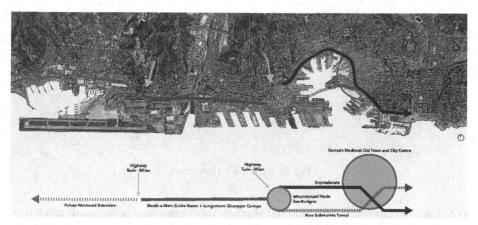

Fig. 1. Above: satellite view of Genoa with tracing of the present and future axes through the city. Below: schematic example of the same routes with relation Overpass-Submarine tunnel. Dashed lines indicate a planned and not yet realized infrastructure work.

4   Methods

The dual system methods may therefore be seen as an interesting example to implement sustainability assessment both to existing and new infrastructures. Firstly, a participated approach was brought forward to develop multiple scenarios, in order to identify most suitable use addressing sustainability and life-quality for residents and tourists. At the same time, a multi-dimensional scoring methodology provided by Italian Ministry for Infrastructures and Transports was applied to sub-marine tunnel project to include and assess environmental and social issues.

Secondly, the learning-by-case method will be used to identify which approaches are most suitable for the upgrading of the causeway. This takes place in a little-debated context in which the sustainable redevelopment of an urban infrastructure is mainly based on design experience. The aim of this activity is to develop potential further scenarios to frame re-functionalization alternatives.

Finally, the two methods of scenario design and learning-by-cases are combined to refine the results achieved.

4.1   Scenario Design for Up-Scaling Sustainability Assessment

To widen sustainability assessment approach, first necessary step was to define local infrastructural scenarios, that could constitute the reference basis to develop multi-dimensional sustainability assessment (Fig. 2):

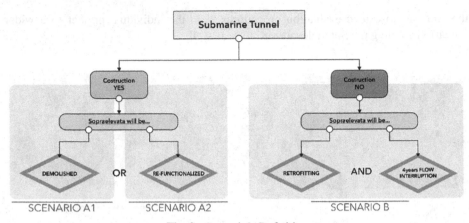

Fig. 2. Scenario's Definition.

- Submarine Tunnel construction and Sopraelevata demolition or re-functionalization. Second hypothesis includes the construction of the new tunnel, together with the prevision that the Sopraelevata will not constitute a traditional transport infrastructure any longer. This open question may hint both at its demolition or its regeneration and re-functionalization as a green linear balcony over the city, or a pedestrian or bicycle dedicated infrastructure.
- Sopraelevata maintenance, structural intervention and retrofitting. New infrastructure is not to be built, thus requiring the existing one to be up-dated and innovated to be able to carry contemporary traffic flows in a more sustainable, effective and efficient way. In this scenario, four years of construction operations are considered with consequent impacts on traffic flows changes and interruptions.

Once scenarios have been defined, they were later mainstreamed within SIMS assessment flow, being each of them evaluated according to a four-dimensions approach: (a) Financial and economic; (b) Environmental; (c) Social; (d) Institutional and governance.

Each dimension was further framed thanks to a wide range of domains and sub-indicators (Table 1), thus enabling to assess infrastructural scenarios impacts on multiple urban and community factors.

Table 1. Multi-dimensional Domains and Indicators applied to the assessment of infrastructure sustainability, as SIMS guideline.

Dimension	Domain	Indicator
a) Financial and Economic	a.1. Financial Analysis	*a.1.1. Investment Cost*
		a.1.2. Operating Costs

(continued)

Table 1. (*continued*)

Dimension	Domain	Indicator
	a.2. Cost-Benefit Analysis	*a.2.1. Economic Internal Rate of Return*
		a.2.2. Economic Net Present Value
	a.3. Economic Development Impacts	*a.3.1. Tourist Attraction Impacts*
b) Environmental	b.1. Six Environmental Goals Contribution-Environmental Issues	*b.1.1. Population and Human Health*
		b.1.2. Biodiversity
		b.1.3. Soil, Land-Use and Agricultural Heritage
		b.1.4. Geology and Water
		b.1.5. Air and Climate
		b.1.6. Landscape, Cultural and Material Heritage
	b.2. Six Environmental Goals Contribution-Physical Agents Issues	*b.2.1. Noise*
		b.2.2. Vibrations
		b.2.3. Non-Ionic Radiations
		b.2.4. Light Pollution
		b.2.5. Ionic Radiations
c) Social	c.1.Accessibility	*c.1.1. Average Site Accessibility*
		c.1.2. Fair and equal access to job opportunities
	c.2. Employment	*c.2.1. New construction-related employment*
	c.3 Beneficiaries	*c.3.1. Supplied Demand*
	c.4. Other Social Impacts	*c.4.1. Other social impacts-Construction Phase*
		c.4.2. Other social impacts-Operational Phase
d) Institutional and Governance	d.1. Programs and Plans Compliance	*d.1.1. Compliance to EU, National and Regional development strategies*

(*continued*)

Table 1. (*continued*)

Dimension	Domain	Indicator
		d.1.2. Compliance to EU, National and Regional urban development strategies
		d.1.2. Compliance to EU, National and Regional road infrastructures development strategies
	d.2. Stakeholders Involvement	*d.2.1. Community acceptance*

Following present scheme, scenarios could be given scores and be compared, too. Nevertheless, scenarios' setting procedure had been developed according to a tunnel-centered perspective. This is to say that first scenario was defined independently from the Sopraelevata future, whether it would be demolished or re-functionalized, while the second one, dealing with merely technical and engineering solutions, was described since the initial hypothesis were drawn.

This procedure, nevertheless, could prove to be more critical to apply to existing infrastructures, where ex-post evaluations are ineludible.

4.2 Learning by Cases for Sopraelevata Re-functionalization and Retrofitting

As seen above, the evolution of an urban infrastructure into a sustainable infrastructure is an untrodden path; all the more so when considering an evolution from grey to green infrastructure. Therefore, in order to be able to imagine a possible re-functionalization of the Sopraelevata, independently of the realization or not of the submarine tunnel, it was decided to proceed through a learning-by-cases method.

This approach is based on a search for case studies that have already dealt with this issue and a subsequent critical analysis of them. With regard to the case study of the causeway, this was done by researching sustainable redevelopment projects of urban infrastructures around the world, e.g. the High Line in New York and the Promenade Plantée in Paris; subsequently, the research was extended to projects involving new urban infrastructures in which the planners have adopted a medium- and long-term sustainable approach in all its facets: social, economic and environmental, e.g. Minimetrò in Perugia, Minhocao in Sao Paulo. This research resulted in 28 case studies to be critically compared and analyzed (see Table 2).

As can be seen from the table above, most of the interventions identified concern projects realized after the 2010s. These interventions are mainly located in the city center and only 7 of them are new developments. By critically analyzing each project, the main design tendencies used in the realization were identified. Four different design approaches emerged from the critical analysis, regardless of the boundary conditions that distinguish each case study. It should be noted that the four approaches identified are rarely exclusive to a project, but often co-exist; in these cases, the most representative

Table 2. Summary table on the 28 cases identified during the learning-by-cases method.

Project Name	City	Year	Urban Location	Project	Status
Ring Road	Amsterdam	2016	Metropolitan Area	Renovation	Study Phase
Te Ara I Whiti	Auckland	2016	Periphery	Redevelopment	Realized
Rambla de Sants	Barcelona	2016	Periphery	Renovation	Realized
Sagrera Linear Park	Barcelona	2011	Periphery	Redevelopment	Study Phase
Simone Veil Bridge	Bordeaux	2024	Periphery	New Project	Construction Phase
Riverwalk	Chicago	2016	Downtown	New Project	Realized
London Garden Bridge	London	2014	Downtown	New Project	Never Realized
Madrid Rio	Madrid	2011	Downtown	Renovation	Realized
Carnaige	Melbourne	2019	Metropolitan Area	Renovation	Realized
Underline	Miami	2015	Metropolitan Area	Renovation	Study Phase
High Line	New York	2009	Downtown	Redevelopment	Realized
Brooklyn	New York	2020	Periphery	Redevelopment	Study Phase
BQ-Park	New York	2019	Periphery	Redevelopment	Study Phase
Bjorvika Tunnel	Oslo	2010	Downtown	New Project	Realized
Prominade Plantée	Paris	1988	Downtown	Redevelopment	Realized
New Deal	Paris	2019	Metropolitan Area	Renovation	Study Phase
Minimetrò	Perugia	2008	Downtown	New Project	Realized
Reading Viaduct	Philadelphia	2018	Downtown	Redevelopment	Partly Realized
Luchtsingel	Rotterdam	2012	Downtown	New Project	Realized
Salesforce Transit Center	San Francisco	2018	Downtown	New Project	Realized
Minhocao	San Paulo	2019	Downtown	Temporary	Realized
Jardines de Pereda	Santander	2017	Downtown	Redevelopment	Realized

(continued)

Table 2. (*continued*)

Project Name	City	Year	Urban Location	Project	Status
Seoullo 7017	Seoul	2017	Downtown	Redevelopment	Realized
Cheonggye	Seoul	2005	Downtown	Redevelopment	Realized
Xuhui Park	Shanghai	2020	Periphery	Redevelopment	Realized
Goods Line	Sydney	2015	Downtown	Redevelopment	Realized
Bentway	Toronto	2018	Downtown	Redevelopment	Realized
A8erna	Zaanstadt	2003	Downtown	Redevelopment	Realized

approach has been attributed to the reference case. Each project approach has been named according to its characteristics:

- Greenery: This category includes those types of interventions that are related to climate resilience, that include green strategies for adaptation and response to climate change such as: biodiversity protection, environmental regeneration and connectivity, e.g. Xuhui Park in Shanghai and Madrid Rio in Madrid. This reference to the benefits of GI is also reflected in the green regeneration projects of grey urban infrastructure, e.g. the High Line in New York that transforms an industrial railway through Manhattan into a human-scale linear park. The term green regeneration refers to a series of interventions of urban integration of the existing building stock with urban greenery.
- Up and Down: is a design theme that enhances the development on different levels and in full respect of the existing infrastructure, two dimensions are defined on a spatial level: the covering of the infrastructure and the urban valorization of the spaces underneath the existing infrastructure. The covering has the dual purpose of an aesthetic value on an element of low quality, e.g. Rambla de Sants in Barcelona, and as a tool through which to solve certain problems that inhibit the proper use of an infrastructure, e.g. protection from the effects of flooding in Underline in Miami. The design of Underline spaces focuses on giving new quality uses to low-value urban spaces, e.g. a park in Bentway in Toronto or a new square in Zaanstadt.
- Junction: The theme of connections is closely linked to functionality, the common need to connect different places within the urban context and also the re-evaluation of the areas that are put in relation, providing new opportunities for use. As in the case of Soullo 7017, in which an old motorway viaduct is converted into a pedestrian park and used as a link between the two parts of the city separated by the railway It is an essential aspect of making the city accessible and liveable, through the creation of continuous paths in harmony and coherence with the infrastructure and the urban context. The intrinsic link between the infrastructure and the city is maintained, but it is given a new type of user, e.g. the new design for Brooklyn Bridge.
- Smart Mobility: All cases focusing on new forms of mobility have been included in this project approach. This vision can be declined either through the realization of new infrastructures that do not involve the private vehicle and guarantee easy mobility through the city, e.g. Minimetrò in Perugia; or through projects that imagine

a revolution of mobility within large urban centers and capable of changing their forms and spaces, e.g. New Ring Road in Amsterdam and New Deal in Paris. Finally, we also highlight cases of projects aimed at enhancing soft mobility on a human scale, such as the conversion of a motorway junction surrounding downtown Auckland, New Zealand, into a cycle path (Te Ara i Withi), or the temporary pedestrianization of the Minhocao in Sao Pauolo, Brazil, which on weekends becomes an urban park for family entertainment.

5   Results and Discussion

The last step was to cross-reference the two methods used: scenario design and learning-by-cases. For each of the three scenarios identified: construction of the submarine tunnel and demolition of the elevated causeway (A1), construction of the tunnel and redevelopment of the elevated causeway (A2) and redevelopment of the elevated causeway only (B); a degree of affinity is attributed to the project line of the identified case studies (see Fig. 3).

This solution is useful to understand the commonalities that emerge from the application of two opposing methodologies, but which share the starting point and the final objective, the design of a sustainable infrastructure. In fact, the first method is based on the validation of a standardized and recognized procedure with the active involvement of the citizens themselves who will benefit from the infrastructure. The second method, on the other hand, is useful in defining a hypothetical imaginary on which to build a win-win and shareable design process with the community, in order to initiate a path of active design involvement.

In different disciplinary circles, the use of a learning by-case methodology, in which the confrontation and analysis of different case studies is required, is now a recognized and validated procedure [59]; moreover, basic driving principles for future project development are identified. In this paper, the qualitative assessment adopted made it possible to define four potentially applicable project scenarios that do not depend on the characteristics of the assets to be reconverted but rather rely on the political, governance will and actions that will be in a position to adopt them. The four design approaches identified from the analysis of the 28 projects can be traced back to four reference domains for sustainable urban planning of a Smart City: Greenery to Green Planning; Junction to Accessibility; Smart Mobility to Mobility; and Up-and-Down to Strategic Urban Spatial Planning. Indeed, the combined effect of driving forces such as accessibility, urbanization, globalization and impact is different in each period and able to influence the pace of change as well as people's perception of the landscape [34]. Instead, using scenario design in the urban environment allows one to analyze the future outcomes of decisions that are made in the present, in order to identify the most effective option [60] and able to coordinate the simultaneous presence of multiple surrounds in a decision-making process involving numerous random variables [61, 62].

As far as two previous methodologies' intersection is concerned, some considerations need to be drawn. Approximately one out of four considered case-studies (27%) proves to be not-suitable for the application of the approach provided. On the other hand, more than 46% of them appears to fit in.

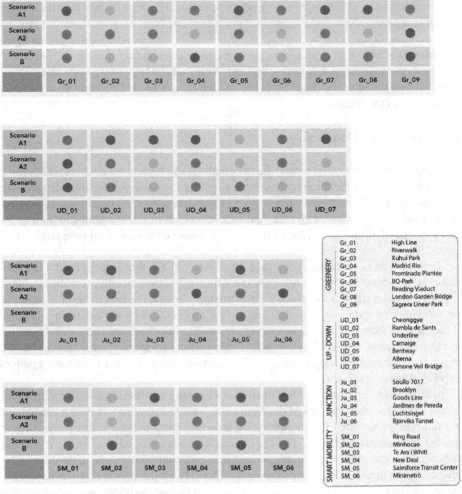

Fig. 3. Image cross-referencing the results of the Scenario Design methodology with those of Learning-by-Cases in assessing the applicability of each in respect of the case study. Green: approach possible; Yellow: approach to be evaluated; Red: approach not applicable. Each case study was given a design approach as shown in the figure. (Color figure online)

Major criticalities concern Up-and-Down approach, despite similar percentage of non-suitable cases can be traced within the four considered domains, while higher shares of "green lights" can be found among Smart Mobility and Greenery domains.

6 Conclusions

Present contribution focuses indeed on potential benefits descending from the application of a double methodology based on Scenario-design and Learning-by-Cases approach to the evaluation of new-borne and existing infrastructures' sustainability.

From the intersection of the two methods, a new process is identified, through the definition of future scenarios that can concretize visions for the city's future and, consequently, allows for greater citizen involvement and participation in the city's decision-making process. The design of a sustainable infrastructure expressly requires a participatory process of involvement of various territorial stakeholders, also external to the work. A technical, quantitative approach should be therefore integrated with a qualitative approach that can foreshadow the future vision also for those who are not among experts in this specific field [60, 63]. Evidently, this can also be done through the adoption of reference case studies that can ensure greater involvement in the public debate, thus allowing local stakeholders to evaluate also surrounding context elements that may help sustainability assessment and evaluation.

Significant challenges will be represented by the need of standardization and transferability of the methodology provided, both in the scenario definition step as well as in terms of considered urban domains framing reference case-studies.

Extending assessment perimeter and test-bed applications would therefore constitute a further validation for this methodology as far as new infrastructures insertion within consolidated urban fabrics and outdated infrastructures re-use and sustainable regeneration are concerned.

It is therefore clear that reaching sustainability goals as well as coping with Climate Change challenges will therefore require to act both intensively and diffusely within urban layered settlements and boundaries. In this direction, proposed methodology would play an extremely pivotal role in terms of supporting indicator-based and scoring methodologies implementation within complex, dense and ramified infrastructural networks, that uneasily could be included and mainstreamed into quantitative and synthetic assessment procedure, thus implying a more holistic approach towards integrated evaluation.

References

1. Raicu, S., Costescu, D., Popa, M., Dragu, V.: Dynamic intercorrelations between transport/traffic infrastructures and territorial systems: from economic growth to sustainable development. Sustainability 13(21), 11951 (2021). https://doi.org/10.3390/su132111951
2. Geurs, K.T., Van Wee, B.: Accessibility evaluation of land-use and transport strategies: review and research directions. J. Transp. Geogr. 12(2), 127–140 (2004). https://doi.org/10.1016/j.jtrangeo.2003.10.005
3. Cheng, J., Bertolini, L.: Measuring urban job accessibility with distance decay, competition and diversity. J. Transp. Geogr. 30, 100–109 (2013). https://doi.org/10.1016/j.jtrangeo.2013.03.005
4. Yan, X.: Toward accessibility-based planning. J. Am. Plann. Assoc. 2021(87), 409–423 (2021). https://doi.org/10.1080/01944363.2020.1850321
5. Deboosere, R., El-Geneidy, A.M., Levinson, D.: Accessibility-oriented development. J. Transp. Geography 70, 11–20 (2018). https://doi.org/10.1016/j.jtrangeo.2018.05.015
6. Shi, Y., Blainey, S., Sun, C., Jing, P.: A literature review on accessibility using bibliometric analysis techniques. J. Transp. Geogr. 87, 102810 (2020). https://doi.org/10.1016/j.jtrangeo.2020.102810
7. Dobre, F., Pauna, V., Vasilescu, A.C., Buzoianu, O.A.C.: The impact of globalization on transport investment. In: SHS Web of Conferences, vol. 129, p. 11002, EDP Sciences (2021). https://doi.org/10.1051/shsconf/202112911002

8. NextGenerationEU Homepage, https://next-generation-eu.europa.eu. Accessed 2023/03/09

9. Dia, H.: Four strategies for reducing urban transport emissions and improving health: avoid, shift, share and improve. J. Transport Health **14**, Supplement, 100683, ISSN 2214-1405 (2019). https://doi.org/10.1016/j.jth.2019.100683

10. Banister, D.: Cities, mobility and climate change. J. Transp. Geogr. **19**(6), 1538–1546 (2011). https://doi.org/10.1016/j.jtrangeo.2011.03.009

11. Roberto, R., Zini, A., Felici, B., Rao, M., Noussan, M.: Potential benefits of remote working on urban mobility and related environmental impacts: results from a case study in Italy. Appl. Sci. **13**(1), 607 (2023). https://doi.org/10.3390/app13010607

12. Allam, Z., Nieuwenhuijsen, M., Chabaud, D., Moreno, C.: The 15-minute city offers a new framework for sustainability, liveability, and health. Lancet Planetary Health **6**(3), e181–e183 (2022). https://doi.org/10.1016/S2542-5196(22)00014-6

13. Gaglione, F., Gargiulo, C., Zucaro, F., Cottrill, C.: Urban accessibility in a 15-minute city: a measure in the city of Naples. Italy. Transportation Res. Procedia **60**, 378–385 (2022). https://doi.org/10.1016/j.trpro.2021.12.049

14. Ferrer-Ortiz, C., Marquet, O., Mojica, L., Vich, G.: Barcelona under the 15-minute city lens: Mapping the accessibility and proximity potential based on pedestrian travel times. Smart Cities, **5**(1), 146–161 (2022). doi.https://doi.org/10.3390/smartcities5010010

15. Malekpour, S., Brown, R.R., de Haan, F.J.: Strategic planning of urban infrastructure for environmental sustainability: Understanding the past to intervene for the future. Cities **46**, 67–75 (2015). https://doi.org/10.1016/j.cities.2015.05.003

16. Zhu, L., Ye, Q., Yuan, J., Hwang, B.G., Cheng, Y.: A scientometric analysis and overview of research on infrastructure externalities. Buildings **11**(12), 630 (2021). https://doi.org/10.3390/buildings11120630

17. Bröcker, J., Korzhenevych, A., Schürmann, C.: Assessing spatial equity and efficiency impacts of transport infrastructure projects. Transp. Res. Part B: Methodological **44**(7), 795–811 (2010). https://doi.org/10.1016/j.trb.2009.12.008

18. Cavill, N., Kahlmeier, S., Rutter, H., Racioppi, F., Oja, P.: Economic analyses of transport infrastructure and policies including health effects related to cycling and walking: a systematic review. Transp. Policy **15**(5), 291–304 (2008). https://doi.org/10.1016/j.tranpol.2008.11.001

19. Dobes, L., Leung, J.: Wider economic impacts in transport infrastructure cost-benefit analysis-A bridge too far?. Agenda: A J. Policy Anal. Reform **22**(1), 75–95 (2015)

20. Sierra, L.A., Yepes, V., Pellicer, E.: A review of multi-criteria assessment of the social sustainability of infrastructures. J. Clean. Prod. **187**, 496–513 (2018). https://doi.org/10.1016/j.jclepro.2018.03.022

21. Thacker, S., et al.: Infrastructure for sustainable development. Nature Sustainability **2**(4), 324–331 (2019). Doi:https://doi.org/10.1038/s41893-019-0256-8

22. Adshead, D., Thacker, S., Fuldauer, L.I., Hall, J.W.: Delivering on the sustainable development Goals through long-term infrastructure planning. Glob. Environ. Chang. **59**, 101975 (2019). https://doi.org/10.1016/j.gloenvcha.2019.101975

23. Leal Filho, W., et al.: An assessment of requirements investments, new technologies, and infrastructures to achieve the SDGs. Environ. Sci. Eur. **34**(1), 1–17 (2022). https://doi.org/10.1186/s12302-022-00629-9

24. López, E., Monzón, A.: Integration of sustainability issues in strategic transportation planning: a multi-criteria model for the assessment of transport infrastructure plans. Comput.-Aided Civil Infrastructure Eng. **25**(6), 440–451 (2010). https://doi.org/10.1111/j.1467-8667.2010.00652.x

25. Zimmermann, R. K., Skjelmose, O., Jensen, K.G., Jensen, K.K., Birgisdottir, H.: Categorizing building certification systems according to the definition of sustainable building. In IOP Conference Series: Materials Science and Engineering, vol. 471, No. 9, p. 092060. IOP Publishing (2019). https://doi.org/10.1088/1757-899X/471/9/092060

26. Singh, R.K., Murty, H.R., Gupta, S.K., Dikshit, A.K.: An overview of sustainability assessment methodologies. Ecol. Ind. **9**(2), 189–212 (2009). https://doi.org/10.1016/j.ecolind.2011.01.007
27. Giama, E., Papadopoulos, A.M.: Sustainable building management: overview of certification schemes and standards. Adv. Build. Energy Res. **6**(2), 242–258 (2012). https://doi.org/10.1080/17512549.2012.740905
28. Nguyen, B.K., Altan, H.: Comparative review of five sustainable rating systems. Procedia Eng. **21**, 376–386 (2011). https://doi.org/10.1016/j.proeng.2011.11.2029
29. Bueno, P.C., Vassallo, J.M., Cheung, K.: Sustainability assessment of transport infrastructure projects: a review of existing tools and methods. Transp. Rev. **35**(5), 622–649 (2015). https://doi.org/10.1080/01441647.2015.1041435
30. Hainsch, K., et al.: Energy transition scenarios: what policies, societal attitudes, and technology developments will realize the EU Green Deal? Energy **239**, 122067 (2022). https://doi.org/10.1016/j.energy.2021.122067
31. Cardoso de Matos, A., Lourencetti, F.D.L.: Reusing railway infrastructures in the spirit of circular theory. A contribution to an operational concept (2021). https://doi.org/10.4995/vitruvio-ijats.2021.15487
32. Hartley, K.: Infrastructure and SDG localization: the 21st century mandate. Environ. Res. Infrastructure Sustainability **2**(1), 013001 (2022). https://doi.org/10.1088/2634-4505/ac442a
33. Kyrkou, D., Karthaus, R.: Urban sustainability standards: predetermined checklists or adaptable frameworks? Procedia Eng. **21**, 204–211 (2011). https://doi.org/10.1016/j.proeng.2011.11.2005
34. Antrop, M.: Why landscapes of the past are important for the future. Landsc. Urban Plan. **70**(1–2), 21–34 (2005). https://doi.org/10.1016/j.landurbplan.2003.10.002
35. Amico, A. D., Currà, E.: The role of urban built heritage in qualify and quantify resilience. specific issues in Mediterranean City. Procedia Econ. Finance **18**, 181–189 (2014). https://doi.org/10.1016/S2212-5671(14)00929-0
36. European Union Publication Homepage. https://op.europa.eu/en/publication-detail/-/publication/738d80bb-7d10-47bc-b131-ba8110e7c2d6. Accessed 2023/03/09
37. Osmond, P., Wilkinson, S.: City planning and green infrastructure: embedding ecology into urban decision-making. Urban Planning https://doi.org/10.1038/s41893-019-0256-86(1), 1–4 (2021). https://doi.org/10.17645/up.v6i1.3957
38. Sturiale, L., Scuderi, A.: The role of green infrastructures in urban planning for climate change adaptation. Climate **7**(10) (2019). https://doi.org/10.3390/cli7100119
39. Wilk, B.: Guidelines for co-design-ing and co-implementing green infrastructure in urban regeneration processes Work package: 2 Dissemination level: PU Lead partner: ICLEI. www.proGIreg.eu, (2020)
40. Hong, G., Tan, C., Qin, L., Wu, X.: Identification of priority areas for UGIoptimisation under carbon neutrality targets: Perspectives from China. Ecological Indicators **148**, 110045 (2023). Doi: https://doi.org/10.1016/j.ecolind.2023.110045
41. Iungman, T., et al.: Cooling cities through urban green infrastructure: a health impact assessment of European cities. The Lancet **401**(10376), 577–589 (2023). https://doi.org/10.1016/S0140-6736(22)02585-5
42. Planas-Carbonell, A., Anguelovski, I., Oscilowicz, E., Pérez-del-Pulgar, C., Shokry, G.: From greening the climate-adaptive city to green climate gentrification? Civic perceptions of short-lived benefits and exclusionary protection in Boston, Philadelphia, Amsterdam and Barcelona. Urban Climate, 48 (September 2022), (2023). https://doi.org/10.1016/j.uclim.2022.101295
43. Francis, R., Bekera, B.: A metric and frameworks for resilience analysis of engineered and infrastructure systems. Reliab. Eng. Syst. Saf. **121**, 90–103 (2014). https://doi.org/10.1016/j.ress.2013.07.004

44. Navarro, I.J., Yepes, V., Martí, J.V.: A review of multicriteria assessment techniques applied to sustainable infrastructure design. Adv. Civil Eng. (2019). https://doi.org/10.1155/2019/613 4803

45. Bartesaghi Koc, C., Osmond, P., Peters, A.: Towards a comprehensive green infrastructure typology: a systematic review of approaches, methods and typologies. Urban Ecosystems **20**(1), 15–35 (2016). https://doi.org/10.1007/s11252-016-0578-5

46. Escobedo, F.J., Giannico, V., Jim, C.Y., Sanesi, G., Lafortezza, R.: Urban forests, ecosystem services, green infrastructure and nature-based solutions: nexus or evolving metaphors? Urban Forestry Urban Green. **37**, 3–12 (2018). https://doi.org/10.1016/j.ufug.2018.02.011

47. Albert, C., Von Haaren, C.: Implications of applying the green infrastructure concept in landscape planning for ecosystem services in peri-urban areas: an expert survey and case study. Plann. Prac. Res. **32**, 227–242 (2014). https://doi.org/10.1080/02697459.2014.973683

48. Wang, J., Banzhaf, E.: Towards a better understanding of green infrastructure: a critical review. Ecol. Indic. **85**, 758–772 (2018). https://doi.org/10.1016/j.ecolind.2017.09.018

49. Austin, G.: Green Infrastructure for Landscape Planning: Integrating Human and Natural Systems. Routledge, New York, NY (2014)

50. Davies, C., MacFarlane, R., McGloin, C., Roe, M.: Green Infrastructure Planning Guide. University of Newcastle Upon Tyne, Tyne and Wear, UK (2006)

51. Sturiale, L., Scuderi, A.: The evaluation of green investments in urban areas: A proposal of an eco-social-green model of the city. Sustainability (Switzerland) **10**(12) (2018). https://doi.org/10.3390/su10124541

52. Lamond, J., Everett, G.: Sustainable Blue-Green Infrastructure: A social practice approach to understanding community preferences and stewardship. Landscape Urban Plann. **191** (2019). https://doi.org/10.1016/j.landurbplan.2019.103639

53. Matsler, A. M., Meerow, S., Mell, I., Pavao-Zuckerman, M.: A 'green' chameleon: exploring the many disciplinary definitions, goals, and forms of green infrastructure. Landsc. Urban Plan. **214** (2021). https://doi.org/10.1016/j.landurbplan.2021.104145

54. Morris, R.L., Konlechner, T.M., Ghisalberti, M., Swearer, S.E.: From grey to green: Efficacy of eco-engineering solutions for nature-based coastal defence. Glob. Change Biol. **24**(5), 1827–1842 (2018). https://doi.org/10.1111/gcb.14063

55. Ugolini, P., Pirlone, F., Spadaro, I., Candia, S.: Waterfront and sustainable mobility. The case study of Genoa. In Transport Infrastructure and Systems, 661–668 (2017). https://doi.org/10.1201/9781315281896

56. Delponte, I.: La Sopraelevata di Genova e le dimensioni di un'opera. Trasporti e cultura **35**, 32–39 (2013)

57. Beltrametti, L., Bottasso, A., Conti, M., Ferrari, C., Piana, M.: Effetti della caduta del Ponte Morandi sull'economia. Rivista di economia e politica dei trasporti **1**(2), 1–7 (2018)

58. Homepage Comune di Genova. http://www.urbancenter.comune.genova.it/node/557. Accessed 2023/03/19

59. Alfieri, L., Timothy J. Nokes-Malach, T.J., Schunn, D.C.: Learning through case comparisons: a meta-analytic review, Educ. Psychol. **48**(2), 87-113 (2013). doi.https://doi.org/10.1080/004 61520.2013.775712

60. Chakraborty, A., McMillan, A.: Scenario planning for urban planners: Toward a practitioner's guide. J. Am. Plann. Assoc. **81**(1), 18–29 (2015). https://doi.org/10.1080/01944363.2015.103 8576

61. Hopkins, L.D., Zapata, M.: Engaging the future: Forecasts, scenarios, plans, and projects. Lincoln Institute of Land Policy, Cambridge, MA (2007)
62. Shipley, R., Hall, B., Feick, R., Earley, R.: Evaluating municipal visioning. Plan. Pract. Res. 19(2), 193–207 (2004). https://doi.org/10.1080/0269745042000284412
63. Ratcliffe, J., Krawczyk, E.: Imagineering city futures: the use of prospective through scenarios in urban planning. Futures 43(7), 642–653 (2011). https://doi.org/10.1016/j.futures.2011.05.005

Virtual Reality and Augmented Reality and Applications (VRA 2023)

An Exploration Towards Sustainable Metaverse Systems for e-Learning by Student Designers: A Meta-analysis

Chien-Sing Lee[1,2,3](✉) (iD)

[1] School of Engineering and Technology, Sunway University, Subang Jaya, Malaysia
chiensingl@sunway.edu.my, csleester@gmail.com
[2] Universiti Tunku Abdul Rahman, Petaling Jaya, Malaysia
[3] Malaysian Invention and Design Society, Petaling Jaya, Malaysia

Abstract. The metaverse has caught the imagination and investments of many. However, in developing countries, the metaverse may raise more questions, than answers. As such, this study aims to investigate first, student-designers' perceptions towards what and how they want the metaverse to be like, and whether students would prioritize information flow; second, the efficacy of triangulating 3 usability-HCI questionnaires; third, whether student-designers would be more interested, creative, and be more confident in designing and developing for interconnecting (non) metaverse (eco)systems. Findings from alpha-beta user testings of Figma prototypes indicate preference for balance between structure and freedom/creativity, enhanced by user feedback and open ecosystems. Mind maps, sequencing of chain of effects in descending order, and the derived hierarchical relationship reflect centralities in design, and continuums in notions of what sustainable interconnected systems in the metaverse may be like. They are influenced by how perspectives, objectives, utility functions, and evaluation criteria, dynamically affect shifts in these centrality of design (dy/dx) over time (dy/dt), based on demographics. Loosely coupled pointer-based systems, are thus viable complements to integration.

Keywords: Interest · Student designers · Information theory · Flow · Design thinking · Computational thinking · Metaverse · Complementary interconnected ecosystems · Future knowledge management · Recommender

1 Introduction

Artificial Intelligence (AI) simulates human intelligence. Four types of AI systems have evidenced much growth in popularity: a) classifier systems, e.g. to classify whether texts from social media are positive or negative; b) recommender systems, e.g. Scratch 3.0's surprise or Lazada's interest-based recommendations; c) predictive systems, e.g. observation of data (non)random to formulate patterns, and predictions, or to integrate data from (co)curricula with curricula to predict student's performance; d) generative systems, which assemble/transform based on given parameters or metrics.

Arising partly from challenging saturated markets, the metaverse is a new frontier and testbed for AI. Zuckerberg [1] envisions the metaverse, as interconnected, loosely coupled ubiquitous (eco) systems, rather than tightly coupled giant integrated enterprise resource planning systems. Similarly, [2] views the metaverse as a culmination/epitome of atomistic building blocks. It interconnects socially, emotionally and cognitively, with other dimensions/worlds. Hence, what, how and the need for or the degree of integration in an interconnected universe with diverse technologies, is of interest.

[3] point out that emerging technologies, can be viewed from four quadrants. The top-bottom quadrants are augmentation and simulation, and the left-right quadrants are external and intimate. Augmentation focuses on the interface (e.g. Augmented Reality/ Virtual Reality) and interconnecting objects/networks/worlds. Simulation builds virtual models and can be (non)immersive (e.g. *SecondLife*, metaverse). External (sensors, everyware), bridges virtual-real worlds. Intimate is more personal, e.g. lifelogging/personalization; resulting in increased socio-cultural research on identity.

1.1 Problems and Objectives

With a looming global recession, we need to figure out how the real world and the metaverse, can co-exist, with different lenses. Internationally, companies e.g. JP Morgan, McDonald's, Disney, Hyundai, Gucci and Nike, have ventured into the metaverse, e.g. Decentraland and Sandbox [4]. Most sell non-fungible tokens (NFTs) and virtual experiences, e.g. games and concerts. [4] adds that in Malaysia, companies, are either selling NFTs to members of their community, which then enables access to exclusive experiences and merchandise, or are encouraging customers to virtually explore, order products, and earn points by playing games.

However, popular successful examples, e.g. Lazada and Shoppee's innovative design thinking business model, planning, and flexible/agile architecture and processes, with optional user feedback and reviews after each purchase-delivery, indicate that the notion of interconnected systems, may not require heavy investments in technologies.

So, how can the metaverse and other worlds co-exist? In line with Zuckerberg's [1] vision, an analogical parallel [5] may provide insights. In the database world, should we design based on the more structured SQL vs. the pointer-based NoSQL, or based on SQL-noSQL [6]? What is necessary in the developing world?

Problem 1: Well-formulated AI considers context, goals, tasks and evaluation, in order to proceed as planned, or to recalibrate/refine. Given the broad but fuzzy evolutions in trends, if we are to venture into the metaverse, how would they want to interact with the metaverse? What are the requirements?

Objective 1: Based on design thinking, we need to investigate students' and users' perceptions towards what they would want the metaverse to be like, and how they would want to interact with the metaverse.

Second, [7] has emphasized that above and beyond coding, we need to teach and empower children to think; to equip them for "a greater and more articulate mastery of the world," (knowledge and communicative clarity) with "a sense of the power of applied knowledge," (application, translation and transformation of knowl-edge) and "a self-confidently realistic image of themselves as intellectual agents" (self-efficacy/becoming). Confucius aptly puts it as teaching a person to fish, rather than giving him/her a fish.

These concepts have partly given rise to [8]'s problem-based learning meets case-based reasoning, [9]'s wide walls creative society, [10]'s adapted driving questions, [11]'s editorial on creativity scaffolds for sustainable design development, [12]'s learning-sciences-decision support approach for 123greetings.com card design, [13]'s series of studies on developing dispositions for social innovations and design thinking-based interconnected physical-digital media among undergraduate creative industries students in Malaysia, and subsequently, [14]'s Scratch fractal study, and [15]'s digital media for open synergistic refactoring.

Regionally, the Interest-Driven Creator (IDC) theory [16] for K-12 schools is more well-known. This research also shares common concerns with [17]'s trajectories study, but is less mathematical. In this paper's spirit of loosely-connected (eco)systems, this study and the latter are (eco)systems, which point to each other, but are context-sensitive in each respective ecosystem, and at different levels of maturity.

Problem 2: Since the metaverse is relatively new in Asia, how to prepare students to develop, direct and enhance an AI/automated-augmented world, in line with [7], continuing from [11]'s editorial.

To traverse, context-goals-tasks-evaluation-adjustments direct search and retrieval, (dis)assembly, integration. [17, 18] have postulated that if we view the influence of information- and system-related characteristics on perceived ease of use, users are more likely to regard the system as relevant to their jobs. Moreover, with high output qual-ity/better result demonstrability, perceived usefulness and technology adoption are more likely to increase.

Furthermore, if we think along [19]'s information flow as the key mediator/director in design, it may be easier to identify what are important in each subspace, reduce informa-tion dimensions, and the degree of dependencies during design in each problem-solving subspace. Thus, [20] posits that emergence and self-organization are more beneficial, in more diverse problem-solving subspaces.

Objective 2: In line with [7]'s vision, to investigate how to guide information design and structural data-driven design using information flow and usability-HCI metrics.

Weighted evaluation methods/criteria are considered to direct search/retrieval/ trans-formation. Furthermore, the Technology Acceptance Models (TAM) 1, 2 and 3 [18, 22, 23], have guided much of systems analysis and design, as TAM covers system factors (TAM 1), social factors (TAM 2) and human factors (TAM 3). Information design-science is implicit in TAM. Hypothetically, if student-designers regard evaluation questionnaires, e.g. Heuristic Evaluation (HE), Computer System Usability Questionnaire (CSUQ), User Experience Questionnaire (UEQ) as complementary evaluation/explanatory/ predictive instruments, they should be able to discover what information-systems analysis and design means, and address one of the challenges of outcome-based learning, i.e., how to balance between flexibility and structure?

Objective 2a: To investigate the efficacy of triangulating usability-Human-Computer Interaction (HCI) evaluation instruments, to enhance requirements engineering, refine design interventions and interpretation of data.

Objective 2b: To investigate whether students would prioritize information flow and reduce dimensions in systems analysis and design.

Objective 2c: To investigate what student-designers and users perceive as important from usability-HCI evaluation questionnaires (HE, CSUQ, UEQ).

Objective 3: To investigate whether students would be more interested, creative, and more confident in designing and developing for interconnecting (non) metaverse (eco)systems.

2 Related Work

2.1 Technology Acceptance Models 1, 3

[18]'s comparison of the effects of 2 TAM constructs, reveals that perceived usefulness is able to explain more than 50% of the variance in behavioural intentions, over a period of 14 weeks (Table 1). Statistically, these are naturally expected, across Gaussian populations/samples. Moreover, though significantly influencing intentions, they find that perceived ease of use's effect is small, moderated mainly by experience, and partially mediated by attitude. Hence, we next refer to HCI evaluation instruments, to enrich/triangulate TAM constructs.

Table 1. [18]'s explanatory and predictiveness of TAM 1, 3

Perceived Usefulness		Perceived Ease of Use
Explaining, Predicting	TAM 3 explains between 52–67% of variance across different time periods as well as models. Experience moderates the effect of perceived ease of use on perceived usefulness	TAM 3 explains between 43–52% of variance in perceived ease of use across different points of time, and models

2.2 HCI Questionnaires

Popular usability-HCI questionnaires are [24]'s Heuristic Evaluation (HE), [25]'s Computer System Usability Questionnaire (CSUQ), and [26]'s User Experience Questionnaire (UEQ). HE provides a broad preliminary assessment of the usability of the system, with regards to user interface design. The constructs *match with the real world*, as well as *aesthetic and minimalist design, visibility, recognition; control and freedom, flexibility and efficiency; consistency, and error prevention*, reflect common but significant user challenges. Concerned with satisfaction, CSUQ's first question assesses users' overall satisfaction with ease of use, and the final question, overall satisfaction with the system. In-between questions cover HE's constructs, weighing more on clarity and quality of interaction.

[26] extend beyond usability of the interface and system, to user experience. They have defined user experience as ultimately, about attractiveness. Often regarded as an emotional/ affective reaction, [26]'s UEQ (Table 2 right), characterizes attractiveness as comprising of two complementary qualities, i.e., pragmatic (functional/practical) and hedonic (sensorial). These states change over time, with changes in context, goals, demographics, and technologies.

Pragmatic aspects encompass goals and tasks. Contributing aspects to perceived pragmatic quality are perspicuity, efficiency and dependability. *Perspicuity* corresponds with TAM's ease of use, clarity/ease to understand and thus, ease to learn. *Efficiency* and *dependability* correspond with TAM's output demonstrability. These three aspects correspond with TAM's anchor and adjustment, influencing user confidence/control. Hedonic quality aspects are oriented towards *stimulation* (exciting, enjoyable) and *novelty*.

Table 2. UEQ (top left), HE (bottom left), CSUQ (right) with UEQ-CSUQ-HE categorizations

Attractiveness (Pragmatic Quality / Hedonic Quality → Perspicuity / Stimulation → Efficiency / Novelty → Dependability)		Clarity, Ease of use, Productivity, (Perspicuity, Efficiency, Attractiveness)	Visibility of system status
			Match between system and the real world
			User control and freedom, Flexibility and efficiency of use
			Consistency and standards, Recognition rather than recall
		Error handling (Dependability)	Consistency and standards
			Recognition rather than recall
			Error prevention, Help users recognize, diagnose, recover from errors, Help and documentation
		Aesthetics (Stimulation)	Match between system and the real world, Aesthetic and minimalist design
		Enjoyment (Stimulation)	Match between system and the real world, User control and freedom, Flexibility and efficiency of use
		Satisfaction (Attractiveness)	Match between system and the real world, User control and freedom, Flexibility and efficiency of use, Recognition rather than recall

3 Methodology

The main methodology is [27]'s multiple case study, with adaptations from [10]'s adapted spiral cascading scaffolding and adaptations from [28]. The project is part of the Human-Computer Interaction (HCI) course assignment (August 2022 semester). The course HCI, is undertaken by the computer science, software engineering, information technology, computer networking and security and recently, the data analytics programs. Hence, balancing flexibility and structure is important. Learning is framed within the United Nations' Sustainable Development Goals (UN SDG). The inquiry-based systems analysis and design project-assignment, is divided into three parts, each simulating design thinking's iterative divergence, and convergence (Table 3).

Table 3. Assignment structure, guided mainly by CMU's systems analysis and design rubrics

Assignment Part I (problem-solving subspace 1, iteration 1)	Assignment Part II (problem-solving subspace 2, iteration 2)	Assignment Part III (problem-solving subspace 3, iteration 3)
• identify trends - Google Trends (divergence), • identify SusA's possible social, technological, environmental, economic, and individual benefits and prioritize in descending order (convergence)	• review literature, market research (divergence), • SWOT and UML (convergence)	• Design & develop (Figma), alpha-beta testing • presentation

The design challenge is based on [1]'s atomistic vision of the metaverse, which component they should connect and how, and [29]'s 7 layers. Scaffolds are Google Trends, local and global metaverse examples, SWOT, [30]'s chain of effects (simplified, with the addition of prioritization in descending order), SDLC, design patterns, adapted short version of the 2018 ACM CHI student design competition rubrics [31], and Carnegie Mellon University's (CMU) systems analysis and design rubrics [32]. Adaptations are due to cultural differences.

The 3 evaluation questionnaires are HE, CSUQ and UEQ. Since the metaverse is new to them, students choose at every stage, from the options they are given/have discovered from Google Trends and literature review, including whether to experiment with what the metaverse should be like, or to design and develop for non-metaverse systems.

4   Results and Discussion

This study is a meta-analysis. Hence, three examples of good performing student-designers' Figma prototypes (Figs. 1a, b, 3, 5) and another layer of analysis, re-representation, and interpretation to students' alpha-beta testing results are presented.

Objective of Group 1: "A one-stop solution for learners to evolve into employees, combining education, e-commerce, and a job recruitment system. The online learning system is both entertaining and educational for users, and provides users with the opportunity to connect with each other, post and seek relevant job opportunities, and purchase necessary items, in one integrated interlinked system". (extracted from students' report).

4.1　Sample

The sample respondents' brief demographics are presented in Table 4 below.

Table 4.　Respondents' demographics (in %)

Age	19	20	21	22	24	25	From Sunway	Not Sunway
Alpha testing	18.8	18.8	37.5	6.3		18.8	31.3	68.8
Beta testing	23.5	17.6	11.8	41.2	5.9		58.8	41.2

Screenshots of their Figma prototype are presented in Figs. 1a and b.

a　　　　　　　　　　　　　　　　　　　b

Figs. 1.　**a** E-learning-job opportunities interconnection **b** E-learning-e-commerce interconnection.

4.2　Findings

Although given the choice of choosing 1 or 2 or 3 of the evaluation questionnaires, the first group of student-designers have chosen [23]'s HE, [24]'s CSUQ and [25]'s UEQ.

4.2.1　Alpha Testing

The HE alpha testing findings are presented in Table 5. The summation of percentages for Likert scales 6 and 7, are analyzed, as these represent the upper quartile. From Table 5, based on the summed percentages, the criteria, which score the highest are related to consistency and standards; followed by user control and freedom, flexibility and efficiency of use and aesthetic and minimalist design; and help and documentation, in third place. All criteria are pragmatic criteria, except aesthetic and minimalist design, which is a hedonistic prerequisite/consequent of pragmatic considerations.

　　As error prevention and system feedback have lower scores, student-designers have included buttons to text fields to prevent errors, and system feedback prompts, in beta.

　　Interestingly, students have compressed the CSUQ and UEQ questionnaires to only three questions, i.e., to what they really wish to know/highlight (Table 6). Students indicate in their report that user preference for the second-ranked criteria in Table 6, makes the interlinked system design challenge sensible to them.

Table 5. HE alpha testing findings (in %) (n = 16)

No	HE evaluation criteria	Likert scale							Rank
		2	3	4	5	6	7	6 + 7	
1	Visibility of system status			18.8	25.0	31.3	25.0	56.3	
2	Match between system and real world			12.5	25.0	25.0	37.5	62.5	
3	*User control and freedom*		6.3	12.5	6.3	31.3	43.8	75.1	2
4	*Consistency and standards*			12.5	6.3	50.0	31.3	81.3	1
5	Error prevention	6.3		37.5	25.0	12.5	18.8	31.3	
6	Recognition rather than recall			25.0	12.5	43.8	18.8	62.6	
7	*Flexibility and efficiency of use*			18.8	6.3	18.8	56.3	75.1	2
8	*Aesthetic and minimalist design*	6.3		6.3	12.5	56.3	18.8	75.1	2
9	Help users recognize, diagnose, recover from errors		6.3	25.0	37.5	12.5	18.8	31.3	
10	*Help and documentation*		6.3	6.3	18.8	37.5	31.3	68.6	3

Table 6. Students' perceived significance of CSUQ-UEQ to the evaluation of their prototype, (in %) (n = 16)

No	Evaluation questions	Likert scale						Rank
	CSUQ-UEQ	3	4	5	6	7	6 + 7	
1	System has an organized and clear layout/interface (design clarity)	6.3		6.3	31.3	56.3	87.6	1
2	Users' interaction with the system with proper messages and feedback (user control, error handling, efficiency)		25.0	18.8	37.5	18.8	56.3	3
3	System has innovative, engaging design		6.3	18.8	31.3	43.8	75.1	2

The student-designers have also added a question, which is not in both CSUQ-UEQ questionnaires, i.e., whether the respondents prefer a third party for each of the subsystems (education, e-commerce, and a job recruitment system), or an integrated system. Approximately two-thirds of the respondents (68.6%) prefer an integrated system. Integration is mainly due to discovery of and easier supply chain management, convenience and data analytics. This indicates courage, self-efficacy, and deeper learning, to experiment and investigate what they really want to know (amidst the possibility of questionnaire fatigue), and more focused requirements.

4.2.2 Beta Testing

Students have made the hypothesis that *"each topic is inherently different from one another. Therefore, a uniform interface and structure for every subject are not viable"*, but ease of use is still primary. Hence, students have the confidence to make their own assumptions, and to experiment, how to design for "innovative and engaging" interactions.

Table 7 presents the CSUQ beta testing results. To be consistent with Tables 5 and 6, ranking is based on the summed percentages of Likert scales 6 and 7, i.e., the third quartile. From Table 7, satisfaction has increased from 82.4% for ease of use, to 88.30% overall. The second highest percentage of 82.40% is equally divided between hedonistic (e.g. Q16 on pleasant interface) and pragmatic considerations (e.g. Q18 on availability of expected functions/functional usefulness, Q4, 5 on productivity). The bridge/main human factor is information clarity (e.g. Q12, 13, 14). These result in comfort in UX (e.g. Q6). Hence, there is increased importance to information flow.

Table 7. Beta testing results based on CSUQ (in %, with n = 17), alpha ranking in ()

No	CSUQ beta testing evaluation criteria	Likert scale					Rank
		4	5	6	7	6 + 7	
1	Overall, I am satisfied with how easy it is to use the system	11.8	5.9	41.2	41.2	82.4	2 (2)
2	It was simple to use this system	11.8	17.6	35.3	35.3	70.6	
3	I can effectively complete my work using this system	11.8	17.6	20.4	41.2	61.6	
4	I am able to complete my work quickly using this system	11.8	11.8	41.2	35.3	76.5	3 (3)
5	I am able to efficiently complete my work using this system	11.8	11.8	41.2	35.3	76.5	3 (3)
6	I feel *comfortable* using this system	11.8	5.9	47.1	35.3	82.4	2 (2)
7	It was easy to learn to use this system	5.9	17.6	29.4	47.1	76.5	3 (3)
8	I believe I became productive quickly using this system	17.6	5.9	41.2	35.3	76.5	3 (3)
9	The system gives error messages that clearly tell me how to fix problems	23.5	5.9	29.4	41.2	70.6	
10	Whenever I make a mistake using the system, I recover easily and quickly	17.6	17.6	29.4	35.3	64.7	
11	The information (such as online help, on-screen messages, and other documentation) provided with this system is clear	5.9	35.3	23.5	35.3	58.8	
12	It is easy to find the *information* I needed	5.9	11.8	47.1	35.3	82.4	2 (2)

(continued)

Table 7. (*continued*)

No	CSUQ beta testing evaluation criteria	Likert scale					Rank
		4	5	6	7	6 + 7	
13	The information provided for the system is easy to understand	5.9	17.6	35.3	41.2	76.5	3 (3)
14	The *information* is effective in helping me complete the tasks and scenarios	5.9	11.8	41.2	41.2	82.4	2 (2)
15	The organization of information on the system screens is clear	0	23.5	29.4	47.1	76.5	3 (3)
16	The interface of this system is pleasant	11.8	11.8	47.1	29.4	76.5	3 (3)
17	I like using the interface of this system	5.9	11.8	47.1	35.3	82.4	2 (2)
18	The system has all the functions and capabilities I expect	5.9	11.8	41.2	41.2	82.4	2 (2)
19	Overall, I am satisfied with this system	0	11.8	47.1	41.2	88.3	1 (1)

The questions students have chosen for UEQ for beta testing, are as short as alpha testing's. Students have decided to overcome modelling challenges, by reducing the problem-solving subspace's degree of dependencies, and dimensionality.

Clarity and feedback in Table 7 contribute to about 50% of factors ranked 2. From Table 8, UEQ's ranking corresponds with that of CSUQ's, with organized and clear interface first, followed by ease of use and creativity. Tables 7 and 8 concur with [18]'s information gain/flow. The switch between the second and third-ranking factor in beta (Table 8) compared to Table 6 (alpha), indicates that students perceive ease of use with feedback, as more important to sustainability, as feedback refines requirements gathering/design thinking.

Table 8. UEQ (results in%), with n = 17, alpha ranking in ()

No	CSUQ and UEQ evaluation criteria								Rank
		2	3	4	5	6	7	6 + 7	
1	System is creative		11.8	5.9	23.5	17.6	41.2	58.8	3 (2)
2	System is easy to use, with feedback for improvement	5.9		11.8	17.6	23.5	41.2	64.7	2 (3)
3	System has an organized and clear layout/interface	5.9		5.9	11.8	29.4	47.1	76.5	1 (1)

Since the triangulation between HE, CSUQ and UEQ support each other, the ranking is supported. A possible hierarchical relationship among these constructs is presented in Fig. 2a. Moreover, shifts in centrality of design (dy/dx over dy/dt), involves identifying which evaluation criteria matters based on utility policies, at dy/dt, and subsequently, retrieving or pointing to the best or most suitable options. The three criteria in Fig. 2b, are examples of such evaluation criteria.

Hence, dimension reduction by identifying more significant contributing factors dynamically over time, is not necessarily promoting lossy-like compression (discard non-representative samples), but involves which variables/factors/criteria to hide, and which to activate at a certain point in time, based on the criteria and utility function at that certain point in time. Hence, integration may not always be the best solution for all. There may be a need for complements, with loosely coupled (eco)systems.

The degree of integration should be with regards to bridging certain aspects, while each retains its own unique value propositions, to freely explore opportunities for growth semi-independently, and more richly computationally, over time. Porter's (1979) five forces, i.e., competition amongst players in the industry, potential of new players in the industry, suppliers' power, customers' power and threat arising from substitute products. Ultimately, due to bounded rationality, dy/dx over dy/dt is not likely to shift much, unless the objective/utility functions, and evaluation criteria change, e.g., in trends/ cultural changes.

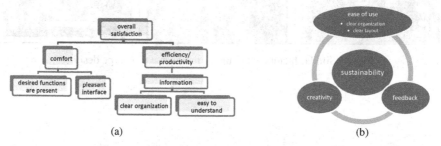

(a)   (b)

Fig. 2. Inferred hierarchy of factors contributing to overall satisfaction/attractiveness based on CSUQ (a) and highlights from CSUQ-HE-UEQ (b), with information as the bridge, and derived three key factors, as mediators and moderators, over time

4.2.3   Similarities Between Groups 1 and 2

Interestingly, the two groups' prototypes, exemplify not only modular-based design, but also open/close networks/interconnections, random starting points, and episodicity. These reflect semi-structured information stacks from the back-end. Stacks are foundations/the "thread" for quantum computing.

Furthermore, similar hierarchical relationships are found in Group 2's designs (Fig. 3), but with greater emphasis on engaging and creative. Group 2's alpha testing involves respondents, who are aged between18 to 24 years old (94.9%). Most of the participants (78.4%) are Malaysians, while 21.6% are non-Malaysians. Beta testing involves respondents aged 18 to 24 years old (90.5%), and the rest, between 25–34 years old, and 35 to 44 years old. Most participants (76.2%) are Malaysians and 23.8% non-Malaysians. Student-designers' report indicate 5/5 for *match with real world, control and freedom, and error prevention* for HE, 5/5 for all UEQ criteria.

The difference lies in prioritization in the chain of effects. Group 1's report prioritizes chain of effects as individual first, followed by social, economic, technological and environmental. Possible reasons are found in their mind map (Fig. 4a). Group 2 (Fig. 4b) prioritizes social, technological, environmental, economic, individual. Both groups recognize that sustainability supports other aspects, but is hard-earned, and needs to be developed over time. Progression in students' model evolutions (alpha to beta), and complexity reduction via identifying the essence in questionnaires, indicate students have grasped what are important to their design, and how to communicate these.

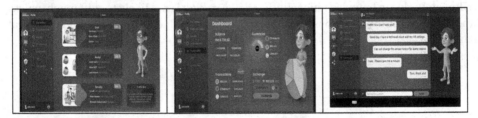

Fig. 3. Similar factors in Group 2's metaverse prototype design

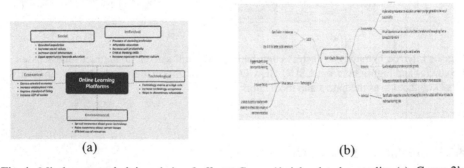

(a)   (b)

Fig. 4. Mind maps underlying chain of effects: Group 1's job-related centrality (a), Group 2's engagement-varied ability/age-user centrality (b)

Students' iterative subspace solutions attest to computational thinking's decomposition, algorithmic logic/information flow, [33]'s perspectives, concepts and practice, and [34]'s computer science-computational thinking, as avenue for connecting with real-world challenges. Pattern recognition is via design patterns' consistency and recognition rather than recall. Abstraction is possible with big data. Findings also support the

Learning Sciences' proposition that emergence and self-organization are more beneficial, in more diverse problem-solving subspaces and [6]'s pointer-connected information stacks, emulating LISP.

5 Comparison With E-Commerce Figma Prototype In Same Class

Students' Objective: To explore an interlinked system and attempt to relate these systems to the metaverse. According to Google Trends, there is an increasing trend regarding e-wallet and cryptocurrency in Malaysia. Cryptocurrency is included as there are also many people interested in investing in cryptocurrency, but do not know how or where to start investing. Therefore, we decided to design a digital wallet named Cryptollar that works as an e-wallet and crypto wallet.

5.1 Sample

The sample respondents' demographics is Gaussian, presented in Table 9.

Table 9. Sample respondents' demographics

Age	19–24	< 18, > 40	N	Male	Female
Alpha testing	91.9	8.1	37	51.4	48.6
Beta testing	91.7	5.6	36	52.8	47.2

Screenshots of the students' Figma prototype are presented in Fig. 5.

Fig. 5. Screenshots of the Cryptollar Figma prototype

5.2 Findings

The student designers have chosen HE for alpha testing, and for beta testing, HE and CSUQ. The HE results are presented in Tables 10, 11 and CSUQ in Tables 12, 13, with rankings, in the right most column. From Table 10, *user control and freedom* and *flexibility and efficiency of use* are ranked first, followed by *recognition rather than recall*. In Table y, however, there is a shift in centrality from loosely structured to more tightly structured. There is a drastic change in preference for *Visibility of system* status (unranked in alpha to rank 1 in beta) and *Consistency and standards* (ranked 5 in alpha, to rank 1 in beta) to enhance ease of use and efficiency (productivity). This is possibly due to the increased number of functions in the beta prototype, where other daily popular functions (Table 3a) are included, on top of e-wallet, crypto and NFT. Consequently, in beta, *recognition rather than recall* and *flexibility and efficiency of use* are ranked second, *user control and freedom,* fourth.

5.2.1 HE Alpha Testing

Table 10. HE alpha testing findings (in %) (n = 37)

No	HE evaluation criteria	Likert scale						Rank
		1	2	3	4	5	4 + 5	
1	Visibility of system status		2.7	29.7	40.5	27.0	67.50	
2	Match between system and the real world			24.3	43.2	32.4	75.60	3
3	*User control and freedom*			18.9	37.8	43.2	81.00	1
4	Consistency and standards			29.7	43.2	27.0	70.20	5
5	Error prevention		2.7	40.5	37.8	18.9	56.70	
6	*Recognition rather than recall*			21.6	59.5	18.9	78.40	2
7	*Flexibility and efficiency of use*			18.9	48.6	32.4	81.00	1
8	Aesthetic and minimalist design	2.7	10.8	21.6	43.2	21.6	64.80	
9	Help users recognize, diagnose, recover from errors		2.7	21.6	51.4	24.3	75.70	3
10	Help and documentation		2.7	24.3	56.8	16.2	73.00	4

5.2.2 HE Beta Testing

Table 11. HE beta testing, findings (in %) (n = 36)

No	HE evaluation criteria	1	2	3	4	5	4 + 5	Rank
1	*Visibility of system status*			13.9	44.4	41.7	86.1	1
2	Match between system and the real world		2.8	16.7	36.1	44.4	80.5	4
3	User control and freedom			19.4	47.2	33.3	80.5	4
4	*Consistency and standards*			13.9	50.0	36.1	86.1	1
5	Error prevention			30.6	44.4	25.0	69.4	
6	*Recognition rather than recall*			16.7	52.8	30.6	83.4	2
7	*Flexibility and efficiency of use*			16.7	30.6	52.8	83.4	2
8	Aesthetic and minimalist design			19.4	44.4	36.1	80.5	4
9	Help users recognize, diagnose, recover from errors			16.7	38.9	44.4	83.3	3
10	Help and documentation			16.7	36.1	47.2	83.3	3

5.2.3 CSUQ Alpha Findings

For alpha, overall satisfaction with ease of use is 62.1%. Overall satisfaction with the system, at 72.9%, indicates improved satisfaction of 10.8% due to other factors (Table 12). Efficiency (Q5), easy to learn (Q6), and adequate and clear information for productivity (Q14) are ranked second. Hence, the sample respondents are mainly concerned with productivity. Ease of use (Q2), easy to understand information (Q13), pleasant interface (Q16) and adequate functions (Q17) are ranked third. Hence, compared to Group 1's e-learning prototype, which has less risks, Group 3's e-wallet-crypto-NFT prototype, indicates caution due to real-time, actual financial rewards/loss.

The students have also reported that respondents' most common positive comments in CSUQ's qualitative section, are the interface is easy to navigate, and is clear. Respondents mention that the navigation method is similar to what the respondents are familiar with. The second aspect is the integration of functions commonly found in other apps, and the number of functions available in the prototype. Respondents find integrating crypto-wallet features and NFTs in one app creative.

Table 12. Alpha testing CSUQ findings (in %)

No	Evaluation criteria	Likert scale Rank							
		2	3	4	5	6	7	6 + 7	
1	Overall, I am satisfied with how easy it is to use the system			16.2	21.6	40.5	21.6	62.1	
2	It was simple to use this system			13.5	21.6	32.4	32.4	64.8	3
3	I can effectively complete my work using this system	2.7		13.5	21.6	35.1	27.0	62.1	
4	I am able to complete my work quickly using this system			13.5	27.0	35.1	24.3	59.4	
5	*I am able to efficiently complete my work using this system*			13.5	18.9	37.8	29.7	67.5	2
6	I feel comfortable using this system		2.7	16.2	24.3	35.1	21.6	56.7	
7	*It was easy to learn to use this system*	2.7	2.7	8.1	18.9	35.1	32.4	67.5	2
8	I believe I became productive quickly using this system		2.7	16.2	24.3	40.5	16.2	56.7	
9	The system gives error messages that clearly tell me how to fix problems	5.4	27.0	29.7	21.6	16.2	37.8		
10	Whenever I make a mistake using the system, I recover easily and quickly		2.7	21.6	24.3	29.7	21.6	51.3	
11	The information (such as online help, on-screen messages, and other documentation) provided with this system is clear	5.4	13.5	27.0	27.0	27.0	54.0		
12	It is easy to find the information I needed			13.5	27.0	37.8	21.6	59.4	
13	The information provided for the system is easy to understand	2.7		8.1	24.3	40.5	24.3	64.8	3
14	*The information is effective in helping me complete the tasks and scenarios*			13.5	18.9	48.6	18.9	67.5	2
15	The organization of information on the system screens is clear		2.7	16.2	18.9	37.8	24.3	62.1	
16	The interface of this system is pleasant		5.4	16.2	13.5	43.2	21.6	64.8	3
17	I like using the interface of this system		5.4	18.9	16.2	35.1	24.3	59.4	
18	This system has all the functions and capabilities I expect it to have			13.5	21.6	32.4	32.4	64.8	3
19	Overall, I am satisfied with this system			16.2	10.8	45.9	27.0	72.9	1

5.2.4 CSUQ Beta Testing Findings

The positive feedback that student-designers have received is that the users are happy with the interface (Q6), the added new features (Q13), and the colour scheme. For alpha and beta testing, overall satisfaction with the system is ranked first. Second (Q6, Q12) and third-ranked (Q13) criteria are related to information (Table 13). Another similarity is the increase of about 10% between Q1 and Q19 in the alpha and beta CSUQ findings, and 7.6% increase between Q19 of alpha and beta. The similarity reflects the degree of variance to which CSUQ enriches HE, in approximating the percentage of contribution by non-ease-of-use factors more specifically.

Table 13. Beta testing CSUQ findings (in %)

No	Questionnaire's evaluation criteria	Likert scale					Rank
		4	5	6	7	6 + 7	
1	Overall, I am satisfied with how easy it is to use the system	11.1	27.8	22.2	38.9	61.1	
2	It was simple to use this system	8.3	22.2	30.6	38.9	69.5	4
3	I can effectively complete my work using this system	8.3	27.8	19.4	44.4	63.8	
4	I am able to complete my work quickly using this system	11.1	30.6	19.4	38.9	58.3	
5	I am able to efficiently complete my work using this system	8.3	33.3	19.4	38.9	58.3	
6	*I feel comfortable using this system*	8.3	13.9	36.1	41.7	77.8	2
7	It was easy to learn to use this system	8.3	25.0	27.8	38.9	66.7	
8	I believe I became productive quickly using this system	5.6	27.8	27.8	38.9	66.7	
9	The system gives error messages that clearly tell me how to fix problems	13.9	36.1	11.1	36.1	47.2	
10	Whenever I make a mistake using the system, I recover easily and quickly	13.9	27.8	25.0	33.3	58.3	
11	The information (such as online help, on-screen messages, etc. provided with this system is clear	8.3	25.0	27.8	38.9	66.7	
12	It is easy to find the information I needed	8.3	19.4	36.1	36.1	72.2	3
13	*The information provided for the system is easy to understand*	8.3	13.9	27.8	50.0	77.8	2
14	The information is effective in helping me complete the tasks and scenarios	5.6	25.0	19.4	50.0	69.4	4
15	The organization of information on the system screens is clear	5.6	27.8	13.9	50.0	63.9	
16	The interface of this system is pleasant	5.6	25.0	25.0	44.4	69.4	4
17	I like using the interface of this system	11.1	19.4	30.6	38.9	69.5	4

(continued)

Table 13. (*continued*)

No	Questionnaire's evaluation criteria	Likert scale Rank					
		4	5	6	7	6 + 7	
18	This system has all the functions and capabilities I expect it to have	11.1	19.4	25.0	44.4	69.4	4
19	Overall, I am satisfied with this system	5.6	13.9	33.3	47.2	80.5	1

These findings are almost identical to that of Groups 1 and 2, indicating that the respondents' demographics are rather homogeneous. Differences are minimal. Hence, Figs. 2a and b apply to all three groups, with slightly different weightage based on centrality in design, adapted to the respective demographics' capability maturity, risk acceptance and expectations.

6 Contributions

Contributions are:

1) the scaffolds for enhancing computational thinking skills, adding on to [36], the meta-analysis, which leads to the derived hierarchy of pragmatic and hedonistic factors based on CSUQ and CSUQ-HE-UEQ and that the chain of effects' descending order, reflected in the underlying mind maps and cultural adaptations are the intertwining DNA;
2) identification of approximate percentage that (non)ease-of-use factors account for via CSUQ;
3) ontological awareness and its possible potential have increased, along the SQL-noSQL and SQL vs. noSQL lines of thought. Hence, the SQL-vs. noSQL and SQL-noSQL analogy, which requires dynamic semi-structured evaluation, and loosely-coupled (dis)assembly.

7 Conclusion

This study has investigated three groups of students' perceptions towards what's important in design, via information systems analysis, design and development of prototypes, and via HE, CSUQ, UEQ evaluations. Student-designers have managed to identify key criteria in alpha testing, and refined their design correspondingly, in beta. Though rankings differ slightly, students are able to identify factors contributing to sustainability for the specific demographic. Findings reflect shifts in centralities of design and models at different points over time. These two groups' designs also reflect continuums and spectrums in notions of what sustainable interconnected systems in the metaverse may be like. Their artefacts and reports also indicate increased interest, and self-efficacy/confidence in designing and developing for interconnecting (non) metaverse (eco)systems.

There are however, limitations to the findings, as the sample size is small. Nevertheless, these findings point to problem-solving subspaces in atomistic contexts as viable, only when and media-rich and ontologically and loosely interconnected, to enable diverse refactoring; similar to Lazada and Shoppee's success with e-commerce. Future work will include diverging frameworks, technologies and assessments.

Acknowledgement. The author thanks the Fulbright Commission for funding/supporting the 2009 research into creativity scaffolds [10], the 2011 editorial on sustainable design-development with Georgia Tech's Prof. Janet L. Kolodner, Prof. Ashok K. Goel [11] and this paper, Prof. Kolodner and Prof. Goel's acceptance of the series of research todate; Prof. Bo Jiang for proofreading, and suggesting the addition of generative systems in the introduction, and for funding the 2019 Scratch fractal study [14] [China NSF]; the IEEE and IEEE Smart Cities initiative; Prof. Hean-Teik Chuah, Prof. Hong-Tat Ewe, for prior foundations in engineering education and computing/informatics, Prof. Yashwant Prasad Singh for past AI foundations; Dr. K. Daniel Wong, for past design thinking and computational thinking studies; Prof. Jari Porras and his team's SusA framework, Tan Sri Augustine Ong (Malaysian Invention and Design Society), for approving the 2022 (first) metaverse article, and Sunway University. Special thanks to Sunway University's mostly Computer Science HCI student-designers for their efforts and inspiring prototypes: Cheryl Qiao-Rou Toh, Wei-Xiang Yap, Yen-Ting Teo, Jesrene Ka-Yan Cheoy, Sharifah Hannah Zahra binti Syed Azaman Shah (IT), Yohen Sheraun a/l Regu, Jun-Yang Fong, Jia-Le Soong; Kambar Mirmanov, Yslam Orazov, Egor Voronianskii, Guan-Wei Yong, Li-Siang Tan, Wen-Jian Koay, Elginaid Elshami, Zhi-Khai Choong, Hao-Zhan Tsang, Agileshwaran Sivasakthi Balan; Boon-Wee Tan, Yao-Xian Chua, Jia-Qian Lee, Chloe Pei-Yu Chiew, Suet-Li Yeoh, Le-Xuan Tan, Kah-How Liong (IT), Yee-Zhen Chong (IT), Vinesh s/o R. Mahendran.

References

1. The Verge: Exclusive: Mark Zuckerberg on the Quest Pro, future of the metaverse, and more (2022). https://www.youtube.com/watch?v=gV50hpSKHFQ
2. Gartner: What is a Metaverse? (2022). https://www.weforum.org/agenda/2022/03/hour-a-day-in-metaverse-by-2026-says-gartner/
3. Bridges, C., et al.: Metaverse Roadmap: A Cross-Industry Public Foresight Project (2009). https://www.metaverseroadmap.org/
4. Tan, Z.Y.: Time to enter the metaverse. Digital Edge, The Edge Malaysia Weekly, May 9, 2022 - May 15 (2022)
5. Goel, A.K.: Design, analogy and creativity. IEEE Expert, pp. 62–70 (1997)
6. Ling, T.W.: Conceptual modelling views on relational databases vs big data. Keynote speech. In: International Conference on Frontiers of Artificial Intelligence and Statistics, December 2–4, 2022. Beijing, China
7. Papert, S.: Mindstorms: Children. Basic Books, NY, Computers and Powerful Ideas (1980)
8. Kolodner, J.L., Hmelo, C.E., Narayanan, N.H.: Problem-based learning meets case- based reasoning. In: International Conference on Learning Sciences, July 25-27, 1996, pp. 188–195 (1996)
9. Resnick, M.: Designing for wide walls. (2005). https://design.blog/2016/08/25/mitchel-resnick-designing-for-wide-walls/
10. Lee, C.S.: Scaffolding everyday creativity: A spiral cascaded development approach. World Conference on Educational Multimedia, Hypermedia and Telecommunications, Honolulu, HI, USA, June 22–26, pp. 770–775 (2009)
11. Lee, C.S., Kolodner, J.L., Goel, A.K.: Creative design: scaffolding creative reasoning and meaningful learning. Educ. Technol. Soc. **14**(1), 1–2 (2011)
12. Lee, C.S.: Scaffolding systemic and creative thinking: a hybrid learning sciences-decision support approach. e-Journal Bus. Educ. Scholarship Teach. **5**(1), 47–58 (2011)

13. Lee, C.S., Wong, K.D.: Developing a disposition for social innovations: an affective-socio-cognitive co-design model. In: International Conference on Cognition and Exploratory Learning in Digital Age, October 24–26, 2015, Ireland, pp. 180–186 (2015)
14. Lee, C.S., Jiang, B.: Assessment of Computational Thinking (CT) in Scratch fractal projects: Towards CT-HCI scaffolds for analogical-fractal thinking. In: International Conference on Computer-Supported Education, Crete, Greece May 2–4, 2019, pp. 192–199 (2019)
15. Lee, C.S., Wong, K.D.: Comparing computational thinking in Scratch and non-Scratch Web design projects: A preliminary meta-analysis study. International Conference on Computers in Education, Thailand, November 22–26, 2021, vol. II, pp. 457–462 (2021)
16. Chan, T.W., Looi, C.K., Chen, W., et al.: Interest-driven creator theory: towards a theory of learning design for Asia in the twenty-first century. J. Comput. Educ. 5, 435–461 (2018)
17. Jiang, B., Zhao, W., Zhang, N., Qiu, F.: Programming trajectories analytics in block-based programming language learning. Interact. Learn. Environ. 30(1), 1113–1126 (2022)
18. Venkatesh, V., Bala, H.: Technology acceptance model 3 and a research agenda on interventions. Decis. Sci. 39(2), 273–315 (2008)
19. Liang, X.S., Kleeman, R.: Information transfer between dynamical system components. Phys. Rev. Lett. 95, 244101 (2005)
20. Liang, X.S.: Liang-kleeman information flow: theory and applications. Entropy 15, 327–360 (2013)
21. Valacich, J., George, J., Hoffer, J.: Essentials of Systems Analysis and Design, 6th edn. Pearson (2015)
22. Davis, F.: Perceived usefulness, perceived ease of use, and user acceptance of information technology. MIS Q. 13(3), 319–340 (1989)
23. Davis, F., Bagozzi, R., Warshaw, P.: User acceptance of computer technology: a comparison of two theoretical models. Manage. Sci. 35, 982–1003 (1989)
24. Nielsen, J.: 10 Usability Heuristics for User Interface Design (1995). https://www.nngroup.com/articles/tenusability-heuristics/
25. Lewis, J.R.: IBM Computer Usability Satisfaction Questionnaires: Psychometric evaluation and instructions for use. International Journal of Human-Computer Interaction, 7(1), 57–78. (1995). https://garyperlman.com/quest/quest.cgi
26. Schrepp, M., Hinderks, A., Thomaschewski, J.: Design and evaluation of a short version of the user experience questionnaire (UEQ-S). Int. J. Interact. Multimed. Artif. Intell. 4(6), 103–108 (2017)
27. Stake, R.E.: Multiple case study analysis. Guilford Publications, New York (2006)
28. Lee, C.S., Singh, Y.P.: Student modeling using principal component analysis of SOM clusters. In: IEEE International Conference on Advanced Learning Technologies, IEEE Computer Society Press, Joensuu, Finland, August 30-September 1, pp. 480–484 (2004)
29. Radoff, J.: Measuring the value chain. In Muse, D. (2022). Understanding-the-7-layers-of -the-metaverse. https://venturebeat.com/enterprise/understanding-the-7-layers-of-the-metaverse/
30. Penzenstadler, B., et al.: The SusA Workshop - improving sustainability awareness to inform future business process and systems design. (Version 1). Zenodo (2021). https://doi.org/10.5281/zenodo.3632486
31. ACM CHI student design competition (2018). https://chi2018.acm.org/authors/student-design-competition/
32. Eberly Centre for Teaching Excellence. Systems Analysis and Design rubrics. Carnegie Mellon University (2015)
33. Brennan, K., Resnick, M.: New frameworks for studying and assessing the development of computational thinking. Annual meeting of the American Educational Research Association (2012)
34. Wing, J.: Computational thinking. Commun. ACM 49(3), 33–36 (2006)

Design and Develop of a Smart City Digital Twin with 3D Representation and User Interface for What-If Analysis

Lorenzo Adreani, Pierfrancesco Bellini, Marco Fanfani, Paolo Nesi$^{(\boxtimes)}$, and Gianni Pantaleo

DISIT Lab, University of Florence, Florence, Italy
{lorenzo.adreani,pierfrancesco.bellini,marco.fanfani,paolo.nesi,
gianni.pantaleo}@unifi.it
https://www.disit.org, https://www.sanp4city.org

Abstract. Digital Twins of Smart Cities are fundamental tools for decision makers since they can provide interactive 3D visualizations of the city enriched with real-time information and connected to actual complete digital model of the entities with all their heterogeneous data/info. Such a technology can be exploited to observe the status of the city, and to perform analysis and simulations, and thus to develop strategies. Indeed, such solutions must satisfy a series of requirements spanning from the 3D construction to the interactive functionality of user interface for the decision makers. In this paper, a Smart City Digital Twin model and tools are presented, which satisfy a wide range of requirements. The principles at the basis of the design and development are reported and discussed. The solution has been developed on top of Snap4City platform and validated on Florence City case (Italy), in CN Mobility of Ministry. Finally, a comparison among several different Smart City Digital Twin solutions is offered.

Keywords: Digital Twin · Smart City · 3D City Model

1 Introduction

Nowadays Smart City Digital Twins, SCDTs, are becoming ever more relevant in academic, government, and industrial fields since they can offer a virtual context that replicates a real city with high fidelity, typically exploiting 3D models of the buildings enriched with structural and contextual information coming from IoT (Internet of Things) sensors, heatmaps, analytic services, building information modelling, etc. [1]. Such solutions can provide a fundamental tool for city decision makers and stakeholders which can observe in real-time the status of the city, and perform analysis and simulations in different application domains like urban planning, mobility and transport, energy, disaster analysis and prevention, air pollution monitoring, city planning, etc.

On the one hand, in the past years several works addressed the problem of 3D city modelling in order to create realistic virtual visualizations of the city structure. Clearly,

---

The original version of this chapter was revised: Reference [18] has been corrected so that its form is now compatible with Scopus. The correction to this chapter is available at
https://doi.org/10.1007/978-3-031-37126-4_45

O. Gervasi et al. (Eds.): ICCSA 2023 Workshops, LNCS 14111, pp. 531–548, 2023.
https://doi.org/10.1007/978-3-031-37126-4_34

since such 3D models must cover city-wide areas, both the production of the 3D models, as well as their handling and processing pose a challenging task still to be solved [2]. With the purpose of defining an adequate format for the data to be displayed on a web interface, CityGML [3] proposed a series of requirements according to different Level of Details (LoD) covered by the model. Five LoD have been defined: LoD0 includes 2D maps and 3D terrain only, LoD1 introduce simple box-like 3D building models that are enhanced with 3D roof structures in LoD2. LoD3 introduces realistic textures, and finally LoD4 describes building interiors. In CityGML3.0, Building Information Modelling (BIM) are included using the Industrial Foundation Class (IFC) format [4].

On the other hand, a SCDT must include information about Point of Interest (POI) locations, IoT Sensor positions and readings, heatmaps to show for example the dispersion of pollutants, paths (e.g., cycling paths) and areas (e.g., city districts). To enhance the 3D model with this kind of knowledge, the SCDT should be embedded into an adequate platform capable to model any data kind, and capable to ingest, manipulate, and index static and real-time data that can then be retrieved using specific API.

In this paper, firstly, a series of requirements for SCDT are reported and discussed in Sect. 2 expanding those presented in [5] considering the required data to be included into a SCDT, and taking into account the users' interaction functionalities that the SCDT interface should provide, and some additional operative requirements that should be satisfied in order to enhance the functionalities offered by a SCDT. Then, we present our SCDT solution describing, in Sect. 3, the development phases; in Sect. 4, how the 3D building models were obtained, and, finally in Sect. 5, how the web interface was developed to integrate all the data and distribute proposed SCDT on a web browser. In Sect. 6, the case of study for Florence (Italy) is presented, showing the possibility of performing What-If analysis via the 3D visual interface. Section 7 provides a comparison with other SCDT and 3D city representations on the basis of the identified requirements. Finally, in Sect. 8, conclusions are drawn and future work highlighted.

2 Requirement Analysis

In this section, the requirements that a SCDT should satisfy are reported and discussed. Clearly, the quality of the 3D representations of buildings is a key aspect of a SCDT. For example, in [3] different levels of detail (LoD) were proposed. However, a SCDT must comply with additional requirements that take into account the 3D representation and the integration of additional massive data to provide a complete tool at support of decision makers. In [5], a list of requirements was proposed to specify which elements should be visualized on a 3D representation for SCDT, and to point out the interactivity aspects to be addressed to guarantee a suitable user experience.

In this paper, we strongly revised and further expanded the requirement list considering aspects related to the data management, advanced interactivity, costs and licensing aspects. Hereafter, a revised and augmented list of requirements is reported. Firstly, requirements on data are presented, then the requirements to offer interactive controls to the user are reported. Finally, the most relevant operative requirements are included.

Requirements on data (RD) to be included in a SCDT are:

RD1. Buildings of the city. Each single building should be represented with details in terms of shape (facades, roof, towers, cupolas, etc.), and **patterns on facades and roofs**. Multiple representations at different LoD could be included. For example, (i) LoD1 structure obtained by extruding the building plans up to the heights of the eaves, or (ii) higher LoD structure represented as 3D meshes, and (iii) BIM should be included.

RD2. Ground information as road shapes and names, names of squares and localities, etc., exploiting the so called Orthomaps, with eventual real aerial view patterns, and the actual graph road information for picking and connecting elements. Orthomaps are typically provided in terms of multi resolution tiled images from GIS systems using WMS protocol, while the road graph can be coarsely recovered from Open Street Map or from institutional cadastre.

RD3. Heatmaps are typically superimposed (with variable transparency) on the ground level without overlapping the buildings. For example, to represent temperature, traffic flow, pollutant distribution, people flow, noise, humidity, etc. In this case, they are typically provided in term of multi resolution geolocated tiled images, provided by GIS using WMS protocol. In some cases, a time sequence of heatmap can be used to show the evolution of the distribution over time. This aspect adds complexity to the model, because the heatmap can be shaped, calibrated with colormaps, and compounded by different elementary blocks of any shape, or points.

RD4. Paths and areas shapes can be super-imposed over the ground and heatmaps levels without overlapping the buildings. Such data can be used to describe perimeters of gardens, cycling paths, trajectories, border of gov areas, elements of origin destination matrices, etc. This information is quite specific and must be produced on the basis of information recovered from some Open Data. Once recovered it can be distributed by using GIS in WFS/WMS protocols.

RD5. PINs marking the position of services, IoT Devices, Point of Interest (POI), Key Performance Indicator (KPI), etc., and providing clickable information according to some data model which may provide access to Time Series, shapes, etc. This information is quite specific and can be produced on the basis of the information recovered from Private and/or Open Data.

RD6. Terrain information and elevation: the elevation of each single building has to be taken into account and thus the skyline of the city may include surrounding mountains, in city hills, etc. This means that the buildings and Orthomaps should be placed according to the terrain elevation, the so-called Digital Terrain Model, DTM. The DTM can be distributed via WMS from GIS.

RD7. Additional 3D entities for completing the realism of the scenario, such as: (i) trees, benches, fountains, semaphores, digital signages, luminaries, and any other city furniture, etc.; and (ii) water bodies should be included into the digital twin to better represent rivers, lakes, fountains, etc.

In addition, the framework used to present the SCDT must met some requirements of interactivity with the model and the 3D elements (RI):

RI1. Map controls to change the point of view by zooming, rotating, tilting, and panning the scene. Changing the light source position, simulating different times of day/night, should be possible. This should lead to produce shades projected by buildings on ground and other buildings, and a different illumination from direct to indirect exposition to daylight, eventual reflections, and transparencies. Picking on map to recover position and eventual information associated with the city structure and road graph.

RI2. Dynamic sky to show different sky conditions according to the time of the day, weather, and/or weather forecast.

RI3. PIN data access to show data associated with IoT Devices, POI, KPI, etc., including real time and historical data, time series, or detailed information, and corresponding drill down facilities.

RI4. Building picking/manipulation: to provide the possibility to select single building to: (i) show detailed information associated with the building, or (ii) move into a BIM view of the building, with the possibility of navigating into the building structure, and again to access the internal data associate to PINs into the building, or (iii) to change the building 3D model with a new one to have an evolution over time.

RI5.Twin management as independent element management loading to have the possibility to hide, show, replace specific element as entities modelled as Digital Twins, for example to disable the building view to see only the city PINs, or to load different heatmaps or paths.

RI6. Business logic call-back to provide the possibility of selecting an element (3D, PIN, ground, heatmap) to provoke a call back into a business logic tool for provoking events and actions in the systems, at which the developers may associate intelligence activities, analytics, other views, etc.

RI7. Underground and elements inspection to provide the possibility of selecting and inspecting specific areas and see detailed 3D elements placed underground or inside the buildings, such as water pipes, metro lines, etc. And interacting with complex elements for example, traffic flow, cycling paths, scenarios, city decors, etc.

RI8. Virtual 3D structures as dynamic PIN changing colour and/or size/shape according to some data value, OD flows with jumps/arcs, etc. Dynamic pins as SVG shape and colour by changing with some real time value. Dynamic pins as 3D solids changing colour or size according to some real time value.

Finally, there are some operative requirements (RO) that must be met to guarantee an accessible, integrated, and affordable SCDT solution:

RO1. Data analytic processes must be available to let the user develops and/or execute specific data analytics.

RO2. Smart Data Model compatibility to guarantee interoperable and replicable Smart Cities, interoperability at level of data formats, federation at level of protocols and APIs.

RO3. Logics for data ingestion and transformation required to ingest data from IoT sensors, and other sources and transform them into different data models and formats.

RO4. Dynamic data management to have new PINs or elements to be automatically reported in the SCDT as soon as they are included in the platform, event driven rendering of data.

RO5. Integration with workflow management systems for ticket management. For example, when an event of a streetlamp fault is detected, in the SCDT the faulty streetlamp is highlighted together with its connection to the electric infrastructure in order to ease the maintenance work.

RO6. Web player: (i) the SCDT must be accessible thought a web browser without additional plugins, and (ii) the player must be released with open or free license.

RO7. No reloading: changes in the SCDT must be rendered without the needs of a full reload of the map.

RO8. Automatic 3D building construction: (i) 3D buildings must be created automatically, to be able to scale and replicate the SCDT framework; and (ii) the used software must be released with open or free license.

In the following sections, our solution is presented and described wrt the defined requirements. Then, in Sect. 7 a comparison among a selection of the most diffuse SCDT solutions is reported highlighting for each solution the satisfied requirements.

3   SCDT Development Phases

In order to develop a SCDT solution capable to fulfil the above requirements, we identified the following main phases:

A. **Data acquisition**: city graph, IoT sensor/actuators, POIs, orthomaps, paths, digital surface model (DSM) and terrain elevation (DTM), images, etc.
B. **Production**: Heatmaps computation, traffic flow reconstruction, OD productions, 3D building construction, etc.
C. **Integration and distribution**: acquired and produced data are integrated into a global digital twin model and rendered as 3D multi-data map and distributed as an interactive web interface.

Phases A, and B are those that mainly respond to reach the data requirements (RD1 – RD7), while phase C must be designed in order to satisfy the requirements on the interactivity (RI1 -RI8). Instead, the operative requirements are mainly addressed by the IoT platform on top of which the SCDT is built on. In our case, the Snap4City platform [6, 7] – an open-source platform developed at DISIT Lab, University of Florence (https://www.snap4city.org/) – was used. The platform includes Data Analytics processes to perform analyses and simulations (RO1), is compatible with a large number of protocols and format and with FIWARE Smart Data Model (RO2), integrates IoT Apps, based on Node-RED, for data ingestion and transformations (RO3), and, thanks to the semantically indexing of data in an RDF Knowledge Base, offers dedicated APIs to query the stored data and to model the road graph and related elements, heatmaps, OD matrices, traffic, scenarios, etc. (RO4).

The developed 3D multi-data map is an open-source web interface (RO6), created as a dashboard in the Snap4City platform. It can allow the visualization of an interactive 3D reconstruction of the city, with the possibility of showing and inspecting different kinds of entities and related data, such as IoT devices, POI, heatmaps, geometries related to bus routes, cycling paths, traffic flows, etc. In this way, the Snap4City platform allows to exploit a complete open-source framework that can collect, process, and manage all the data needed to obtain a high-fidelity SCDT.

Indeed, phase A is realized exploiting the Snap4City capabilities to ingest, manage, retrieve heterogeneous data: ground information (RD2) and paths and geometry (RD4) from OSM and Open Data, IoT sensors data, POI and KPI (RD5) to be shown as PINs.

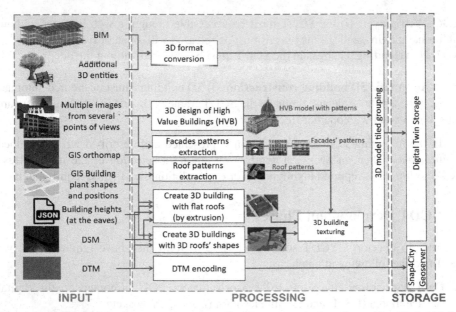

Fig. 1. Proposed production process to create the 3D structures of our Smart City Digital Twin.

In phase B, heatmaps (RD3) are produced from the acquired data using some Data Analytics [8, 9], and the 3D buildings (RD1) and the terrain elevation (RD6) are created following the procedure described in Sect. 4. Note that, the algorithm to create the 3D building structure is completely automatic and released as open source[1], satisfying RO8. Additional 3D entities (RD7) can be obtained from free archives of general 3D models and included into the map. Finally, in phase C, all the data are integrated into an interactive web interface as shown in Sect. 5.

4   3D Data Production

A block diagram depicting the 3D production process is reported in Fig. 1. As can be see, inputs, sub-processing blocks and the final storage in the Snap4City platform are highlighted. Regarding the inputs, the production process requires street-level and aerial (i.e., orthomaps) RGB photos to obtain roof and façade textures and to model possible High Value Buildings (HVB). Additionally, building plant shapes from OSM are used to geographically localize the buildings to be produced. Finally, building height information (in the format of GEOJson files) and DSM data are required to properly model the 3D structures, while the DTM is used to compute a terrain level and to put the building at the right elevation position. BIM and additional 3D entities are considered, possibly requiring some format conversion. Hereafter, more details on the sub-processing blocks are reported.

---

[1] Available at https://github.com/disit/3d-building-modelling.

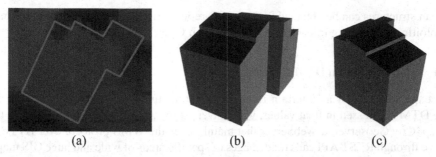

| (a) | (b) | (c) |

Fig. 2. Example of DSM modelling to obtain building models with 3D rooftops. In (a) the original DSM with superimposed the building plant shape. In (b) and (c) the obtained 3D model from two different views.

To obtain high quality models for the HVBs manual 3D design or automatic computer vision techniques, such as Structure from Motion, can be employed. The obtained models are then put in the right scale, position, and elevation.

Regarding the roof and façade patterns, they are respectively extracted from orthomaps and street level images. In order to obtain an accurate orthomap segmentation to extract the roof texture, a deep net was used [10] to find the similarity transformation required to locally warp the orthomaps and make them accurately fit the building plant shapes. Diversely, façade's patterns are extracted by identifying the building façade into the acquired images and then rectifying them using planar homographies.

3D structure of ordinary buildings can be obtained with two different approaches. Flat-roof buildings are obtained by extrusion from the building plant shapes using the building height. Such height attribute can be obtained from manual measurements of the eave heights, or by evaluating the average height of the DSM samples included into the building plant shape. Differently, 3D-roof buildings are obtained by analysing the DSM and fitting on its samples planar primitives to describe the different roof slopes. Such a process includes spatial clustering using region growing [11] and HDBSCAN [12], multiple line model regression [13] and finally robust plane fitting. In Fig. 2, an example of input DSM and output model is provided. Both flat-roof and 3D-roof building models can be put at the right terrain elevation exploiting the information encoded in the DTM, and roof and façade texture are then applied to the 3D models using the Python Blender API.

To guarantee a fast model loading through by the browser interactive web interface we exploited a tiled approach (see Sect. 5). The complete city map was divided in non-overlapping tiles and for each building we computed the tile it belongs considering the building plant centroid to uniquely assign a building to a tile. All the building 3D textured models falling into the same tile, considering HVB when available, were then collected into a single folder and saved into the Snap4City 3D Storage, following a hierarchical Z/X/Y folder organization used by most of GIS applications like OSM, QGIS, etc. Z is the zoom factor (fixed at 18 for our tiles) that describe the tile dimension, while X and Y are the tile coordinates. Note that, even if the models are grouped in tiles, each single building is represented as a separate entity in order to enable the picking functionality (RI4). Additional 3D entities (RD7) such as tree, streetlamp or other minor urban structures can be obtained from free 3D repositories and then placed into the map exploiting positioning information obtained from Open Data.

4.1 High Resolution DTM Encoding

To exploit the DTM as a terrain level in our interactive user interface (see Sect. 5), the DTM, expressed in float values, was converted to RGB format and deployed in the Snap4City Geoserver, a WebServer that mainly uses the WMS protocol over HTTP to serve through REST API calls tiled images of specific areas of wide and huge GIS maps. In order to accomplish the DTM conversion, we use the following mapping function:

$$\begin{cases} R = \left\lfloor \frac{100000 + 10v}{256^2} \right\rfloor \\ \left\lfloor \frac{100000 + 10v}{256} \right\rfloor - 256R \\ \lfloor 100000 + 10v \rfloor 256^2 R - 256G \end{cases}$$

where $v \in R$ is the DTM raw value. In this way we can obtain an RGB image able to encode elevation differences up to 0.1 m. Then, the encoded DTM is loaded into the Snap4City GeoServer to be retrieved in real-time.

5 Interactive Web Interface

The general architecture developed for distributing the SCDT as a 3D multi-data map dashboard in the Snap4City platform is able to distribute and reassemble all the data required by the requirements RD1-RD7: different version of 3D models of buildings (LoD1, LoD3, BIM) and additional entities, heatmaps (for traffic flow, pollutant dispersion, etc.), PINs (IOT, POI, etc.), 3D terrain from DTM, sky pattern, ground information, paths and areas. The architecture implements a client-side business logic that exploits a series of REST API calls to load the data independently on user demand (as requested by RI5). For example, the 3D tiled representations are retrieved via HTTPS protocol, as well as data for POI, IoT devices, paths, etc. obtained with specific geographic queries on the SuperService Map of Snap4City [14]. Differently, heatmaps (static or animated) and the encoded DTM are retrieved via WMS protocol over HTTPS by querying the Snap4City GeoServer, limited to the portion of the map visualized by the user. The hierarchical layered structure depicted in Fig. 3 and described in this section is used to model and represent the different kinds of information provided.

The rendered solution has been implemented via layered WebGL and APIs, in order to access to the GPU thanks to the passthrough available in Web Browsers without the needs of plugin, to satisfy RO6, exploiting the open-source library Deck.gl. Deck.gl offers some default layers that we used to display 3D elements. And, in order to handle specific needs, specific layers were modified and/or completely implemented from scratch. All layers are loaded at runtime on user demand. Thanks to the multi-layer structure of Deck.gl, layers were implemented individually with their own safe context, to avoid reciprocal interferences. Every layer has its own scope, managing its own data type.

First, the Deck.gl application has been realized by using a custom implementation and management of the ViewState object, in which the geographical information for the

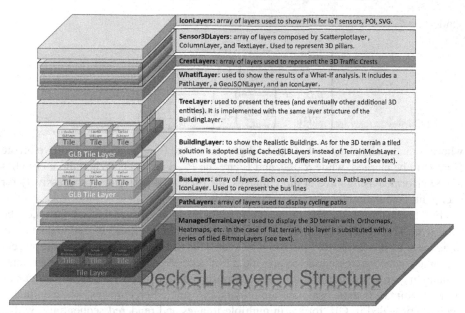

Fig. 3. Hierarchical layers structure of the interactive web interface. Mapping of the Digital Twin model on layer structure on rendering on the client.

map (such as latitude, longitude, zoom, etc.), are defined. We implemented a custom rendering system in order to add features like SkyBox – to be able to include a sky representation into the 3D map – that needs direct access to the WebGL context. The solution is able to handle two different kinds of terrains, in order to respond at the requirement RD6. The first one uses a flat model, while the second one instead exploits a three-dimensional terrain with accurate elevation (referring to them as flat or elevated). Note that, each of them uses different layers and structures, as reported in Fig. 3. The terrain called ManagedTerrainLayer is displayed in tiles using the default TileLayer, with every tile loading different resources from the WMS servers using business logic call-back (RI6). The most important data source is the encoded DTM of the tile, that is used to generate the mesh of the terrain using the Martini tessellation algorithm. Note that, it possible to mix multiple DTM files, for example with different resolutions: in such a case one of the DTM has higher priority over the others. The terrain texture is instead created by merging multiple images: the base image is the Orthomap of the terrain, over which different heatmaps can be shown on user demand. This data integration forms a layer called TerrainMeshLayer. The texture merging process is carried out directly inside the GPU in order to have maximum performance. In order to handle the opacity level selected, we used the following equations to merge different texture inside the fragment shader:

$$
\begin{cases}
mix_\alpha = 1 - (1 - \alpha_2) * (1 - \alpha_1) \\
mix_R = \left(\frac{R_2 * \alpha_2}{mix_\alpha} \right) + \left(\frac{R_1 * \alpha_1 * (1 - \alpha_2)}{mix_\alpha} \right) \\
mix_G = \left(\frac{G_2 * \alpha_2}{mix_\alpha} \right) + \left(\frac{G_1 * \alpha_1 * (1 - \alpha_2)}{mix_\alpha} \right) \\
mix_B = \left(\frac{B_2 * \alpha_2}{mix_\alpha} \right) + \left(\frac{B_1 * \alpha_1 * (1 - \alpha_2)}{mix_\alpha} \right)
\end{cases}
$$

where α_i is the alpha channel of the background image ($i = 1$), and the additive image ($i = 2$) to be merged, while R_i, C_i, and B_i are the RGB channels. When the merge has to be performed using three or more images, the process is performed progressively for each pair, cumulating the next on the first couple merged.

For the flat terrain, the background Orthomaps are implemented through tiles, i.e., the TileLayer. The mesh is a flat square, and, in this case, a single bitmap is used to display an image as a texture exploiting the BitmapLayer. This method has been used to represent heatmaps, which are essentials to provide a fast access/representation to large amounts of data. In both cases, data are automatically retrieved from GeoServer. Heatmaps can be static or animated: static heatmaps are provided as single PNG images, while animated ones are provided in GIF format in multiple images and rendered sequentially with a custom delay.

For the implementation of data coming from different sources like IoT devices, trajectories, cycling paths, etc., various layers with a specific JSON mapping have been implemented. To display paths and geometries, different layers depending on the type of geometry to be displayed have been used - e.g., PathLayer for the cycling path or the BusLayer to show bus routes.

Two 3D representations of buildings are used: Extruded (i.e., LoD1 model) and Realistic (including textured LoD3 models, and HVB). The Realistic representation can be retrieved as a monolithic file or divided in different non overlapping tiles. Extruded buildings are provided as GeoJSON and loaded in GeoJSONLayer. Differently, Realistic buildings can be loaded as both SceneGraph and 3D tiles. In the case of Realistic building in glTF/GLB format the SceneGraphLayer is used. This type of integration works well to achieve impressive visualization without impacting too much on the application performances. In the case of monolithic representation, the model is loaded and shown as it is regardless of the ViewState. Differently, in the tiled case, the CachedGLBTileLayer is used, and models are loaded taking into account the viewing position and angle. Models are loaded from the nearest to the farthest w.r.t the point of view. Note that it is possible to define a limit to the amount of tile that to be displayed in order to avoid GPU overloading. This dynamic loading of the building ensures that only the amount of resource needed to display the current scene are used, since the buildings outside the ViewState cannot be processed. This is particularly useful when dealing with Smart City composed by a huge number of buildings. Trees and additional 3D entities are shown in separate layers with a structure similar to the one used to represent the 3D buildings.

IoT devices and POIs are displayed as pickable PINs on the map. If the terrain is elevated PINs are raised according to the elevation of the terrain. When a user selects one of them, a popup is shown with the relative information (static attributes as well as real-time data, if available), satisfying the requirement RI3. Whenever the sensor provides real-time data, they can be displayed on dedicated widgets, such as time trends. A relevant feature refers to the visualization of dynamic pins (RI8). Dynamic pins allow to graphically represent sensor markers changing shape and/or colour depending on the value of the metric to which they are associated with. In this way, dynamic pins enable a fast and immersive data-driven and event-driven visualization of data coming from physical or virtual sensors. Multiple views for different types of sensors can be exploited, ranging from dynamic SVG to 3D column representations of real-time data values. When a SVG is selected for PIN visualization, the dynamic PIN is created dynamically in the backend; then it is retrieved and displayed by using the IconLayer. In the case of a 3D column representing a device attribute value, a composite layer, called Sensor3DLayer, is generated to recreate a thermometer effect: it can display the value of any sensors with a 3D cylinder shape whose height is proportional to the considered metric while the actual value is reported in textual form on top of the cylinder. The colour of the column typically represents the category of the sensors, and all these elements can be customized by the user.

The light effects have been modelled with two types of lights: an ambient light to affect all the scene, and a directional light to model the position of the sun. In order to calculate the position of the sun, the formula given by the Astronomy Answer articles about "the position of the sun" [15] was used. This process created the lights and shadows of the scene, and it is useful to simulate when a particular area is well illuminated or not.

It should be noted that, most of the features working on the 2D representation of data needed to be revised or completely modified to pass at the 3D representation environment. For instance, in 2D traffic flow representations are typically represented by coloured lines in the map that are marginally visible into the 3D representation. Therefore, in order to provide a 3D visualization of traffic flows density a new layer called CrestLayer has been developed. In this layer, traffic density is displayed as raised crests (with amplitude proportional to the computed traffic density values) following the terrain elevation. The crests are coloured using a standard colour map that can be defined by the user. Due to the nature of the problem, traffic flow polylines can be fragmented. Therefore, a data pre-process is performed to have a smoother representation. Every crest segment is created from three points: a middle point, in which the value is the traffic density of the specific road segment, and two extrema ones, where densities are obtained considering the average of all density values of roads connected to it.

A key functionality for urban planning and management that can be offered by a SCDT is the possibility to observe the effects produced by a change in the contextual environment modelled in terms of RDF coding of the road graph. For example, to observe how vehicle routing can change due to a scenario in which an area is blocked to traffic. Such a functionality is called a What-If analysis [18]. To implement various scenarios, the platform needs to offer the user the capability of drawing different shapes. In such a way a street or multiple areas can be blocked to traffic in the road network for hours and days: which is the definition of a so called What-If scenario. Then, the results of the What-If analysis can be shown to the user together with the defined shapes using the new WhatIfLayer. For example, after having selected a city area to be traffic free, the What-If analytic provides the SCDT with novel routing possibilities that do not enter into the zones defined in the scenarios (which may be constrained according to a set of different descriptors). This can be applied to different kinds of analysis to understand the impact of these scenarios to traffic flow, possible routing approaches, pollutant diffusions, people flows, etc.

6 Case of Study: Florence City, Italy

To validate the proposed SCDT solution, we selected as case of study the city of Florence in Italy. Our SCDT encompass the full Florence municipality (as shown in Fig. 4) covering an approximate extension of 151 km2 (wider than the area of the Florence municipality of 102 km2). Our SCDT of Florence, freely accessible through a web interface[2] and presented in Fig. 5, includes LoD1 and LoD3 3D building models, and terrain elevation.

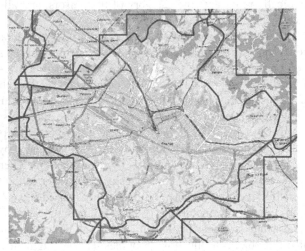

Fig. 4. Extension of the modelled Florence area. In blue the administrative border of Florence municipality; in red the area covered by our Digital Twin. This map is shown in the EPGS:3003 coordinate system.

The DSM and DTM data used in this work to model respectively the buildings and the terrain were kindly provided by the "Sistema Informativo Territoriale ed Ambientale" of Tuscany Region. They were obtained from a LiDAR survey and are composed by several tiles covering the city of Florence, with a resolution of 1 square meter. 3D building models were enhanced with roof textures obtained from orthomaps of the city of Florence. The RGB photos are tiles with a resolution of 8200x6200 pixels, with partial overlap and rough geo-localization in the EPSG 3003 (Monte Mario / Italy zone 1) coordinate system. The SCDT includes PIN indicating position of POI and IoT Sensors. Thanks to the semantic indexing of data offered by the Snap4City Knowledge Base, different PINs can be represented with specific icons according to their semantic category [16, 17].

---

[2] https://www.snap4city.org/dashboardSmartCity/view/Gea-Night.php?iddasboard=MzQ5OA
= =

Information associated with a specific sensor or city element can be accessed by simply clicking on the device PIN: a popup is shown to the user presenting static attributes and, when available, real-time and historical data. Moreover, heatmaps can be loaded at user demand to show for example real-time dispersion of pollutant, and traffic reconstruction representations are shown as animated 3D crest.

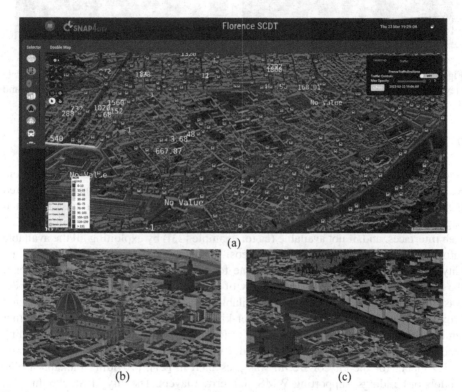

(a)

(b)   (c)

Fig. 5. Snap4City dashboard showing the Smart City Digital Twin of Florence. In (a) the dashboard is presented with LoD3 and HVB models shown together with PINs, 3D Crests for traffic, heatmaps, 3D Cylinders, trees. In (b) a close-up view of the Florence city center. In (c) another close-up showing entities correclty elevated according to the 3D terrain (textured with satellite orthomaps). To try our SCDT of Florence the reader is invited to visit the following link https://www.snap4city.org/dashboardSmartCity/view/Gea-Night.php?iddasboard=MzQ5OA = =

In order to show the capability of our SCDT system to let the user carry out simulation and analysis on routing, controls for What-If analysis [18] were implemented into the web interface. By clicking on the map, the user can select specific points or areas to simulate a traffic restriction. Then the routing algorithm produces trajectories between any start and end position considering the defined restriction. An example of What-If on routing is presented in Fig. 6: as can be seen an area was selected to ban traffic from the enclosed streets and the updated routing is shown to the user.

(a)   (b)

Fig. 6. Example of What-If analysis on vehicle routing. In (a) the intial routing, shown as a purple elevated line. In (b) a What-If scenario is enabled: a blue polygon highlight the blocked area and the updated routing is shown to the user.

7   SCDT Solution Comparison

According to the requirements identified in Section 2, a comparison among different SCDT solutions has been carried out. To produce the comparison, we manually inspected the available information of a set of other solutions: except for [3] who has associated papers describing it, the other solutions have been studied mainly by analysing their 3D web interfaces, and, if not available (as for example [23]) by exploiting all the available information such as web pages and videos. In this comparison, we included at first CityGML [3] in order to define a baseline for SCDT solutions. Then we considered the following cases: the SCDT of the city of Helsinki, that includes LoD3 city model was implemented and made publicly available [19]. However, such a system does not provide integration with IoT data or other kinds of city related information. Another similar solution was proposed by the city of Rotterdam [20], exploiting LoD2 building models, without integrating neither any decoration elements nor elevation of terrain. A 3D model for the city of Berlin was presented in [21], providing pickable LoD2 models of buildings, supporting WMS and terrain layers. The city of Stockholm [22] implemented many aspects of the Digital Twin concept, such as POI, LoD3 buildings, either with 3D tiles and modelled ones, and others 3D entities. However, the solution lacks in the implementation of WMS heatmaps. More recently, a SCDT of Wellington was proposed [23]. Powered by the Unreal Engine, such a solution can offer LoD3 building models, paths, sensor data, terrain elevation, and additional 3D entities. However, the usage of the Unreal Engine can limit the accessibility of such a solution. Finally, in the scope of the DUET project [24], Digital Twins of Flanders, Athens, and Pilsen were produced in a project not actually accessible. Such solutions implement building models with different LoD, terrain elevation, heatmaps, and additional 3D elements. However, this solution seems to be a work in progress, with several test cases with a public web interface very limited. In Table 1, the full comparison is reported w.r.t. the previously defined requirements. As can be seen, most of the solutions are able to satisfy the data requirements (RD1 – RD7). Differently, the interactivity requirements seem to be more difficult to be respected, in particular those that are related to the dynamic change of some models (RI4.ii, RI4.iii) and for the underground inspection (RI7). For the interactive requirements, the most advanced solution appear to be [23]: in our opinion, this is due to the fact that is the only solution powered by Unreal Engine. Indeed, such a 3D engine can offer additional functionality respect to simpler 3D engine/web player, and it requires higher computational resources, at least from server-side, since the 3D web interface (that should be based on Pixel Streaming) requires the 3D rendering be carried out on the server while the client receive only a video stream of the 3D scene. Finally, the operative requirements (RO1 – RO8) seem to be the hardest ones to be meet by all the compared approaches except for our solution since our SCDT is embedded into the IoT platform Snap4City. The platform offers business logic, data ingestion and manipulation capabilities, data analytics, etc., enhancing the geospatial data rendered in the 3D map with a plethora of additional information and services, realizing a complete Smart City Digital Twin.

8 Conclusions

In this paper, the processes used to develop a Smart City Digital Twin were described. Firstly, a series of requirements were presented and discussed. Then the development phases, guided by the previously defined requirements, were presented. Data and processes used to build the 3D structure to be included into the Digital Twin model infrastructure were described, as well as the layered structured used on client-side rendering on interactive web interface. In order to include additional information - e.g., IoT sensor data, POI locations, heatmaps, paths, etc. - our solution has been implemented into the Snap4City platform, to exploit specific API calls to retrieve the data and show them on the map on specific layer loaded on user demand. The implementation of the Digital

Table 1. Comparison of SCDT platforms: (*) defines only the building model, (**) functionality implemented in CESIUM but without any model placed underground, (x) use CESIUM, it could be possible, (C) based on CESIUM.

	CityGML [3]	Helsinki [19]	Rotterdam [20]	Berlin [21]	Stockholm [22]	Wellington [23]	DUET [24]	Snap4City (our)
RD1.i	Yes	No	No	No	No	No	Yes	Yes
RD1.ii	Yes (LoD3)	Yes	Yes (LoD2)	Yes (LoD2)	Yes (LoD3)	Yes (LoD3)	Yes (LoD2/LoD3)	Yes
RD1.iii	No	No	No	No	No	Probably	No	Yes
RD2	No	Yes	Yes (C)	Yes (C)	Yes	Yes	Yes	Yes
RD3	No	No	No	Yes	No	Probably	Yes	Yes
RD4	No	Yes (C)	Yes (C)	No (x)	Yes	Yes	No	Yes
RD5	No	No	No	No	Yes	Yes	No	Yes
RD6	Yes	Yes	No	No	Yes	Yes	Yes	Yes
RD7.i	Yes	Yes	No	No	Yes	Yes	Yes	Yes
RD7.ii	Yes	No	No	No	No	Yes	No	No
RI1	No (*)	Yes	Yes	Yes	Yes	Yes	Yes	Yes
RI2	No (*)	No	No	No	No	Yes	No	Yes
RI3	No (*)	No	Yes	No	Yes	Yes	No	Yes

(*continued*)

Table 1. (*continued*)

	CityGML [3]	Helsinki [19]	Rotterdam [20]	Berlin [21]	Stockholm [22]	Wellington [23]	DUET [24]	Snap4City (our)
RI4.i	Not clear (maybe)	Yes (s)	Yes	Yes	No	Probably	No	Yes
RI4.ii	No	No	No	No	No	Probably	No	No
RI4.iii	No	No	No	No	No	Yes	No	No
RI5	No	No	No	Yes	No	Yes	No	Yes
RI6	No (*)	No	No	No	Yes	No	Yes	Yes
RI7	No (*)	Yes (**)	Yes (**)	No (x)	No	No	No	No
RI8	No	No	No	No	Yes	Yes	No	Yes
RO1	No	No	No	No	No	No	No	Yes
RO2	No	No	No	No	No	No	No	Yes
RO3	No	No	No	No	No	No	No	Yes
RO4	No	No	No (not specified)	No	No (not specified)	No (not specified)	No	Yes
RO5	No	No	No	No	No	No	No	No
RO6.i	No	Yes	Yes	Yes	Yes	Yes	Yes	Yes
RO6.ii	n/a	Non-free	Free	Free	Non-free	Non-free	Non-free	Free
RO7	No	Yes	Possible (x)	Possible (x)	Possible	Yes	Possible	Yes
RO8.i	No	Yes	Yes	No	Yes	Yes	Not clear	Yes
RO8.ii	n/a	Non free	Non free	n/a	Non free	Non free	Not clear	Yes

Twin of the Florence city – publicly available at https://www.snap4city.org/dashboard
SmartCity/view/Gea-Night.php?iddasboard=MzQ5OA = = – was discussed as a case
of study, showing in particular some of the most complex functionalities offered such as
the possibility to perform What-If analysis on demand. Finally, a comparison with other
state of the art Digital Twin solutions was carried out, showing that our approach can
offer a more complete solution, considering in particular the interactive and the operative
requirements as reported in Table 1.

In future works, the digital twin and its 3D representation will be further enriched with
additional kind of models, and novel functionalities will be introduced in our interactive
web inter-face. Moreover, the Snap4City knowledge base (Km4City) will be further
expanded considering all the entities included into the Digital Twin to be able to perform
semantic, relational, temporal and geographical queries to handle and retrieve all the data
to be presented in our Smart City Digital Twin.

Acknowledgement. The authors would like to thank the MIUR, the University of Florence and
the companies involved for co-founding the national Center on Sustainable Mobility, MOST. A
thanks to the many developers on snap4city platforms. Snap4City (https://www.snap4city.org) is
open technologies of DISIT Lab.

References

1. Mylonas, G., Kalogers, A., Kkalogeras, G., Anagnostopoulos, C., Alexakos, C., Muñoz, L.: Digital twins from smart manufacturing to smart cities: a survey. IEEE Access **9**, 143222–143249 (2021). https://doi.org/10.1109/ACCESS.2021.3120843
2. Shahat, E., Hyun, C.T., Yeom, C.: City digital twin potentials: a review and research agenda. MDPI, p. 3 (2021)
3. Gröger, G., Plümer, L.: "CityGML Interoperable semantic 3D city models. ISPRS J. Photogrammetry Remote Sens., 16–21 (2012)
4. Jovanovic, D., et al.: Building virtual 3d city model for smart cities applications: a case study on campus area of the university of novi sad. ISPRS Int. J. Geo-Information, 16–21 (2020)
5. Adreani, L., et al.: Digital twin framework for smart city solutions. In: Proceedings of the 28th International DMS Conference on Visualization and Visual Languages (DMSVIVA 2022) (2022)
6. Han, Q., Nesi, P., Pantaleo, G., Paoli, I.: Smart city dashboards: design, development and evaluation. In: Proceedings of the IEEE ICHMS 2020, International Conference on Human Machine Systems, September 2020. http://ichms.dimes.unical.it/
7. Garau, C., Nesi, P., Paoli, I., Paolucci, M., Zamperlin, P.: A big data platform for smart and sustainable cities: environmental monitoring case studies in europe. In: Gervasi, O., et al. (eds.) ICCSA 2020. LNCS, vol. 12255, pp. 393–406. Springer, Cham (2020). https://doi.org/10.1007/978-3-030-58820-5_30
8. Bilotta, S., Nesi, P.: Traffic flow reconstruction by solving indeterminacy on traffic distribution at junctions. Futur. Gener. Comput. Syst. **114**, 649–660 (2021)
9. Bilotta, S., Collini, E., Nesi, P., Pantaleo, G.: Short-term prediction of city traffic flow via convolutional deep learning. IEEE Access **10**, 113086–113099 (2022). https://doi.org/10.1109/ACCESS.2022.3217240
10. Girard, N., Charpiat, G., Tarabalka, Y.: Aligning and updating cadaster maps with aerial images by multi-task, multi-resolution deep learning. In: Jawahar, C.V., Li, H., Mori, G., Schindler, K. (eds.) ACCV 2018. LNCS, vol. 11365, pp. 675–690. Springer, Cham (2019). https://doi.org/10.1007/978-3-030-20873-8_43
11. Pal, N.R., Pal, S.K.: A review on image segmentation techniques. Pattern Recogn. **26**(9), 1277–1278 (1993). https://doi.org/10.1016/0031-3203(93)90135-J
12. Campello, R.J.G.B., Moulavi, D., Sander, J.: Density-based clustering based on hierarchical density estimates. In: Pei, J., Tseng, V.S., Cao, L., Motoda, H., Xu, G. (eds.) PAKDD 2013. LNCS (LNAI), vol. 7819, pp. 160–172. Springer, Heidelberg (2013). https://doi.org/10.1007/978-3-642-37456-2_14
13. Toldo, R., Fusiello, A.: Robust multiple structures estimation with j-linkage. In: Forsyth, D., Torr, P., Zisserman, A. (eds.) ECCV 2008. LNCS, vol. 5302, pp. 537–547. Springer, Heidelberg (2008). https://doi.org/10.1007/978-3-540-88682-2_41
14. Badii, C., Bellini, P., Cenni, D., Difino, A., Nesi, P., Paolucci, M.: Analysis and assessment of a knowledge based smart city architecture providing service APIs. Futur. Gener. Comput. Syst. **75**, 14–29 (2017)
15. https://www.aa.quae.nl/en/reken/zonpositie.html
16. Nesi, P., et al.: An integrated smart city platform. Semantic Keyword-based Search on Structured Data Sources. Springer, Cham (2017). https://doi.org/10.1007/978-3-319-74497-1_17
17. Bellini, P., Bugli, F., Nesi, P., Pantaleo, G., Paolucci, M., Zaza, I.: Data flow management and visual analytic for big data smart City/IOT. In: 19th IEEE Int. Conf. on Scalable Computing and Communication, IEEE SCALCOM 2019, Leicester, UK. https://www.slideshare.net/paolonesi/data-flow-management-and-visual-analytic-for-big-data-smart-cityiot

18. Bellini, P., Bilotta, S., Palesi, A.L.I., Nesi, P., Pantaleo, G.: Vehicular traffic flow reconstruction analysis to mitigate scenarios with large city changes. IEEE ACCESS **10**, 131061–131075 (2022). https://doi.org/10.1109/ACCESS.2022.3229183
19. Helsinki 3D city model. https://kartta.hel.fi/3d/#/
20. Rotterdam 3D. https://www.3drotterdam.nl
21. Berlin 3D, 3dcitydb. https://www.3dcitydb.org/3dcitydb-web-map/1.7/3dwebclient/index. html?title=Berlin_Demo&batchSize=1&latitude=52.517479728958044&longitude=13.411 141287558161&height=534.3099172951087&heading=345.2992773976952&pitch=-44. 26228062802528&roll=359.933888621294&layer_0=url%3Dhttps%253A%252F%252 Fwww.3dcitydb.org%252F3dcitydb%252Ffileadmin%252Fmydata%252FBerlin_Demo% 252FBerlin_Buildings_rgbTexture_ScaleFactor_0.3%252FBerlin_Buildings_rgbTexture_c ollada_MasterJSON.json%26name%3DBrlin_Buildings_rgbTexture%26active%3Dtrue% 26spreadsheetUrl%3Dhttps%253A%252F%252Fwww.google.com%252Ffusiontables% 252FDataSource%253Fdocid%253D19cuclDgIHMqrRQyBwLEztMLeGzP83IBWfEtKQ A3B%2526pli%253D1%2523rows%253Aid%253D1%26cityobjectsJsonUrl%3D%26m inLodPixels%3D100%26maxLodPixels%3D1.7976931348623157e%252B308%26maxS izeOfCachedTiles%3D200%26maxCountOfVisibleTiles%3D200
22. Stockholm Opencities Planner. https://eu.opencitiesplanner.bentley.com/stockholm/stockh olmvaxer
23. Wellington DT. https://buildmedia.com/work/wellington-digital-twin
24. DUET Project. https://www.digitalurbantwins.com/

Numerical Simulations of 1461 and 1762 San Pio delle Camere (L'Aquila) Earthquakes Using 3D Physic-Based Model

Donato Pera[1](✉), F. Di Michele[2], E. Stagnini[3], B. Rubino[1], R. Aloisio[3,4], and P. Marcati[3]

[1] Department of Information Engineering, Computer Science and Mathematics, University of L'Aquila, via Vetoio, loc. Coppito, I, L'Aquila, Italy
donato.pera@univaq.it
[2] Istituto Nazionale di Geofisica e Vulcanologia, via Alfonso Corti 12, Milan, Italy
[3] Gran Sasso Science Institute (GSSI), via M. Iacobucci 2, L'Aquila, Italy
[4] INFN-Laboratori Nazionali del Gran Sasso, Via G. Acitelli 22, Assergi, AQ, Italy

Abstract. The aim of this paper is to propose a physics-based simulation of the two earthquakes that hit the surrounding area of the city of L'Aquila (Abruzzo central Italy) in 1461 and 1762, with magnitudes 6.4 Mw and 6.0 Mw, respectively. Both events are placed, by the available literature, on the fault structure named San Pio delle Camere [11]. The physical parameters characterizing the earthquake such as fault plane, epicenter, and magnitude are considered to be fixed. Starting from them three stochastic rupture scenarios are generated from each earthquake using three different slip distributions. The scenarios were evaluated in relation to the possibility to reproduce the macroseismic intensity field available from the historical catalogs. The simulated values of peak velocity are used to derive the value of the macrosiesmic intensity obtained by a suitable empirical relationship specifically derived for Italy.

For the numerical simulations we used a three-dimensional soil model used and validated in a previous study related to the 2009 L'Aquila earthquake. The considered slip distributions are able to reproduce quite well the macroseismic effect of the 1461 earthquake. While none of the three scenarios developed satisfactorily reproduce the 1762 earthquake.

1 Introduction

Abruzzo (central Italy) is a region of high seismic risk, having been hit by numerous earthquakes in the past, the most recent in 2009 [7,20]. For many of them, however, which occurred in the pre-instrumental era, available information are often lacking and/or inaccurate. Therefore physical based (PB) numerical simulations represent a valuable tool to increase the understanding of the area, both from a geological and historical point of view.

The 27th November 1461 and 6th October 1762 earthquakes, object of this study, are just two of the several seismic events that hit L'Aquila in the past. Both of them, according to the available literature, were caused by the San Pio delle Camere fault system [11].

O. Gervasi et al. (Eds.): ICCSA 2023 Workshops, LNCS 14111, pp. 549–565, 2023.
https://doi.org/10.1007/978-3-031-37126-4_35

In addition to historical interest, this work may be useful in assessing the effect of future earthquakes that may occur on the same fault. Before analysing the results of the simulation we shortly introduce the two events, summarising the (few) available information.

According to the available literature, the 1461 earthquake had epicenter at Lat 42.314-Lon 13.5429 and estimated magnitude 6.4 Mw. As reported in the *Catalogo dei forti terremoti in Italia 461A.C.-1997 e dell'area mediterranea 760A.C-1500* from mid-November 1461 to the end of March 1462, the area of the Abruzzo Apennines, where L'Aquila was one of the most important cities, was hit by a sequence of earthquakes. On November 16, 1461, a shock was felt in L'Aquila which did not cause any damage. A few days later, on the night of 27 November, preceded by strong underground noises, two strong tremors struck the L'Aquila area. These earthquakes seriously affected all the buildings in the city of L'Aquila: a quarter of the houses collapsed entirely and all the others suffered partial collapses and very serious injuries. The north-western area of the city was the most damaged with about 75 houses destroyed. The north-eastern area of the city was less damaged than the others. Many of the very numerous towers of the city also collapsed. For the city of L'Aquila it is possible to have a detailed list of damage to churches and public buildings in the urban area. According to chronicle sources, 46 monuments in the city were hit. There were collapses, partial collapses, or damage to churches and bell towers, monasteries, palaces and hospitals. The dead were numerous: about 80 or 100 depending on the sources, many of whom were overwhelmed by the collapse of the vaults of the main hospital (S.Salvatore). The effects of the earthquake were worsen by fire and, later, by the abundant snowfalls that occurred in January 1462. In the area surrounding L'Aquila, made up of a total of over 80 forti-fied villages, the following were seriously affected: Onna (I_{MCS} 10), where all the houses collapsed causing the death of many of the inhabitants; Sant'Eusanio Forconese (I_{MCS} 10) which was almost entirely destroyed, including the recently built castle, there were many victims. The Castelnuovo (I_{MCS} 9.5) village col-lapsed almost entirely, including the towers of the walls and there were 28 dead. The Castelvecchio Calvisio (I_{MCS} 9) suffered the collapse of many houses and there were 12 dead, also Poggio Picenze (I_{MCS} 9) collapsed almost entirely. This earthquake was felt without damage in a very large area in particular in other cities as Perugia and Rome. On December 11, 1461, the most intense phase of the seismic sequence ended, up to that day, about a hundred seismic events were felt in L'Aquila.

The 1762 earthquake had an estimated epicenter at Lat 42.308 Lon 13.585 and moment magnitude Mw 6.0. Also for this second earthquake, we can report the description of *Catalogo dei forti terremoti in Italia 461A.C.-1997 e dell'area mediterranea 760A.C-1500*. According to it, the main shock occurred on 6 Octo-ber 1762 around 13 o'clock "Italian" time and violently struck two villages near L'Aquila, named Castelnuovo (I_{MCS} 9.5) and Poggio Picenze (I_{MCS} 9), causing the total or partial collapse of most of the houses. Many buildings suffered the fall of the roofs or the untying of the load-bearing walls, described by witnesses as irreparably damaged and on the verge of falling. The general condition of the two villages, which emerges from the detailed contemporary sources, is that of two almost completely uninhabitable sites. The earthquake was strongly felt in the nearby towns of Barisciano (I_{MCS} 4.5) and San Demetrio ne' Vestini (I_{MCS} 4.5), where no damage is reported finally in L'Aquila (I_{MCS} 7), where it caused injuries and caused chimneys to fall. This earthquake was felt lightly also in Rome.

Recently, massive technological advances related to the development of High Performance Computing (HPC) technologies [42] have made it possible to simulate complex earthquake events at local and regional scales [1,3,12,13,15,34, 41,48]. In the last decades, Physical Based Simulations (PBS) techniques have been extensively used to simulate earthquakes that occurred in the recent past [13,15,34,47], but limited efforts have been devoted to the numerical reconstruction of historical earthquakes for which no recordings are available. As an example, in [32] a stochastic finite-fault method model is applied to simulate the 1939 Erzincan Earthquake (Ms 7.8). The model has validated comparing the computed macroseismic intensity, obtained according to [10], with those provided by the historical catalogs. Moreover some plausible scenarios of the 1895 Ljubljana earthquake are presented in [52].

Within this paper numerical simulations are performed using a numerical simulation tool named SPEED based on the Discontinuous Galerkin Spectral Element Method [36] (http://speed.mox.polimi.it). As we say before for both the earthquakes we are considering, the epicenter is probably located on the San Pio delle Camere fault. However the related slip distribution is obviously unknown. To overcome this problem we use a suitable tool for stochastic slip distribution generation, derived according to [31] and actually embedded on SPEED.

We consider three different realizations of the slip distributions for both the 1461 and 1762 earthquakes. Then the PGV values, provided by each simulations, are employed to get an estimate of the macroseismic intensity (I_{MCS}) value using the empirical model recently proposed by [37]. The simulated values of the I_{MCS} are then compared with those made available by the CFTI5Med and CPTI15 catalogs [27,28,45,46]. More details that we use for the comparison of I_{MCS} values of 6 villages for 1461 earthquake and 5 villages for the 1762 events are reported as in Table 3 and 4. We just point out as only the villages located inside our computational domain are considered.

The paper is organized as follows. In Sect. 2 we briefly describe the workflow related to the construction of the computational domain, the mathematical formulation of the problem and empirical model employed to correlate PGV and MCS intensities. In Sect. 3 we present and discuss our results. Finally, in the last section, we summarize our conclusions and present some possible developments of this study.

2 Computational Model and Mathematical Tools

Seismic waves propagation during seismic events are influenced by geological structures such as alluvial basins, passive fault structures, and cavities as well as by the topography and the human constructions (see eg., [8,12,14,22,29,33,43,44,53] and references therein). The goal of a PBS model is to get seismic ground shaking scenarios that are realistic and sufficiently close to seismic records, when they are available. For this purpose, it is essential to have an accurate *digital twin* of the studied seismic area, which requires geophysical information that are not always available. Luckily for the earthquakes related to this work thanks to the work of *Microzonazione sismica* of Central Italy, realized by the *Protezione Civile italiana* after the 2009 L'Aquila earthquake, a large amount of data are available, according to this collected data a reconstruction of the geological stratigraphy of the subsoil is possible. Our computational domain extends about 67.2 km × 59.7 km in the East-West and North-South directions respectively and for 20.1 km in depth. The horizontal layered crustal model contains four layers with different thicknesses as in [13,15], the thickness and the mechanical properties for each earth-crust layer are reported in Table 1. To account for the local application, we also include a detailed three dimensional reconstruction of the quaternary L'Aquila - San Demetrio sedimentary basin (see Fig. 2) validated in [13].

Fault	Mesh Features	Domain Image
L=16.2 Km W=10.5 Km Strike=127° Dip=50° Rake=270°	Size=(67.2,59.7,20.1Km N. Elements=1660440 Spectral Degree=3 N. Mesh Nodes=1838615 Δt=0.0003s Duration=30s	

Fig. 1. In the first two columns we report the main characteristics of the fault plane and the computational domain. In the last column, we show a 3D representation of the computational domain, the projection of the fault zone in the top surface (green color) is highlighted in red. (Color figure online)

According to [15], the velocity and the quality factor inside the basin are modelled using a depth-dependent profile as follows:

$$V_S = 300 + 36 \cdot z^{0.43}(\text{m/s}), \ V_P = V_S\sqrt{4.57}, \ Q_S = 0.10V_S, \tag{1}$$

whereas the density is constant: $\rho = 1.9(\text{g/cm}^3)$.

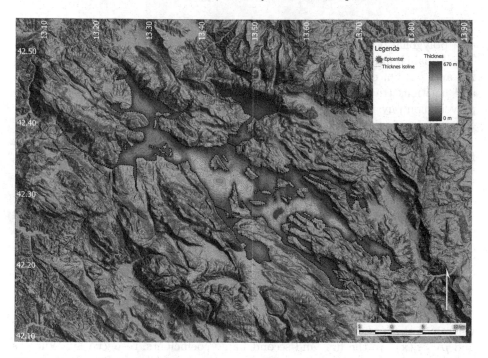

Fig. 2. Map of the Quaternary L'Aquila - San Demetrio sedimentary basin (geological model available as in [13]). The observed microcosmic intensity, according to the CFTI5Med catalogue, and the position of the epicenter are also reported

Table 1. Mechanical properties of the crustal layers.

Layer	Depth(km)	V_S(m/s)	V_P(m/s)	ρ(g/cm^3)	Q_S
1	0–1	1700	3160	2.5	100
2	1–2	2600	4380	2.5	200
3	2–5	3100	5760	2.84	200
4	5–20	3500	6510	3.18	200

The topography that forms the surface layer of our model has been realized using the python tool introduced in [35], starting from a dataset made available by the project TINITALY [49–51]. The seismogenic fault plane corresponding to the fault of San Pio delle Camere, has been constructed according to the database DISS (Database of Individual Seismogenic Sources) [9]. This fault plane has dimensions of 16.2 km in length and 10.5 km in width, whereas strike, dip, and rake angles are respectively 127°, 50° and 270° (cf. Fig. 1).

The position of the hypocenters are obtained using epicenter position and fault geometry. We got respectively $z_{hypo} = 6.16$ km for the 1461 earthquake and $z_{hypo} = 4.38$ km for the 1762 earthquake. The computational domain is meshed using *CUBIT* (https://coreform.com/products/coreform-cubit/) getting $1.66 \cdot 10^6$ elements, having a size ranging from 130 m (top layer) to max 1 Km (bottom layer).

From the mathematical point of view the computational domain is modelled as a polygonal bounded domain $\Omega \subset \mathbb{R}^3$ with outward pointing normal unit $\mathbf{n}$. The domain boundary is decomposed into three disjoint surfaces, with names Γ_D, Γ_N and Γ_A. On each considered surfaces we assign the displacement, traction, and fictitious traction values respectively. The fictitious traction is needed to prevent non physical reflections on the boundaries, whereas on Γ_N we prescribe free surface conditions.

The displacement at the soil level $\mathbf{u}(\mathbf{x}, t) = (u_1, u_2, u_3)(\mathbf{x}, t)$ will be described, for the values $t \in [0, T]$ and $\mathbf{x} \in \Omega$, as

$$\rho \partial_{tt}^2 \mathbf{u} + 2\rho\xi\partial_t \mathbf{u} + \rho\xi^2 \mathbf{u} - \nabla \cdot \sigma(\mathbf{u}) = \mathbf{f}, \tag{2}$$

where $\mathbf{f}$, $\rho = \rho(\mathbf{x}) > 0$ and σ are the external applied load, the mass density and the stress tensor respectively. We define the stress tensor as a function of the displacement using the formula:

$$\sigma_{ij} = \mu\left(\frac{\partial u_i}{\partial x_j} + \frac{\partial u_j}{\partial x_i}\right) + \lambda \sum_{k=1}^{3} \frac{\partial u_k}{\partial x_k}\delta_{ij}, \quad \text{for } i, j = 1, 2, 3 \tag{3}$$

where δ is the Kronecker symbol. The positive and bounded functions $\lambda = \lambda(\mathbf{x})$ and $\mu = \mu(\mathbf{x})$ are the first and second Lamé coefficients, respectively. Whereas ξ always defined in (2) is a decay factor $\xi = \xi(x) > 0$ that models the viscosity of the media [6] and has dimension $[1/sec]$. In this work, this parameter has been defined using an a-dimensional quality factor $Q = Q_0 f / f_0$ where f_0 is a reference frequency and $Q_0 = \pi f_0 / \xi$.

The boundaries conditions are defined as: $\mathbf{u} = \mathbf{0}$ on Γ_D, $\sigma\mathbf{n} = \mathbf{0}$ on Γ_N, $(\sigma\mathbf{n})^* = \mathbf{0}$ on Γ_A. We refer to [6] for the complete definition of $(\sigma\mathbf{n})^*$.
We set $\mathbf{u}(\mathbf{x}, 0) = \mathbf{0}$ $\partial_t \mathbf{u}(\mathbf{x}, 0) = \mathbf{0}$ as initial condition. We report also the useful formula to compute the *compressional* and *shear* wave velocities from the Lamé coefficients and the mass density.

$$V_P = \sqrt{(\lambda + 2\mu)/\rho} \qquad V_S = \sqrt{\mu/\rho}.$$

For the body force distribution $\mathbf{f}$ we consider $\mathbf{f}(\mathbf{x}, t) = \nabla \cdot \mathbf{m}(\mathbf{x}, t)$, as in [17], where $\mathbf{m}(\mathbf{x}, t)$ is the seismic moment tensor as reported in [2]. The method used to approximate equation (2) is the spectral element method in space coupled with the leap-frog scheme in time according to SPEED software tool used in this work [36]. Finally for the stability and convergence of the used numerical method we refer to [4,5,21]. We refer also to [30,38–40,47] for other interesting applications in computational seismology. Using the mentioned above mathematical model and computational domain we performed for each seismic event three numerical simulations named as scenario 1,2 and 3 (SC1, SC2 and SC3 in the following). For each simulated scenario we generate a stochastic slip distributions as reported in Fig. 3, using the basic geophysical parameters reported above. The considered simulation time for each scenario it is equal to 30 s with a time step $\Delta t = 0.0003$ s (see Fig. 1). All numerical simulations have been executed in the Linux High Performance Computing cluster Caliban located in the High-Performance Computing Laboratory of the Department of Information Engineering, Computer Science and Mathematics (DISIM) at the University of L'Aquila. Each single simulation ran using 128 MPI processes on DELL PowerEdge C6400-4-blades-C6525 servers equipped with 2x CPU AMD EPYC 7282 2.7GHz and 128GB Ram per blade. As mentioned above each used server is located inside the DISIM Caliban HPC cluster based on Rocks Cluster 7.0 (Manzanita) (http://www.rocksclusters.org/). The computational time required for a single run it is equal to 34 h (run-time execution).

After running simulations, for each scenario it is necessary to derive the relative values of I_{MCS} to compare with available historical data.

In the literature, different empirical relationships have been proposed to correlate the macroseismic intensity I_{MCS} with selected ground-motion intensity measures, such as peak ground velocity and peak ground acceleration. Models specific designed and validate for the Italian territory had been, for example, proposed in [16, 18, 23, 24]. They are based on the statistical fitting of data from past earthquakes, and are very useful to estimate the damage due to past or potential future earthquakes, although it is recognized that they suffer high uncertainties.

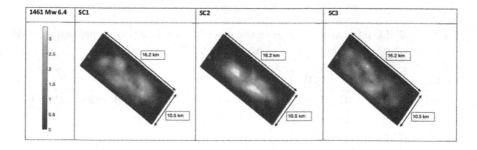

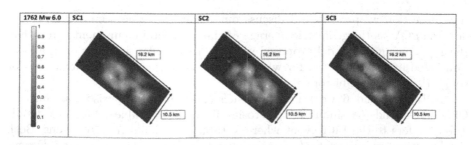

Fig. 3. Slip distributions provided by the rupture model generator introduced by [31] and available in the SPEED pre-processing tool, for the four hypothetical earthquake scenarios considered in this study for the 1461 Mw6.4 (top) 1762 earthquake Mw 6.0 (bottom.)

Among the many empirical relationships available in the literature, here we will consider the most recent model proposed in [37]. In this paper, the authors correlate peak ground velocity (PGV), peak ground acceleration (PGA) and spectral acceleration (SA) at 0.3, 1.0 and 3.0 s with the macroseismic intensity (I_{MCS}). Both the European Macroseismic (EMS-98) and the Mercalli-Cancani-Sieberg (MCS) scales are considered. The (invertible) relations are derived using the orthogonal distance regression technique, already applied for a similar purpose in [18, 19]. The working dataset contains earthquakes that occurred in Italy between 1972 and 2016 and a quadratic correlation between the intensity and the base-10 logarithm of I_{MCS} has been considered, instead of the linear one often employed in other studies.

In other words, the authors assume

$$I = a + b \log_{10} I_{MCS} + c(\log_{10} I_{MCS})^2, \qquad (4)$$

where the coefficients a, b, and c are derived for each couple of the dependent-independent variables.

For the purpose of this paper we just consider the relation linking microcosmic intensity in the Mercalli-Cancani-Sieberg scale ad PGV reported in Table 2. In fact, the frequency resolution of the model is 2 Hz, which is not sufficient to ensure accurate estimation of PGA and spectral acceleration values.

Table 2. Available relationships between the macroseismic intensity, expressed in MCS scale, and peak ground velocity (PGV) according to [37]

Model	PGV
Oliveti et al. (2022) [37]	$I_{MCS} = 4.31 + 1.99 * \log_{10} PGV + 0.58 + (\log_{10} PGV)^2$

3   Results and Discussion

In this section we present and discuss our result. For each scenario we calculate the PGV as the geometric average of the horizontal components, and then the I_{MCS} using the model proposed in [37]. In particular we focus on the location listed in Table 3 and 4, for which the values of the I_{MCS} are available for comparison from the historical catalogues.

In Tables 5 and 6 we report for each scenario a comparison among the CFT15Med and the simulated macrosiesmic intensity values. In more details Table 5 refers to the 1461 event whereas Table 6 is related to 1762 event. Both the historical and estimate I_{MCS} are reported. In the column named *Err* we report, for each scenario, the difference between the simulated value and the historical one.

As mentioned in the introduction, the 1461 and 1762 seismic events were felt by the population and certainly caused damage to the buildings. According

Table 3. Macroseismic intensity in MCS scale for the 1461 earthquake related to 6 towns included in the computational domain. In the last two columns the geographical coordinates and the distance from the estimated epicenter are reported.

I_{MCS}	Name	Lat-Lon	Epicentral Distance (km)
X	Onna (AQ)	42.328–13.479	5.5
X	San'Eusanio Forconese (AQ)	42.288–13.524	3.3
IX-X	Castelnuovo (AQ)	42.295–13.628	7.3
IX	Castelvecchio Calvisio (AQ)	42.311–13.688	11.9
IX	L'Aquila (AQ)	42.356–13.396	13.0
IX	Poggio Picenze (AQ)	42.321–13.541	0.8

Table 4. Macroseismic intensity in MCS scale for 1762 earthquake related to 5 towns included in the computational domain. In the last two columns the geographical coordinates and the distance from the estimated epicenter are reported.

I_{MCS}	Name	Lat-Lon	Epicentral Distance (km)
IX-X	Castenuovo (AQ)	42.295–13.628	3.8
IX	Poggio Picenze (AQ)	42.321–13.541	3.9
VII	L'Aquila (AQ)	42.356–13.396	16.4
IV-V	Barisciano (AQ)	42.326–13.592	2.1
IV-V	San Demetrio ne' Vestini (AQ)	42.289–13.558	3.1

Table 5. Macroseismic intensity in MCS scale for the 6 towns included in the computational domain comparison between estimated and simulated data earthquake 1461.

Name	I_{MCS}	I_{MCS} SC1	I_{MCS} SC2	I_{MCS} SC3	ErrSC1	ErrSC2	ErrSC3
Onna	10	8.60	7.65	8.68	−1.39	−2.35	−1.32
Sant'Eusanio Forconese	10	8.85	8.3	8.61	−1.14	−1.69	−1.39
Castelnuovo	9.5	11.10	10.02	11.46	1.60	0.52	1.96
Castelvecchio Calvisio	9	10.53	8.56	8.86	1.53	−0.43	−0.14
L'Aquila	9	7.28	6.34	6.82	−1.72	−2.66	−2.17
Poggio Picenze	9	9.77	8.51	8.92	0.77	−0.48	−0.08

to the CFT15Med Catalogue the 1461 seismic event had I_{MCS} with a range from 9 to 10 with the maximum (10) in Onna (AQ) and Sant'Eusanio Forconese (AQ). While the 1762 earthquake had I_{MCS} with a range from 4.5 to 9 with the maximum (9) in Castelnuovo.

To get a quantitative measure of the performance of each scenario and understand which one provides better results, we introduce the two metrics described below

$$E_{max} = \max |I_{MCS}(i) - I_{MCS,real}(i)|, \tag{5}$$

Table 6. Macroseismic intensity in MCS scale for the 5 towns included in the computational domain comparison between estimated and simulated data earthquake 1762.

Name	I_{MCS}	I_{MCS} SC1	I_{MCS} SC2	I_{MCS} SC3	ErrSC1	ErrSC2	ErrSC3
Castenuovo	9.5	7.81	8.84	8.03	−1.69	−0.66	−1.47
Poggio Picenze	9.0	5.78	6.55	6.98	−3.22	−2.45	−2.02
L'Aquila	7	4.82	5.65	5.57	−2.18	−1.35	−1.43
Barisciano	4.5	6.20	7.46	6.54	1.7	2.96	2.04
San Demetrio ne' Vestini	4.5	7.65	8.68	8.47	3.15	4.18	3.97

$$E_{mean} = E_{tot}/N \quad \text{where} \quad E_{tot} = \sum_{i=1}^{N=k} |I_{MCS}(i) - I_{MCS,real}(i)|, \qquad (6)$$

where $I_{MCS}(i)$ and $I_{MCS,real}(i)$ are, respectively, the ith value I_{MCS} of the calculated using [37] and provided by the catalogue CFT15Med. Here $k = 6$ and $k = 5$ for 1461 and 1762 seismic event, respectively. The values of the maximum error (5) and the mean error (6) are displayed in Tables 7, for both the considered seismic events. Point values of damage calculated at specific sites are necessary for model evaluation and validation. The advantage of physical-based simulations is that they provide detailed information about the entire area affected by the earthquake, taking into account the geology and topography of the area. Simulations, in other words, can be useful to supplement, refute and validate available historical data. Therefore for both the earthquakes we also analyze the spatial distribution of the macroseismic intensity obtained and the PGV for the best scenario.

Table 7. Maximum and average errors on the evaluation of the I_{MCS} using PGV for the IM models and the scenario for 1461 and 1762 events

	SC1		SC2		SC3	
	E_{max}	E_{mean}	E_{max}	E_{mean}	E_{max}	E_{mean}
1461	1.72	1.36	2.66	1.35	2.17	1.18
1762	3.22	2.39	2.96	2.32	3.97	2.19

Figure 4 shows the maps PGV obtained using best score scenario for the 1461-SC1 in (a) and 1762-SC2 in (b). The PGV has been calculated as the geometric mean of the maximum horizontal component obtained from the numerical simulations.

Figure 5 shows the I_{MCS} maps obtained from PGV values using the scenarios with a lower average error, for the 1461-SC1 in (a) and 1762-SC2 in (b).

From the PGV and I_{MCS} maps we can see as for both the considered seismic events we got the highest values in the south-east region of the alluvional basin.

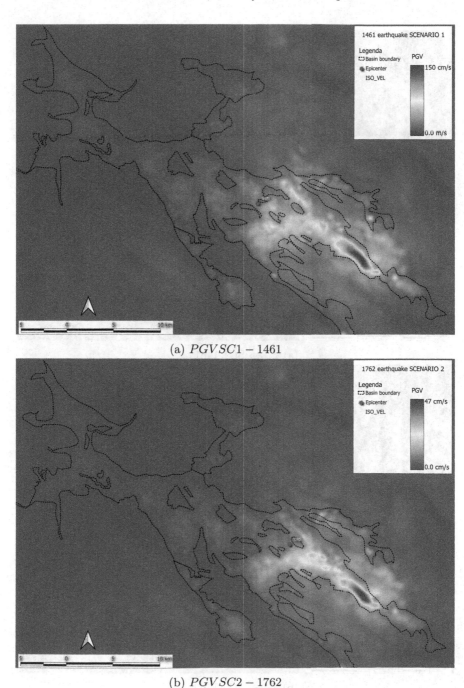

(a) $PGVSC1 - 1461$

(b) $PGVSC2 - 1762$

Fig. 4. PGV maps: peak ground velocity maps calculated using the best scenario, namely SC1 for 1461 (a) and SC2 for 1762 (b). In both cases, the peak velocity in correspondence with the southeastern region of the alluvial basin

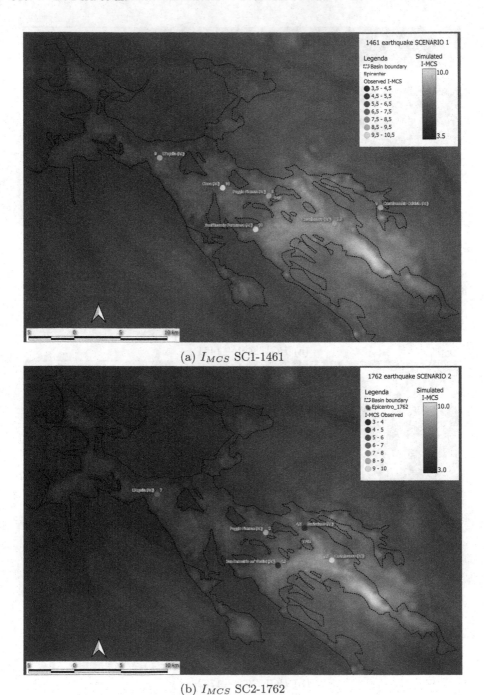

(a) I_{MCS} SC1-1461

(b) I_{MCS} SC2-1762

Fig. 5. Microcosmic Intensity maps: I_{MCS} obtained starting from the best score scenario namely SC1 for 1461(a) and SC2 for 1762 (b).

This behavior is probably due to the superposition of two effects. On the one hand, in this region between present-day San Pio delle Camere and Navelli, there is a local maximum in the thickness of the sedimentary basin (see Fig. 2), which amplifies the seismic signal. On the other hand, the slip distributions corresponding to SC1 for 1461 and SC2 for 1762 (Fig. 3) show a peak in the in the south zone of the fault structure in correspondence with the PGV peak observed in Fig. 4. In more detail analyzing both the maps and the relative errors, we can say that for the 1461 earthquake: SC2 appears to be the worst scenario. SC1 and SC3 have a quite satisfactory behaviour in all considered villages with the best fitting data in Poggio Picenze and the wrost in L'Aquila city. SC1 shows a good agreement between the real and simulated data also in the part of the domain where the other scenarios fail. Finally for the all scenarios we got the wrost results in L'Aquila and Onna locations. Although all scenarios acceptably reproduce the considered seismic event, according to the previous analysis, we can conclude that the best scenario is SC1, having the highest slip distribution in the south region of the fault. The less accurate results are instead provided by SC2, for which the maximum asperity path is located in the central part of the fault structure. For the 1762 earthquake: SC3 appears to be the worst scenario. SC1-SC2 also doesn't have in general a quite satisfactory behaviour also if we are able to get good results in Castelnuovo location. SC2 shows the best agreement between the real and simulated data with the best results in Castelnuovo and the wrost in San Demetrio dei Vestini. Finally we found that all scenarios fail in reproducing the damage in San Demetrio dei Vestini and Poggio Picenze locations. Therefore according to the previous analysis, we can conclude that the best scenario among the three considered is SC2, having the highest slip distribution in the central-south region of the fault. The less accurate results are instead provided by SC3, for which the maximum asperity path is located in the north part of the fault structure. In general, however, none of the scenarios satisfactorily reproduce this event.

4   Conclusions

In this article, we present some plausible scenarios for two earthquakes occurring in the Aterno valley region on 27 November 1461 and 6 October 1762. We reconstructed a computational domain with an extends of 67.2 km × 59.7 km in the East-West and North-South directions respectively and for 20.1 km in depth centered in L'Aquila city and realized using the CUBIT Coreform meshing tool. For both the simulated earthquakes each scenario has been simulated using SPEED tool with fixed values of Magnitude (6.4 Mw and 6.0 Mw for 1461 and 1762, respectivetly), fault plane and epicenter, but different slip distributions. For each scenario, we computed the PGV values and then the I_{MCS} using the model available from the literature defined in [37]. Among the available simulations SC1 better reproduce the 1461 earthquake. It is characterized by a localized slip distribution in the south part of the fault structure, which could be a plausible slip distribution for the 1461 earthquake. Concerning the 1762, no scenario can satisfactorily reproduce the (few) information available. However the SC2, characterized by a localized slip distribution in the central-south part of the fault structure, is the one that shows better performance. In summary, we can say that the 1461 earthquake is acceptably reproduced by all slip distributions considered, whereas the results are less satisfactory for 1762. Although three scenarios are few to draw conclusions, it is possible to assume that the available information is not sufficient and/or accurate enough to model this event. It is in our opinion necessary to develop a more accurate analysis that not only considers more scenarios, but also investigates the location of the epicenter and possibly the fault structure. Finally, we recall the lack of other reconstructions relating to the simulation of the earthquakes considered in this article and the possibility of extending the domain reconstruction and earthquake simulation techniques to other historical earthquakes for the definition and study of risk plans related to the Italian territory. Some other simulations based in the same area are available on platform https://www.opendatalaquila.it, together with much other information about the L'Aquila area and the reconstruction process after the 2009 earthquake, [25, 26].

Acknowledgements. This paper is part of a larger project focused on the post-earthquake reconstruction of the city of L'Aquila (see https://www.opendatalaquila.it) and was partially supported by the GSSI "Centre for Urban Informatics and Modelling" (CUIM). This paper received financial support from ICSC - Centro Nazionale di Ricerca in High Performance Computing, Big Data and Quantum Computing, funded by European Union - NextGenerationEU (ref. Prof. B. Rubino and Dr. D. Pera. University of L'Aquila). All numerical simulations have been realized on the Linux HPC cluster Caliban of the High Performance Parallel Computing Laboratory of the Department of Information Engineering, Computer Science and Mathematics (DISIM) at the University of L'Aquila.

References

1. Abraham, J.R., Smerzini, C., Paolucci, R., Lai, C.G.: Numerical study on basin-edge effects in the seismic response of the Gubbio valley, central Italy. Bull. Earthquake Eng. **14**(6), 1437–1459 (2016)
2. Aki, K., Richards, P.G.: Quantitative seismology (2002)
3. Antonietti, P.F., et al.: Three-dimensional physics-based earthquake ground motion simulations for seismic risk assessment in densely populated urban areas. Math. Eng. **3**(2), 1–31 (2021). https://doi.org/10.3934/mine.2021012, https://www.aimspress.com/article/doi/10.3934/mine.2021012
4. Antonietti, P.F., Ayuso de Dios, B., Mazzieri, I., Quarteroni, A.: Stability analysis of discontinuous Galerkin approximations to the elastodynamics problem. J. Sci. Comput. **68**–1, 143–170 (2016)
5. Antonietti, P.F., Mazzieri, I., Quarteroni, A., Rapetti, F.: Non-conforming high order approximations of the elastodynamics equation. Comput. Meth. Appl. Mech. Eng. **209**, 212–238 (2012)
6. Antonietti, P., et al.: Numerical modeling of seismic waves by discontinuous spectral element methods. ESAIM: Proc. Surv. **61**(1–37) (2018)

7. Anzidei, M., et al.: Coseismic deformation of the destructive April 6, 2009 l'aquila earthquake (central Italy) from GPS data. Geophy. Res. Lett. **36**(17) (2009)

8. Baron, J., Primofiore, I., Klin, P., Vessia, G., Laurenzano, G.: Investigation of topographic site effects using 3D waveform modelling: amplification, polarization and torsional motions in the case study of arquata del tronto (italy). Bull. Earthquake Eng. **20**(2), 677–710 (2022)

9. Basili, R., et al.: Database of individual seismogenic sources (diss), version 3.3. 0: A compilation of potential sources for earthquakes larger than m 5.5 in Italy and surrounding areas (2021)

10. Bilal, M., Askan, A.: Relationships between felt intensity and recorded ground-motion parameters for turkey. Bull. Seismolog. Soc. Am. **104**(1), 484–496 (2014)

11. Boncio, P., Lavecchia, G., Pace, B.: Defining a model of 3D seismogenic sources for seismic hazard assessment applications: the case of central Apennines (Italy). J. Seismolog. **8**, 407–425 (2004)

12. Di Michele, F., et al.: On the possible use of the not-honoring method to include a real thrust into 3D physical based simulations. In: 2021 21st International Conference on Computational Science and its applications (ICCSA), pp. 268–275. IEEE (2021)

13. Di Michele, F., et al.: Spectral element numerical simulation of the 2009 L'aquila earthquake on a detailed reconstructed domain. Geophys. J. Int. **230**(1), 29–49 (2022)

14. Di Michele, F., et al.: Fault shape effect on SH waves using finite element method. J. Seismol. 1–21 (2022)

15. Evangelista, L., et al.: Physics-based seismic input for engineering applications: a case study in the Aterno river valley, central Italy. Bull. Earthq. Eng. **15**(7), 2645–2671 (2017)

16. Faccioli, E., Cauzzi, C.: Macroseismic intensities for seismic scenarios estimated from instrumentally based correlations. In: Proceedings of the First European Conference on Earthquake Engineering and Seismology, paper. No. 569 (2006)

17. Faccioli, E., Maggio, F., Paolucci, R., Quarteroni, A.: 2D and 3D elastic wave propagation by a pseudo-spectral domain decomposition method. J. Seismolog. **1**(3), 237–251 (1997)

18. Faenza, L., Michelini, A.: Regression analysis of MCS intensity and ground motion parameters in Italy and its application in Shakemap. Geophys. J. Int. **180**(3), 1138–1152 (2010)

19. Faenza, L., Michelini, A.: Regression analysis of MCS intensity and ground motion spectral accelerations (SAS) in Italy. Geophys. J. Int. **186**(3), 1415–1430 (2011)

20. Falcucci, E., et al.: The paganica fault and surface coseismic ruptures caused by the 6 April 2009 earthquake (L'aquila, central Italy). Seismol. Res. Lett. **80**(6), 940–950 (2009)

21. Ferroni, A., Antonietti, P.F., Mazzieri, I., Quarteroni, A.: Dispersion-dissipation analysis of 3-D continuous and discontinuous spectral element methods for the elastodynamics equation. Geophys. J. Int. **211**–3, 1554–1574 (2017)

22. Gao, Y., Zhang, N.: Scattering of cylindrical SH waves induced by a symmetrical v-shaped canyon: near-source topographic effects. Geophys. J. Int. **193**(2), 874–885 (2013)

23. Gomez Capera, A., Albarello, D., Gasperini, P., et al.: Aggiornamento relazioni fra l'intensità macrosismica e pga. progetto ingv-dpc s1, deliverable d11 (2007)

24. Gomez Capera, A., et al.: Macroseismic intensity to ground motion empirical relationships for Italy. In: Proceedings, vol. 37, pp. 289–291 (2018)

25. GSSI: Open data L'aquila (2019). https://www.opendatalaquila.it/
26. GSSI: Open data ricostruzione (2019). https://opendataricostruzione.gssi.it/home
27. Guidoboni, E., et al.: Cfti5med, the new release of the catalogue of strong earthquakes in Italy and in the Mediterranean area. Sci. Data **6**(1), 1–15 (2019)
28. Guidoboni, E., et al.: Cfti5med, catalogo dei forti terremoti in italia (461 ac-1997) e nell'area mediterranea (760 ac-1500) (2018)
29. Imperatori, W., Mai, P.M.: The role of topography and lateral velocity heterogeneities on near-source scattering and ground-motion variability. Geophys. J. Int. **202**(3), 2163–2181 (2015)
30. Infantino, M., Mazzieri, I., Özcebe, A.G., Paolucci, R., Stupazzini, M.: 3d physics-based numerical simulations of ground motion in Istanbul from earthquakes along the Marmara segment of the north Anatolian fault. Bull. Seismol. Soc. Am. **110–5**, 2559–2576 (2020)
31. J. Schmedes, R.J.A., Lavallée, D.: A kinematic rupture model generator incorporating spatial interdependency of earthquake source parameters (2013)
32. Karimzadeh, S., Askan, A.: Modeling of a historical earthquake in erzincan, turkey (ms⁻ 7.8, in 1939) using regional seismological information obtained from a recent event. Acta Geophysica **66**(3), 293–304 (2018)
33. Lewis, M., Peng, Z., Ben-Zion, Y., Vernon, F.: Shallow seismic trapping structure in the san Jacinto fault zone near Anza, California. Geophys. J. Int. **162**(3), 867–881 (2005)
34. Magnoni, F., et al.: Spectral-element simulations of seismic waves generated by the 2009 L'aquila earthquake. Bull. Seismol. Soc. Am. **104**(1), 73–94 (2013)
35. May, J., Pera, D., Di Michele, F., Rubino, B., Aloisio, R., Marcati, P.: Fast cubit-python tool for highly accurate topography generation and layered domain reconstruction. In: 29th International Meshing Roundtable (2021)
36. Mazzieri, I., Stupazzini, M., Guidotti, R., Smerzini, C.: Speed: spectral elements in elastodynamics with discontinuous galerkin: a non-conforming approach for 3D multi-scale problems. Int. J. Numer. Meth. Eng. **95**(12), 991–1010 (2013)
37. Oliveti, I., Faenza, L., Michelini, A.: New reversible relationships between ground motion parameters and macrosesmic intensity for Italy and their application in shakemap. Geophys. J. Int. **231**(2), 1117–1137 (2022)
38. Paolucci, R., Evangelista, L., Mazzieri, I., Schiappaterra, E.: The 3D numerical simulation of near-source ground motion during the marsica earthquake, central Italy, 100 years later. Soil Dyn. Earthq. Eng. **91**, 39–52 (2016)
39. Paolucci, R., Mazzieri, I., Özcebe, A.G., Smerzini, C.: Anatomy of strong ground motion: near-source records and three-dimensional physics-based numerical simulations of the mw 6.0 2012 may 29 Po plain earthquake, Italy. Geophysical Journal International 203–3, 2001–2020 (2015)
40. Paolucci, R., Mazzieri, I., Piunno, G., Smerizni, C., Vanini, M., Özcebe, A.G.: Earthquake ground motion modeling of induced seismicity in the Groningen gas field. Earthquake Eng. Struct. Dyn. **50–1**, 135–154 (2021)
41. Paolucci, R., Evangelista, L., Mazzieri, I., Schiappapietra, E.: The 3d numerical simulation of near-source ground motion during the Marsica earthquake, central Italy, 100 years later. Soil Dyn. Earthq. Eng. **91**, 39–52 (2016)
42. Pera, D.: Design and performance evaluation of a Linux HPC cluster. Task Quart. **22**(2), 113–123 (2018)
43. Pilz, M., Parolai, S., Stupazzini, M., Paolucci, R., Zschau, J.: Modelling basin effects on earthquake ground motion in the santiago de chile basin by a spectral element code. Geophys. J. Int. **187**(2), 929–945 (2011)

44. Rodriguez-Plata, R., Ozcebe, A., Smerzini, C., Lai, C.: Aggravation factors for 2d site effects in sedimentary basins: the case of Norcia, central Italy. Soil Dyn. Earthq. Eng. **149**, 106854 (2021)

45. Rovida, A., Locati, M., Camassi, R., Lolli, B., Gasperini, P.: The Italian earthquake catalogue cpti15. Bull. Earthq. Eng. **18**(7), 2953–2984 (2020)

46. Rovida, A., Locati, M., Camassi, R., Lolli, B., Gasperini, P., Antonucci, A.: Catalogo parametrico dei terremoti italiani (cpti15). versione 4.0. Istituto Nazionale di Geofisica e Vulcanologia (INGV). Italy (2022)

47. Smerzini, C., Villani, M.: Broadband numerical simulations in complex near-field geological configurations: the case of the 2009 m w 6.3 L'aquila earthquake. Bull. Seismol. Soc. Am. **102**(6), 2436–2451 (2012)

48. Stupazzini, M., Infantino, M., Allmann, A., Paolucci, R.: Physics-based probabilistic seismic hazard and loss assessment in large urban areas: a simplified application to Istanbul. Earthquake Eng. Struct. Dyn. **50**(1), 99–115 (2021)

49. Tarquini, S., et al.: Tinitaly/01: a new triangular irregular network of Italy. Ann. Geophys. (2007)

50. Tarquini, S., Nannipieri, L.: The 10 m-resolution Tinitaly dem as a transdisciplinary basis for the analysis of the Italian territory: current trends and new perspectives. Geomorphology **281**, 108–115 (2017)

51. Tarquini, S., Vinci, S., Favalli, M., Doumaz, F., Fornaciai, A., Nannipieri, L.: Release of a 10-m-resolution dem for the Italian territory: Comparison with global-coverage Dems and anaglyph-mode exploration via the web. Comput. Geosci. **38**(1), 168–170 (2012)

52. Tiberi, L., Costa, G., Jamšek Rupnik, P., Cecić, I., Suhadolc, P.: The 1895 Ljubljana earthquake: can the intensity data points discriminate which one of the nearby faults was the causative one? J. Seismolog. **22**(4), 927–941 (2018)

53. Veeraraghavan, S., Coleman, J.L., Bielak, J.: Simulation of site and topographic effects on ground motion in los alamos, nm mesas. Geophys. J. Int. **220**(3), 1504–1520 (2020)

Graphical Visualization of Phase Surface of the Sprott Type A System Immersed in 4D

Eder Escobar[1], Flabio Gutierrez[1(✉)], Edwar Lujan[2], Rolando Ipanaque[1], Cesar Silva[1], and Lemin Abanto[1]

[1] Universidad Nacional de Piura, Urb. Miraflores s/n, Castilla, Piura, Peru
{eescobarg,flabio,ripanaques,csilvam,labantoc}@unp.edu.pe
[2] Universidad Católica de Trujillo, Panamericana Norte Km. 555, Moche, Trujillo, La Libertad, Peru
elujan@uct.edu.pe

Abstract. When formulating a system of differential equations, the main objective is to determine their solutions, in addition to visualizing the phase surface to observe the behavior of the physical phenomenon. In this work an algorithm is developed to graph phase surfaces and perform qualitative analysis to a four-dimensional (4D) system. The algorithm is implemented in the scientific software Octave obtaining the program called SystemSprott4D, which is applied to the Sprott type A system in 4D to be able to graph, phase surfaces, limit cycle and trajectories of initial conditions of the system. A qualitative analysis of the system is performed, such as symmetry of the vector field, sensitivity in the initial conditions, Lyapunov exponents, fractal dimension and limit cycle. It is found that it is a non-equilibrium system, this means that the 4D chaotic system can exhibit attracting limit cycles, these limit cycles are found by selecting different initial points. The program can be used to analyze non-linear 4D systems from various disciplines such as electronics, telecommunications, biology, meteorology, economics, medicine, etc.

Keywords: Sprott type A hyper attractor · Chaotic system · Geometric visualization · Octave software

1 Introduction

Chaos is a broad and universal phenomenon that exists in several nonlinear systems and has been confused with noise for a long time. In 1980, the engineering field officially announced chaos existence in electrical systems. Chaotic systems have sensitivity to initial conditions. Small changes in initial conditions can lead to significant changes in the systems' behavior. The coexisting hidden attractors of a chaotic system can be found by selecting different initial conditions. Chaotic systems are used to model various physical phenomena; for example, Lorenz systems are used to model climate behavior. The Sprott simple systems were created to simplify the Lorenz systems of equations that model climate behavior globally.

O. Gervasi et al. (Eds.): ICCSA 2023 Workshops, LNCS 14111, pp. 566–582, 2023.
https://doi.org/10.1007/978-3-031-37126-4_36

Previous work on the Sprott system type A in four-dimensional space (4D) is presented in [5]; the authors analyzed the energy cycle of the Sprott-A system transforming it to a Kolmogorov type system, then based on the energy analysis of the Sprott-A system, a new conservative 4D chaotic system with constant Hamiltonian energy is obtained. The study presents four static images of the phase surface. Still, it doesn't show a qualitative analysis of the 4D system or deliver a complete phase surface to be analyzed.

Currently, to visualize phase surfaces and limit cycles of 4D systems, they are projected in three dimensions (3D), making zero any of the coordinate axes, resulting in four surfaces to analyze (for examples, see [1–10]). Researchers can overcome this analysis limitation by applying the Velezmoro and Ipanaque model that allows the visualization of 4D objects in a 3D system (see Sect. 2.2) by obtaining a single surface that can be rotated from different angles, allowing a better analysis of what happens in a 4D system of equations.

This study presents an Octave program called SistemaSprott4D that allows the visualization of phase surfaces and limit cycles of nonlinear systems immersed in a 4D system. The SistemaSprott4D includes the Velezmoro and Ipanaque model to visualize phase surfaces of a chaotic Sprott system type A immersed in the fourth dimension. It can be used to analyze nonlinear 4D systems from various disciplines such as electronics, telecommunications, biology, meteorology, economics, medicine, etc.

2 Preliminaries

In this Section, the necessary mathematical concepts for the work are defined, the definitions of, sensitivity in the initial conditions, chaotic invariant set and strange attractor are fundamental characteristics for a system to be chaotic. In addition, mention is also made of the Velezmoro and Robert model that allows to visualize in 3D objects that are in 4D.

2.1 Dynamical Systems

Definition 1 (Sensitive dependence on initial conditions) [13]. The flow $\phi(t, x)$ is said to possess a sensitive dependence on initial conditions in Λ (invariant compact set under $\phi(t, x)$) if there exists $\varepsilon > 0$ such that for any $x \in \Lambda$ and any neighborhood U of x, there exist $y \in U$ and $t > 0$ such that $|\phi(t, x) - \phi(t, y)| > \varepsilon$.

Definition 2 (Chaotic Invariant Set) [13]. Λ Is said to be chaotic if:

1. $\phi(t, x)$ has a sensitive dependence on initial conditions in Λ.
2. $\phi(t, x)$ is topologically transitive in Λ.
3. The periodic orbits of $\phi(t, x)$ are dense in Λ.

Definition 3 (Strange attractor) [12]. Suppose that $A \subset R^n$ is an attractor. Then A is called a strange attractor if it is chaotic.

2.2 Velezmoro and Ipanaque Immersion Model

Ricardo Velezmoro and Robert Ipanaque [11], proposed a new mathematical model that allows 4D objects to be graphed in 3D following the same method for visualizing 3D objects on a 2D screen. The mathematical model is built using a 3D hologram projector.

Consider a two-unit length cube whose center of gravity is the coordinate origin of the 3D Cartesian system. Four coordinate axes, x, y, z, and w are arranged in the cube shown in Fig. 1.

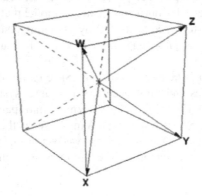

Fig. 1. Arrangement of the coordinate axes x, y, z, and w in three-dimensional space.

Consider the unit vectors:

$$e_1 = \left(\frac{1}{\sqrt{3}}, -\frac{1}{\sqrt{3}}, -\frac{1}{\sqrt{3}}\right) \quad e_2 = \left(\frac{1}{\sqrt{3}}, \frac{1}{\sqrt{3}}, -\frac{1}{\sqrt{3}}\right)$$

$$e_3 = \left(\frac{1}{\sqrt{3}}, \frac{1}{\sqrt{3}}, \frac{1}{\sqrt{3}}\right) \quad e_4 = \left(\frac{1}{\sqrt{3}}, -\frac{1}{\sqrt{3}}, \frac{1}{\sqrt{3}}\right)$$

In the direction of the x, y, z, and w axes (see Fig. 2).

From the unit vectors, an immersion is defined as ψ, constituting the method for graphing 4D objects in a 3D environment.

Let's define immersion $\psi : R^4 \rightarrow R^3$ such that,

$$\psi(p) = p_1 e_1 + p_2 e_2 + p_3 e_3 + p_4 e_4, \text{ for all } p \in R^4.$$

Immersion ψ can be written in the form,

$$\psi(p) = \frac{1}{\sqrt{3}}(p_1 + p_2 + p_3 + p_4, -p_1 + p_2 + p_3 - p_4, -p_1 - p_2 + p_3 + p_4), \forall p \in R^4$$

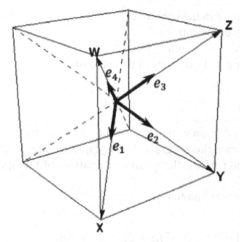

Fig. 2. Unit vectors, e_i, $i = 1, 2, 3, 4$, from which immersion ψ is defined.

3 Results and Discussion

In this section, the new Sprott type A system is shown in 4D. Also, an algorithm to plot phase surfaces and perform qualitative analysis is shown, then the algorithm is applied to the new Sprott type A system in 4D. In addition, a qualitative analysis of the system is also made and a scenario of the different hidden attractors is shown by varying the initial conditions.

3.1 Nonlinear Sprott Type A 4D System

Equation (1) is a system without equilibrium, its trajectories form attractive limit cycles. The system (1) represents the new Sprott type A system in 4D. This system is nonlinear in the second and third equations, also it has a positive control parameter and four state variables x, y, z, w as shown below:

$$\begin{cases} x' = y \\ y' = -x + ayz \\ z' = -y^2 + 1 \\ w' = -z \end{cases} \tag{1}$$

3.2 Steps to Graph Phase Surfaces and Perform Qualitative Analysis to a 4D System

Step 1. Solve the 4D system using a numerical method.
Step 2. Use the Velezmoro and Ipanaque immersion model to visualize a phase surface graph of the system that is in 4D in 3D.
Step 3. Perform a qualitative analysis of the system:

Step 3.1. Symmetry.

Step 3.2. Sensitivity in initial conditions.
Step 3.3. Lyapunov exponents.
Step 3.4. Lyapunov - Yorke dimension.
Step 3.5. Dissipation and existence of the attractor.

3.3 SystemSprott4D

The SystemSprott4D program is an implementation of the algorithm of Sect. 3.2 in the
Octave scientific software, this program allows graphing, phase surfaces and trajectories
of initial conditions, to perform the qualitative analysis of the Sprott type A system in
4D.
Case Study to the New 4D Sprott Type 1.

```
a=1;
func=@(t,x)[x(2);-x(1)+a*x(2)*x(3);1-x(2)*x(2);-x(3)];
x0=[-0.0561 1.5652 1.0484 1.0543]; % condiciones iniciales.
t=linspace(0,300,10000);
[t, x]=ode45(func,t,x0);
x(1:20,:) % vector que muestra las 20 primeras iteraciones.
```

Implementation of Step 2.

```
a=1;
func=@(t,x)[x(2);-x(1)+a*x(2)*x(3);1-x(2)*x(2);-x(3)];
x0=[-0.0561 1.5652 1.0484 1.0543];
t=linspace(0,300,10000);
[t,x]=ode45(func,t,x0);
z=[x(:,1) x(:,2) x(:,3) x(:,4)];
p1=(1/sqrt(3)).*[z(:,1)+z(:,2)+z(:,3)+z(:,4)];
p2=(1/sqrt(3)).*[-z(:,1)+z(:,2)+z(:,3)-z(:,4)];
p3=(1/sqrt(3)).*[-z(:,1)-z(:,2)+z(:,3)+z(:,4)];
disp([p1(1:20,:),p2(1:20,:),p3(1:20,:)]);
plot3(p1,p2,p3,'b','linewidth',2).
xlabel('X'); ylabel('Y'); zlabel('Z').
```

Implementation of Step 3.
Subprogram that allows visualizing the trajectories by varying the first component.

```
sistem4D=@(t,x)[x(2);-x(1)+x(2)*x(3);-x(2)^2+1;-x(3)];
x0=[-0.0561 1.5652 1.0484 0];
X0=[-0.2561 1.5652 1.0484 0];
t=linspace(0,80,800);
[tout,xout]=ode45(sistem4D,t,x0);
plot(tout,xout(:,1),'b').
hold on.
[tout,Xout]=ode45(sistem4D,t,X0);
plot(tout,Xout(:,1),'k').
xlabel('time').
```

ylabel('X vs x').
grid.

Subprogram that allows visualizing the trajectories by varying the second component.

```
sistem4D=@(t,x)[x(2);-x(1)+x(2)*x(3);-x(2)^2+1;-x(3)];
x0=[-0.0561 1.5652 1.0484 0];
X0=[-0.0561 1.9652 1.0484 0];
t=linspacc(0,100,1000);
[tout,xout]=ode45(sistem4D,t,x0);
plot(tout,xout(:,2),'b').
hold on.
[tout,Xout]=ode45(sistem4D,t,X0);
plot(tout,Xout(:,2),'k').
xlabel('time').
ylabel('Y vs y').
grid.
```

Subprogram that allows visualizing the trajectories by varying the third component.

```
sistem4D=@(t,x)[x(2);-x(1)+x(2)*x(3);-x(2)^2+1;-x(3)];
x0=[-0.0561 1.5652 1.0484 0];
X0=[-0.0561 1.5652 1.1884 0];
t=linspace(0,100,1000);
[tout,xout]=ode45(sistem4D,t,x0);
plot(tout,xout(:,3),'b').
hold on.
[tout,Xout]=ode45(sistem4D,t,X0);
plot(tout,Xout(:,3),'k').
xlabel('time').
ylabel('Z vs z').
grid.
```

Subprogram that allows visualizing the trajectories by varying the fourth component.

```
sistem4D=@(t,x)[x(2);-x(1)+x(2)*x(3);-x(2)^2+1;-x(3)];
x0=[-0.0561 1.5652 1.0484 0];
X0=[-0.0561 1.5652 1.1884 0.123];
t=linspace(0,100,1000);
[tout,xout]=ode45(sistem4D,t,x0);
plot(tout,xout(:,4),'b').
hold on.
[tout,Xout]=ode45(sistem4D,t,X0);
plot(tout,Xout(:,4),'k').
xlabel('time').
ylabel('W vs w').
grid.
```

Subprogram to calculate the Lyapunov exponents.

```
Function[Texp,Lexp]=lyapunov(n,rhs_ext_fcn,
fcn_integrator,tstart,stept,tend,ystart);
n1=n; n2=n1*(n1+1);
%  Number of steps
nit = round((tend-tstart)/stept);
% Memory allocation
y=zeros(n2,1); cum=zeros(n1,1); y0=y;
gsc=cum; znorm=cum;
% Initial values
y(1:n)=ystart(:);
for i=1:n1 y((n1+1)*i)=1.0; end;
t=tstart;
% Main loop
for ITERLYAP=1:nit
% Solution of extended ODE system
[T,Y] = feval(fcn_integrator,rhs_ext_fcn,[t t+stept],y);
 t=t+stept;
  y=Y(size(Y,1),:);
for i=1:n1
    for j=1:n1 y0(n1*i+j)=y(n1*j+i); end;
  end;
znorm(1)=0.0;
  for j=1:n1 znorm(1)=znorm(1)+y0(n1*j+1)^2; end;
znorm(1)=sqrt(znorm(1));
for j=1:n1 y0(n1*j+1)=y0(n1*j+1)/znorm(1); end;
 for j=2:n1
    for k=1:(j-1)
       gsc(k)=0.0;
       for l=1:n1 gsc(k)=gsc(k)+y0(n1*l+j)*y0(n1*l+k); end;
    end;
    for k=1:n1
       for l=1:(j-1)
          y0(n1*k+j)=y0(n1*k+j)-gsc(l)*y0(n1*k+l);
       end;
    end;
    znorm(j)=0.0;
    for k=1:n1 znorm(j)=znorm(j)+y0(n1*k+j)^2; end;
    znorm(j)=sqrt(znorm(j));
    for k=1:n1 y0(n1*k+j)=y0(n1*k+j)/znorm(j); end;
  end;
for k=1:n1 cum(k)=cum(k)+log(znorm(k)); end;
for k=1:n1
    lp(k)=cum(k)/(t-tstart);
  end;
```

```
% Output modification
 if ITERLYAP==1
   Lexp=lp;
   Texp=t;
 else
   Lexp=[Lexp; lp];
   Texp=[Texp; t];
 end;
 for i=1:n1
   for j=1:n1
     y(n1*j+i)=y0(n1*i+j);
   end;
 end;
end;


function f=exp_lyapunov4(t,X)
   x=X(1); y=X(2); z=X(3);w=X(4);
   Y= [X(5), X(9), X(13),X(17); X(6), X(10), X(14), X(18);...
     X(7), X(11), X(15), X(19); X(8), X(12), X(16), X(20)];
   f=zeros(16,1);
   f(1) = y;
   f(2) = -x+y*z;
   f(3) = -y^2+1;
   f(4) = -z;
   Jac=[0 1 0 0;-1 z y 0;0 -2*y 0 0;0 0 -1 0];
   f(5:20)=Jac*Y;
end


[T,Res]=lyapunov(4,@exp_lyapunov4D,@ode45,0,0.5,200,[0.0561,1.5652,1.0
484,0);
plot(T,Res(:,1),'r','linewidth',1);
hold on
plot(T,Res(:,2),'b','linewidth',1);
plot(T,Res(:,3),'k','linewidth',1);
plot(T,Res(:,4),'g','linewidth',1);
xlabel('Tiempo'); ylabel('Exponentes de Lyapunov');
Res(length(Res),:)
```

Subprogram that shows different scenarios for different values of a.

```
% a=[0.01, 0.1, 0.5, 1, 10] different values of the parameter a to obtain the.
% phase surfaces.
a=1;
func=@(t,x)[x(2);-x(1)+a*x(2)*x(3);1-x(2)*x(2);-x(3)];
x0=[-0.0561 1.5652 1.0484 1.0543];
t=linspace(0,300,10000);
[t,x]=ode45(func,t,x0);
```

```
z=[x(:,1) x(:,2) x(:,3) x(:,4)];
p1=(1/sqrt(3)).*[z(:,1)+z(:,2)=z(:,3)+z(:,4)];
p2-(1/sqrt(3)) *[-z(:,1)+z(:,2)+z(:,3)-z(:,4)];
p3=(1/sqrt(3)).*[-z(:,1)-z(:,2)+z(:,3)+z(:,4)];
disp([p1(1:20,:),p2(1:20,:),p3(1:20,:)]);
plot3(p1,p2,p3,'b','linewidth',2);
xlabel('X'); ylabel('Y'); zlabel('Z').
```

3.4 Applying the Algorithm as a Case Study to the New 4D Sprott Type A System

In [5], a new 4D Sprott type A system was proposed (see Eq. 2)

$$\begin{cases} x' = y \\ y' = -x + yz \\ z' = -y^2 + 1 \\ w' = -z \end{cases} \quad (2)$$

We solve the new system of Sprott type A in 4D using the numerical method of Runge Kutta (library ode45 in Octave). Table 1 shows the approximate solution for the first 20 iterations.

Table 1. Numerical solution of the system (3.2)

N°	x	y	z	w
1	-5.6100e-02	1.5652e+00	1.0484e+00	1.0543e+00
2	-8.3853e-03	1.6151e+00	1.0025e+00	1.0235e+00
3	4.0793e-02	1.6627e+00	9.5190e-01	9.9419e-01
4	9.1359e-02	1.7075e+00	8.9668e-01	9.6645e-01
5	1.4322e-01	1.7489e+00	8.3704e-01	9.4043e-01
6	1.9627e-01	1.7866e+00	7.7325e-01	9.1626e-01
7	2.5038e-01	1.8199e+00	7.0565e-01	8.9407e-01
8	3.0542e-01	1.8485e+00	6.3466e-01	8.7395e-01
9	3.6125e-01	1.8718e+00	5.6080e-01	8.5601e-01
10	4.1769e-01	1.8896e+00	4.8463e-01	8.4032e-01
11	4.7458e-01	1.9016e+00	4.0676e-01	8.2695e-01
12	5.3174e-01	1.9075e+00	3.2787e-01	8.1593e-01
13	5.8898e-01	1.9072e+00	2.4864e-01	8.0727e-01
14	6.4613e-01	1.9006e+00	1.6981e-01	8.0099e-01
15	7.0297e-01	1.8879e+00	9.2110e-02	7.9706e-01
16	7.5934e-01	1.8690e+00	1.6216e-02	7.9544e-01
17	8.1506e-01	1.8442e+00	-5.7237e-02	7.9607e-01
18	8.6995e-01	1.8139e+00	-1.2766e-01	7.9886e-01
19	9.2385e-01	1.7783e+00	-1.9450e-01	8.0371e-01
20	9.7661e-01	1.7378e+00	-2.5727e-01	8.1050e-01

With the application of the Velezmoro and Ipanaque model, the 4D phase surface is displayed in 3D (see Fig. 3).

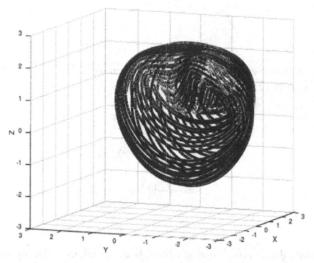

Fig. 3. Phase surface of the chaotic Sprott type A system immersed in 4D.

3.5   Qualitative Analysis of the System

3.5.1   Symmetry

The coordinate transformation is applied to the system of Eqs. (2), if the equations of state remain unchanged, it means that the system is symmetric with respect to the analyzed axis.

- Symmetry with the x-axis: It exists because when replacing $-y$ by y, $-z$ by z, and $-w$ by w in the system (2), equality is obtained.

$$x' = y = -y = -x'$$

$$y' = -x + (-y)(-z) = y'$$

$$z' = -(-y)^2 + 1 = z'$$

$$w' = -(-z) = -w'$$

- Symmetry with the y-axis: It exists because when replacing $-x$ by x, $-z$ by z, and $-w$ by w in the system (2), equality is obtained.

$$x' = y = x'$$

$$y' = -(-x) + y(-z) = -y'$$

$$z' = -y^2 + 1 = z'$$

$$w' = -(-z) = -w'$$

- Symmetry with the z-axis: It exists because when replacing –x by x, -y by y, and –w by w in the system (2), equality is obtained.

$$x' = -y = -x'$$

$$y' = -(-x) + (-y)z = -y'$$

$$z' = -(-y)^2 + 1 = z'$$

$$w' = -z = w'$$

- Symmetry with the w axis: It doesn't exist, because when replacing –x by x, -y by y, and –z by z in the system (2), equality is not obtained.

$$x' = -y = -x'$$

$$y' = -(-x) + (-y)(-z) \neq -y'$$

$$z' = -(-y)^2 + 1 = z'$$

$$w' = -(-z) = -w'$$

The analysis shows that the vector field of the system (2) has symmetry with respect to the axes x, y, z and it has no symmetry in the w-axis. When the flow of the system of equations crosses the axes x, y, z, the state variable w is canceled, i.e., $w' = 0$. This result indicates that every orbit that passes through the axes x, y, z cannot leave it; therefore, the system is invariant.

3.5.2   Sensibility in Initial Conditions

A characteristic of a chaotic system is sensitivity to initial conditions (see Definition 1). This work graphically shows that small variations in systems' initial conditions produce significant variations in their trajectories.

In Fig. 4, a small variation from -0.0561 to -0.2561 was made in the first component of the initial condition x_0. The varying trajectory is shown in black color and the non-varying trajectory is shown in blue color. The results show that black and blue color trajectories remain close to the value of $x_0 = 40$. For values of x_0 greater than 40, the black color trajectory diverges, thus showing sensitivity in this component.

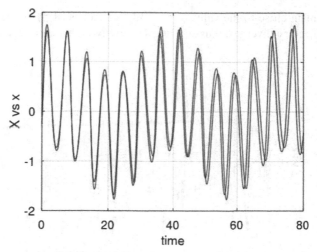

Fig. 4. The blue color trajectory corresponds to the first component without variation and the back color trajectory corresponds to the component's variation. (Color figure online)

In Fig. 5, a small variation from 1.5652 to 1.9652 was made in the second component of the initial condition y_0. The varying trajectory is shown in black color and the non-varying trajectory is shown in blue color. The results show that black and blue color trajectories remain close to the value of $y_0 = 40$. For values of y_0 greater than 40, the black color trajectory diverges, thus showing sensitivity in this component.

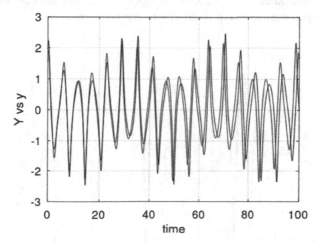

Fig. 5. The blue color trajectory corresponds to the second component without variation and the back color trajectory corresponds to the component's variation. (Color figure online)

In Fig. 6, a small variation from 1.0484 to 1.1884 was made in the third component of the initial condition z_0. The varying trajectory is shown in black color and the non-varying trajectory is shown in blue color. The results show that black and blue color trajectories remain close to the value of $z = 30$. For values of z_0 greater than 30, the black color trajectory diverges, thus showing sensitivity in this component.

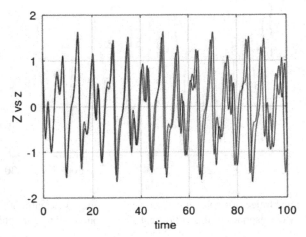

Fig. 6. The blue color trajectory corresponds to the third component without variation and the back color trajectory corresponds to the component's variation. (Color figure online)

In Fig. 7, a small variation from 0 to 0.123 was made in the fourth component of the initial condition w_0. The varying trajectory is shown in black color and the non-varying trajectory is shown in blue color. The results show that black and blue color trajectories remain close to the value of $w = 20$. For values of w_0 greater than 20, the black color trajectory diverges, thus showing sensitivity in this component.

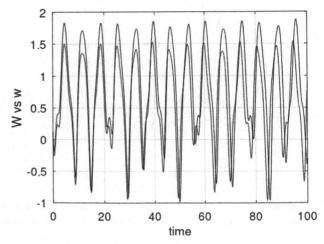

Fig. 7. The blue color trajectory corresponds to the fourth component without variation and the back color trajectory corresponds to the component's variation. (Color figure online)

3.5.3 Lyapunov Exponents

In system (2) the initial condition is $(x, y, z, w) = (-0.0561, 1.5652, 1.0484, 0)$; the Sprott System type A in the fourth dimension, presents three negative and one positive Lyapunov exponents.

$$\lambda_1 = 0.016635, \lambda_2 = -0.0004872, \lambda_3 = -0.0032606y, \lambda_4 = -0.016125$$

3.5.4 Lyapunov-Yorke Dimension

The Lyapunov-Yorke dimension of the hyper-chaotic attractor is fractional with initial conditions $(x, y, z, w) = (0.0561, 1.5652, 1.0484, 0)$.

$$D_{LY} = j + \frac{1}{|\lambda_{j+1}|} \sum_{i=1}^{j} \lambda_i$$

$$D_{LY} = 3 + \frac{1}{|-0.016125|}(0.016635 - 0.0004872 - 0.0032606)$$

$$D_{LY} = 3.7992$$

3.5.5 Dissipation and Existence of the Attractor

System (2) divergence is defined by:

$$\nabla V = \frac{\partial x'}{\partial x} + \frac{\partial y'}{\partial y} + \frac{\partial z'}{\partial z} + \frac{\partial w'}{\partial w}$$

and it measures how quickly the volume changes under the flow of the system.

$$\nabla V = z$$

$$V(t) = V(0)e^{zt}$$

When $t \to \infty$ and $z < 0$, the volume is exponentially reduced to zero. Any flow that enters the attractor will remain in time.

3.5.6 4D Type A Sprott System Scenarios

When the parameter the $a = 0.01$, the trajectories rotate forming a closed surface, the flow of the vector field forms an attractor limit cycle. By varying a, different phase surfaces are obtained (see Figs. 8, 9, 10, 11 and 12).

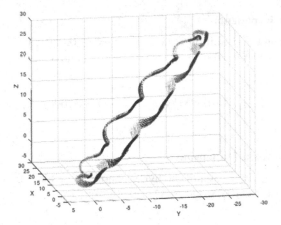

Fig. 8. When $a = 0.01$, the flow of the vector field rotates around an attractor limit cycle.

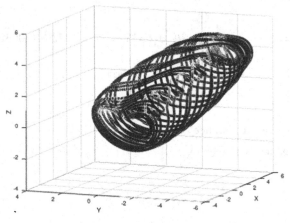

Fig. 9. When the $a = 0.1$, the flow of the vector field is compact and invariant.

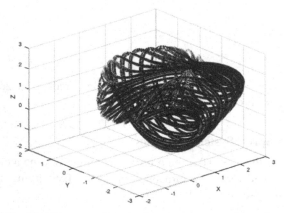

Fig. 10. When $a = 0.5$, the flow is compact and invariant

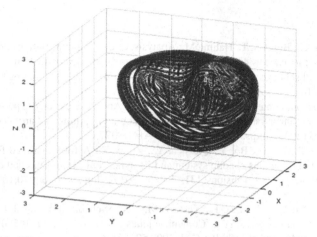

Fig. 11. When $a = 1$, a compact and invariant, and chaotic flow is observed.

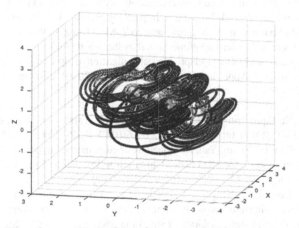

Fig. 12. When the $a = 10$, the flow of the vector field is invariant and chaotic.

4 Conclusions and Recommendations

The SystemSprott4D program implemented in Octave allowed graphical visualization of the phase surfaces of the Sprott type A system in four dimensions. In addition, the program allows graphing trajectories of initial conditions, attractor limit cycles to later observe the qualitative behavior of the system flow.

The Sprott system type A in 4D shows sensitivity in the initial conditions, presents three negative and one positive Lyapunov exponents, and has a fractional dimension. When a = 0.0, the flow forms a limit cycle, and when the parameter a values approach one, the flow is compact and invariant, and its volume is maximum. The flow is invariant for values a > 1, and its volume tends to zero for values of $z < 0$.

References

1. Benkouider, K., Bouden, T., Halimi, M.: Analysis, circuit implementation and active control synchronization of a new 4D chaotic system with two quadratic nonlinearities. Cuarta conferencia mundial sobre sistemas complejos 4(N° 1), 1–6 (2019). https://doi.org/10.1109/ICoCS.2019.8930718
2. Escobar, E., Abramonte, R., Aliaga, A., Gutierrez, F.: An octave package to perform qualitative analysis of nonlinear ystems immersed in 4D. Machine Learning and artificial intelligence., pp. 136–145 (2020). https://doi.org/10.3233/FAIA200775
3. Fei, Y., Lei, G., Ke, G., Bo, Y., Qiuzhen, W., Zhou, Z.: A fully qualified four-wing four-dimensional autonomous chaotic system and its synchronization. Enriched data. Enhanced analytics. Evidence-led decisions 131, 79–88 (2017). https://doi.org/10.1016/j.ijleo.2016.11.067
4. Guan, L.L., Xi, Y.C., Feng, C.L., Xian, M.M.: Hyper-chaotic Canonical 4-D Chua's Circuit. Conferencia Internacional de Comunicaciones, Circuitos y Sistemas 2009, pp. 820–823 (2009). https://doi.org/10.1109/ICCCAS.2009.5250380
5. Hongyan, J., Wenxin, S., Lei, W., Guoyuan, Q.: Energy analysis of Sprott-A system and generation of a new Hamiltonian conservative chaotic system with coexisting hidden attractors. Chaos, Solitons Fractals 133, 1–9 (2020). https://doi.org/10.1016/j.chaos.2020.109635
6. Jahanshahi, H., Yousefpour, A., Munoz-Pacheco, J. M., Moroz, I., Wei, Z., Castillo, O.: A new multi-stable fractional-order four-dimensional system with self-excited and hidden chaotic attractors: dynamic analysis and adaptive synchronization using a novel fuzzy adaptive sliding mode control method. Appl. Soft Comput. J. 87, 1–15 (2020). doi.https://doi.org/10.1016/j.asoc.2019.105943
7. Shirin, P., Viet, T.P., Karthikeyan, R., Olfa, B., Sajad, J.: A New Four-Dimensional Chaotic System With No Equilibrium Point. Avances recientes en sistemas caóticos y sincronización (págs., pp. 63–76 (2019). https://doi.org/10.1016/B978-0-12-815838-8.00004-2). Elsevier
8. Si Gang, Q., Cao, H., Zhang Yan, B.: A new four-dimensional hyperchaotic Lorenz system and its adaptive control. Sociedad Física China e IOP Publishing Ltd, vol. 20(N° 1), pp. 1–9 (2011). https://doi.org/10.1088/1674-1056/20/1/010509
9. Tamba, V.K., Kengne, R., Kingni, S.T., Fotsin, H.B.: A four-dimensional chaotic system with one or without equilibrium points: dynamical analysis and its application to text encryption. Avances recientes en sistemas caóticos y sincronización, pp. 277–300 (2019). https://doi.org/10.1016/B978-0-12-815838-8.00014-5
10. Vaidyanathan, S., Tlelo-Cuautle, E., Muñoz-Pacheco, J.M., Sambas, A.: A new four-dimensional chaotic system with hidden attractor and its circuit design. In: IEEE 9th Latin American Symposium on Circuits & Systems, pp. 1–4 (2018). https://doi.org/10.1109/LASCAS.2018.8399900
11. Velezmoro, R., Ipanaqué, R.: Un modelo para visualizar objetos en 4D con el Mathematica. ECIPerú, Vol. 12(N° 2), pp. 12–18 (2015). http://reddeperuanos.com/revista/eci2015vrevista/02matematicavelezmoro.pdf
12. Kuznetsov, Y.A.: Elements of applied bifurcation theory, vol. 112. Springer (1998)
13. wiggins, S.: Introduction to applied nonlinear Dynamical systems and chaos, 2 edn., vol. 2. Springer (2003). https://doi.org/10.1007/b97481

Open Metaverse with Open Software

Damiano Perri[1,2], Marco Simonetti[1,2], Sergio Tasso[2],
and Osvaldo Gervasi[2]

[1] Department of Mathematics and Computer Science, University of Florence,
Florence, Italy
[2] Department of Mathematics and Computer Science, University of Perugia, Perugia,
Italy
osvaldo.gervasi@unipg.it

Abstract. The metaverse is an increasingly popular social interaction, gaming, and education platform. In recent years there has been a growing interest in the Metaverse by various commercial firms in order to promote economic transactions and the development of applications in the world of digital and virtual interaction. With the widespread adoption of the metaverse concept, there is a growing need for open standards and open-source code related to the metaverse to ensure interoperability and enable innovation. Open standards enable different systems to communicate and share data, while open-source code promotes collaboration and transparency in development. This manuscript describes the importance of open standards and open-source code for developing metaverse technologies. We discuss the benefits of open standards for interoperability and innovation and examine case studies of successful open-source metaverse projects. We also discuss challenges in implementing open standards and open source code in metaverse development, including intellectual property concerns and governance issues. The open standards and open source code are essential for the metaverse's growth and sustainability. The developers and policymakers should prioritize these principles to ensure a the development of inclusive and open virtual environment. Our work aims to generate immersive, multiverse reality scenarios using dedicated graphics platforms for generating virtual environments.

Keywords: Metaverse · Augmented Reality · Virtual Reality · Blender · Unity · Virtual environment

1 Introduction

The metaverse is a complex and dynamic system that requires a high degree of interoperability to function effectively. Without open standards, developers must create custom solutions for each platform, resulting in a fragmented and siloed ecosystem. Open standards like those developed by the Khronos Group and the W3C enable different platforms to communicate and share data, reducing friction and promoting innovation. Similarly, open-source code is critical for metaverse development. By making code freely available, developers can collaborate

O. Gervasi et al. (Eds.): ICCSA 2023 Workshops, LNCS 14111, pp. 583–596, 2023.
https://doi.org/10.1007/978-3-031-37126-4_37

and build on each other's work, leading to faster and more robust development. Open source code also promotes transparency and accountability, as developers can inspect the code to ensure it is secure and performs as intended. Several successful metaverse projects like OpenSimulator and Second Life have been built on open-source code and open standards. These projects have benefited from the contributions of a large and diverse community of developers, resulting in rich and engaging virtual worlds. However, implementing open standards and open-source code in metaverse development can be challenging. Intellectual property concerns can limit the adoption of open standards, while governance issues can arise when multiple stakeholders are involved in development. Additionally, concerns arise about the sustainability of open-source projects, as volunteer developers may need more resources to maintain the code long-term. Despite these challenges, open standards and open-source code are essential for the growth and sustainability of the metaverse. As the metaverse continues to evolve and expand, policymakers and developers should prioritize these principles to ensure an open and inclusive virtual environment.

2 Related Works

The term Metaverse first appeared in author Neal Stephenson's 1992 science fiction novel Snow Crash [1,2]. Regarding this novel, the author describes a sort of virtual world in which it is possible to access the whole world and in which the main characters, human beings, enter and live in a parallel virtual world through a transformation into software, in which one acts in the form of Digital Avatars, through the use of Virtual Reality (VR) equipment, to carry out actions of daily life.

Inside the virtual world, there are Digital Avatars which are the digital representation of human users within the Metaverse, where a user can create various Digital Avatars which can be of different types to each other such as, for example, they can be human Avatars, animal avatars, imaginary creature avatars. Subsequently, the Digital Avatar gradually transforms into an ideal form, which mirrors the outward appearance and reflects the ego of the human user and acquires a well-defined social role [3–5]. As regards the construction of the Digital Avatar, this is defined by the user; indeed, a reasonable reconstruction of the face is significant. It is generally based on a 3D Morphable model [6–8] generated by the Principal Component Analysis (PCA) algorithm; only the performance is limited by the amount of data and the difficulty of facial expression. In recent years, the development of deep learning technology has made it possible to subsequently improve the degree of realism of the Digital Avatar to obtain highly photo-realistic 3D face models.

Concerning a 3D body reconstruction, many techniques are possible [9–11]. One of the most famous models is MANO, which adapts to the deep learning network to prevent, when scanning or acquiring data of the whole body, the low quality of the reproduction of the hands, as they are tiny [12]. By manipulating the Digital Avatar, the user creates its animation, thanks to the real-time mapping of the user's movements, thus creating interactions [13,14]. Creating the virtual 3D scene [15] within the Metaverse is possible using two alternative ways: *physics-based construction* or *design-based construction*; both include the initialization phase, modelling and rendering. By studying in detail the construction of the virtual scene based on physics, laser scans are used to create digital twins whose name turns out to be 3D reconstructions [16].

Inside the Metaverse, there are two fundamental sources of information: one turns out to be the information from inputs from the real world, such as the information captured in the real world and visualized in the virtual world, and the information from the outputs of the virtual worlds, such as the information which the Digital Avatars, various digital objects and services of the virtual world generate. Considering the large amount of data, there is a need for authentication and access control, as well as data reliability, traceability and data privacy within the Metaverse [17,18]. From this, it is deduced that information is the central resource of the Metaverse and that it will eventually allow the coexistence of the virtual world with that of the real world. Social networks with mutual interactions between human beings interconnect human society [19]. Thus, the Metaverse shows singular characteristics that fully define it.

- *Immersivity*: it allows the user to feel completely immersed in the virtual world created by the computer in real-time. At the same time, it is essential to access the Metaverse through any device and browser [20], which respects the established specification (client-based rendering), and to allow more Digital Avatars to interact with other Avatars digital assets on multiple servers and allow users to search, view, trade and delete digital assets. In order to fortify the concept of greater immersion, some accessories are presented, for the future, which will allow more incredible sensation within the Metaverse to allow greater immersion [21]. Many companies are working on various innovations, such as the creation of a Metaskin [22,23]; this accessory enhances sensory sensation; this involves the use of a rubber containing a magnetic molecule, which is combined with Artificial Intelligence (AI) to allow the tactile sensation; this type of innovation is also extremely expensive today and in the development stage. Subsequently, the Meta bracelet is presented; when worn, this tool continuously traces the communication of the human nerve between the brain and the nerve. This tool is also based on Artificial Intelligence (AI). For a more excellent tactile sensation, meta gloves have been designed to improve the sensation of perception of objects or things touched. However, all these accessories are currently undergoing further studies and improvements.
- *Hyperspatiability*: it refers to breaking the limitations of time and space, as each user can move freely through various worlds with different spatiotemporal characteristics, thus allowing the experimentation of several different timelines, such as being able to experience set in past periods of history to experiences set in futuristic environments.
- *Sustainability*: it turns out to be particularly full of challenges, as, for one part, it should be an open economic cycle to allow the continuous interest

or curiosity of the user for the creation of new digital content or new digital innovations; on the other hand it should be a decentralized system to allow persistence over time and prevent it from being controlled exclusively by some entities [24].

- *Interpolarity*: it means that virtual world users can freely move through any sub-Metaverse simultaneously in different scenes and with different modes of interaction without interrupting the virtual experience [25, 26].
- *Scalability*: it concerns the ability to manage multiple users and Virtual Avatars simultaneously, from the complexity of the scenes and the various modes of interaction, all with efficiency [27–31].
- *Heterogeneity*: it includes all the distinct implementations, distinct interfaces, types of data, communications, such as cellular and satellite communications, and the diversity of the human psyche of every human being [32].

Therefore, all these characteristics lead to a new space for social communication, with a high degree of freedom and a highly immersive view of the world. Virtual reality (VR) and Augmented reality (AR) are pillars in constructing the new world of Metaverse and have a wide range of applications across different fields. Some of the most common uses of VR include:

- *Gaming*: It provides an immersive experience to gamers, allowing them to feel as if they are a part of the game world. Indeed, one of the most popular uses of VR is in gaming [33].
- *Education and training*: VR can be used for educational [34, 35] and training purposes [36, 37].
- *Tourism and travel*: VR can be used to provide virtual tours of places that are difficult to access or that no longer exist. This includes virtual tours of historical sites, museums, and even space [38, 39].
- *Sports*: VR can be used to simulate different sports environments, allowing athletes to train in a more realistic and immersive setting [40].
- *Architecture and design*: VR can be used to create 3D models of buildings and structures, allowing architects and designers to visualize their projects in a more immersive way [41, 42].
- *Therapy and mental health*: VR can be used to treat anxiety disorders, phobias, and PTSD by creating a safe and controlled environment for patients to face their fears [43, 44] but even to help patients in rehabilitation [45, 46].
- *Marketing and advertising*: VR can be used to create immersive experiences for consumers, allowing them to interact with products and services in a more engaging way [47].
- *Art and entertainment*: VR can be used to create interactive art installations and immersive theatrical experiences.

3   The Proposed Solution

The development of Virtual Reality and Augmented Reality applications is constantly increasing. Creating a virtual world that is tangible to users and easy to manage requires special hardware/software tools and trained professionals who are able to develop and then over time maintain the IT and software infrastructure needed to deliver services to users. The main software that developers must use when creating virtual worlds is the Video Game Engine, i.e. an application that allows the management of three-dimensional models, the simulation of lighting in real time and not, the use of any special graphic or sound effects, and above all the possibility of making the user interact with this virtual world using various input devices. These softwares are mainly used for the creation of video games, but can also be used for cinema, advertising and much more. Moreover, the video game product itself respects many of the characteristics sought in the Metaverse, making it the perfect base from which to start and then customise it according to each case.

Today, there are many graphics engines that can be adapted to the different needs of developers. The characteristics of a graphics engine vary depending on the target group you want to reach and the type of applications you want to realise. For the creation of complex three-dimensional virtual environments, the most widely used graphics engines are Unity[1] and Unreal Engine[2], which offer a complete development environment to manage the resources needed to create interconnected and customisable environments. The two engines have aspects in common and some differences. Both make it possible to create interactive virtual worlds and to take care of both the graphical aspects and the aspects of interaction with the scenario and ambient sound. If one wants to achieve a very high degree of graphical detail, Unreal Engine, particularly in the recently released version 5, allows for excellent results, but it will be necessary to take into account that users will have to be equipped with very high level hardware to fully enjoy the gaming experience realised. Unity, on the other hand, has a lower learning curve, a larger community, and allows the creation of applications with a very good graphic quality, suitable for both mobile applications and native applications for users' operating systems. Very high graphical results can also be achieved with Unity, but the time developers will have to dedicate to this will usually be greater. Preferences between graphics engines will depend on the implementation choices and objectives of the final product. Unity is suitable for the creation of complex environments and interactions using the programming language C# and offers several paid and/or free addons that can be downloaded from the official store. Unreal Engine, on the other hand, departs from its flexibility with programming languages in favour of complex and layered functions that maintain high graphical fidelity and an expensive but extremely realistic lighting system.

These graphics engines either do not offer any tools for the creation of three-dimensional models or offer simplified solutions that are only useful for a few special cases. Therefore, they will necessarily have to be flanked by professional three-dimensional modelling software in order to be able to create the 'physical' appearance of the environment in question using simple import-export

---

[1] https://unity.com/.
[2] https://www.unrealengine.com.

mechanisms of the available resources. Programs such as Blender[3], Cinema 4D[4], Autodesk Maya[5] and ZBrush[6] belong to this category, and are among the most well-known and used in the sector, both at a professional and amateur level. Thanks to the synergetic use of these tools, it is possible to obtain most of the virtual products available on the market, including video games, professional and non-professional simulators, illustrations and animated sequences in film or television series format.

With a view to creating increasingly complex environments, developers should take into account the enormous potential offered by the open source world. Among the aforementioned software, Blender is in fact distributed free of charge and under an Open Source licence by the *Blender Foundation*, and has been providing developers with a stable and reliable environment to create their works since 1998. Open source software plays a crucial role in the development of the metaverse and other three-dimensional environments. One example of this is the popular virtual world platform Second Life[7], which was released with open source code. Second Life was developed by Linden Lab, the teams has made their entire client software open source, allowing developers to create their own modifications and extensions. This has led to a thriving community of developers who have built everything from custom avatar animations to entire regions within the virtual world. The openness of the Second Life platform has not only fostered innovation and creativity but has also ensured the longevity of the platform by allowing it to evolve with changing technology and user needs.

Another example of the importance of open source in the metaverse is the OpenSimulator project[8]. OpenSimulator is an open-source software platform that allows users to create their own virtual worlds, similar to Second Life. However, unlike Second Life, OpenSimulator is completely open source, meaning that anyone can modify and improve the code. This has resulted in a diverse ecosystem of virtual worlds, each with its own unique features and user community. Moreover, the open nature of the OpenSimulator project has encouraged collaboration between developers and users, resulting in a community-driven platform that is responsive to user needs.

Allowing developers and students to freely access and modify the existing code of the metaverse projects, open source software can reduce barriers to entry and encouraged innovation. This will led to a proliferation of new virtual world platforms and applications, each with its own strengths and weaknesses. Morehover, this competition will led to better software for users, as developers are incentivized to create more user-friendly and feature-rich platforms.

Another key advantage of open source software in the metaverse is the ability to audit and verify the code. Because the source code is freely available,

---

[3] https://www.blender.org/.
[4] https://www.maxon.net/it/cinema-4d.
[5] https://www.autodesk.it/products/maya/overview.
[6] https://pixologic.com/.
[7] https://secondlife.com/.
[8] http://opensimulator.org.

the communities can inspect the code to ensure that it is secure and free from malicious code. This will help to prevent security breaches and other issues that could compromise user data or the stability of the virtual environment.

Today, a number of large companies and multinationals, such as Meta, are investing large amounts of capital in the development of hardware and software for virtual worlds. It is important to reflect and ponder on the implications these environments will have on people's lives and social relationships. Is it really acceptable to immerse ourselves in environments where there is no control over the privacy of our data and where we are unable to know what is being done with what is being collected in real time by the hardware being used?

Our research group pushes and coordinates many students both within the Bachelor's degree courses and in the thesis courses that aim to realise three-dimensional environments and works. First of all, it must be kept in mind that there is a big difference between the licence under which a graphics engine is released and the licence under which an application (such as a Metaverse) is released. Even if the graphics engines used have closed or partially closed source codes, we feel it is important to teach students the importance of sharing the source code of the projects with appropriate licences such as the GPL or MIT via secure and reliable platforms such as GitHub[9].

4   Case Studies

We present some use cases of metaverses developed by our research team also in collaboration with students in the Virtual Reality Systems course of the Computer Science degree program at the University of Perugia[10].

Although such projects are developed by young students who do not yet have the maturity of professional developers, they show how it is possible to implement very interesting use cases, often related to individual hobbies and passions, that introduce the realisation of metaverses at zero cost and with a very high degree of portability. The use of commercial software, if it is deemed appropriate to adopt it, will enable these young people to achieve higher quality standards and to embark on a successful professional life.

4.1   Virtual Theatre

This use case is extremely interesting and suggestive and originated from the passion for dance and classical music culture. It was implemented using Blender for the creation of shapes and models, which were then imported into Unity for movement and interaction management. Figure 1 shows some images of the scenario and a dancer performing dancing to a piece of classical music.

---

[9] https://github.com/.

[10] The course has been delivered since 2000 and introduces students to the realisation of virtual worlds with Web3D, Blender and Unity technologies. Particular attention is paid to achieving high quality standards in terms of scene realism, navigation speed and effective user interaction, optimising all aspects of project development.

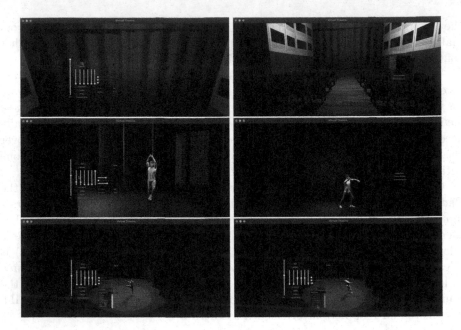

Fig. 1. Scenes of the virtual theatre and of a boy dancing.

This metaverse allows user interaction in the playback of the music track, having all the tools to control the various parameters and control the dancer's movements.

4.2   Monuments and Landscape Views

Metaverses that reproduce landscape views, physical meeting corners in cities, and areas with monuments, constitute extremely stimulating scenarios where virtual visitors can experience pleasant interactions. These environments also lend themselves very well to conveying important social and cultural messages and keeping traditions and cultures alive, which over time tend to disappear due to changed habits and lifestyles.

This approach allows for the development of digital culture. It favours the digitization process of cultural heritage, which would bring significant advantages on a national scale, particularly in Italy and Europe.

4.3   Rooms and Places of Entertainment

During the period of the COVID-19 pandemic, some students recreated home environments such as virtual rooms, living rooms or offices and tried to recreate social and entertaining situations, as it was not possible to go to social venues due to government restrictions. The Fig. 2 shows 4 projects realised during the Virtual Reality course at the University of Perugia.

Fig. 2. Scenes of Virtual environments developed during the COVID-19

The realisation of an interactive environment must necessarily include the integration of features that enable users to communicate such as text and/or voice chat. In one project, which we have made publicly available on GitHub[11],

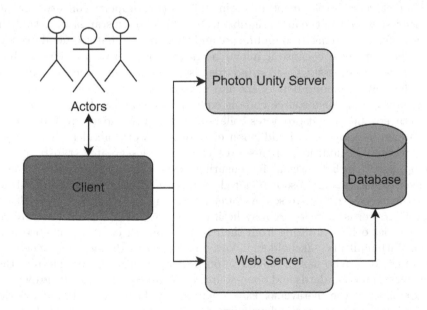

Fig. 3. Metaverse infrastructure

---

[11] https://github.com/DamianoP/openMetaverse.

we have created an environment where users can connect and communications are managed by a backend server with a MySQL database.

A significant piece of the application is shown in Fig. 3.

Users use a client, which is generated by the compilation of the metaverse from the Unity project. The client connects to an Apache Webserver on which PHP code is executed. The Webserver allows users to authenticate themselves with a username and password and checks that they are registered users within the database. If users are authenticated, they access the metaverse. Voice chat and text chat are then provided by a second server called Photon Unity Server.

5   Conclusions and Future Work

The metaverse is a digital realm that has become increasingly popular for social interaction, gaming, and education. The widespread adoption of the metaverse concept has created a growing interest among various commercial firms to promote economic transactions and the development of applications in the world of digital and virtual interaction. However, in order to ensure interoperability and enable innovation, there is a need for open standards and open-source code related to the metaverse. This article has discussed the importance of open standards and open-source code for developing metaverse technologies. We have highlighted the benefits of open standards for interoperability and innovation and examined case studies of successful open-source metaverse projects. In addition, we have discussed challenges in implementing open standards and open-source code in metaverse development, including intellectual property concerns and governance issues. One of the more significant benefits of open standards is that they enable different systems to communicate and share data. That is crucial for developing the metaverse because it allows users to move between different virtual environments seamlessly. Open standards also promote innovation by encouraging collaboration among developers and allowing for the creation of new tools and technologies. Open-source code is equally essential for the development of the metaverse because it promotes collaboration and transparency. Open-source code allows developers to build upon each other's work, accelerating the pace of innovation. In addition, open-source code provides greater transparency in development, which is crucial for ensuring the security and privacy of users. However, challenges are also associated with implementing open standards and open-source code in metaverse development. One major challenge is intellectual property concerns. Developers may hesitate to share their work if they are concerned about others profiting from their ideas. Another challenge is governance issues. With multiple stakeholders involved in metaverse development, there may be conflicts over who has the final say on development decisions. Despite these challenges, open standards and open-source code are essential for the growth and sustainability of the metaverse. Developers and policymakers should prioritise these principles to ensure the development of inclusive and open virtual environments. Our work aims to generate immersive, multiverse reality scenarios using dedicated graphics platforms to develop virtual environments. By incorporating open standards and open-source code into the development of the metaverse, we hope to create a more collaborative and transparent environment that will promote innovation and benefit users.

Acronyms

The following acronyms are used in this manuscript:

AI Artificial Intelligence
AP Application Programming Interface
AR Augmented Reality
GPL GNU General Public License
IT Information Technology
JS JavaScript
KB KiloByte
MB MegaByte
MIT Massachusetts Institute of Technology
PCA Principal Component Analysis
PTSD Post-traumatic stress disorder
VR Virtual Reality
W3C World Wide Web Consortium

References

1. Neal Stephenson. Snow crash: A novel. Spectra (2003). ISBN 0-553-08853-X
2. Mystakidis, S.: Metaverse. Encyclopedia **2**(1), 486–497 (2022)
3. Park, S.-M., Kim, Y.-G.: A metaverse: taxonomy, components, applications, and open challenges. IEEE Access **10**, 4209–4251 (2022)
4. Lee, L.-H., et al.: All one needs to know about metaverse: a complete survey on technological singularity, virtual ecosystem, and research agenda. arXiv preprint arXiv:2110.05352 (2021)
5. Duan, H., Li, J., Fan, S., Lin, Z., Wu, X., Cai, W.: Metaverse for social good: a university campus prototype. In: Proceedings of the 29th ACM International Conference on Multimedia, pp. 153–161 (2021)
6. Wang, P., Tong, X., Du, Y., Li, J., Hu, W., Zhang, Y.: Augmented makeover based on 3d morphable model. In: Proceedings of the 19th ACM International Conference on Multimedia, pp. 1569–1572 (2011)
7. Zheng, Y., et al.: Im avatar: implicit morphable head avatars from videos. In: Proceedings of the IEEE/CVF Conference on Computer Vision and Pattern Recognition, pp. 13545–13555 (2022)
8. Ploumpis, S., et al.: Towards a complete 3D morphable model of the human head. IEEE Trans. Pattern Anal. Mach. Intell. **43**(11), 4142–4160 (2020)
9. Barmpoutis, A.: Tensor body: real-time reconstruction of the human body and avatar synthesis from RGB-D. IEEE Trans. Cybern. **43**(5), 1347–1356 (2013)
10. Jiang, B., Hong, Y., Bao, H., Zhang, J.: Selfrecon: self reconstruction your digital avatar from monocular video. In: Proceedings of the IEEE/CVF Conference on Computer Vision and Pattern Recognition, pp. 5605–5615 (2022)

11. Dong, J., et al.: Totalselfscan: learning full-body avatars from self-portrait videos of faces, hands, and bodies. In: Advances in Neural Information Processing Systems (2022)

12. Chen, X., Wang, B., Shum, H.-Y.: Hand avatar: free-pose hand animation and rendering from monocular video. arXiv preprint arXiv:2211.12782 (2022)

13. Shum, H.P.H., Komura, T., Yamazaki, S.: Simulating interactions of avatars in high dimensional state space. In: Proceedings of the 2008 Symposium on Interactive 3D Graphics and Games, pp. 131–138 (2008)

14. Shum, H.P.H., Komura, T., Yamazaki, S.: Simulating competitive interactions using singly captured motions. In: Proceedings of the 2007 ACM Symposium on Virtual Reality Software and Technology, pp. 65–72 (2007)

15. Wang, Y., et al.: A survey on metaverse: fundamentals, security, and privacy. IEEE Commun. Surv. Tutor. (2022)

16. Ning, H., et al.: A survey on metaverse: the state-of-the-art, technologies, applications, and challenges. arXiv preprint arXiv:2111.09673 (2021)

17. Fernandez, C.B., Hui, P.: Life, the metaverse and everything: an overview of privacy, ethics, and governance in metaverse. In 2022 IEEE 42nd International Conference on Distributed Computing Systems Workshops (ICDCSW), pp. 272–277. IEEE (2022)

18. Pietro, R.D., Cresci, S.: Metaverse: security and privacy issues. In: 2021 Third IEEE International Conference on Trust, Privacy and Security in Intelligent Systems and Applications (TPS-ISA), pp. 281–288. IEEE (2021)

19. Cheng, R., Wu, N., Varvello, M., Chen, S., Han, B.: Are we ready for metaverse? a measurement study of social virtual reality platforms. In: Proceedings of the 22nd ACM Internet Measurement Conference, pp. 504–518 (2022)

20. Lee, L.-H., Zhou, P., Braud, T., Hui, P.: What is the metaverse? An immersive cyberspace and open challenges. arXiv preprint arXiv:2206.03018 (2022)

21. Tayal, S., Rajagopal, K., Mahajan, V.: Virtual reality based metaverse of gamification. In: 2022 6th International Conference on Computing Methodologies and Communication (ICCMC), pp. 1597–1604. IEEE (2022)

22. Tong, L., et al.: An acoustic meta-skin insulator. Adv. Mater. **32**(37), 2002251 (2020)

23. Yang, S., Liu, P., Yang, M., Wang, Q., Song, J., Dong, L.: From flexible and stretchable meta-atom to metamaterial: a wearable microwave meta-skin with tunable frequency selective and cloaking effects. Sci. Rep. **6**(1), 21921 (2016)

24. Jauhiainen, J.S., Krohn, C., Junnila, J.: Metaverse and sustainability: Systematic review of scientific publications until 2022 and beyond. Sustainability **15**(1), 346 (2023)

25. Hashash, O., Chaccour, C., Saad, W., Sakaguchi, K., Yu,T.: Towards a decentralized metaverse: synchronized orchestration of digital twins and sub-metaverses. arXiv preprint arXiv:2211.14686 (2022)

26. Rawat, D.B., Alami, H.E.: Metaverse: requirements, architecture, standards, status, challenges, and perspectives. IEEE Internet Things Mag. **6**(1), 14–18 (2023)

27. Perri, D., Simonetti, M., Gervasi, O.: Deploying efficiently modern applications on cloud. Electronics **11**(3) (2022). ISSN 2079-9292. https://doi.org/10.3390/electronics11030450.https://www.mdpi.com/2079-9292/11/3/450

28. Perri, D., Simonetti, M., Gervasi, O., Tasso, S.: Chapter 4 - high-performance computing and computational intelligence applications with a multi-chaos perspective. In: Karaca, Y., Baleanu, D., Zhang, Y.-D., Gervasi, O., Moonis, M. (eds.) Multi-Chaos, Fractal and Multi-Fractional Artificial Intelligence of Different Complex Systems, pp. 55–76. Academic Press (2022). ISBN 978-0-323-90032-4. https://doi.org/10.1016/B978-0-323-90032-4.00010-9. https://www.sciencedirect.com/science/article/pii/B9780323900324000109
29. Dionisio, J.D.N., Burns III, W.G., Gilbert, R..: 3D virtual worlds and the metaverse: current status and future possibilities. ACM Comput. Surv. (CSUR) **45**(3), 1–38 (2013)
30. Lim, W.Y.B., et al.: Realizing the metaverse with edge intelligence: a match made in heaven. IEEE Wirel. Commun. (2022)
31. Perri, D., Simonetti, M., Tasso, S., Ragni, F., Gervasi, O.: Implementing a scalable and elastic computing environment based on cloud containers. In: Gervasi, O., et al. (eds.) ICCSA 2021. LNCS, vol. 12949, pp. 676–689. Springer, Cham (2021). https://doi.org/10.1007/978-3-030-86653-2_49
32. Tang, F., Chen, X., Zhao, M., Kato, N.: The roadmap of communication and networking in 6g for the metaverse. IEEE Wirel. Commun. (2022)
33. Santucci, F., Frenguelli, F., De Angelis, A., Cuccaro, I., Perri, D., Simonetti, M.: An immersive open source environment using Godot. In: Gervasi, O., et al. (eds.) ICCSA 2020. LNCS, vol. 12255, pp. 784–798. Springer, Cham (2020). https://doi.org/10.1007/978-3-030-58820-5_56
34. Simonetti, M., Perri, D., Amato, N., Gervasi, O.: Teaching Math with the Help of Virtual Reality. In: Gervasi, O., et al. (eds.) ICCSA 2020. LNCS, vol. 12255, pp. 799–809. Springer, Cham (2020). https://doi.org/10.1007/978-3-030-58820-5_57
35. Perri, D., Simonetti, M., Tasso, S., Gervasi, O.: Learning mathematics in an immersive way. In: Castro, L.M., Cabrero, D., Heimgärtner, R. (eds.) Software Usability, chapter 1. IntechOpen, Rijeka (2021). https://doi.org/10.5772/intechopen.96533.URL https://doi.org/10.5772/intechopen.96533
36. Gervasi, O., Perri, D., Simonetti, M.: Strategies and system implementations for secure electronic written exams. IEEE Access **10**, 20559–20570 (2022). https://doi.org/10.1109/ACCESS.2022.3150860
37. Perri, D., Simonetti, M., Gervasi, O.: Synthetic data generation to speed-up the object recognition pipeline. Electronics **11**(1) (2022). ISSN 2079–9292. https://doi.org/10.3390/electronics11010002. https://www.mdpi.com/2079-9292/11/1/2
38. Gervasi, O., Perri, D., Simonetti, M., Tasso, S.: Strategies for the digitalization of cultural heritage. In: Gervasi, O., Murgante, B., Misra, S., Rocha, A.M.A.C., Garau, C. (eds.) Computational Science and Its Applications - ICCSA 2022 Workshops, pp. 486–502. Springer, Cham (2022). https://doi.org/10.1007/978-3-031-10592-0_35. ISBN 978-3-031-10592-0
39. Yung, R., Khoo-Lattimore, C., Potter, L.E.: Virtual reality and tourism marketing: Conceptualizing a framework on presence, emotion, and intention. Current Issues in Tourism **24**(11), 1505–1525 (2021)
40. Neumann, D.L., et al.: A systematic review of the application of interactive virtual reality to sport. Virtual Real. **22**, 183–198 (2018)
41. Frost, P., Warren, P.: Virtual reality used in a collaborative architectural design process. In: 2000 IEEE Conference on Information Visualization. An International Conference on Computer Visualization and Graphics, pp. 568–573. IEEE (2000)
42. Racz, A., Zilizi, G.: VR aided architecture and interior design. In: 2018 International Conference on Advances in Computing and Communication Engineering (ICACCE), pp. 11–16. IEEE (2018)

43. Perri, D., Simonetti, M., Gervasi, O.: Deploying serious games for cognitive reha- bilitation. Computers **11**(7) (2022). ISSN 2073–431X. https://doi.org/10.3390/ computers11070103. https://www.mdpi.com/2073-431X/11/7/103

44. Perri, D., Simonetti, M., Gervasi, O., Amato, N · A mobile app to help people affected by visual snow. In: Gervasi, O., Murgante, B., Misra, S., Rocha, A.M.A.C., Garau, C. (eds.) Computational Science and Its Applications - ICCSA 2022 Work- shops, pp. 473–485. Springer, Cham (2022). ISBN 978-3-031-10592-0. https://doi. org/10.1007/978-3-031-10592-0_34

45. Perri, D., Fortunelli, M., Simonetti, M., Magni, R., Carloni, J., Gervasi, O.: Rapid prototyping of virtual reality cognitive exercises in a tele-rehabilitation context. Electronics **10**(4) (2021). ISSN 2079–9292. https://doi.org/10.3390/ electronics10040457. https://www.mdpi.com/2079-9292/10/4/457

46. Benedetti, P., Perri, D., Simonetti, M., Gervasi, O., Reali, G., Femminella, M.: Skin cancer classification using inception network and transfer learning. In: Gervasi, O., et al. (eds.) ICCSA 2020. LNCS, vol. 12249, pp. 536–545. Springer, Cham (2020). https://doi.org/10.1007/978-3-030-58799-4_39

47. Ryan, C.: Virtual reality in marketing. Direct Mark. **63**(12), 57–57 (2001)

Aerial and Terrestrial LiDAR: Comparisons and Accuracies

Gabriele Garnero(✉)

Interuniversity Department of Regional and Urban Studies and Planning,
Politecnico e Università degli Studi di Torino, Turin, Italy
gabriele.garnero@unito.it

Abstract. Based on the availability of data produced during the activities carried out for the creation of the new topographic database [DBT] of the Municipality of Genoa, the integration methods between aerial laser scanner and terrestrial laser scanner surveys are evaluated for a comprehensive modeling of the territory.

In the recent past, methodologies for acquiring territorial data that generate point clouds have become available: aerial and terrestrial laser scanning, SLAM acquisitions, and the production of point clouds obtained through photogrammetric correlation.

The purpose of this paper is to highlight, based on the conducted experiences and available data, the activities carried out that involve the potential for mutual integration between aerial and terrestrial LiDAR surveys.

The mutual accuracies and the merging methods between the available datasets are also assessed.

Keywords: ALS · TLS · LiDAR

1 Introduction

Within the National Operational Programme for Metropolitan Cities PON METRO 2014–2020 - Axis 1 "Metropolitan Digital Agenda," co-financed with European Union resources (European Structural and Investment Funds) and national resources (Agency for Territorial Cohesion), the Municipality of Genoa has initiated the modernization of its territorial database, aiming to integrate all the information concerning the entity's territorial objects.

This project involves the implementation of a computerized service system for the exposure/use of the information stored in various subsystems, including management systems, linked through certified unique identifiers based on the properly re-engineered and updated Topographic Database of the entity.

To carry out the aforementioned, it is necessary to have an updated Topographic Database, which is an essential support for activities related to intervention planning, prevention of hydrogeological disasters, and overall knowledge of the territory.

Therefore, the production of the Topographic Database at a scale of 1:1000 for urban areas and 1:2000 for extra-urban territory has been initiated. This entails an update starting from the available database, which was previously converted according to the specifications of the DM 10.11.2011 "Technical rules for defining the content specifications

O. Gervasi et al. (Eds.): ICCSA 2023 Workshops, LNCS 14111, pp. 597–607, 2023.
https://doi.org/10.1007/978-3-031-37126-4_38

of geotopographic databases" (Official Gazette no. 48 of 27/02/2012 - Supplementary ordinary no. 37).

2 Aerial and Terrestrial LiDAR

Aerial LiDAR involves the use of laser sensors mounted on aircraft, typically planes or helicopters. These sensors emit laser pulses towards the ground and measure the time taken for the laser to reflect back. Using this time information, along with the aircraft's position data, it is possible to create a three-dimensional model of the terrain with extensive coverage. Aerial Lidar is particularly suitable for large-scale acquisitions such as land mapping, digital elevation model generation, and identification of topographic features on a large scale. It offers fast coverage and high resolution, but accuracy can vary depending on the point density and the precision of the aircraft's orientation and positioning.

On the other hand, terrestrial lidar involves the use of lidar instruments mounted on tripods or ground vehicles, which are positioned on the ground at regular intervals. These instruments directly measure laser reflection points within their range, creating a high-density point cloud in three dimensions. Terrestrial lidar is particularly suitable for detailed and highly precise acquisitions, such as surveying buildings, monuments, infrastructure, and specific areas of interest. It offers high accuracy due to the close distance between the instrument and the object being measured, but the coverage is limited to the area where the instrument is positioned.

The accuracy of lidar depends on various factors, including the point density, the precision of the positioning and orientation system, the accuracy of point coordinate calculations, and the correction of systematic errors. In general, both aerial and terrestrial lidar can provide high measurement accuracies, with errors ranging from a few centimeters to a few decimeters, depending on the project specifications and operational conditions.

In addition, it should be noted that transitioning from a traditional aerial view to a ground-level view produces a change in the quantity and level of detail of the captured features. Therefore, it is currently appropriate to proceed with a true integration of acquisitions, each capable of capturing specific objects:

- on one hand, aerial LiDAR captures extensive territorial surfaces, roads, and building roofs but lacks details on facades related to capture geometry aspects;
- on the other hand, ground surveys (static or SLAM-based) capture details at eye level, where many specific features necessary for technical applications are present.

3 Characteristics of the Production in the City of Genoa

Within the mentioned specifications, the production in question has distinctive characteristics related to the use of innovative tools and methodologies. It involves the creation of cartographic materials, including unconventional ones, for which it is currently recognized that the City of Genoa has the most up-to-date and innovative database at the national level.

The production in Genoa has served as inspiration for ongoing productions in other important cities at the national level, such as Milan, Turin, and others.

The production was carried out by a Temporary Grouping of Companies composed of *SIT - Servizi di Informazione Territoriale* S.r.l. (lead company based in Noci - BA, now Mermec), *Corvallis SpA a socio unico* (Padua), *Arcadia Sistemi Informativi Territoriali S.r.l.* (Milan), and *Aerosigma S.r.l. a socio unico* (Grottaglie - TA).

3.1 Aerial Photogrammetric Surveys and Aerial LiDAR

The project specification included an integrated aerial photogrammetric survey combined with an aerial LiDAR survey, with the latter being crucial for accurate terrain modeling in vegetated areas and for generating digital surface models (DSMs) and digital terrain models (DTMs) needed for hydrogeological studies. This was one of the main objectives of the project due to the well-known challenges posed by the municipal territory and the Liguria region as a whole.

The aerial survey was conducted using a *Vexcel UltraCam Eagle Mark 3* photogrammetric camera mounted on a *Vulcanair P68 Victor B* twin-engine aircraft (Fig. 1).

Approximately 5000 RGBN photographs were captured, with a ground sampling distance (GSD) of 5 cm for a scale of 1:1000 and 9 cm for the remaining area. The survey achieved high overlaps, ranging from 80–90% in the longitudinal direction and 60% in the transverse direction, due to the unique geographical features and the presence of a large and densely populated urban core.

The LiDAR survey, on the other hand, was carried out using a *Riegl LMS-Q1560* sensor. The point density was set at 55 points per square meter for urban areas and 40 points per square meter for the rest of the territory.

Fig. 1. Main devices used for the photogrammetric and LiDAR acquisitions: *Vexcel UltraCam Eagle Mark 3* and *Riegl LMS-Q1560*

The high quality of the employed sensors allowed for achieving accuracies on the checkpoints of less than 10 cm for photogrammetry and residuals in the Z-axis (vertical) of approximately 5 cm for the LiDAR strips. These values are entirely compatible with the requirements of the project specifications and align with the standards stated in international literature (Fig. 2).

The achieved accuracies demonstrate the effectiveness and precision of the data acquisition process. The photogrammetric outputs, with accuracies below 10 cm on the checkpoints, indicate the reliability of the generated orthophotos, digital surface models (DSMs), and digital terrain models (DTMs). Similarly, the LiDAR residuals in the Z-axis within the range of 5 cm affirm the accuracy and vertical precision of the captured LiDAR point clouds.

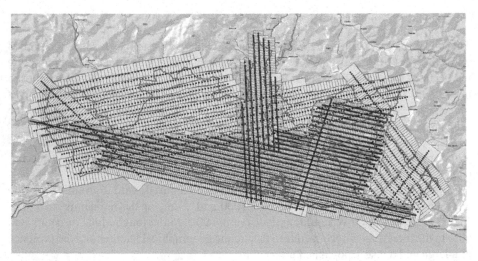

Fig. 2. Index of aerial shots taken in the territory of the Municipality of Genoa: capture centers and frame overlaps

These accuracies are in line with the industry standards and reflect the adherence to the specified requirements, ensuring the reliability and usability of the acquired data for various applications and analyses.

3.2   MMS Survey

MMS (Mobile Mapping System) surveys refer to a geospatial data acquisition system carried out using vehicles equipped with advanced sensors and positioning technologies. These vehicles are equipped with high-resolution cameras, LiDAR systems, and GPS/IMU to accurately record the 3D geometry of the surrounding environment as the vehicle moves along a designated trajectory.

During MMS surveys, the vehicle collects data from multiple sources simultaneously. The cameras capture high-resolution images that can be used to generate orthophotos and detect objects and details in the environment. LiDAR sensors emit laser pulses to measure the distance to surrounding objects and create high-density three-dimensional point clouds. The GPS/IMU system records the real-time position and orientation of the vehicle, allowing for georeferencing of the collected data.

MMS surveys are widely used for mapping roads, urban areas, infrastructure, and other complex environments in an efficient and accurate manner. This data acquisition approach enables extensive and detailed coverage, facilitating in-depth analysis and the creation of precise three-dimensional models of the surrounding environment.

The dense nature of the urban territory led the Municipal Administration to request an MMS (Mobile Mapping System) survey using a vehicle (*Videocar*) equipped with a *Riegl Vux1* LiDAR sensor integrated with GNSS/IMU apparatus (Fig. 3).

The acquisition density on the facades of urban buildings reached approximately 4,000 to 5,000 points per square meter. Additionally, a *Ladybug* spherical camera (with an 8,000 × 3,000 pixel sensor) was used for 360° panoramic photography, covering all city road sections (Figs. 4 and 6).

During the survey production, these devices were supplemented with more manageable equipment to account for the unique morphology of the territory, such as pedestrian areas and narrow alleys ("*caruggi*"):

- the narrowest alleys were surveyed using backpack-mounted equipment provided by Gexcel. Leveraging SLAM (Simultaneous Localization and Mapping) technology, laser data was acquired using a *Velodyne* sensor, resulting in point densities of approximately 3,000 to 4,000 points per square meter;
- in areas inaccessible to the Videocar, where SLAM technology would not yield optimal results due to the distance from the details to be surveyed, a static Leica scanner was employed. The scanner stations were repeated every 20–30 m, resulting in point densities reaching 20,000 to 30,000 points per square meter, which were subsequently thinned out for final delivery. A high-resolution reflex camera (20,000 × 10,000 pixels) was used to acquire information for coloring the point cloud.

Fig. 3. Main devices used for MMS (Mobile Mapping System) acquisitions: Videocar equipped with the *Vux1* LiDAR sensor and the *Ladybug* camera (on the left) and the *Gexcel Backpack* with the *Velodyne* LiDAR sensor (on the right)

Fig. 4. Tracks of acquisition trajectories from Videocar

4 Cartographic Products

The elaborations have led to the creation of traditional cartographic outputs:

- Digital Base Map (DBT) according to the shared specifications of the ex D.M. 10/11/2011;
- Digital Surface Model (DSM) level 6 for extra-urban areas and level 7 for urbanized areas (Fig. 5);
- True orthophoto.

The focus of this document is not so much the description of traditional products but the analysis of innovative supports that are not yet widely used in the national territory, except for prototypical implementations. However, these innovative supports are extensively applied throughout the entire municipal territory.

4.1 Integration Between Aerial and Terrestrial LiDAR Point Clouds

The integration of aerial and terrestrial LiDAR point clouds is a process that combines data acquired from LiDAR sensors mounted on aircraft and ground-based devices. This integration allows for extensive and detailed coverage of the terrain by combining three-dimensional information from different sources.

In the integration process, aerial and terrestrial LiDAR point clouds are registered and aligned in a common reference coordinate system. This involves correcting systematic errors, processing positioning data, and identifying common reference points between the two data sources.

Once the point clouds have been integrated, the combined data can be used to create a comprehensive and accurate three-dimensional model of the terrain. This model can

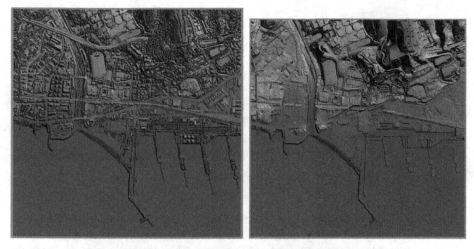

Fig. 5. DSM (Digital Surface Model) e DTM (Digital Terrain Model)

Fig. 6. Example of acquisition from Videocar

be applied in various ways, such as urban planning, land management, terrain analysis, and 3D visualization.

The integration of aerial and terrestrial LiDAR point clouds leverages the strengths of both acquisition techniques, providing a more complete and detailed view of the surrounding environment (Fig. 7).

Fig. 7. Overall point cloud

The availability of point clouds acquired from both aerial and mobile vehicle means allows for a highly detailed geometric description, but only for areas where acquisition was possible or for roads and public areas. This description incorporates the characteristics of the different acquisition points:

- on one hand, aerial LIDAR enables optimal acquisition of road surfaces and coverings.
- on the other hand, mobile LIDAR, in addition to road surfaces, provides significant coverage of building facades facing streets and public spaces, excluding private areas and roof coverings (Figs. 8, 9 and 10).

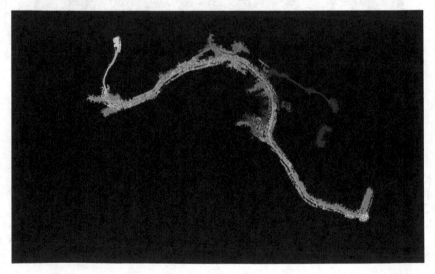

Fig. 8. Set of colored ground runs for acquisition mission: total of 21 runs - Porto Antico area.

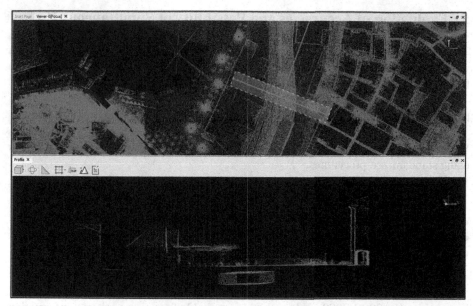

Fig. 9. Overlap between aerial (purple) and ground (orange) point clouds. (Color figure online)

Fig. 10. Overlap between aerial (purple) and ground (orange) point clouds - area of the elevated road in front of the "Bigo". (Color figure online)

5 Evaluation of Accuracies and Possibility of Simultaneous Use

The simultaneous use of different acquisitions is clearly possible only after appropriate verification activities regarding their correct georeferencing and the resulting residuals following their merging (Figs. 6 and 7).

Therefore, a significant precision analysis activity has been initiated, based on which the production of tiles obtained from the merge of different acquisitions was possible.

The accuracy analysis was performed using the dedicated tools of the Trimble Real-Works environment (version 12.4), which allowed evaluating "cloud to cloud" distances using standardized procedures.

The validation of integration possibilities between point clouds led to the following results, assessed on a significant sample across different territorial areas:

- mean planimetric residuals between different *Videocar* acquisitions: ± 2 cm
- mean altimetric residuals between different *Videocar* acquisitions: ± 2 cm
- mean altimetric residuals between *Videocar* acquisitions and aerial LiDAR acquisitions: ± 6 cm

These accuracies are highly compatible with the usual cartographic tolerances of large scales (1:1000/1:2000) and are therefore suitable for use in territorial information systems at those scales.

Acknowledgments. We would like to thank the working group SIT Applications of the Municipality of Genoa for providing the material for the experimentation of this work.

References

1. Frías, E., Previtali, M., Díaz-Vilariño, L., Scaioni, M., Lorenzo, H.: Optimal scan planning for surveying large sites with static and mobile mapping systems. ISPRS J. Photogram. Remote Sens. **192**, 13–32 (2022). ISSN 0924-2716, https://doi.org/10.1016/j.isprsjprs.2022.07.025
2. White, G., Zink, A., Codecà, L., Clarke, S.: A digital twin smart city for citizen feedback. Cities **110**, 103064 (2021). ISSN 0264-2751, https://doi.org/10.1016/j.cities.2020.103064
3. Shaohua, G., Kailun, Y., Hao, S., Kaiwei, W., Bai, J.: Review on panoramic imaging and its applications in scene understanding. IEEE Trans. Instrum. Meas. **71**, 1–34 (2022)
4. Terrone, M., Piana, P., Paliaga, G., D'Orazi, M., Faccini, F.: Coupling historical maps and LiDAR data to identify man-made landforms in urban areas. ISPRS Int. J. Geo Inf. **10**, 349 (2021). https://doi.org/10.3390/ijgi10050349
5. Chen, W., et al.: SLAM overview: from single sensor to heterogeneous fusion. Remote Sens. **14**, 6033 (2022). https://doi.org/10.3390/rs1423603
6. Schade, S., et al.: Geospatial information infrastructures. In: Guo, H., Goodchild, M.F., Annoni, A. (eds.) Manual of Digital Earth, pp. 161–190. Springer, Singapore (2020). https://doi.org/10.1007/978-981-32-9915-3_5
7. Breunig, M., et al.: Geospatial data management research: progress and future directions. ISPRS Int. J. Geo-Inf. **9**(2), 95 (2020). https://doi.org/10.3390/ijgi9020095
8. Sammartano, G., Spanò, A.: Point clouds by SLAM-based mobile mapping systems: accuracy and geometric content validation in multisensor survey and stand-alone acquisition. Appl. Geomatics **10**(4), 317–339 (2018). https://doi.org/10.1007/s12518-018-0221-7

9. Schrotter, G., Hürzeler, C.: The digital twin of the city of Zurich for urban planning. PFG – J. Photogram. Remote Sens. Geoinf. Sci. **88**(1), 99–112 (2020). https://doi.org/10.1007/s41 064-020-00092-2

10. Zhu, J., Wan, J., Wang, X., Tan, Y.: Chapter 19: An economical approach to geo-referencing 3D model for integration of BIM and GIS. In: Innovative Production and Construction, pp. 321– 334 (2019). https://doi.org/10.1142/9789813272491_001

11. Bresson, G., Alsayed, Z., Yu, L., Glaser, S.: Simultaneous localization and mapping: a survey of current trends in autonomous driving. IEEE Trans. Intell. Veh. **2**, 194–220 (2017)

12. Taheri, H., Xia, Z.C.: SLAM, definition and evolution. Eng. Appl. Artif. Intell. **97**, 104032 (2021)

13. Jack Dangermond Fall 2013, The Power of GIS is Transforming Our World, Esri International User Conference

14. White, G., Zink, A., Codecà, L., Clarke, S.: A digital twin smart city for citizen feedback. Cities **110**, 103064 (2021). ISSN 0264-2751, https://doi.org/10.1016/j.cities.2020.103064

15. Schrotter, G., Hürzeler, C.: The digital twin of the city of Zurich for urban planning. PFG – J. Photogram. Remote Sens. Geoinf. Sci. **88**(1), 99–112 (2020). https://doi.org/10.1007/s41 064-020-00092-2

16. D'Orazi, M., Garnero, G., Traverso, S., Vertamy, E.: The new geodatabase of the municipality of Genoa: innovative aspects and applications. In: Borgogno-Mondino, E., Zamperlin, P. (eds.) ASITA 2021. CCIS, vol. 1507, pp. 216–229. Springer, Cham (2022). https://doi.org/10.1007/ 978-3-030-94426-1_16

Workshop on Advanced and Computational Methods for Earth Science Applications (WACM4ES 2023)

Exploring the Signature of the Apollo Medicane in the Central Mediterranean Sea Through Multi-source Data Analysis: Satellites, Radar HF, Marine Buoys, and Seismic Data in October 2021

Luca Piroddi[1]([✉]) [iD], Adam Gauci[1] [iD], Rami Kalfouni[1] [iD], Matthew R. Agius[1] [iD], Davide Melfi[2], Alfio Marco Borzì[3] [iD], Andrea Cannata[3,4] [iD], Flavio Cannavò[4] [iD], Vittorio Minio[3] [iD], Arianna Orasi[5] [iD], Salvatore Aronica[6] [iD], Giuseppe Ciraolo[7] [iD], and Sebastiano D'Amico[1] [iD]

[1] Department of Geosciences, University of Malta, Msida, Malta
Lucapiroddi@yahoo.it, sebastiano.damico@um.edu.mt
[2] Italian Air Force Meteorological Service - CNMCA, Rome, Italy
[3] Dipartimento di Scienze Biologiche, Geologiche ed Ambientali - Sezione di Scienze della Terra, Università degli Studi di Catania, Catania, Italy
[4] Istituto Nazionale di Geofisica e Vulcanologia - Sezione di Catania, Osservatorio Etneo, Catania, Italy
[5] Centro Nazionale per la Caratterizzazione Ambientale e la Protezione della Fascia Costiera, la Climatologia Marina e l'Oceanografa Operativa, Italian National Institute for Environmental Protection and Research, Rome, Italy
[6] Consiglio Nazionale delle Ricerche, Via del Mare, 3 Torretta Granitola, 91021 Fraz. Campobello di Mazara, Tp, Italy
[7] University of Palermo, Palermo, Italy

Abstract. In the last decades, the frequency of extreme weather and marine events has drastically increased. During the last week of October 2021 an intense Mediterranean hurricane (Medicane), named Apollo, affected many countries on the Mediterranean coasts. Eight people died as a consequence of the floodings from the cyclone in the countries of Tunisia, Algeria, Malta, and Italy. A preliminary search for possible signatures of the Apollo Medicane by meteorological satellite, radar HF, marine buoy, and seismic data is performed. This was done in a framework of an international collaboration between Italian and Maltese partners for the monitoring of the sea state in scenarios of climate change. The experimental results confirm, at this preliminary stage, the possibility and the usefulness of jointly looking at such phenomena with multiple aims of retrieving a more robust characterization, having a backup alternative in case a primary monitoring network gets failure, and pathing the way to heuristic and data-driven analytical and predictive approaches to Medicanes issues.

Keywords: Apollo Medicane · Seismic Noise · Marine Buoy

O. Gervasi et al. (Eds.): ICCSA 2023 Workshops, LNCS 14111, pp. 611–623, 2023.
https://doi.org/10.1007/978-3-031-37126-4_39

1 Introduction

1.1 Apollo Medicane

In past decades, due to climate change, the frequency of extreme weather and marine events has increased significantly [1]. During the last week of October 2021 an intense Mediterranean hurricane (Medicane), named Apollo by a consortium of European meteorological services, affected many countries on the Mediterranean coasts. The deaths toll peaked up to 8 people, due to flooding from the cyclone in the countries of Tunisia, Algeria, Malta, and Italy [2]. The Apollo Medicane persisted over such areas for about one week (24 October–30 October 2021, Fig. 1) and produced very intense rainfall phenomena and widespread flash flood and flood episodes, especially over eastern Sicily on 25–26 October 2021 [2].

A Medicane can manifest different characteristics at the different stages of its life cycle. It typically starts with features of extra-tropical cyclones that are frequently observed in the middle latitudes, but under certain conditions, it can evolve into phenomena like hurricanes that develop in the tropical belts of the Atlantic, Pacific, and Indian oceans [3]. It is generally triggered by a strong temperature difference between the upper layers of the atmosphere (colder) and those low and close to the earth's surface (warmer) [3, 4]. Evolution into a tropical-like cyclone occurs when there is enough exchange of heat and moisture between the sea and the lower atmosphere, that fuels the development of massive storm clouds [3, 4]. Typical characteristics of mature events are nearly circular symmetry, a deep warm core, a closed eye in its center with spiral cloud coverage around it, and maximum 10 m s^{-1} wind speed at 20–30 km from its center [3].

A recent study examines the interplay between the Apollo atmospheric cyclone and a cyclonic gyre located in the western Ionian Sea [5]. During the event, the temperature in the core of the cold gyre dropped dramatically. The resulting biogeochemical impacts included an increase in oxygen solubility, chlorophyll concentration, productivity at the surface, and decreases in the subsurface layer [5]. Their analysis demonstrated how a coordinated, multi-platform observing system integrated to an operational model in the Mediterranean Sea, dedicated to monitoring ocean and atmospheric parameters would be beneficial to improve our knowledge of the complex processes that may be linked to the Medicanes intensification, their impacts and/or to other extreme events [5].

1.2 Damages Caused by Apollo - Impacts of Apollo Medicane

The storm in study was named as Medicane Apollo on October 28th when it was located in the Ionian Sea, offshore Sicily. This low-pressure system was isolated near the Balearic Islands around the 22nd of October and then moved on the Central Mediterranean Sea producing self-regenerating thunderstorms in Catania on the 24th of October [7]. Figure 2 displays the track of the cyclone along its most intense life cycle. During the tropical phase of Apollo at least 8 people were killed by the storm in Sicily, Malta, Algeria and Tunisia. The highest wind gusts were measured on October 29th (104 km/h) and the pressure minimum value was estimated to 999 hPa [7]. From the convective precipitations associated with Apollo, the Sicilian Meteorological service SIAS measured > 200 mm rain around Syracuse on the same date [7]. Apollo weakened on 30th October 2021

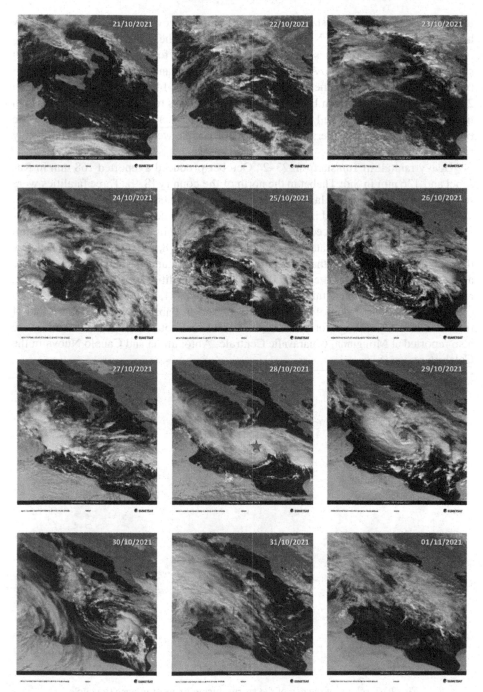

Fig. 1. Tracking of the eye of the cyclone over the RGB Natural Colour Enhanced product from Eumetsat [6] across the Central Mediterranean.

landfalling near Bayda and stayed inland until emerging over the Mediterranean a few hours later. Then, on 2nd of November, it dissipated off the coast of Turkey [7].

More than 100 properties were flooded in Algeria, following heavy rains which started on 23 October [8, 9]. Algiers, Boumerdes, Chlef and Tizi Ouzou were some of the worst hit provinces. Algiers city received more than 140 mm of rain in 24 h from 23–24 October [8, 9]. In Ain Benian, 246 mm of rain was reported, which is more than five times the average rainfall for October (13, MKWeather, 2021). Two fatalities were reported in south-west Algiers, where dozens of people were rescued following heavy rains [8, 10].

Heavy rainfall in Tunisia from 23–24 October produced a reported 168 mm in Ras Jebel and 136 mm in Sidi Thabet in the north of the country [8, 9]. Three fatalities were recorded in Tunisia. In Thala, northwest Tunisia, two fatalities were reported, whilst another fatality was reported in Borj Chakir, near the capital Tunis [8, 11].

Eastern Sicily experienced the highest levels of rainfall, with a total of 520 mm reported at Linguaglossa, Catania, from 24–26 October [8, 12]. On 24 October, heavy downpours produced more than 300 mm of rain near Catania, which is nearly half the average annual rainfall for the island [8, 9, 13]. Two fatalities were reported in Catania region on 24 October and a third one on 26 October [8, 14, 15].

In Calabria, 440.2 mm of rainfall was reported in Fabrizia, which is more than 4 times the monthly average for October [8, 16]. Rainfall totals exceeding 300 mm were also reported at Mongiana, Chiaravalle Centrale, Antonimina and Canolo Nuova in the Calabria region [8].

Fig. 2. Tracking of the eye of the storm during its most intense life cycle.

2   The i-waveNET Framework

Extreme events cause significant impacts on exposed territories, and it is expected that they may have even greater impacts in next future, especially on coastal areas. Consequently, the level of risk associated with sea storms must be continuously monitored and characterized with a view to implementing increasingly targeted and effective mitigation actions [17]. The i-waveNET project, in which this research is conducted, is carried out by Sicilian and Maltese partners and sets up an integrated monitoring system based on numerous synergistic technologies (Fig. 3), consisting of HF radars, marine buoys, seismic stations, weather stations, and tide indicators [17].

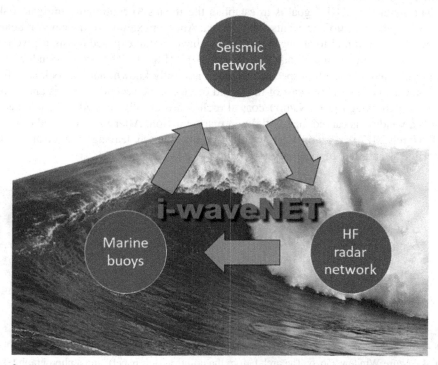

Fig. 3. Sketch of the synergistic marine monitoring networks in the context of the i-waveNET collaborative project.

In the Malta-Sicily Channel, several monitoring systems were already deployed, and this monitoring infrastructure is reinforced and integrates the available technologies by means of i-waveNET.

New weather stations and a new HF radar in strategic points are a first expansion of the operational networks. The permanent seismic networks – managed by Istituto Nazionale di Geofisica e Vulcanologia (INGV) and Seismic Monitoring and Research Group, within the Department of Geosciences, University of Malta [18, 19] – is strengthened through the installation of new sensors close the HF radar sites. All these data will be harmonized and analyzed to ensure integration with meteo-marine data.

In the context of the i-waveNET project machine learning algorithms to characterize the sea state through microseism data are implemented. The forcing of a spectral wave model with data also flowing from the monitoring network ensures a real-time sea state monitoring at a regular spatial-temporal grid over a larger domain [17].

Finally, these instrumental networks, integrated with numerical models, supply the input data to a Decision Support System (DSS) in a GIS environment, capable of producing information in line with the conventions of the various stakeholders involved and to influence regional planning activities. Consequently, the i-waveNET project will result in a homogeneous and continuous dataset of measured data, the creation of a dataset on the state of the sea modelled on a regular grid and finally a real-time monitoring system of the physical state of the sea [17].

The main i-waveNET goal is to establish the means to continually mitigate risks due to extreme catastrophic events from the sea. Another example of the environmental effects that even a mid-to-strong sea storm can have on the exposed coasts is given by the collapse of the Azure Window in March 2017 (Fig. 4). The Azure Window was the popular name given to a spectacular, internationally known, natural rock arch that stood on the northwestern coast of the island of Gozo, the second largest island of the Maltese archipelago [20]. Natural coastal arches are usually formed in headlands in which a window is carved mainly through marine action. After years of rapid erosion, on 8 March 2017 the Azure Window collapsed into the sea, leaving no trace above the waterline as an effect of a marine storm with wave heights of 3 m.

Fig. 4. Azure Window, Gozo: The arch before the collapse (left panel), and a photograph taken from the same point after the collapse (right panel). The boundary between the upper (B) and lower (A) geological stratigraphy is marked with a dashed line. The area highlighted with dots is a block that detached in 2012. After [20]

3   Experimental Datasets

This paper provides a preliminary analysis of the integrated monitoring datasets, looking at the possible qualitative detection of signatures of the Apollo Medicane phases on the experimental datasets. In Fig. 5, the locations of three different kinds of sensors are shown: the three-component seismic station WDD, a digital broadband seismometer located south of Malta in Wied Dalam [19]; the two-components HF radar sensor SOPU, and the marine wave-buoy SOPU, co-located in Sopu, east coast of Gozo.

Fig. 5. Localization of the environmental monitoring stations: the three-component seismic station WDD, a digital broadband seismometer located south of Malta in Wied Dalam; the two-component HF radar sensor SOPU, and the marine wave-buoy SOPU, co-located in Sopu, east coast of Gozo

3.1 Wave Buoy vs HF Radar

As a first attempt to detect possible signatures of the Apollo Medicane, in Fig. 6, a graphical comparison of wave buoy and radar data for the site of SOPU during the period from 21 October to 2 November is shown. The buoy data are strongly influenced by the drifting of the sensor progressively out of the national waters for the strong winds and wave movements, that happened on 23 October at the beginning of the cyclone not yet a medicane. Nevertheless, in this event the two time-series of wave amplitude show a common behavior with a background wave height of about half a meter and a progressive increase to two meters on 23 October, just before the buoy started drifting. Until the 2 November (last day in the plot) the sea conditions at the two sensors remained quite similar indicating that the buoy had not yet reached positions too far from the observational ring of the HF radar (6 km distance for the plotted data).

Another important result of the HF radar monitoring is the strong correlation between the waves directionality (orange dots in Fig. 6.a) and the position of the eye of Apollo

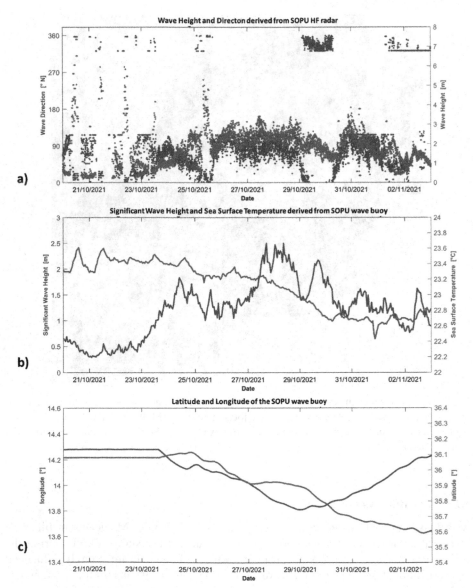

Fig. 6. Graphical comparison of HF radar and buoy data for the site of SOPU. In the top panel, the radar data are plotted for the dates from 21 October to 2 November (a): in orange the wave height in meters, while in blue the related angles of the velocity vector. In the middle panel (b), the buoy data are plotted, indicating in blue the wave height and in orange the sea temperature. In the bottom panel, the two geographical coordinates of the buoy are plotted, showing on 23 October the beginning of the buoy movement out of place which, in the dates out of our graph, lead the buoy to the North African sea. (Color figure online)

(Fig. 2.a). In fact, it is possible to observe the trends to about $-15°/345° \pm 20°$ on the days of 25 and 29 October, when the location of the center of the Apollo perturbation was at its most northern and closest position to Malta.

3.2 Wave Buoy vs Seismic Noise

In the framework of the i-waveNET project, the relation between seismic noise and the state of the sea has been and is being investigated [21, 22].

Borzì *et al.* [21] propose the monitoring extreme meteo-marine events in the Mediterranean area using the microseism, in particular the Apollo Medicane. They investigated the microseism accompanying this extreme Mediterranean weather event, and its relationship with the sea state retrieved from hindcast maps and wave buoys. The spectral and amplitude analyses of the seismic data showed the space–time variation of the microseism amplitude. In addition, they tracked the position of Apollo during the time using two different methods: (i) a grid search method; (ii) an array analysis, obtaining a good match between the real position of Apollo and the location constraint by both seismic methods.

Kalfouni *et al.* [22] derive insights into the state of the sea from seismic noise in the wake of the i-waveNET project. There, the measured wave height at marine buoys is correlated with the vertical component of the seismic noise velocity measured at the seismic monitoring stations with appropriately long time-series. Figure 7 shows a

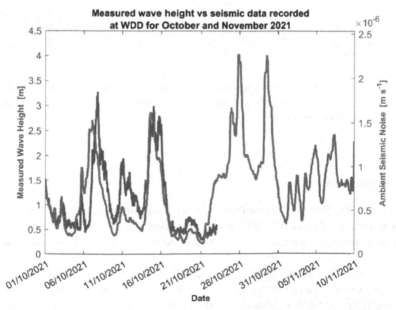

Fig. 7. Graphical overlay of the vertical component of the ambient seismic noise at the WDD station in Wied Dalam (orange plot) and the measured wave height by the SOPU buoy in Gozo (blue plot), until it abandoned the original measuring location. Notice the good correlation between the two datasets. (Color figure online)

graphical overlay of the sea wave height measured at SOPU buoy until it started drifting due to the early phases of Apollo storm (blue) versus the ambient noise velocity at WDD station. Even with this short time period it is possible to notice the strong correlation between the two datasets, and, on the basis of the robust relation obtained on the long datasets, in Fig. 8 the sea wave height at the original SOPU position is reconstructed from the seismological monitoring data using a linear regression model.

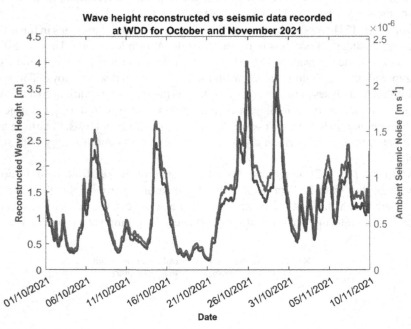

Fig. 8. Graphical overlay of the vertical component of the ambient seismic noise at the WDD station in Wied Dalam (orange plot) and the estimated sea wave height reconstructed using the same dataset. (Color figure online)

3.3 Satellite Data

Geostationary satellite multispectral data are becoming an important tool for monitoring many environmental risks [23–28]. This is particularly true for the study and forecast of strong meteorological events [29–31] in which the thermal infrared bands are extremely useful.

In Fig. 9, a time series of the European HRV-RGB (E-view) for the Apollo case study is presented. The E-View product is an RGB (Red, Green, Blue) composite based upon data from the SEVIRI instrument. It is dedicated to detailed cloud monitoring of the European region and is based on data from the SEVIRI High Resolution Visible (panchromatic) channel combined with data from the IR10.8 channel that provides the temperature information (blue component) [32]. This RGB type concentrates on high cloud monitoring. Thin and thick high clouds have good color contrasts with each other,

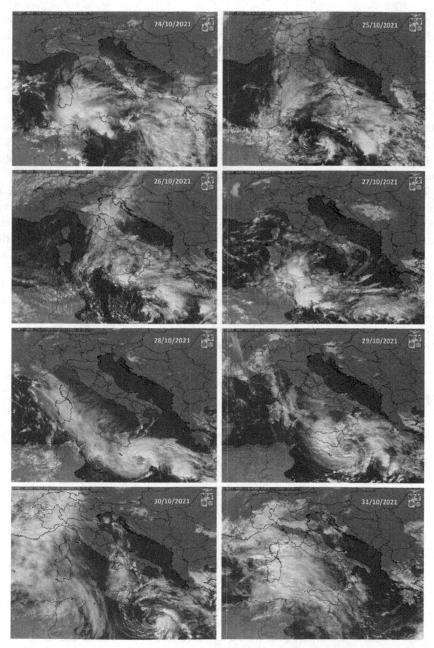

Fig. 9. European HRV-RGB (E-view) for the Apollo Medicane. The white-blue tones indicate the high, coldest and thickest clouds, representative of the mature phases of the storm. (Color figure online)

from lower-level clouds, and from cloud-free regions (including snow/ice) [31]. Intense (and/or long-lived) overshooting tops, gravity waves, long-lived cold U/V and cold rings are indicators of strong updrafts and possibly severity [32].

4 Concluding Remarks

In this paper a preliminary search for a signature of the Apollo Medicane by satellite, radar HF, marine buoy, and seismic data is performed. This is done in a framework of an international collaboration between Italian and Maltese partners for the monitoring of the sea state in scenarios of climate change.

The experimental results here presented, together with the collateral research already published and in the phase of publication, confirm the possibility and the usefulness of jointly looking at such phenomena with multiple aims of retrieving a more robust characterization. This allows to have a backup alternative in case a primary monitoring network gets failure, and to path the way to heuristic and data-driven analyses and monitoring techniques.

Acknowledgement. The authors acknowledge the financial support of i-waveNET project "Implementazione di un sistema innovativo di monitoraggio dello stato del mare in scenari di cambiamento climatico", cod. C2 3.2 106, Program INTERR EG V A Italia-Malta 2014 2020 (Interreg V-A Cross Border Cooperation Italia–Malta projects).

References

1. Swain, D.L., Singh, D., Touma, D., Diffenbaugh, N.S.: Attributing extreme events to climate change: a new frontier in a warming world. One Earth **2**(6), 522–527 (2020)
2. EUMEeTrain, https://eumetrain.org/resources/complete-meteo-hydrological-chain-support-early-warning-systems-weather-scenarios-flooded. Accessed 20 Mar 2023
3. Lagasio, M., et al.: A Complete meteo/hydro/hydraulic chain application to support early warning and monitoring systems: the Apollo Medicane use case. Remote Sens. **14**(24), 6348 (2022)
4. Emanuel, K.: Genesis and maintenance of "Mediterranean hurricanes." Adv. Geosci. **2**, 217–220 (2005)
5. Menna, M., et al.: A case study of impacts of an extreme weather system on the Mediterranean Sea circulation features: Medicane Apollo (2021). Sci. Rep. **13**(1), 3870 (2023)
6. https://pics.eumetsat.int/viewer/index.html
7. https://xaida.eu/medicane-apollo/
8. https://www.jbarisk.com/products-services/event-response/medicane-apollo/
9. https://floodlist.com/africa/algeria-tunisia-italy-medicane-floods-october-2021
10. https://themaghrebtimes.com/floods-in-algeria-the-toll-is-growing/
11. https://www.sott.net/article/459914-Three-killed-in-Tunisia-flash-floods?utm_source=rss&utm_medium=MINT+Social&utm_campaign=RSS
12. https://www.severe-weather.eu/europe-weather/medicane-tropical-cyclone-sicily-italy-malta-flooding-mediterranean-mk/
13. Levantesi, S.: Assessing Italy's Climate risk, Nature Italy. https://doi.org/10.1038/d43978-021-00136-0

14. https://www.bbc.co.uk/news/world-europe-59048809
15. http://www.nimbus.it/eventi/2021/211031TempestaApolloSicilia.htm
16. https://www.worldweatheronline.com/fabrizia-weather-averages/calabria/it.aspx
17. Aronica, S., et al.: The i-waveNet project and the integrated sea wave measurements in the Mediterranean sea. In: 2022 IEEE International Workshop on Metrology for the Sea; Learning to Measure Sea Health Parameters (MetroSea), pp. 484–487. IEEE, October 2022
18. Ferretti, R., et al.: Analysis of the development mechanisms of a large-hail storm event, on the Adriatic Sea using an atmosphere-ocean coupled model (COAWST) (No. EGU22–12876). Copernicus Meetings (2022)
19. Galea, P., Agius, M.R., Bozionelos, G., D'Amico, S., Farrugia, D.: A first national seismic network for the Maltese Islands—the Malta seismic network. Seismol. Res. Lett. **92**, 1817–1831 (2021). https://doi.org/10.1785/0220200387
20. Galea, P., Bozionelos, G., D'Amico, S., Drago, A., Colica, E.: Seismic signature of the Azure window collapse, Gozo, central Mediterranean. Seismol. Res. Lett. **89**(3), 1108–1117 (2018)
21. Borzì, A.M., et al.: Monitoring extreme meteo-marine events in the Mediterranean area using the microseism (Medicane Apollo case study). Sci. Rep. **12**(1), 21363 (2022)
22. Kalfouni, R., Agius, M.R., D'Amico, S., Gauci, A., Galea, P.: Deriving insights into the state of the sea from seismic noise in the wake of the i-WaveNET project. Appl. Sci. (2023, in prep.)
23. Jones, S., Hally, B., Reinke, K., Wickramasinghe, C., Wallace, L., Engel, C.: Next generation fire detection from geostationary satellites. In: IGARSS 2018–2018 IEEE International Geoscience and Remote Sensing Symposium, pp. 5465–5468. IEEE, July 2018
24. Vu, B.N., Bi, J., Wang, W., Huff, A., Kondragunta, S., Liu, Y.: Application of geostationary satellite and high-resolution meteorology data in estimating hourly PM2. 5 levels during the Camp Fire episode in California. Remote Sens. Environ. **271**, 112890 (2022)
25. Liew, S.C.: Detecting active fires with himawari-8 geostationary satellite data. In: IGARSS 2019–2019 IEEE International Geoscience and Remote Sensing Symposium, pp. 9984–9987. IEEE, July 2019
26. Piroddi, L., Ranieri, G.: Night thermal gradient: a new potential tool for earthquake precursors studies. An application to the seismic area of L'Aquila (central Italy). IEEE J. Sel. Top. Appl. Earth Observ. Remote Sens. **5**(1), 307–312 (2011)
27. Piroddi, L., Ranieri, G., Freund, F., Trogu, A.: Geology, tectonics and topography underlined by L'Aquila earthquake TIR precursors. Geophys. J. Int. **197**(3), 1532–1536 (2014)
28. Piroddi, L.: From high temporal resolution to synthetically enhanced radiometric resolution: insights from Night Thermal Gradient results. Eur. Phys. J. Spec. Top. **230**(1), 111–132 (2021). https://doi.org/10.1140/epjst/e2020-000247-x
29. McNally, T., Bonavita, M., Thépaut, J.N.: The role of satellite data in the forecasting of Hurricane Sandy. Mon. Weather Rev. **142**(2), 634–646 (2014)
30. Knapp, K.R., Kossin, J.P.: New global tropical cyclone data set from ISCCP B1 geostationary satellite observations. J. Appl. Remote Sens. **1**(1), 013505 (2007)
31. Ciardullo, G., Primavera, L., Ferrucci, F., Lepreti, F., Carbone, V.: New investigation of a tropical cyclone: observational and turbulence analysis for the Faraji hurricane. Remote Sens. **15**(5), 1383 (2023)
32. https://data.eumetsat.int/product-navigator/product/EO:EUM:DAT:MSG:EVIEW

(Pseudo-)3D Inversion of Geophysical Electromagnetic Induction Data by Using an Arbitrary Prior and Constrained to Ancillary Information

Nicola Zaru[1], Matteo Rossi[2], Giuseppina Vacca[1] (iD), and Giulio Vignoli[1,3(✉)] (iD)

[1] University of Cagliari, 09124 Cagliari, Italy
gvignoli@unica.it
[2] Lund University, 22100 Lund, Sweden
[3] GEUS, 8000 Aarhus, Denmark

Abstract. Electromagnetic induction (EMI) methods are often used to map rapidly large areas with minimal logistical efforts. However, they are limited by a small number of frequencies and by their severe ill-posedness. On the other hand, electrical resistivity tomography (ERT) results are generally considered more reliable, with no need for specific calibration procedures and easy 2D/3D inversion. Still, ERT surveys are definitely more time-consuming, and, ideally, an approach with the advantages of both EMI and ERT would be optimal. The present research addresses this issue by incorporating realistic constraints into EMI inversion, going beyond simplistic spatial constraints like smooth or sharp regularization terms, while taking into consideration the ancillary information already available about the investigated site. We demonstrate how additional pre-existing information, such as a reference model (i.e., an existing ERT section) can enhance the EMI inversion. The study verifies the results against observations from boreholes.

Keywords: Electromagnetic Induction · Spatially Constrained Inversion · Realistic Prior Distribution

1 Introduction

Geophysical techniques refer to (quasi-)non-invasive methods employed to infer the physical properties of the subsurface. Among these techniques, electrical resistivity tomography (ERT) and electromagnetic induction (EMI) are frequently used to recover the electrical characteristics - mainly, the electrical resistivity - of the medium.

ERT data are collected through a series of electrodes galvanically coupled to the ground. Nowadays, ERT data are routinely inverted with 2D/3D forward modeling. Conversely, EMI measurements can be collected without any physical contact with the surface, and, in most cases, the data are inverted via simple 1D forward modeling. Hence, the collection of ERT data generally requires much more effort than the acquisition of EMI measurements [1, 2] because of the necessity for the electrodes' direct contact with

O. Gervasi et al. (Eds.): ICCSA 2023 Workshops, LNCS 14111, pp. 624–638, 2023.
https://doi.org/10.1007/978-3-031-37126-4_40

the ground. On the other hand, EMI methods can be used to reconstruct the 3D resistivity volume of extremely large areas in a very limited amount of time; in this respect, there even exist EMI systems designed to be mounted on helicopters/airplanes [3–6]. Despite being more troublesome to collect than EMI observations, ERT measurements do not need special calibration procedures as their observations can be readily checked against test resistances [7–11]. In addition, the capability of 2D/3D inversion contributes to the reduction of artifacts due to the unavoidable presence of coherent noise (i.e.: the modelling error). However, modelling error will always be present (even sophisticated 3D tools are mere approximations of real phenomena) and it should be taken into account to avoid misleading overinterpretation of the data. Clearly, the standard, simplistic, 1D strategies adopted for the EMI inversion are more prone to be negatively affected by this kind of coherent noise [12, 13].

In another respect, to enforce some level of spatial coherence between the 1D inversion results and, in this way, contribute further to tackling effectively the ill-posedness of the problem, regularization terms acting both vertically and laterally have been utilized during the inversion of large EMI datasets. Over the years, various options for both lateral and vertical regularization terms have been investigated and implemented: in addition to the commonly used L2-norm - which promotes solutions that minimize the spatial variation of the model parameters [14–16] - other stabilizer terms, such as the Minimum Support (MS) stabilizer, have gained popularity [17–21]. The MS stabilizers favor the selection of solutions characterized by abrupt resistivity changes, and this, in many cases, might better reflect the investigated geologies. Similar arguments apply to the ERT inversion: also in this case, several stabilizers have been proposed to address the severe ill-posedness of the problem and to correctly formalize the available a priori information [22–26].

The newest deterministic approaches, based on the minimization of Tikhonov's objective function and formalizing the a priori information via the regularization terms, are still quite successful in exploring the solution space [27]. However, probabilistic approaches are becoming more and more frequent as they are capable of assessing the solution uncertainty in a very natural way and of being fed with arbitrary (realistic) prior [28–30].

For the specific field dataset investigated here, we needed a pragmatic strategy capable: 1) of incorporating realistic prior distribution ensuring that the individual 1D EMI reconstructions were compatible with specific expectations about the studied subsurface (so, not, simply, blocky or smooth vertical resistivity models) and 2) of guaranteeing that, laterally, the solutions were consistent with the pre-existing knowledge of the site (i.e., alternatively: a previous 2D ERT section or its corresponding 2D geological interpretation).

2 Methodology

The aim of this research is to incorporate as much prior information as possible into the inversion of EMI datasets. Electromagnetic data are typically acquired with some ideas of the pursued target or with other geophysical measurements available. In this study, the EMI data are inverted by making use of the ERT results (either directly or through their interpretations) obtained along a single acquisition line crossing the investigated area. The objective is to spread the information from the ERT 2D section throughout the entire 3D volume of the EMI survey

EMI inversion is extremely ill-posed due to the limited number of observations, noise in the data (caused, for example, by unwanted inclinations of the instrumentation), and the nonlinearity of the forward modelling. So, in a deterministic inversion, some level of regularization is required to get a unique and stable solution. Regularization picks the unique and stable solution amongst all possible models fitting the data within the level sets by the estimated noise in the data. In most cases, the regularization is enforced via the minimization of the stabilizer

$$s(\boldsymbol{m}) = \|\boldsymbol{m} - \boldsymbol{m}_{apr}\|, \tag{1}$$

in which: $\boldsymbol{m}$ is the vector of the model parameters - in this specific case, the resistivity of each layer - and $\boldsymbol{m}_{apr}$ is a reference model.

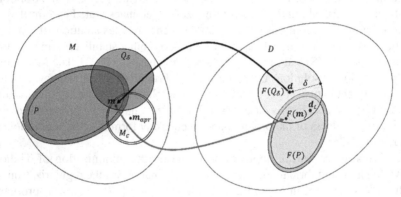

Fig. 1. $\boldsymbol{d}$ is the measurements' vector consisting of the summation of the true data vector $\boldsymbol{d}_t$ and the noise $\boldsymbol{\delta}$. F is the forward modelling used to calculate the response $\boldsymbol{d}$ associated with the model $\boldsymbol{m}$. Hence, the set of all possible models consistent with the data is $Q_\delta = \{\boldsymbol{m} | \boldsymbol{m} \in M \text{ and} \|F(\boldsymbol{m}) - \boldsymbol{d}\| \leq \|\boldsymbol{\delta}\| = \delta\}$. In general, the solution of the inverse problem is the minimizer of the regularizer $s(\boldsymbol{m}) = \|\boldsymbol{m} - \boldsymbol{m}_{apr}\|$ (defining the correctness set M_c [31]) that, also, belongs to Q_δ. Here, instead, the set of all possible solutions is no longer defined uniquely by δ, but rather by the intersection $Q_\delta \cap P$, in which the set P consists of the samples of the prior distribution. D is the set of all possible measurements. (Color figure online)

Given a noise vector $\boldsymbol{\delta}$ associated to the vector of the measurements $\boldsymbol{d}$, the subset of all possible models compatible with the observed data is defined as

$$Q_\delta = \{\boldsymbol{m} | \boldsymbol{m} \in M \text{ and} \|F(\boldsymbol{m}) - \boldsymbol{d}\| \leq \|\boldsymbol{\delta}\| = \delta\}, \tag{2}$$

where F is the forward modelling and M is the model space. The regularizer $s(\boldsymbol{m})$ selects from Q_δ the specific solution $\boldsymbol{m}$ that minimizes $s(\boldsymbol{m})$.

In the stochastic approaches, the a priori information is also provided via the selection of the appropriate prior distribution P: the samples of P are models defined in agreement with our expectations about the possible resistivity models. The stochastic solution consists of the a posteriori distribution populated by the models compatible with the prior and associated with their probability of being the actual model generating the observed data - clearly, this probability is a function of their corresponding data fitting.

The present approach can be considered a mixture of the deterministic and stochastic perspectives as the inversion solution is found as the minimizer m of Eq. 1 belonging at the intersection $Q_\delta \cap P$ between the prior ensemble and the set of possible models fitting the data (rather than simply at Q_δ).

In this way, we can search for the solutions (Fig. 1) with some specific (very general and arbitrarily complex) characteristics (defining the samples of P) and as close as possible to some reference models (possibly, defined by other ancillary information, consisting, for example, of the presence of 2D ERT models).

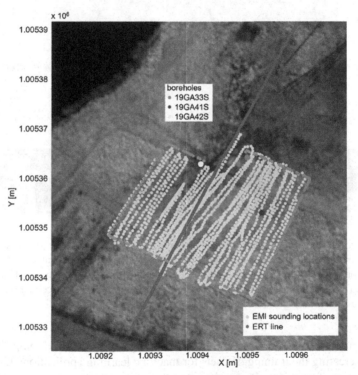

Fig. 2. The available boreholes are indicated by the large yellow, orange, and blue dots, while the EMI soundings are represented by light blue color. The ERT line is shown as a red line, and the perimeter of the area is highlighted by green dots. The coordinates are not the real ones. (Color figure online)

In our specific case, the set P has been defined via 20×10^6 samples (consisting of 1D resistivity profiles characterized by 31 layers with logarithmically increasing thicknesses; the depth of the top of the last layer is at 30 m depth). The samples have been designed in order to be representative of the variability of the physical properties of the investigated site. Across the investigated site (Fig. 2), both EMI and ERT data have been collected. Specifically, one 2D ERT line crosses the 3D EMI survey. A portion of the result of the 2D inversion of the ERT [32] is shown in Fig. 3a. The representativeness of the EMI prior samples has been verified a posteriori by checking how well the prior samples could fit the retrieved ERT section [33]. The prior models best fitting the ERT results are shown in Fig. 3b. Hence, Fig. 3c (showing the model misfit between the Fig. 3a and 3b resistivity distributions) demonstrates how the typical resistivities characterizing the investigated site (Fig. 3a) can be reproduced by the possible candidates (i.e., the best fitting elements of P - in Fig. 3b) to be the solutions of the EMI inversion.

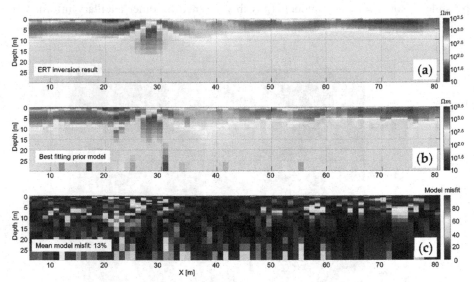

Fig. 3. Check of the prior models representativeness. (a) The 2D resistivity distribution obtained via the ERT inversion of the data along the profile crossing the investigated area (Fig. 2, red line). The only portion shown corresponds to the part overlapping the EMI survey. (b) The 2D section obtained via the best fitting 1D models of the prior distribution. (c) The percentage relative misfit between the ERT model and the best fitting one. (Color figure online)

From an alternative perspective, the underlying logic for developing the prior is similar to creating the training datasets for machine learning applications [34]: in both cases, the sets of pairs (m, d), consisting of the prior models and the associated electromagnetic responses, and making up the training dataset, are generated based on the stationary assumption. As a result, it is essential for the pairs in the training dataset - as well as those in the prior ensemble P and its associated image in D: $F(P)$ (in Fig. 1) - to be independent and identically distributed (i.i.d.) random variables [35].

Once P is populated, and the responses in $F(P)$ calculated, it is straight forward to select the models belonging to the subset $P \cap Q_\delta$ and whose data are compatible with the field observations. Subsequently, the model of the intersection $P \cap Q_\delta$ which is also the minimizer of $s(m)$ is selected as the final solution to the inverse problem.

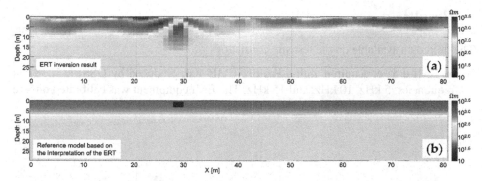

Fig. 4. The two electrical resistivity distributions used as alternative reference models for the EMI inversion. (a) The 2D resistivity from the ERT data (Fig. 2, red line, and Fig. 3a). (b) The interpretation of the ERT result. (Color figure online)

The proposed method can be viewed as a progression from the standard spatially constrained inversion technique [6, 14]. Unlike the former, the vertical regularization in the proposed strategy is not confined to a mere demand for maximum smoothness. Instead, in this new approach, vertical spatial coherence is ensured by the selected model being an element of the prior ensemble P. Therefore, the similarity to the spatially constrained inversion concerns only the formalization of lateral constraints, opening up the possibility of reconstructing much more realistic geological structures (consistent with the prior knowledge). Of course, whereas the EMI survey profiles adjacent to the ERT section (or, in general, to any other available source of prior information) are directly constrained by the ERT resistivity values, the EMI profiles that are further distant from the ERT section are uniquely bound to the closest EMI profiles. Thus, during the EMI inversion process, moving away from the ERT section, the influence of the initial ERT information competes with the one provided by the EMI measurements themselves, and gradually weakens. This is coherent with the expectation that, as we move away from the ERT section, there would be a reduced resemblance between the electrical and electromagnetic outcomes.

From a computational perspective, the proposed method is only seemingly costly. In reality, for comparable geological settings, the elements of P can be pre-computed, and, since the forward response is independent for each 1D model, the process is highly parallelizable. Furthermore, all the challenges associated with minimizing the objective function of standard deterministic approaches (such as selecting Tikhonov's parameter [36]) are automatically eliminated and everything is reduced to simply calculating the norm of the model distance with respect to m_{apr} (Eq. 1).

In the following, we investigate the possibility to use, to guide the inversion, not just the ERT result, but, as an alternative, its interpretation based on additional information. So, we will check the consequences of using the resistivity section in Fig. 4b and compare that result against the one obtained via the distribution in Fig. 4a.

3 Results

The field data available on the test site consist of:

- the EMI dataset acquired with a Profiler EMP-400, produced by GSSI [37, 38], at frequencies: 5 kHz, 10 kHz, and 15 kHz. The EMI equipment was calibrated on-site following the standard manufacturer's prescription.

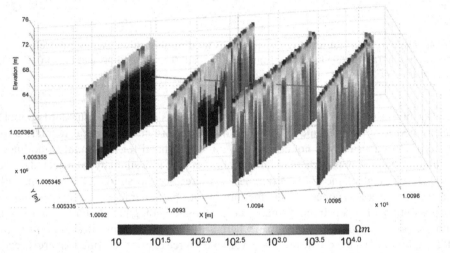

Fig. 5. Vertical slices of the 3D EMI unconstrained inversion. The purple solid line indicates where the probable pipeline's location. (Color figure online)

- an ERT line passing, in the middle, the EMI survey area (red line in Fig. 2). The ERT was performed with a Terrameter LS2 (GuidelineGeo), with 81 electrodes 1 m apart. The acquisition protocol was a gradient nested array producing 1603 individual measurements. The contact electrical resistance was always less than 1 KΩ. The ERT inversion was performed utilizing pyGIMLi [32] and, e.g., it is shown in Fig. 4a (just the portion overlapping the EMI survey area). In that Figure, at around X = 29 m, the conductive evidence of an existing pipe is clear.

In the following, we compare the EMI inversion results, respectively:

- relying uniquely on the data and the information provided by the prior distribution (Fig. 5). In what follows, we will refer to this result as the Unconstrained result.
- incorporating the information from the 2D ERT section (Fig. 6). We call this result the ERT-constrained result.
- based on the interpretation of the ERT section as it is shown in Fig. 4b. We generally call it Model-constrained result (Fig. 7).

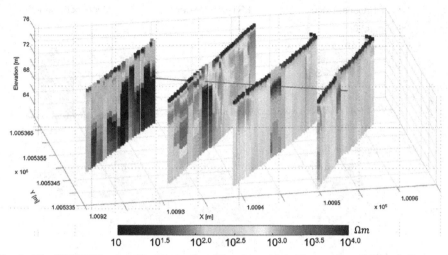

Fig. 6. The EMI ERT-constrained inversion (Figs. 2a and 3a). The purple solid line indicates the supposed pipeline's location. (Color figure online)

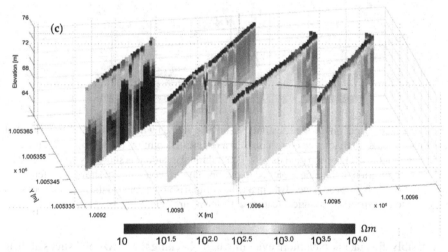

Fig. 7. The EMI Model-constrained inversion (Fig. 3b). The purple solid line indicates the supposed pipeline's location. (Color figure online)

By comparing Figs. 5, 6 and 7, it is easy to notice that incorporating the additional information either from the ERT section or its interpretation generates results that are more spatially coherent, decreasing the spurious variations between different adjacent 1D models, which are characterizing the Unconstrained result.

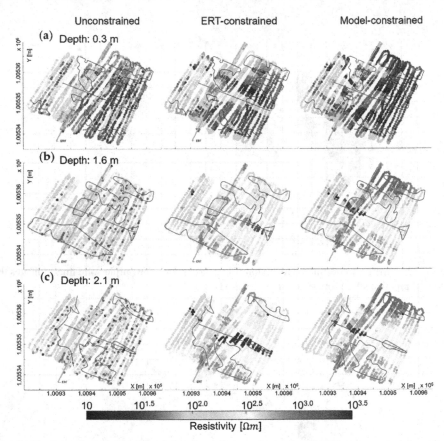

Fig. 8. Horizontal sections of the resistivity volumes obtained with different constraining strategies (Figs. 5, 6 and 7). Each row corresponds to a different depth: (a) 0.3 m; (b) 1.6 m; (c) 2.1 m. The location of the ERT section (and its geoelectrical interpretation) is shown as a green solid line. The assumed position of the pipe is plotted in purple. The red contours are shown as references to the anomalies; their purpose is merely to make the comparisons easier, and they are not necessarily connected to any specific geological features. (Color figure online)

Possibly, this fact is even more evident when checking the horizontal slices at different depths of the (pseudo-)3D EMI volumes as in Figs. 8 and 9. In particular, the ERT - and Model-constrained results in Figs. 8 and 9 highlight clearly the presence of the non-metallic pipe known to be crossing the area (whose location is shown in Figs. 8 and 9 as a purple solid line). The presence of the pipeline at around 2.4 m depth is confirmed by means of other investigations.

The Model-constrained inversion seems to better retrieve the actual resistivity distribution even compared against the ERT-constrained result as the pipe reconstruction is more coherent with its most probable location; in this respect, for example, in Figs. 9b–c, the Model-constrained reconstruction shows no traces of the conductive pipe deeper than 2.6 m (where, indeed, it should not appear since it is shallower than that).

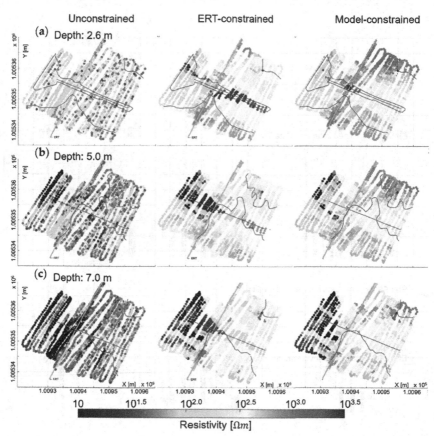

Fig. 9. Horizontal sections of the resistivity volumes obtained with different constraining strategies (Figs. 5, 6 and 7). Each row corresponds to a different depth: (a) 2.6 m; (b) 5.0 m; (c) 7.0 m. The location of the ERT section (and its geoelectrical interpretation) is shown as a green solid line. The assumed position of the pipe is plotted in purple. The red contours are shown as references to the anomalies; their purpose is merely to make the comparisons easier, and they are not necessarily connected to any specific geological features. (Color figure online)

In addition to the verification against the pipeline presence and location, the vertical sections of the retrieved EMI volumes have been checked also against the available borehole logs, whose locations are plotted in Fig. 1 (c.f. the yellow, orange, and blue large dots [39]).

634   N. Zaru et al.

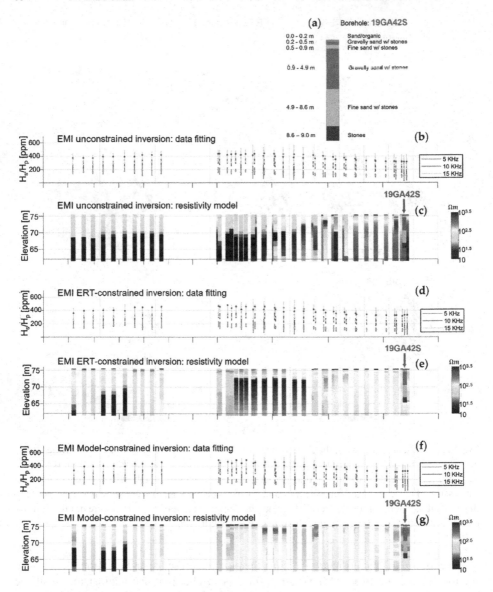

Fig. 10. Vertical sections of the EMI inversions performed by utilizing different ancillary information. (a) Description of borehole no. 19GA42S (Fig. 1). (b–c) Data fitting and model for the Unconstrained inversion. (d–e) Data fitting and model for the ERT-constrained in-version. (f–g) Data fitting and model for the Model-constrained inversion.

On this matter, Fig. 10 shows the vertical sections of the three 3D EMI inversions are compared against the corresponding stratigraphy of the nearest borehole (19GA42S): these significantly different results further demonstrate the necessity of including the proper ancillary information during the inversion; also the ERT - and Model-constrained

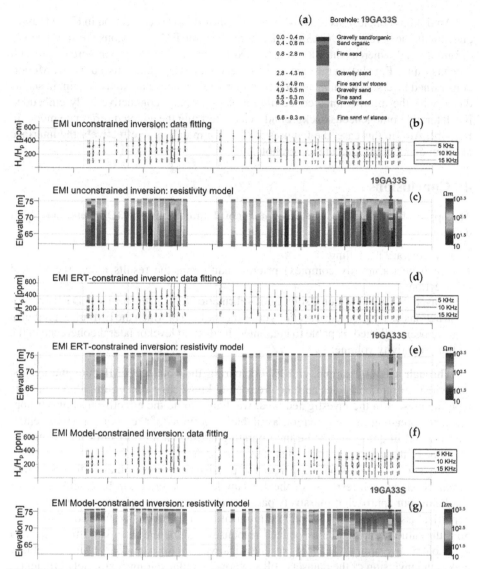

Fig. 11. Vertical sections of the EMI inversions performed by utilizing different ancillary information. (a) Description of borehole no. 19GA33S (Fig. 1). (b–c) Data fitting and model for the Unconstrained inversion. (d–e) Data fitting and model for the ERT-constrained in-version. (f–g) Data fitting and model for the Model-constrained inversion.

results are quite different (Figs. 10e and 10g) even if the data fitting is clearly equally good for all the cases (Figs. 10b, d and f). Furthermore, concerning the borehole stratigraphy, not only the EMI results can match the conductive shallow layers in the well, but the Model-constrained inversion can correctly identify the interface at 8.6 m depth visible in the log.

636   N. Zaru et al.

Analogous conclusions can be drawn from the other vertical section in Fig. 11, associated with the borehole 19GA33S. Also here, the three EMI inversions are significantly different. And, whereas the ERT-constrained reconstruction shows (in agreement with its constraint - Fig. 4a), in the center of the section, a deep conductive unit, the Model-constrained inversion is characterized by a sharper conductive anomaly (again, in accordance with the information - concerning a blocky square conductive body embedded in a laterally homogeneous background - characterizing the adopted reference model in Fig. 4b). Also in this case, the features in Fig. 11g match more effectively the interface at 6.6 m depth noticeable in the borehole.

4 Conclusions

The approach we propose here concerns a novel strategy for the 3D inversion of EMI data making use of:

- a 1D forward modelling;
- a realistic (arbitrarily complex) prior, conditioning the results along the vertical direction;
- the availability of additional sources of information (e.g., in the form of 2D ERT reconstructions or 2D geological sections crossing the area in which the EMI measurements have been collected) capable to guarantee the desired level of lateral coherence in the final resistivity volume.

Through a field example, and by comparing the obtained EMI outcome against the evidence from boreholes and the preexisting knowledge concerning a non-metallic pipeline present in the investigated area, we demonstrate the effectiveness of our approach in spreading the information available in portions of the area across the entire volume, and in doing that while incorporating additional a priori information via the selection of the appropriate prior distribution models.

The new approach is only apparently expensive from a computational perspective. In reality, since each response of the 1D samples of the prior can be calculated independently, our approach is massively parallelizable, moreover, it is immune from all the numerical issues connected with the minimization of the objective functional. In addition, the same prior (and its associated responses) can be pre-calculated for areas that are geologically similar (i.e., that are, statistically speaking, stationary); this possibility makes the inversion of the datasets collected over similar settings extremely efficient.

Acknowledgments. The authors are very grateful to Dr. Henning Persson (Geological Survey of Sweden, SGU) for his support during the survey and for providing the background material. In addition, many thanks are due to the Engineering Geology Division of Lund University for its logistical support.

References

1. Guillemoteau, J., Christensen, N.B., Jacobsen, B.H., Tronicke, J.: Fast 3D multichannel deconvolution of electromagnetic induction loop-loop apparent conductivity data sets acquired at low induction numbers. Geophysics **82**(6), E357–E369 (2017)

2. Koganti, T., Van De Vijver, E., Allred, B.J., Greve, M.H., Ringgaard, J., Iversen, B.V.: Mapping of agricultural subsurface drainage systems using a frequency-domain ground penetrating radar and evaluating its performance using a single-frequency multi-receiver electromagnetic induction instrument. Sensors **20**(14), 3922 (2020)
3. Karshakov, E.V., Podmogov, Y.G., Kertsman, V.M., Moilanen, J.: Combined frequency domain and time domain airborne data for environmental and engineering challenges. J. Environ. Eng. Geophys. **22**(1), 1–11 (2017)
4. Yin, C., Hodges, G.: 3D animated visualization of EM diffusion for a frequency-domain helicopter EM system. Geophysics **72**(1), F1–F7 (2007)
5. Won, I.J., Oren, A., Funak, F.: GEM-2A: A programmable broadband helicopter-towed electromagnetic sensorGEM-2A HEM Sensor. Geophysics **68**(6), 1888–1895 (2003)
6. Dzikunoo, E.A., Vignoli, G., Jørgensen, F., Yidana, S.M., Banoeng-Yakubo, B.: New regional stratigraphic insights from a 3D geological model of the Nasia sub-basin, Ghana, developed for hydrogeological purposes and based on reprocessed B-field data originally collected for mineral exploration. Solid Earth **11**(2), 349–361 (2020)
7. Thiesson, J., Kessouri, P., Schamper, C., Tabbagh, A.: Calibration of frequency-domain electromagnetic devices used in near-surface surveying. Near Surface Geophys. **12**(4), 481–491 (2014)
8. Foged, N., Auken, E., Christiansen, A.V., Sørensen, K.I.: Test-site calibration and validation of airborne and ground-based TEM systems. Geophysics **78**(2), E95–E106 (2013)
9. Ley-Cooper, Y., Macnae, J., Robb, T., Vrbancich, J.: Identification of calibration errors in helicopter electromagnetic (HEM) data through transform to the altitude-corrected phase-amplitude domain. Geophysics **71**(2), G27–G34 (2006)
10. Triantafilis, J., Laslett, G.M., McBratney, A.B.: Calibrating an electromagnetic induction instrument to measure salinity in soil under irrigated cotton. Soil Sci. Soc. Am. J. **64**(3), 1009–1017 (2000)
11. Minsley, B.J., Smith, B.D., Hammack, R., Sams, J.I., Veloski, G.: Calibration and filtering strategies for frequency domain electromagnetic data. J. Appl. Geophys. **80**, 56–66 (2012)
12. Bai, P., Vignoli, G., Hansen, T.M.: 1D stochastic inversion of airborne time-domain electromagnetic data with realistic prior and accounting for the forward modeling error. Remote Sensing **13**(19), 3881 (2021)
13. Hansen, T.M., Cordua, K.S., Jacobsen, B.H., Mosegaard, K.: Accounting for imperfect forward modeling in geophysical inverse problems—exemplified for crosshole tomography. Geophysics **79**(3), H1–H21 (2014)
14. Viezzoli, A., Auken, E., Munday, T.: Spatially constrained inversion for quasi 3D modelling of airborne electromagnetic data–an application for environmental assessment in the Lower Murray Region of South Australia. Explor. Geophys. **40**(2), 173–183 (2009)
15. Brodie, R., Sambridge, M.: A holistic approach to inversion of frequency-domain airborne EM data. Geophysics **71**(6), G301–G312 (2006)
16. McLachlan, P., Blanchy, G., Binley, A.: EMagPy: open-source standalone software for processing, forward modeling and inversion of electromagnetic induction data. Comput. Geosci. **146**, 104561 (2021)
17. Vignoli, G., Fiandaca, G., Christiansen, A.V., Kirkegaard, C., Auken, E.: Sharp spatially constrained inversion with applications to transient electromagnetic data. Geophys. Prospect. **63**(1), 243–255 (2015)
18. Klose, T., Guillemoteau, J., Vignoli, G., Tronicke, J.: Laterally constrained inversion (LCI) of multi-configuration EMI data with tunable sharpness. J. Appl. Geophys. **196**, 104519 (2022)
19. Vignoli, G., Sapia, V., Menghini, A., Viezzoli, A.: Examples of improved inversion of different airborne electromagnetic datasets via sharp regularization. J. Environ. Eng. Geophys. **22**(1), 51–61 (2017)

20. Ley-Cooper, A.Y., et al.: Airborne electromagnetic modelling options and their consequences in target definition. Explor. Geophys. **46**(1), 74–84 (2015)

21. Klose, T., Guillemoteau, J., Vignoli, G., Walter, J., Herrmann, A., Tronicke, J.: Structurally constrained inversion by means of a Minimum Gradient Support regularizer: examples of FD-EMI data inversion constrained by GPR reflection data. Geophys. J. Int. **233**(3), 1938–1949 (2023)

22. Pagliara, G., Vignoli, G.: Focusing inversion techniques applied to electrical resistance tomography in an experimental tank. In: XI International Congress Proceedings of the International Association for Mathematical Geology, Liege, Belgium (2006)

23. Thibaut, R., Kremer, T., Royen, A., Ngun, B.K., Nguyen, F., Hermans, T.: A new workflow to incorporate prior information in minimum gradient support (MGS) inversion of electrical resistivity and induced polarization data. J. Appl. Geophys. **187**, 104286 (2021)

24. Fiandaca, G., Doetsch, J., Vignoli, G., Auken, E.: Generalized focusing of time-lapse changes with applications to direct current and time-domain induced polarization inversions. Geophys. J. Int. **203**(2), 1101–1112 (2015)

25. Karaoulis, M., Revil, A., Tsourlos, P., Werkema, D.D., Minsley, B.J.: IP4DI: a software for time-lapse 2D/3D DC-resistivity and induced polarization tomography. Comput. Geosci. **54**, 164–170 (2013)

26. Zhou, J., Revil, A., Karaoulis, M., Hale, D., Doetsch, J., Cuttler, S.: Image-guided inversion of electrical resistivity data. Geophys. J. Int. **197**(1), 292–309 (2014)

27. Vignoli, G., Guillemoteau, J., Barreto, J., Rossi, M.: Reconstruction, with tunable sparsity levels, of shear wave velocity profiles from surface wave data. Geophys. J. Int. **225**(3), 1935–1951 (2021)

28. Hansen, T.M.: Efficient probabilistic inversion using the rejection sampler - exemplified on airborne EM data. Geophys. J. Int. **224**(1), 543–557 (2021)

29. Hansen, T.M., Minsley, B.J.: Inversion of airborne EM data with an explicit choice of prior model. Geophys. J. Int. **218**(2), 1348–1366 (2019)

30. Mosegaard, K., Tarantola, A.: Monte Carlo sampling of solutions to inverse problems. J. Geophys. Res. Solid Earth **100**(B7), 12431–12447 (1995)

31. Tikhonov, A.N., Arsenin, V.Y.: Solutions of Ill-Posed Problems, 1st edn. V. H. Winston & Sons, Washington, U.S.A. (1977)

32. Rücker, C., Günther, T., Wagner, F.M.: pyGIMLi: an open-source library for modelling and inversion in geophysics. Comput. Geosci. **109**, 106–123 (2017)

33. Høyer, A.S., Vignoli, G., Hansen, T.M., Vu, L.T., Keefer, D.A., Jørgensen, F.: Multiple-point statistical simulation for hydrogeological models: 3-D training image development and conditioning strategies. Hydrol. Earth Syst. Sci. **21**(12), 6069–6089 (2017)

34. Bai, P., Vignoli, G., Viezzoli, A., Nevalainen, J., Vacca, G.: (Quasi-) real-time inversion of airborne time-domain electromagnetic data via artificial neural network. Remote Sens. **12**(20), 3440 (2020)

35. Neal, R.M.: Bayesian Learning for Neural Networks, vol. 118. Springer, Germany (2012). https://doi.org/10.1007/978-1-4612-0745-0

36. Zhdanov, M.S., Vignoli, G., Ueda, T.: Sharp boundary inversion in crosswell travel-time tomography. J. Geophys. Eng. **3**(2), 122–134 (2006)

37. Haynie, K.L., Khan, S.D.: Shallow subsurface detection of buried weathered hydrocarbons using GPR and EMI. Mar. Pet. Geol. **77**, 116–123 (2016)

38. Rashed, M., Niyazi, B.: Environmental impact assessment of the former Al-Musk lake wastewater dumpsite using electromagnetic induction technique. Earth Syst. Environ. **1**(1), 1–10 (2017)

39. Torin, L., Davidsson, L., Nilsson, M.: Inledandeprojektering av Nisses kemtvätt i Osby. Report for Sveriges Geologiska Undersökning by WSP Environmental Sverige, Sweden (2021)

Transportation Infrastructures Exposed to Seismic Risk: Evaluation of Social Costs for Resilience Design

Mauro D'Apuzzo[1]([✉]) [iD], Azzurra Evangelisti[1] [iD], Giuseppe Cappelli[1],
Vittorio Nicolosi[2] [iD], Rose-Line Spacagna[1], and Luca Paolella[1]

[1] University of Cassino and Southern Lazio, Via G. di Biasio 43, 03043 Cassino, Italy
{dapuzzo,giuseppe.cappelli1,rlspacagna,paolella}@unicas.it
[2] University of Rome "Tor Vergata", via del Politecnico 1, 00133 Rome, Italy
nicolosi@uniroma2.it

Abstract. Seismic risk assessment and management of civil infrastructure systems are prominent topic for researchers. Different methods and approaches were proposed in the past and in this study, a methodology to evaluate social cost due to reduction or loss of serviceability of road network caused by catastrophic event as the liquefaction phenomenon, was developed. The strategy involves the combination of hazard, vulnerability and exposure of the transportation network by means of geotechnical and traffic analyses.

The methodology was applied to the Municipality of Terre del Reno (Italy), that in 2012 was hit by a strong seismic sequence which caused severe liquefaction phenomena on the territory.

Five different seismic events with increasing seismic intensity were simulated and, according to the damage level occurred, a grade of serviceability to the road network, was assigned. For each scenario, a traffic analysis, to evaluate the travel time, was performed and the social cost in terms of Over Delay Cost were evaluated.

The results show an increasing Over Delay Cost as the seismic intensity increases, until the isolation of the Municipality, when a reduction was observed. It can be due a huge number of daily trips forcibly suppressed.

Although the methodology refers to damage caused by liquefaction phenomena, it is simply adaptable to any catastrophic event.

Keywords: Seismic Resilience · Transportation Network · Social Cost · Embankments · Serviceability · Liquefaction

1 Introduction

The long and forced coexistence with the global pandemic has led to rethink the modern societies and innovative economies by improving speed and multi-level communications: information, knowledges, services, goods, people move more quickly than before. Reliability, efficiency, and safety are key aspects required to both emerging and

O. Gervasi et al. (Eds.): ICCSA 2023 Workshops, LNCS 14111, pp. 639–649, 2023.
https://doi.org/10.1007/978-3-031-37126-4_41

traditional communication networks, especially when extreme and disastrous scenarios happen. Catastrophic phenomena, as liquefaction induced by earthquakes, affecting conventional transportation systems as rail or road networks, can cause both direct and indirect economic losses. In fact, several events in the world (as Christchurch 2010, 2011 and 2016; Tohoku Oki, 2011; Emilia Romagna, 2012; Kumamoto, 2016) have shown the destructive potential and economical damages of liquefaction due to seismic events.

From early nineties, several national and international projects and methodologies have been promoted with the aim to estimate the potential losses induced by catastrophic events [1–5]. As far as transportation networks and infrastructures are concerned, the most significant researches and projects, with their main features, are summarized in the Table 1.

Table 1. Summary of the main research projects/methodologies for losses estimation.

Project/ methodology	Ref.	Hazard type	Losses Estimation	Transportation Analysis
AllTraIn	[6]	Natural, Man-made	Element level	No
STRIT	[7]	Natural	Element level	No
HAZUS	[8]	Natural	Network level	No
SYNER-G	[9]	Natural	Network level	Yes
Molarius et al	[10]	Natural	Network level	No
SecMan	[11]	Man-made	Network level	No
SeRoN	[12]	Man-made	Network level	Yes
Seville et al.	[13]	Natural	Network level	Yes
REDARS 2	[14]	Natural	Network level	Yes
Chang L.	[15]	Natural	Network level	Yes

It is understandable that as far as catastrophic risk assessment and mitigation interventions decision-making on transportation systems are concerned, the element level (bridges, tunnels, …) analysis is insufficient and, at least the network-level analysis within a long-term period, is required. According to the transportation network analysis classification [9], summarized in the Table 2, the *Capacity Analysis* seems represent a minimum requirement for guaranteeing reliable results in terms of socio-economic impacts related to the traffic flows rearrangement.

Table 2. Summary of the transportation network analysis classification [9].

Transportation network analysis type	Description
Vulnerability	related to the damage level of each single element of the transportation network (as bridge, tunnel, embankment, etc.), according to a specific post-seismic scenario
Connectivity	according to a specific post-earthquake scenario, evaluates the accessibility to specific or strategic areas when the loss of service of some connections occurs
Capacity	related to the network capacity to accommodate traffic flows, provides direct and indirect losses due to damage levels occurred of the whole network
Serviceability	provides a more realistic estimate of total loss on the long-term period, considering both direct and indirect impacts on the economic sectors

Follow this direction the main aim of this study is to present a methodological approach for the evaluation of social losses due to liquefaction damage suffered by a transportation system and its application on a case study.

2 Methodology

The probability of occurrence of the risk of liquefaction is associated with the seismic intensity, the motion of the soil, the susceptibility to subsurface liquefaction, the response to infrastructure, physical damage, and socio-economic losses. The assessment of the risk of liquefaction can therefore be summarized as follows (1):

$$LR = f\{H, V, E\} \tag{1}$$

where:
  LR = Liquefaction Risk;
  H = Hazard;
  V = Vulnerability;
  E = Exposure.

The factors necessary for the occurrence of liquefaction are:

- The seismic event;
- Sand with limited fine content;
- Low density;
- Saturation.

According to the proposed methodology, the coupled approach for the subsoil is proposed - the infrastructural responses, customizing the formula of Karamitros et al. [16], which was then applied to estimate the settlements of the road embankment [17].

Table 3. Definition of damage state for Roadway embankments [18].

Damage State	Permanent Ground Deformation [m]			Damage description	Road Network Serviceability
	min	max	mean		
Minor	0.02	0.08	0.05	Surface slide of embankment at the top of slope; minor cracks on road surface; minor track displacement	Useful road with speed reduction
Moderate	0.08	0.22	0.15	Deep slide or slump of embankment; medium cracks on road surface and/or settlement; medium track displacement	Partially open during repair works (alternating direction of travel)
Extensive	0.22	0.58	0.40	Extensive slump and slide of embankment; extensive cracks on road surface and/or settlement; extensive tracks displacement	Unusable

As regards the assessment of the vulnerability of road embankments, the SYNER-G classification for the definition of damage status limits has been adopted [18]. The main features have been summarized in Table 3:

A catastrophic event causes damage to the transport network, which can be assessed as a sum of direct losses (such as the cost of repair or repositioning of damaged elements) and indirect (reduction or interruption of the transport network service and its impact on society and the economy). In this methodology the *Capacity Analysis,* which represents a satisfying approach to evaluate socio-economic impacts related to the mobility in the post-seismic scenario, has been performed to evaluate the indirect losses in terms of the *Total Delay Cost, TDC.*

In fact, the reduction/loss of serviceability of the transportation networks, which can mainly depend on the features of the transportation system and the traffic demand, has as principal consequence the impact on the traffic flows and the trips of the study area. Assuming that the *Generalized Transport Cost, GTC,* is a measure of the overall cost (including travel time cost) that is "paid" by each transport user in a specific study area, the *TDC* can be evaluated by means of the following expression (2):

$$TDC = GTC_{post} - GTC_{pre} \tag{2}$$

where:

TDC = Total Delay Cost computed daily.

GTC_{post} = Generalized Transport Cost in the post-seismic scenario;

GTC_{pre} = Generalized Transport Cost in the pre-seismic scenario.

The TDC multiplied by the number of days needed to ensure the restoration of the situation pre-event provide the total social cost defined by the acronym *OSC*.

This social cost represents the cost to the population of the affected area.

The Capacity analysis requires the development and implementation of the *Travel Demand Forecasting Model, TDFM*.

A TDFM [19] is a model consisting of four sub-models.

It is defined cascading because the output of the previous model becomes the input of the next model.

These sub-models essentially define the origin and destination of travel, the route chosen by the user, the means of transport and the time taken to make the travel. It is worth noting that, although the methodology refers to damage caused by liquefaction phenomena, it is replicable and adaptable for any destructive event or calamity.

3 Case Study

The Emilian Po Valley (Italy) has been subject to two major seismic events that have caused a total of 27 victims, about 400 injured, over 15,000 displaced people and significant damage to the cultural and economic heritage of the area. Furthermore, due to the conditions of the subsoil, widespread liquefaction phenomena have been observed. In the municipalities of San Carlo, Sant'Agostino and Mirabello, (see in Fig. 1) along the old riverbed of the Reno River, the greatest concentration of liquefaction evidence, have been detected [20]. These urban areas and their relative road networks have been built near the paleo-channel and paleo-levees of the Reno River where the subsoil can be categorized into (from the top to down): fluvial channel deposits; a stratum of fine-grained materials (swamps) and Pleistocene alluvial plain. Finally, in order to protect the territories against flooding, the artificial silty sand layers have been built along the old riverbed.

Due to the importance of the series of seismic events and the numerous and relevant observations of liquefaction phenomena, the area of the municipalities of S. Carlo,

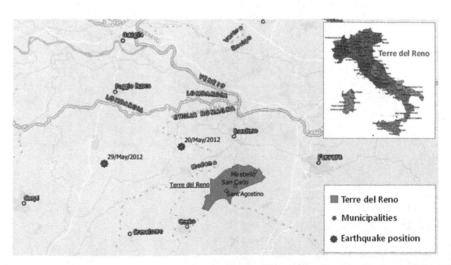

Fig. 1. The Terre del Reno areas, the municipalities of Sant'Agostino, San Carlo and Mirabello and the position of the two major seismic events occurred in 2012. [26]

Sant'Agostino and Mirabello, called Terre del Reno, has been therefore selected as the case study in the analysis of resilience due to liquefaction damage on the road network.

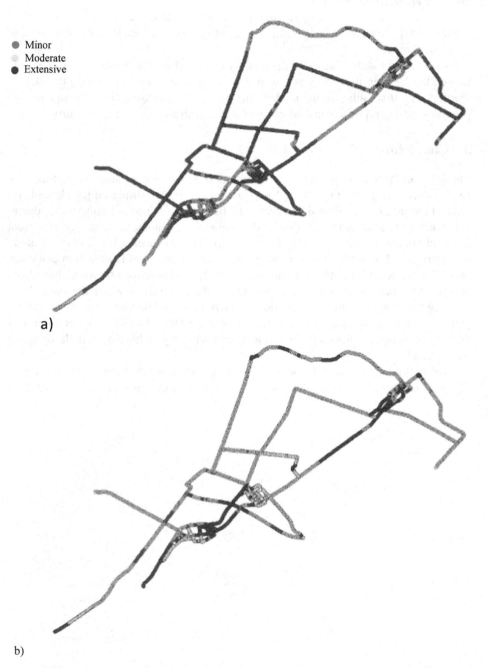

● Minor
● Moderate
● Extensive

a)

b)

Fig. 2. Maps of the embankment damage levels for a) RP 30Y and b) RP 975Y.

3.1 Liquefaction Phenomenon and Damage Evaluation

According to the liquefaction risk assessment proposed in [21], the coupled approach for subsurface and infrastructure resettlement has been adopted. Indeed, from a comparison with an effective stress calculation using an advanced numerical model [17], the formula of Karamitros et al. [16] has been adapted to calculate the sets induced by the liquefaction of the banks of Terre del Reno. To apply a probabilistic approach, four increasing seismic events have been simulated for the road network damage evaluation. Return Periods (RPs) of 30, 50, 475 and 975 years, have been selected.

By way of example in the b).

Figure 2 is reported the road network damage level for RP 30 years and 975 years.

3.2 Travel Demand Forecasting Model of Terre del Reno

A Terre del Reno TDFM was developed which, after sensitivity analysis [22] was calibrated and experimentally validated in a 60 km radius buffer area around a rural area in the Terre del Reno district [22]. In the Fig. 3 the graph of the study area has been reported.

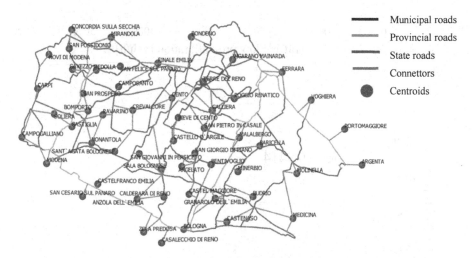

Fig. 3. Graph of the Study area [26].

In particular, the scenarios chosen for the case study are divided according to different "schedules":

- "Peak" which occurs mainly in two-time bands (from 7:00 to 9:00 and from 17:00 to 19:00)
- "Median peak" (12:00 to 14:00)
- "Off-peak" for the rest of the day.

The O/D matrix was assessed from the commuting data provided by ISTAT [23] and then calibrated with traffic counts provided by the Emilia - Romagna region [24].

As an example, in Fig. 4 the results of the TDFM calibration have been reported, in terms of traffic flows for the morning peak hours.

To convert the traffic delay into Overall Social Cost, a cost of 45€ for heavy vehicles and 12€ for the others, has been applied.

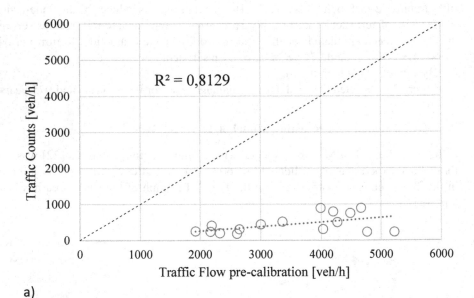

a)

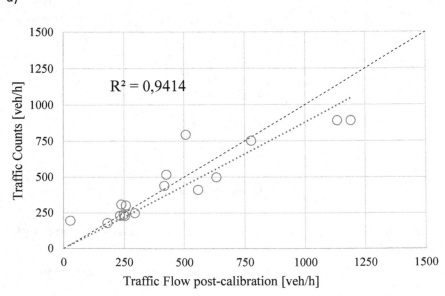

b)

Fig. 4. Comparison of Traffic Counts VS Predicted Traffic Flow a) pre-calibration and b) post-calibration [26].

4 Results

For each scenario, including the actual scenario of May 2012, the infrastructure damage incurred was assessed and identified in the TDC and OSC both expressed in the Eq. (2). The results in terms of traffic and OSC can be seen in Table 4.

Table 4. Summary of the results in terms of traffic delay and OSC, suffered by Terre del Reno, for different return periods.

Return Period	Traffic Delay [h]	Overall Social Cost [€]
30 Years	1014	34.354.989
50 Years	1118	38.003.367
May 2012 Event	1636	62.481.661
475 Years	1063	46.689.300
975 Years	1019	48.569.595

As it is possible to see in the summary of For each scenario, including the actual scenario of May 2012, the infrastructure damage incurred was assessed and identified in the TDC and OSC both expressed in the Eq. (2). The results in terms of traffic and OSC can be seen in Table 4.

Table 4, in the last two analyzed return periods, a reduction, in terms of both traffic delay and OSC, has been highlighted. While it may seem counterintuitive, the reduction is correctly related to the damage level suffered by the road network. In fact, in the last two return period scenarios, a complete isolation of the Municipality of Terre del Reno occurred. In these cases, a considerable number of trips, which generally take place the territory of Terre del Reno, is suppressed. These lost trips are also a cost suffered by the community which must renounce to the movements of its normal everyday life.

5 Conclusions

A liquefaction risk assessment methodology to estimate the social cost suffered by a community after a seismic event has been presented. The strategy involves the evaluation and combination of the territorial distribution of hazard, vulnerability, and exposure also by means of geoinformatics [25].

A probabilistic approach has been performed on the Municipality of Terre del Reno, by simulating five different seismic events with increasing return periods. The relative liquefaction damage levels suffered by the road network have been evaluated and, for each scenario, a traffic analysis, to evaluate the travel time, has been performed.

The analysis shows that traffic delays suffered by the population increase considerably as the seismic intensity of the event increases.

This implies, at a given intensity of event, also the isolation of the Municipality.

This in isolation would appear to decrease the amount of traffic on the network but, generates additional costs that the community faces. Further analyses are needed to quantify in a proper way, the economic value of the suppressed trips due to the loss of accessibility to the Municipality.

Acknowledgement. The authors would like to thank the EU funded project LIQUEFACT "Assessment and mitigation of liquefaction potential across Europe: a holistic approach to protect structures/infrastructures for improved resilience to earthquake-induced liquefaction disasters", project ID 700748 funded under the H2020-DRS-2015. This study was also carried out within the MOST – Sustainable Mobility Center and received funding from the European Union Next-GenerationEU (PIANO NAZIONALE DI RIPRESA E RESILIENZA (PNRR) – MISSIONE 4 COMPONENTE 2, INVESTIMENTO 1.4 – D.D. 1033 17/06/2022, CN00000023). The research leading to these results has also received funding by Project "Ecosistema dell'innovazione Rome Technopole" financed by EU in NextGenerationEU plan through MUR Decree n. 1051 23.06.2022 - CUP H33C22000420001. This manuscript reflects only the authors' views and opinions, neither the European Union nor the European Commission can be considered responsible for them.

References

1. Applied Technology Council project ATC-25. Seismic Vulnerability and Impact of Disruption of Lifelines in the Conterminous United States, Applied Technology Council. USA (1991)
2. Risk Assessment Tools for Diagnosis of Urban Areas against Seismic Disasters, RADIUS project. Assessment Tools for Diagnostic of Urban Areas against Seismic Disasters. Secrétariat IDNDR (International Decade for Natural Disaster Reduction). United Nations. (1996). http://www.geohaz.org/radius/
3. GEMITIS-Nice Projet, Fort-de-France; Evaluation du risquesismique: programme d'étude (1997)
4. RISK-UE project. "An advanced approach to earthquake risk scenarios, with applications to different European cities" (2001–2004). http://www.risk-ue.net
5. Japan International Cooperation Agency, JICA project. The study on earthquake disaster mitigation in the Kathmandu Valley. Nippon Koei Co LTD, Final report, Kingdom of Nepal (2002)
6. All-Hazard Guide for Transport Infrastructure. © Copyright 2013–2015. The AllTraInConsorsium. http://www.alltrain-project.eu/
7. STRIT project Homepage. http://www.stress-scarl.com/it/innovazione/i-progetti-nazionali/strit.html. Accessed 15 Feb 2020
8. Multi-hazard Loss Estimation Methodology Earthquake Model HAZUS®MH MR4 Technical Manual. National Institute of Building Sciences. (NIBS). Washington, DC. (2004). http://www.fema.gov/hazus/
9. Systemic Seismic Vulnerability and Risk Analysis for Buildings, Lifeline Networks and Infrastructures Safety Gain (2014). ISBN 978-92-79-33135-0, https://doi.org/10.2788/23242, http://www.vce.at/SYNER-G/files/project/proj-overview.html
10. Molarius, R., et al.: Systemic vulnerability and resilience analysis of electric and transport network failure in cases of extreme winter storms. In: Beer, M., Au, S.-K., Hall, J.W. (eds.) Vulnerability, Uncertainty, and Risk: Quantification, Mitigation, and Management, pp. 608–617. American Society of Civil Engineers (ASCE), Reston (2014)
11. SECURITY MANUAL FOR EUROPEAN ROAD INFRASTRUCTURE. Copyright: SecMan Consortium (2013). www.secman-project.eu

12. Deliverable D400: Importance of the structures for the traffic network. © Copyright 2009–2012. The SeRoN Consortium (2012)
13. Seville, E., Nicholson, A.: Risk and impact of natural hazards on a road network. J. Transp. Eng. (ASCE) **127** (2001). https://doi.org/10.1061/(ASCE)0733-947X(2001)127:2(159)
14. Werner, S.D., et al.: REDARS 2 methodology and software for seismic risk analysis of highway systems. Special Report MCEER-06-SP08. Federal Highway Administration (2006)
15. Chang, L.: Transportation system modeling and applications in earthquake engineering. Doctoral thesis in the Graduate College of the University of Illinois at Urbana-Champaign (2010)
16. Karamitros, D.K., Bouckovalas, G.D., Chaloulos, Y.K.: Seismic settlements of shallow foundations on liquefiable soil with a clay crust. Soil Dyn. Earthq. Eng. **46**, 64–76 (2013)
17. Modoni, G., Spacagna, R.L., Paolella, L., Salvatore, E., Rasulo, A., Martelli, L.: Liquefaction risk assessment: lesson learned from a case study. In: Proceedings of the VI International Conference of Earthquake Geotechnical Engineering, Rome (2019)
18. Pitilakis, K., Crowley, H., Kaynia, A.M. (eds.): SYNER-G: Typology Definition and Fragility Functions for Physical Elements at Seismic Risk. GGEE, vol. 27. Springer, Dordrecht (2014). https://doi.org/10.1007/978-94-007-7872-6
19. Cascetta, E.: Transportation Systems Analysis. Models and Applications. 2nd edn, pp. 1–752. Springer, Heidelberg (2009). https://doi.org/10.1007/978-0-387-75857-2
20. Fioravante, V., et al.: Earthquake geotechnical engineering aspects: the 2012 Emilia Romagna earthquake (Italy). In: Seventh International Conference on Case Histories in Geotechnical Engineering, 29th April–4th May 2013. Chicago (US) (2013)
21. D'Apuzzo, M., et al.: Strategies for the assessment of risk induced by seismic liquefaction on road networks. In: Beer, M., Zio, E. (eds.) 29th European Safety and Reliability Conference. Copyright ©2019 by ESREL2019 Organizers, pp. 1651–1658. Published by Research Publishing, Singapore (2019). https://doi.org/10.3850/978-981-11-2724-3_0589-cd
22. D'Apuzzo, M., et al.: Simplified approach for liquefaction risk assessment of transportation systems: preliminary outcomes. In: Gervasi, O., et al. (eds.) ICCSA 2020. LNCS, vol. 12255, pp. 130–145. Springer, Cham (2020). https://doi.org/10.1007/978-3-030-58820-5_10
23. Italian Institute of Statistic (ISTAT). https://www.istat.it/it/archivio/139381
24. Emilia-Romagna Region. https://servizissiir.regione.emilia-romagna.it/FlussiMTS/
25. Spacagna, R.L., Rasulo, A., Modoni, G.: Geostatistical analysis of settlements induced by groundwater extraction. In: Gervasi, O., et al. (eds.) ICCSA 2017. LNCS, vol. 10407, pp. 350–364. Springer, Cham (2017). https://doi.org/10.1007/978-3-319-62401-3_26
26. D'Apuzzo, M., et al.: Seismic resilience assessment strategy for social and sustainability impact evaluation on transportation road network: a seismic liquefaction-induced damage application. Sustainability **14**(14), 8411 (2022)

Low-Cost Geomatics Surveys for Emergency Interventions on Cultural Heritage. The Case of Historic Wall in Cagliari

Giuseppina Vacca$^{(\boxtimes)}$ ⓘ and Andrea Dessi

Department of Civil and Environmental Engineering and Architecture, University of Cagliari, 09123 Cagliari, Italy
vaccag@unica.it

Abstract. The documentation and metric knowledge of cultural heritage is becoming an increasingly important need, especially concerning the state of degradation of some historical assets. In this context, the metric documentation of the investigated heritage becomes fundamental for a complete knowledge of the asset to support architects and engineers in the restoration process. Recently, methods and geomatics instrumentation have been developed for the survey of cultural heritage aiming at optimizing costs and time. For example, the Apple has integrated, into its devices, a LiDAR sensor capable of providing a 3D model of spaces and objects. The paper presents the studies of their potential about the study and metric documentation of cultural heritage, in particular in cases of extreme urgency and danger of the architectural asset where the speed of survey and non-contact with it becomes relevant.

We focused on the case study of a perimeter wall of a historical building. The survey was performed with two fast and expeditious geomatics methods such as the Close Range Photogrammetry (CRP) and with the LiDAR Apple sensor of the iPad Pro. The wall was also surveyed with Terrestrial Laser Scanner methodology for the validation of the results.

Keywords: Low-cost LiDAR sensor · 3D model · cultural heritage

1 Introduction

The documentation and metric knowledge of the cultural heritage are becoming crucial if we consider the state of degradation of the major part of the historical built heritage and the associated restoration interventions. For these valuable architectures, in-depth metric documentation is fundamental for an overall understanding of these structures, and, in turn, to support architects and engineers in optimizing restoration, conservation, safeguarding and artifact enhancement [1–4]. Recently, however, public funding intended for geometric investigations has been reduced, leading stakeholders and researchers to develop low-cost geomatic tools and methodologies to tackle this necessity, without compromising too much the metric accuracy [5]. In this respect, among the low-cost

O. Gervasi et al. (Eds.): ICCSA 2023 Workshops, LNCS 14111, pp. 650–664, 2023.
https://doi.org/10.1007/978-3-031-37126-4_42

geomatic techniques, multi-image photogrammetry [6–8] is certainly the most effective in facilitating the democratization of the metric documentary process and, thus, in contributing to a wider involvement of users without any specific geomatics expertise.

Via multi-image photogrammetry, it is possible to obtain complete and exhaustive 3D metric surveys with a rapid and intuitive approach [9, 10]. Several examples on this matter are reported in the literature: ranging from architectural applications [11–13] to control and monitoring of structures [14, 15], or environmental and forestry assessments [16–19]. Structure-from-Motion (SfM) algorithm, used in multi-image photogrammetry, produces accurate point clouds with good repeatability [20] and are well suited for the production of metric documentation.

For 3D metric surveys, new miniaturized and low-cost sensors have recently paved the way to cost-effective survey and 3D modeling of buildings or historical-cultural heritage assets. Among the most interesting tools, the laser scanning sensor implemented, since 2020, in Apple devices IPhone (from 12 Pro) and IPad Pro is worth to be mentioned. The complete technical specifications of this sensor - recommended mostly for Augmented Reality (AR) and Virtual Reality (VR) - is not available, but, from the scientific literature, it seems that it consists of a solid-state LiDAR (SSL), i.e. a type of LiDAR which, unlike traditional sensors, does not use motorized mechanical parts (ensuring greater reliability) [21, 22]. The points measured by the LiDAR sensor are combined with the information provided by the RGB camera present in the device and the range declared by Apple is 5 m. Furthermore, from various studies, it seems that there are no differences between the LiDAR sensors mounted on the iPhone and the iPad [23].

The use of the Apple LiDAR sensor is possible only through the dedicated apps that can be downloaded from the App Store. Their combined use allows, in addition to the acquisition of the points, exporting the point cloud and the mesh in various formats. For many apps, it exists: 1) a free-of-charge version, which makes it possible to export merely the mesh and/or point cloud, and 2) a paid version (with a monthly or yearly fee) with more advanced functions targeting mainly metric documentation.

Since the advent of the LiDAR sensor in Apple devices, several apps have been developed and research carried out by research groups to study the geomatic potential and functions of both the sensor and the dedicated apps.

In [24], researchers demonstrate the potential and functionality of both sensors in the IPhone and IPad and of some iOS applications (SiteScape, 3DScanner App, EveryPoint). Accuracies are investigated in different relevant scenarios such as: indoor and outdoor, static or dynamic configuration, and in different types of cultural and architectural heritage (e.g., statues, decorated rooms, and external facades). In addition, concerning heritage documentation, Murtiyos et al. [25] studied the potential of the sensor with respect to multi-image photogrammetry and Terrestrial Laser Scanning on a small object, a facade and a 3D space, using two apps: Every Point and SiteScape. On the other hand, in [26], some geometric aspects of the surveys with the Apple sensor have been addressed: local precision, global correctness and surface coverage for indoor and outdoor environments.

In [27] the accuracy achieved with 4 different apps (among the most used for cultural heritage) are studied on the different assets.

The work presented is a part of a broader research on low-cost geomatics methodologies for the survey of cultural heritage. We focused on the case study of a perimeter wall of a historical building. The survey was performed with two low-cost and fast geomatics methods such as the Close Range Photogrammetry (CRP) by means of a Structure from Motion approach (SfM) and with the LiDAR Apple sensor of the iPad Pro using the app Polycam [28]. The wall was also detected with Terrestrial Laser Scanner methodology for the validation of the results.

2 Materials and Methods

The paper presented is part of a broader research on geomatic methodologies for the survey of cultural heritage with low cost geomatics methodologies. In this context, a perimeter wall of the Institute of Normal Human Anatomy of the University of Cagliari was used as a case study. The building dating back to the early '900 is surrounded by historic walls that, in January 2023, presented cracks that forced the municipality of Cagliari to close the adjacent road. This road is an important access to the historic center of the city. Its closure has created considerable inconvenience to city mobility and therefore the urgent procedure for the restoration of the perimeter wall of the building was immediately activated.

The perimeter wall has a length of about 43 m and for our study 2 distinct parts were chosen called Part 1 (Fig. 1) made of stone without plaster, free of support structures; and Part 2 (Fig. 2), plastered, is the most compromised supported by an iron structure.

Fig. 1. The case study – Part 1

Fig. 2. The case study – Part 2

The property is bound by the Archaeological Superintendence of Fine Arts and Landscape for the metropolitan city of Cagliari and the provinces of Oristano and South Sardinia as a historical-artistic asset and therefore required that all interventions for the safety and restoration of the wall do not modify neither the structure, nor the materials, nor the shape of the wall. The municipality of Cagliari required a fast intervention to speed up the reopening of the road. The works, which started with the urgent procedure, included a geomatic survey of the parts of the wall subject to intervention to document metrically and photographically the parts subject to restoration.

The survey was performed with two fast and expeditious geomatic methods such as the Close Range Photogrammetry (CRP) by means of a Structure from Motion approach (SfM) and with the LiDAR sensor inserted in the iPad Pro, using the Polycam app. The wall was also detected with Terrestrial Laser Scanner methodology for the validation of the two methods. The validation of the point clouds of the LiDAR sensor was performed by means of the CloudCompare software [29].

2.1 Terrestrial Laser Scanner

In order to evaluate the accuracy of the scans performed with the LiDAR sensor, the case study was surveyed with the Faro Focus 3D Terrestrial Laser Scanner.

The Faro Focus 3D Terrestrial Laser Scanner is a compact scanner characterized by an operative range spanning between 0.6 and 120 m, with a ranging error of ± 2 mm for scanner–object distances between 10 and 25 m.

The scans were processed by using the JRC Reconstructor software v. 3.1.0 by Gexcel Ltd [30]. All clouds from the apps were aligned to those from the TLS by using the JRC Reconstructor software.

For the design of the scans, we started by thinking about the geometry of the wall and the scale of restitution. The presence of architectural details and the situation of the deformations to be detected were considered. From these considerations, it was decided to perform the scans at a resolution of ¼, with 3x quality, which corresponds to a resolution of 7 mm / 10 m. To ensure an overlap between the scans of at least 30%, 4 scans we made.

Figures 3 and 4 show the point clouds of the two parts of the wall under study. The Point cloud Part 1 had 6.703.748 points, while Point Cloud Part 2 had 9.023.013 points.

Fig. 3. TLS point cloud – Part 1

Fig. 4. TLS point cloud – Part 2

2.2 Apple LiDAR sensor Survey

For the geomatics survey with the Apple LiDAR sensor was used the iPad Pro. It has the following specifications: 11" Liquid Retina display, weight of 468 g, 512 GB of memory, 8-core CPU, 8 GB RAM and iOS 15.0.2 software version. It is equipped with a 12MP wide-angle and 10MP ultra-wide-angle RGB camera system and a LiDAR sensor.

Polycam app (version 2.3.9 by charge—Fig. 5) was used for survey. It allows to scan objects by choosing between the LiDAR and ROOM options. This last option allows obtaining, in addition to the point cloud of the scanned room, the horizontal section in dxf format. In the point cloud processing phase, it is possible to choose between Fast (allowing for fast processing for acquisition verification), Space (designed for space scans), Object (for object scans) and Custom modes. For the Custom mode, it is possible to choose the Depth Range (from 0.1 to 6 m), the Voxel Size (from 3 mm to 27 mm) and the simplification to be applied to the mesh (in percentage). Polycam was purchased, at a cost of $6.99/month, allowing us to export the point clouds in different formats (a possibility prevented in the free version, which is capable of ex-porting only the mesh in glTF format). The two parts of the wall were taken over separately. The survey was carried out by holding iPad always parallel to the wall object of the survey and at distance about 2 m. The scan was processed in the "Space" mode.

In Fig. 6 it can be seen how, especially for Part 1, the scan was not able to include the entire height of the wall. This is due to the Apple LiDAR sensor's range of only 5m. To get the whole scan of Part 1 we will have to use a ladder or other support to pick up the Ipad Pro from the ground. Figure 7 shows the complete Part 2 scan.

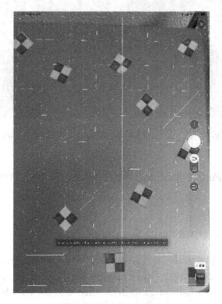

Fig. 5. Polycam App

Fig. 6. Apple LiDAR sensor point cloud – Part 1

Fig. 7. Apple LiDAR sensor point cloud – Part 2

The Point cloud Part 1 had 651.409 points, while Point Cloud Part 2 had 2.830.747points.

2.3 Close Range Photogrammetry Survey

The wall was also surveyed with the Close Range Photogrammetry technique.

The low-cost Close Range Photogrammetric (CRP) system included non-professional digital camera Canon EOS M3 with a sensor CMOS 22.3x14.9 mm and a 24.2 Megapixel resolution; objective EF-S 18–55 mm; the output data formats are Exif 2.3 (JPEG) and RAW (CR2 Canon original). The images were processed with the Metashape commercial software by Agisoft That implements the Structure from Motion (SfM) algorithm. The SfM is a low-cost photogrammetric method for high-resolution topographic reconstructions. The SfM operates under the same basic tenets of the stereoscopic photogrammetry. However, they fundamentally differ because in SfM the geometry of the scene, camera positions and orientation are solved automatically without points known. In the other method, instead, points are solved simultaneously using a highly redundant, iterative bundle adjustment procedure, based on a database of features automatically extracted from a set of multiple images with a high degree of overlap [31].

The Metashape workflows consist in the following main steps: image import, image alignment, generation of the sparse point cloud, optimization of image alignment, georeferenced, generation of the dense point cloud, generation DEM and generation orthophoto.

Photogrammetric surveys were carried out for both parts of the wall by taking images with the optical axis as orthogonal to the wall as possible. A total of 66 images were taken for the Part 1 and 55 images for the Part 2.

The image processing workflow follows the standard steps of SfM software with the solution of the Bundle Adjustment on sparse point cloud, external orientation of the block and generation of the dense point cloud. All images have been elaborated in Medium mode, in fact, as verified in [1] the accuracy does not vary with respect to UltraHigh mode and processing times are reduced.

The Point Cloud 1 had 2,470,590 points (Fig. 8), while Point Cloud 2 had 4,325,094 points (Fig. 9).

The CRP point cloud was georeferenced using 6 GCPs extracted from the TLS point cloud. The global RMS of georeferencing was about 2 cm.

Fig. 8. CRP point cloud – Part 1

Fig. 9. CRP point cloud – Part 2

3 Results

Point clouds from the Appel LiDAR sensor and CRP were compared with each other and validated with the point cloud from TLS.

The validation of the point clouds was performed by means of the CloudCompare software [29] and, specifically, using Cloud-to-Cloud Distance (C2C) tool. Cloud-to-cloud (C2C) analysis calculates the minimal distance between every point of the models using the nearest neighbour algorithm. Furthermore, the software allows the evaluation of statistical parameters, such as the minimal distance, maximal distance, average distance, and standard deviation.

Below are the results of the comparisons made between point clouds.

3.1 Apple LiDAR Sensor vs CRP

The first comparison is between the survey Apple LiDAR point cloud and the CRP point cloud. Table 1 shows the statistical parameters associated to these comparisons.

Figures 10 and 11 show the results of this comparison.

Table 1. C2C analysis - Statistical parameters of the comparisons between the Apple LiDAR sensor and the CRP point clouds.

	Part 1	Part 2
Min (m)	0	0
Max (m)	0.199	0.709
Mean (m)	0.005	0.056
Dev. Stand (m)	0.030	0.128

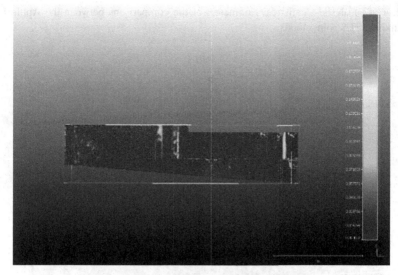

Fig. 10. Discrepancy (m) map between Apple LiDAR and the CRP point clouds – Part 1.

Fig. 11. Discrepancy (m) map between Apple LiDAR and the CRP point clouds – Part 2.

3.2 Apple LiDAR Sensor vs TLS

The second comparison performed is between the survey with the Apple LiDAR sensor and the Terrestrial Laser Scanner. To evaluate the accuracy of the point clouds, they were compared via the Cloud-to-cloud (C2C) analysis. Table 2 shows the statistical parameters associated to these comparisons. Figures 12 and 13 show the results of this comparison.

Table 2. C2C analysis - Statistical parameters of the comparisons between the Apple LiDAR sensor and the TLS point clouds.

	Part 1	Part 2
Min (m)	0	0
Max (m)	0.629	0.287
Mean (m)	0.005	0.011
Dev. Stand (m)	0.038	0.037

Fig. 12. Discrepancy (m) map between Apple LiDAR and the TLS point clouds – Part 1

Fig. 13. Discrepancy (m) map between Apple LiDAR and the TLS point clouds – Part 2

3.3 TLS Vs CRP

The third comparison performed is between the survey with the Terrestrial Laser Scanner and the Close Range Photogrammetry. To evaluate the accuracy of the point clouds, they were compared via the Cloud-to-cloud (C2C) analysis.

Table 3 shows the statistical parameters associated to these comparisons.

Figures 14 and 15 show the results of this comparison.

Table 3. C2C analysis - Statistical parameters of the comparisons between the TLS and the CRP point clouds.

	Part 1	Part 2
Min (m)	0	0
Max (m)	0.660	0.316
Mean (m)	0.006	0.006
Dev. Stand (m)	0.039	0.027

Fig. 14. Discrepancy (m) map between TLS and the CRP point clouds – Part 1.

Fig. 15. Discrepancy (m) map between TLS and the CRP point clouds – Part 2.

4   Discussion and Conclusion

We investigated the accuracy of the low cost geomatics methodologies and techniques, in particular we studied the potential of Apple Lidar sensor incorporated into the latest generation of Apple iPad and the Close Range Photogrammetry with low cost digital camera for the 3D models acquisition of historical, cultural, and architectural heritage assets.

From these results we dare to assert that, in line with other research, both CRP and Apple LiDAR geomatics methodologies can be a valuable tool for the 3D models creating of architectural and cultural heritage [32], providing the possibility to contribute to the metric documentation required in the process of knowledge of the asset. However, it is necessary to pay particular attention to survey mode, especially for the Apple LiDAR sensor. This attention is due to the range of the Apple LiDAR sensor of only 5 m. This limitation, in fact, provides for the use of survey supports in order to access the upper parts of the architectural asset such as stairs or elevators and to provide more scans that must subsequently be joined. This attention will allow you to survey assets wider than the range provided by Apple.

From these researches it therefore seems that these new devices and associated opportunities pave the way for faster production of metric documentation which can be crucial, for example, in emergencies and with limited funds available.

References

1. Barsanti, S.G., Remondino, F., Fenández-Palacios, B.J., Visintini, D.: Critical factors and guidelines for 3D surveying and modelling in cultural heritage. Int. J. Heritage Digital Era **3**(1), 141–158 (2014)
2. Munumer, E., Lerma, J.L.: Fusion of 3D data from different image-based and range-based sources for efficient heritage recording. Digital Heritage **2015**, 83–86 (2015)

3. Deidda, M., Musa, C., Vacca, G.: A GIS of Sardinia's coastal defense system (XVI – XVIII Century). Int. Arch. Photogramm. Remote Sens. Spatial Inf. Sci. **XL-4/W7**, 17–22 (2015). https://doi.org/10.5194/isprsarchives-XL-4-W7-17-2015

4. Giannattasio, C., Grillo, S.M., Vacca, G.: Interdisciplinary study for knowledge and dating of the San Francesco convent in Stampace, Cagliari – Italy (XIII-XXI Century). ISPRS Ann. Photogramm. Remote Sens. Spatial Inf. Sci. **II-5/W1**, 139–144 (2013). https://doi.org/10. 5194/isprsannals-II-5-W1-139-2013

5. Nocerino, E., et al.: A smartphone-based 3D pipeline for the creative industry – the replicate EU project. Int. Arch. Photogramm. Remote Sens. Spatial Inf. Sci. **XLII-2/W3**, 535–541 (2017). https://doi.org/10.5194/isprs-archives-XLII-2-W3-535-2017

6. Vacca, G.: UAV photogrammetry for volume calculations. a case study of an open sand quarry. In: Gervasi, O., Murgante, B., Misra, S., Ana, M.A., Rocha, C., Garau, C. (eds.) Computational Science and Its Applications – ICCSA 2022 Workshops: Malaga, Spain, July 4–7, 2022, Proceedings, Part VI, pp. 505–518. Springer International Publishing, Cham (2022). https:// doi.org/10.1007/978-3-031-10592-0_36

7. Brandolini, F., Patrucco, G.: Structure-From-Motion (SFM) photogrammetry as a non-invasive methodology to digitalize historical documents: a highly flexible and low-cost approach? Heritage **2**, 2124–2136 (2019). https://doi.org/10.3390/heritage2030128

8. Parrinello, S., Dell'Amico, A.: Experience of documentation for the accessibility of widespread cultural heritage. Heritage **2**, 1032–1044 (2019). https://doi.org/10.3390/heritage2010067

9. Janiszewski, M., Torkan, M., Uotinen, L., Rinne, M.: Rapid photogrammetry with a 360-degree camera for tunnel mapping. Remote Sens. **14**, 5494 (2022). https://doi.org/10.3390/rs14215494

10. Teppati Losè, L., Chiabrando, F., Giulio Tonolo, F.: Documentation of complex environments using 360° cameras. The Santa Marta Belltower in Montanaro. Remote Sens. **13**, 3633 (2021)

11. Vacca, G., Dessi A.: Geomatics supporting knowledge of cultural heritage aimed at recovery and restoration. Int. Arch. Photogramm. Remote Sens. Spatial Inf. Sci. 43, 909–915 (2022)

12. Grillo, S.M., Pilia, E., Vacca, G.: Integrated study of the Beata Vergine Assunta dome with Structure from Motion and diagnostic approaches. Int. Arch. Photogramm. Remote Sens. Spatial Inf. Sci. **XLII-2/W11**, 579–585 (2019). https://doi.org/10.5194/isprs-archives-XLII-2-W11-579-2019

13. Aita, D., Barsotti, R., Bennati, S., Caroti, G., Piemonte, A.: 3-dimensional geometric survey and structural modelling of the dome of Pisa cathedral. Int. Arch. Photogramm. Remote Sens. Spatial Inf. Sci. XLII-2/W3, 39–46 (2017). https://doi.org/10.5194/isprs-archives-XLII-2-W3-39-2017

14. Park, G., Lee, J.H., Yoon, H.: Semantic structure from motion for railroad bridges using deep learning. Appl. Sci. **11**, 4332 (2021). https://doi.org/10.3390/app11104332

15. Mandirola, M., Casarotti, C., Peloso, S., Lanese, I., Brunesi, E., Senaldi, I.: Use of UAS for damage inspection and assessment of bridge infrastructures, Int. J. Disaster Risk Reduction, **72**, 102824, ISSN 2212-4209 (2022). https://doi.org/10.1016/j.ijdrr.2022.102824

16. Garcia Millan, V.E., Rankine, C., Sanchez-Azofeifa, G.A.: Crop loss evaluation using digital surface models from unmanned aerial vehicles data. Remote Sens. **12**, 981 (2020). https:// doi.org/10.3390/rs12060981

17. Hasheminasab, S.M., Zhou, T., Habib, A.: GNSS/INS-assisted structure from motion strategies for UAV-based imagery over mechanized agricultural fields. Remote Sens. **12**, 351 (2020). https://doi.org/10.3390/rs12030351

18. Grottoli, E., Biausque, M., Rogers, D., Jackson, D.W.T., Cooper, J.A.G.: Structure-from-motion-derived digital surface models from historical aerial photographs: a new 3D application for coastal dune monitoring. Remote Sens.13, 95 (2021). https://doi.org/10.3390/rs13010095

19. Vacca, G.: Estimating tree height using low-cost UAV. Int. Arch. Photogramm. Remote Sens. Spatial Inf. Sci. **XLVIII-M-1–2023**, 381–386 (2023). https://doi.org/10.5194/isprs-archives-XLVIII-M-1-2023 381-2023

20. De Marco, J., Maset, E., Cucchiaro, S., Beinat, A., Cazorzi, F.: Assessing repcatability and reproducibility of structure from-motion photogrammetry for 3D terrain mapping of riverbeds. Remote Sens. **13**, 2572 (2021). https://doi.org/10.3390/rs13132572

21. García-Gómez, P., Royo, S., Rodrigo, N., Casas, J.R.: Geometric model and calibration method for a solid-state LiDAR. Sensors **20**, 2898 (2020)

22. Wang, D., Watkins, C., Xie, H.: MEMS mirrors for LiDAR: a review. Micromachines **11**, 456 (2020)

23. Luetzenburg, G., Kroon, A., Bjørk, A.A.: Evaluation of the Apple iPhone 12 Pro LiDAR for an application in geosciences. Sci. Rep. **11**, 22221 (2021)

24. Teppati Losè, L., Spreafico, A., Chiabrando, F., Giulio Tonolo, F.: Apple LiDAR sensor for 3D surveying: tests and results in the cultural heritage domain. Remote Sens. **14**, 4157 (2022). https://doi.org/10.3390/rs14174157

25. Murtiyoso, A., Grussenmeyer, P., Landes, T., Macher, H.: First assessments into the use of commercial-grade solid state lidar for low cost heritage documentation. Int. Arch. Photogramm. Remote Sens. Spatial Inf. Sci. XLIII-B2–2, 599–604 (2021)

26. Díaz-Vilariño, L., Tran, H., Frías, E., Balado, J., Khoshelham, K.: 3D mapping of indoor and outdoor environments using Apple smart devices, Int. Arch. Photogramm. Remote Sens. Spatial Inf. Sci. XLIII-B4–2022, 303–308 (2022). https://doi.org/10.5194/isprs-archives-XLIII-B4-2022-303-2022

27. Vacca, G.: 3D Survey with Apple LiDAR Sensor—test and assessment for architectural and cultural heritage. Heritage **6**, 1476–1501 (2023). https://doi.org/10.3390/heritage6020080

28. PolyCam https://poly.cam/. Accessed 5 Oct 2022

29. https://www.cloudcompare.org/main.html

30. https://gexcel.it/it/software/reconstructor

31. Szeliski, R.: Computer vision: algorithms and applications. Springer, London (2010). https://doi.org/10.1007/978-1-84882-935-0

32. Vacca, G., Quaquero, E.: BIM-3D GIS: an integrated system for the knowledge process of the buildings. J. Spatial Sci. **65**(2), 193–208 (2019). https://doi.org/10.1080/14498596.2019

AGEO: Advanced Citizens' Observatory for Atlantic Geohazard Risk Management

Eleni Mangina[1]([✉]) [iD], Levent Görgü[1] [iD], Kieran Parker[2], Kirstin Lemon[2], and Eoghan Holohan[3] [iD]

[1] School of Computer Science, University College Dublin, Dublin, Ireland
eleni.mangina@ucd.ie
[2] British Geological Survey, Belfast, Northern Ireland
[3] School of Earth Sciences, University College Dublin, Dublin, Ireland

Abstract. AGEO (Atlantic Geohazard Risk Management) platform has been employed from several pilots in Europe within the INTERREG AGEO project as Citizens' Observatory on geohazards. The aim was to demonstrate how citizens' involvement in geohazard risks prevention can strengthen regional and national risk management systems. Parallel with this activity AGEO fosters an efficient uptake of Copernicus data, products, and services on regional level. A combination of these two actions can result the improved geohazard risk prevention and resilience to natural disasters in the Atlantic region. National and regional authorities are directly involved in the project and have been in charge for the project outputs' development with the help of solution providers and facilitators. Public stakeholders (civil society and individuals) have been directly engaged with locally and on a regional, interregional, and national level. The requirements of all stakeholders have been considered in a combined effort to address the individual needs of each group to the satisfaction of everyone. Within this paper we aim to describe the AGEO platform for earth science application, with participatory sensing capability to facilitate the capture of citizen observations through the provision of an online catalogue of citizen science resources (best practice, software tools, datasets, usability trials, citizen engagement studies).

Keywords: Citizens' observatory · Geohazard Risk Management · Decision Support platform and mobile applications

1 Introduction

1.1 AGEO INTERREG

AGEO project is part of the INTERREG Atlantic Area Priority on "Strengthening the territory's resilience to risks of natural, climate and human origin, with the objective to strength risk management systems" [1]. AGEO has launched several Citizens' Observatory (CO) pilots on geohazards according to regional priorities [2]. The aim was to engage with local communities to actively participate in risk preparedness and monitoring and incorporate local capacities into risk management systems. Experiences gained during the implementation of the CO pilots have been used to formulate recommendations for the creation of future observatories in response to the widest range of hazards (both natural and human-induced) in the Atlantic region. Specific objectives within the project include the following actions:

- Create a cooperation and resource platform on Atlantic geohazards risk assessment, preparedness, mitigation, and prevention.
- Deliver concrete case studies to confirm the capacities of Citizens' Observatories in improving risk management systems.
- Encourage the regional-level uptake and use of products and services provided by European spatial data infrastructures (i.e., Copernicus [3]).

AGEO demonstrates a new form of engagement between civil society and local authorities for geohazards-related local capacity building and encourage the local use of innovative Earth Observation (EO) products and services [4] provided by European data infrastructures, in particular Copernicus. AGEO helps to empower citizens to initiate change by actively participating in geohazard risk preparedness actions. This will result in more informed decision making and new forms of social mobilization, facilitated by new ways of communicating and assessing information on natural hazards. COs are playing an increasingly important role in addressing social-technological challenges, primarily by allowing citizens and policymakers access to new forms of data-driven assessment of the problems at hand. The resulting effects on equal opportunities are numerous, covering security, demographics, socioeconomics, and sustainable development including the following:

- Enabling all actors of society to participate in making their community safer and stronger, including otherwise disadvantaged groups, senior citizens, or people with disabilities.
- Providing equal access to complementary training and experience related to natural hazards, data processing, use of mobile technologies.
- Creating more local support for bottom-up initiatives and entrepreneurship that could create new employment directly or indirectly related to AGEO objectives (for example environmental monitoring startups, drone-tech companies, other citizens' science initiatives).
- Create temporary occupational tasks for people on unemployment benefit, keeping them active and valuable contributors of their local community.
- Orient young people towards taking up scientific and engineering careers related to geosciences, information technologies, telecommunications.
- The AGEO CO pilots enable data-driven engagement on geohazards, creating the basis for more targeted future interventions and enhanced collaboration between the public and the authorities. This will not only contribute to the creation of more secure and inclusive local communities but will also support the creation of new jobs and economic development opportunities for groups facing employment and/or integration problems.

National and regional authorities are directly involved in the project and have been in charge for the development of the main project outputs with the help of solution providers and facilitators (members of the AGEO INTERREG Consortium [1]). The requirements of all stakeholders have been considered in a combined effort to address the individual needs of each group for the outputs designed and delivered to meet stakeholder needs. During the final months of the project stakeholder satisfaction has been assessed as a part of the evaluation of the pilots. This helped to anticipate future stakeholder needs of follow-up projects and replication of results.

1.2 AGEO INTERREG Platform

AGEO platform [5] can be used from citizens, to report, monitor, review and examine their observations. The main purpose behind AGEO Citizens' Observatory Platform's goals is to bring citizens and authorities together and enable communication and interaction between each other. The AGEO Platform allows authorities to manage citizens' observations by enabling the platform managers to direct citizens' observations to the correct facilities and take timely action.

AGEO CO Platform's development involved studying in detail any bottlenecks and risks to a more meaningful engagement with society via COs. Concrete cases, success stories, and existing initiatives have been discussed, analysed, and mapped, including cooperation and national projects with telecommunication companies and civil society initiatives. Information has been collected via surveys and concrete actions, recommendations, and a roadmap of exploitation either for the AGEO platform or the AGEO mobile applications [6, 7] were also developed. Several critical issues were addressed carefully in the software development and the resulting platform ensures data masking by adopting anonymization or pseudonymization in line with GDPR requirements. It also delivers a viewing metaphor that adopts a map-based interface using Google Maps as the vehicle which enables data to be viewed collectively. Provision for multimedia data collection is offered and this is stored in a cloud-based service. However, the software includes a rudimentary data quality filter that thwarts poor quality, incomplete or malicious/rogue data polluting the integrity of the data corpus.

2 Advanced Citizens' Observatory for Atlantic Geohazard Risk Management

AGEO platform is simple and easy to use with participatory sensing capability to facilitate the capture of citizen observations through the provision of an online catalogue of citizen science resources (best practice, software tools, datasets, usability trials, citizen engagement studies). A map-based interface [5] for social engagement through which citizens can observe the collective citizen observed geohazard data. An online catalogue of citizen science resources (best practice, software tools, datasets, usability trials, citizen engagement studies) collects relevant resources to stimulate the effective use of Citizens' Observatories for geohazards monitoring under operational conditions as integral part of regional/national risk management systems. Within this project Copernicus data (available products, services, uptake efficiency, recent use-cases) in the participating Atlantic regions have been reviewed and AGEO promotes the development of sustainable supply chains for new, geohazards-EO products and services with demonstrated value/importance for the stakeholders and communities in the Atlantic region. As a result, there is increased engagement with citizens in the validation and improvements of EO products, processes/services via new generation mobile applications, encouraging them to actively participate in geohazards monitoring in their communities. Studies were carried out on a national/regional level within each five countries mobilizing national and regional clusters and stakeholders. The software tools developed [6–8], prioritize ease of use, and immediate accessibility for the citizen. The software ensures data masking adopting anonymization or pseudonymization in line with GDPR requirements. It delivers a viewing metaphor that adopts a map-based interface using open street maps as the vehicle which will enable data to be viewed collectively. Provision for multi-media data collection is offered through a cloud-based service. The software includes a rudimentary data quality filter that thwarts poor quality, incomplete or malicious/rogue data polluting the integrity of the data corpus. Concrete cases, success stories, existing initiatives have been mapped, including cooperation and national projects with telecommunication companies and civil society initiatives.

2.1 Functionality of Citizens' AGEO Observatory

AGEO observatory includes two distinct basic web interfaces, one as a search/data extraction tool and map based (Fig. 1). Additional major elements, such as a sophisticated map-based interface that uses Google Maps API and a managerial dashboard that allows viewing, forwarding, responding to, and extracting data from geohazard occurrences, have been created. A sophisticated implementation of RESTful API is in place, which can accept requests regarding events based on date and type and returning the results in JSON format is also necessary. The platform includes a dashboard with user login, sign in and the search/download tool, an advanced map-based interface implementation, an advanced RESTful API implementation, database updates/conversion, some graphic design, integration, and navigation work. AGEO Citizen Observatory Web Platform can be used to report various events (Wildfire, Tsunami, Earthquake, Rockfall, Sinkhole, Eruption, Landslide, River Flooding, Marine Flooding, Coastal Erosion, Building Settlement). The development of the observatory is available for inclusion of further events to cover any other geohazard the society finds suitable for inclusion.

Users can view all the event reported plotted on a map view. Users can pan and zoom through the map for looking at different events. The map will be anchored around Europe by default. If the user allows location access, the map will get anchored to the user's location. Each event is represented by a separate pin. Multiple pins are clustered together and the total number of clustered pins (Fig. 2).

The Web platform allows admin and managers to download the event data in different format (JSON format supports complete event data dumping; Excel and CSV format allows only structured data download and custom event questionnaire answers are not included). The users can view all the event reported in a tabular view and sort data on various fields with search and selection functionality (Fig. 3).

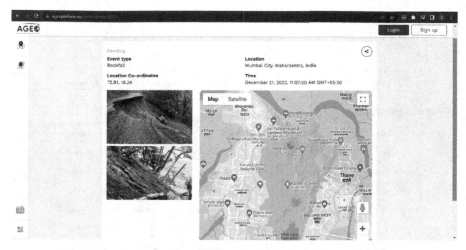

Fig. 1. Event review at the AGEO web platform: Pending Rockfall event

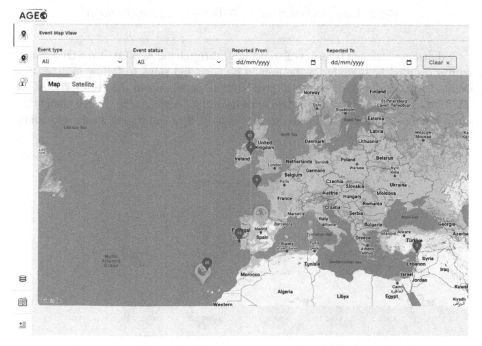

Fig. 2. Event pinned at the AGEO web platform map.

670   E. Mangina et al.

AGEO

Event Management

Event Id	Event Type	Location	Date & Time	Event Status
SKHL3	Sinkhole	Lisboa, Portugal	December 27, 2022, 4:11:00 PM GMT+00:00	Pending
TSNM2	Tsunami	Lisboa, Portugal	December 28, 2022, 12:13:00 PM GMT+00:00	Pending
LNSL3	Landslide	Lisboa, Portugal	December 27, 2022, 10:09:00 AM GMT+00:00	Pending
BDST2	Building Settlement	Lisboa, Portugal	December 27, 2022, 4:09:00 PM GMT+00:00	Pending
ETQK3	Earthquake	Lisboa, Portugal	December 27, 2022, 3:52:00 PM GMT+00:00	Pending
RKFL6	Rockfall	Lisboa, Portugal	December 27, 2022, 10:06:00 AM GMT+00:00	Pending
TSNM1	Tsunami	Lisboa, Portugal	December 27, 2022, 10:03:00 AM GMT+00:00	Pending
SKHL2	Sinkhole	Lisboa, Portugal	December 27, 2022, 10:02:00 AM GMT+00:00	Pending
ETQK2	Earthquake	Lisboa, Portugal	December 27, 2022, 10:05:00 AM GMT+00:00	Pending
RVFL1	River Flooding	Lisboa, Portugal	December 27, 2022, 3:54:00 PM GMT+00:00	Pending

Fig. 3. Example of event data - AGEO pilot in Lisbon (Portugal).

Educational content (Fig. 4) is also available through the AGEO Citizen Observatory with a detailed help guide for the user to prepare and steps to follow in case of an event. The educational content also gives further details about the event. The AGEO platform also supports the plugin facility of local data stations (Fig. 5). All content and information to login an event and view live logs of data can be accessible through the mobile application (Fig. 6).

Fig. 4. AGEO Platform Educational Content

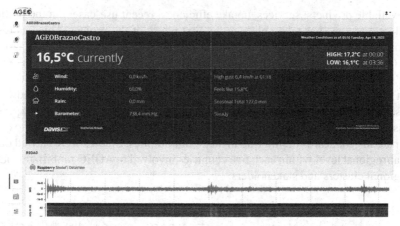

Fig. 5. Example of Madeira based data station within AGEO web platform.

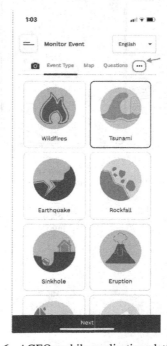

Fig. 6. AGEO mobile application platform.

2.2 Provision of Satellite-Derived Multi-temporal Interferometry of Synthetic Aperture Radar (InSAR) Data for the AGEO Citizen Observatory Pilots

Copernicus products and services are expected to be a key component of many future COs on geohazards [9]. Within AGEO project, the review of the use of Copernicus data (available products, services, uptake efficiency, recent use-cases) in the participating Atlantic regions has taken place at the first phase of the project. This has resulted the provision of satellite-derived multi-temporal Interferometry of Synthetic Aperture Radar (InSAR) data for the AGEO Citizen Observatory Pilots (Fig. 7) to enhance the region's stakeholders' (including SMEs) potential to take advantage of present and future market opportunities offered by Copernicus. This task also created the groundwork for increased engagement with citizens in the validation and improvements of EO products, processes/services via new generation mobile applications, encouraging them to actively participate in geohazards monitoring in their communities. Studies were carried out on a national/regional level within each five countries involved in AGEO mobilizing national and regional clusters and stakeholders.

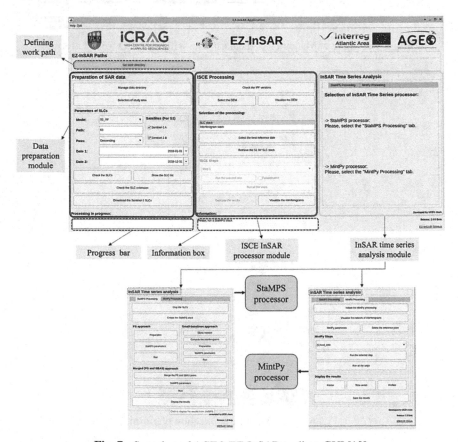

Fig. 7. Snapshot of AGEO EZ-InSAR toolbox GUI [10].

The level and efficiency of the use of Copernicus (including Copernicus EMS) in geohazards risk reduction in the participating Atlantic regions has been reviewed taking into account existing reviews [11–13] aiming to understand the level of user engagement and the scalability of Copernicus solutions on a regional scale for a range of geohazards: landslides, floods, tsunamis, earthquakes, volcanic activity, cascading events that may include other types of natural hazards (such as forest fires) and human-induced geohazards (e.g. induced seismicity or surface subsidence). The activities included development and build up on the open access data policy of Copernicus and ensure that the evolution of services considered the specific needs of the Atlantic region with regards to evolving user needs and services; regional investments and priorities, and the identified challenges related to geohazard risks. Another aim is to further develop the geohazard dimension of Copernicus to enable its response to evolving user needs, from the Atlantic region. The results of these activities include:

- Provision of satellite-derived multi-temporal Interferometry of Synthetic Aperture Radar (InSAR) data for the AGEO Citizen Observatory Pilots (Fig. 8)
- Provision of an easy-use, open-source, multi-temporal InSAR processing tool for future (post-AGEO) geohazard monitoring [14].

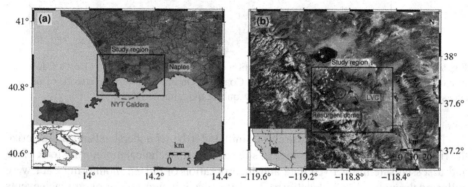

Fig. 8. Sample of Satellite maps, provided by Google Earth, of the test site Campi Flegrei volcano (a) and Long Valley caldera (b). The rectangles are the coverage of the Regions of Interest. The red dashed lines are the NYT caldera boundary in (a) and LVC boundary in (b). The solid blue line within LVC outlines the Resurgent Dome.

3   AGEO Pilot (Northern Ireland)

The Northern Ireland CO located on the Causeway Coast, County Antrim (Fig. 9), consists of two individual sites: Giants Causeway and Carrick-a-rede. The Giants Causeway is a designated UNESCO World Heritage Site (WHS) with Carrick-a-rede located 14km east. Both sites hold significant geological, cultural, and commercial status. The objectives of the pilot were to

1. Carry out routine monitoring of the sites.
2. Engage local communities and stakeholders to provide them with education awareness of geohazards.
3. Encourage their active participation in hazard monitoring through a mobile application developed by the AGEO project.

4. Evaluate satellite data from the Copernicus programme as a geohazard monitoring tool and
5. Promote better understanding of geohazard risk to stakeholders to enhance risk management at the sites using evidence-based information.

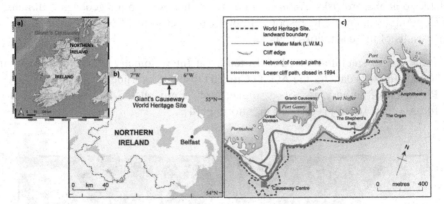

Fig. 9. Northern Ireland AGEO Pilot: a) Location of the Causeway Coast and Giant's Causeway in Northern Ireland. b) Map of the Causeway Coast. c) Outline map of the network of publiuc access routes at Giants Caiseway (source, www.qub.ac.uk/geomaterials).

To meet these objectives, research was initiated to better understand and characterize the risk through carrying out geological site survey; geotechnical monitoring took place and assessed satellite derived data and incorporation of citizen monitoring data were collected through the AGEO platform. The pilot also initiated a series of outreach events within the local communities to raise awareness of geohazard and the participatory role citizens could take in monitoring their landscape using the AGEO platform. The work carried out resulted in the recording of numerous landslide events including images of each event leading to an increased understanding of the areas and exposure of risk across the sites. Citizen involvement was achieved through local engagement and collection and evaluation of citizen data as a means of geohazard monitoring to enhance risk management of the sites. The use of the AGEO platform was the first of its type in Northern Ireland to utilize such a public application to assist in geohazard monitoring. National Trust staff, who manage both sites, were provided with training on its use and a series of public workshops was delivered to promote citizen involvement through using the application. Between September 2022 and January 2023, a total of ninety-three (93) citizen monitoring images, identifying recent slope failures, were uploaded to the AGEO platform (Fig. 10).

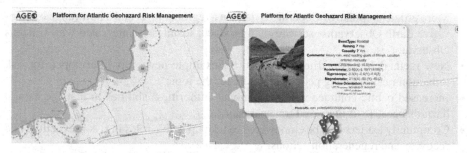

Fig. 10. AGEO online platform applied for Northern Ireland pilot

4 Conclusions

The Citizens' Observatories that have been delivered are the immediate outputs of the project, also constituting the basis of a long-term result i.e., direct involvement of citizens in natural hazards monitoring and risk preparedness along the Atlantic region. AGEO, apart from the web platform of the citizens' observatory, has delivered:

- Five (5) Citizens' Observatories covering geohazards of regional importance: landslides, rockfalls, floods, seismic risks. A comprehensive toolbox that facilitates the deployment of the Citizens' Observatories to be also used in follow-up projects.
- Information leaflets and dissemination materials.
- A project website and social media channels for direct engagement with citizens and the professional community.
- Several high-impact conferences and workshops organized on a national and international level with the aim of stakeholder engagement and the mobilization of external expertise.
- A Platform dedicated to long-term cooperation and information sharing on geohazards.
- An evaluation of the AGEO Citizens' Observatories and recommendations for the future regional use of Copernicus products and recommendations for the future.
- Overarching recommendations for the development of new policies and measures in view of improving the resilience of land and maritime areas to climate and nature changes.

All these results will help regional authorities and stakeholders be better prepared to facing potential risks occurring in the Atlantic territory of natural or anthropogenic origin. AGEO platform has tangible contribution towards increased resilience of society against natural hazards with better capacity in disaster risk reduction based on the principle of public engagement. The project is designed with the objective to create permanent links amongst partners using a cooperation platform supported by an easy to maintain social media presence. Within the next decade the following are anticipated:

- Citizens' Observatories will become a regular component of risk management systems at local, regional, and national levels.
- Stronger public awareness for the importance of geohazard risk prevention and a strong social license for the implementation of new measures.

- More efficient uptake of Copernicus data on a regional level and a new range of innovative Earth Observation services and products seamlessly integrated with Citizens Observatories.
- New methodologies and technologies (for example new Apps) developed for risk reduction raising young people's interest for the topic.
- Increased public confidence in the regional authorities' abilities to manage natural hazards because of increased transparency.
- Community leaders will be empowered to take up active roles in risk prevention, and recovery and regeneration actions.

AGEO has contributed to the development of a proactive and socially licensed risk management approach that takes into consideration vulnerability, capacity, exposure of persons and assets, hazard characteristics and the environment. The platform and the mobile apps can be utilized for disaster risk governance especially for the north-east Atlantic area at the transnational, regional and local levels, which is very important for prevention, mitigation, preparedness, response, recovery, and rehabilitation. Investment in disaster risk prevention and reduction through structural and non-structural measures are important for the economic, social, health and cultural resilience of persons, communities, countries and their assets. The project has strengthened disaster preparedness for response, take action in anticipation of events, and ensure capacities are in place for effective response and recovery at all levels through proper policy making based on the stakeholders' requirements and transnational and regional interrelations. AGEO acts as a catalyst among the so far limited regional policy initiatives and cooperation.

References

1. INTERREG AGEO Homepage. https://ageoatlantic.eu/
2. AGEO Citizens' Observatory pilots on geohazards Homepage. https://ageoatlantic.eu/pilots/
3. Schubert, A., Miranda, N., Geudtner, D., Small, D.: Sentinel-1A/B combined product geolocation accuracy. Remote Sens. **9**(6), 607 (2017). https://doi.org/10.3390/rs9060607
4. Görgü, L., O'Grady, M., Mangina, E., O'Hare, G.M.P.: Participatory risk management in the smart city. In: 2022 IEEE International Smart Cities Conference (ISC2), Pafos, Cyprus, pp. 1-6 (2022).https://doi.org/10.1109/ISC255366.2022.9922040
5. AGEO Citizens' Observatory Web Platform Homepage. https://ageoplatform.eu
6. AGEO Mobile Observatory on Google Play Store (for Android devices). https://play.google.com/store/apps/details?id=eu.ageoplatform.app
7. AGEO Mobile Observatory on Apple AppStore (for iOS devices). https://apps.apple.com/ie/app/id6444765392
8. Wang, X., Hrysiewicz, A., Holohan, E.P.: EZ-InSAR: an easy-to-use open-source toolbox for mapping ground surface deformation using satellite interferometric synthetic aperture radar. In: 2022, American Geophysical Union Fall Meeting, Chicago, G42D-0259. https://agu.confex.com/agu/fm22/meetingapp.cgi/Paper/1081352
9. Spataro, F., Pavia, P., Roscigno, R., Torres, R., Bibby, D., Cossu, M.: AIS P/L on SAR satellite: the Copernicus Sentinel-1 solution. In: EUSAR 2021; 13th European Conference on Synthetic Aperture Radar (2021)
10. Hrysiewicz, A., Wang, X., Holohan, E.P.: EZ-InSAR: an easy-to-use open-source toolbox for mapping ground surface deformation using satellite interferometric synthetic aperture radar. Earth Sci Inform (2023). https://doi.org/10.1007/s12145-023-00973-1

11. Lee, K.A., Lee, J.R., Bell, P.: A review of citizen science within the earth sciences: potential benefits and obstacles. Proc. Geologists' Assoc. **131**(6), 605–617 (2020). https://doi.org/10.1016/j.pgeola.2020.07.010

12. Mazzoleni, M., et al.: Exploring the influence of citizen involvement on the assimilation of crowdsourced observations: a modelling study based on the 2013 flood event in the Bacchiglione catchment (Italy). Hydrol. Earth Syst. Sci. **22**, 391–416 (2018). https://doi.org/10.5194/hess-22-391-2018

13. Mazumdar, S., et al.: Citizens observatories for effective Earth observations: the WeSenseIt approach. Environ. Scient. **25**, 56–61 (2016)

14. EZ-InSAR toolbox GitHub. https://github.com/alexisInSAR/EZ-InSAR

Multidisciplinary Research at the Castle of Santapau (Licodia Eubea, Italy): New Data for the Research, Protection and Enhancement of the Site

Rodolfo Brancato[1](✉) ⓘ, Marilena Cozzolino[2] ⓘ, Vincenzo Gentile[2] ⓘ, and Sergio Montalbano[3] ⓘ

[1] Department of Humanities, University of Naples Federico II, Via Nuova Marina 33, 80133 Napoli, Italy
rodolfo.brancato@unina.it
[2] Department of Agriculture, Environment and Food, University of Molise, Via De Sanctis Snc, 86100 Campobasso, Italy
[3] Department of Biological, Geological and Environmental Sciences, University of Catania, Piazza Università 2, 95131 Catania, Italy

Abstract. Since 2019, a multidisciplinary research project is in progress at the Castle of Santapau (Licodia Eubea, Italy). Different non-invasive investigation techniques, such as proximity remote sensing (UAV) and geophysical prospecting (GPR, electromagnetic, geoelectric and seismic surveys), were integrated in order to enrich the knowledge of the site. The results will be the starting point to plan and develop restoration projects for the protection and enhancement of the castle.

Keywords: Castle of Santapau · Archaeological survey · Proximity remote sensing · GPR · Electromagnetic · geoelectric and seismic surveys

As part of the research on the archaeological landscapes of the Hyblaean Plateau, on the edges of Ragusa and Catania districts (Sicily, Italy) (Fig. 1a), a multidisciplinary project aimed at the reconstruction of the ancient topography of the Castle of Santapau (Licodia Eubea, Catania) has been launched in 2019 (Figs. 1b and 2). The castle stands on a hill (Colle Castello, 582 m asl) in a perched position in the hinterland of south-eastern Sicily. For centuries, the site was one of the most important fortresses of the Sicilian feudal system in the western sector of the Hyblaean region. Positioned along the road that led towards the Etna area, from its top the view ranges from the Dirillo valley to the Gela Plain and even sees the African Sea.

The fortress appears in the official documents of the Angevin Statute of the Sicilian castles of 1274. However, there are numerous hypotheses in the literature relating to its relevance to an older castrum, from the Middle Ages [1]. A possible occupation of the Byzantine era, suggested by the numerous testimonies that emerged during the research conducted in the urban area and in particular along the slopes of the hill [2–4], was probably obliterated in the years of the Islamic conquest (late 9th century) [5]. However, from the sources, the military vocation of the hill emerges only starting from the

O. Gervasi et al. (Eds.): ICCSA 2023 Workshops, LNCS 14111, pp. 678–693, 2023.
https://doi.org/10.1007/978-3-031-37126-4_44

aforementioned documents of the 13th century, when Licodia was an important military post of the Angevin kingdom. Indeed, at the time of Charles I of Anjou, the place assumed the name of *Castrum Licodiæ*, closely connected to the network of fortification works, which militarized the landscape of the island's hinterland, aimed in particular for the control of the major routes communication. From the complex history of the castle, it is possible to reconstruct the pertinence to the fiefdoms of great noble families: from the Santapau family, Spaniards who gave the castle its name, the property passed to the Ruffos of Calabria, related to the first, who maintained control of the monument until 1812. The castle had actually been reduced to a state of ruins by the disastrous earthquake of 1693. Structures that survived until the beginning of the 20th century were demolished during the Fascist period due to the danger of collapse [6].

Thanks to the project launched, a new interpretation of the ruins visible today has been possible. The data on the elevations has been integrated with what is known of the underground structures of the hill of which the most interesting element is certainly constituted from the axis of an ancient aqueduct, to be traced back to the inhabited area of the Greek age [7], partly adapted in the Roman age and in the following phases [8]. The Angevin castle is characterized by an irregular plan, similar to a pentagon on whose southern side a rectangular body is flanked.

As already tested by the excavations and prospecting [4], the site presents an interesting multi-stratification largely still not adequately investigated. Covered by the ruins of the castle, the top of the hill was identified with the acropolis of the Hellenized Sicilian settlement largely known from funerary contexts [4–9]. However, on the western side of the hill investigations identified the traces of the aforementioned underground aqueduct, pertinent to this phase, but also numerous elements relating to the history of the settlement in Roman and early medieval times late antique burial grounds and Byzantine underground buildings near the church mother, in the northern slopes [4]. The project at the base of the Spanish castle exploits the peculiar geomorphology of the hill, taking advantage of its natural defendability and rocky overhangs, occupying the entire top: the walls insist on the rock and its general layout is still legible. It consists of mighty rectilinear walls and circular towers (originally, a total of six); almost the entire wall circuit remains visible even if for a modest elevation. The most consistent part is found in the portion of the walls, which includes the two twin towers placed at the southern corner. The construction technique is of the sack type with external masonry in stone ashlars; in the surviving towers, there are string courses and a summit cordon. Inside the area, there are legible traces of environments whose destination is unknown: most of the structures are, however, covered by thick layers of debris accumulated due to the collapses and filled up intentionally to consolidate the structures, as well as confirmed by recently conducted investigations.

This paper presents the first results of the surveys carried out on the hill of Licodia Eubea. The research was conducted through the integrated application of different non-invasive investigation methodologies, i.e. remote and proximity remote sensing (UAV) and geophysical prospecting (GPR, electromagnetic, geoelectric, seismic refraction induction). The study aims to support the enhancement of the monument and the engagement of the local community.

680   R. Brancato et al.

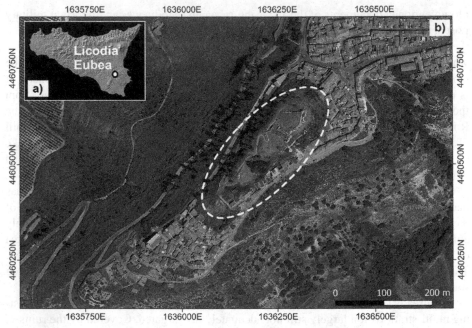

Fig. 1. Location of Licodia Eubea on a Google Earth™ satellite image of Sicily (a) and a detail of the Castle of Santapau (b).

Fig. 2. Colle Castello (Licodia Eubea), view of the southern structures of the Santapau Castle.

1 Methodology

The survey project of the historic hill of Licodia Eubea and of the structures was carried out through the integrated application of different non-invasive investigation methodologies. In recent years, scientific disciplines as geophysics and geomatics are widely applied in archaeological surveys for representing all that is visible with what is hidden into the surfaces. Geophysics, in particular, plays today an important role in site evaluation, mapping of soil and fill layers, foundation design, detection of cavities and underground structures. Methods such as seismic prospections [10, 11], induced electromagnetic method (EMI) [12, 13], electrical resistivity tomography (ERT) [14, 15], GPR surveys [16, 16] and magnetometry [17, 18] are very efficient for these purposes. On the other hand, geomatics allows the acquisition of highly accurate point clouds that represent the reference basis for all the information acquired in the evaluation process of a site. In the last decade, the use of close-range aerial photography using platforms operating at low altitude have grown impressively in terms of instrumentation, information handling, representation strategies, as well as processing and combined systems. A comprehensive overview has been published by Vernoeven [19], while in Campana [20] a summary of the available platforms, along with their main merits and disadvantages, is proposed. However, masts, poles, booms, towers, kites, balloons and blimps seem to have less intense use in recent years due to the development of UAVs. The latter applications has shown considerable progress in the field of aerial photography for documenting archaeological excavations [21–23], three-dimensional survey of monuments and historic buildings [24–27], the survey of archaeological sites and landscapes [28, 29]. In a recent comprehensive literature review [30] the technological developments in UAVs and in lightweight sensors operating with visible (VIS), near-infrared (NIR), thermal-infrared (TIR), multi-spectral (MS) and hyperspectral (HS) cameras, laser and radar sensors are analyzed. RGB cameras are often used in combination with other sensors and, in general, studies report the implementation of multiple devices [31–34].

In this work, an integration of geophysical and geomatic methods is applied for the study of the hill of Licodia Eubea. The drafting of the archaeological, digital and multiscalar documentation of the site was conducted through the integration of traditional survey techniques and remote/ proximal sensing for aerial and terrestrial photogrammetry, exploiting the potential of each method in order to maximize the final result [20]. Two UAVs (DJI av6v S900 hexacopter and the DJI Mavic Due Pro quadcopter) equipped with RGB and thermal sensors have been used for a large-scale sensing of the area of research. The first step was the planning of several aerial photogrammetric surveys to understand the extent of the site and to analyze the relationships between the different sectors of the complex. The UAV-Based High Resolution Thermal Imaging for the archeo-architectural anomalies detecting in vegetation was performed through the use of a FLIR Vue Pro R 640 camera.

The photographic datasets were obtained by flying over the area at low altitude (about 30 m above ground level) while maintaining a high frontal and lateral overlap between shots ($\geq$ 80%) and making use of Ground Control Points (hereafter GCP) on the ground, surveyed using a GNSS antenna in RTK (Real Time Kinematic) mode. The survey of GCPs was performed with Topcon Hyper V Differential GPS. Data processing of images was performed with Agisoft Metashape software (LLC. St. Petersburg, Russia) using the Structure from Motion (SfM) technique (Fig. 3) [35].

Fig. 3. 3D model of the hill and camera positions at frame capture.

As regards geophysical prospections, considering the typology of searched targets (archaeological remains, geological layers, cavities), their supposed depth (from centimeters to 5 m), their constitutive material (stones, landfills), their physical properties (density, conductivity, susceptibility) and their geometry (punctual targets, stretched objects, layers) the proper method that is suitable for solving the goal of the research has been chosen. Thus, seismic refraction tomography (SRT), EMI, ERT and GPR prospections were preferred over other methods.

Seismic Refraction Tomography had as its purpose the measurement of the difference in density of the different lithological and sedimentary layers that overlap below the surface, and therefore the measurement of the average thickness of the upper sediment layer in the various unexcavated segments. During the research, in collaboration with the Geophysical Institute of Israel, five refraction prospections were conducted using the Geometrics, Geode seismic recorder (Fig. 4, Area A, green lines). Each spread consisted of 34–45 geophones and source points every second geophone (2 m). The location of the lines was chosen by the department of archaeology and were surveyed using an RTK GPS for each line edge. Data was recorded and saved in the industry standard for refraction surveys – SEG-2. In each shot point, a sledgehammer hitting a metal plate was used. The data recorded was analyzed using the Geometrics - SeisImager program. Each shot was examined, and some basic processing procedures were applied when needed such as AGC/Gain, Filter etc. (refraction surveys usually do not need processing due to its short offsets and good signal to noise ratio). The QC procedure also included geometry check to ensure shots were located correctly along the spread. After the QC procedure, the first arrival time for each shot was picked and saved for interpretation. The interpretation process utilized the Intercept Time method to create an initial model (velocity and depth). After the initial model is created, a travel time tomography procedure is initiated [36]. This process attempts to minimize the difference between the observed (picked arrival times) and the calculated (model calculated arrival times). Each spread had appx 100 iterations done to achieve relative low error values. Error here refers to the difference between the observed travel time to the calculated.

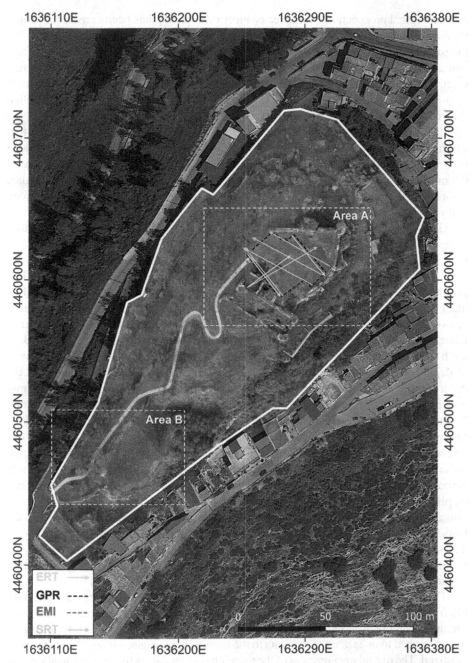

Fig. 4. RGB image obtained thought aerial photogrammetric survey with indication of the geophysical survey.

ERT was carried out using a multi-electrode resistivity meter, the A3000E (M.A.E. s.r.l., Frosolone, Italy). For ERT, three profiles with a length of 32 m were measured. The electrode spacing was in any case set to 1 m (Fig. 4, Area A, light blue lines). Regarding archaeological prospections, the selected electrode spacing has been considered proper to reach supposed large deep walls. A dipole-dipole (DD) configuration was used. The measured apparent resistivity datasets were processed in order to remove dragging effects that are typical of DD array and model the survey targets converting the values in real electrical resistivity values displayed as a function of depth below surface. To this end, data-adaptive probability-based ERT inversion (PERTI) method [37] has been applied for imaging the sources of anomalies into the analyzed grounds.

EMI prospections were conducted utilizing the GSSI Profiler EMP-400 [38]. Measurements were collected in continuous mode using frequencies in the range 5–16 kHz with vertically oriented dipoles. The investigation area was covered by profiles spaced 0.5 m inserted in a regular grid (Fig. 4, Area A and B, red dotted polygons). During data elaboration the measured values of conductivity were transformed in values of resistivity and visualized in 2D maps through a contouring software.

GPR was implemented through an IDS Georadar (IDS GeoRadar s.r.l., Pisa, Italy), equipped with a multi-frequency TRMF antenna (200–600 MHz). All radar reflections were recorded digitally in the field as 16-bit data, 512 samples per radar scan at 25 scan s^{-1} (1 scan approximately corresponds to 0.025 m). Half meter equally spaced GPR profiles were acquired in grids adapted to the available areas (Fig. 4, Area A and B, black dotted polygon). As the interpretation of each section can lead to underestimation or overestimation of the reflected signals and makes it not easy to identify the effect of lateral bodies present in the subsoil, all sections were processed together using standard methodological approaches in order to obtain 2D horizontal maps at a different range of depth (GPR-SLICE 7.0 software) [39]. Data were converted by subtracting out the dc-drift (wobble) in the data, and at the same time adding a gain with time of 20. A time-zero correction was determined to designate the starting point of the wave and the center frequency of the antenna was matched. Then the bandpass filter and the background removal were respectively applied to reduce noise from oscillating components that had a regular frequency cycle in the frequency domain and to remove striation noises that occurred at the same time. Processed radargrams were subsequently corrected with an automatic gain function applied to each trace based on the difference between the mean amplitude of the signal in the time window and the maximum amplitude of the trace. Thus, horizontal sections (time slices) were processed considering the whole dataset. Data were gridded using the inverse distance algorithm, which includes a search of all data within a fixed radius of 0.75 m of the desired point to be interpolated on the grid and a smoothing factor of two. Grid cell size was set to 0.01 m to produce high resolution images.

The management of the data collected during the activities took place through a GIS platform: all the topographic and archaeological data, in fact, were georeferenced (photographs, photoplans, lines and polygons of the anomalies) and managed through a geodatase created to integrate the new data to the mass of legacy data surveyed and specially digitized. The digital management of the research project data is the premise to allow real accessibility for the purposes of research, protection and enhancement of the Mediterranean archaeological heritage, whose documentation is traditionally heterogeneous, because created with different and often obsolete documentation technologies.

2   Results and Discussion

As is known, in the context of archaeological research, proximal remote sensing allows the contextual reading of non-adjacent architectural elements, making clear the possible topographical relationships that exist between elements visible on the surface of the recognized areas (areas of fragments, outcropping structures, etc.). In Fig. 4 a detailed orthophoto of the castle is shown, while in Fig. 5 the thermal image is displayed which

Fig. 5. Aerial thermal image.

highlights the ground cover, soil composition, or the depth and character of archaeological features. The Digital Elevation Model (DEM) obtained from the data processing
highlights the current state of the structures of the Santapau Castle in three dimensions
(Fig. 6).These images support the design of direct surveys to be programmed and the
graphic rendering of the site plan of the Castle. Moreover, the oblique shots taken during
the reconnaissance were of great use, not only because they allowed us to grasp some
anomalies from above that are not visible from the ground but also because they allow
us to ascertain the state of conservation of the castle structures.

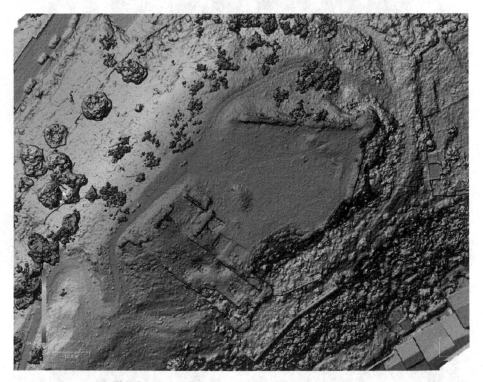

Fig. 6. Digital Elevation Model (DEM) of the Castle.

Thanks to the management of data in the GIS environment, it was therefore possible
to contextually analyze the archaeographic data that emerged from archive research,
such as the partly unpublished surveys [4] and the new topographical documentation
produced (graphic survey; photogrammetry; geophysical survey).

The management of data in the GIS environment has therefore allowed the production of updated and scalable cartography available to the Municipality and the Superintendency based on protection and enhancement needs. On the other hand, the data collected form the basis of the analysis geo-spatial analysis (vieshed analysis and least path coast analysis) also useful for archaeological research. In fact, the recomposition of the original volumes of the structures of the modern age, and the ratio of the current height of the top of the hill with respect to the original walking surface, which can be inferred from the surveys refraction geophysics, allow a new reading of the topography of the hill and its relationship with the territory. This is fundamental for understanding its diachronic function in the context of the fortified landscape already in ancient times, still perpetuated in the Middle Ages and modern times.

Fig. 7. Area B, horizontal section of electrical resistivity obtained through EMI prospecting at the frequency of 8 kHz.

Figure 7 shows the horizontal section of electrical resistivity obtained through EMI prospecting in the southern area (Area B) relative to the 8 kHz frequency. The results highlight two groups of resistive anomalies. In the eastern area, the anomalies clearly show the continuation of the section of the wall partially brought to light by the recent excavations underground and define a probable room of considerable size whose major septum has a NNO-SSE orientation. In the eastern area, the inhomogeneities with clear regular contours are distributed with a similar orientation to the southern circuit of the castle.

Inside the castle walls (Area A), the EMI surveys (Fig. 8) and GPR (Fig. 9) highlight, albeit with different resolutions, different areas with atypical values compared to the average values measured (nn. 1‑4 in Figs. 8 and 9). In particular, around the recently discovered cistern, the anomalies define the probable size of the cavity, partially filled with backfill material, which appears to be approximately 7 m x 6 m in size (n.4 in Figs. 8 and 9). Elsewhere, while the EMI investigations broadly indicate areas of high resistivity, the GPR investigation returns a detailed image of probable buried environments, some of which are clearly connected to the partially excavated structures.

Fig. 8. Area A, horizontal section of electrical resistivity obtained through EMI prospecting at the frequency of 8 kHz.

The three tomographic sections confirm, in the anomalous points found with the EMI and GPR investigations, the presence of surface resistive anomalies (indicated with black arrows in Fig. 10, right) attributable to buried archaeological structures. Furthermore, ERT 2 defines the depth of the tank at approximately 3 m in the x-axis range between 14 m and 16 m.

Fig. 9. Area A, GPR slice relative to 0.5 m in depth.

The seismic tomographies confirm, in the anomalous points found with the EMI and GPR investigations, the presence of surface resistive anomalies attributable to buried archaeological structures (Fig. 11). The results comprise of a 2D section of the spread, showing the velocity layers and their respective depth from the surface. Since the study area is relatively flat, no elevation information was gathered. Line L5 that does show minor elevation changes in its first few meters (appx. 1.5 m above the rest of the survey even surface). Each section shows a dotted line representing the limit for the interpretation. This is done since the short length and 1m spacing limits the penetration of seismic waves ray path (a ray path needs to travel from the source to the receiver).

The examination of the final velocity profiles indicates that a shallow layer with a velocity of ~ 200 m/sec exists in from the surface to 2–4 m. This layer could be attributed to the upper loose ground. The layer is sometimes very thin and perhaps not present (Line 4 around 25 m and line 3 around 30–35 m). There are two velocities interpreted beneath the first layer, one with a velocity of appx 600–800 m/sec and the second with appx 1000–1200 m/sec. It is hard to give a good interpretation of the material that is indicative of the velocities observed since no data exists to define the subsurface geology. In any case, these velocities are not indicative of a massive bed rock and are generally indicative of weathered rock or consolidated soil. The higher the velocity, the harder the soil/rock are. To give some interpretation to the results we can assume that two scenarios can be thought of. The first, is that higher velocities are indicative of a man-made structure. In that case, areas with higher velocities are structures or walls in the subsurface. The other assumption could be that the lower velocities are soil filled "chambers" and the surrounding are the natural undisturbed soil. In any case, these are assumptions that need to be examined both by the archaeologist findings, and by other investigation tools.

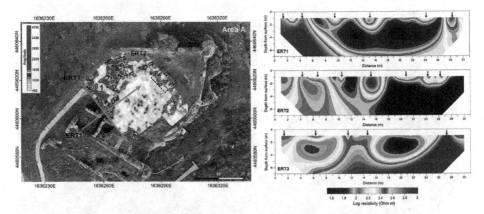

Fig. 10. Location of ERT surveys overlaid on the GPR slice (left) and ERT sections (right) with indication of shallow anomalies.

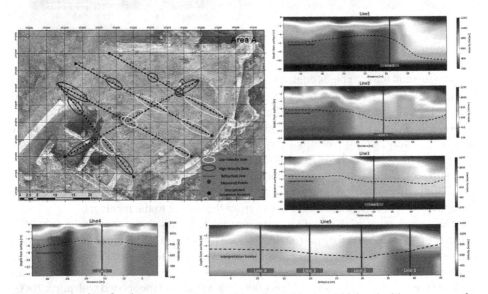

Fig. 11. Seismic refraction tomographies and location of low and high velocities zones on the map of the castle.

3 Conclusions

The preventive assessment of the archaeological interest through non-invasive geophysical diagnosis at the Castle of Licodia Eubea was carried out using different geomatic and geophysical methodologies. Beyond the differences in the operating principles, in the type of instrumentation involved in the measurements, in the type of response provided and in the fields of applicability of the various prospecting techniques used, the common objective was to provide as many elements as possible for a general evaluation of the sites being researched.

In some points the environmental conditions of the places to be investigated possessed logistic features, which allowed the application of a single method of investigation. Individually, the three methods have guaranteed satisfactory results and, in particular, it has been possible to reconstruct, in a rapid and totally non-invasive way, the distribution in three-dimensional space of the structures buried in archaeological environments known or vaguely suspected of containing objects of anthropic nature. The supports provided by the prospecting represented valid information for planning in advance systematic excavations or enhancement of the relevant elements. In the areas where it was possible, a multi-methodological approach was followed with the aim of obtaining high-quality information through a global assessment of the convergence of data subject to different physical factors. Thanks to the integration of several techniques, the same geophysical anomalies were found which, despite having been detected through various physical behaviours, identified the same buried object. However, direct verification with archaeological excavations is necessary for the complete study of the sites.

Acknowledgments. We are extremely grateful to dr. Maria Turco of the Superintendence of Archeology of Catania for the authorization for the research and to Maurel et Prom Italia s.r.l for the financial support.

Author Contribution. Writing-original draft preparation: Introduction (Rodolfo Brancato); Methodology (Rodolfo Brancato, Marilena Cozzolino); Results and Discussion (Rodolfo Brancato, Marilena Cozzolino, Vincenzo Gentile, Sergio Montalbano); Conclusions (Marilena Cozzolino).

References

1. Arcifa, L.: Dinamiche insediative nel territorio di mineo tra tardoantico e bassomedioevo il castrum di monte catalfaro. MEFRAM **113**, 269–311 (2001)
2. Patane, A.: Licodia Eubea, in F. Privitera, U. Spigo (eds.), Dall'Alcantara agli Iblei, Reg. Siciliana, Palermo: 133–135 (2005)
3. Bonacini, E.: Il borgo cristiano di Licodia Eubea, Trento: ed. Uniservice (2008)
4. Brancato, R.: Topografia della Piana di Catania. Quasar, Rome (2021)
5. Arcifa, L.: Dinamiche insediative e grande proprietà nella Sicilia bizantina. Uno sguardo archeo-logico. In: Martin, J.M., Peter-Custot, A., Prigent, V., (eds.), L'héritage byzantin en Italie (VIIIe-XIIe siècle). IV. Habitat et structure agraire, (Roma 17-18 dicembre 2010), Collection de l'Ecole Française de Rome 531, Rome: 237–267 (2017)
6. Cannizzo, P.M.: Licodia Eubea: le sue origini e la sua storia nel contesto della storia della Sicilia (1995)
7. Orsi, P.: Licodia Eubea, in Notizie Scavi di Antichità, pp. 435–440 (1904)
8. Politano, F.: La "Specus Immensus" di Licodia Eubea. Agora **52**(15), 85–91 (2015)
9. Camera, M.: La ceramica di Licodia Eubea, Bari (2018)

10. Tsokas, G.N., Papazachos, C.B., Vafidis, A., Loukoyiannakis, M.Z., Vargemezis, G., Tzimeas, K.: The detection of monumental tombs buried in tumuli by seismic refraction. Geophysics **60**(6), 1735–1742 (1995)
11. Barone, I., Cassiani, G., Ourabah, A., Boaga, J., Pavoni, M., Deiana, R.: Comparison and Integration of active and passive 3D surface wave measures around the Scrovegni Chapel. In: 83rd EAGE Annual Conference & Exhibition, vol. 2022(1), pp. 1–5, European Association of Geoscientists & Engineers (2022)
12. Scollar, I.: Electromagnetic prospecting methods in archaeology. Archaeometry **5**, 146–153 (1962)
13. Bozzo, E., Merlanti, F., Ranieri, G., Sambuelli, L., Finzi, E.: EM-VLF soundings on the eastern hill of the archaeological site of Selinunte. Boll. Geofis. Teor. Appl. **34**, 132–140 (1991)
14. Al-Saadi, O.S., Schmidt, V., Becken, M., Fritsch, T.: Very-high-resolution electrical resistivity imaging of buried foundations of a Roman villa near Nonnweiler Germany. Archaeol. Prospection **25**(3), 209–218 (2018)
15. Cozzolino, M., Caliò, L.M., Gentile, V., Mauriello, P., Di Meo, A.: The discovery of the theater of Akragas (Valley of Temples, Agrigento, Italy): an archaeological confirmation of the supposed buried structures from a geophysical survey. Geosciences **10**(5), 161 (2020)
16. Cozzolino, M., Gentile, V., Giordano, C., Mauriello, P.: Imaging buried archaeological features through ground penetrating radar: the case of the ancient saepinum (Campobasso, Italy). Geosciences **10**(6), 225 (2020)
17. Caldara, M., Ciminale, M., De Santis, V., Noviello, M.: A multidisciplinary approach to reveal and interpret 'missing' archaeological features at the masseria pantano site in apulia. Archaeol. Prospect. **21**(4), 301–309 (2014)
18. Urban, T.M., et al.: Magnetic detection of archaeological hearths in Alaska: a tool for investigating the full span of human presence at the gateway to North America. Quatern. Sci. Rev. **211**, 73–92 (2019)
19. Verhoeven, G.: Providing an archeological bird'seye view - an overall picture of ground-based means to execute low-altitude aerial photography (LAAP) in Archeology. Archaeol. Prospect. **16**(4), 233–249 (2009)
20. Campana, S.: Drones in archaeology state-of-the-art and future perspectives. Archaeol. Prospection **24**(4), 275–296 (2017)
21. Seitz, C., Altenbach, H.: Project Archeye – the quadrocopter as the archaelogist's eye, ISPRS Zurich 2011 Workshop, 14–16 September 2011, Zurich. Int. Arch. Photogramm. Remote Sens. Spatial Inf. Sci. XXXVIII (1/C22), 297–302 (2011)
22. Remondino, F., Barazzetti, L., Nex, F., Scaioni, M., Sarazzi, D.: UAV photogrammetry for mapping and 3D modelling – current status and future perspectives, ISPRS Zurich 2011 Workshop, 14–16 September 2011, Zurich. Int. Arch. Photogramm. Remote Sens. Spatial Inf. Sci. XXXVIII (1/C22), 25–31 (2011)
23. Rinaudo, F., Chiabrando, F., Lingua, A., Spanò, A.: Archaeological site monitoring: UAV photogrammetry could be an answer. Int. Arch. Photogramm. Remote. Sens. Spat. Inf. Sci. **39**(5), 583–588 (2012)
24. Fiorillo, F., Jiménez Fernández-Palacios, B., Remondino, F., Barba, S.: 3D surveying and modelling of the archaeological area of Paestum Italy. Virtual Archaeol. Rev. **4**(8), 55–60 (2013)
25. Pueschel, H., Sauerbier, M., Eisenbeiss, H.: A 3D model of castle Landenberg (CH) from combined photogrammetric processing of terrestrial and UAV-based images. Int. Arch. Photogramm. Remote. Sens. Spat. Inf. Sci. **XXXVII**(B6b), 93–98 (2008)
26. Cozzolino, M., Gabrielli, R., Galatà, P., Gentile, V., Greco, G., Scopinaro, E.: Combined use of 3D metric surveys and non-invasive geophysical surveys for the determination of the state

of conservation of the Stylite Tower (Umm ar-Rasas, Jordan). Ann. Geophys. **62**(3), SE339 (2019)

27. Sonnemann, T.F., Malatesta, E.H., Hofman, C.L.: Applying UAS photogrammetry to analyze spatial patterns of indigenous settlement sites in the northern Dominican Republic. Archaeology in the Age of Sensing, Forte, M., Campana S (eds), Springer, New York (2016). https://doi.org/10.1007/978-3-319-40658-9_4

28. Orihuela, A., Molina-Fajardo, M.A.: UAV photogrammetry surveying for sustainable conservation: the case of mondújar castle (Granada, Spain). Sustainability **13**, 24 (2021)

29. Cozzolino, M., Di Meo, A., Gentile, V.: The contribution of indirect topographic surveys (photogrammetry and the laser scanner) and GPR investigations in the study of the vulnerability of the Abbey of Santa Maria a Mare, Tremiti Islands (Italy). Ann. Geophys. **62**(3), (2019)

30. Adamopoulos, E., Rinaudo, F.: UAS-based archaeological remote sensing: review, meta-analysis and state-of-the-art. Drones **4**, 46 (2020)

31. Agudo, P., Pajas, J., Pérez-Cabello, F., Redón, J., Lebrón, B.: The potential of drones and sensors to enhance detection of archaeological cropmarks: a comparative study between multi-spectral and thermal imagery. Drones **2**, 29 (2018)

32. Brooke, C., Clutterbuck, B.: Mapping heterogeneous buried archaeological features using multisensor data from unmanned aerial vehicles. Remote Sens. **12**, 41 (2019)

33. Liu, C., Cao, Y., Yang, C., Zhou, Y., Ai, M.: Pattern identification and analysis for the traditional village using low altitude UAV-borne remote sensing: multifeatured geospatial data to support rural landscape investigation, documentation and management. J. Cult. Herit. **44**, 185–195 (2020)

34. Parisi, E.I., Suma, M., Güleç Korumaz, A., Rosina, E., Tucci, G.: Aerial platforms (UAV) surveys in the VIS and TIR range. Applications on archaeology and agriculture. Int. Arch. Photogramm. Remote Sens. Spatial Inf. Sci. **XLII-2/W11**, 945–952 (2019). https://doi.org/10.5194/isprs-archives-XLII-2-W11-945-2019

35. Remondino, F., Spera, M.G., Nocerino, E., Menna, F., Nex, F.: State of the art in high density image matching. Photogrammet. Rec. **29**, 144–166 (2014)

36. Zhang, J., Ten Brink, U., Toksöz, M.: Nonlinear refraction reflection travel time tomography. J. Geophys. Res. **103**, 29743–29757 (1998)

37. Mauriello, P., Patella, D.: A data-adaptive probability-based fast ERT inversion method. Prog. Electromagn. Res. **97**, 275–290 (2009)

38. Geophysical Homepage (2023). www.geophysical.com. Accessed 28 Mar 2023

39. Goodman, D.: GPR-SLICE. Ground penetrating radar imaging software, user's manual. Geophysical Archaeometry Laboratory, Los Angeles, CA, USA (2004)

Correction to: Design and Develop of a Smart City Digital Twin with 3D Representation and User Interface for What-If Analysis

Lorenzo Adreani, Pierfrancesco Bellini, Marco Fanfani,
Paolo Nesi, and Gianni Pantaleo

Correction to:
Chapter 34 in: O. Gervasi et al. (Eds.): *Computational Science and Its Applications – ICCSA 2023 Workshops*, **LNCS 14111,**
https://doi.org/10.1007/978-3-031-37126-4_34

The original version of the book was inadvertently published with an incorrect form of reference [18] in Chapter 34, it was not compatible with Scopus. This has been corrected.

The updated version of this chapter can be found at
https://doi.org/10.1007/978-3-031-37126-4_34

Author Index